THE ST. MARTIN'S
SOURCEBOOK
FOR WRITING TUTORS

THE ST. MARTIN'S SOURCEBOOK FOR WRITING TUTORS

FOURTH EDITION

Christina Murphy
MARSHALL UNIVERSITY

Steve Sherwood
TEXAS CHRISTIAN UNIVERSITY

BEDFORD / ST. MARTIN'S

BOSTON ◆ NEW YORK

For Bedford/St. Martin's

Developmental Editor: Nicholas McCarthy
Associate Production Editor: Kellan Cummings
Production Associate: Samuel Jones
Marketing Manager: Marjorie Adler
Copy Editor: Fran Weinberg
Permissions Manager: Kalina Ingham Hintz
Art Director: Lucy Krikorian
Composition: Greg Johnson/Textbook Perfect
Printing and Binding: Haddon Craftsmen, Inc., an RR Donnelley & Sons Company

President: Joan E. Feinberg
Editorial Director: Denise B. Wydra
Editor in Chief: Karen S. Henry
Director of Development: Erica T. Appel
Director of Marketing: Karen R. Soeltz
Director of Production: Susan W. Brown
Associate Director, Editorial Production: Elise S. Kaiser
Managing Editor: Shuli Traub

Library of Congress Control Number: 2010943154

Manufactured in the United States of America.

6 5 4 3 2
f   e   d   c

For information, write: Bedford/St. Martin's, 75 Arlington Street, Boston, MA 02116 (617-399-4000)

ISBN: 978-0-312-66191-5

Acknowledgments

CONTENTS

Part III. Resources for Further Inquiry 375

THE ST. MARTIN'S
SOURCEBOOK
FOR WRITING TUTORS

I

The Tutoring Process: Exploring Paradigms and Practices

We begin *The St. Martin's Sourcebook for Writing Tutors* with the principal ideas that will guide our discussion of the tutoring process and the tutor's role in writing instruction:

- *Tutoring is contextual.* Tutoring takes place in a number of sociocultural and interpersonal contexts that lend richness and complexity to the tutor's role. An understanding of these contexts extends the tutor's technical skill.
- *Tutoring is collaborative.* Tutoring is grounded in interpersonal transactions; it is, fundamentally, a *relationship* more than a body of techniques or even a body of knowledge. In the tutoring session, two people work together toward a common goal; they collaborate. The purpose of the collaboration is to assist writers in their own development. The dialogue between tutor and student—a conversation with a definite purpose—is the basis on which tutors and students build a supportive working relationship. Thus, tutoring offers a conceptual and interpersonal framework for the sharing of ideas.
- *Tutoring is interpersonal.* Tutors must draw upon extensive interpersonal skills to work effectively with students who bring a range of educational and cultural backgrounds and a variety of learning styles to their tutoring sessions. Tutors need effective interpersonal skills because the purpose of tutoring is to meet the needs of individual writers.
- *Tutoring is individualized.* If there is any one truth about tutoring, it is that no single method of tutoring, no one approach, will work effectively with every student in every situation. Each tutor develops a style of tutoring primarily from experience, and experience is always a dynamic process of change. Tutoring sessions are as unique and individual as the students who come to be tutored.

With tutoring's complex philosophical background and its rich interpersonal dynamic, you might wonder, "Can I be an effective tutor?" The answer is "yes"—because you are already engaged in the essence of tutoring, which is

conversation. With your instructors and fellow students, you have had numerous discussions of the writing process and of how writers learn to improve
their work. Now, as a writing center tutor, you will build on these discussions
with new thoughts and ideas from conversations with your fellow tutors and
your writing center mentors. You will also have this sourcebook to enhance
your understanding of the tutoring process.

The St. Martin's Sourcebook for Writing Tutors is not a philosophical treatise
that separates theory from practice. Nor is it a how-to book of procedures and
tactics. Such a simple technique-driven approach would be inadequate for
operating in the fluid, unpredictable, give-and-take atmosphere of the tutorial. While tutoring is generally logical, it is seldom tactical; that is, it is not
possible to learn a single method and apply it in all instances. Such a scenario
fails to describe the complexity and richness of the encounters between tutor
and writer.

Rather than a single scenario, then, we have chosen to present multiple
views of tutorials and multiple commentaries on the learning experiences those
tutorials embody. The essays here represent a valuable body of knowledge for
both the novice and the experienced tutor. In them, we hear many voices
commenting on the practice of tutoring—the hows, whys, why nots, shoulds,
and should nots—together with the lines of reasoning and the personal experiences that support these viewpoints. We hear of success and failure and
starting over again—of the continual rediscovery that tutoring represents as
both a learning and a teaching experience. We hear the voices of theorists
who are accomplished professionals in the field, as well as those of veteran
tutors and of beginning tutors who are new to the field. We hear the voices of
students who have come to tutors seeking knowledge, assistance, and reassurance. Above all, we hear the essence of tutoring: *conversation*. And we begin
to realize that there is a broad, interdisciplinary, and theoretical conversation
surrounding the practice of tutoring—a conversation this sourcebook invites
you to join.

TUTORING AND THE PARADIGMS OF WRITING INSTRUCTION

As a method for teaching writing, tutoring has been influenced by the *paradigms*
that have shaped writing instruction during the past several decades. Tutoring
has also been instrumental in shaping those paradigms, largely because writing
center tutorials provide practical opportunities to test theoretical assumptions
about how students develop as writers.

Theories in Writing Instruction

Since writing centers first appeared on the U.S. higher-education scene in
the 1930s, three paradigms have predominated as models of how writing
should be taught: current traditional rhetoric, expressivism (also sometimes

called expressionism), and social constructionism. These three models held sway over writing instruction and tutoring until well into the 1980s, after which cultural studies, postcolonial, postmodern, and postprocess theories of composition also had an increasing influence on composition instruction and on writing center tutorials. In the twenty-first century, the emergence of information technology on a global scale has reshaped our understandings of communication and even our definitions of *writing* itself. Many composition and rhetoric scholars view the design of documents that combine film, video, sound, and other effects—with or without text—as a form of writing, and many writing centers are already offering, or gearing up to offer, tutorials on these documents. There is no question that the vast introduction of information technology via electronic media adds another level of complexity to tutoring, and one that will continue to become a significant component of writing center work in the twenty-first century.

Current traditional rhetoric focuses almost exclusively on the writer's text and its formal dimensions of grammatical correctness. Writing center tutors who adopt this approach would concern themselves with isolating errors and formal weaknesses in a student's text and providing information on how to correct those problems.

Because writing centers emerged at a time when current traditional rhetoric was the dominant paradigm, they often tended to take on the role of providing this kind of remedial help to students. As a consequence, writing centers became known, early on, as grammar "fix-it shops," as Stephen M. North puts it in "The Idea of a Writing Center" (p. 44). In his essay, North opposes limiting writing center instruction to issues of grammatical correctness. Instead, he favors giving more attention to the writer than to the text—especially, to how the writer can learn to become more fluent in expressing ideas. He describes a model for such a perspective, one based on the philosophy of expressivism.

Expressivism, represented by the works of Peter Elbow, Donald Murray, and Ken Macrorie, dominated writing instruction from the 1970s to the mid-1980s. In this paradigm, writing is viewed as a means of self-discovery. By exploring language as a mode of self-expression, students come to know themselves and to develop an "authentic voice" in their writing. Expressivists tend to value the individual writer as a solitary creator who communicates ideas through personal explorations of language, experience, and individual identity.

[handwritten margin note: Expressivists]

An expressivist tutor explores the student's understanding of the writing process, particularly the stages of invention and drafting, in which the writer generates ideas and seeks an authentic voice. Expressivist tutors often employ "the Socratic dialogue," asking heuristic, or exploratory, questions as a way of getting the student to discover and think about ideas and how they can best be communicated.

North's essay and Jeff Brooks's "Minimalist Tutoring: Making the Student Do All the Work" (p. 128) discuss in detail the philosophy of expressivist tutoring and the tutor's role within a Socratic dialogue. However, as you will discover in Andrea Lunsford's "Collaboration, Control, and the Idea of a Writing Center," not all theorists view expressivism as a genuinely liberating form of writing instruction. Lunsford, for example, argues that the Socratic dialogue of the expressivist tutor can *seem* to be a freely structured exploration of ideas when, in fact, the tutor's so-called heuristic questions are actually leading questions — ones that lead the student toward conclusions already known and valued by the tutor. Lunsford also contends that expressivism places too much emphasis on the individual writer while minimizing or ignoring the social dimensions of language, knowledge, and writing. As a consequence, she argues against the limited scope of expressivism in favor of the philosophy of social constructionism.

While current traditional rhetoric emphasizes the writer's text and expressivism emphasizes the writer's creative processes, *social constructionism* focuses on the sociocultural and historical settings in which writers develop their understanding of language and knowledge. Social constructionism began to influence writing instruction in the mid-1980s and has since become one of the dominant paradigms. The most noted advocates of social constructionism are Kenneth A. Bruffee, Marilyn M. Cooper, James Berlin, and Patricia Bizzell.

As Lunsford's essay indicates, social constructionists do not believe in the romantic image of the writer as a solitary genius who only has to look inward to find the truth of self-expression. They maintain that knowledge, rather than being "found" uniquely through self-discovery, is "made" by agreement, or consensus, within discourse communities. For example, we as tutors come to have similar ways of talking (and thinking) about our work; other groups form other discourse communities.

The writing center practice advocated by social constructionists involves extensive use of peer-group critiquing to reflect the workings of discourse communities and to downplay the role of the tutor as an authority figure or the single source of knowledge. Thus, collaboration and collaborative learning play an important role in social-constructionist writing instruction. The tutor's voice is only one of many the writer will hear, and the tutor and writer are co-learners who collaborate to negotiate meanings and construct knowledge.

Recent Innovations in Composition Theory

Cultural-studies pedagogies, influenced by the ideas of Paulo Freire, Ira Shor, Jacques Derrida, and Mikhail Bakhtin, take social constructionism a step further, asking writers and writing tutors to acknowledge the public and political nature of their work. Cultural studies proponents argue that writing center tutors often act as unthinking agents of acculturation for the dominant culture as represented in the discursive practices of the academy. As Nancy Grimm argues in "The Regulatory Role of the Writing Center: Coming to Terms with a Loss of Innocence," tutors who see themselves as neutral helpers in reality "reinforce the status quo, to support the teacher and the institution" (11) and promote a "fixed notion of literacy, a singular standard," which not only "closes down meaning" (22) but supports a disguised "racist and classist agenda" (19). Marilyn M. Cooper makes a similar argument in "Really Useful Knowledge: A Cultural Studies Agenda for Writing Centers." Cooper calls on tutors to adopt a subject position from which they can critique (and seek to reform) not only the dominant social order but also their own practices. In this view, the goal of writing tutorials should not be the simple improvement of student writing. Instead, the goal is to give student writers a heightened awareness of the social injustice perpetrated by the dominant culture's racist, sexist, and classist agendas and to empower these writers to resist these agendas (98, 106). In short, the goal of such tutoring is to make better citizens of both tutors and student writers.

In a similar vein, proponents of *postmodern*, *postcolonial*, and *postprocess* theories of composition call for approaches to tutoring that emphasize plural perspectives, identities, and processes. In *Good Intentions: Writing Center Work for Postmodern Times*, Nancy Grimm argues that contemporary universities operate in a modernist framework that privileges essential truths and a stable notion of reality. Writing center tutors are positioned to challenge modernist notions, Grimm says, because "in the postmodern encounters of a writing center, essential truths come under questioning, 'reality' changes with a shift in perspective, one's identity shifts in response to different situations, and the coherence of an essay comes at the expense of complexity" (2). In *Noise from the Writing Center*, Elizabeth H. Boquet discusses the potential of noise (or feedback distortion) and chaos for generating ideas and more closely reflecting the complex composing processes of writers in the midst of their work. Rather than embracing a model of writing center practice rooted in the relative neatness of process theory, Boquet says, "I much prefer thinking of the work of the writing center as random chaos, or maybe controlled chaos, instead" (83). She invokes comparisons between musical improvisation, or jazz, and the work tutors do. In general, postmodern approaches, such as those of Grimm and Boquet, tend to value and support writers' plural identities and processes.

Postcolonial views of the writing center derive from both the cultural-studies and postmodern movements. As Anis Bawarshi and Stephanie Pelkowski explain in "Postcolonialism and the Idea of a Writing Center," most writing centers — especially, those with a current traditional or expressivist orientation — are in the business of acculturating students, not fostering multiple perspectives on writing (42).

Bawarshi and Pelkowski contend that nontraditional students, upon receiving their first exposure to academic writing, often feel as if they are losing something in the transformation — giving up a level of complexity and an awareness of alternative perspectives in order to fit their ideas into frameworks acceptable to the university. To avoid this situation, and help students resist acculturation, Bawarshi and Pelkowski propose "a writing center strategy in which under-prepared students, especially those marginalized by race, class, and ethnicity, are encouraged to adopt critical consciousness as a means of functioning within the university and its discourses" (44). The aim of this critical consciousness is to help students succeed in the university without surrendering their sense of who they are. This important aim is also endorsed by Meg Woolbright in "The Politics of Tutoring: Feminism within the Patriarchy." Woolbright contends that tutorials often reflect hidden or overt agendas of political and social power that favor patriarchal values. This focus on imposing one set of values on the tutoring session and its outcomes can undermine a student's sense of self. To avoid this destructive consequence, Woolbright urges a self-reflective practice for tutors that engages them in examining the power dynamics involved in their tutorials so that their practice can become more egalitarian (17, 22–27).

A number of theorists, clustered under the heading of the *postprocess* school, share with the postmodernists similar assumptions about the fragmented, highly contextual, and contingent nature of human perspectives on reality and therefore on writing. Because each piece of writing is situated in a specific rhetorical context, these theorists claim, the composition processes a writer uses will vary widely from one act of writing to the next. After the fact, a writer may be able to trace a series of steps he or she took in arriving at the finished piece, but this process may have no application to the writing of another piece. Therefore, postprocess theorists object to the "one size fits all" approach they claim is at the heart of process theory. As Thomas Kent says, "Post-process theorists hold—for all sorts of different reasons—that writing is a practice that cannot be captured by a generalized process or Big Theory" (1). Gary A. Olson agrees with Kent in saying that "writing—indeed all communication—is radically contingent, radically situational. Consequently, efforts to pin down some version of 'the writing process' are misguided, unproductive, and misleading" (8–9). In light of these insights, postprocess theorists are, David Foster says, "deeply skeptical of a writing pedagogy that assumes regularity and transferability in writing behavior . . . ." (152). Postprocess theorists agree that the composition classroom is not an effective or appropriate site for learning how to write. Instead, what universities need are approaches to writing instruction that make allowances for changing circumstances, purposes, and needs. While postprocess theorists make no specific recommendations for reforming composition programs, most prefer an approach based on experiential learning in highly specific settings—such as writing in the disciplines or in an apprenticeship on the job.

Writing center practices, as they have evolved during the past two decades, match up well with postmodern, postcolonial, and postprocess theories. By working with student writers from multiple disciplines and cultures, tutors generally develop a sensitivity to the contingent, contextual nature of writing, which requires them to respond to each writer's needs and sensibilities. Tutors realize that each piece of writing has a different audience, purpose, and set of rhetorical expectations—and quite possibly multiple processes through which the writer could succeed. Working with multiple disciplines and genres, and adopting multiple perspectives each day, tutors cultivate an unusual and valuable "mental agility" (Grimm, *Good Intentions* 2). As Grimm says:

> Writing centers are often places where people develop what scholars call *postmodern skills*: the ability to simultaneously maintain multiple viewpoints, to make quick shifts in discourse orientation, to handle rapid changes in information technology, to work elbow to elbow with people differently positioned in the university hierarchy, to negotiate cultural and social differences, to handle the inevitable blurring of authorial boundaries, and to regularly renegotiate issues of knowledge, power, and ownership. This ability to work the border between tradition and change, to simultaneously entertain multiple—often conflicting—perspectives is a valuable survival skill for the turn of the century. (2)

Perhaps no other development has had a more dramatic effect on composition theory and writing center tutoring than technology, especially the rise of multimodality. The transformation of writing centers into multiliteracy centers greatly adds to the range of skills and the knowledge base that tutors will need to operate effectively in the twenty-first century writing center. As David M. Sheridan writes in his introduction to *Multiliteracy Centers: Writing Center Work, New Media, and Multimodal Rhetoric*, communication is changing fundamentally:

> Salient among the many changes currently transpiring is the increasing reliance on the integration of multiple semiotic components that span across aural, visual, and verbal modes: written words, spoken words, music, still images, moving images, charts, graphs, illustrations, layout schemes, navigation schemes, colors, ambient noises, and so on. Further, these components are not neatly separable; communication is not the result of one element merely being added to another, but of the *interaction* among the different elements. (1–2)

Sheridan states that "the constellation of cultural and technological dynamics" that has "shaped this shift to multimodality" includes the following (2):

- *Increasing proliferation of multimodal media*. "Old media" forms like radio, TV, film—and ever-more sophisticated print media—flourished beginning in the early twentieth century, to be joined at the century's end by "new media" forms such as web pages, digital videos, and digital animations.
- *Increasing access to the tools of multimodal production and distribution*. Many entry-level computers now come bundled with easy-to-use digital video applications. These applications enable a kind of video production that only a few years ago would have required expensive and arcane equipment. Moreover, videos can now be distributed over the Internet at little or no cost (consider, for example, YouTube).

- *Increasing cultural acceptance of multimodal compositions as "serious" and useful forms of communication.* In public, professional, and personal contexts, multimodal forms are increasingly understood to be not just entertainment but essential ways of getting work done, whether that work is publicizing a nonprofit organization or presenting a proposal to the board of directors.

Sheridan concludes that "these transformations affected language-related fields in substantial ways." In terms of writing instruction and tutoring, these changes call for and require a "broadening of mission" to embrace "all kinds of texts" including those of "new media" (3).

Sheridan is in agreement with Cynthia Selfe, a leading theorist on multi-literacy issues, who stated in 2004: "To make it possible for students to practice, value, and understand a full range of literacies—emerging, competing, and fading—English composition teachers have got to be willing to expand their own understanding of composing beyond conventional bounds of the alphabetic. And we do have to do so quickly or risk having composition studies become increasingly irrelevant" (54).

Of course, we would add writing center practitioners to Selfe's call for understanding the "full range of literacies." And we would argue, too, that writing centers and writing center tutorials are especially conducive environments for this progression to occur. For example, in 1996, prominent futurist theoretician Don Tapscott predicted in *The Digital Economy: Promise and Peril in the Age of Networked Intelligence* that the emergence of communication technology, particularly the Internet, would redefine societal interactions as we have known them—resulting in a "revolution as significant as any other in human history" (xiii). Tapscott goes on to discuss "twelve themes" that will reshape communication and social interaction, including individualization or, in this context, the process by which nearly all aspects of communication and commodification could be designed to meet the specific interests and needs of each person (44–67). As Tapscott predicted, individualization has become a primary social fact and factor in such technologies as the iPod, which enables the user to select music that appeals to his or her sensibilities, or publishing-on-demand (POD), which permits the creation of books and other publications for a specific person or audience. Both inventions reshaped the music industry and the publishing business and thus people's individualized access to information.

We hypothesize that Tapscott's vision of the future is particularly relevant to writing centers, which have been shaped by their ability to work with students on an individual basis. Tutoring is largely an individual experience with no one tutorial likely to be the same as another but with each tutorial committed to addressing the student's needs. Thus, it is not surprising that the writing center is once again redefining individualization in tutoring as information technology transforms the twentieth-century writing center into the twenty-first–century multiliteracy center.

The proliferation of theories over the past few decades and their related practices might seem intimidating as you begin your tutoring practice. However,
you will discover ways to interpret these theories and to apply them. As a
tutor, you will discover, too, that tutorials are rarely, if ever, exclusively the
product of any one paradigm. Instead, they are often a creative, and highly
individual, mix of approaches, as the needs of the student dictate. This philosophical complexity adds richness and challenge to the tutor's role and provides ongoing learning experiences through which to refine and personalize a
tutoring style.

THE TUTOR'S ROLE: DEVELOPING AN
INFORMED PRACTICE

We believe in the idea of an informed tutoring practice, and we hope this
book will serve as a source of information and insight. A tutor who develops
a sufficiently broad interpretive frame for understanding his or her own work
can apply this knowledge to new situations. In the absence of such a perspective, the tutor has only hit-or-miss, trial-and-error experimentation to rely
on—often at the student's expense. On the other hand, a tutor who draws on
an experience informed by insight and an evolving personal philosophy can
bring to the tutoring session the technical skill and creativity needed to teach
writing successfully.

This approach suggests a reflective practice, one in which the tutor views
rules as guidelines and guidelines as avenues to further refinement of aptitude,
or know-how. The know-how of good tutors comes from a willingness to
reflect on their efforts and to keep learning. Such tutors are eager both to confirm what they do well and to question any practices that impede productive
interactions with students. Ultimately, successful tutors are willing to modify
their views and procedures as new insights emerge.

The capacity for reconceptualizing is also one of the most significant means
for improving writing skills that we as tutors can offer a student. To be a
capable writer, a student needs to shift perspective from that of the writer who
generated the text to that of an objective reader able to assess his or her own
text and its methods of communicating to an audience. Many of the students
we work with, though, have had little experience with reconceptualizing their
own writing in this way.

Often students cannot think about their writing in meaningful and productive ways because they are unpracticed at extensive revision. They may see
revision as tedious and frustrating. After all, expressing their ideas was probably difficult enough the first time; doing it again in a revised form can seem
overwhelming. Guiding such students through drafting and revising can be of
enormous help. By modeling the act of revision, we are demonstrating the process of reflecting on their ideas and written work. In the process, we also provide the "moral support" that can help sustain motivation. As Muriel Harris,

one of the most respected and influential figures in writing center theory and the author of *Teaching One-to-One: The Writing Conference*, says:

> Writers also need another kind of help when revising—some support and encouragement—because the messiness of working and reworking a paper can lead to surprise and dismay as a topic falls apart or changes direction during writing. Novice writers need to learn how to persist, and they need some encouragement to do so. (8)

In emphasizing the interpersonal dimensions of the working relationship between tutor and student, Harris shows how tutoring functions as an assistive process. Tutors have been described as mentors, teachers, therapists, editors, midwives, coaches, grammarmeisters, nurturers, diagnosticians, guides, facilitators, rescuers, advisors, consultants, and allies. Perhaps we are all these. But, primarily, tutors are collaborators: we assist writers in achieving their goals. Among the many traits effective tutors share are strong writing and editing skills, flexibility, an eagerness to help, an analytical yet creative mind, a dedication to excellence, good listening skills, an ability to be supportive yet honest, a willingness to work hard, a sense of humor, sensitivity to others, careful judgment, patience, and a dedication to collaborative learning. Tutors need all these traits because solving problems and motivating others are key interpersonal activities in the tutoring process.

DIMENSIONS OF THE TUTORIAL

Writing center tutorials are multifaceted in nature and can take place in a range of settings using a number of approaches and methods that support the tutor's interpersonal skills, knowledge, and commitment to working with the student. Some tutorials take place in face-to-face, sit-down conversations in the writing center, and some take place online using asynchronous email or using a software option like Wimba, which enables synchronous audio and visual interaction between the tutor and student. Some tutorials focus on the student's print-based text, and some tutorials focus on the student's digital text, which uses new media to include video, audio, digital animation, and graphic design and illustration in addition to print-based text.

Thus, our use of the terms *text* and *textual* is not limited to print-based documents but extends to new media "texts" that are multimodal and may include visual, aural, and verbal modes. The development of multimodal communication has reconfigured the way terms like *texts, documents, manuscripts,* and even *writing* itself are understood in our culture—and no less so in composition studies and in the writing center. Some of the dynamics of tutorials will change to meet the needs of students writing digital texts, but, in spite of such differences and in spite of the diversity of texts and situations a tutor will encounter, tutorials will still tend to share common patterns. We have chosen to call these shared activities the pretextual, textual, and posttextual dimensions of the tutorial, and we have divided the tutorial into separate dimensions for discussion purposes. We are aware that tutorials do not always involve all these dimensions. And we know that tutorials do not always progress in a linear fashion. Instead, tutorials tend to be recursive and move fluidly back and forth and within these various dimensions. A tutor should not feel bound by any sense that she or he must proceed lockstep through these dimensions. Tutoring is a multifaceted learning and instructional experience, and no single description of it can capture the individual character of all tutorials. As the discussion that follows indicates, however, we do believe that there are conceptual contours offering important insights that tutors can explore to enrich their understanding of tutoring.

The Pretextual Dimension

In the pretextual dimension, tutor and student begin the process of developing the interpersonal relationship that will guide their collaborations. Education theorists tell us that interpersonal relationships are exceptionally important because they provide a context for interactive learning. In the past, theorists did not place much emphasis on context because they viewed the mind of the learner as an object to be filled with information. The method of presenting that information was important but the context in which it occurred was not. Now the mind of the learner is viewed as a process of meaning-making activities. This process is highly influenced by contexts—especially interpersonal ones. As psychologist and learning theorist Richard G. Tiberius writes:

> Effective teachers form relationships that are trustful, open and secure, that involve a minimum of control, are cooperative, and are conducted in a reciprocal, interactive manner. They share control with students and encourage interactions that are determined by mutual agreement. Within such relationships learners are willing to disclose their lack of understanding, rather than hide it from their teachers; learners are more attentive, ask more questions, are more actively engaged. Thus, the better the relationship, the better the interaction; the better the interaction, the better the learning. (1–2)

Most writing center theorists tend to agree with Tiberius in stressing the quality of the interpersonal relationship between tutor and student. For example, in "Freud in the Writing Center: The Psychoanalytics of Tutoring Well," Christina Murphy maintains that the mutual trust and rapport between tutor and student determine how successful the tutorial as a whole will be. To achieve this level of reciprocal learning, Murphy contends, tutors often need to break through psychological barriers that might otherwise impede collaboration (13–15).

In establishing an interpersonal relationship, the tutor must respond to various personality and learning styles and be sensitive to differences in gender, age, ethnicity, cultural and educational backgrounds, and attitudes toward writing. The ways in which individuals process information must always be taken into account, too, as people tend to interpret, understand, and evaluate ideas in diverse ways. Consequently, tutors need to engage in what Harris calls "perception checking" or "guessing the student's basic message and asking for affirmation of that guess" (*Teaching One-to-One* 57). In a similar vein, Emily Meyer and Louise Z. Smith claim that tutors "must listen carefully to distinguish underlying meanings in writers' comments" (9) and work diligently to ascertain that those meanings are understood. Tutors should strive to understand, not judge, the student and to recognize the importance of the student's problems and feelings. Students vary in levels of autonomy, sensitivity to criticism, ego strength, personal maturity, motivation, and perseverance. Relating to the student as an individual and empathizing with his or her particular personality and character traits will go a long way toward forming a special trust, one that provides the motivation, energy, and direction for the tutorial itself.

When individuals choose to work together, their transactions should be based on a shared dialogue. Too often collaborations that seem democratic may actually be autocratic and controlling, as Andrea Lunsford indicates in her essay on collaboration and control (p. 70). Sometimes in a tutorial we need to overcome an assumed hierarchy of power, with the tutor in command and the student acting as a subservient petitioner. A good question for tutors to ask ourselves is, "Who has the power in the collaboration and how is that power used?" Are we, for example, truly interested in what the student has to say, or are we too quick to announce our opinions? Are we acting as collaborators or as authority figures? Do our comments invite responses and show respect for the student's ideas, or do they foreclose further interaction and leave the student feeling intimidated? Carol Severino points out that tutors can analyze a collaboration rhetorically by considering how the agenda for the conference is decided, the length of each person's contributions to the discussions, and the rhetorical functions of verbal exchanges and of body language (56). As Elizabeth H. Boquet says in "Intellectual Tug-of-War: Snapshots of Life in the Center," tutorials involving difficult interpersonal conflicts—with students or fellow tutors—can sometimes leave a tutor feeling "simply at a loss" and call into question his or her sense of "progress toward becoming the 'ideal' writing center tutor" (16). Boquet suggests that such questioning is an important part of peer tutors' development because it can lead them to become "dynamic forces within their workplaces" (21), reflecting on and possibly changing for the better aspects of their practice or work environment.

Clearly, one component of a tutor's reflective practice is responsiveness to the ethical issues that often emerge in tutoring sessions. Students often express ideas and opinions on social, political, and moral issues that run counter to the tutor's own views. Knowing how to handle such conflicts wisely for the benefit of the tutor and the student alike is a challenging aspect of tutoring practice. Advocates of nondirective tutoring might urge a largely objective, if not distant, role for the tutor in dealing with such students and situations.

Others, like Stacey Freed in "Subjectivity in the Tutorial Session: How Far Can We Go?" and Steve Sherwood in "Censoring Students, Censoring Ourselves: Constraining Conversations in the Writing Center," challenge the nondirective principle common to tutoring practice in which tutors are urged to remain neutral on social and political issues. Freed says that tutors have not only a right but an obligation to challenge students' ill-conceived and sometimes morally questionable ideas. She claims that "we would be doing the students a disservice by not voicing our own opinions" (40) and thus not forcing them to scrutinize their work. To do so, "we must make students aware of other points of view that may be 'disturbing' to them and may 'distress' them; and we should, if we believe an individual case warrants it, overstep the boundaries and be subjective—without being judgmental—in expressing these views" (42–43). Sherwood claims the idea that the tutor can remain ethically neutral in all tutoring sessions is naive. He contends that the "ostensibly objective devil's advocate role" (53) tutors are expected to play while responding to a student's text has to be balanced against broader concerns for the student's best interests that may require the tutor to adopt an interventionist strategy.

All these approaches to tutoring are available for your investigation during tutorials. Self-reflection can assist you in assessing your interpersonal transactions and in responding to students' needs. In "'Whispers of Coming and Going': Lessons from Fannie," Anne DiPardo discusses another dimension of interpersonal sensitivity—an appreciation of diversity. The students you tutor will come from different backgrounds, often different cultures. Their ways of looking at the world and interpreting experience may be strikingly different from yours, though equally valid. As DiPardo notes, we can serve students best by avoiding stereotypical and preconceived ideas and by being curious about how their ways of thinking differ from ours. Appreciating the multiplicity of perspectives encountered among students will add to our skill as tutors. As examples of this diversity, consider the following scenarios based on actual writing center interactions.

Darren and Yaroslav Darren worked with Yaroslav, a Russian student, on an assignment for his composition class to write a letter to the editor to argue against changes in governmental policies. From their initial conversations, Darren saw that Yaroslav was a bright, articulate, and highly motivated student. Yet there seemed to be a problem. Yaroslav was reluctant to discuss the requirements of the assignment and to work with Darren toward a rudimentary outline or draft.

Darren was patient and continued to ask Yaroslav questions related to the assignment. Did he understand the requirements of a paper that asked for a writer to take a stand on an issue? Had he ever written a similar paper before? With that question, Yaroslav suddenly became very animated. "In my country," he said, " you do not write letters to the editor to complain about the government."

Thus, Darren discovered that the issues that had made the tutorial difficult to that point did not result from Yaroslav's weaknesses as a writer or from a lack of motivation to complete his assignment. Rather, they arose from a cultural difference that had to do with the freedom of an individual to be politically active in one society versus another.

Had Darren not patiently addressed the resistance he sensed in Yaroslav, he might have merely assumed that Yaroslav was scattered, disorganized, or not ready to begin and might have sent him off to work on his own for a while. As it turned out, his sensitivity created a supportive atmosphere in which Yaroslav was able to talk through his fears and realize that what would be an unimaginable and terrifying act in his culture was an everyday, safe occurrence in Darren's culture. Darren encouraged Yaroslav to shift perspectives and imagine the political freedom to express negative opinions about governmental policies. What would this be like? What actions would Yaroslav want to take? What would he most want to change politically? Eventually, because Darren had made his discussions with Yaroslav nonjudgmental and nonthreatening, Yaroslav began the process of drafting his essay. The understanding Darren and Yaroslav had achieved made the tutorial successful.

Patrick and Sabah Patrick worked with Sabah, a graduate student from Singapore, for several tutoring sessions on a paper Sabah was assigned on an event or experience in her life which she was most proud of. Sabah had difficulty choosing a topic, and Patrick had talked with her about her life and work experiences. He learned that Sabah had been a teacher for three years in her home country, working with elementary school children. Patrick asked Sabah about these experiences and was delighted to discover how quickly Sabah brightened with enthusiasm and fondness as she discussed her students and how she had enjoyed teaching them.

"So you were a good teacher?" Patrick inquired.

Sabah hesitated, and her mood became less effusive. Patrick was puzzled. He asked again, taking a different approach.

"I would think, from what you say, that you were an excellent teacher and one who had a great influence on the children's lives."

Again Sabah seemed to hesitate, and then she became quite embarrassed. Patrick was now even more confused and also worried that he had offended her in some way. Then it occurred to him to ask Sabah about what she was feeling and what might be troubling her.

"Is this awkward for you?" he asked. "Were there problems with your teaching?"

Sabah was relieved and grateful for the chance to unburden her feelings.

"No," Sabah said. "There were no problems. It's just that in my country it is considered inappropriate and too prideful to brag on oneself. It is very difficult for me to say that I was an excellent teacher—even though . . ."

Sabah paused, and Patrick saw a good opening for reducing the tension of the conversation.

"Even though you were," he said, smiling.

Sabah, too, smiled and laughed. "Yes," she said, "even though I was."

What Patrick learned from this tutoring session was a greater appreciation for cultural differences. As an American, Patrick could boast of an accomplishment, or even take justifiable pride in his achievements, but the same was not true for Sabah as a native of Singapore. Instead, her culture advocated restraint in discussing one's achievements and held that one should not claim excellence but rather let the listener deduce one's qualities and talents from the conversation itself. Prior to his interaction with Sabah, it had never occurred to Patrick that cultural norms might make it difficult for a student to accept a compliment or to take pride in an achievement. He learned from this encounter to broaden his understanding of cultural attitudes and expectations. He also learned that he might strengthen his tutoring style by not starting with assumptions—as in his statement, "So you were a good teacher?"—but by letting the conversation itself provide him with contextual clues so that the speaker could help shape the direction or flow of the discussion. In essence, he learned not to think "just like an American," with no other sense of audience than an American one, and he also learned to be a more empathetic and skilled listener and speaker. Because it became clear to him that telling Sabah how she should feel about her experiences was not a productive way to proceed with the tutorial, he adopted the strategy of getting Sabah herself to talk about her work as a teacher and to place the events she described into a narrative structure. His role was to locate the most important, vivid, moving, and persuasive details in the stories Sabah was telling about her teaching and then help her develop a framework that would highlight those experiences and enable them to lead inductively to an overall insightful experience for the reader. Patrick experienced, as a tutor, a shift in his frame of reference. His role was not to tell Sabah what type of teacher she was but, instead, to help her tell her own stories about being a teacher in a way that would convey the nature and the "feel" of the events in a meaningful way to Sabah's readers.

Laura and Ted Laura worked with Ted in a number of tutorials before he confided in her that he had a learning disability. He showed her his letter of accommodation from the coordinator for academic services and talked about how he usually could do well on tests if given a little extra time. Laura was surprised to discover that Ted had a learning disability. At that moment, in thinking about Ted in a new light, she realized that she had held a stereotypical view of students with learning disabilities as "slower" than "normal" students. Yet here was Ted, so hardworking and zipping through his computer science courses with high grades. He didn't seem "slow" at all. In fact, he seemed bright and talented.

"I can't read," Ted said, laughing. "At least not the way you do. I have dyslexia. Letters kind of tumble around on the page—you know, upside down, backwards, the whole bit. But if I take my time and work with my colors, I can manage pretty well."

When Ted mentioned his colors, a lot became clear to Laura. She remembered the way Ted marked up his drafts in highlighter colors of green, yellow, pink, and orange. When they talked, Ted always took notes and then highlighted sections of the notes in the various colors.

Laura didn't think much about it at the time. She assumed that Ted had his own way of organizing his work. Now, as Ted explained his system, she realized that he was using his enormous visual memory to compensate for his difficulties in processing symbols. Ted could literally see his paper in his mind once he had the paper coded to show its organization and to emphasize certain stylistic techniques.

"It's all about neurological processing," he said. "Some of us do it differently."

At that moment, Laura felt embarrassed. She remembered that on her campus students with learning disabilities were not referred to as "disabled" but as "differently abled." She realized that she had never really understood that term as more than a slogan. Now Ted had made it real for her. He was exceptionally "abled," and he went about his learning and information processing in a different way. She admired his motivation and drive. Ted had to work many times harder and longer than the "normal" student, yet he persevered and actually became quite creative in finding new ways to learn and to succeed.

"You know, I was kind of hesitant to tell you I had a learning disability," Ted said. "Sometimes people can't handle it. They freak out and start treating you differently, or they assume you're a basket case and start doing everything for you. Or worse yet, they start distancing themselves from you, like you're some kind of freak they just can't cope with. It's no fun."

"I can imagine," Laura said.

"But I wanted to be honest," Ted said. "I wanted you to know me for who I am. And I wanted to thank you."

Laura was a bit surprised.

"You've always been very patient with me. When I needed something explained more than once, you always would. You went through your explanations step by step, and that helped me a lot. Like I said, I can usually do pretty well if I have a little extra time—and a little extra encouragement."

When Laura reviewed her tutorials with her peer-tutoring coordinator, she told him she was dismayed to discover how unenlightened her attitude toward students with learning disabilities had been. "I had just a superficial knowledge," she said. "And lots of stereotypical thinking. I really learned a lot from Ted about encouraging people to speak openly about themselves and about not prejudging anybody."

Laura's tutorials with Ted confirm Julie Neff's views in "Learning Disabilities and the Writing Center." Neff believes that students with learning disabilities may amass a wealth of specific knowledge about a discipline but have trouble accessing that knowledge without assistance. Such students may need help brainstorming about topics, with the tutor asking probing questions and writing down the students' answers. Others may have difficulty at the strategic level. Because of the variety of learning disabilities, Neff suggests that tutors remain open-minded and modify tutoring techniques to meet individual student writers' specific needs. Tutors can best work with students who have learning disabilities by discovering and encouraging each student's own way of processing information. Doing so allows the tutor to provide commentary relevant to the student's particular learning style.

Paul and Leonard Leonard had been the manager of a trucking company for over twenty years before being laid off. Now he was returning to the university to get a degree in engineering and pursue another career. Leonard was highly motivated, organized, and very sure of his abilities—except when it came to expressing himself in writing.

"I haven't had an English class in about thirty years," he said to Paul during their first tutorial. "Now I have to write a personal essay for my composition class, and I'm not even sure what a personal essay is. All I know is I have to write something about my experiences, and I can't seem to get started."

"Are you experiencing writer's block?" Paul asked.

"I guess I am."

"Are you kind of a perfectionist? I mean, do you expect to get everything right the first time?"

Leonard nodded. "When you're in the trucking business, you'd better get it right the first time."

"I'm sure that's true, but did it always work out that way?"

After some thought, Leonard conceded that the more complex the task, the greater the probability of error. As they talked, Paul sensed that Leonard liked his world to be clear-cut—simple, neat, and organized. Paul realized that his first priority was showing Leonard that the writing task could be more manageable than it seemed, but he also realized that Leonard would probably still experience setbacks along the way. He explained the drafting and revision stages. He also explained that most writers feel some measure of self-doubt, especially in the early stages of coming up with ideas and finding a way to express them. Paul said, "It seems to me that, since you were in the trucking business, you should have a lot of material for writing a personal essay."

Leonard's face brightened. "You mean I could write about my old job?"

"Sure. Why not? That's personal, isn't it?"

"Yeah, very." Leonard thought for a moment. "Oh I see," he said. "Personal—like from my life."

Paul asked Leonard, "If you were going to write about your old job, what would you want a reader to know?"

"The first thing I'd want to tell them is that you can work for a company for twenty years, do your best and put your life's blood into the business, but, when times get tough, you get the ax anyway."

"Could we set this up as a scene? You know, like a story—a narrative—so that people could experience this from your point of view?"

As the two discussed options for the essay, Paul suggested the idea of beginning the narrative with strong visual imagery and perhaps some dialogue. This idea appealed to Leonard because his last conversation with his ex-boss was still fresh in his mind. As he told Paul, it was raining and bitterly cold the night he lost his job. He had driven to the dispatch office and brought his thermos of coffee in from the car. He still remembered how cold the metal thermos had felt, even after he had stepped into the warm office. Then he saw his boss's pained expression. Even though Leonard suspected what was coming, he still couldn't believe it when it happened.

"What you've just told me is very vivid," Paul said. "I can feel the coldness of the thermos, too. Why don't we begin with that scene and perhaps the conversation you and your boss had that night?"

Leonard liked this approach and began brainstorming with Paul to come up with more details he could include. In a short while, the two had begun work on a preliminary outline, and the idea of a personal essay no longer seemed so mysterious or intimidating to Leonard.

Paul helped build Leonard's confidence as a writer by making him aware of competencies he already had. He pointed out to Leonard how strong the sensory details in his descriptions were and how he could use this talent to his advantage in a personal essay. He also helped Leonard see that his past experiences were relevant now.

As Paul's work with Leonard affirms, tutoring nontraditional students often means that "the best we can do to help students learn is to connect what we say to their previous experience and knowledge" (Tiberius 1).

Each of the preceding tutorials demonstrates the power of the interpersonal relationship to accommodate diversity, foster communication, and allow the student to take positive action in this supportive environment:

- The tutor can help reduce the student's anxieties, self-doubts, and insecurities that can lead to writer's block, a sense of failure, and poor self-esteem.
- The tutor can help the student break a writing project of intimidating size and scope into smaller pieces (or stages) that the student can more easily manage.
- The student can get his or her ideas out in the open where they can be reacted to, examined, discussed, clarified, tested, and, if necessary, revised.

- The student has an opportunity to practice collaborative problem solving with an experienced writer who has the student's best interest in mind.
- The student can observe, reflect on, and perhaps internalize the invention processes of the tutor.

Ultimately, a positive interpersonal relationship built in an early meeting allows for a fluid transition to a consideration of the student's text.

The Textual Dimension

Students bring to the writing center the types of issues faced by writers at all levels of ability. They suffer from writer's block or from not knowing when to stop writing; they have something they want to say but can't quite put into words; or their most beloved passages are incomprehensible to their readers. In addition, they often have problems with grammar, style, syntax, logic, organization, tone, diction, and focus. In the case of multimodal texts, they may be unsure whether the combination of words, images, sounds, and layout clearly conveys their central idea—or they may lack the technical skill to make all these features work smoothly together. To find solutions that remain true to a student's style and intent, a tutor must learn to address the student's needs while also creating a collaborative space where confidence and skills can flourish.

The goal of most tutors is to assist students in making long-term improvements in their writing. In "Provocative Revision," Toby Fulwiler argues that teaching writers how to improve involves teaching them how to revise. He adds that revision is the primary way that both thinking and writing evolve, mature, and improve" (190). Many students, though, identify tutoring with proofreading, or simple error detection and correction. They may be primarily interested in making sure their writing is grammatically and mechanically correct and only secondarily interested in a tutor's assessment of the quality of their ideas and the effectiveness of their organization. This attitude can put tutor and student at cross-purposes, creating a central dilemma for the tutor about how much to intervene in the student's overall writing processes. In essence, when critiquing a student's writing and offering assistance, should we serve as editors of basic errors or as commentators on larger concerns?

This dilemma arises in nearly all tutoring situations. As you will see in Jeff Brooks's essay (p. 128), some tutors attempt to resolve this dilemma by taking a hands-off, or *minimalist*, approach to the text. They focus on global issues such as thesis, structure, diction, tone, and the logical development or presentation of ideas. Students read their texts aloud; the tutor comments. As commentators, minimalist tutors assist students in solving their own problems. They ask heuristic questions—questions that encourage students to analyze their work and seek solutions to the difficulties the writing presents. Questions such as "Are you aware of the many simple sentences you use throughout your essay and the monotonous effect this can produce for a reader?" and "Have you thought about reorganizing your ideas along another line?" might prove more beneficial to a student's growth as a writer than simply correcting errors and sending the student off to reproduce a clean, error-free copy to hand in to the instructor. Minimalist tutors believe that proofreading and editing must be understood in the broader context of the writing process. Basic grammatical or mechanical errors may be symptomatic of deeper problems with text development, and just correcting those errors for the student will not resolve the larger issues.

Minimalist tutoring can present its own set of difficulties, however. A tutor who listens to a student read a text aloud and does not look at the text might not be able to detect certain types of formal errors that may affect meaning. For example, the sentence "The auditors role is to evaluate financial statements and certify that the statements have been fairly presented without material error" sounds correct when read aloud. But when viewed as a written text, the sentence's apostrophe error becomes apparent.

The difference between spoken and written text is further demonstrated by the interaction between Steve, a tutor, and Shafik, an ESL student who came to the writing center with a paper on the Muslim religion. Shafik asked for help in expressing his ideas clearly. Steve had him read his paper aloud and listened to the most polished, well-organized essay he had come across in weeks. "Your ideas seem clear enough to me," Steve said.

"When I speak them, yes," Shafik said as he handed Steve the manuscript, "but I have a slight problem with English grammar."

It turned out that Shafik's essay was a single paragraph, ten pages long, punctuated haphazardly, with a comma roughly every fifty words and a period every hundred. What Shafik needed and wanted was a close editing of the grammatical errors in his text. This meant that Steve, as the tutor, had to decide whether to follow his training in nondirective tutoring or address Shafik's specific needs by proofreading his paper. Shafik's case points to at least one problem a strictly minimalist approach can lead to. It can fail to help students like Shafik, who come to a tutorial with expectations that differ from those of native writers. As Muriel Harris states in "Cultural Conflicts in the Writing Center: Expectations and Assumptions of ESL Students":

> For ESL students, finding their own answers rather than being told what the answer is or what they must learn can be a new process. As tutors, we have to suppress any discomfort with ESL students who seem to want us to tell them how to fix their papers. There is a cross-cultural problem in the clash between ESL students who sit with pencil poised, waiting to write down what we tell them, and us, as we keep trying to return responsibility for revision to the writer. When the tutor asks, "What is the connection between these two sentences?" or "Is there a word missing there?" and the polite student waits for the tutor to answer the question, the two parties are acting out assumptions and expectations from very different worlds. (225)

Like Harris, Sharon A. Myers casts doubt on the value of minimalist, or nondirective, tutoring for ESL students (p. 284). In fact, Myers argues that a tutor should feel free to work on so-called sentence-level errors with ESL students since these errors often point to problems with creating and processing meaning. By helping ESL students correct these errors, the tutor can guide students toward deeper knowledge of English syntax—an important step in their becoming better readers and writers of the language. As she says, "The central insight in foreign language pedagogy in the last thirty years is that, in fact, language acquisition emerges from learners wrestling with meaning in acts of communicating or trying to communicate. That is exactly what ESL students are doing in writing centers, person to person." Such learning often takes a long time—"years, not months"—and may not become immediately apparent to either the student or the tutor. By refusing to work with ESL students' grammar and style errors, she suggests, tutors may unwittingly slow the students' progress toward second-language acquisition.

Not all tutors, of course, object to editing a student's text. Some consider modeling this part of the revision process for the student a significant aid to comprehension. Linda K. Shamoon and Deborah H. Burns (p. 133), for example, challenge nondirective tutoring orthodoxy, or "pure tutoring," and call for a reexamination of writing center ideology to permit direct intervention in students' writing when necessary. As they point out, in disciplines such as music, master artists work with various levels of students in a highly directive manner. "The tutorial typically begins with one student's performance; then the master teacher works over a section of the piece with the student, suggesting different ways to play a passage. . . . On occasion, the master teacher will play the passage herself and ask the student to play it with her or immediately after her." In what amounts to a direct, hierarchical handing down of technique, the master demonstrates, and the student imitates—and neither questions the ethics of this transaction. As Shamoon and Burns say, "Rather than assuming that this imitation will prevent authentic self-expression, the tutor and the student assume that imitation will lead to improved technique, which will enable freedom of expression." While they do not make an unqualified endorsement of directive tutoring, Shamoon and Burns argue that it is an appropriate response to a number of tutoring situations, especially in helping novices learn writing skills related to specific disciplines. They point out the weaknesses of expressivist and social constructionist viewpoints and suggest that writing center scholars reexamine mentorship and directive tutoring, accommodating such practices if they make knowledge and achievement more accessible to students.

For many tutors, the dilemma of how much help to give can be personally troubling. This dilemma intensifies as the definition of *help* shifts in the many contexts of tutoring and in the full range of the tutor's responsibilities. The natural tendency to be helpful and supportive may conflict with a sense that doing too much of the student's work will not produce the desired result of improving his or her writing abilities and critical-thinking skills. A related issue is the question of how candid to be in critiquing a student's work. Some students are mature enough to deal with having their work critiqued. Other students are far more fragile. As Peter Elbow says in *Writing with Power*, "Some people are terrified no matter how friendly the audience is, while others are not intimidated even by sharks" (184–85).

With the complex of problems, needs, ego strengths, and personality styles students bring to the tutoring situation, what courses of action should the tutor pursue to be effective? The following ideas might prove helpful:

- *Give a candid opinion of the strengths and weaknesses of the work in progress; in the process, be sensitive to the student's reactions.* Such candor can be difficult, but honesty about the problems you detect with the reasoning, structure, or content of a text is essential for improvement. This is not to say that criticism doesn't hurt. It sometimes does. But anything short of a truthful—but also sensitive—appraisal is a betrayal of the student's trust.
- *Suggest ways to enhance the strengths and minimize the weaknesses in the student's writing.* A tutorial that focuses exclusively, or even primarily, on weaknesses can leave a student feeling demoralized. Noting strengths and achievements in the writing can build a student's confidence and set the tone for comments and suggestions that follow.
- *Recognize that every text and every writer is a work in progress.* Writers progress at different rates, but they do progress—in part because they acquire greater intellectual maturity and in part because writing is an ongoing learning experience. Writers learn to be better writers by striving to improve. The issue is not whether they will make mistakes—because they will; the issue is whether they will learn from those mistakes or be defeated by them. Here the tutor can be instrumental. As a supportive ally and a candid critic, a tutor can encourage progress by fostering potential.

The Posttextual Dimension

The posttextual dimension has two major functions: it provides a sense of closure for the tutorial and it offers a template, or model, for future learning experiences. The most helpful tutorials do not simply end—they are brought to a satisfactory conclusion. Tutor and student seek an overview that brings the strategic insights of the tutorial into focus and clarifies what work still remains to be done. Ultimately, this perspective contributes to the student's ease in working with a tutor and makes future tutoring sessions seem natural extensions of an ongoing learning process.

Bringing tutorials to a graceful yet productive conclusion can also contribute to students' feelings of empowerment, providing them with the confidence they need to take the insights they have gained and apply them in new writing situations. Among other goals, you should encourage self-motivated and independent learning styles for the student as a way of preventing the student from becoming overly dependent on your help. You can accomplish this objective in several ways: first, by leaving the student with a clear sense of where to go from here; second, by letting the student know that revision is well within the limits of his or her abilities; third, by providing a perceptive audience for the student's future work; and fourth, by refusing to be satisfied with anything less than the student's best effort. Not all students will respond to your demands for their best work. Those who do will grow as a result of learning to push themselves rather than settling for the easy solution. Eventually, if they internalize these expectations, they can become their own best audience.

As an example of a tutorial that was successful in encouraging independent learning, consider Barbara, a student who came to the writing center with a paper about William Faulkner's *Sanctuary*. During the initial "reading" of the student to establish a working relationship, Steve, the tutor, interviewed Barbara to learn a number of key pieces of information. He learned, for instance, that her instructor had refused to grade Barbara's essay, saying that she needed help at all stages of her writing. Steve also learned that Barbara, a mother of three, had quit college as a sophomore nine years earlier and was now trying to pick up where she had left off. Barbara admitted she was feeling discouraged, saying, "It's been ten years since I've taken a writing course, and I've lost the knack. Anyway, my professor has a problem with the way I write. I'm worried about this paper," she said, "but I'm more worried about what's going to happen next year if I don't improve my writing."

Barbara moved the tutorial into the textual dimension by showing Steve a heavily marked-up manuscript. "My instructor says I need to make a point and that I have problems with sentence structure," she said. She read her essay aloud, and Steve primarily noted rough transitions and a general lack of organization. In the essay, Barbara tended to repeat herself, to think in circles rather than systematically developing her main idea. Steve told Barbara that, circular or not, her ideas were good and that she had something interesting to say on Faulkner's motives for writing about particular characters. Together, they worked out a tentative essay structure. Since Barbara's main stylistic and mechanical errors were short, choppy sentences, errors of diction, and sentence fragments, Steve also went over individual sentences, asking Barbara to add the necessary elements.

Toward the end of the tutorial, Steve reviewed what they had accomplished, gave Barbara some words of encouragement, and then sent her away to write. Three days later, Barbara returned. Her paper had taken a new direction, and, though the paper occasionally wandered off the point, Steve felt it might work with some adjustments. He encouraged Barbara to rewrite along the lines they had discussed.

Steve did not see Barbara for over a week; then she returned to say she had received a B+ on the essay. "The best thing is, I did most of the work on my own," she said proudly. She was feeling independent and ready to face the challenges of future assignments. Through discussion, questioning, and being open both to small corrections and major changes in thinking, Barbara had gained at least an initial sense of her composing process.

Stimulating independent learning is an important aspect of the tutoring process and is the primary objective of the posttextual dimension. When the posttextual phase of a tutorial is successful, students work to develop their own strengths separately from those of the tutor, taking what they can from the more experienced member of the relationship and adding this knowledge to an already-existing repertoire of technique and understanding. In so doing, they build a knowledge indebted to, but independent of, their tutor's. As Wallace Stegner, a noted author and creative writing teacher, says, "Something unpredictable has happened in your head or on your typewriter, and no teacher did it—though a teacher may have helped it along" (19).

As a tutor, you can help foster independent learning and writing by

- letting students do what they can for themselves
- reminding students of any challenges they have conquered on their own or with minimal help
- recognizing and praising any steps they take toward independence in their writing
- refusing to let students credit you with their successes
- letting them know that, while you value their increasing independence, you will gladly help them cope with future challenges they might feel unable to face alone

As Christina Murphy states, "a good tutor function[s] to awaken individuals to their potentials and to channel their creative energies toward self-enhancing ends" (16).

TUTORING ONLINE

Many of the principles of effective tutoring apply to all tutorials—whether face-to-face, via electronic mail, or in multimodal settings that involve virtual conferencing software—although both email and multimodal tutorials present tutors with fresh opportunities and challenges.

Asynchronous online tutorials take place primarily at the textual stage. When a tutorial occurs via email, with delays between submission and response, and when it involves a writer and tutor who have never met, the tutor may find it hard to establish a personal relationship with the writer. The interaction often consists of exchanges of text messages—disembodied language—with the accompanying danger of misinterpretation of tone or wording, both of which may get in the way of establishing a helpful rapport with the writer. As Michael Spooner argues in "A Dialogue on OWLing in the Writing Lab: Some Thoughts about Online Writing Labs," such essential aspects of the writing conference as facial expressions, tone of voice, gestures, and pauses for thought are lost in online tutorials (6–8). In making judgments about what advice to give a writer, the tutor must depend on the implied rhetorical context surrounding the piece of writing, the implied personality of the writer embodied in the "voice" of the piece, and any information a writer volunteers. Tutors who enjoy the interpersonal aspects of face-to-face tutoring are sometimes reluctant, at first, to engage in email tutorials. In "The Anxieties of Distance: Online Tutors Reflect," David Á. Carlson and Eileen Apperson-Williams observe, "For us, the face-to-face relationship is one of the joys, as well as a reason for success in a tutoring session. With online tutoring, this relationship is severed. The tutoring table is replaced with a computer screen: cold, sterile, and, to many, uninviting" (129).

Despite such drawbacks, tutoring via email has some definite advantages. As Carlson and Apperson-Williams suggest, email tutorials do away with some of the personal anxieties that accompany face-to-face meetings and "foreground students' texts instead of the mediated relationships between tutors and students" (134). Similarly, David Coogan argues that the anonymity of email tutoring allows the tutor to speak more frankly about what he or she sees in a writer's text. In "E-mail Tutoring: A New Way to Do New Work," he says, "E-mail enabled me to perform close readings of student work—or more precisely, of the student—without the old fear of 'how will the student react?' What seems like a disadvantage (not seeing the student) can at times be an advantage" (176). Coogan concludes that focusing on email text puts the emphasis of tutoring where it belongs—back on the writing itself.

Of course, such a focus raises ethical concerns about whether an online tutor, unable to engage in a timely dialogue, might simply revise student writers' papers, making the OWL a drop-off editing service. For this reason, a number of experienced online tutors recommend limiting commentary to general issues, such as structure, development of ideas, and overall impressions, rather than to specific issues, such as punctuation and sentence errors—limitations that may run counter to student writers' needs. Other experienced tutors suggest using the "comment" function of their word processor to give student writers feedback without changing the text itself. Such feedback can range from remarks about structure and content to instructions on how to correct simple errors in punctuation, and tutors often find themselves in the same dilemmas they confront in face-to-face tutorials—forced to decide to what extent they should be directive or nondirective. In "Protocols and Process in Online Tutoring," George Cooper, Kara Bui, and Linda Riker advise tutors to set a friendly, informal tone at the start of the tutorial, thus beginning the process of building an interpersonal relationship with the writer. They also suggest that tutors make frequent use of questions to encourage a dialogue with the writer—and to make it clear that much of the responsibility for the piece of writing rests with the writer. To help students improve grammar and style without resorting to proofreading, tutors should identify patterns of error in a piece of writing and make sample corrections that guide revision. Finally, to leave a student writer feeling confident in his or her ability to revise, they recommend closing asynchronous online tutor-ing sessions by summarizing strengths and weaknesses in the student's text and restating plans for revision (92–97).

Synchronous tutoring through an online environment that permits a tutor and a student to interact virtually in real time may help writing centers avoid the drawbacks of email while retaining most of the interpersonal features of face-to-face tutoring. Some writing centers use Second Life, an electronic envi-ronment in which the avatars of tutor and student can meet, review a paper, and discuss options for revision (Carpenter and Griffin 8–12). Others make use of Adobe Connect, Wimba Pronto, WCOnline, or other software pro-grams that offer various levels of video, audio, and text-sharing capabilities (McKinney 11–12). In a 2008 *Kairos* article, "Expanding the Space of f2f," Melanie Yergeau, Katie Wozniak, and Peter Vandenberg dub synchronous online interactions "audio-video-textual conferencing," or AVT tutoring. As they argue, "AVT recovers the interpersonal connection so difficult to con-struct in asynchronous methods. It does so by sustaining the paralinguistic channels of communication operative in a f2f setting—gesticulation, tone of voice (which enables more accurate expression and interpretation of emotion), facial expression, and so on." AVT conferences, they add, do not fully replicate the dynamics of a face-to-face session, but they do allow a more immediate and complete dialogue between tutor and student than asynchronous tutoring. On the other hand, both tutors and students must become well acquainted with the features of the conferencing program before they can effectively inter-act. One advantage of Wimba is that it permits tutoring sessions to be recorded and archived. This function allows students to keep a copy of the tutorial for future reference—an advantage in that the student can focus more on the original tutorial and less on note taking or other attempts to recall the tutor's comments. Wimba records in MP4 files that can be transmitted to a number of sources, such as iPhone Video, iPod, cell phones, thus making them readily accessible to the student in a number of communication venues. In addition, Wimba's MP4 files can be saved and archived by the writing center, so a large number of recorded actual tutorials can be used in tutor training.

Although video and audio conferencing offers a closer approximation of face-to-face tutoring, some writing centers elect to use only the audio and text-sharing features of AVT programs. Shareen Grogan, director of the Writing Centers at National University, says, "We don't use the video feature—band-width is already an issue without adding that burden. . . . And my tutors balked at the idea—they work from home, and they said they wanted to stay in their pajamas and not have to clean their rooms. I couldn't argue with that. So we use audio, doc sharing, and text-chats" ("Message"). Grogan recently took the writing centers she directs, which serve multiple campuses in California, 100 percent online. Her tutors now offer only synchronous audio-textual tutori-als to maintain the spontaneity of face-to-face sessions yet avoid some of the pitfalls of email tutoring. As Grogan explains:

> We had online tutoring as a supplement to our face-to-face tutoring, and I always made it synchronous to avoid the whole specter of a drop-off center. I maintained that stance as we went completely online. . . . It's not that I think asynchronous tutoring can't be helpful—I just find it already hard enough to make clear what we do, to get students involved in the hard work of revising. ("Message")

One of the major benefits of synchronous tutoring, she adds, is that "once students are familiar with the platform, our sessions are highly interactive and democratic" ("Review" 6).

Whether via email or an AVT program, online tutoring is perhaps most appropriate in academic settings in which face-to-face tutoring is impractical or inconvenient. Sometimes the physical space of a writing center can be filled to the maximum by a large number of tutorials, and students must either wait in line for a tutoring session or sign up days ahead of time for an appointment. Obviously, this overcrowding can limit the time and number of interactions a student can work with a tutor, and it can affect the timeliness of the tutorial for the assignment the student is completing. Online tutoring can help address these issues in many instances. Then, too, online tutoring allows distance learners to access academic support that might be unavailable to them otherwise. Universities with a single campus and a relatively small student population will perhaps continue to offer primarily face-to-face tutorial services. In any case, the extent to which a writer benefits from either online or face-to-face tutoring will depend not only on his or her attitude and energy but also on the training, insight, and enthusiasm the tutor brings to the tutorial.

MULTIMODAL TUTORING

One of the most significant changes in writing center work during the first decade of this century was the transformation of the writing center into the multiliteracy center that focuses on multimodal communication. Communication has changed dramatically since the introduction of the Internet and has generated "an increasing reliance on multiple semiotic components" (Sheridan 1).

The multiliteracy center responds to these "multiple semiotic components" as "occasions for further textuality" (Scholes 16) and the opportunity for a "broadening of mission" as "rhetorical theory is being reformulated to account for multimodality" (Sheridan 3). As David Sheridan states:

> In short, our culture is changing; the academy is changing; English studies, rhetorical studies, literacy studies, and composition studies are all changing. Nearly every sector and institution is participating in a shift that involves a more capacious embrace of semiotic possibility: an embrace that comprehends images, words, and sounds. What about writing centers? How are we responding to these changes? (4)

One of the ways writing centers are responding to these changes is through an expansion of the role of the tutor to include multimodal tutoring. Christina Murphy and Lory Hawkes in "The Future of Multiliteracy Centers in the E-World: An Exploration of Cultural Narratives and Cultural Transformations" envision the multimodal tutor as a "digital content specialist" who is versed in the e-literacies of "(a) digital technology (digital literacies), (b) images and design (visual literacies), (c) using the Internet to search for information (information literacies), and (d) the capacity to work electronically in international settings and groups (global literacies)." As Murphy and Hawkes contend, "Decidedly, the future of the Writing Center will be shaped by its digital awareness and the contributions of digital content specialists to student engagement and instruction via electronic methods" (p. 362).

For some tutors, the idea of multimodal tutoring and working as a "digital content specialist" might seem overwhelming. The thought of being well versed in multiple literacies might seem alien, at best, to almost everything the tutor is used to doing in traditional tutorials on print-based texts. What is reassuring, though, is that multimodal tutoring shares a great deal in common with traditional tutoring. The tutor still creates an interpersonal relationship with the writer. The tutorial is highly individualized. The focus remains on the writer and his or her strategies to design, develop, and structure a means to communicate ideas and experiences to an audience. The tutor's role is assistive and should be identified by the writer with opportunities for the tutor and writer to explore options and generate ideas for shaping the tutorial in productive ways.

Even with the added dimensions of multimodal tutoring, some tutors find the idea of using the e-literacies to complement and extend traditional tutoring very exciting. As Murphy and Hawkes point out, this new model is empowering in what it adds to redefining the paradigm of writing instruction. There are new skills, ideas, practices, and approaches for the tutor to learn, and that challenge in itself can be very engaging. Many tutors find the idea of being on the cutting edge in learning how to tutor with new media a gratifying experience because it meets the needs of writers in contemporary academic, professional, and personal settings. As Luke, a junior tutor in a writing center that is beginning to implement multimodal tutoring, said, "It's a whole new world out there."

A Multimodal Tutorial

Clark came to the writing center with a project for his senior-level American Legal History class. His instructor's assignment called for a discussion of a twentieth-century Supreme Court case. Students were to analyze the cultural setting of the case and its ramifications and do so using a range of electronic media as a complement to their written work.

His tutor, Alicia, began by asking Clark about his understanding of the assignment. Specifically, she was interested in how Clark saw the multimedia aspects of his assignment fitting into his research and his writing. She wanted to be sure that Clark conceptualized the multimedia components not as add-ons but as integral parts of how Clark would communicate his ideas and perspectives.

Clark said he knew everything needed to fit together. "It's like a puzzle. I have to make all the parts work together in order to get my ideas across well."

Alicia explained that three components would likely impact the work Clark was doing. The first was rhetoric — or all the elements involved in writing in a clear and organized manner that conveyed his knowledge of the subject and that structured his argument for the reader. The second was cultural interpretation, which involved heuristic thinking about how the cultural and historical context influenced the issues in this Supreme Court case and its outcomes.

"So far, we're in the realm of any traditional written assignment," she said. "And although it's important to remember that your written analysis is the most important thing, the multimedia sources you use should not just function as ancillaries but as tools integral to the primary goal of communicating your ideas effectively."

"Got it," Clark said.

"Now, because you're using multimedia sources, what would the third aspect be?"

"Working them in well," Clark replied.

"Yes, and that involves elements of visual design," Alicia said. "The integration of the multimedia components has to be done in a way that adds to, not detracts from, the flow of the text itself. This involves layout issues as well as ease of access and of use within the document."

Clark said that of the various cases and historical eras he studied in the class, the ones that caught his attention most were those from the civil rights movement of the 1950s and 60s. He especially was drawn to cases that challenged the Civil Rights Act of 1964 — the most interesting one, to him, being *Katzenbach v. McClung* in 1964, which challenged the constitutionality of the act's public accommodations section.

"Tell me about that case," Alicia said.

"Well," Clark replied, "the Civil Rights Act of 1964 outlawed segregation in schools and public places like restaurants and hotels. Almost the minute the Civil Rights Act was passed, there were legal challenges to its right to impose regulations on public businesses. Ollie McClung owned a barbecue restaurant in Birmingham, Alabama, that did not permit blacks to enter and be waited on. And McClung sued saying the government had no right to tell him how to conduct the private business he owned. The Supreme Court said, though, in a unanimous decision that it did have that right because over 50 percent of the food McClung used in his restaurant was from suppliers outside Alabama.

Therefore, McClung's actions in discriminating against blacks in his restaurant placed an undue burden on interstate commerce in terms of the movement of goods, people, and information from one state to another."

"So how do you intend to present your ideas on this case?" Alicia asked.

"Well, I have to discuss the racial climate of the 1960s and why the Civil Rights Act of 1964 was enacted. Then I need to lay out the issues that created the challenge from Ollie McClung and discuss how people responded to the public accommodations issues in Title II of the Act, which was the basis for the decision in *Katzenbach v. McClung*. Some people thought basing the decision on the interstate commerce issue weakened the decision and that the case should have been decided on equal protection under the law—just like the landmark *Brown v. Board of Education* case was in 1954. I have to talk about the implications of this decision on other cases and on American society itself."

"Good. You seem to have the structure for your work clearly in mind," Alicia said. "What types of writing do you think you will need in your paper?"

"Well, I have to summarize the case, presenting both sides of the argument. And I have to be able to evaluate the influence of the case on society."

"Okay," Alicia said, "but since this is going to be a multimedia project, what are your ideas on that? What types of media do you intend to use, and how will you integrate them into your writing?"

Clark planned to add links to several research databases, including www. oyez.org, a multimedia database that compiles information on Supreme Court cases; the Civil Rights Archives Digital Library; and the Television News of the Civil Rights Era archive at the University of Virginia. He also planned to use the *New York Times* archives, the iTunes Podcast Library, which contains interviews with civil rights leaders, and YouTube, which has a large number of videos to which he could direct readers.

"So from these sources, you would have text, video, audio, and photographs that would give insights into the civil rights era. What are your thoughts on how to work all this information into your project and make it accessible to your readers?"

"I'm not as clear on that. I was hoping you could discuss that with me and give me some guidelines."

"Sure. You're covering an enormous amount of information here, even if you narrow your project down to a focus on the *Katzenbach v. McClung* case and its implications. One advantage of using multimedia in your writing is that it enables you to provide links to information as a complement to the ideas in your text. The reader can choose to follow the links or not."

"Right. I like that part a lot," Clark said. "Everybody can read this paper differently, depending on the links each person follows."

"Now let's talk about some practical aspects of creating a multimedia document," Alicia said. "It's important that the resources you use enhance your narrative. You don't want to direct people away from your text to links that do not really advance your ideas. You want to be sure the information is relevant and on point. And you want to try out all your links to be sure not only that they work and are active but also that the sites are easy to navigate. It's not going to help your project if you link to a site where people will have a time-consuming and frustrating experience trying to locate the information you want them to find. Ease of use and accessibility are important."

"I understand."

"And of course," Alicia said, "you want to be sure that all of your references to links are properly labeled and identified with the date, source, and so forth. Also, it sounds like everything you will be referencing is in the public domain or available for free use, but be sure to check on that with every reference you create. Some sites have copyrighted material and images that cannot be copied—even into a document like yours that will not be for public use. And if you plan to post any or all of your information to a blog or similar site in the future, this copyright issue becomes very important."

"Right."

"Visual placement in your text is important, too. You don't want to overburden your text with hundreds of links. This makes for difficult reading and can break up the flow of your argument. Use the links judiciously. One thing I recommend is to run short teaser statements in sidebars alongside the text and to make each teaser itself a hyperlink."

"Could you give me an example?"

"Let's say you're writing about the civil rights efforts in the South to integrate public facilities. You could insert a pull quote right next to that section of your text that would quote Martin Luther King Jr., commenting on this issue. The quotation itself would be a hyperlink to a resource or database that would provide even more information."

"I like that idea."

"But you don't have to restrict yourself to words for your hyperlinks. You can have pictures of people or images of historical documents open up into a video or audio through the links you create."

"If I do this right, I could have lots of ways for people to experience these ideas."

"That's right, Clark. It would be a very interesting and in-depth document to read. I'm sure I would enjoy reading it myself—although the term *reading* isn't quite right, is it? I would enjoy reading, viewing, listening, and interacting with your project."

"Thanks, Alicia. This has given me some great ideas. After I get my first draft together, can I bring it back here and show it to you—you know, get some feedback?"

"Of course. And also if you decide you need some help even as you are creating your draft, just come on back, and we will work on it together."

"Great. That's wonderful to know. I hope to be seeing you with a draft soon."

"I'll look forward to it, Clark."

A tutor in the writing center for five years, Alicia began as a sophomore undergraduate tutor and worked through her junior and senior years. When she assisted Clark, she had been a graduate tutor for two years as she completed her master's degree in chemistry. In reflecting on her experiences through follow-up conversations with her writing center director, she said what struck her most was how common it was becoming to tutor students working on multimedia projects:

"It used to be that this was a rare event, and I remember how nervous I felt the first time this occurred. The idea of talking with students on how to integrate various media and electronic resources into their writing was rather scary at first. But I began to realize that this was the way of the future, and I wanted to be a part of it, even if I was a bit out of my element at first.

It's definitely a generational thing. When I started tutoring five years ago as a sophomore, Facebook was not the phenomenon it is now, and Twitter did not even exist. Five years ago, the kids who are in college now as freshmen were maybe thirteen years old, and, even then, they knew more about using computers and other technologies than a lot of us know today. When a new batch of freshmen arrives five years from now, their sense of how one communicates in this world may well be entirely digital—they will read books and newspapers on a Kindle or another such device, communicate via Facebook, Twitter, and blogs, research and write through electronic sources, and on and on. Many communication technologies that don't exist now will be important and customary five years from now. That's how rapidly this all is changing, and writing centers can be an important contributor to helping students progress in their communication skills. Really, tutoring for multimedia is, in many ways, like tutoring for more conventional texts. You still have to have a good idea, communicate it in a clear and effective way, be organized in your thinking, and have a good command of the conventions of your genre. You still have to be creative as a writer—and as a tutor, too."

ON BECOMING AN EFFECTIVE TUTOR

We hope that investigating the tutoring process from a number of perspectives has revealed to you its philosophical complexity, interpersonal richness, and educational significance. We also hope that it has intensified both your desire to be a tutor and your willingness to continue learning how to improve your craft. Actually, tutoring is more than a craft; it is also an art form—one that will continue to evolve as you acquire more experience and wisdom. Everyone who has ever tutored has stood where you stand now—at the beginning of the journey into tutoring or a little bit further down the road. We assume you have started on that journey because you believe in the value of your work as a tutor. That value is often hard to measure in a quantitative sense, but it is exceptionally easy to experience as personal satisfaction when the work you do is helpful to another. We believe that assisting others is best achieved in an informed practice that blends experience, theory, and reflection. We hope this sourcebook will assist you in developing a philosophy and style of your own and, ultimately, in achieving your full potential as a tutor.

Works Cited

Bawarshi, Anis, and Stephanie Pelkowski. "Postcolonialism and the Idea of a Writing Center." *Writing Center Journal* 19.2 (1999): 41–58. Print.

Boquet, Elizabeth H. "Intellectual Tug of War: Snapshots of Life in the Center." *Stories from the Center: Connecting Narrative and Theory in the Writing Center.* Ed. Lyn Craigue Briggs and Meg Woolbright. Urbana, IL: NCTE, 2000. Print.

---. *Noise from the Writing Center.* Logan, UT: Utah State UP, 2002. Print.

Carlson, David A., and Eileen Apperson-Williams. "The Anxieties of Distance: Online Tutors Reflect." *Taking Flight with OWLs: Examining Writing Center Work.* Ed. James A. Inmon and Donna M. Sewell. Mahwah: Lawrence Erlbaum. 129–40. Print.

Carpenter, Russell, and Meghan Griffin. "Exploring Second Life: Recent Developments in Virtual Writing Centers." *Writing Lab Newsletter* 34.7 (2010): 8–12. Print.

Coogan, David. "E-mail Tutoring: A New Way to Do New Work." *Computers and Composition* 12 (1995): 171–81. Print.

Cooper, George, Kara Bui, and Linda Riker. "Protocols and Process in Online Tutoring." *A Tutor's Guide: Helping Writers One to One.* Ed. Ben Rafoth. Portsmouth: Boynton/Cook, 2000. 129–39. Print.

Cooper, Marilyn. "Really Useful Knowledge: A Cultural Studies Agenda for Writing Centers. *Writing Center Journal* 14.2 (1994): 97–111. Print.

Elbow, Peter. *Writing with Power: Techniques for Mastering the Writing Process.* New York: Oxford UP, 1981. Print.

Foster, David. "The Challenge of Contingency: Process and the Turn to the Social in Composition." *Post-Process Theory: Beyond the Writing-Process Paradigm.* Ed. Thomas Kent. Carbondale: Southern Illinois UP, 1999. 149–62. Print.

Freed, Stacey. "Subjectivity in the Tutorial Session: How Far Can We Go?" *Writing Center Journal* 10.1 (1989): 39–43. Print.

Fulwiler, Toby. "Provocative Revision." *Writing Center Journal* 12.2 (1992): 190–204. Print.

Grimm, Nancy. *Good Intentions: Writing Center Work for Postmodern Times.* Portsmouth: Heinemann, 1999. Print.

---. "The Regulatory Role of the Writing Center: Coming to Terms with a Loss of Innocence." *Writing Center Journal* 17.1 (1996): 5–29. Print.

Grogan, Shareen. Message to Steve Sherwood. 30 June 2010. E-mail.

---. "A Review of iLinc, A Voice and Video over the Internet Protocol (VOIP) Conferencing System." *Writing Lab Newsletter* 32.6 (2008): 6–7. Print.

Harris, Muriel. "Cultural Conflicts in the Writing Center: Expectations and Assumptions of ESL Students." *Writing in Multicultural Settings.* Ed. Carol Severino, Juan C. Guerra, and Johnnella E. Butler. New York: Modern Language Association, 1997. 220–33. Print.

---. *Teaching One-to-One: The Writing Conference.* Urbana: NCTE, 1986. Print.

Kent, Thomas, ed. *Post-Process Theory: Beyond the Writing-Process Paradigm.* Carbondale: Southern Illinois UP, 1999. Print.

McKinney, Jackie Grutsch. "Geek in the Center: Audio-Visual-Textual Conferencing Options." *Writing Lab Newsletter* 34.9/10 (2010): 11–12. Print.

Meyer, Emily, and Louise Z. Smith. *The Practical Tutor*. New York: Oxford UP, 1987. Print.

Murphy, Christina. "Freud in the Writing Center: the Psychoanalytics of Tutoring Well." *Writing Center Journal* 10.1 (1989): 13–18. Print.

Olson, Gary A. "Toward a Post-Process Composition: Abandoning the Rhetoric of Assertion." *Post-Process Theory: Beyond the Writing-Process Paradigm*. Ed. Thomas Kent. Carbondale: Southern Illinois UP, 1999. 7–15. Print.

Scholes, Robert. *Textual Power: Literary Theory and the Teaching of English*. New Haven: Yale UP, 1985. Print.

Selfe, Cynthia. "Students Who Teach Us: A Case Study in a New Media Designer." *Writing New Media: Theory and Applications for Expanding the Teaching of Composition*. Ed. Anne Frances Wysocki, et al. Logan: Utah State UP, 2004. 43–66. Print.

Severino, Carol. "Rhetorically Analyzing Collaboration(s)." *The Writing Center Journal* 13.1 (1992): 53–64. Print.

Sheridan, David M. Introduction. *Multiliteracy Centers: Writing Center Work, New Media, and Multimodal Rhetoric*. Ed. David M. Sheridan and James A. Inman. Cresskill: Hampton, 2010. 1–16. Print.

Sherwood, Steve. "Censoring Students, Censoring Ourselves: Constraining Conversations in the Writing Center." *Writing Center Journal* 20.1 (1999): 51–60. Print.

Spooner, Michael. "A Dialogue on OWLing in the Writing Lab: Some Thoughts about Online Writing Labs." *Writing Lab Newsletter* 18.6 (1994): 6–8. Print.

Stegner, Wallace. *On the Teaching of Creative Writing*. Hanover: UP of New England, 1988. Print.

Tapscott, Don. *The Digital Economy: Promise and Peril in the Age of Networked Intelligence*. New York: McGraw-Hill, 1996. Print.

Tiberius, Richard G. "The Why of Teacher/Student Relationships." *Teaching Effectiveness: Toward the Best in the Academy* 6.1 (1994–95): 1–2. Print.

Wollbright, Meg. "The Politics of Tutoring: Feminism within the Patriarchy." *Writing Center Journal* 13.1. (1992): 16–30. Print.

Yergeau, Melanie, Katie Wozniak, and Peter Vandenberg. "Expanding the Space of f2f." *Kairos* 13.1 (2008): n. pag. Web. 25 June 2010.

PART

II

Readings: Entering the
Professional Conversation

These groups of essays introduce you to many of the ideas and issues currently defining the practice of tutoring. In a sense, they provide a body of knowledge about the function of tutoring in the broader context of education theory.

The theorists and practitioners whose work is presented here examine the role of the tutor, speculate on the types of instructional and interpersonal transactions that occur in tutorials, consider tutoring in relation to current ideas about composition instruction, discuss the significance of multicultural issues in tutoring, and review the benefits and pitfalls of tutoring in virtual environments.

We have grouped these essays into four sections that reflect the key ideas and common concerns structuring each: (1) "Theoretical Constructs," a selection of essays that introduces and explores some of the underlying philosophies of instruction in the writing center; (2) "What We Talk about When We Talk about Tutoring," a selection that investigates the interpersonal dynamics of tutoring and offers different approaches to critiquing students' texts; (3) "Affirming Diversity;" and (4) "Explorations: The Multimodal Writing Center," a group of essays that explores the difficulties and advantages of online tutoring and tutoring in multimodal settings using a broad range of electronic media.

You will find that the readings in the *Sourcebook* are a blend of classic essays that have had a lasting influence on writing center scholarship and of newer essays that address contemporary challenges and also consider future directions for the writing center and its primary work of tutoring. The essays span essentially the last quarter of a century in writing center scholarship from 1984 through 2010. We believe that the range of topics discussed, the dialectics involved in point and counterpoint investigations of major theories and practices, and the philosophical and practice-oriented speculations on what transformations the writing center and tutoring will continue to undergo provide an insightful look into the writing center discipline. Most importantly, the readings in the *Sourcebook* offer you the opportunity to explore major ideas in writing center scholarship and develop your own interpretation of their relevance and application to your work as a tutor.

THEORETICAL CONSTRUCTS

Stephen M. North's "The Idea of a Writing Center" and Andrea Lunsford's "Collaboration, Control, and the Idea of a Writing Center" examine the paradigms, or models, of composition instruction that have shaped writing center tutorials. As discussed in the previous section, such paradigms include current traditional rhetoric, expressivism, and social constructionism. In responding to the constraints of current traditional rhetoric, North rejects the stereotypical image of the writing center as a "fix-it shop" and "skills center" for remediation. Instead, he validates the principles of expressivism in viewing the writing center as an instructional site in which "the object is to make sure that writers, and not necessarily their texts, are what get changed by instruction." As tutors, "our job is to produce better writers, not better writing," North claims, moving the focus of writing center instruction from the text to the writer. Lunsford provides an overview of how writing centers have progressed from the "storehouses" of current traditional rhetoric, to the "garrets" of expressivism, to the "Burkean parlors" of social constructionism. Like North, she finds limited value in the emphases of current traditional rhetoric, but she also challenges expressivism's belief in the interiority of knowledge and its romantic view of the writer as a solitary creator. In an interesting philosophical twist, in "Revisiting 'The Idea of a Writing Center,'" North returns a decade later to reevaluate his original essay and discovers that his earlier views of tutoring may have reflected a naiveté bordering on romanticism. In "Revisiting," he expresses his reservations about his earlier "Idea" and offers new perspectives by investigating three relationships: (1) tutor and writer, (2) tutor and instructor, and (3) tutor and institution.

Peter Vandenberg's "Lessons of Inscription: Tutor Training and the 'Professional Conversation'" and Steve Sherwood's "Portrait of the Tutor as an Artist: Lessons No One Can Teach" are reflections on what best prepares tutors to fulfill their roles. Vandenberg discusses two approaches to tutor training: (1) tutoring manuals that emphasize skill sets that tutors need as well as guidelines to follow in tutorials and (2) collections of scholarly readings in the discipline that introduce tutors to the major ideas that underlie writing center theory and practice. Vandenberg is critical of the tutoring-manual approach as reductive, at best, and too simplistic, at worst. However, he directs his strongest criticism toward preparing tutors through readings in the discipline. He finds little value in introducing beginning tutors to the "most painful and factious" points of contention in the field, and, second, he argues that turning peer tutors into "miniprofessors" stifles their instinctual abilities and their personal efforts to discover meaningful tutoring methods that resonate with their own understanding and values.

Steve Sherwood's essay is a philosophical counter to Vandenberg's argument that a knowledge of leading ideas and even controversial ideas in writing center scholarship stifles a tutor's growth into his or her own style of tutoring.

The opposite is true, Sherwood argues. Knowledge enriches practice and can be liberating in opening the tutor's mind to new ideas. Drawing upon classical rhetoric, Sherwood distinguishes between the tutor as an "artisan" and an "artist." The "artisan" tutor understands tutoring as a set of rules and skills that can be applied in a range of tutorials. The "artist" tutor draws upon a triad of abilities: knowledge, experience, and talent. The "artist" tutor knows that tutoring itself is an "art" form in that no one set of rules or skills can be applied in all situations. Instead, the tutor must draw on all the tools at his or her disposal and be open to improvising, synthesizing, and creating from knowledge, experience, and talent in order to respond to the challenges inherent in each tutorial.

WHAT WE TALK ABOUT WHEN WE TALK ABOUT TUTORING

In 1991, Jeff Brooks's essay "Minimalist Tutoring: Making the Student Do All the Work" was published in *Writing Lab Newsletter* and instantly became both an iconic and a controversial piece whose ideas continue to reverberate through the writing center discipline to this day. Brooks's essay revealed a divide among writing center professionals over directive and nondirective tutoring. Brooks's minimalist, or nondirective, method advocated a hands-off approach by the tutor. The tutor was to do none of the work for the student of proofreading, revising, and so forth. Instead, the tutor was to engage the student in a series of Socratic questions that brought the student toward the insights necessary to write effectively. As Brooks stated: "Fixing flawed papers is easy; showing the students how to fix their papers is complex and difficult."

Many writing center professionals cheered Brooks's approach, seeing it as the answer to the negative "fix-it shop" view of the writing center that Stephen North described. Now tutors could do what North had called for—focus on improving the writer and not the writing. Others, though, challenged Brooks's ideas as too formulaic and simplistic and even, in some instances, unethical. Was it ethical, some asked, for tutors to withhold the help and information an individual student might need?

Challenges to minimalist, nondirective tutoring were many, including several contained in this section. Linda K. Shamoon and Deborah H. Burns in "A Critique of Pure Tutoring" find value in both approaches and argue that tutors should be encouraged to explore both directive and nondirective practices in their tutoring in order to be the most effective instructors for their students. They state that the result of such a synthesis "would be an enrichment of tutoring repertoires, stronger connection between the writing center and writers in other disciplines, and increased attention to the cognitive, social, and rhetorical needs of writers at all stages of development."

Steven J. Corbett in "Tutoring Style, Tutoring Ethics: The Continuing Relevance of the Directive/Nondirective Instructional Debate" provides an overview of the issues that continue to reverberate in writing center circles since the publication of Brooks's essay. Corbett states that, not surprisingly, the directive/nondirective debate represents not just instructional but also political issues. It touches such issues as tutor authority, tutor–tutee trust, philosophies of tutor training, and writing process versus product theories and practices. Corbett encourages a reassessment of the implications of both directive and nondirective tutoring and states that "tutors need to be aware of the rhetorical complexity—both interpersonal and intertextual—that any given tutorial can entail." He urges viewing tutoring as a "practice along a continuum of instructional choices both socially collaborative and individually empowering."

Carl Glover in "*Kairos* and the Writing Center: Modern Perspectives on an Ancient Idea" also explores the "individually empowering" components of tutoring practice that Corbett discusses. Glover finds in the classical idea of *kairos* an opportunity to view the tutoring session as one that draws on improvisation in the truest sense of being creative in the moment. Each tutorial is a rhetorical situation that is unique and that cannot be repeated. In a sense, the tutor and student create the moment, and, much like a jazz riff, the creative energy of the moment shapes the contours of the tutorial's interactions. *Kairos* is being "in the moment" and appreciating its potential. Like Steve Sherwood's tutor as "artist," Glover, too, emphasizes looking at the creative aspects of tutoring and the potential for responding to each writer on an individual basis rather than in terms of rules, guidelines, or polarities like those inherent in the directive/nondirective divide. Glover's focus is on how tutors can interpret and respond to opportune moments of insight in discovering new directions for writing center work.

The history of writing center practice reveals an extensive examination of ethics in relation to writing center values and outcomes. As an instructional act, tutoring is conceptualized and carried out in a complex network of ethical issues that extends to all the constituencies the writing center serves. In "Identifying Our Ethical Responsibility: A Criterion-Based Approach," David Bringhurst points out that writing center professionals "are often explicitly or implicitly asked to defend our conduct and even our existence to one or more constituencies at any given time." This is especially true of tutoring, which is freighted with considerations of tutor authority and the tutor's possible usurping of the instructor's role. To aid tutors and directors in responding to these issues, Bringhurst proposes a criterion-based approach that is grounded in the realization that "any solutions we propose to ethical problems must include an ethical response to each of the constituencies affected or we risk a response that is ethical for one constituent but unethical for another."

As Bringhurst points out, the question of tutor authority is a complex issue and one that can be viewed from multiple perspectives, many of which can be controversial. Peter Carino in "Power and Authority in Peer Tutoring" explains that the idea of "peership" in peer tutoring has served writing centers well in presenting themselves as "nonhierarchical and nonthreatening collaborative environments." But is the idea of "peership" what it seems, or are there issues of power and authority, however subtle and however hidden, within this construct? Carino explores the dynamics of the tutoring relationship by focusing on what is often unacknowledged in the idea of "peership"—that tutor and tutee often share unequal relationships in terms of "rhetorical knowledge and academic success." Carino's analysis of "power and authority" in peer tutoring extends to an analysis of the implications of these factors in shaping the potential for collaboration in the peer tutor and tutee relationship.

Terese Thonus and Neal Lerner explore the concepts of success and effectiveness by examining different aspects of writing centers and of writing tutorials. In "Tutor and Student Assessments of Academic Writing Tutorials: What Is 'Success'?" Thonus questions what we know about success in tutorials and how the claims of various models of tutoring actually do stand up to assessment. Among the views Thonus questions as more *ethos* than reality are (1) the view that writing centers remain neutral and separated from the evaluation of writing (a perspective espoused by North in "The Idea of a Writing Center") and (2) the view that there is equality of status between tutor and the tutee in peer tutoring. Both positions might seem to tilt tutorials in the direction of nondirective tutoring. However, as Thonus argues, "many studies of tutorial effectiveness lack adequate analyses of tutorial talk" in order to determine which modes of tutorial interaction are most effective. Thonus uses the framework of sociolinguistics and ethnographic research to examine the implications of "tutorial talk" and to provide greater insight into the psychodynamics and possible hidden agendas in tutorials. Neal Lerner in "Writing Center Assessment: Searching for the 'Proof' of Our Effectiveness" provides a historical, theoretical, and methodological overview of assessment research in writing centers, including specific areas and methods for studying "effects." Lerner considers writing center assessment in the context of "the larger assessment movement in higher education" and finds not only useful tools that can be adapted to writing centers but also "important cautions about the nature of assessment work and its pitfalls." Lerner's primary intent is to provide a clearer understanding of research on writing center "effects" and "to put into a critical context the common call to investigate how well we are doing."

Two essays explore the range and versatility of the writing center through two models of outreach in tutoring. In "Exporting Writing Center Pedagogy: Writing Fellows Programs as Ambassadors for the Writing Center," Carol Severino and Megan Knight describe a program they established at the University of Iowa in which Writing Fellows from the writing center are assigned to instructors across the curriculum to work with students in their classes on drafts of two course papers. The relationship established between the writing center and instructors across the curriculum via the Writing Fellows enforces good will and positive connections, introduces instructors and students to the ways tutoring works and thus its numerous benefits, and serves as a means for connecting and promoting the writing center to the broader campus. Jacob S. Blumner in "A Writing Center–Education Department Collaboration" describes a model of "active professional development" that targets students who would "most benefit from the experience of being tutors." Blumner considers education majors from all disciplines as an important target population because "education students stand uniquely to benefit from the experiences of tutoring in a writing center. Once these students become teachers, they will need to work individually with their students." Thus, the experience they get in tutorials will help prepare them for individual work with students and also expand their interpersonal and instructional skills.

AFFIRMING DIVERSITY

Diversity is a central principle and reality of writing centers, which consistently interact with a broad range of students, faculty, staff, alumni, and community members from different backgrounds. Issues of culture, race, ethnicity, age, sexual-orientation, gender, religion, and socioeconomic status are aspects of tutorials for both the tutor and the tutee. Physical and learning disabilities and learning styles are also aspects of many tutorials.

The ways tutors conceptualize, understand, and respond to diversity are highly important components of tutoring effectively. Modern and postmodern theorists on writing instruction consider the epistemological, or knowledge-related, issues that define tutorials to be influenced strongly by diversity issues—a point of view expressed by the authors in this section. Anne DiPardo in "'Whispers of Coming and Going': Lessons from Fannie" examines the interpersonal dynamics involved in the tutor's role. She presents the tutor–student relationship in terms of multicultural sensitivity, emphasizing how tutors can facilitate successful interactions with students from diverse cultural backgrounds. She tells of Fannie, a Native American student, and of the dialogues through which Fannie and her tutor negotiated a working relationship sensitive to the "hidden corners" of a student's cultural heritage. As DiPardo states, "Often placed on the front lines of efforts to provide respectful, insightful attention to these students' diverse struggles with academic discourse, writing tutors likewise occupy multiple roles, remaining learners even while emerging as teachers, perennially searching for a suitable social stance. . . ."

Julie Neff in "Learning Disabilities and the Writing Center" explores through case histories and narrative examples the value of tutoring as a one-to-one, individual process. Neff focuses on the educational and sociocultural backgrounds of students with learning disabilities that can factor into the tutoring process, and she presents narratives that affirm the value of shared assumptions when working with students who are differently abled.

Sharon A. Myers in "Reassessing the 'Proofreading Trap': ESL Tutoring and Writing Instruction" shares Neff's view of sensitivity to differences—in this case, cross-cultural differences that may influence the quality and effectiveness of tutorials when tutors work with ESL students. Myers challenges the common practice of focusing tutoring sessions for ESL writers on proofreading for surface-level errors while overlooking ways to enhance the intellectual development of ESL students as writers. She also takes on the issue of minimalist, nondirective tutoring by questioning whether this is the best approach—or even an effective approach—when working with ESL students.

The authors in "Affirming Diversity" are united by the view that tutors need to develop a critical consciousness when working with students from diverse backgrounds. The aim of this critical consciousness is to help students succeed in the university without surrendering their sense of who they are. This important aim is also endorsed by writing center theorists who explore the social and political implications of gender, identity, and racial differences and who contend that tutorials can reflect hidden or overt agendas of political and social power that favor majority values. This focus on imposing one set of values on the tutoring session and its outcomes can undermine a student's sense of self. To avoid this destructive consequence, theorists of identity politics urge a self-reflective practice for tutors that engages them in examining the power dynamics involved in their tutorials so that their practice can become more egalitarian.

Harry Denny extends this critique in "Queering the Writing Center" by urging centers to adopt the insights and methods of queer theory. As he argues, writing centers that alert student writers to the role language plays in constructing knowledge and social identity can help the writers "gain a modicum of agency" in using language to construct their own knowledge and identity. In this approach, Denny explains, tutors empower a student writer to express ideas that defy, critique, or clash with those held by privileged members of the academic culture, including the tutors themselves. Ideally, by "queering sessions—seeking strategic occasions to subvert conventional dynamics," a tutor and a student collaborate in the discovery of creative ways to meet professors' writing assignments without betraying the student's own vision. Contemporary writing center and queer theorists share key goals, Denny contends, including their ongoing effort to bring to light the normalizing forces of society and to equip people with different perspectives or identities to resist these forces.

In a similar vein, Nancy Barron and Nancy Grimm call on writing centers to resist the subtle forms that institutional racism can take in tutorials. In "Addressing Racial Diversity in a Writing Center: Stories and Lessons from Two Beginners," Barron and Grimm discuss their attempts, during training sessions, to raise awareness of racism among their writing coaches. As they contend, most writing centers practice—in the tradition of liberal education—a type of institutional "colorblindness" that views students as homogeneous and ignores their differences, including those of class and race. Such a practice, Barron and Grimm argue, not only perpetuates a falsehood but also can silence students of color, preventing them from voicing legitimate criticisms or unusual perspectives and cutting them off from personal experiences and truths that are crucial to writers. Their training efforts confirmed the continuing existence of racism in writing center interactions but also highlighted the difficulties of discussing the issue in tutor training. Some of their "mainstream" coaches "reacted in defense of their schooling, their domination, their identities. They became defensive at the idea of systemic domination and injustice. Many covered their uncomfortable views through denial." In spite of an initial failure to raise the consciousness of their writing coaches, Barron and Grimm continue to view the writing center as a "space for hope, a place to begin" this work. They emphasize the need to address institutional racism in "multidirectional ways" and over extended periods of time.

EXPLORATIONS: THE MULTIMODAL WRITING CENTER

The most significant theoretical movement in contemporary rhetoric and composition, and therefore in writing centers, has resulted from innovations in computer technologies that are leading scholars to redefine what it means to "write." A widespread ability to create and instantly publish on the Internet "texts" that combine words, still images, video, sound effects, and hypertext links has revolutionized communication, including the writing done in or for the classroom. Prominent theorists at work redesigning the field of composition to embrace the new media (also called digital or multimodal media) include Cynthia Selef, Gail Hawisher, Cheryl Ball, Kathleen Blake Yancey, and Andrea Lunsford. They argue that composition specialists must expand their notion of writing to embrace student writers' rhetorical uses of visual and auditory features along with written language to entertain, inform, or persuade an audience.

Long invested in providing online tutorials, writing center professionals are likewise responding—or getting set to respond—to a growing demand from student writers for help with digital texts. A number of scholars, in fact, see the shift from paper to new media as inevitable and argue that writing centers must also make the shift in order to stay relevant. In "The Future of Multiliteracy Centers in the E-World: An Exploration of Cultural Narratives and Cultural Transformation," Christina Murphy and Lory Hawkes contend that writing tutors will soon become "digital content specialists" who continually retool and retrain to stay on the cutting edge of communication technologies. Such digital content specialists not only will assist students with multimodal writing projects, they argue, but also will find new ways to use technology to design interactive learning experiences for students. Murphy and Hawkes also discuss the emergence of multiliteracy centers in the context of a "new historicism" cultural narrative in which the writing center shapes, and is shaped by, the realities of global communication in the e-world of the twenty-first century.

In "Words, "Images, Sounds: Writing Centers as Multiliteracy Centers," David Sheridan, the director of the writing center at Michigan State University, discusses how he already recruits and trains "digital writing consultants" to assist students with multimodal writing projects. As he observes, "In new media, the semiotic whole is greater than the sum of its parts. Words are inextricably linked to other media elements, making it difficult to talk about them in isolation. A multiliteracy consultant . . . would embrace the chance to explore the rhetorical dimensions of all elements, including photographs, color, layout, and navigational scheme." Most writing centers, even those that employ tutors trained to work with digital texts, still do a majority of their work with traditional paper texts, since instructors continue to value and assign them. But as Jackie Grutsch McKinney argues in "New Media Matters: Tutoring in the Late Age of Print," "Writing has evolved with new composing technologies and media, and we must evolve, too, because we are in the writing business." McKinney asserts that we are witnessing in writing centers—as in society as a whole—a "fundamental change in the textual climate" as increasingly nearly all composition is done on screens and is multitextual.

Certainly, the move toward online and multimodal writing invites consideration of the impact of such changes on tutoring. Lisa Bell in "Preserving the Rhetorical Nature of Tutoring When Going Online" contends that the nature of the tutoring relationship has always been based on collaboration. Yet what are the parameters of that collaboration and the implications for interpersonal relationships between tutor and tutee when tutorials are conducted online? Most writing centers now offer tutoring in virtual environments, and with this relatively new approach have come some challenges and concerns. One challenge facing online tutors is how to build interpersonal relationships with student writers. Bell questions whether the personal nature and the rhetorical function of the writing center can be retained in online tutoring, and she offers valuable insights for responding to this challenge when a conventional writing center goes electronic.

The authors in this section explore the transformation of the writing center to the multiliteracy center. The changes they envision for writing centers and for tutoring are widespread. The changes are also under way in a number of writing centers where "digital rhetoric" and "digital media" continue to emerge as the leading means of communication and of writing instruction in the twenty-first century. McKinney perhaps best makes the case for the types of changes that writing centers will need to undertake. She states that "it would be foolish" not to prepare tutors to work with digital texts. And she concludes, "What I have come to believe is that accepting new media texts necessitates rethinking our dominant writing center ideas and revising our common practices."

THEORETICAL CONSTRUCTS

The Idea of a Writing Center

Stephen M. North _____
STATE UNIVERSITY OF NEW YORK AT ALBANY

Stephen M. North contends that many students, writing instructors, and faculty in other disciplines do not understand the role of the writing center. They tend to view the writing center as a "skills center" or "fix-it shop" for grammar correction and writer remediation rather than as a place of active learning and student enrichment. North directs tutors toward examining a student's text as an indicator of the processes that produced it, rather than as a product that must be reworked to meet accepted standards of form and correctness. In this fashion, and in his assertion that tutoring should be student-centered rather than text-oriented, he endorses the primary tenets of expressivism in writing center pedagogy. A classic essay, frequently quoted and cited in writing center scholarship, "The Idea of a Writing Center" is important for tutors in contrasting two models of writing center instruction—one that stresses "the correction of textual problems" and another that focuses on the writer's intellectual and personal involvement in the creation of texts. North's essay is also important for its examination of the tutor's role within a "student-centered" pedagogy in which the writing center's "primary responsibility" and "only reason for being" is "to talk to writers." This essay originally appeared in 1984 in College English.

This is an essay that began out of frustration. Despite the reference to writing centers in the title, it is not addressed to a writing center audience but to what is, for my purposes, just the opposite: those not involved with writing centers. Do not exclude yourself from this group just because you know that writing centers (or labs or clinics or places or however you think of them) exist; "involved" here means having directed such a place, having worked there for a minimum of 100 hours, or, at the very least, having talked about writing of your own there for five or more hours. The source of my frustration? Ignorance: the members of my profession, my colleagues, people I might see at MLA or CCCC or read in the pages of *College English*, do not understand what I do. They do not understand what does happen, what can happen, in a writing center.

Let me be clear here. Misunderstanding is something one expects—and almost gets used to—in the writing center business. The new faculty member in our writing-across-the-curriculum program, for example, who sends his students to get their papers "cleaned up" in the writing center before they

MIS.

hand them in; the occasional student who tosses her paper on our reception desk, announcing that she'll "pick it up in an hour"; even the well-intentioned administrators who are so happy that we deal with "skills" or "fundamentals" or, to use the word that seems to subsume all others, "grammar" (or usually "GRAMMAR")—these are fairly predictable. But from people in English departments, people well trained in the complex relationship between writer and text, so painfully aware, if only from the composing of dissertations and theses, how lonely and difficult writing can be, I expect more. And I am generally disappointed.

What makes the situation particularly frustrating is that so many such people will vehemently claim that they do, *really*, understand the idea of a writing center. The non-English faculty, the students, the administrators—they may not understand what a writing center is or does, but they have no investment in their ignorance, and can often be educated. But in English departments this second layer of ignorance, this false sense of knowing, makes it doubly hard to get a message through. Indeed, even as you read now, you may be dismissing my argument as the ritual plaint of a "remedial" teacher begging for respectability, the product of a kind of professional paranoia. But while I might admit that there are elements of such a plaint involved—no one likes not to be understood—there is a good deal more at stake. For in coming to terms with this ignorance, I have discovered that it is only a symptom of a much deeper, more serious problem. As a profession I think we are holding on tightly to attitudes and beliefs about the teaching and learning of writing that we thought we had left behind. In fact, my central contention—in the first half of this essay, anyway—is that the failure or inability of the bulk of the English teaching profession, including even those most ardent spokespersons of the so-called "revolution" in the teaching of writing, to perceive the idea of a writing center suggests that, for all our noise and bother about composition, we have fundamentally changed very little.

Let me begin by citing a couple of typical manifestations of this ignorance from close to home. Our writing center has been open for seven years. During that time we have changed our philosophy a little bit as a result of lessons learned from experience, but for the most part we have always been open to anybody in the university community, worked with writers at any time during the composing of a given piece of writing, and dealt with whole pieces of discourse, and not exercises on what might be construed as "subskills" (spelling, punctuation, etc.) outside of the context of the writer's work.

We have delivered the message about what we do to the university generally, and the English department in particular, in a number of ways: letters, flyers, posters, class presentations, information booths, and so on. And, as long as there has been a writing committee, advisory to the director of the writing program, we have sent at least one representative. So it is all the more surprising, and disheartening, that the text for our writing program flyer, composed and approved by that committee, should read as follows:

> The University houses the Center for Writing, founded in 1978 to sponsor the interdisciplinary study of writing. Among its projects are a series of summer institutes for area teachers of writing, a resource center for writers and teachers of writing, *and a tutorial facility for those with special problems in composition.* (My emphasis)

I don't know, quite frankly, how that copy got past me. What are these "special problems"? What would constitute a regular problem, and why wouldn't we talk to the owner of one? Is this hint of pathology, in some mysterious way, a good marketing ploy?

But that's only the beginning. Let me cite another, in many ways more common and painful instance. As a member, recently, of a doctoral examination committee, I conducted an oral in composition theory and practice. One of the candidate's areas of concentration was writing centers, so as part of the exam I gave her a piece of student writing and asked her to play tutor to my student. The session went well enough, but afterward, as we evaluated the entire exam, one of my fellow examiners—a longtime colleague and friend—said that, while the candidate handled the tutoring nicely, he was surprised that the student who had written the paper would have bothered with the writing center in the first place. He would not recommend a student to the center, he said, "unless there were something like twenty-five errors per page."

People make similar remarks all the time, stopping me or members of my staff in the halls, or calling us into offices, to discuss—in hushed tones, frequently—their current "impossible" or difficult students. There was a time, I will confess, when I let my frustration get the better of me. I would be more or less combative, confrontational, challenging the instructor's often well-intentioned but not very useful "diagnosis." We no longer bother with such confrontations; they never worked very well, and they risk undermining the genuine compassion our teachers have for the students they single out. Nevertheless, their behavior makes it clear that for them, a writing center is to illiteracy what a cross between Lourdes and a hospice would be to serious illness: one goes there hoping for miracles, but ready to face the inevitable. In their minds, clearly, writers fall into three fairly distinct groups: the talented, the average, and the others; and the writing center's only logical *raison d'être* must be to handle those others—those, as the flyer proclaims, with "special problems."

Mine is not, of course, the only English department in which such misconceptions are rife. One comes away from any large meeting of writing center people laden with similar horror stories. And in at least one case, a member of such a department—Malcolm Hayward of the Indiana University of Pennsylvania—decided formally to explore and document his faculty's perceptions of the center, and to compare them with the views the center's staff held.[1] His aim, in a two-part survey of both groups, was to determine, first, which goals each group deemed most important in the teaching of writing; and, second, what role they thought the writing center ought to play in that teaching, which goals it ought to concern itself with.

Happily, the writing center faculty and the center staff agreed on what the primary goals in teaching writing should be (in the terms offered by Hayward's questionnaire): the development of general patterns of thinking and writing. Unhappily, the two groups disagreed rather sharply about the reasons for referring students to the center. For faculty members the two primary criteria were grammar and punctuation. Tutors, on the other hand, ranked organization "as by far the single most important factor for referral," followed rather *mis.* distantly by paragraphing, grammar, and style. In short, Hayward's survey reveals the same kind of misunderstanding on his campus that I find so frustrating on my own: the idea that a writing center can only be some sort of skills center, a fix-it shop.

Now if this were just a matter of local misunderstanding, if Hayward and I could straighten it out with a few workshops or lectures, maybe I wouldn't need to write this essay for a public forum. But that is not the case. For whatever reasons, writing centers have gotten mostly this kind of press, have been represented—or misrepresented—more often as fix-it shops than in any other way, and in some fairly influential places. Consider, for example, this passage from Barbara E. Fassler Walvoord's *Helping Students Write Well: A Guide for Teachers in All Disciplines* (New York: Modern Language Association, 1981). What makes it particularly odd, at least in terms of my argument, is that Professor Walvoord's book, in many other ways, offers to faculty the kind of perspective on writing (writing as a complex process, writing as a way of learning) that I might offer myself. Yet here she is on writing centers:

> If you are very short of time, if you think you are not skilled enough to deal with mechanical problems, or if you have a number of students with serious difficulties, you may wish to let the skills center carry the ball for mechanics and spend your time on other kinds of writing and learning problems. (p. 63)

Don't be misled by Professor Walvoord's use of the "skills center" label; in her index the entry for "Writing centers" reads "See skills centers"—precisely the kind of interchangeable terminology I find so abhorrent. On the other hand, to do Professor Walvoord justice, she does recommend that teachers become "at least generally aware of how your skills center works with students, what its basic philosophy is, and what goals it sets for the students in your class," but it seems to me that she has already restricted the possible scope of such a philosophy pretty severely: "deal with mechanical problems"? "carry the ball for mechanics"?

Still, as puzzling and troubling as it is to see Professor Walvoord publishing misinformation about writing centers, it is even more painful, downright maddening, to read one's own professional obituary; to find, in the pages of a reputable professional journal, that what you do has been judged a failure, written off. Maxine Hairston's "The Winds of Change: Thomas Kuhn and the Revolution in the Teaching of Writing" (*College Composition and Communication*, 33, [1982], 76–88) is an attempt to apply the notion of a "paradigm shift" to the field of composition teaching. In the course of doing so Professor Hairston catalogues, under the subheading "Signs of Change," what she calls "ad hoc" remedies to the writing "crisis":

> Following the pattern that Kuhn describes in his book, our first response to crisis has been to improvise ad hoc measures to try to patch the cracks and keep the system running. Among the first responses were the writing labs that sprang up about ten years ago to give first aid to students who seemed unable to function within the traditional paradigm. Those labs are still with us, but they're still only giving first aid and treating symptoms. They have not solved the problem. (p. 82)

What first struck me about this assessment — what probably strikes most people in the writing center business — is the mistaken history, the notion that writing labs "sprang up about ten years ago." The fact is, writing "labs," as Professor Hairston chooses to call them, have been around in one form or another since at least the 1930s when Carrie Stanley was already working with writers at the University of Iowa. Moreover, this limited conception of what such places can do — the fix-it shop image — has been around far longer than ten years, too. Robert Moore, in a 1950 *College English* article, "The Writing Clinic and the Writing Laboratory" (7 [1950], 388–393), writes that "writing clinics and writing laboratories are becoming increasingly popular among American universities and colleges as remedial agencies for removing students' deficiencies in composition" (p. 388).

   Still, you might think that I ought to be happier with Professor Hairston's position than with, say, Professor Walvoord's. And to some extent I am: even if she mistakenly assumes that the skill and drill model represents all writing centers equally well, she at least recognizes its essential futility. Nevertheless — and this is what bothers me most about her position — her dismissal fails to lay the blame for these worst versions of writing centers on the right heads. According to her "sprang up" historical sketch, these places simply appeared — like so many mushrooms? — to do battle with illiteracy. "They" are still with "us," but "they" haven't solved the problem. What is missing here is a doer, an agent, a creator — someone to take responsibility. The implication is that "they" done it — "they" being, apparently, the places themselves.

   But that won't wash. "They," to borrow from Walt Kelly, is us: members of English departments, teachers of writing. Consider, as evidence, the pattern of writing center origins as revealed in back issues of *The Writing Lab Newsletter*: the castoff, windowless classroom (or in some cases, literally, closet), the battered desks, the old textbooks, a phone (maybe), no budget, and, almost inevitably, a director with limited status — an untenured or non–tenure track faculty member, a teaching assistant, an undergraduate, a "paraprofessional," etc. Now who do you suppose has determined what is to happen in that center? Not the director, surely; not the staff, if there is one. The mandate is clearly from the sponsoring body, usually an English department. And lest you think that things are better where space and money are not such serious problems, I urge you to visit a center where a good bit of what is usually grant money has been spent in the first year or two of the center's operation. Almost always, the money will have been used on materials: drills, texts, machines, tapes, carrels, headphones—the works. And then the director, hired on "soft" money, without political clout, is locked into an approach because she or he has to justify the expense by using the materials.

Clearly, then, where there is or has been misplaced emphasis on so-called basics or drill, where centers have been prohibited from dealing with the writing that students do for their classes—where, in short, writing centers have been of the kind that Professor Hairston is quite correctly prepared to write off—it is because the agency that created the center in the first place, too often an English department, has made it so. The grammar and drill center, the fix-it shop, the first aid station—these are neither the vestiges of some paradigm left behind nor pedagogical aberrations that have been overlooked in the confusion of the "revolution" in the teaching of writing, but that will soon enough be set on the right path, or done away with. They are, instead, the vital and authentic reflection of a way of thinking about writing and the teaching of writing that is alive and well and living in English departments everywhere.

But if my claims are correct—if this is not what writing centers are or, if it is what they are, it is not what they should be—then what are, what *should* they be? What is the idea of a writing center? By way of answer, let me return briefly to the family of metaphors by which my sources have characterized their idea of a writing center: Robert Moore's "removing students' deficiencies," Hairston's "first aid" and "treating symptoms," my colleague's "twenty-five errors per page," Hayward's punctuation and grammar referrers, and Walvoord's "carrying the ball for mechanics" (where, at least, writing centers are athletic and not surgical). All these imply essentially the same thing: that writing centers define their province in terms of a given curriculum, taking over those portions of it that "regular" teachers are willing to cede or, presumably, unable to handle. Over the past six years or so I have visited more than fifty centers, and read descriptions of hundreds of others, and I can assure you that there are indeed centers of this kind, centers that can trace their conceptual lineage back at least as far as Moore. But the "new" writing center has a somewhat shorter history. It is the result of a documentable resurgence, a renaissance, if you will, that began in the early 1970s. In fact, the flurry of activity that caught Professor Hairston's attention, and which she mistook for the beginnings of the "old" center, marked instead the genesis of a center which defined its province in a radically different way. Though I have some serious reservations about Hairston's use of Kuhn's paradigm model to describe what happens in composition teaching, I will for the moment put things in her terms: the new writing center, far from marking the end of an era, is the embodiment, the epitome, of a new one. It represents the marriage of what are arguably the two most powerful contemporary perspectives on teaching writing: first, that writing is most usefully viewed as a process; and second, that writing curricula need to be student-centered. This new writing center, then, defines its province not in terms of some curriculum, but in terms of the writers it serves.

To say that writing centers are based on a view of writing as a process is, original good intentions notwithstanding, not to say very much anymore. The slogan—and I daresay that is what it has become—has been devalued, losing most of its impact and explanatory power. Let me use it, then, to make the one distinction of which it still seems capable: in a writing center the object is to make sure that writers, and not necessarily their texts, are what get changed by instruction. In axiom form it goes like this: our job is to produce better writers, not better writing. Any given project—a class assignment, a law school application letter, an encyclopedia entry, a dissertation proposal—is for the writer the prime, often the exclusive concern. That particular text, its success or failure, is what brings them to talk to us in the first place. In the center, though, we look beyond or through that particular project, that particular text, and see it as an occasion for addressing *our* primary concern, the process by which it is produced.

At this point, however, the writing-as-a-process slogan tends to lose its usefulness. That "process," after all, has been characterized as everything from the reception of divine inspiration to a set of nearly algorithmic rules for producing the five paragraph theme. In between are the more widely accepted and, for the moment, more respectable descriptions derived from composing aloud protocols, interviews, videotaping, and so on. None of those, in any case, represent the composing process we seek in a writing center. The version we want can only be found, in as yet unarticulated form, in the writer we are working with. I think probably the best way to describe a writing center tutor's relationship to composing is to say that a tutor is a holist devoted to a participant-observer methodology. This may seem, at first glance, too passive — or, perhaps, too glamorous, legitimate, or trendy—a role in which to cast tutors. But consider this passage from Paul Diesing's *Patterns of Discovery in the Social Sciences* (Hawthorne, NY: Aldine, 1971):

> Holism is not, in the participant-observer method, an a priori belief that everything is related to everything else. It is rather the methodological necessity of pushing on to new aspects and new kinds of evidence in order to make sense of what one has already observed and to test the validity of one's interpretations. A belief in the organic unity of living systems may also be present, but this belief by itself would not be sufficient to force a continual expansion of one's observations. It is rather one's inability to develop an intelligible and validated partial model that drives one on. (p. 167)

How does this definition relate to tutors and composing? Think of the writer writing as a kind of host setting. What we want to do in a writing center is fit into—observe and participate in—this ordinarily solo ritual of writing. To do this, we need to do what any participant-observer must do: see what happens during this "ritual," try to make sense of it, observe some more, revise our model, and so on indefinitely, all the time behaving in a way the host finds acceptable. For validation and correction of our model, we quite naturally rely on the writer, who is, in turn, a willing collaborator in—and, usually, beneficiary of—the entire process. This process precludes, obviously, a reliance on or a clinging to any predetermined models of "the" composing process, except as crude topographical guides to what the "territory" of composing processes might look like. The only composing process that matters in a writing center is "a" composing process, and it "belongs" to, is acted out by, only one given writer.

It follows quite naturally, then, that any curriculum—any plan of action the tutor follows—is going to be student-centered in the strictest sense of that term. That is, it will not derive from a generalized model of composing, or be based on where the student ought to be because she is a freshman or sophomore, but will begin from where the student is, and move where the student moves—an approach possible only if, as James Moffett suggests in *Teaching the Universe Of Discourse* (Boston: Houghton Mifflin, 1968), the teacher (or tutor in this case) "shifts his gaze from the subject to the learner, for the subject is in the learner" (p. 67). The result is what might be called a pedagogy of direct intervention. Whereas in the "old" center instruction tends to take place after or apart from writing, and tends to focus on the correction of textual problems, in the "new" center the teaching takes place as much as possible during writing, during the activity being learned. and tends to focus on the activity itself.

I do not want to push the participant-observer analogy too far. Tutors are not, finally, researchers: they must measure their success not in terms of the constantly changing model they create, but in terms of changes in the writer. Rather than being fearful of disturbing the "ritual" of composing, they observe it and are charged to change it: to interfere, to get in the way, to participate in ways that will leave the "ritual" itself forever altered. The whole enterprise seems to me most natural. Nearly everyone who writes likes—and needs—to talk about his or her writing, preferably to someone who will really listen, who knows how to listen, and knows how to talk about writing too. Maybe in a perfect world, all writers would have their own ready auditor—a teacher, a classmate, a roommate, an editor—who would not only listen but draw them out, ask them questions they would not think to ask themselves. A writing center is an institutional response to this need. Clearly writing centers can never hope to satisfy this need themselves; on my campus alone, the student-to-tutor ratio would be about a thousand to one. Writing centers are simply one manifestation—polished and highly visible—of a dialogue about writing that is central to higher education.

As is clear from my citations in the first half of this essay, however, what seems perfectly natural to me is not so natural for everyone else. One part of the difficulty, it seems to me now, is not theoretical at all, but practical, a question of coordination or division of labor. It usually comes in the form of a question like this: "If I'm doing process-centered teaching in my class, why do I need a writing center? How can I use it?" For a long time I tried to soft-pedal my answers to this question. For instance, in my dissertation ("Writing Centers: A Sourcebook," Diss. SUNY at Albany, 1978) I talked about complementing or intensifying classroom instruction. Or, again, in our center we tried using, early on, what is a fairly common device among writing centers, a referral form; at one point it even had a sort of diagnostic taxonomy, a checklist, by which teachers could communicate to us their concerns about the writers they sent us.

But I have come with experience to take a harder, less conciliatory position. The answer to the question in all cases is that teachers, as teachers, do not need, and cannot use, a writing center: only writers need it, only writers can use it. You cannot parcel out some portion of a given student for us to deal with ("You take care of editing, I'll deal with invention"). Nor should you require that all of your students drop by with an early draft of a research paper to get a reading from a fresh audience. You should not scrawl, at the bottom of a failing paper, "Go to the writing center." Even those of you who, out of genuine concern, bring students to a writing center, almost by the hand, to make sure they know that we won't hurt them—even you are essentially out of line. Occasionally we manage to convert such writers from people who have to see us to people who want to, but most often they either come as if for a kind of detention, or they drift away. (It would be nice if in writing, as in so many things, people would do what we tell them because it's good for them, but they don't. If and when *they* are ready, we will be here.)

In short, we are not here to serve, supplement, back up, complement, reinforce, or otherwise be defined by any external curriculum. We are here to talk to writers. If they happen to come from your classes, you might take it as a compliment to your assignments, in that your writers are engaged in them enough to want to talk about their work. On the other hand, we do a fair amount of trade in people working on ambiguous or poorly designed assignments, and far too much work with writers whose writing has received caustic, hostile, or otherwise unconstructive commentary.

I suppose this declaration of independence sounds more like a declaration of war, and that is obviously not what I intend, especially since the primary casualties would be the students and writers we all aim to serve. And I see no reason that writing centers and classroom teachers cannot cooperate as well as coexist. For example, the first rule in our writing center is that we are professionals at what we do. While that does, as I have argued, give us the freedom of self-definition, it also carries with it a responsibility to respect our fellow professionals. Hence we never play student-advocates in teacher-student relationships. The guidelines are very clear. In all instances the student must understand that we support the teacher's position completely. (Or, to put it in less loaded terms—for we are not teacher advocates either—the instructor is simply part of the rhetorical context in which the writer is trying to operate.

We cannot change that context: all we can do is help the writer learn how to operate in it and other contexts like it.) In practice, this rule means that we never evaluate or second-guess any teacher's syllabus, assignments, comments, or grades. If students are unclear about any of those, we send them back to the teacher to get clear. Even in those instances I mentioned above—where writers come in confused by what seem to be poorly designed assignments, or crushed by what appear to be unwarrantedly hostile comments—we pass no judgment, at least as far as the student is concerned. We simply try, every way we can, to help the writer make constructive sense of the situation.

In return, of course, we expect equal professional courtesy. We need, first of all, instructors' trust that our work with writers-in-progress on academic assignments is not plagiarism, any more than a conference with the teacher would be—that, to put it the way I most often hear it, we will not write students' papers for them. Second, instructors must grant us the same respect we grant them—that is, they must neither evaluate nor second-guess our work with writers. We are, of course, most willing to talk about that work. But we do not take kindly to the perverse kind of thinking represented in remarks like, "Well, I had a student hand in a paper that he took to the writing center, and it was *still* full of errors." The axiom, if you will recall, is that we aim to make better writers, not necessarily—or immediately—better texts.

Finally, we can always use classroom teachers' cooperation in helping us explain to students what we do. As a first step, of course, I am asking that they revise their thinking about what a writing center can do. Beyond that, in our center we find it best to go directly to the students ourselves. That is, rather than sending out a memo or announcement for the teachers to read in their classes, we simply send our staff, upon invitation, into classes to talk with students or, better yet, to do live tutorials. The standard presentation, a ten-minute affair, gives students a person, a name, and a face to remember the center by. The live tutorials take longer, but we think they are worth it. We ask the instructor to help us find a writer willing to have a draft (or a set of notes or even just the assignment) reproduced for the whole class. Then the writing center person does, with the participation of the entire class, what we do in the center: talk about writing with the writer. In our experience the instructors learn as much about the center from these sessions as the students.

To argue that writing centers are not here to serve writing class curricula is not to say, however, that they are here to replace them. In our center, anyway, nearly every member of the full-time staff is or has been a classroom teacher of writing. Even our undergraduate tutors work part of their time in an introductory writing course. We all recognize and value the power of classroom teaching, and we take pride in ourselves as professionals in that setting too. But working in both situations makes us acutely aware of crucial differences between talking about writing in the context of a class, and talking about it in the context of the center. When we hold student conferences in our classes, we are the teacher, in the writers' minds especially, the assigner and evaluator of the writing in question. And for the most part we are pretty busy people, with conference appointments scheduled on the half hour, and a line forming outside the office. For efficiency the papers-in-progress are in some assigned form—an outline, a first draft, a statement of purpose with bibliography and note cards; and while the conference may lead to further composing, there is rarely the time or the atmosphere for composing to happen during the conference itself. Last but not least, the conference is likely to be a command performance, our idea, not the writer's.

When we are writing center tutors all of that changes. First of all, conferences are the writer's idea; he or she seeks us out. While we have an appointment book that offers half-hour appointment slots, our typical session is fifty minutes, and we average between three and four per writer; we can afford to give a writer plenty of time. The work-in-progress is in whatever form the writer has managed to put it in, which may make tutoring less efficient, but which clearly makes it more student-centered, allowing us to begin where the writers are, not where we told them to be. This also means that in most cases the writers come prepared, even anxious to get on with their work, to begin or to keep on composing. Whereas going to keep a conference with a teacher is, almost by definition, a kind of goal or deadline—a stopping place — going to talk in the writing center is a means of getting started, or a way to keep going. And finally—in a way subsuming all the rest—we are not the teacher. We did not assign the writing, and we will not grade it. However little that distinction might mean in our behaviors, it seems to mean plenty to the writers.

What these differences boil down to, in general pedagogical terms, are timing and motivation. The fact is, not everyone's interest in writing, their need or desire to write or learn to write, coincides with the fifteen or thirty weeks they spend in writing courses—especially when, as is currently the case at so many institutions, those weeks are required. When writing does become important, a writing center can be there in a way that our regular classes cannot. Charles Cooper, in an unpublished paper called "What College Writers Need to Know" (1979), puts it this way:

> The first thing college writers need to know is that they can improve as writers and the second is that they will never reach a point where they cannot improve further. One writing course, two courses, three courses may not be enough. If they're on a campus which takes writing seriously, they will be able to find the courses they need to feel reasonably confident they can fulfill the requests which will be made of them in their academic work. . . . Throughout their college years they should also be able to find on a drop-in, no-fee basis expert tutorial help with any writing problem they encounter in a paper. (p. 1)

A writing center's advantage in motivation is a function of the same phenomenon. Writers come looking for us because, more often than not, they are genuinely, deeply engaged with their material, anxious to wrestle it into the best form they can: they are motivated to write. If we agree that the biggest obstacle to overcome in teaching anything, writing included, is getting learners to decide that they want to learn, then what a writing center does is cash in on motivation that the writer provides. This teaching at the conjunction of timing and motivation is most strikingly evident when we work with writers doing "real world" tasks: application essays for law, medical, and graduate schools, newspaper and magazine articles, or poems and stories. Law school application writers are suddenly willing — sometimes overwhelmingly so — to concern themselves with audience, purpose, and persona, and to revise over and over again. But we see the same excitement in writers working on literature or history or philosophy papers, or preparing dissertation proposals, or getting ready to tackle comprehensive exams. Their primary concern is with their material, with some existential context where new ideas must merge with old, and suddenly writing is a vehicle, a means to an end, and not an end in itself. These opportunities to talk with excited writers at the height of their engagement with their work are the lifeblood of a writing center.

The essence of the writing center method, then, is this talking. If we conceive of writing as a relatively rhythmic and repeatable kind of behavior, then for a writer to improve that behavior, that rhythm, has to change — preferably, though not necessarily, under the writer's control. Such changes can be fostered, of course, by work outside of the act of composing itself — hence the success of the classical discipline of imitation, or more recent ones like sentence combining or the tagmemic heuristic, all of which, with practice, "merge" with and affect composing. And, indeed, depending on the writer, none of these tactics would be ruled out in a writing center. By and large, however, we find that the best breaker of old rhythms, the best creator of new ones, is our style of live intervention, our talk in all its forms.

The kind of writing does not substantially change the approach. We always want the writer to tell us about the rhetorical context — what the purpose of the writing is, who its audience is, how the writer hopes to present herself. We want to know about other constraints — deadlines, earlier experiences with the same audience or genre, research completed or not completed, and so on. In other ways, though, the variations on the kind of talk are endless. We can question, praise, cajole, criticize, acknowledge, badger, plead — even cry. We can read: silently, aloud, together, separately. We can play with options. We can both write — as, for example, in response to sample essay exam questions — and compare opening strategies. We can poke around in resources — comparing, perhaps, the manuscript conventions of the Modern Language Association with those of the American Psychological Association. We can ask writers to compose aloud while we listen, or we can compose aloud, and the writer can watch and listen.

In this essay, however, I will say no more about the nature of this talk. One reason is that most of what can be said, for the moment, has been said in print already. There is, for example, my own "Training Tutors to Talk About

Writing" (*CCC*, 33, [1982], 434–41), or Muriel Harris' "Modeling: A Process Method of Teaching" (*College English*, 45, [1983], 74–84). And there are several other sources, including a couple of essay collections, that provide some insights into the hows and whys of tutorial talk.[2]

A second reason, though, seems to me more substantive, and symptomatic of the kinds of misunderstanding I have tried to dispel here. We don't know very much, in other than a practitioner's anecdotal way, about the dynamics of the tutorial. The same can be said, of course, with regard to talk about writing in any setting—the classroom, the peer group, the workshop, the teacher-student conference, and so on. But while ignorance of the nature of talk in those settings does not threaten their existence, it may do precisely that in writing centers. That is, given the idea of the writing center I have set forth here, talk is everything. If the writing center is ever to prove its worth in other than quantitative terms—numbers of students seen, for example, or hours of tutorials provided—it will have to do so by describing this talk: what characterizes it, what effects it has, how it can be enhanced.

Unfortunately, the same "proofreading-shop-in-the-basement" mentality that undermines the pedagogical efforts of the writing center hampers research as well. So far most of the people hired to run such places have neither the time, the training, nor the status to undertake any serious research. Moreover, the few of us lucky enough to even consider the possibility of research have found that there are other difficulties. One is that writing center work is often not considered fundable—that is, relevant to a wide enough audience—even though there are about a thousand such facilities in the country, a figure which suggests that there must be at least ten to fifteen thousand tutorials every school day, and even though research into any kind of talk about writing is relevant for the widest possible audience. Second, we have discovered that focusing our scholarly efforts on writing centers may be a professional liability. Even if we can publish our work (and that is by no means easy), there is no guarantee that it will be viewed favorably by tenure and promotion review committees. Composition itself is suspect enough; writing centers, a kind of obscure backwater, seem no place for a scholar.

These conditions may be changing. Manuscripts for *The Writing Center Journal*, for example, suggest that writing center folk generally are becoming more research-oriented; there were sessions scheduled at this year's meetings of the MLA and NCTE on research in or relevant to writing centers. In an even more tangible signal of change, the State University of New York has made funds available for our Albany center to develop an appropriate case study methodology for writing center tutorials. Whether this trend continues or not, my point remains the same. Writing centers, like any other portion of a college writing curriculum, need time and space for appropriate research and reflection if they are to more clearly understand what they do, and figure out how to do it better. The great danger is that the very misapprehensions that put them in basements to begin with may conspire to keep them there.

It is possible that I have presented here, at least by implication, too dismal a portrait of the current state of writing centers. One could, as a matter of fact, mount a pretty strong argument that things have never been better. There are, for example, several regional writing center associations that have annual meetings, and the number of such associations increases every year. Both *The Writing Lab Newsletter* and *The Writing Center Journal*, the two publications in the field, have solid circulations. This year at NCTE, for the first time, writing center people met as a recognized National Assembly, a major step up from their previous Special Interest Session status.

And on individual campuses all over the country, writing centers have begun to expand their institutional roles. So, for instance, some centers have established resource libraries for writing teachers. They sponsor readings or reading series by poets and fiction writers, and annual festivals to celebrate writing of all kinds. They serve as clearinghouses for information on where to publish, on writing programs, competitions, scholarships, and so on; and they sponsor such competitions themselves, even putting out their own publications. They design and conduct workshops for groups with special needs — essay exam takers, for example, or job application writers. They are involved with, or have even taken over entirely, the task of training new teaching assistants. They have played central roles in the creation of writing-across-the-curriculum programs. And centers have extended themselves beyond their own institutions, sending tutors to other schools (often high schools), or helping other institutions set up their own facilities. In some cases, they have made themselves available to the wider community, often opening a "Grammar Hotline" or "Grammaphone" — a service so popular at one institution, in fact, that a major publishing company provided funding to keep it open over the summer.

Finally, writing centers have gotten into the business of offering academic credit. As a starting point they have trained their tutors in formal courses or, in some instances, "paid" their tutors in credits rather than money. They have set up independent study arrangements to sponsor both academic and nonacademic writing experiences. They have offered credit-bearing courses of their own; in our center, for example, we are piloting an introductory writing course that uses writing center staff members as small group leaders.

I would very much like to say that all this activity is a sure sign that the idea of a writing center is here to stay, that the widespread misunderstandings I described in this essay, especially those held so strongly in English departments, are dissolving. But in good conscience I cannot. Consider the activities we are talking about. Some of them, of course, are either completely or mostly public relations: a way of making people aware that a writing center exists, and that (grammar hotlines aside) it deals in more than usage and punctuation. Others — like the resource library, the clearinghouse, or the training of new teaching assistants — are more substantive, and may well belong in a writing center, but most of them end up there in the first place because nobody else wants to do them. As for the credit generating, that is simply pragmatic. The bottom line in academic budget making is calculated in student credit hours; when budgets are tight, as they will be for the foreseeable future, facilities that generate no credits are the first to be cut. Writing centers—even really good writing centers—have proved no exception.

None of these efforts to promote writing centers suggest that there is any changed understanding of the idea of a writing center. Indeed it is as though what writing centers do that really matters—talking to writers—were not enough. That being the case, enterprising directors stake out as large a claim as they can in more visible or acceptable territory. All of these efforts—and, I assure you, my center does its share—have about them an air of shrewdness, or desperation, the trace of a survival instinct at work. I am not such a purist as to suggest that these things are all bad. At the very least they can be good for staff morale. Beyond that I think they may eventually help make writing centers the centers of consciousness about writing on campuses, a kind of physical locus for the ideas and ideals of college or university or high school commitment to writing—a status to which they might well aspire and which, judging by results on a few campuses already, they can achieve.

But not this way, not via the back door, not—like some marginal ball-player—by doing whatever it takes to stay on the team. If writing centers are going to finally be accepted, surely they must be accepted on their own terms, as places whose primary responsibility, whose only reason for being, is to talk to writers. That is their heritage, and it stretches back farther than the late 1960s or the early 1970s, or to Iowa in the 1930s—back, in fact, to Athens, where in a busy marketplace a tutor called Socrates set up the same kind of shop: open to all comers, no fees charged, offering, on whatever subject a visitor might propose, a continuous dialectic that is, finally, its own end.

Notes

[1] "Assessing Attitudes toward the Writing Center," *The Writing Center Journal* 3, no. 2 (1983): 1–11.

[2] See, for example, *Tutoring Writing: A Sourcebook for Writing Labs*, ed. Muriel Harris (Glenview, IL: Scott Foresman, 1982); and *New Directions for College Learning Assistance: Improving Writing Skills*, ed. Phyllis Brooks and Thom Hawkins (San Francisco: Jossey-Bass, 1981).

Revisiting "The Idea of a Writing Center"

Stephen M. North _____
STATE UNIVERSITY OF NEW YORK AT ALBANY

Ten years after "The Idea of a Writing Center" became the iconic article on writing centers, Stephen North looks back at his seminal article and finds some of his assumptions and statements were inaccurate and idealistic even if passionate in conviction. In "Revisiting," North reconsiders three relationships central to writing center work: (1) tutor and writer, (2) tutor and instructor, and (3) tutor and institution. As part of an honest reassessment of writing center work, North calls for a move away from "the rather too grand 'Idea' proposed in that earlier essay" and toward more realistic goals.

I need to begin this essay—somewhat obliquely, I confess—by invoking the 1989 film *Dead Poets Society*. That movie, as those of you who saw it may recall, tells the story of a group of boys who attend an exclusive private preparatory school called Welton Academy (located in what John Danaher, to whom I am indebted for this line of argument, calls eternally autumnal New England). Set in the early 1960s, the film focuses in particular on how the boys' lives are affected by their English teacher, himself a graduate of Welton: one John Keating (a name chosen, perhaps, for its Romantic resonances), played by Robin Williams.

Keating is the pivotal character in the film. Not the protagonist—in that sense, this really is the boys' story—but clearly the catalyst, the agent for change, the voice of freedom in a one-hundred-year-old boarding school whose four "pillars"—Tradition, Discipline, Honor, Excellence—are represented less as holding the school up than as weighing its students down. Thus, while Mr. Keating is not featured in all that many scenes, the ones he does appear in take on enormous significance, and none more so than the classroom scenes, three of the most crucial of which I'll sketch here.

The first of these—the students' introduction to Keating on the first day of classes—is set up by what amounts to a highlight film (or, more aptly, a lowlight film) of the other classes the boys attend before they arrive for English at what appears to be the end of the school day. All those classes are taught, as was English until Keating arrived to replace a now-revered retiree, by older men, dour, serious, strict men: the chemistry teacher who not only lays out an intimidating workload for the year, but who announces—with something close to a smirk—that the twenty questions at the end of Chapter One are due tomorrow; the trigonometry teacher who calls for "precision" above all else, and warns that every missed homework assignment will cost one point off the final grade ("Let me urge you now not to test me on this point"); the pointer-wielding Scot of a Latin teacher who leads his charges again and again through the declensions of "agricola."

Keating is presented to us in an entirely different way. We see him first peeking at his students from the doorway of his office at the head of the classroom. Then he begins whistling—the *1812 Overture*—and walks, still whistling, through the classroom to the hallway door, and on out. There is a pause, a moment of student (and audience) puzzlement, until he sticks his head back in the doorway: "Well, come on!" The boys (and camera) follow him into the school's vestibule where, after urging the "more daring" of them to call him "O captain, my captain" (after Whitman on Lincoln, as he tells them), he turns their attention to the trophy case photos of Welton graduates past. These pictured boys-turned-men-turned-moldering-corpses, Keating tells his lads, have a message. "Go on," he tells them, "lean in. Hear it?" And when they are leaning in, the camera panning alternately over intent faces and ancient photos, he offers a kind of ventriloqual whisper: "Caaarpe! Caaarpe! Carpe diem! Seize the day, boys! Make your lives extraordinary!"

The second and third of these key classroom scenes serve to further flesh out this image of the English teacher as liberator, as Romantic—or (given the New England setting and the prominence of Thoreau's phrase about "sucking the marrow out of life") transcendentalist—revolutionary. In the second, he asks a student to read the textbook's Introduction to Poetry, written by one J. Evans Pritchard, Ph.D. (a name which, it's worth noting, Williams manages to pronounce with considerable derision). It features a formula for computing poetic "greatness" [G = I(mportance) x P(erfection)] that prompts Keating to declare "Excrement!" and to insist that the boys tear the page out and, when they have done that, to keep going, to tear out not only that page, but the entire Introduction: "Rip! Rip it out! We're not laying pipe; we're talking about poetry here." And in the third key classroom scene—after we have seen Keating bring Shakespeare to life with vintage Robin Williams impressions of Marlin Brando as Brutus and John Wayne as Macbeth—he climbs atop his desk to dramatize our need to always, always try to see things from a new perspective. Again, he invites the boys to join him, as he invited them to join him in hearing voices and tearing textbooks; and we see in their ready agreement that his teachings are really beginning to take hold.

I don't want to be too hard on this film. In fact, I enjoyed it, in its way, and find it quite moving. Still, as a teacher—and particularly as a teacher of English—I find it annoying, disturbing, irritating. I won't say that no teacher has ever played any version of this John Keating role in a classroom where I was a student; in limited ways, various teachers have, or at least I cast them in it. Nor would I say that I have never assumed such a role—invited, or at least accepted, the kind of teacher-student relationship Keating invites when he urges the "more daring" to call him, not Mr. Keating, but "O captain, my captain."

But teaching English, at least for me, is not generally about grand entrances or grand gestures—neither dramatically tearing up textbooks, nor standing on top of desks. Certainly there is, or at least can be, an element of theater, something of the performance, in any teaching. The "scene" of teaching in our culture—our conceptions of knowing, the conversational dynamics of larger groups, and so on—pretty much guarantees that. *Dead Poets Society* sets up, or perhaps plays into, a grandiose, idealized version of that scene that is potentially dangerous for everyone involved—students, teachers, parents, administrators—especially as that idealization is allowed to embody expectations. Film is a wonderful, captivating medium, but it deals in illusion. Classroom life doesn't come scripted or specially lit; there are no second or third takes, no sound track, no score, no editing. In a film like this, the dynamics of teaching are magically compressed; a few minutes of well- chosen footage can evoke a month or more of classroom interaction. In a real classroom, the teacher's John Wayne impression doesn't necessarily last any longer, but the action doesn't end when the cameras stop rolling.

The reason I bring all this up in the context of writing centers, as you may have guessed from my title, is that I think my essay "The Idea of a Writing Center" (1984) has performed . . . well, let us call it an equally ambivalent service for those of us in the writing center business: offered a version of what we do that is, in its own way, very attractive; but one which also, to the extent that it is a romantic idealization, presents its own kind of jeopardy. I don't want to be too hard on this essay, either. Like *Dead Poets Society*, it was directed—explicitly—at a larger public: those, it says, not involved with writing centers; those who have not directed such a place, worked there a minimum of 100 hours, or talked about their own writing there for 5 hours or more (433). And just as the film no doubt affected (however briefly) the image of English teachers in this country, I think the essay was reasonably effective for its audience: placed prominently in *College English*, it gave lots of essentially ignorant but well-meaning people pause. Tactically speaking, in other words, it worked pretty well.

Nevertheless, its more lasting impact has almost certainly been on us, on writing center people. More to the point here, it has come back—a highly visible version of our mythology, a public idealization—to haunt us in much the same way *Dead Poets Society* comes back to haunt us as English teachers. Indeed, the situation is probably worse with a document like "The Idea of a Writing Center." We can at least partly free ourselves from having to perform in the shadow of Robin Williams' John Keating by pointing out that we were not consulted about the script, and that we would never endorse the film's realism. By contrast, we are bound by "The Idea of a Writing Center" to the extent to which we have endorsed it: asked training tutors to read it, cited it in various writings or talks, used it in arguments with administrators, and so on. And there is plenty of evidence, I think, that we have indeed endorsed it—to good effect, often, and in ways that have provided me with moments of tremendous gratification—but also (therefore) in ways that make it harder for us to disown or renounce what may be its less desirable legacies.

So the primary object of this essay—the point of revisiting "The Idea of a Writing Center"—is to contribute in my own peculiar way to the work of reimagining of writing centers already well under way in such venues as *The Writing Center Journal* and *Writing Lab Newsletter* (see, e.g., Grimm, Woolbright, Joyner, and many others). To do that, I'm going to go behind the scenes, as it were, to critique and/or amend a selection of the public-directed images the essay offers, relying in particular on my sense of the lived experience of writing centers such images can be said to conceal.

Specifically, I'm going to work from four passages, looking in particular at how they characterize three relationships: the tutor and the writer (passages 1 and 2); the tutor and the teacher (passage 2); and the tutor and the institution (passages 3 and 4, and combining, albeit somewhat awkwardly, such entities as the English department and larger administrative units). I'll then conclude by seeing what directions I think such amendments suggest for the future of writing centers.

A. Tutor and Writer

Passage 1:

> Writers come looking for us because, more often than not, they are genuinely, deeply engaged with their material, anxious to wrestle it into the best form they can: they are really motivated to write. (443)

To test the face validity of this claim, I have read it on more than one occasion to a live audience of writing center people, and then paused. The reaction—to the passage, to the pause, to (likely) my raised eyebrows—is telling: people laugh. It isn't, of course, that the writers we see—students, for the most past—*aren't* motivated. They are. But not in the uncomplicated way this passage would suggest. They will, rather, be motivated to (say) finish writing; to be finished with writing; to have their writing be finished. They will be motivated to have the writing they submit for a class win them a good grade, whatever they imagine that will take: for it to be mechanically correct, or thoroughly documented, or to follow the instructor's directions to the letter. (Or, to invoke the most extreme example in my experience, they'll be motivated to satisfy the "sentence" imposed on them by the Student Conduct Committee, which found them "guilty" of Plagiarism, Third Degree [unpremeditated].)

This isn't to be cynical about the possibilities for "genuine" or "deep" engagement. It is, rather, to contextualize such notions, to (re)situate them in the school culture, and indeed the larger culture, that this passage tends to erase. And it is to do so especially, in this case, for the sake of any number of tutors I have talked with—undergraduates, in particular—who, taking this passage pretty much at face value, tend to blame themselves (or, just as problematically, the writers they work with) when their tutorials don't seem to be so unproblematically driven. After all, it does come as a shock when, having been led by your training to expect some deep, unalloyed, genuine engagement—some eager wrestler-of-texts—you meet instead a frightened freshman who seems only to want a super proofreader; a sophomore who seems preoccupied by her fear that the instructor doesn't like her; a senior who seems concerned with doing just enough to pass an S/U course, but not a whit more; or any of the other very complicated, very human creatures who find their way to writing centers. This passage from "The Idea of a Writing Center," whatever its strategic value for other purposes, can lay an unnecessarily heavy burden on such tutors and such writers.

Passage 2:

Think of the writer writing as a kind of host setting. What we want to do in a writing center is fit into—observe and participate in—this ordinarily solo ritual of writing. To do this, we need to do what any participant-observer must do: see what happens during this "ritual," try to make sense of it, observe some more, revise our model, and so on indefinitely, all the time behaving in a way that the host finds acceptable. For validation and correction of our model, we quite naturally rely on the writer, who is, in turn, a willing collaborator in—and, usually, beneficiary of—the entire process. (439)

Sure (imagine a brogue here) and it's a charming image, this tutor of enormous restraint, endless curiosity, heightened sensitivities—antennae all atremble—self-lessly and unobtrusively joining our unself-conscious freshman as she undertakes (deeply and genuinely engaged) her assignment to . . . oh, write a paper on some feature of "A Rose for Emily." Okay, so maybe she isn't so entirely unself-conscious; maybe we make her a little nervous. Okay, maybe she isn't entirely a willing collaborator; maybe she came because she got a C or D on an earlier assignment, or because the instructor insisted she come to the Writing Center. Okay, so maybe you were tired or busy or are habitually a little abrupt (I am in confessional mode now) and your greeting was something like "What is it!?!"

Whatever Margaret Mead may have been doing all those years ago (if it is, indeed, the Mead image of anthropology this invokes), and whatever conceptual leverage such an image provides (it was intended, obviously, to emphasize the centrality of the writer and her composing in the tutoring process), it too can offer a curious and troublesome legacy for tutors— especially new ones—who take it at anything like face value. On the one hand, it makes them feel handcuffed (or perhaps gagged): "I better sit here quietly, unobtrusively, not so much a coach or a consultant as a human recorder of some kind, committed above all to my belief in the intrinsic wholeness-as-writers of the people I tutor." On the other, it tends to blind them to, or deny for them, the extent to which they are (always) already enmeshed in a system or systems—educational, political, economic, social, and so on—in ways that render such innocence (and I think that's the right word) impossible. Think of it this way. It isn't only—as might happen with the Mead-image anthropologist—that this low-profile participant-observer might carry into the visited environment a virus which proves dangerous, or even lethal, to the observed. In the (purportedly) analogous writing center situation, the performer-of-the-ritual is enticed (or coerced or whatever) to leave her usual scene of writing, and to perform it instead in . . . well, the analogy would lead me here to say "hospital," and I'm reluctant to do that. But you see my point. Staging the tutorial in the writing center space—even if it is, as we would no doubt put it, for the writer's good (and not merely, say, logistically convenient)—constitutes an alteration, not to say invasion, of this "ordinarily solo ritual" that no practiced tutorial (bedside) manner can overcome.

B. Tutor and teacher

Passage 3:

> In all instances the student must understand that we support the teacher's
> position completely. Or, to put it in less loaded terms— for we are not teacher
> advocates either—the instructor is simply part of the rhetorical context in
> which the writer is trying to operate. We cannot change that context: all we
> can do is help the writer learn how to operate in it and other contexts like it. In
> practice, this rule means that we never evaluate or second-guess any teacher's
> syllabus, assignments, comments, or grades. If students are unclear about any
> of those, we send them back to the teacher to get clear. Even in those instances
> I mentioned above—where writers come in confused by what seem to be
> poorly designed assignments, or crushed by what appear to be unwarrantedly
> hostile comments—we pass no judgment, at least as far as the student is con-
> cerned. We simply try, every way we can, to help the writer make constructive
> sense of the situation. (441)

The language of this passage always makes me want to ask people to raise
their right hand and recite it as a pledge: "I promise never ever to evaluate or
second-guess any teacher's syllabus, assignments, comments, or grades" and
then start a series of big-tent revivals for those who fail to scrupulously live
up to such a pledge. I am, moreover, reminded of things I learned working in
our writing center over the years: of one colleague, now retired, who used four
different colors of ink in responding to student papers, always marked every
feature he deemed worth commentary, *and* provided totals ("You have 64 separate errors in this paper, Mr. Johnson."). And then there was another, also
now retired, who would not—as a matter of *policy*—talk with her students.
Instead, she said, if they wanted to talk about their work, they could bring it
to the Writing Center. Every year at Christmas time, though, she would send
the Center a two-pound box of chocolates.

The fact is that, from the admittedly peculiar vantage point provided by
our centers, we very often get to view our institutions—and especially *teaching* in our institutions—in the way that, say, the police or journalists get to
view our larger communities: day in and day out, year in and year out, we
see (and participate in) a range of teacher-student interactions very few other
members of the institution can match. There are certainly delights and advantages to this, stories we can tell of commitment and learning and kindness
and happy endings. But we also see what we at least construe as the seamier
side of things—probably, again like the police and journalists, more of the
seaminess than most other vantage points would provide. In any case, it adds
up and in cumulative form puts a lot of pressure on the sort of tutor-teacher
détente proposed by the passage quoted above. And it doesn't help in handling
such pressure that, despite the gradual improvement of working conditions for
writing center people, they still tend to be viewed as—or at least to feel that
they are viewed as—lower in institutional pecking orders than the teachers

whose practices the passage pledges them to uphold, especially when differentials in paychecks, workload, or job security reinforce such feelings.

C. Tutor and institution

Passage 4:

> I think . . . writing centers [can be] the centers of consciousness about writing on campuses, a kind of physical locus for the ideas and ideals of college or university or high school commitment to writing—a status to which they might well aspire and which, judging by results on a few campuses already, they can achieve. (446)

Of the four passages I've presented here, this one is likely both the most accurate and, at the same time, the most genuinely laughable. It is the most accurate because what was true when I first wrote those words would appear to be even truer now. Many centers can, in fact, claim such a status, do serve their respective campuses as that institutional node to which primary responsibility for writing is ceded, both functionally and symbolically. They are responsible, then, not only for tutoring the "underprepared" student writers who have so often been understood to be their sole province, but—to offer a sample listing—for any writer, student or otherwise, interested in talking about his or her writing; for the direction and execution of writing-across-the-curriculum programs; for publishing student writing, faculty newsletters, and the like; for training T.A.s; for placement and assessment procedures; for research.

What makes this apparent success, this fulfillment of my essay's prophecy, laughable—and I do apologize for the harshness of that term—are two factors: scale and image. The problems created by scale are, I think, fairly obvious. It may be that on smaller campuses a writing center can establish a tutor-to-student and staff-to-faculty ratio that makes these notions of a physical locus and a center of consciousness loosely plausible. There aren't any magic formulas here, but suppose a campus of 1,400 students and 25 full-time faculty has a center with 5 more or less full-time people (i.e., faculty members with part of their load in the center), and 15 undergraduate tutors. That represents 1–70 tutor–student and 1–5 staff–faculty ratios; people could, in fact, talk with and know one another.

As we move up the scale in institutional size, though, these ratios seem to get swamped pretty quickly. Our center, for example—of which I remain stubbornly proud—nevertheless has something like the staff I just described: six or seven more or less full-time people, and maybe fourteen undergraduate tutors. Unfortunately, our middle-sized research university enrolls some 16,000 students (12,000 undergraduate, 4,000 graduate) and has in the neighborhood of 700 faculty (not to mention a raft of T.A.s, lecturers, and people teaching in various part-time capacities). The resulting ratios help explain, I hope, my use of the term laughable: 1–800 for tutor–student, 1–70 staff–faculty. If we are called upon to be this center of consciousness and physical locus—and, indeed, we are—the image that springs to mind comes from all those dinosaur books I read as a child (ignoring, for the moment, their paleontological accuracy): the university as this huge, lumbering stegosaurus, say, with a brain so physically small that it needs a second neural node just to operate its hindquarters; and for which "consciousness," if it can be called that, seems to consist of little more than the awareness of a perpetual hunger, a visceral knowledge that the organism has grown so huge that it must be constantly about the work of eating simply to stay alive. (But imagine the size of the center if we wanted to preserve the ratios I offered above: it would require some 230 tutors, of whom 140 would have to be staff people! Our largest departments rarely reach 50.)

The problems presented by image may be even more acute, not least because they can arise even where problems of scale are not so severe. Michael Pemberton, borrowing from Michel Foucault, has traced in the language of and about writing centers three of the more widely held representations: the center as hospital, prison, and madhouse. I would add to these, on a slightly more metaphysical plane—and as an alternative to the notion of a "center of consciousness"—the center as institutional *conscience*, that small nagging voice that ostensibly reminds the institution of its duties regarding writing. Whichever image one opts for, the point is essentially the same. Regardless of the commitment by a writing center staff to reforming the larger institution, the tendency seems not for the center to become the locus of any larger consciousness. On the contrary, there is a very strong tendency for it to become the place whose existence serves simultaneously to locate a wrongness (in this case, illiteracy, variously conceived) *in* a set of persons (and in that sense to constitute language differences *as* a wrong-ness); to absolve the institution from further consideration of such persons, in that they have now been named ("basic," "remedial," "developmental") and "taken care of"; and, not incidentally, to thereby insulate the institution from any danger to its own configuration the differences such persons are now said to embody might otherwise pose. In short—and to put it in the most sinister terms—this particular romanticization of the writing center's institutional potential may actually mask its complicity in what Elspeth Stuckey has called the violence of literacy.

So where does this critique of "The Idea of a Writing Center" leave me... or take us? In keeping with the less Keating-esque image I have been trying to move toward in this essay, I am obliged to confess (albeit with considerable relief) that institutional arrangements seem to me too idiosyncratic, and writing centers' political visions too varied, for me to tell you where I think "we"—all writing center people—are going. But I *can* say where I'm hoping *our* writing center will head. I have to begin by explaining a bit about where our undergraduate writing program as a whole is heading. Specifically, we are no longer interested in moving each of our 2,000 freshmen per year through a composition course or two. I have never had much faith in those courses as they were institutionalized at Albany (and, to be candid, elsewhere), i.e., understood as pre-college, or pre-disciplinary, literally extracurricular, some sort of literacy inoculation program. It is common enough for people to claim that they want these courses—administrators, parents, faculty, legislators, etc.—but at least in my history with our particular institution (and from what I know of lots of others), *nobody ever wants to pay for them*, so that they have been and still are nearly always taught by the underpaid, the overworked, the undertrained (see, e.g., Connors, Miller).

So, no more. We don't offer them. In their place, I favor—and we have now formally adopted—what an increasing number of other programs are moving toward (see, e.g., Jenseth): a writing track through the English major, in this case one called "Writing: Rhetoric and Poetics," which combines what used to be called (and isolated as) "composition," "creative writing," "expository writing," "practical writing," and so on. What we're after is a long-term commitment founded primarily upon the full-time, tenure-track faculty the institution is *in fact* willing to support and a proportionate number of students. Together, this group of teachers and students will teach and learn writing over a four-year cycle of courses.

My amended idea of a writing center, then, runs along similar lines. The general ideal, perhaps, can still be said to hold. I believe—I want to say that I *know*—that an hour of talk about writing at the right time between the right people can be more valuable than a semester of mandatory class meetings when that timing isn't right. But I no longer believe that our energies are really best applied trying to live up to—*real*-ize—the rather too grand "Idea" proposed in that earlier essay. I'll frame my alternative proposal in terms of the points of critique above:

(1) I want a situation in which writers are, in fact, motivated about, engaged in, their writing because they are self-selectively enrolled in a program—a coherent, four-year sequence of study—that values writing. (It is crucial to note, however, that our Writing Sequence imposes no admission requirements. We will provide advisement—much of it in the Writing Center—so that students will, indeed, be able to make informed decisions about whether to enroll. But actual entrance is on a first-come, first-served basis, up to the limits of our resources.)

(2) I want a program in which we've gotten to know the writers and the writers have gotten to know us; a situation, in short, in which talk-about-writing is so common that we can, in fact, carry on such talk, get better at and even fluent in it—not fence, or be forever carrying on those quickie fix-it chats between people who talk twice for a total of an hour . . . and then never again.

(3) I want a situation in which we are *not* required to sustain some delicate but carefully distanced relationship between classroom teachers and the writing center, not least because the classroom teachers are directly involved with, and therefore invested in the functioning of, that center. I don't want to substitute another idealization here by suggesting that the center constituted along

these lines would achieve perfect harmony. Far from it: bringing center and classroom, teaching and tutoring, into this tighter orbit would surely generate as many new tensions as new opportunities, and I foresee plenty of stormy politics and raised voices. (Indeed, we've had them already, just in planning the program.) But at least these won't be distant and delicate negotiations; students will play a much greater role in them; and the energy involved—for better and for worse (I'm willing to take my chances)—will return mostly to the center and to the program, and not be dissipated throughout the bureaucratic structures of a large campus, where it has heretofore had little visible or (given the rate of personnel turnover) lasting effect. And if this seems like an attractive model—if other programs, other majors, other departments want to provide such centers for their students—I would urge them to follow the same principles.

(4) I want a situation in which the writing center's mission matches its resources and, to whatever extent possible, its image. Perhaps my favorite portion of the New Testament is the account of the loaves and fishes. So far as I've been able to tell, though, tutorial time does not extend to meet—let alone exceed—the needs of the faithful. Instead, in those all-too-common situations in which workload far exceeds resources, everyone—teachers, tutors, students—just gets weary. Moreover (to pursue the New Testament connection a little further), I do not believe it is finally a good thing for a writing center to be seen as taking upon its shoulders the whole institution's (real or imagined) sins of illiteracy, either: to serve as conscience, savior, or sacrificial victim.

For our purposes, the best way to create this situation is to tie the Center directly to our Writing Sequence through the English major: to make it the center of consciousness, the physical locus—not for the entire, lumbering university—but for the approximately 10 faculty members, the 20 graduate students, and the 250 or so undergraduates that we can actually, sanely, responsibly bring together. They can meet there, and talk about writing.

As I have tried to argue here, images of the kind offered in *Dead Poets Society* and "The Idea of a Writing Center" can be wonderfully inspiring, but they can outlive their usefulness, too, and come back to haunt us: mislead us, delude us or, as seems to be particularly the case in these two instances, lock us into trajectories which—should we persist in following them—are likely to take us places that we don't really want to go. At the end of the Williams film, you may recall, his Keating character has been fired, made the scapegoat for the suicide of a student who, acting on Keating's advice, played Puck in a local production against his father's vehemently expressed opposition. In the final scene—set appropriately in the English classroom, where Keating has been replaced by the repressive headmaster who engineered his dismissal—Keating has come to collect his belongings. As the class carries on (a student is reading aloud the excised Introduction to Poetry by J. Evans Pritchard), Keating walks, visibly dejected, past the rows of desks toward the back of the room. Just as he reaches the doorway, though, his shyest defender finally cries out at the injustice of it all: he is sorry, he declares, and it isn't fair; the students were forced to sign the statement that led to Keating's dismissal. Ordered to silence by the outraged headmaster, the lad instead climbs atop his desk and chants, with all sorts of poignant resonance, "O captain, my captain." Soon other boys, one by one, climb atop their desks, too, and pick up the chant. Keating stands in the doorway drinking in this tribute until, visibly heartened, he finally thanks his young men and then, head high, leaves Welton forever.

It's a wonderful cinematic moment, to be sure — nary a dry eye in the house — and not least because it arrives with such tragic and symmetrical inevitability: Keating has been headed unerringly toward it since we first saw him make that same walk, whistling Tchaikovsky, a latter-day Pied Piper. As the finishing touch on the film's image of the English teacher, however, it is rather more problematic. I mean, what's the message? That the inevitable fate of the truly talented, truly in-tune, truly committed English teacher — indeed, the litmus test of that commitment — is a kind of institutional martyrdom? Which means, in turn, that those of us who (like the repressive headmaster) stay on are . . . what, exactly?

The trajectory plotted by "The Idea of a Writing Center" may be less tragic in a technical sense, in that it does not require that the protagonist be expelled. Nevertheless, it threatens to lead just as surely to an analogous brand of institutional martyrdom — a version of what Susan Miller has so aptly termed the "sad women in the basement" (121 ff.) (or, in the case of writing centers, the sub-basement) — and, perhaps more to the point, to create just as powerful a tactical disadvantage: that is, agreeing to serve as the (universal) staff literacy scapegoat gives us no more power to alter what we believe are flawed institutional arrangements than Keating's departure gives him to affect Welton, and indeed lacks even the short-term power of his grand gesture.

Of course, where we *do* have the advantage over Keating is in still being able to alter that trajectory, to rewrite the script. As I suggested earlier, the amended idea of a writing center I have recommended here will by no means guarantee a happy ending. On the contrary: while this fairly radical restructuring of both writing curriculum and writing center will certainly address some very important problems of writing program life, it will likely also both intensify any number of extant difficulties *and* produce new ones, as-yet unforeseen byproducts of these alternative institutional arrangements. Nevertheless, I believe that it represents a crucial move — albeit a somewhat hard-nosed one — in our long-term campaign to renegotiate the place of writing in postsecondary education.

Notes

[1] My thanks to Deb Kelsh, Anne DiPardo, and John Trimbur for their thoughtful readings of and responses to this essay.

Works Cited

Connors, Robert J. "Rhetoric in the Modern University: The Creation of an Underclass." *The Politics of Writing Instruction: Postsecondary*. Ed. Richard Bullock and John Trimbur. Portsmouth: Boynton/Cook, 1991. 55–84. Print.

Danaher, John. "Extended Acquaintance with Seemingly Small Matters: A Teacher's Stories." Diss. SUNY Albany, 1992. Print.

Dead Poets Society. Dir. Peter Weir. Perf. Robin Williams. Buena Vista, 1989. Film.

Grimm, Nancy. "Contesting 'The Idea of a Writing Center': The Politics of Writing Center Research? *Writing Lab Newsletter* 17.1 (1992): 5–6. Print.

Jenseth, Richard. "Surveying the Writing Minor: ¿Qué Es Eso?" Paper presented at CCCC. Boston. 22 Mar. 1991.

Joyner, Michael. "The Writing Center Conference and the Textuality of Power." *The Writing Center Journal* 12.1 (1991): 80–89. Print.

Miller, Susan. *Textual Carnivals: The Politics of Composition*. Carbondale: Southern Illinois UP, 1991. Print.

North, Stephen. "The Idea of a Writing Center." *College English* 46.5 (1984): 433–46. Print.

Pemberton, Michael. "The Prison, the Hospital, and the Madhouse: Redefining Metaphors for the Writing Center." *Writing Lab Newsletter* 17.1 (1992): 11–16. Print.

Stuckey, Elspeth. *The Violence of Literacy*. Portsmouth, NH: Boynton/Cook, 1991. Print.

Woolbright, Meg. "The Politics of Peer Tutoring: Feminism within the Patriarchy." *The Writing Center Journal* 13.1 (1992): 16–30. Print.

Collaboration, Control, and the Idea of a Writing Center

Andrea Lunsford _____

STANFORD UNIVERSITY

Andrea Lunsford has helped define for writing instructors the significance of collaborative learning and the social construction of knowledge. In this essay, Lunsford extends her discussion to writing center pedagogy. As she shows us, collaborative writing centers pose "a threat as well as a challenge to the status quo in higher education" by challenging the firmly held notion of authorship as a solitary activity and knowledge as "individually derived, individually held." Lunsford argues that writing centers are excellent sites for undertaking the difficult task of "creating a collaborative environment" that "promotes excellence" and "encourages active learning." Her essay, which originally appeared in 1991 in The Writing Center Journal, is especially helpful for tutors in providing an overview of social constructionism and its impact on writing center philosophies. In essence, the essay establishes a theoretical context for the work tutors do by contrasting the collaborative writing center with earlier writing center models, shaped by expressivism and current traditional rhetoric.

The triple focus of my title reflects some problems I've been concentrating on as I thought about and prepared for the opportunity to speak last week at the Midwest Writing Centers Association meeting in St. Cloud, and here at the Pacific Coast/Inland Northwest Writing Centers meeting in Le Grande. I'll try as I go along to illuminate—or at least to complicate—each of these foci, and I'll conclude by sketching in what I see as a particularly compelling idea of a writing center, one informed by collaboration and, I hope, attuned to diversity.

As some of you may know, I've recently written a book on collaboration, in collaboration with my dearest friend and coauthor, Lisa Ede. *Singular Texts/Plural Authors: Perspectives on Collaborative Writing* was six years in the research and writing, so I would naturally gravitate to principles of collaboration in this or any other address.

Yet it's interesting to me to note that when Lisa and I began our research (see "Why Write . . . Together?"), we didn't even use the term "collaboration"; we identified our subjects as "co- and group-writing." And when we presented our first paper on the subject at the 1985 CCCC meeting, ours was the only such paper at the conference, ours the only presentation with "collaboration" in the title. Now, as you know, the word is everywhere, in every journal, every conference program, on the tip of every scholarly tongue. So—collaboration, yes. But why control? Because as the latest pedagogical bandwagon, collaboration often masquerades as democracy when it in fact practices the same old authoritarian control. It thus stands open to abuse and can, in fact, lead to poor teaching and poor learning. And it can lead—as many of you know—to disastrous results in the writing center. So amidst the rush to embrace collaboration, I see a need for careful interrogation and some caution.

We might begin by asking where the collaboration bandwagon got rolling. Why has it gathered such steam? Because, I believe, collaboration both in theory and practice reflects a broad-based epistemological shift, a shift in the way we view knowledge. The shift involves a move from viewing knowledge and reality as things exterior to or outside of us, as immediately accessible, individually knowable, measurable, and shareable—to viewing knowledge and reality as mediated by or constructed through language in social use, as socially constructed, contextualized, as, in short, the product of *collaboration*.

I'd like to suggest that collaboration as an embodiment of this theory of knowledge poses a distinct threat to one particular idea of a writing center. This idea of a writing center, what I'll call "The Center as Storehouse," holds to the earlier view of knowledge just described—knowledge as exterior to us and as directly accessible. The Center as Storehouse operates as [an] information station or storehouse, prescribing and handing out skills and strategies to individual learners. They often use "modules" or other kinds of individualized learning materials. They tend to view knowledge as individually derived and held, and they are not particularly amenable to collaboration, sometimes actively hostile to it. I visit lots of Storehouse Centers, and in fact I set up such a center myself, shortly after I had finished an M.A. degree and a thesis on William Faulkner.

Since Storehouse Centers do a lot of good work and since I worked very hard to set up one of them, I was loath to complicate or critique such a center. Even after Lisa and I started studying collaboration in earnest, and in spite of the avalanche of data we gathered in support of the premise that collaboration is the norm in most professions (American Consulting Engineers Council, American Institute of Chemists, American Psychological Institute, Modern Language Association, Professional Services Management Association, International City Management Association, Society for Technical Communication), I was still a very reluctant convert.

Why? Because, I believe, collaboration posed another threat to my way of teaching, a way that informs another idea of a writing center, which I'll call "The Center as Garret." Garret Centers are informed by a deep-seated belief in individual "genius," in the Romantic sense of the term. (I need hardly point out that this belief also informs much of the humanities and, in particular, English studies.) These Centers are also informed by a deep-seated attachment to the American brand of individualism, a term coined by Alexis de Tocqueville as he sought to describe the defining characteristics of this Republic.

Unlike Storehouse Centers, Garret Centers don't view knowledge as exterior, as information to be sought out or passed on mechanically. Rather they see knowledge as interior, as inside the student, and the writing center's job as helping students get in touch with this knowledge, as a way to find their unique voices, their individual and unique powers. This idea has been articulated by many, including Ken Macrorie, Peter Elbow, and Don Murray, and the idea usually gets acted out in Murray-like conferences, those in which the tutor or teacher listens, voices encouragement, and essentially serves as a validation of the students' "I-search." Obviously, collaboration problematizes Garret Centers as well, for they also view knowledge as interiorized, solitary, individually derived, individually held.

As I've indicated, I held on pretty fiercely to this idea as well as to the first one. I was still resistant to collaboration. So I took the natural path for an academic faced with this dilemma: I decided to do more research. I did a *lot* of it. And, to my chagrin, I found more and more evidence to challenge my ideas, to challenge both the idea of Centers as Storehouses or as Garrets. Not incidentally, the data I amassed mirrored what my students had been telling me for years: not the research they carried out, not their dogged writing of essays, not *me* even, but their work in groups, their *collaboration*, was the most important and helpful part of their school experience. Briefly, the data I found all support the following claims:

1.   Collaboration aids in problem finding as well as problem solving.
2.   Collaboration aids in learning abstractions.

3. Collaboration aids in transfer and assimilation; it fosters interdisciplinary thinking.

4. Collaboration leads not only to sharper, more critical thinking (students must explain, defend, adapt), but to deeper understanding of *others*.

5. Collaboration leads to higher achievement in general. I might mention here the Johnson and Johnson analysis of 122 studies from 1924–1981, which included every North American study that considered achievement or performance data in competitive, cooperative/collaborative, or individualistic classrooms. Some 60% showed that collaboration promoted higher achievement, while only 6% showed the reverse. Among studies comparing the effects of collaboration and independent work, the results are even more strongly in favor of collaboration.
Moreover, the superiority of collaboration held for all subject areas and all age groups. See "How to Succeed Without Even Vying," *Psychology Today*, September 1986.

6. Collaboration promotes excellence. In this regard, I am fond of quoting Hannah Arendt: "For excellence, the presence of others is always required."

7. Collaboration engages the whole student and encourages active learning; it combines reading, talking, writing, thinking; it provides practice in both synthetic and analytic skills.

Given these research findings, why am I still urging caution in using collaboration as our key term, in using collaboration as the idea of the kind of writing center I now advocate?

First, because creating a collaborative environment and truly collaborative tasks is damnably difficult. Collaborative environments and tasks must *demand* collaboration. Students, tutors, teachers must really need one another to carry out common goals. As an aside, let me note that studies of collaboration in the workplace identify three kinds of tasks that seem to call consistently for collaboration: high-order problem defining and solving; division of labor tasks, in which the job is simply too big for any one person; and division of expertise tasks. Such tasks are often difficult to come by in writing centers, particularly those based on the Storehouse or Garret models.

A collaborative environment must also be one in which goals are clearly defined and in which the jobs at hand engage everyone fairly equally, from the student clients to work-study students to peer tutors and professional staff. In other words, such an environment rejects traditional hierarchies. In addition, the kind of collaborative environment I want to encourage calls for careful and ongoing monitoring and evaluating of the collaboration or group process, again on the part of all involved. In practice, such monitoring calls on each person involved in the collaboration to build a *theory* of collaboration, a theory of group dynamics.

Building such a collaborative environment is also hard because getting groups of any kind going is hard. The students', tutors', and teachers' prior experiences may work against it (they probably held or still hold to Storehouse or Garret ideas); the school day and term work against it; and the drop-in nature of many centers, including my own, works against it. Against these odds, we have to figure out how to constitute groups in our centers; how to allow for evaluation and monitoring; how to teach, model, and learn about careful listening, leadership, goal setting, and negotiation—all of which are necessary to effective collaboration.

We must also recognize that collaboration is hardly a monolith. Instead, it comes in a dizzying variety of modes about which we know almost nothing. In our books, Lisa and I identify and describe two such modes, the hierarchical and the dialogic, both of which our centers need to be well versed at using. But it stands to reason that these two modes perch only at the tip of the collaborative iceberg.

As I argued earlier, I think we must be cautious in rushing to embrace collaboration because collaboration can also be used to reproduce the status quo; the rigid hierarchy of teacher-centered classrooms is replicated in the tutor-centered writing center in which the tutor is still the seat of all authority but is simply pretending it isn't so. Such a pretense of democracy sends badly mixed messages. It can also lead to the kind of homogeneity that squelches diversity, that waters down ideas to the lowest common denominator, that erases rather than values difference. This tendency is particularly troubling given our growing awareness of the roles gender and ethnicity play in all learning. So regression toward the mean is not a goal I seek in an idea of a writing center based on collaboration.

The issue of control surfaces most powerfully in this concern over a collaborative center. In the writing center ideas I put forward earlier, where is that focus of control? In Storehouse Centers, it seems to me control resides in the tutor or center staff, the possessors of information, the currency of the Academy. Garret Centers, on the other hand, seem to invest power and control in the individual student knower, though I would argue that such control is often appropriated by the tutor/teacher, as I have often seen happen during Murray or Elbow style conferences. Any center based on collaboration will need to address the issue of control explicitly, and doing so will not be easy.

It won't be easy because what I think of as successful collaboration (which I'll call Burkean Parlor Centers), collaboration that is attuned to diversity, goes deeply against the grain of education in America. To illustrate, I need offer only a few representative examples:

1. Mina Shaughnessy, welcoming a supervisor to her classroom in which students were busily collaborating, was told, "Oh . . . I'll come back when you're teaching."
2. A prominent and very distinguished feminist scholar has been refused an endowed chair because most of her work had been written collaboratively.

3. A prestigious college poetry prize was withdrawn after the winning poem turned out to be written by three student collaborators.
4. A faculty member working in a writing center was threatened with dismissal for "encouraging" group-produced documents.

I have a number of such examples, all of which suggest that—used unreflectively or *uncautiously*—collaboration may harm professionally those who seek to use it and may as a result further reify a model of education as the top-down transfer of information (back to The Storehouse) or a private search for Truth (back to The Garret). As I also hope I've suggested, collaboration can easily degenerate into busy work or what Jim Corder calls "fading into the tribe."

So I am very, very serious about the cautions I've been raising, about our need to examine carefully what we mean by collaboration and to explore how those definitions locate control. And yet I still advocate—with growing and deepening conviction—the move to collaboration in both classrooms and centers. In short, I am advocating a third, alternative idea of a writing center, one I know many of you have already brought into being. In spite of the very real risks involved, we need to embrace the idea of writing centers as Burkean Parlors, as centers for collaboration. Only in doing so can we, I believe, enable a student body and citizenry to meet the demands of the twenty-first century. A recent Labor Department report tells us, for instance, that by the mid-1990s workers will need to read at the 11th grade level for even low-paying jobs; that workers will need to be able not so much to solve prepackaged problems but to identify problems amidst a welter of information or data; that they will need to reason from complex symbol systems rather than from simple observations; most of all that they will need to be able to work with others who are different from them and to learn to negotiate power and control (Heath).

The idea of a center I want to advocate speaks directly to these needs, for its theory of knowledge is based not on positivistic principles (that's The Storehouse again), not on Platonic or absolutist ideals (that's The Garret), but on the notion of knowledge as always contextually bound, as always socially constructed. Such a center might well have as its motto Arendt's statement: "For excellence, the presence of others is always required." Such a center would place control, power, and authority not in the tutor or staff, not in the individual student, but in the negotiating group. It would engage students not only in solving problems set by teachers but in identifying problems for themselves; not only in working as a group but in monitoring, evaluating, and building a theory of how groups work; not only in understanding and valuing collaboration but in confronting squarely the issues of control that successful collaboration inevitably raises; not only in reaching consensus but in valuing dissensus and diversity.

The idea of a center informed by a theory of knowledge as socially constructed, of power and control as constantly negotiated and shared, and of collaboration as its first principle presents quite a challenge. It challenges our ways of organizing our centers, of training our staff and tutors, of working with teachers. It even challenges our sense of where we "fit" in this idea. More importantly, however, such a center presents a challenge to the institution of higher education, an institution that insists on rigidly controlled individual performance, on evaluation as punishment, on isolation, on the kinds of values that took that poetry prize away from three young people or that accused Mina Shaughnessy of "not teaching."

This alternative, this third idea of a writing center, poses a threat as well as a challenge to the status quo in higher education. This threat is one powerful and largely invisible reason, I would argue, for the way in which many writing centers have been consistently marginalized, consistently silenced. But organizations like this one are gaining a voice, are finding ways to imagine into being centers as Burkean Parlors for collaboration, writing centers, I believe, which can lead the way in changing the face of higher education.

So, as if you didn't already know it, you're a subversive group, and I'm delighted to have been invited to participate in this collaboration. But I've been talking far too long by myself now, so I'd like to close by giving the floor to two of my student collaborators. The first—like I was—was a reluctant convert to the kind of collaboration I've been describing tonight. But here's what she wrote to me some time ago:

> Dr. Lunsford: I don't know exactly what to say here, but I want to say something. So here goes. When this Writing Center class first began, I didn't know what in the hell you meant by collaboration. I thought—hey! yo!—you're the teacher and you know a lot of stuff. And you better tell it to me. Then I can tell it to the other guys. Now I know that you know even more than I thought. I even found out I know a lot. But that's not important. What's important is knowing that knowing doesn't just happen all by itself, like the cartoons show with a little light bulb going off in a bubble over a character's head. Knowing happens with other people, figuring things out, trying to explain, talking through things. What I know is that we are all making and remaking our knowing and ourselves with each other every day—you just as much as me and the other guys, Dr. Lunsford. We're all—all of us together—collaborative re-creations in process. So—well—just wish me luck.

And here's a note I received just as I got on the plane, from another student/collaborator:

> I had believed that Ohio State had nothing more to offer me in the way of improving my writing. Happily, I was mistaken. I have great expectations for our Writing Center Seminar class. I look forward to every one of our classes and to every session with my 110W students [2 groups of 3 undergraduates he is tutoring]. I sometimes feel that they have more to offer me than I to them. They say the same thing, though, so I guess we're about even, all learning together. (P.S. This class and the Center have made me certain I want to attend graduate school.)

These students embody the kind of center I'm advocating, and I'm honored to join them in conversation about it, conversation we can continue together now.

Works Cited

Corder, Jim W. "Hunting for Ethos Where They Say It Can't Be Found." *Rhetoric Review* 7 (1989): 299–316. Print.

Ede, Lisa S., and Andrea A. Lunsford. *Singular Texts/Plural Authors: Perspectives on Collaborative Writing*. Carbondale: Southern Illinois UP, 1990. Print.

---. "Why Write . . . Together?" *Rhetoric Review* 1 (1983): 150–58. Print.

Heath, Shirley Brice. "The Fourth Vision: Literate Language at Work." *The Right to Literacy*. Ed. Andrea A. Lunsford, Helen Moglen, and James Slevin. New York: Modern Language Association, 1990. Print.

Khon, Alfie. "How to Succeed Without Even Vying." *Psychology Today* Sept. 1986: 22–28. Print.

Lessons of Inscription: Tutor Training and the "Professional Conversation"[1]

Peter Vandenberg

DEPAUL UNIVERSITY

Peter Vandenberg discusses the political, philosophical, and practical implications of tutor roles and tutor training in academic institutions committed to particular (and often dominant) views of literacy education. Vandenberg questions what model of tutor training serves tutors better. Is it the "practical" job-training manual that many books on tutoring offer, or is it the "professional approach" that "establishes awareness of the specialized discourse of writing center scholarship as a standard of tutor competence"? Aware of the limitations of the "practical approach" as providing an overly facile sense that tutoring is guided by a "set of skills," Vandenberg is also critical of the "professional approach" in its efforts to transform peer tutors into "mini-professors." By immersing peer tutors in the "professional approach," we involve peer tutors in our most "painful and factious" debates about the meaning of theory while devaluing the purposes of personal agency—or each tutor's highly individual effort to bring his or her special abilities into the tutoring moment. Vandenberg's concern is that the "professional approach" provides the stamp of "institutional legitimacy" in tutor training while undercutting efforts by each tutor to question the legitimacy of hegemonic institutional practices in writing instruction. This essay originally appeared in 1999 in The Writing Center Journal.

> *Because power circulates in the normalized writing practices of the institution, it cannot be challenged. As this power becomes inscribed in our teaching and learning relationships, we assume responsibility for our own subjugation.*
>
> *—Nancy Grimm*

If the pages of *The Writing Center Journal* are any kind of barometer, a dark cloud has been gathering over writing center work. Recent critical, self-reflexive *WCJ* articles by Terrance Riley and Stephen North, according to Lisa Ede, explore "sites of discomfort and controversy" (112), and Ede finds these essays intimately related to disciplinary development in composition studies and growing concern about its implications. The flowering of the National Writing Centers Association—and its national and regional conferences, press, and journals—suggest that to identify with writing centers is increasingly to contend with traditional disciplinary practices and academic professionalism. Removed as it must be from the day-to-day, location-bound activities of writing centers, the written "professional conversation" generalizes tutoring and writing-center administration in a wider, communal context, one recently drawn dark around the edges. While Riley warns that writing centers may face an unpromising future, Nancy Grimm implicates them already in what she calls "the regulatory power" of institutionalized writing practices (7). Writing center scholarship is beginning to question whether writing centers ever did or ever can occupy the academy's anti-space. The last several volumes of *WCJ* seem to indicate the aptness of this Grimm trope for the current state of professional discourse about writing centers: "A Loss of Innocence."

While I do not intend to predict in this essay where precisely writing centers are headed, I am interested in what lies along the horizon for writing centers as are Riley, Ede, North, and Grimm. And I am concerned that the collective "we" of our professional discourse is groping toward it without a great deal of regard for the largest contingent among us—our student tutors. My concern is that as we conceptualize directions for writing centers—the actual ones we work in and the virtual, generalized figures of our scholarship—our understanding of tutors as "students" and our interaction with them as "education" may mask the ways they sometimes serve simply and without reflection as extensions of values and desires written deeply into the institution, into us. Teaching, of course, is the act of transmitting values, and as writing teachers we implicitly grade most writing students on their ability to approximate our values—those of the institution and the dominant culture—and they often arrive and leave resistant to that project. On the other hand, we typically expect student tutors to replicate dominant institutional and literate values and to reproduce them in others as a condition of employment. Comparatively speaking, they accomplish this with little or no resistance at all; they arrive at the writing center door with commitments to academic discipline and a belief in the transformative potential of literacy, but what they often lack is an awareness of the institutional function of the "tutor position," its implication in what Grimm identifies as regulatory power. Our increasing attention to what Ede calls "sites of discomfort," then, might recommend that we vigorously promote a self-reflexive attitude among our tutors and implicate *ourselves* in the web of power structures that attempt to control them. This, of course, is not always "practical."

I am concerned here with formulations of "the practical" in writing center work, particularly as they relate to student tutors and their relationship to published scholarship. In this essay I consider the evolution of writing tutor pedagogies, from the job-specific training of tutorial-centered "practical" manuals (Harris; Meyer and Smith) to the professionalizing approach that establishes awareness of the specialized discourse of writing center scholarship as a standard for tutor competence (Murphy and Sherwood). By appealing to them as "professionals" (Simard) and "experts" (Clark), this new approach incorporates student tutors into our struggle for what Riley calls "academic credibility"; yet with limited potential to engage in the discourse that governs their activities and few opportunities to construct themselves within it, the "professional approach" offers student tutors much in common with their faculty counterparts who struggle under heavy teaching loads. As I will go on to show, my own experience training student tutors with the professional approach suggests that it also writes them into our most painful and factious debates—about the meanings and uses of theory and the possibilities for personal agency through writing within institutions hierarchized by writing. In part by elaborating Writing Center Theory and Pedagogy, the course required of all student tutors at my institution, I go on to suggest that the professional approach makes explicit the complex and undeniable relationship between authority and authorship in university culture.

From the "Practical" to the Professional in Tutor-Training Textbooks

Beginning around 1984, when Kenneth Bruffee and Stephen North wrote the first of what are now published as "landmark essays" about writing centers, business as usual in many writing centers, including the one at DePaul, was disrupted by remarkably persuasive theorizing about writing as process. When the dizzy feeling went away, many had shifted attention from *text* to *context*. Writing was no longer conceived as *only* a set of skills, but as a slippery and intricate set of recursive practices interdependent with readers' reactions. What once was practical in tutor training was no longer. The standard for effective training became decidedly more complex; an activity once dependent almost exclusively on grammarians was suddenly informed by rhetoricians, critical theorists, psychologists, sociologists, and biologists.

Muriel Harris' *Teaching One-to-One: The Writing Conference* emphasizes the shift in attention away from the written product toward the processes of its production and interpretation. Still in print more than a decade after it appeared, and widely used as a tutor-training manual, the book devotes just 15 of its 135 pages to "Grammar and Correctness." Another influential tutor-training text, Emily Meyer and Louise Z. Smith's *The Practical Tutor*, which announces itself as "a practical guide to tutoring composition," mandates the exploration of invention heuristics, critical analysis, concept formation, and the reciprocity between reading and writing. The tremendous range of theoretical constructs that inform *The Practical Tutor* and Harris' *Teaching One-to-One*, however, can easily be harnessed to the rather conservative cultural work that many writing centers (such as the one at DePaul) were established to do, and Meyer and Smith's title reflects how quickly a ragged theoretical landscape can be worn smooth. Together these two training manuals constitute a dominant approach to tutor training: "the newly practical."

These books widened the theory base for tutoring writing outside of the English department's "current-traditional" concern with surface correctness; at the same time, however, they reified or concretized unsettled and competing theories into a new conception of "the practical." These books helped widen the focus of tutor training from text to context; at the same time, however, they limited the concerns of tutor training *to* the tutorial. Neither book offers a consideration of tutoring activity within a wider social or institutional context or questions the assumptions, values, or motives that necessitate and sustain writing tutorials to begin with—whatever they are said to be. Indeed, by advertising *The Practical Tutor* in the "Introduction" as a complete course design, Meyer and Smith appear to imply that any wider context is unnecessary. The extent to which these books shape or reflect the views of most writing center directors and scholars is open to question, of course. Yet it has not been uncommon, on the listserv WCENTER and in some periodicals, to see a wide and unruly collection of constructs, "skills," and procedures naturalized as "practical" as opposed to something distant, onerous, and unreliable labeled "theory."

Writing center scholars have worried on behalf of tutors, though, about the limitations associated with the newly practical. As Roger Munger, Ilene Rubenstein, and Edna Barrow maintain, strong student writers come from typically uniform cultural orientations, and practical training "is often too brief to expect much-needed conversations and reflections to take place" (3). When tutor training does not encourage or demand such reflection—something that may come only from considering tutor-tutee interaction within wider institutional and cultural contexts—"academic elitism and cultural egocentricity" may be the *de facto* result (2). When tutors are trained exclusively or primarily in what Linda Bannister-Wills calls a "learning by doing environment" (132), directors risk exploiting the will to insider status and the novice's tendency to rigidity (Simard). They risk failing to encourage in student tutors a critical awareness of their own privileged literate position in the social and institutional hierarchy. When that happens, they are simply disciplined as instruments of a system they haven't been invited to consider.

Writing center directors are, of course, painfully aware of the friction between their responsibilities as administrators and their options as teachers. According to Munger and others, budget constraints limit most directors to "orientation-type" training programs that, out of necessity, teach the tutorial rather than the tutor. Since credit-bearing training courses are often a "luxury" (Capossela 2), some directors, who may be judged directly or indirectly on the basis of retention and classroom success (Denton), often train tutors within the narrow context of the tutorial. To satisfy short-term goals, many directors are trapped in a cold, pragmatic banking model of tutor training that violates Paulo Freire's first principle of liberatory pedagogy; ignorant of their locations in institutional and disciplinary politics, tutors have little choice but to adapt to and support the limited view their training offers them.[2] I will not dispute Lisa Ede's agreement with Jennifer Gore: "there are no *inherently* liberating practices or discourses" (Gore qtd. in Ede 126, my emphasis). Yet when a teacher wears a writing center director's hat in the tutor-training classroom, teaching can become a more pure form of surveillance and control. Conflict among competing discourses can become something to be managed and suppressed rather than explored. What Bobbie Silk identifies as the director's "dual pedagogical charge"—"we must encourage growth in the tutor as well as the writer" (84)—is often overrun by the instinct to professional self-preservation.

This dual charge has typically, and not unexpectedly, centered on writing; as Bruffee has it, "tutors refine their own writing abilities as well as learn to help others develop their writing skills" (Bruffee qtd. in Bannister-Wills 132). Student tutors clearly do benefit as writers from their tutoring activity and training. I am advocating that we explicitly encourage growth in student tutors by assuring what Tilly Warnok and John Warnock assume, that once they "develop a critical consciousness toward their own writing, they will very likely have developed such consciousness toward the context for that writing, the world they live in" (18). Fear of the "botched job or . . . disgruntled customer" (Capossela 1–2) necessitates that many directors, however unconsciously, construct tutors as employees in need of narrow, job-specific training rather than as students who deserve encouragement toward the self-examination and reflection Munger and others identify.

A bold step forward, Christina Murphy and Steve Sherwood's *St. Martin's Sourcebook for Writing Tutors* appears to offer tutors the kind of situated awareness lacking in newly practical training pedagogies. Murphy and Sherwood present their edited collection of writing center scholarship as a resource "that will allow [tutors] to see tutoring as an ongoing, evolving process that they will help define" (v). The editors announce "a broad, interdisciplinary, and theoretical conversation surrounding the practice of tutoring—a conversation this sourcebook invites you to join" (2). This slim volume fully realizes Simard's early-1980s request that tutoring be considered a "new professional role," and Murphy and Sherwood establish tutors as professionals in the fashion one would expect within the academy. They explicitly bifurcate writing center work into "the practice of tutoring" and participation in a "conversation" that surrounds it by "inviting" students to join the latter. "Informed tutors," they declare, are those "aware of the ongoing professional conversation that contributes to defining writing center practice" (21). Unlike the newly practical manuals, this claim clearly yokes student tutors' competence to their awareness of published scholarship; further, it establishes a hierarchical relationship between "writing center practice" and the authoritative discourse that "contributes" to it by separating the "informed" from their opposites.

Writing center work has gained some degree of institutional legitimacy in the same fashion as the wider field of composition studies. Employing rather conventional disciplinary methods of inscription—conference papers, a press, academic journals, specialized dissertations, and training curricula—writing center scholars have constructed a written discourse and claimed its necessity to tutor effectively. Murphy and Sherwood provide the relief from which the newly practical can be viewed in all its narrowness. What "Part I" of their *Sourcebook* does best, however, though the editors do not acknowledge it, is illustrate the way in which academic hierarchies are constructed and maintained via the privilege of written discourses.

Hierarchy and authority in the academy are inscribed, written. Just as "theorists" and "practitioners" are stratified by writing (Vandenberg), so are newly professionalized tutors and the students they work with. Along with Irene Clark, who suggests that effective "writing conferences do not simply 'happen'[,] . . . they occur because tutors have become experts in the field" (qtd. in Munger and others 3), Murphy and Sherwood effectively erase the romantic possibilities of tutor-student interaction as status-equal "collaborative peers" (Bruffee; Kail and Trimbur), a matter on which I will elaborate in this essay's final section. Constructed as professionals in the conventional academic sense, tutors are implicitly identified as authorities separated from clients by their awareness of and participation in a specialized discourse that helps shape appropriate (professional) interaction with clients. While the professional approach clarifies the hierarchized difference between tutors and tutees based on familiarity with a specialized discourse, tutors remain oddly suspended in this economy of production as the informed rather than as informers.

Murphy and Sherwood's invitation is a truncated one; they implicitly call out to student tutors as readers of the professional discourse, as obedient clients of the cadre of *writers* who authorize it. Unable to negotiate the specialized discourse with any degree of proficiency, student tutors, particularly undergraduate student tutors, as I will go on to show, have little hope of doing more than "listening" to the conversation. As in the wider field of composition studies, the activity of producing a professional, authoritative discourse escapes definition as a practice itself, and the result is a perceived opposition between "theory" and "practice," "research" and "teaching." The professional approach declares student tutors "experts," but with no capacity to produce the *capital* of expertise, tutors fall to the degraded pole of the research/teaching opposition. Like many writing faculty and the "basic writers" with whom they typically meet, newly professionalized student tutors are oppressed by literacy standards they are prevented from attaining.[3]

The professional approach to tutor training explodes the narrow focus of tutorial-based training, but in so doing it merely foregrounds tutors as manipulable, agency-free objects in what Grimm calls the "regulatory function" of writing centers. As I attempt to elaborate in the remainder of this article, as it does to those constructed as "practitioners" across the academy, the professional approach offers student tutors just one opportunity to escape their subjugated role. They must write their way out, and they must do it in and on the terms they have been given—this means an unavoidable encounter with *theory*.

Breaking Down Theory

In "Writing Centers and the Politics of Location," Lisa Ede engages the most distressing dilemma for directors who introduce student tutors to the professional discourse, the "theory-practice" opposition. By refiguring "what has often been termed a theory-practice conflict to be a practice-practice conflict," Ede demonstrates her awareness of the "discursive and material practices of those constructed as theorists over those constructed as practitioners" (114). As Ede implies here, the negative differential between these two constructs is enforced by the academic reward structure that frames academics' workplace activities. Those who engage primarily in publishing theory about writing (or writing centers) are rewarded more favorably than those who primarily theorize about writing with students in the context of the classroom or the writing center. This arrangement diminishes the work of teaching and tutoring, and assumes a professional-client relationship between those who primarily publish and those who primarily teach.

Ede loses this "practice-practice" distinction almost immediately, however, when she conflates "those constructed as theorists" with "theory": "I have learned," she writes, "to be suspicious of the claims that theory often makes for itself" (114). Instead of renegotiating the dilemma by differentiating practical activities, Ede reinscribes it, despite her awareness that the problem is one of inequitably rewarding people engaged in different, yet important, activities—the "practice-practice" conflict. Ede inadvertently strengthens the imbalance by making "theory" itself the marker of privilege rather than "discursive and material practices," such as writing books, articles, and conference papers, that are favored over teaching in a pattern of reward. This move throws her into contradiction; she is suspicious of "a reliance upon binaries and the construction of taxonomies" (114), yet cannot "reconceive the relationship of theory and practice" without relying on them. As Susan Jarratt suggests, to imagine the escape from binary thinking is to imagine transcendence. Ede's analysis inevitably demonstrates, as she allows, that she cannot escape the "theoretical strategies" she resists; further, "theory" remains something opposed to, different from, and privileged over "practice." In this formulation, "theory" is both the oppressor and the only route out of oppression—those who have no privilege are said to lack the very thing that Ede demonstrates they need: "theory."

Any published attempt to reconceive "the nature and relationship of theory and practice in the academy" (Ede 127) in terms of the opposition is destined to maintain it, and inadvertently privilege one over another. Sticking with Ede's initial move—to retheorize the theory-practice conflict as a practice-practice conflict—offers a more promising opportunity to rethink the ways practices are acknowledged, rewarded, and motivated. It demands that we see any institutionalized hierarchy of practices as an imposed order rather than a natural one. Until we are able to dismantle inequitable and unethical hierarchies of practice, we must take care not to blame the processes of constructing concepts (theory), but the power structures that disproportionately reward different modes of constructing or *disseminating* theory—publication, say, over teaching and tutoring. Until we find ways to transcend the binary thinking that worries Ede, our best effort to counter its hegemonic potential is to explore the possibility that two constructs can be "opposed" only if they are already interrelated. And if we do not actively encourage tutors to investigate "theory," we can hardly expect them to understand or consciously shape their practice.

If theorizing is something like examining the relationships among concepts, definitions, and propositions for the purpose of explaining or predicting, one can hardly walk across the street without theorizing, let alone conceptualize a practice-practice conflict or tutor self-critically. Examining relationships among concepts for the purpose of explaining or predicting appears to be what Andrea Lunsford means by *theory* when she contends that an effective monitoring of any "collaborative environment" such as a writing center" calls on *each person involved* in the collaboration to build a theory of collaboration" (39).[4] It appears to be what Hey and Nahrwold mean by *theory* when they argue in *The Writing Lab Newsletter* that "only theory makes higher order concerns (HOCs) visible and discussable" (4). When defined this way, the relationship of theory to tutoring is obvious. *It is by way of theory that we determine the "practical."*

Tutors need *theory* in the sense that Hey and Nahrwold use the term, as a way of explaining and predicting; but to assume an informed, critical stance to their location in the disciplinary and institutional web that defines writing centers, tutors need theory as Ede implicitly defines it, as a privileged discourse we sometimes call *Theory*, the ownership of which defines teachers' and tutors' expertise in institutional terms.[5] Tutors need theory (to explain or predict), then, to understand the *Theory* (as privileged discourse) they need. Without an awareness of theorizing as an active way of making sense of what they hear and read, student tutors are likely to engage the professional discourse as a confusing and unfinished quest for a final Truth rather than as the "conversation" that Murphy and Sherwood promote. As skeptical of the "strategies of theory" as Ede rightfully suggests we all ought to be, it seems to me we cannot in good conscience avoid foregrounding and exploring them with the student tutors we ask to engage in any sort of "practice."

In his *College Composition and Communication* article, "Composition Theory in the 1980s," Richard Fulkerson offers a taxonomy of theory; he breaks *Theory* down into related yet discrete categories of concepts, definitions, and propositions. Some aspects of Fulkerson's article were not popular with poststructural critics for obvious reasons. Further, no taxonomy can be a lens without a binder. However, Fulkerson's categories will seem particularly attractive to those who train tutors because they are born of misgivings similar to those

Ede expresses. Fulkerson is not a champion of *theory* for *Theory's* sake; the chief value of his taxonomy is that it can help student tutors begin to untangle and diagram the often contradictory and confused theoretical syntax of writing center *Theory* as they struggle to make it relevant to their tutorial practice.

Fulkerson begins with the problem that dogs use of the term *theory* almost wherever it appears; when used "to refer to any general propositions about writing and its teaching," the term obscures more than it explains (410). He goes on to suggest that such general propositions typically arise out of four categories of theory, and that by observing and acting along this taxonomy one can both detect and evade overt theoretical contradiction:

- *Theories of value:* "what we want student writers to achieve as a result of effective teaching" (Fulkerson 411). A writing teacher or tutor's primary theory of value is typically a conception of what constitutes good writing, but it may have little to do with writing. Jacqueline Glasgow, for example, contends in *The Writing Lab Newsletter* that the "bottom line" in her tutor training is this: "how you treat people is more important than what you know" (2). A teacher might value self-esteem, multicultural awareness, competent participation, or even his own popularity over some conception of writing. For Eric Hobson, it might be "to help students understand the systems of power in which they function" (4). In any case, as Fulkerson suggests, a theory of value represents the standard by which progress may be judged.
- *Theories of knowledge:* "teaching writing involves teaching epistemology" (Fulkerson 411), the study of what knowledge is and how it is "made." Teaching or tutoring writing depends on assumptions about how we know what we know. Knowledge might be conceived of as the result of social interaction, the product of solitary genius, the gift of a benevolent god, and so on.
- *Theories of procedure:* A writing teacher needs a working theory of how people do, or as Fulkerson suggests "should," go about creating texts. "That is," a teacher or tutor must also theorize about "the *means* by which writers can reach the *ends*" specified by her theory of value. By foregrounding a conception of procedure as theory, Fulkerson reminds us that "the writing process" is not an objective fact, but a cover term for a diverse set of theories relating to procedure that has been fixed or hardened through repetition and acceptance like a dead metaphor (411).
- *Theories of pedagogy:* "Some perspective about classroom procedures and curricular designs suitable for enabling students to achieve" what is valued. Pedagogical theory "also concerns means, but the teacher's means rather than the writer's" (411).

When I ask my tutors to "enter the theoretical conversation surrounding the practice of tutoring," it is not with the unquestioned assumption that having read the professional discourse will necessarily make them better tutors. I am asking them to *contend* with theories of value, knowledge, procedure, and pedagogy as a way of "developing an informed practice" (Murphy and Sherwood 2, 4). Moreover, I'm asking them to recognize that their practical activities are suspended in a web of practical activities such as publishing *Theory*, administering institutions, and conforming to socially accepted standards for literacy and its teaching. Fulkerson's taxonomy of theory supports this effort in two important and related ways.

It breaks down *Theory* to reveal the work of *theories*. New tutors asked to understand Fulkerson's taxonomy are less likely to think of theory exclusively as a set of oppressive, exclusive discursive practices than as a set of interrelated concepts we all use to develop, explain and, most important, change ways we act in the world. Fulkerson implies a method for interrogating *Theory*; it provides tutors with the capacity to recognize and explore the diversity of values, procedures, epistemologies and pedagogies at work in writing center scholarship. More important, it allows them to map and explain their confusion when the theorists they read confuse one category of theory and its concerns with another, or uncritically oppose "theory" to "practice." As a reading strategy, Fulkerson's taxonomy allows even undergraduate tutors to quickly offer meaningful answers to Eric Hobson's question: "Writing Center Practice Often Counters Its Theory. So What?" Further, by classifying theories of pedagogy, value, and procedure alongside theories of knowledge, Fulkerson implicitly invites students to recognize and critique the preoccupation with epistemology at work in the professional scholarship.

Fulkerson's taxonomy enables tutors' agency as readers *and* as composers—of both *Theory* and of tutoring praxis. It encourages them to make conscious their assumptions about tutoring writing by providing them with a heuristic, a vocabulary with which they can develop answers, and a framework for testing the coherence of their own combinations of value, procedure, epistemology, and pedagogy. Upon understanding how and why publishing authors use theory to promote change through their own practices, student tutors are more likely to take active responsibility for developing and defending their own tutorial practice. Moreover, they are more likely to understand the differential between authoring *Theory* and enacting pedagogy as a "practice-practice" split rather than as a division between "theory" and "practice."

Write On! Layering "The Conversation"

My use of Fulkerson's taxonomy when introducing student tutors to *Theory* reflects my adherence to a social epistemology—I find the conception of knowledge as a consequence of social interaction to be powerfully persuasive. Who and what we are, what we are likely to "invent" or "discover" is intricately tied to what we've agreed to accept by using language with others. I do not promote a social epistemology as fact, therefore, but as a belief, and it has a powerful impact on what I value for my students, what I ask them to do, and how I encourage them to do it. My belief in a social epistemology leads me to align my own theorizing about values, pedagogy, and procedure.

To introduce new tutors to professional discourse—that of writing center scholars or the wider field of rhetoric and composition—is not necessarily to introduce students to the possibility of constructing their own theory. Asking tutors to read articles by faceless scholars and talk about them in the classroom may satisfy my understanding of knowledge production as an intertextual transaction; however, new tutors are hard pressed to relate their literal interpretation of *conversation* to reading and writing. Tutors new to epistemological theory are likely to interpret *conversation* as C. J. Singley and H. W. Boucher do—"the form of communication we use for tutoring sessions." And they are likely to assume, as Singley and Boucher do, that it "should structure all aspects of a peer tutoring program" (11). The value of *conversation* as a trope for the authorization of knowledge through literate scholarly activity does not come as readily to new student tutors as it does to practiced scholars. As Simard argues, tutors tend to "define their new role rigidly and can become inflexible in both their stance and attitude" (198). By contrast, their perception of published scholarship as dense, fixed, and distant can make it seem irreconcilable with the immediacy of the talk-based tutorials they are intensely motivated to manage. Without a pedagogy that actively encourages the role of literate activity in the social construction of knowledge, directors who ask students to read the professional discourse may be simply underscoring a perception of the "theory/practice" division most students bring with them to tutor training.

A truncated social epistemology centered on talk may not encourage tutors to develop values for their tutees centered on writing, and it may do little to promote awareness of the tutor's institutional and social roles. Training pedagogy that complements "talk" with intensely interactive reading and writing widens the context of training beyond the tutorial to the textual "conversation" that informs it, and the social and institutional attitudes and expectations for literacy that necessitate the tutorial to begin with. A pedagogy consistent with a Western social epistemology ought to model and encourage procedures by which students come to recognize the production and interpretation of text as central to the process of authorizing knowledge. E-mail listservs offer such an opportunity.

The use of electronic fora in composition courses is well documented, yet its possibilities for tutor training have been elaborated only recently. In the "Special Issue" of *Computers and Composition* dedicated to writing centers and electronic technology, Virginia Chappell and Ellen Strenski each explain the integration of E-mail listservs in tutor training programs. My own reasons for establishing a course listserv parallel theirs in many ways. Like Strenski, I hoped that the listserv, *WriteOn*, would become more than another channel for the top-down distribution of "information," a community-building apparatus that encouraged boundary-crossing participation. Like Chappell, I wanted to promote movement beyond the isolated, student-teacher transaction of most course-based writing and give students the opportunity to see each other's writing and the immediate impact of their rhetorical choices. Mostly, though, like Chappell, I'd hoped that a listserv would make "real" the relationship between published *Theory* and tutors' situated experiences, and allow them to recognize the role of literate transactions in constructing authoritative knowledge.

Such understanding is not a *de facto* result of asking students to read excerpts from the professional discourse. Photocopied articles and essay collections appear to student tutors as static or frozen icons of their teachers' authority rather than tentative and contingent propositions in an ongoing "conversation." When presented with published scholarship, but not the opportunity to contend with it and each other, "students have the option of accepting or rejecting that authority but are not likely to take on the responsibility of scrutinizing or modifying it" (Chappell 230). In an institutional context that literally equates *authority* with *authorship*, student tutors must be authorized to author; in an institutional context that depends on written debate to modify ideas and ultimately confer acceptance or rejection, student tutors must become response-able.

Ironically, perhaps, the most effective way to encourage students' capacity to author is for the teacher to author less. Like Chappell, I wanted to set the listserv in place, periodically stress its relationship to the professional discourse and, then, "move myself out of the way" (229). Unlike Strenski, however, it did not occur to me that "the director can participate in the conversation as a listserv member rather than as the director" (252). Well aware that students would detect my presence as both the "overall orchestrator of class activity" (Chappell 230) and a committed "lurker," I developed a protocol statement for *WriteOn*, and structured my expectations in line with the values that motivated me toward the listserv: I wanted students to form whatever electronic association they would by cooperatively engaging the published professional discourse.

Fearful that too many lengthy posts, and my stipulation that the list was required reading, would turn *WriteOn* into an unwanted obligation, I asked students to be direct, and limit their posts to 300 words. In my second "question" of the term, I asked contributors to "compare and contrast" a couple of readings for the week. This was more direction than they wanted, and in the following class they let me know it. They realized what I did not: *WriteOn* was in danger of becoming just another way of turning in assignments. After that, I handed over the process of posting discussion starters to student tutors, maintaining the "professional approach" implicitly by stipulating only that "questions" encourage consideration of published scholarship. Students were left to contend with *Theory* and each others' theories in an evolving and unsettled dialectic.

As one student tutor who took the course, Kathryn Giglio, explained to the National Writing Centers Association conference in Park City, Utah, the evolution of this electronic community and its relationship to the professional, published discourse was elastic and uncertain, precisely the kind of "ongoing theorizing" (233) that Chappell reports. Slowly, writing emerged as both the object of the student-tutors' study and the agent that simultaneously held them together and threatened to pull them apart. Giglio's essay demonstrates that via *WriteOn* student tutors did not simply mimic via e-mail the published discourse they read, they constructed a hybrid particular to their circumstances, one capable of "helping itself," of "re-center[ing] institutional writing center knowledge as something personal, social, and cultural" (9).

Yet Giglio demonstrates that the course listserv also functioned as a location for the virtual inscription and maintenance of conventional academic hierarchies grounded in what she calls "theoretical literacies":

> Although tempted to immediately embrace the surfaces of cyber-rebellion, it became clear to me that no discourse, not even that of writing consultants, can exist outside the ideological constructs of institutional power and control. It can be argued that while online technologies demonstrate the power of peer collaboration, collaborative efforts are too easily broken apart on the precarious landscape of language and power. (5)

In a close reading of the *WriteOn* archives, Giglio shows the ways that a field's knowledge — its professional "conversation" — functions *as* institutional authority, and how "collaborative activity" among tutors effectively constructs tutors "as guardians of this knowledge" (6):

> Not all [threads] were communally inclusive, nor were they communally productive. One thread focused on the term "ideology," but only four, second-year graduate students actually "collaborated" about the word's implications. As one of the guilty co-creators of the thread, I never once stopped to define the term for others, nor attempted to apply it directly to the common ground of writing center theory. Users of this term formed an exclusive sub-group, and, not meaning to, pushed the postings of our undergraduate and first-year graduate classmates to the margins. The "specialized" talk that we had learned in the academy threatened to divide the discussion. (7–8)

Interrupting the "Conversation"

Perhaps in spite of the messaging protocol I established initially, and the listserv's implicit location in the performance-evaluation schema written into every credit-bearing course, *WriteOn* became the fluid mechanism Giglio describes, a forum for students to at once try on and actively resist published scholarship's disciplining voice of mastery. Situated as a kind of middle ground between their "private" discourses and circulated *Theory*, the listserv compelled student tutors to contend with each other and with the professional scholarship of writing center studies. Bound less by the sometimes rigid expectations for form, style, and textual evidence that typify published scholarship, listserv discourse can be "a roundabout way of adopting and adapting to conventions" (Welch 18).

As the description implies, though, *WriteOn* and its participants existed in a space removed from yet dependent on the professional discourse. Student tutors raised fascinating questions, offered considered responses, and engaged in lively critique, yet this discursive interaction had no influence upon writing center studies writ large. *WriteOn* presented the possibility that tutors could engage outside the *tutorial* in another, different writing center *practice*, but it had no way to sustain *that* possibility beyond the boundaries of the class.

In the second ten-week quarter of the course, then, during which student tutors met every *other* week, I encouraged them to interrupt the "conversation" and introduce themselves. I asked them to pick one of two brief (500–1500 words) "discussion papers" they had written during the first ten weeks, and develop it into a form appropriate to a specific audience of writing center practitioner-theorists. Undergraduates, for example, might write a paper to be read at an undergraduate conference or to be published in *The Dangling Modifier* [published nationally for undergraduate tutors at Penn State University] or *The Writing Lab Newsletter*. Graduate students might write for a graduate-student or professional conference, or a professional journal that includes longer arguments written from sources.

Students divided themselves into groups of four, and each group devised its own draft-due schedule. In the second-term syllabus, under the heading "What You'll Do This Quarter," I offered (or imposed upon) them a loom on which to weave their collaborative activity:

> At the beginning of each class meeting, one member of your group will present a copy of her paper to each group member. Ideally, she will include a "cover sheet" explaining her paper's rhetorical situation whom she has written for (a particular journal audience, a particular conference audience); what limitations she is under (length, documentation styles, etc.); any specific rhetorical choices she has made in anticipation of her audience (for example, she might explain that she assumes her audience is familiar with a given text or idea). This *informal* cover sheet might also explain, briefly, any specific issues or points within the paper that the author would like members of the group to consider. Your group should take 10–15 minutes to read and discuss this cover sheet to assure that a context for critique (the paper's rhetorical situation) has been established.

I asked members of each group to e-mail each author a commentary that would "reflect a careful reading of the paper's argument, a consideration of the appropriateness of the author's rhetorical choices to her audience, and specific, useful suggestions for revision that are oriented to the author's purpose and audience." Further, I asked each group to set its own agenda for workshopping the papers at the following meeting. Depending on the draft they were reviewing, and what kind of work they thought it needed, students planned a range of workshop activities from research to editing.

By the standards of Fulkerson's taxonomy, this seemed to me coherent praxis. My pedagogy reflected the values I had for my students, in Fulkerson's terms what "students are to achieve as a result of effective teaching" (411): I wanted them to be active participants in their own learning and explore the ways tutoring situated them within the larger institution. The practice remained consistent with a social epistemology, and encouraged a procedure whereby students could realize the values I promoted on their behalf—by "collaborating" with each other *and* with the scholarly field that claims to inform their practice.

Independent of class requirements, but not without my encouragement, many of the twenty-five students authored proposals developed from these papers, and eleven have been accepted to speak at conferences—from student meetings in Pittsburgh and New Orleans to the NWCA convention in Park City to the CCCC in Chicago. This level of "success" suggests that they learned a great deal about crossing from the discursive middle ground of *WriteOn* to the professional expectations for the conference abstract. However, what exposure to the written "professional conversation" taught some students best, the capacity of a power discourse to index participants along its literacy standard, was learned at some cost. One of writing center scholarship's most hallowed ideals, the possibility of a hierarchy-free "collaboration" of equal peers, crumbled as they came to grips with the inviolable relationship between authority and authorship in the academy.

Authority and Authorship

In summarizing the "Critical Debate Over Collaborative Learning," Alice Gillam demonstrates that writing center scholarship in large measure has unfolded around questions of *authority*. The word's root suggests its critical significance to the study of writing, and "virtually every segment of composition studies" is inscribed within competing definitions of the term (Clough 22). To introduce new student tutors to the professional "conversation" is to embrace "the challenge" for those engaged in tutor training: to help "tutors negotiate the paradoxes of authority" (Chappell 229). Authority is destined to remain paradoxical in writing center studies precisely because our most impassioned attempts to dismiss or destroy it are themselves products of it. Efforts to theorize *authority* out of the picture—by declaring it "voluntary social interaction" in "semi-autonomous space" (Kail and Trimbur 206–7) or a concept made moot by peership (Bruffee)—depend on a conceptual sleight-of-hand that leaves institutionalized, "functional categories" of authority right in front of us even as it appears to blind us to them.

Writing centers are sites of authority as expertise. Directors are chosen, most often, because they are deemed experts along local standards. Such standards for writing center expertise might range from scholarly reputation in the field to some conception of "experience." Students are chosen to tutor, typically, because as writers they have met a standard of expertise recognized by their directors. The key here is that while we can theorize authority in multiple ways with multiple effects, directors and tutors are always themselves products of institutional authority. They do not author themselves, their positions, or their workspace — whether they work in a center, the pages of the field's professional literature, or both. While they may well challenge "the traditional reward system, with its emphasis on individual performance and competition among students for grades and faculty esteem" (Kail and Trimbur 207), they are themselves always already the result of this system, and their best efforts to change it maddeningly demonstrate its capacity for appropriation. The system ultimately authorizes and absorbs its own critique.

By no means am I suggesting that change cannot or does not occur; however, the possibilities for change outside institutionally determined standards of authority — whatever they may be — have yet to be articulated. Student tutors who read, say, Kail and Trimbur, on the direction of a teacher dedicated to "lead students to substitute idealized versions of authority for the real forms of power that dominate their lives" have hardly "removed themselves from official structures" or achieved "detachment from the influence of authority" (208–9). They have simply traded one conception of authority for another, the new perhaps all the more authoritative because it comes packaged under the title, *Landmark Essays.* Tutors, directors, and publishing scholars are not "free" to divest themselves of power *through* functional categories of authority — tutoring, directing, publishing.

Peter Mortensen and Gem Kirsch maintain that "authority can finally only be defined and negotiated according to the circumstances in which it occurs" (567). Here Mortensen and Kirsch remind us that collaboration never begins like a game of Monopoly, with all the participants lined up at "Go" following an equal distribution of means. And, further, that individual agents are always preceded by the institutional contexts in which they interact; while change is inevitable, it is never authorized independent of a given context's conventions of authority.

The experiences of one member of my class, Gretchen Woertendyke-Rohde, demonstrate that student tutors arrive for tutor training *already* authorized along a standard of authorship, and they are motivated by institutional reward to maintain and increase that authority. In a paper also delivered at the NWCA Conference in Park City, titled "When Tutors Are Peers: Authority as a Prerequisite to Collaboration," Woertendyke-Rohde chronicles the process of unlearning a "naive" belief in "Bruffee's notion of collaborative learning . . . [in which] each participant brings 'separate but equal' knowledge to the group's collaborative efforts" (1). As her title suggests, Woertendyke-Rohde now believes that "institutional authority may be a prerequisite to collaborative learning in small group settings" (2). She begins by pointing out that collaboration — in my class and in her writing center tutoring — is never "voluntary" but always part of a pre-existing script, and that each "collaborative" context is already layered with institutional authority. Unlike a writing center tutorial, however, where levels of authority are implied by the setting and therefore imperceptible and seemingly inoperative, collaboration among student tutors in this mixed graduate-undergraduate classroom setting was, for a junior English major like Woertendyke-Rohde, a persistent deference to authority defined outside the context of the collaboration:

> The written responses [to my draft], while negative in tone, were immensely helpful. I took them as important critical viewpoints, even if my ego was wounded . . . . The classroom workshopping of my paper, however, fell far short of my expectations for peer collaboration . . . . While I did receive suggestions of where to locate appropriate sources for my research, I was left feeling more irrelevant than helped. The suggestions came at the end of too many questions about my paper, and not enough of an attempt to determine what I was trying to say. When my groupmates collaborated on my paper, I felt little attempt on their part to contribute to the final product, little investment in my project.

As Woertendyke-Rohde argues, the primary effect of the collaboration was to confirm the strata of authority in place at the beginning of the process:

> The varying degrees by which each of us could employ the conventions of academic writing reflected our variable institutional status; we were realistic collaborators because we were unequal, but we were hardly the idealized, equal collaborators we'd read about.

Further, she argues that if the end result of collaboration is, as she takes Bruffee to imply, Rorty's definition of normal discourse—when "everyone agrees on the 'set of conventions about what counts as a relevant contribution, what counts as a question, what counts as having a good argument for that answer or a good criticism of it'" (92)—then collaboration toward this end must begin with the following:

> an implicit inequality between students; while some are already a part of the "knowledge community," others are accepted into it only after they have mastered the "normal discourse," the conventions of the field. This concept of collaboration is vastly different from Lunsford's notion that "collaborative environments and tasks must demand collaboration. Students, tutors, teachers must really need one another to carry out common goals" (111). Lunsford's assertion led me to ask myself if my group members really needed me to carry out their goals? The answer, of course, is no. However, I desperately needed them to learn the normal discourse and gain admittance into this knowledge community.
> . . . [C]ollaboration, in practice, was a lesson in conforming to the expected language and conventions of academic writing in the field of composition. . . . In our group workshop, once I accepted and began to incorporate normal discourse, our status as co-learners began, allowing collaboration on my paper to take place. This happened only after the rules, the conventions, were en forced by the graduate students, and I accepted them. In discussing the role of tutors in the writing center, Bruffee points out that as peer tutors, "our task must involve engaging students in conversation at as many points in the writing process as possible and that *we should contrive to ensure that that*

conversation is similar in as many ways as possible to the way we would like them eventually to write" (my emphasis, 91). Bruffee's proposal that we "contrive to ensure"—that is, that we understand the conversation or collaborative process well enough to control it and encourage a specific outcome—destabilizes collaborative learning as dependent upon both parties being equal peers, and questions the assumption that knowledge is a product of status-equal or "voluntary" collaboration. On the whole, Bruffee's statements—and my own group workshop experience—suggest that established authority is a prerequisite to collaborative learning.

How much Woertendyke-Rohde learned "collaboratively" about the professional discourse of writing center studies was ultimately judged by the profession itself. Abstracts of both papers that she wrote for this class—the one workshopped by her group and the critique of that experience excerpted here—were accepted for reading at a national conference.

The ultimate implication of the professional approach's invitation to "join the conversation" is to harden the relationship between authority and authorship, to ask student tutors to produce "submissions" and submit them(selves) to authorities who will authorize them. As Giglio and Woertendyke-Rohde demonstrate, the professional approach to tutor training does nothing quite so well as normalize for student tutors the stratification of institutional work into a competitive, exclusionary, and sometimes violent hierarchy of discursive practices. Through the professional approach, the dominant practices associated with writing centers—pedagogy and scholarship—are unified in what Grimm calls "a regulatory function."

Lessons of Inscription

The students we train as tutors are so enjoyable to work with because they come to us free of the resistance to writing that marks so many of our students. Our student tutors are "good writers" not only because they write with fewer errors than their fellow students but because their ideals already approximate ours. They come to us predisposed to academic discipline, typically in our own field, structured in the pattern of reward that aligns authority with authorship. Yet often they arrive innocent of how they are situated in a culture and institution that uses literacy, in a variety of conceptions, as a yardstick for competence; full of the passion, romance, and transformative potential of the written word, they are idealized (and much younger) versions of ourselves.

As writing center scholars continue to question the innocence and unrealized idealism of our "landmark" essays, readers will be less and less satisfied with agendas of all stripes that exploit tutors as a compliant, multipurpose work force. As tutor trainers grow increasingly uncomfortable with scholarship that denies the implication of hierarchy in writing center practices, we will continue to interrogate the ethical dimensions of token professionalism and training models that construct tutors as the practically mute. A return to the "newly practical," tutorial-centered approach that can "blind" tutors to the ways they are "enmeshed in a system or systems" (North 12) may not be an option. And as faculty grow less and less accepting of a professional "career template" that ensures the failure of those engaged primarily in teaching rather than publication (Sosnoski), we will become more and more reflective about the implications of ensnaring student tutors within that same model.

We may not be free to liberate ourselves or our student tutors from the institutional structures that both unify and stratify, and yet remain a collective that "we" would recognize. "We" are already inscribed within the institutional discourse that calls out to us as a community. Those who develop training pedagogies can, however, "invite" student tutors to consciously explore their implication in an intensely competitive economy of literacy that both distributes rewards and exacts costs. We might make explicit the lessons of inscription. The alternative is to encourage tutors, those who often strive most to be like us, to replicate our worst self-image.

Notes

[1] I want to acknowledge the 1996-97 students of Writing Center Theory and Pedagogy—a twenty-week, two-quarter seminar required of all graduate and undergraduate student tutors—who struggled with and against my attempts to professionalize them: Derek Boczkowski, Beth Ann Bryant-Richards, HonorC line, Patricia Trimnell Doss, Liana Waugh Fitch, Kate Giglio, Nellie Greely, Richard Harper, Mark King, Karen Kopelson, Theresa Lesh, Jennifer Marie Marcus, Michele Mohr, Margaret O'Brien, John Pendell, Debbie Pinkston, Elisa Ridley, Riki Robson, Gretchen Woertendyke-Rohde, Tim Sheehan, Katie Smolik, Cedric Stines, Diane Snezlecki, Todd Zuniga.

[2] See *Pedagogy of the Oppressed*, especially Chapter 2.

[3] See James Sosnoski's description of the "token professional" in literary studies and my exploration of the "ideology of research" in "Composing Composition Studies."

[4] John Pendell interprets Lunsford's claim as a call for tutors to discuss the purposes and importance of theory with student writers.

[5] Understanding *theory* in the two senses I have proposed here might be developed best by considering the range of meanings the term has been used to signify, both in the wider culture (see Williams) and the field of composition studies (see Heilker and Vandenberg).

Works Cited

Bannister-Wills, Linda. "Developing a Peer Tutoring Program." *Writing Centers: Theory and Administration.* Ed. Gary A. Olson. Urbana: NCTE, 1984. 132–43. Print.

Bruffee, Kenneth A. "Peer Tutoring and the 'Conversation of Mankind.'" *Landmark Essays: Writing Centers* Ed. Christina Murphy and Joe Law. Davis: Hermagoras, 1995. 87–98. Print.

Capossela, Toni-Lee. "Collaboration as Triangulation: An Apprenticeship System of Tutor Training." *The Writing Lab Newsletter* 20.6 (1996): 1-4. Print.

Chappell, Virginia. "Theorizing in Practice: Tutor Training 'Live, from the VAX Lab.'" *Computers and Composition* 12.2 (1995): 227–36. Print.

Clark, Irene L. *Writing in the Center: Teaching in a Writing Center Setting.* 2nd ed. Dubuque: Kendall/Hunt, 1992. Print.

Clough, Jennifer A. "Authority." *Keywords in Composition Studies*. Ed. Paul Heilker and Peter Vandenberg. Portsmouth: Boynton/Cook, 1996. 22–25. Print.

Denton, Thomas. "Peer Tutors' Evaluations of the Tutor Training Course and the Tutoring Experience: A Questionnaire." *The Writing Lab Newsletter* 18.3 (1993): 14–16. Print.

Ede, Lisa. "Writing Centers and the Politics of Location: A Response to Terrance Riley and Stephen M. North." *The Writing Center Journal* 16.2 (1996): 111–30. Print.

Freire, Paulo. *Pedagogy of the Oppressed*. New York: Continuum, 1990. Print.

Fulkerson, Richard. "Composition Theory in the 1980s: Axiological Consensus and Paradigmatic Diversity." *College Composition and Communication* 41.4 (1990): 409–29. Print.

Giglio, Kathryn. "Cyber-Communities and Collaboration: Elements of Authority in a Writing Center Listserv." National Writing Centers Association Convention. Olympia Park Hotel, Park City, UT. 18 Sept. 1997. Print.

Gillam, Alice M. "Collaborative Learning Theory and Peer Tutoring Practice." *Intersections: Theory-Practice in the Writing Center*. Ed. Joan A. Mullin and Ray Wallace. Urbana: NCTE, 1994. 39–53. Print.

Glasgow, Jacqueline N. "Training Tutors for Secondary School Writing Centers." *The Writing Lab Newsletter* 20.3 (1995): 1–6. Print.

Grimm, Nancy. "The Regulatory Role of the Writing Center: Coming to Terms with a Loss of Innocence." *The Writing Center Journal* 17.1 (1996): 5–29. Print.

Harris, Muriel. *Teaching One-to-One: The Writing Conference*. Urbana: NCTE, 1986. Print.

Heilker, Paul, and Peter Vandenberg. Introduction. *Keywords in Composition Studies*. Ed. Paul Heilker and Peter Vandenberg. Portsmouth: Boynton/Cook, 1996. Print.

Hey, Phil, and Cindy Nahrwold. "Tutors Aren't Trained-They're Educated: The Need for Composition Theory." *The Writing Lab Newsletter* 18.7 (1994): 4–5. Print.

Hobson, Eric H. "Writing Center Practice Often Counters Its Theory. So What?" *Intersections: Theory-Practice in the Writing Center*. Ed. Joan A. Mullin and Ray Wallace. Urbana: NCTE, 1994. 1–10. Print.

Jarratt, Susan. "Response to John Poulakos." *Rhetoric Society Quarterly* 22.2 (1992): 68–70. Print.

Kail, Harvey, and John Trimbur. "The Politics of Peer Tutoring." *Landmark Essays: Writing Centers*. Ed. Christina Murphy and Joe Law. Davis: Hermagoras, 1995. 203–10. Print.

Lunsford, Andrea. "Collaboration, Control, and the Idea of a Writing Center." *Landmark Essays: Writing Centers*. Ed. Christina Murphy and Joe Law. Davis: Hermagoras, 1995. 36–42. Print.

Meyer, Emily, and Louise Z. Smith, eds. *The Practical Tutor*. New York: Oxford UP, 1987. Print.

Mortensen, Peter, and Gesa E. Kirsch. "On Authority in the Study of Writing." *College Composition and Communication* 44.4 (1993): 556–72. Print.

Munger, Roger H., Ilene Rubenstein, and Edna Barrow. "Observation, Interaction, and Reflection: The Foundation for Tutor Training." *The Writing Lab Newsletter* 21.4 (1996): 1–5. Print.

Murphy, Christina, and Steve Sherwood, eds. *The St. Martin's Sourcebook for Writing Tutors*. New York: St. Martins, 1995. Print.

North, Stephen M. "The Idea of a Writing Center." *Landmark Essays: Writing Centers*. Ed. Christina Murphy and Joe Law. Davis, CA: Hermagoras, 1995. 71–86. Print.

---. "Revisiting 'The Idea of a Writing Center.'" *The Writing Center Journal* 15.1 (1994): 7–19. Print.

Pendell, John. "Toward True Collaboration: Co-Theorizing in the Writing Center." National Writing Centers Association Convention. Olympia Park Hotel, Park City, UT. 20 September 1997. Print.

Riley, Terrance. "The Unpromising Future of Writing Centers." *The Writing Center Journal 15.1* (1994): 20–34. Print.

Silk, Bobbie. "Review of *The St. Martin's Sourcebook for Writing Tutors* and *The Bedford Guide for Writing Tutors*." *The Writing Center Journal* 16.1 (1995): 81–85. Print.

Simard, Rodney. "Assessing a New Professional Role: The Writing Center Tutor." *Writing Centers: Theory and Administration*. Ed. Gary A. Olson. Urbana: NCTE, 1984. 197–205. Print.

Singley, C. J., and H. W. Boucher. "Dialogue in Tutor Training: Creating the Essential Space for Learning." *The Writing Center Journal* 8.2 (1998): 11–22. Print.

Sosnoski, James J. *Token Professionals and Master Critics: A Critique of Orthodoxy in Literary Studies*. Albany: SUNY P, 1994. Print.

Strenski, Ellen, and TA-TALKers. "Virtual Staff Meetings: Electronic Tutor Training with a Local E-Mail Listserv Discussion Group." *Computers and Composition* 12.2 (1995): 247–55. Print.

Vandenberg, Peter. "Composing Composition Studies: Scholarly Publication and the Practice of Discipline." *Under Construction: Working at the Intersections of Composition Theory, Research, and Practice*. Ed. Christine Farris and Chris M. Anson. Logan: Utah State UP, 1998. 19–29. Print.

Warnock, Tilly, and John Warnock. "Liberatory Writing Centers: Restoring Authority to Writers." In *Writing Centers: Theory and Administration*. Ed. Gary A. Olson. Urbana: NCTE, 1984. 16–23. Print.

Welch, Nancy. "Migrant Rationalities: Graduate Students and the Idea of Authority in the Writing Center." *The Writing Center Journal* 16.1 (1995): 5–23. Print.

Williams, Raymond. *Keywords: A Vocabulary of Culture and Society*. Revised Edition. New York: Oxford UP, 1983. Print.

Woertendyke-Rohde, Gretchen. "When Tutors Are Peers: Authority as a Prerequisite to Collaboration." National Writing Centers Association Convention. Olympia Park Hotel, Park City, UT. 20 Sept. 1997. Print.

Portrait of the Tutor as an Artist: Lessons No One Can Teach

Steve Sherwood
TEXAS CHRISTIAN UNIVERSITY

Citing the Greek rhetorician Isocrates, Steve Sherwood argues in this essay—originally published in The Writing Center Journal in 2007—that, like writing itself, tutoring is a rhetorical art form whose mastery combines talent, training, and experience. To become artists rather than artisans who base their craft on repetitive, rule-bound techniques, tutors must come to the work already equipped with a high aptitude for writing, speaking, and interacting with people. Tutor training courses often provide a crucial, yet insufficient, stage in the development of these aptitudes—insufficient because training courses cannot anticipate or expose tutors to many of the

challenges they will face as they work with writers. To complete their shift
from artisan to artist, tutors must go beyond their training and maximize
the lessons they learn from experience by cultivating a taste for surprise,
developing a sensitivity to kairos *(the rhetorical situation), practicing their*
ability to improvise solutions to unfamiliar problems, and applying a height-
ened awareness to tutorials by viewing each as a potentially unique event.
In the process, they learn valuable lessons about writers, themselves, and
the rhetorical arts of writing, speaking, and tutoring that a course alone
cannot teach them.

A university employee, Nancy, recently brought to me an idea for a nonfiction book about coping with thyroid cancer. In remission and awaiting
word on her latest diagnostic scan, Nancy began our tutorial by excitedly
reviewing the many and sometimes amusing lessons about life and family she
had learned from her ordeal. As she explained, the book gave her a chance to
explore her long-dormant writing skills, work on a project worthy of her time,
and pass along what she had learned to other cancer victims. Her personal
investment in the project was high, and the intensity with which she listened to
my every word of encouragement and advice certainly raised the stakes for me.
As we discussed where to begin and the book's potential commercial appeal,
I felt edgy and alert—a condition heightened by Nancy's sudden jumps from
idea to idea. I wanted to offer support but not build false hope, so I tried to
balance any assurance that she had good ideas with a realistic assessment. She
asked hard questions about working in a mixed genre—in her case, autobi-
ography combined with elements of a "how-to" manual that might eventually
become a sort of humorous *Chicken Soup for the Cancer Survivor's Soul.* Some
of her questions I simply could not answer, in part because many of her ideas
remained half-formed and success would hinge on her persistence and writing
ability. But I improvised suggestions based on some experience with creative
nonfiction, a slight familiarity with "how-to" books, and secondhand knowledge of cancer-survival stories. Nancy left our ninety-minute brainstorming
session with an attitude of eager determination to continue working. As good
sessions sometimes do, this one left me feeling used up but exhilarated—an
intellectual version of runner's high.

I mention Nancy because our session was far from a routine tutorial—if
there is such a thing—and because she prompted me to push myself creatively and intellectually, growing in the process of trying to help her grow.
Writing center practitioners, including peer tutors, often experience the elusive, artistic aspects of writing and tutoring while struggling to make sense of
the insensible, so we know the difficulty writers have in trying to capture the
ideas and images that flash into their minds. In this essay, I want to explore
the artistic aspects of tutoring that we can learn but that no one can simply
teach us. It's a topic few writing center scholars write about—at least by that
name—perhaps because "artistic" sounds ill-defined and expressionistic.[1] But

if we accept the claim, made long ago by Isocrates, that learning a complex art such as rhetoric requires talent, training, and experience,[2] we should also accept that we learn the rhetorical art of tutoring in much the same way. To become artists at the job, we must begin with a certain amount of talent for writing, speaking, and interacting with people. A lot of the learning that goes into our development as writing tutors involves direct training, aimed at helping us handle specific situations and categories of writers, writing assignments, and rules of engagement. But the ultimate teacher, experience, often pushes us into unknown territory in our efforts to understand what a writer is trying to do and to help him or her succeed. As I will argue, a vital part of our education involves experience in reacting to and learning from four elements of artistry: (1) surprise, (2) circumstance, (3) improvisation, and (4) flow. To become artists, in other words, we must learn to cope with and embrace surprise, to spontaneously meet unexpected circumstances, to improvise appropriate and effective help for writers, and to remain open to what researchers call "flow" experiences. Some peer tutors appear, like beat poets, to come to the job equipped with a jazz-like talent for improvising solutions to novel problems, and developing this talent is perhaps the key to the writing tutor's art. Those who have this ability, I would argue, can ultimately achieve a degree of artistry both related to—and dependent on—their artistry as writers.

What Is "Art"?

Before arguing that the work tutors do in the writing center is equivalent to the work of a poet or sculptor, let me take the time to establish what I mean by "art." Philosopher Larry Shiner, who has examined historical conceptions of "art" and "artistry" says, "Today you can call virtually anything 'art' and get away with it. One reason for the explosion in what counts as art is that the art world itself has taken on the old theme of getting 'art' and 'life' back together. Gestures of this kind have lurched between the innocent and the outrageous" (3). Perhaps I am guilty of committing an outrage by applying the term "art" to the writing tutorial, but I hope not. By "art" I mean something akin to the terms *ars* and *techne*, by which the ancient Greeks and Romans referred to such diverse activities as "carpentry and poetry, shoemaking and medicine, sculpture and horse breaking" (19). *Ars* and *techne* described processes leading to works that had practical application, and the ancients made no distinction between fine art and craft or between artist and artisan (5). As Shiner says, there were "only arts, just as there were neither 'artists' nor 'artisans' but only artisan/artists who gave equal honor to skill and imagination, tradition and invention" (17–18). The distinction between artist and artisan is a recent one, he adds, with the designation of artist usually referring to one to whom the words "inspiration, imagination, freedom, and genius" might apply and that of artisan referring to one to whom the words "skill, rules, imitation, and service" (111) might apply. As these definitions suggest, an artist is a breaker of new ground and a maker of unique works or experiences while a competent artisan follows rules, learns how to perform a particular task repetitively, such as making a wooden bowl, and replicates this performance many times, striving not for uniqueness or originality of expression but for successful imitation of the original product.

The Tutor as Artist vs. Artisan

Applying these terms to the writing center, one can speculate that a tutor who performs as an artisan would take a similar approach to each tutorial, seeing tutoring as a repetitive, rule-bound task she can master through diligence. No doubt all of us act as artisans at some point in the work week, approaching particular tutorials as run-of-the-mill. Some tutorials—for example, a request for help with APA style—might qualify as routine. In fact, much of the training peer tutors undergo prepares them to be artisans—to follow the rules directors set for them (and this training is a necessary part of their development). Consider, for example, the recipes and scripts directors give neophyte tutors to help them survive their early tutorials. One such recipe I use in training divides a tutorial into seven steps: (1) greet the client, (2), discuss the assignment, (3) set a focus for the tutorial, (4) read the paper, (5) evaluate strengths and weaknesses, (6) give suggestions for revision, and (7) end the tutorial gracefully. Such a list, like a standard essay structure in a composition manual, has some value because tutorials will usually include these steps (though not necessarily in this order). But directors expect tutors to develop far beyond the need for such recipes, and those who do not would presumably continue to do the work of artisans.

By contrast, a tutor who performs as an artist would view each tutorial as a potentially unique event, a chance to experience instances of creativity, engage completely in the moment, and effect change in the writer and herself—without ever pretending she could fully master the art. Such a tutor would view any rules laid down during training as flexible rather than binding. Of course, one cannot seriously suggest that rules do not apply to writing center work, so often constrained by the needs and requirements of student writers, professors, the university, the profession, and society itself. A tutor sits at the nexus of conflicting forces involving ethics, practices, and social customs and can never feel quite sure that what she is saying or doing in a given situation is ethically, practically, or socially correct. And yet, in the service of student writers, she must speak and act. Through experience, she will have practiced the art form enough to learn how to navigate safely through these forces and devise a suitable response to a particular rhetorical situation. Postmodern theorist Jean-Francois Lyotard argues that all writers should work as artists do, "without rules in order to formulate rules of what *will have been done*" (qtd. in Vitanza 163, emphasis in original). As Lyotard suggests, rules apply only in hindsight to a specific writer's project and may not apply to the next project or to the work of another writer. Each writer invents her own "rules" through experience and cannot teach them to others. An artistic tutor operates in a similar way, helping writers work through projects in order to gain insights into what they have done and are trying to do. Where elements of the artistic merge with workaday realities, where a tutor relies not only on established rules and existing skills but also on the impromptu creation of an appropriate response to each rhetorical situation, tutoring departs from the recipes of the artisan and attains some of the aspects of a fine art.

Cultivating a Taste for Surprise

One might begin building an artistic approach to tutoring by cultivating a taste for surprise, which has intimate connections to invention, wit, and writing. Indeed, one entry in the *Oxford English Dictionary* defines *wit* as that "quality of speech or writing which consists in the apt association of thought and expression, calculated to surprise and delight by its unexpectedness." Humor theorist Arthur Asa Berger argues that surprise is a necessary element of comic invention, saying, "Humorists, like all creative people, live in a world of chance . . . where random happenings and accidents suggest possibilities to be explored and developed" (171). Sigmund Freud notes the relationship between wit and invention in his discussion of the sudden insights that occur when a person's mind bypasses logic through what amounts to a "short-circuit" (182). As Freud explains, a joke is especially pleasurable when it connects ideas that ordinarily are "remote and foreign" (182). V. K. Krishna Menon cites a similar mechanism—"hopping"—by which humor forges surprising, yet creative and potentially useful, ideas by skipping logical steps and leaping to an association less clearly logical. Hopping allows a person to perceive indirect or metaphorical connections among objects, people, or ideas that a logical approach might miss.

In the haphazard wordplay of the writing center tutorial something similar sometimes happens. There is often an element of surprise in our conversations; things happen that no one can entirely predict. Our give-and-take dialogue can sometimes generate unexpected links between ideas (for example, Arnold Schwarzenegger as radical feminist), which can strike tutor and student writer as amusing yet, in a backhanded way, illuminating. These short-circuits or instances of hopping help create a set of circumstances that may never happen again, but out of which fragmented notions combine in unexpected patterns. And some of these patterns may prove both creative and valuable—at least to the student writer. Last semester, for example, I observed a conversation between a peer tutor and student writer that took a surprising turn thanks to what looks like a case of hopping. Assigned to write an essay on invention processes, the writer was—ironically enough—stuck for an idea. During a collaborative brainstorming session with him, and as if thinking aloud, the tutor asked, "Why do so many people come up with great ideas in the shower?"

Without hesitation, the student said, "Steam."

After a brief silence, the tutor asked, "Steam?" They both laughed, but the student nodded with unshakable confidence and repeated, "Steam."[3]

A discussion followed as the tutor pressed him to elaborate on this absurd notion, and together they drew a cause and effect chain leading from steam to heat, from heat to relaxation, from relaxation to revelation, and from revelation to invention. The student's surprising and illogical leap led to a good paper topic, and I later praised the tutor for being alert and open-minded enough to take pleasure from and run with the student's idea. Such moments may not occur in every tutoring session, but as Truman Capote reveals in a *Paris Review* interview, surprise is an essential element in his own and other writers' creative processes. As he says, "In the working-out, infinite surprises happen. Thank God, because the surprise, the twist, the phrase that comes at the right moment out of nowhere, is the unexpected dividend, that joyful little push that keeps a writer going" (Hill 297). The surprises that occur during tutorials can—if embraced—also bring unexpected dividends for a tutor and student writer, giving them experience with what may become an important element in their artistic processes.

Responding to Contingency and Circumstance

Although saying so may sound paradoxical, surprise is the rule within the contingent, circumstantial setting of the writing tutorial—and in responding to surprise, a tutor must rely to a great extent on her own spontaneity. After all, when she goes to work each day, she has no way to anticipate the sorts of questions she will have to answer or the challenges she will face. Unlike a classroom teacher, a writing tutor cannot rely on lesson plans. And even when she can prepare, thanks to appointments aimed at resolving particular issues, she cannot predict the circuitous paths the conversation will take. Writers may interject, ask unanticipated questions for which the tutor has no definite answer, and express misunderstandings the tutor must attempt to address on the spot. And students are right to put tutors on the spot, to ask questions, to lead the conversation astray, to misunderstand points, and to resist advice, especially when doing so leads them to deeper understanding of their own ideas and writing processes. Students often ask such challenging questions as "If Hemingway can use sentence fragments, why can't I?" Or they bring us essays that may fail to meet a professor's assignment but do so in clever and interesting ways, and these essays put tutors in the uncomfortable position of deciding whether to advise the writers to take the safe or the risky road. Writers also tie themselves into stylistic or ethical knots, which they ask tutors to help untie. Last semester, for instance, a young man came to our center asking for help with a journal assignment due the next day. Twenty minutes into the session, the tutor assigned to work with him came to my office and explained her dilemma, one we had never faced before. For the past three months, the young man—a kinesiology student—should have been keeping a journal of his efforts to use diet and exercise to achieve specific personal fitness goals. His problem, which had become ours, was that he had not written a single entry. He wanted the tutor to help him write them now.

"We can't help him cheat, can we?" she asked.

"No we can't."

"And yet he's so desperate I want to help him somehow."

"What would you do in his place?" I asked.

She made a bad joke about killing herself, and then said, "I guess, I'd write from memory changing pens to make it look like I'd done the journal all semester. But that would be cheating too, wouldn't it? He could go to the professor and beg for mercy. If he tells the truth, maybe the professor will let him write the journal from memory, for partial credit. And that wouldn't he cheating then."

"Not bad," I said, impressed on a number of levels with her thinking. "The professor may fail him anyway, but it's probably the best we can do."

By wrestling with such moral or practical dilemmas, tutors learn to think on their feet. In the process, they become increasingly sensitive to what the ancient Greeks called *kairos*, a rhetorical principle with several definitions, including "'fitness for the occasion'" (Bizzell and Herzberg 44), "opportune moment, right time, opportunity" (Poulakos 57), and "the situational forces that induce, constrain and influence discourse" (Enos, *Roman Rhetoric*, 16). Rhetorical situations tend, like tutorials, to unfold in unique, unpredictable ways and defy prefabricated responses. A sense of *kairos* helps one understand the social context surrounding the act of speaking or writing and provides clues about how to proceed. A tutor who has developed a keen sensitivity to *kairos* is more likely than those without this sensitivity to read a situation well enough to determine the most appropriate response to a particular student writer's work. For example, although some students have no trouble accepting frank criticism of their writing and welcome honesty as a key to revision, others may respond to honesty by suffering an emotional meltdown. In dealing with sensitive students, an artful tutor would walk a line somewhere between honesty and diplomacy, delivering just the right dose of candor. As John Poulakos observes, "Springing from one's sense of timing and the will to invent, *kairos* alludes to the realization that speech exists in time and is uttered both as a spontaneous formulation of and a barely constituted response to a new situation unfolding in the immediate present" (61). A person who understands the contingent nature of discourse, Poulakos says, "addresses each occasion in its particularity, its singularity, its uniqueness" (61), making her "both a hunter and a maker of unique opportunities, always ready to address improvisationally and confer meaning on new and emerging situations" (61). In plainer words, she becomes more adept at improvisation, and her process comes to resemble those of the mid-twentieth-century beat poets, like Alan Ginsberg and Jack Kerouac, who claim to have done their best work in bursts of spontaneous composition. As Rick Moody writes, the beat poets shared "a devotion to spontaneity" (qtd. in Plimpton xi) and considered their first, raw words to be poetry—"the only requirement being that the poetry *was not to be rewritten*. First thought, best thought" (emphasis in original, ix). Writing centers exist because of a widespread belief in the power of revision. And in this way, our ultimate goal could not differ more from that of the beat poets. But by engaging student writers in conversation, and giving them advice, we often rely on the principle of "first thought, best thought" (ix), drawing on a repertoire of techniques and experience, and using our creativity and our "ear" to improvise a response that sounds right in a given situation.

Improvisation as a Key to Artistry

Improvisation is, as Donald A. Schön has observed, an essential aspect of professional artistry in nearly any field. Facing a problem that goes beyond her experience, a professional improvises a solution in a way similar to the process of jazz musicians, who, by "listening to one another, listening to themselves, . . . 'feel' where the music is going and adjust their playing accordingly" (30). Elizabeth H. Boquet makes a similar observation in *Noise from the Writing Center*, where she applies the metaphor of musical improvisation to tutoring. As she says, "The most interesting improvisations work because they are always on the verge of dissonance. They are always just about to fail. They are risky. But when they work well, they are also really, really fun. They leave you wide-eyed" (76). Opportunities for improvisation, and for such wide-eyed moments, occur often in tutorials thanks to the continual need to react to changing circumstances. A tutor's preparation for such work comes primarily from her regular experience with improvisation — a capacity Quintilian calls "the crown of all our study and the highest reward of our long labours" (X.vii.2–3). However, to provide such experience, several writing center directors use exercises invented by famed improvisational acting groups such as the Groundlings — both in their work with student writers and in tutor training. For instance, in "From Stage to Page: Using Improvisational Acting to Cultivate Confidence in Writers," Adar Cohen recounts how she has used improv exercises to stimulate creativity and bolster confidence in struggling writers. At Boise State University, Michael Mattison uses a number of improvisational exercises he picked up in theatre classes to prepare tutors to react constructively to the unexpected. These exercises include

> a free-wheeling, risk-taking, community-building, expectation-dropping, laugh-inducing series of skits that prepare us as a group to role play in mock consultations and then move on to real consultations. It is a first step in the process of educating consultants to trust in themselves and their instincts and to take some risks in their consultation work. (11)

These skits often hinge on "what if" questions that lead to scenarios that could unfold in the writing center, Mattison says, such as "What if a student has plagiarized?" or "What if someone hits on me?"(12). These improvised scenes and other exercises, he says, "lead to more freedom and creativity in our consulting work and also help us better connect with one another" (13).[4]

A key to effective improvisation is riveting one's attention on what is occurring in the moment. Patricia Ryan Madson, author of *Improv Wisdom: Don't Prepare, Just Show Up*, says, "To improvise, it is essential that we use the present moment efficiently. An instant of distraction—searching for a witty line, for example—robs us of our investment in what is actually happening. We need to know everything about the moment" (36). An artistic tutor must also bring to each moment an awareness of and investment in what is actually happening. Consider, for instance, what might occur when a student writer brings to the center a project that, on the surface, looks like a simple, well-defined exercise but—in concept or execution—is actually complex and difficult. Such a situation might occur because a writer is trying to push beyond his or her current ability level or beyond the boundaries of a particular genre. Or it might occur because a teacher has issued an assignment that sounds straightforward hut, on reflection, is a complex tangle. And sometimes students come up with quirky ideas that make a certain amount of sense, such as one student's comparison of J. D. Salinger's Holden Caulfield to Shakespeare's Hamlet. A distracted tutor who fails to recognize the hidden complexity and difficulty in a project may attempt to use tutoring or writing strategies that have worked on past projects—only to share in the writer's puzzlement and frustration when these strategies founder. The tutor may even assume, since her strategies have proven sound in the past, that the fault lies in the student writer or in the assignment rather than in her failure to attend to and embrace the moment.

On the other hand, a tutor who brings to a tutorial the rapt attention of a beat poet or jazz musician, and who views each encounter with a writer as a potentially unique event, increases her chances of detecting and rising to the challenges posed by a deceptively difficult or complex writing project. An existing technique or combination of techniques may work well. But if the tutor's current repertoire of strategies does not work, she may find herself stretching (or bending) her mind in an effort to understand the problems well enough to help the writer improvise solutions. Madson argues that a heightened awareness helps improvisational actors to surprise themselves with "images, solutions, advice, stories" (36) which may already lurk in their minds or hide in plain view. She urges her readers to surrender to the moment—to "[t]rust your imagination. Trust your mind. Allow yourself to be surprised" (36–37). Those who give in to the moment—or go with the flow—may not only gain a greater sensitivity to *kairos* and become more adept at improvisation but also reap other benefits.

Going with the Flow (Experience)

After all, investing all of one's attention and abilities into a complex task, such as assisting someone with a piece of writing, can lead to what Mihaly Csikszentmihalyi calls an "optimal" or "flow" experience. As Csikszentmihalyi says, "When all a person's relevant skills are needed to cope with the challenge of a situation, that person's attention is completely absorbed by the activity" (53). In such moments, people become so absorbed in what they are doing "that the activity becomes spontaneous, almost automatic; they stop being aware of themselves as separate from the actions they are performing" (53). All the aspects of the task, complex as they are, appear to form a harmonious whole (41). As those who experience flow step outside of themselves and their ordinary concerns to focus on the task, their perception of time warps, either speeding up or slowing down (49). As Csikszentmihalyi says, "The combination of these elements causes a sense of deep enjoyment that is so rewarding people feel that expending a great deal of energy is worthwhile simply to be able to feel it" (49). Flow is, he suggests, why people find enjoyment in work that others find routine and even boring.

Both Richard Leahy and Lynn Briggs have applied the concept of "flow" to the writing center. Leahy looks at flow primarily from the writer's perspective, seeking ways to help student writers recognize and take advantage of their "flow experiences" (155). Briggs applies "flow" directly to the tutorial, seeing a tutor's total absorption in a person or text as akin to meditation—and potentially transformative for both the tutor and writer. As she says, Viktor Frankl's three ways of gaining meaning in life—doing good work, connecting with others, and undergoing personal change—"often intersect in the writing center—writers bring work they have created into a setting where they plan to encounter someone and change themselves (even if the change is only to be a better writer). The writing center is a site where people can use the text they have created to make transformative connections" (88). In her own case, Briggs's close work with a particular writer led to revelations about her practice, feelings of invigoration, and personal growth as a tutor. And I believe my session with Nancy, the cancer survivor, also qualifies as a flow experience. Our conversation became a dance of intellects, a push and pull of wits. Both of us were intensely involved in this act of communication, I trying to understand her ideas well enough to help her analyze, develop, and organize them, and she trying to make clear both what she hoped to do and how much the writing of her "how to" book would mean to her personally. The time passed quickly, and when the session ended, instead of falling back wearily into my chair, I felt refreshed and elated.

The stretching, striving, improvising, and growing I do during tutorials first attracted me to the job and provide a good reason to continue doing it. As far as I'm concerned, the lessons I learn as a writer and tutor from such "flow" experiences are an intended product of tutoring—of lesser importance than the learning of student writers, perhaps, but still important because they keep me vital, engaged, and eager for the next session. As tutors help people achieve their potential as thinkers and writers, after all, the tutors become more adept at these arts themselves. Of course, not every writing center encounter is satisfying or results in a flow experience. Some tutorials are frustrating events—often because either the writer or tutor is unwilling for whatever reason to fully engage in the work. Wayne Booth's observation about the complexities, difficulties, and frustrations of teaching applies to tutoring as well. As Booth says,

> Teaching is impossible to master, inexhaustibly varied, unpredictable from hour to hour, from minute to minute within the hour: tears when you don't expect them, laughter when you might predict tears; cooperation and resistance in baffling mixtures; disconcerting depths of ignorance and sudden unexpected revelations of knowledge or wisdom. And the results are almost always ambiguous. (219)

The fact that Wayne Booth found teaching impossible to master should give the rest of us—even those who have tutored for decades—a sense of the challenges we and our peer tutors face in attempting to master our own rhetorical art form. Writers learn by experimenting, failing, and trying again. And by working alongside student writers in this process, tutors not only learn lessons about writing but also about how to help writers improvise solutions to the often surprising and ambiguous problems they face. This shared adventure onto unfamiliar ground can test a tutor's intellect and abilities, and sometimes he or she will on some level fail. For example, a peer tutor in the writing center I direct recently experimented with humor during a session involving a paper about Flannery O'Connor's use of biblical symbolism. Noting that the student had cited a biblical passage without making a transition back into the paper, the tutor said, "Try to introduce and summarize quotations. As you can see, this one sticks out like a big biblical zit." The writer took offense and complained to her teacher, who complained to me. I suggested that, in the future, this tutor read the students with whom he works a little more carefully to gauge their tolerance for humor, but at the same time I felt a grudging sense of pride. He's a good writer, his advice is nearly always sound, and he cares about his work. What I like about the incident is his attempt to lift a tutorial out of the mundane. This tutor is in the process of becoming, in John Poulakos's words, "both a hunter and a maker of unique opportunities . . . [,] ready to confer meaning on new and emerging situations" (61). His joke qualifies as a surprising, spontaneous act of improvisation, and during the tutorial he obviously engaged fully in the moment. Though his sensitivity to *kairos* could use some tweaking, and his joke did not result in a flow experience, he has many of the qualities—including an ability to learn from failure—that he will need to make a run at becoming an artist.

Portrait of a Budding Artist

That such a tutor can evolve from artisan to artist became clear to me recently after I witnessed such a transformation. Three years ago, I hired Ben Graber—an honors student—based on a very good writing sample and the recommendation of a trusted faculty member. A tall, stocky, introverted young man who always carried a book, Graber struck me initially as only a fair candidate for the job because of his personality. He seldom spoke without prompting and seemed withdrawn, reluctant to meet my eyes when we talked. But he did good work during his first semester—in spite of the untimely death of a close family member. At the start of his second year at the center, when I began to train a new group of tutors, Graber spoke to the group about his experiences in the center with a level of sensitivity and self-assurance that surprised me. And I soon began getting feedback about his work from students who appreciated not only his gentle manner but also his insights into their needs and abilities as writers. He became someone whose intuition I trusted—to the extent that I sometimes let this undergraduate religion major assist graduate students in English, history, and divinity with their writing.

In fact, Graber's responses to writing assignments for our center's tutor training course impressed me enough that I invited him to compose an essay about his experiences as a tutor and present it to a regional writing center conference. In this unpublished essay, which he delivered in April 2006 to a conference of the North Texas Writing Centers Association, he reflects on several tutorials that taught him lessons about his work. During a session with a neuroscience major struggling to make sense of social issues raised in literary works, for example, he realized the problem lay in the young man's inability to go beyond scientific reasoning to discover relations among seemingly unrelated ideas. What the student needed, Graber believed, was to adopt an artistic vision, a way to look *"between the data"* he had gathered in order to forge connections and meaning. As Graber writes, "It's a matter of aesthetics: can you see these data and then look between them and see why they fit together in the way they do? Can you find something beautiful in the way the two authors argue their opposing cases, or how another two came to the same conclusion from such radically different angles? How do you teach that?" As I later told him, experienced writing center professionals often ask such questions.

Although he offers no definite answers, Graber raises similar, and even more insightful, issues about other tutorials, including one involving a student who disclosed in an autobiographical essay for a composition class that, at eleven years of age, she had been the victim of a rape. This disclosure at first stopped Graber cold. As he writes,

> What was I doing reading about this? What business did her professor have knowing this, for that matter? How many people knew this about this girl? But here I was, and she'd brought her paper to me, and now I was within this privileged circle of those to whom she could share this kind of experience, because I was supposed to be helping her to make it read better, to make it seem more real to those who were presumably to try and attach a grade to this revelation[.]

The tutorial raised a number of moral and practical dilemmas. It challenged Graber to respond sensitively to a situation he had never before encountered. It made him wonder about the nature of his role as a tutor. It frightened him—on several levels. And it called into doubt what he thought he knew about his job. As he asks, "Who was I to tell her to think of [the rape] as being *like* something, or as connected to something in a way that is as beautiful and powerful as the original experience was tragic and frightening and cruel and hideous? But that was the only thing I knew how to do." Afterward, he gave this difficult session a lot of thought and realized, among other insights, that tutoring "would not be a safe job; we're in the business of helping people to put their lives on display, or at least to publish their lives for a select audience, and it's something very serious."

In response to the risky and consequential moments he faced on the job, Graber synthesized a tutoring philosophy based in part on his own "commitment to see teaching as the art of conveying the ability to think artistically." As he explains, when meeting challenges with which he cannot cope by using standard techniques,

> I can only hope to be a sort of Zen master, urging the novices to focus, to stare into themselves until inspiration strikes and enlightenment is achieved. There are only so many facts to be learned in writing; once you learn them, you have all the tools of a sculptor but can just as easily end up with a pile of rubble as a recognizable statue when you try to use them.

While presenting this part of his essay Graber paused to glance up at the professionals in the audience and add, "You all probably know this better than I."

Do we? I wondered at the time. Many writing center professionals would hesitate to describe tutoring as a fine art or themselves and their peer tutors as artists. But those who remain aware that tutoring "is impossible to master" (Booth 219) and yet willingly confront, learn from, and exploit the ambiguous moments when ideas unexpectedly unify or fragment do think and act like artists. By embracing surprise, refining their sensitivity to *kairos*, developing a capacity for improvisation, and cultivating a taste for "flow" experiences, they have achieved a high level of *ars* or *techne* and, in the process, gained valuable insights into writing, rhetoric, and human nature. Can these professionals pass their insights along to peer tutors? I'm not entirely sure they can—at least directly. Formal training plays a key role in the development of any artist. Like all of the peer tutors who work in our center, Graber took a noncredit course, read about writing center theory and practice, wrote about his experiences, engaged in mock tutorials, and participated in discussions. Yet he (and several others) moved beyond his formal training and beyond the status of artisan. Graber may have come to the job with a greater potential than most to develop into an artist—thanks, as Isocrates suggests, to talent and an ability to learn from experience. Each tutor possesses a different mix of aptitudes, and no writing center director can anticipate all the quandaries a tutor will face in the writing center, so I doubt we can devise a training program to mass produce artistic tutors. But we can caution them against complacency and help them see ambiguous, frustrating, frightening, or difficult tutorials as chances to explore, improvise, reflect, and grow. And by incorporating practice tutorials and improvisational exercises into training, we can give tutors some preliminary (and safe) experience with unusual and challenging situations. Such stage-managed experiences may, in a limited way, help to prepare them for the real thing—and provide a foundation on which to build their own techniques and philosophies of tutoring. After that, maybe the best we can do for the ones who show artistic promise is to step back and let them make their own discoveries.

Notes

[1] Several scholars write about similar concepts, placing them in the context of Zen philosophy. For example, see Gamache.

[2] In *Against the Sophists*, Isocrates said, "Ability, whether in speech or in any other activity, is found in those who are well endowed by nature and have been schooled by practical experience. Formal training makes such [persons] more skillful and more resourceful in discovering the possibilities of a subject. . . ." (14–15).

[3] The anecdotes and examples in this article are personal observations drawn from day-to-day work in the writing center, not part of a formal, sustained research project.

[4] As sources for improvisational exercises potentially useful in tutoring or tutor training, Mattison, Cohen, and others recommend Keith Johnstone's *Improv*, Milton Polsky's *Let's Improvise*, Viola Spolin's *Improvisation for the Theatre*, and Patricia Ryan Madson's *Improv Wisdom: Don't Prepare, Just Show Up*.

[5] I would like to thank Michael Mattison and Ben Graber for sending me copies of their essays. I would also like to thank the editors of *WCJ*, the reviewers, and my friends at TCU, especially Dave Kuhne and Cynthia Shearer, for reading drafts of my manuscript, suggesting a more apt title, and guiding my revision.

Works Cited

Berger, Arthur Asa. *An Anatomy of Humor*. New Brunswick: Transaction, 1993. Print.

Bizzell, Patricia, and Bruce Herzberg, eds. *The Rhetorical Tradition: Readings from Classical Times to the Present*. Boston: Bedford, 1990. Print.

Booth, Wayne C. *The Vocation of a Teacher: Rhetorical Occasions 1967–1988*. Chicago: U of Chicago P, 1988. Print.

Boquet, Elizabeth H. *Noise from the Writing Center*. Logan: Utah State UP, 2002. Print.

Briggs, Lynn. "Understanding 'Spirit' in the Writing Center." *Writing Center Journal* 19.1 (1998): 87–98. Print.

Cohen, Adar. "From Stage to Page: Using Improvisational Acting to Cultivate Confidence in Writers." *Writing Lab Newsletter* 27.2 (2002): 6–8. Print.

Csikszentmihalyi, Mihaly. *Flow: The Psychology of Optimal Experience*. New York: Harper & Row, 1990. Print.

Enos, Richard Leo. *Roman Rhetoric: Revolution and the Greek Influence*. Prospect Heights: Waveland, 1995. Print.

Freud, Sigmund. *Wit and Its Relation to the Unconscious*. New York: Moffat, Yard, 1916.

Gamache, Paul. "Zen and the Art of the Writing Tutorial." *Writing Lab Newsletter* 28.2 (2003): 1–5. Print.

Graber, Ben. "Three Years in the Writing Center: A Tutor's Retrospective." Unpublished essay, 2006. Print.

Hill, Pati. "Truman Capote." *Writers at Work: The Paris Review Interviews*. New York: Viking, 1958. 283–99. Print.

Isocrates. *Against the Sophists. Works*. Trans. George Norlin. Cambridge: Harvard UP, 1929. Print.

Leahy, Rick. "When the Going Is Good: Implications of 'Flow' and 'Liking' for Writers and Tutors?' *Writing Center Journal* 15.2 (1995): 152–62. Print.

Madson, Patricia Ryan. *Improv Wisdom: Don't Prepare, Just Show Up*. New York: Bell Tower, 2005. Print.

Mattison, Michael. "Mission Improvable: Further Thoughts on Consultant Education." *Writing Lab Newsletter* 31.1 (2006): 10–14. Print.

Menon, V. K. Krishna. *A Theory of Laughter, with Special Relation to Comedy and Tragedy*. London: G. Allen & Unwin, 1931. Print.

Plimpton, George, ed. *Beat Writers at Work: The Paris Review*. New York: Modern Library, 1999. Print.

Poulakos, John. *Sophistical Rhetoric in Classical Greece*. Columbia: U of South Carolina P, 1995. Print.

Quintilian. *The Institutio Oratoria*. Ed. H. E. Butler. New York: G. P. Putnam, 1921. Print.

Schön, Donald. *Educating the Reflective Practitioner: Toward a New Design for Teaching and Learning in the Professions*. San Francisco: Jossey-Bass, 1987. Print.

Shiner, Larry. *The Invention of Art: A Cultural History*. Chicago and London: U of Chicago P, 2001. Print.

Vitanza, Victor. "Three Countertheses: Or, A Critical In(ter)vention into Composition Theories and Pedagogies." *Contending with Words: Composition and Rhetoric in a Postmodern Age*. Ed. Patricia Harkin and John Schilb. New York: MLA, 1991. 139–72. Print.

"Wit" Def. 8a. *The Oxford English Dictionary*. 1970. Print.

WHAT WE TALK ABOUT WHEN WE TALK ABOUT TUTORING

Power and Authority in Peer Tutoring

Peter Carino
INDIANA STATE UNIVERSITY

In this essay, first published in 2003 in The Center Will Hold: Critical Perspectives on Writing Center Scholarship, *Peter Carino examines the ambivalent feelings toward power and authority peer tutors often bring to tutorials as a result of writing centers' widespread acceptance of nondirective tutoring philosophies. As Carino argues, these philosophies, described by Jeff Brooks's article "Minimalist Tutoring" (p. 128), reflect idealistic notions of an equal partnership between a peer tutor and a student writer but fail to acknowledge real, and often crucial, differences in their levels of expertise in writing. Instead of suppressing or denying their authority, Carino suggests tutors should receive training and guidance in the benevolent and effective uses of it. Since nondirective tutoring may contribute to tutors' role confusion, he adds, writing center scholars need to reexamine the ethical soundness of this approach.*

"Power" and "authority" are not nice words, especially to writing centers, who have always advertised themselves as nurturing environments, friendly places with coffee pots and comfy couches for the weary. These words are further muted by calling students who work in writing centers peer tutors, peer writing consultants, or some such formation that includes the word *peer*. The use of undergraduate peer tutors has powerfully shaped writing center practice for more than twenty years, and the idea of peership has served in center scholarship to represent writing centers as the nonhierarchical and non-threatening collaborative environments most aspire to be. As early as 1980, Thom Hawkins, in "Intimacy and Audience: The Relationship between Revision and the Social Dimension of Peer Tutoring," lauded writing center work as "a reciprocal relationship between equals, a sharing in the work of the system (for example, writing papers) between two friends who trust one another" (66). Kenneth Bruffee's model of collaborative learning (1983), which Hawkins cites and many centers adopted, did much to shape initial constructions of the tutor as peer. Though in the 1980s, John Trimbur's "Peer Tutoring: A Contradiction in Terms" called into question the notion of "peerness," pointing to the unequal positions tutor and tutee often hold in terms of rhetorical knowledge and academic success, Trimbur recommended training tutors in nondirective questioning methods to preserve the peer relationship as much as possible and to encourage collaborative learning rather than hierarchical teaching. As

Carrie Leverenz wrote of peer tutors, "it could be said that they are experts in not appearing to be experts" (2001, 54).

Two essays in the *Writing Lab Newsletter* demonstrate tutors' difficulty in always remaining peers. As tutor Jason Palmeri (2000) put it after discussing a session in which a tutee lost confidence in him because he could not show her how to integrate source material as expected in her discipline, "I came to realize that authority is a central part of peer tutoring" (10). Palmeri goes on to lament that once this student lost confidence in his authority, she had far less interest in their sessions. Julie Bokser (2000), a new director, concludes an essay by questioning the purpose of suppressing directive behaviors learned on the job by older tutors who have worked in corporate settings where people are more comfortable in hierarchical arrangements. Bokser issues a call "to resituate discussions about collaboration and peerness within the locus of discussions about power and authority" (9). These complaints, coming from a tutor and new director rather than the community's "name" theoreticians or practitioners, suggest a grassroots problem that tutors face daily and that has remained problematic in center scholarship—the question of tutorial power and authority. This question has had a long and unresolved history in the writing center community, and likely will remain one of the more difficult questions as the community continues to develop. In this paper, I will attempt to sort out why writing centers have been uncomfortable with wielding power and claiming authority, how they have masked these terms in the egalitarian rhetoric of "peerness," how centers might gain by refiguring authority as a usable descriptor in discussing tutorial work, and how tutors might be trained differently to recognize and use their power and authority without becoming authoritarian.

Power, Authority, and the Writing Center's Discontents

Historical work on writing centers, such as that of Beth Boquet, Irene Clark, and Dave Healy, as well as some of my own, has demonstrated that centers have long been uncomfortable with power and authority. First, as instructional sites that require funding and resources but neither generate FTE credit hours nor award grades, centers have always been (and in many cases still are) vulnerable to budget cuts and seen as expensive peripherals for remediating students considered unprepared. Furthermore, as instructional sites but not classrooms, student service units yet instructional (in contrast, say, to the health center or financial aid office), centers have been difficult to classify in the taxonomy of university entities, despite their aspirations to disciplinary status. They are neither fish nor fowl. While their ambiguity makes them hard to define, it also makes them easy to marginalize. The initial positioning of centers figures heavily in their attitudes towards the unfortunate yet unavoidable power relations that govern the large majority of American universities. Having felt the pressure of being on the bottom of hierarchical relationships in the university, centers have been loath to take an authoritative position in their work, preferring a peer tutoring model that promotes a nonhierarchical relationship between tutor and student.

Before proceeding further, however, I would like to say that, like others who work in writing centers, I am certainly no fan of hierarchical relationships. None of us likes to feel less empowered than another in interpersonal relations, and students who enter writing centers should be made to feel as comfortable as possible, if for no other reason than basic human decency. However, to pretend that there is not a hierarchical relationship between tutor and student is a fallacy, and to engineer peer tutoring techniques that divest the tutor of power and authority is at times foolish and can even be unethical. Yet to some degree, that is what writing centers have done. Much tutor training routinely includes community-endorsed noninterventionist dictums, if not dogma, that instruct tutors to never hold the pen, never write on a student's paper, never edit a student sentence or supply language in the form of phrases or vocabulary. Irene Clark and Dave Healy, in "Are Writing Centers Ethical?" (1996), catalogue a number of examples of articles propagating these dictums, most notably Jeff Brooks's "Minimalist Tutoring: Making the Student Do All the Work," a piece originally published in the *Writing Lab Newsletter* (1991) and reprinted in *The St. Martin's Sourcebook for Writing Tutors* (pp. 128–32). Brooks's essay encapsulates nondirective pedagogy in its title, and such instruction is then justified by egalitarian notions of peership that maintain that doing otherwise would be to appropriate the student's text, to take ownership of it. In other words, except for a few notable exceptions, writing center discourse, in both published scholarship and conference talk, often represents direct instruction as a form of plunder rather than help, while adherence to nondirective principles remain the pedagogy *du jour*.

In the past few years, some center scholars have questioned notions of peership and nondirective pedagogy on ethical and political grounds, though they remain in the minority. The beginnings of this line of questioning were adumbrated in 1990 in Irene Clark's "Maintaining Chaos in the Writing Center: A Critical Perspective on Writing Center Dogma." There Clark attempted to dislodge such dicta that the tutor never hold the pen or that the best answers to students' questions are more questions from the tutor. Though Clark's essay appeared in the Tenth Anniversary Issue of the *Writing Center Journal*, it was essentially a lone and unjustifiably ignored voice in a community espousing nondirective pedagogy, though perhaps not being able to implement it consistently given the diverse needs of students and the complexity of tutorials. This latter point is borne out in a 1994 essay by Alice Gillam, Susan Callaway, and Katherine Hennessy Winkoff. Tellingly titled "The Role of Authority and the Authority of Roles in Peer Writing Tutorials," Gillam et al. organize their essay with an opening review of writing center theory, demonstrating the hegemony of nondirective methods based on the tricky notion of peerness. They then move to a section on practice, showing how tutors in their center—often torn between needing to follow the party line and needing to exercise authority—struggle with role conflict, and how students are often confused by the tutors' behavior.

However, published in *The Journal of Teaching Writing*, rather than in a venue more regularly read by center directors and scholars, this essay, despite its high quality, had little or no influence on the community and is not even listed in the Murphy, Law, Sherwood bibliography of 1996.

In 1995, however, the community could no longer ignore challenges to nondirective pedagogy with the publication of Linda Shamoon and Deborah Burns's "A Critique of Pure Tutoring" in the *Writing Center Journal* (see pp. 133–48). Aside from their wickedly subtle pun on "peer tutoring" in the title, they unapologetically attacked writing centers' seemingly unflagging allegiance to a nondirective peer model, characterizing its tenets as a "bible" in the most inflexible sense of the term. They then demonstrated how master-apprentice relationships in music and art constitute a kind of directive tutorial and are an accepted and fruitful practice, arguing that tutorials in these disciplines "are hierarchical: there is an open admission that some individuals have more knowledge and skills than others, and that the knowledge and skills are being 'handed down'" (141). Needless to say, this essay caused much gnashing of teeth and rending of garments on WCenter, the community's online discussion group. A year later, Irene Clark, this time as a co-author with David Healy, attributed the community's long commitment to nondirective peer tutoring not to a saintly sense of egalitarianism, but to writing centers' attempts to mollify faculty who suspect tutoring is a from of plagiarism. Accusing centers of having adopted a "pedagogy of self-defense" (34), Clark and Healy dare centers to stop pretending that tutors do not do some work for students, arguing that directors must educate faculty about postmodern ideas of authorship whereby no single author is fully responsible for any text, and that what goes on in tutorials is no different than what goes on in the production of most professional writing. From a more political stance, Nancy Grimm, in *Good Intentions: Writing Center Work for Post-Modern Times* (1999), has questioned the ethics of nondirective methods, contending that in adopting them centers unwittingly "protect the status quo and withhold insider knowledge, inadvertently keeping students from nonmainstream culture on the sidelines, making them guess about what the mainstream culture expects" (31).

Examined closely, all of this is tough talk. If centers, as Clark and Healy (1995) maintain, embraced nondirective collaborative pedagogy largely as a defense mechanism, then the dominant practices of writing centers in the last twenty-odd years have been little more than a rationalization of the frightened. If Grimm (1999) is right, then centers are not just cowards but dupes, political pawns in some larger power structure they serve unawares. And if Shamoon and Burns (1995) can be believed, centers are immature — unable to face the fact that "some individuals have more knowledge and skills than others," something small children quickly learn. Cowardly? Gullible? Childish? Even if I am engaging in a bit of rhetorical hyperbole in representing the implications of these scholars' positions, these are strong words. They do not describe the writing center directors I know, and I think Healy, Clark, Burns, Shamoon, and Grimm would agree. Nevertheless, their exposure of the problematics of a nondirective collaborative peer model of tutoring helps to account for the anxieties tutors such as Palmeri (2000) and Bokser (2000) articulate.

Unpacking each of these critiques uncovers the issues of power and authority beneath them, issues imbricated in the institutional position of the writing center but carrying over into the pedagogy of peer tutoring. Many accounts of writing centers in the 1970s, as Clark and Healy (1995) demonstrate, show writing centers acceding to a mission of providing grammatical instruction and drill, the fix-it-shop model. These centers were given the authority to deliver this type of instruction perceived by the public and university administrations as necessary to acculturate underprepared students admitted to the academy under open admissions programs. Simultaneously, other centers, influenced by the emerging process pedagogy in composition, began to take authority for more than grammar, tutoring students in rhetorical matters as well and thus engaging in a power struggle with the classroom for the authority to teach students to write, an authority usually reserved for the classroom. This binary arrangement—center for grammar, classroom for rhetoric—never reached detente, as is evident in the anticlassroom rhetoric marking much writing center scholarship of subsequent decades (see Hemmeter 1990), and as remains clear in the fix-it-shop image of centers that still persists for some faculty, administrators, and many students. Rather than a division of authority or acceptance of a compromise position—e.g., both classroom and center teach writing, but just differently—a power struggle ensued that continues today. In terms of institutional positioning, the classroom held and continues to hold the stronger position, given that it generates credit hours and awards grades, the very blood of the university.

While the classroom holds the high ground, the hegemonic position afforded by institutional recognition, writing centers have functioned more like a minority party, recognized as a voice but lacking institutional power, operating pedagogically somewhat clandestinely, while simultaneously attempting to work through the system through extended services—WAC linkages being the most obvious—to increase their authority and power base within the institution. These struggles continue, and while some centers have won strong positions on their campuses, others remain struggling, and laments about marginalization, though sometimes seeming counterproductive to more successful centers, still inflect the community's discourse. Still other centers, though empowered on their campuses, consciously take a subversive stance, seeing as their duty exposing students to what they perceive as the oppressive power structures of the university and society itself (Grimm 1999; Davis 1995).

Although centers vary in institutional power and authority, as well as taking different stances toward their positions, they have almost uniformly maintained their identity as nonhierarchical, friendly places where students can feel welcome. Though many teachers would argue that the same applies to their classrooms, centers have the added luxury of being positioned where they do not have to give grades. This is both an advantage and disadvantage.

As mentioned, their failure to generate credit hours may make centers seem a frill to university administrators. Furthermore, students so acculturated to tangible rewards—they speak of "getting something out of a class," "getting good grades"—may wonder what they "get out of" going to the center, what they "get for" spending an hour of their busy week talking with someone about their writing. For many, the answer is "better grades," an answer that writing centers have often seen as grubbing and vulgar, preferring rather to follow Stephen North's claim that the center's job is "to produce better writers, not better papers" (1984, 438). While this mission has satisfied writing center directors, it is unlikely too many students would accept it, though they may unwittingly become better writers through their work in the center (and thus earn better grades). Thus students sometimes come to the center expecting work to be done for them in exchange for the time they sacrifice, an attitude which further pushes centers toward a nondirective peer pedagogy.

Not having to assign grades, however, also becomes a reason to contrast the center advantageously against the classroom. Students can, it is claimed, feel relaxed and unintimidated as they might not in a teacher's office or in class. They find creature comforts such as the three Cs of writing centers—coffee, cookies, and couches—and they interact with others supposedly like themselves—students. This is the image of the writing center as "safe house" or student sanctuary, a place beyond the competition, evaluation, and grade-grubbing that supposedly marks the classroom. Centers have taken pride in this image in presenting themselves as student advocates, while turning to it for succor when feeling the sting of marginalization (if we lack clout, at least we are nice). But when taken too far, the safe house metaphor has also contributed to an identity that is not only unrealistic, but that also has adversely affected peer tutoring. The "safe house" metaphor rests on maintaining a non-hierarchical environment at all costs, which, though imperative in the atmosphere of the center, in a tutorial can undermine the tutor and lead to dogmatic applications of nondirective peer-tutoring principles. It is these principles that Shamoon and Burns (1995) castigate in their call for more directive tutoring in which the tutor takes more authority, wields more power, and is only a peer in perhaps belonging to the same age group and sharing the status of student.

While I agree with Shamoon and Burns, as well as Grimm (1999) and Clark and Healy (1996), that peer tutoring has been represented by the community and translated into practice, often uncritically, as a largely nondirective egalitarian enterprise, I believe that peer tutoring should not be dismissed, but refigured in terms of the way authority and power play themselves out depending on the players in any given tutorial, a refiguration I will now attempt.

What Do We Mean by Peers?

Peer tutoring has been a powerful pedagogy for writing center teaching and student learning. However, when the word *peer* has been interpreted in the extreme, it has been distorted to support the kind of nondirective tutoring that understandably rankles some center scholars and practitioners. At the same time, the enshrinement of nondirective tutoring is understandable in the context of writing center history. On the one hand, as Clark and Healy (1996) argue, this pedagogy helped deflect charges of plagiarism, but on the other, I would argue that center workers were as concerned about plagiarism as teachers were, and developed nondirective pedagogy not only to deflect criticism, but also because they believed it worked. Based on questioning methods, whether designated Socratic or Rogerian, nondirective tutoring can cue students to recall knowledge they have and construct new knowledge that they do not. Anyone who has worked in writing centers knows that when nondirective tutoring clicks, it is wonderful, and its effectiveness accounts for some of the zealotry of those who endorse it but then impose it upon situations where other strategies are necessary.

An ideal peer tutorial in the nondirective mode proceeds something like this. A third-year chemistry major comes into the center with a draft of a lab report and meets with a tutor, let's say a second-year literature major and skilled writer. The two are peers in that both are students, and both are committed to being good writers:

Tutor: You seem to have your thesis at the end and the first part talks about your steps in the experiment. Is that the way you want it?

Student: Yes, we are supposed to use an inductive pattern and draw a conclusion.

Tutor: Ok, that's good. Now, on the third page you talk about mixing the chemicals and then heating them, but you don't explain why. Do you see what I mean? Could you add a transition to get the reader from one to the other?

Student: Yes, I could say how I mixed the chemicals until they got syrupy, that's how they should be, before I put them on the Bunsen burner, something like "Once the chemicals thickened to a reddish syrupy consistency, they were placed on the Bunsen burner." And then add some stuff about the temperature . . .

Tutor: Yes, that would really help.

This snippet illustrates nondirective peer tutoring at its best. The tutor asks questions; the student answers in ways that lead to improving the writing. The student takes responsibility for the content, which the tutor, a literature major, cannot be expected to know, justifying the placement of her thesis based on knowledge of the rhetorical structure of the lab report, and even takes a step toward becoming a better writer in supplying a concrete example of the tutor's reference to an abstract rhetorical term—*transition*.

This tutorial not only exemplifies the effectiveness of nondirective tutoring, but Bruffian collaborative learning as well, with the tutor learning that a thesis in a lab report (though usually called something else) is more desirable as a conclusion based on induction, something he can file for future reference, just as the student can the definition of transition. Both student and tutor share authority and engage in collaborative operations to improve the text. It is important to remember that in adopting a nonhierarchical pedagogy of peer collaboration, centers were heavily influenced by Kenneth Bruffee's work on collaborative learning (1993), which originated when he was directing the writing center at Brooklyn College. Coupling the mutual benefits to tutor and student with the theoretical underpinning of Bruffian collaborative learning, this tutorial is exactly the way writing centers would like to represent their work—effective in practice and underpinned by theory. In fact, this tutorial works so well that it becomes a myth for self-justification. Unfortunately, the myth is seductive, and directors want to believe such tutorials happen far more often than they do, use them to represent center work, and try to train tutors to approximate, if not attain, them consistently, all the time knowing at heart that such tutorials are rare, many are messier, and most are far messier.

Furthermore, to pretend this tutorial is exemplary is not only to ignore its rarity but to misread Bruffee somewhat. While certainly he placed much faith in students' ability to learn from one another, his sense of collaboration included the assumption that the tutor had some authority. Discussing training tutors at Brooklyn under Bruffee's supervision, Marcia Silver (1978) argues "probably the single most important condition for teaching writing is the willingness on the part of the student writer to accept criticism, and grow as a result of it" (435). This is tough love, not the egalitarian, nonhierarchical presentation of tutor student as "two friends" cited in Hawkins (1980) at the outset of this essay. The tutor is expected to criticize, and the student is expected to have a skin tough enough to put the criticism to good use. However, blind adherence to a nonhierarchical ethic of peer tutoring treats the student as if he or she is a high-strung child, and can also lead to inefficiency if the tutor refuses to take authority when necessary.

Witness this tutorial in which the tutor will not deviate from nondirective principles. This time the tutor is a journalism major minoring in theater; the student, an undeclared freshman writing a review of a campus production for an introduction to theater class:

Tutor: After reading through your paper, I am wondering why you spent the first page writing about you and your friends on the way to the theater.

Student: I don't know. That's what happened. We met in town, then drove to campus, and had a hard time finding a parking space, like I said.

Tutor: Do you think that is important for the reader to know?

Student: Well, I thought I would put it in to get started and I thought it was neat the way we got lucky and got a space just when we thought we'd be late. I wanted to start with something interesting, and I thought the play was really serious, heavy.

Tutor: It is interesting, but how do you see it relating to the play?
Student: I don't know. Should I take it out?
Tutor: That's up to you. What do you think?

Here the tutor continues nondirective questioning to a fault in the name of preserving the peer relationship. It is obvious that the student lacks knowledge of the conventions of a play review, but instead of taking authority for teaching him, the tutor coyly "wonders" about the way the student opens the paper. No one can implicate this tutorial for plagiarism, and the tutor certainly maintains a nonhierarchical peer relationship with the student, but it is doubtful that anything other than adherence to principle has been achieved. If the student does cut the superfluous introduction, it is likely the cut will be more the influence of the tutor's doubts about it than from a writerly decision by the student.

Compare a second version of the same tutorial, in which the tutor draws upon his knowledge in journalism and theater, takes some authority for the text, and exercises some power in directing the student:

Tutor: After reading your paper, I see you have a long part about getting to the theater. Have you ever written a play review before?
Student: No. I put that in because I thought it was interesting the way we got the parking space at the last minute. I wanted to start with something interesting before doing all the stuff on the play, which I thought was really serious, heavy.
Tutor: Yes, it is good to start with something interesting, but did your teacher explain anything about how to write the review?
Student: No, we just have that little sheet I gave you saying we had to write the review, how many pages, and when the play is on.
Tutor: Well, in a play review, you might have a short introduction, but you should start as close to the play as possible because your purpose is to help the reader decide if they want to see the play or not. You need to cut the part about getting to the theater and start with the sentence where you say "*Oleanna* is a play that will make people think." That is a short direct sentence, and it previews what follows.

Clearly, the tutor here takes more authority, is more responsible for the shape the paper will take. In addition, the tutor uses her authority—familiarity with the conventions of play reviews and the rhetorical need to consider audience—to provide instruction that will be useful to the student in completing the paper as well as others in the future. Strict adherents to nondirective methods might argue that the tutor is appropriating the student's paper in directly telling him to cut the long introduction, or wielding too much power over a student who seems to have little himself in terms of this assignment. Although beneath the surface of the first exchanges there may be a slight bit of contentiousness on the tutor's part and defensiveness on the student's, the tutor does not belittle or exclude the student, but uses her authority to transmit knowledge and power to direct the student for the purpose of helping him complete the task. Undoubtedly there is not the sharing of authority seen in the tutorial on the chemistry lab report, where the student is much more knowledgeable, but nevertheless there is a sharing of the work as the student, though lacking authority, remains attentive and explains his motivations to the tutor.

Tutorials, then, I would argue, depend on authority and power; authority about the nature of the writing and the power to proceed from or resist what that authority says. Either tutor and student must share authority, producing a pleasant but rare collaborative peer situation as in the tutorial on the lab report, or one or the other must have it, and in writing centers the one with it is more often the tutor, as is the case in the second tutorial on the play review. Writing centers should not be ashamed of this fact. Of course, there are caveats. In some tutorials, authority may be lacking on both parts, because every tutor cannot be expert in all types of writing. Or power can be misdirected. For example, the student writing the theater review has the power to resist the tutor and not cut the irrelevant introduction. Or the tutor may wield power without authority, misleading the student, as is evident in the following excerpt, again with a literature major tutoring a chemistry student, this one less able, on a lab report:

Tutor:　　You seem to have your thesis at the end and the paper talks about your steps in the experiment. Is that the way you want it?

Student:　I don't know. Why? This is chemistry. I thought thesis sentences were for English papers.

Tutor:　　No, most papers have a thesis and usually it comes at the beginning.

Student:　You mean the part where I say the chemicals turned into a clear gel when heated to a certain temperature.

Tutor:　　Yes, can you put that in the first paragraph so the reader knows what you found?

Student:　Ok, I get it now.

This tutorial goes immediately astray because the tutor lacks authority, in that he misdirects the student based on his own experience of placing the thesis sentence first, something generally not done in lab reports. The student, though somewhat suspicious, does not wield power to resist, because the institution of the writing center and the position of authority it awards the tutor cows him into acting on the tutor's misleading advice. The only benefit of the nondirective technique here is that it somewhat preserves the environment of the center as "safe house," because the tutor's question gently raises the possibility of moving the thesis rather than directly telling the student about the (mis)perceived thesis problem. Yet in the end, the "safe house" is not safe at all because the non-directive method is worthless without some authoritative knowledge on the structure of lab reports. Nor would directive tutoring work in this case, because without the knowledge of the conventions of the lab report, the tutor would be unable to help — to direct — the student about the placement of the thesis.

In this case, the tutor, lacking knowledge, lacks power and authority beyond that conferred by being the tutor — a situation analogous to that which Palmeri (2000) describes when he cannot show the student how to cite sources in her discipline. Granted, the tutorials above are invented, but I would argue that similar tutorials happen regularly. Invented or not, they illustrate the wide variety of tutorials that occur in writing centers every day, a variety conditioned by the degree of power and authority brought into the tutorial by tutor, student, and assignment. All of these tutorials demonstrate that, no matter what techniques are used, both parties (ideally) or one (more commonly) must have some knowledge at hand, must occupy the position of power and authority in a hierarchical relationship. In the first tutorial on the lab report, the student fortuitously had the knowledge and only needed it to be drawn out by the tutor's cues; thus the tutorial worked exceedingly well. In the second, neither knew the conventions of the lab report, and the tutorial went awry because knowledge was not available. In the tutorials on the play review, the first tutor had the knowledge but chose to withhold it in the name of egalitarianism, thus abusing power and authority, while the second exercised them responsibly to instruct the student. I realize here that I am seeming to treat knowledge as an entity, a thing, rather than something constructed, as is readily accepted in postmodern thought, but in many tutorials the knowledge, for student and tutor, is something to be retrieved or transmitted. Though the conventions of the lab report and the play review are constructions in that they are agreed upon by writers and readers of such pieces, for the tutor and student the conventions are fixed and transmittable knowledge, because neither has the authority or power to change them without negative consequences in the situation offered by the assignment and tutorial.

Implications for Tutor Training

Writing center professionals like to point out that every tutorial is different, and the samples discussed illustrate that claim. What they do not like to point out is that very often one tutorial is better than another despite efforts to train tutors. In the twenty-fifth anniversary issue of *The Writing Center Journal*, longtime writing center scholars and practitioners Lil Brannon and Stephen North claim that "If we are honest, we know the quality of the work is uneven" (2000, 11). This is a rare admission, given the protective and defensive stance writing center scholars usually take regarding peer tutors. The party line runs something like this. Tutors are effective because they are peers trained to be nondirective. In this sense, their authority comes from not having any. If they know more than the students, they use nondirective questioning to ensure that they don't end up doing students' work for them. If they know less than the students, they again rely on nondirective questioning to draw out the student's knowledge of the subject. Nondirective tutoring thus becomes the antidote for having too much authority, or too little.

Certainly tutors should continue to be trained to maintain a comfortable environment for students, treating them with kindness, understanding, and respect. Though raising the spectres of power and authority in this essay, my purpose is not to turn the writing center into just another impersonal office on campus. Students must face enough of those already, and, as much as possible, writing centers should maintain the atmosphere of the safe house. At the same time, tutors need to learn that the center is not the local coffee house, and tutorials just a chat about a paper or assignment. In short, a nonhierarchical environment does not depend on blind commitment to nondirective tutoring methods. Instead, tutors should be taught to recognize where the power and authority lie in any given tutorial, when and to what degree they have them, when and to what degree the student has them, and when and to what degree they are absent in any given tutorial.

When they can do so, they can proceed using techniques — nondirective or directive — based on their position in the tutorial. As in the tutorial the play review, the tutor should know to take the lead and be more directive when tutoring an inexperienced freshman in an introductory theater course. To shackle such a tutor by training him or her only in nondirective methods, in the name of maintaining a nonhierarchical peer relationship, is to shortchange the student lucky enough to be paired with him or her, a point Bokser implies when she chafes against the training in nondirective methods that would have her suppress assertive behaviors that would help the student. At the same time nondirective methods should be maintained for situations in which the tutor does not have authority, and needs to draw it from the student. When such is the case, a question such as "Do you want your thesis last?" becomes a real question, and not a ploy to push the student to move it where the tutor thinks it belongs. Similarly, when tutors lack authority in one area — organizational conventions for a particular type of discourse, for instance — they should feel free to move the tutorial in a direction in which they feel more authoritative. The tutor who tells the chemistry student to move the thesis to the beginning would have been better off to direct the student to ask the instructor about the organization and then perhaps move to matters of style and even grammar, raising questions about wordy constructions, vague pronoun references and the like. Unfortunately, writing center orthodoxy would train him or her to reserve those areas for last, or to shun a tutorial that works primarily at the sentence level as the demeaning stuff of the fix-it shop, rather than value it as a service to the student based on the authority available in the tutorial.

In an unpublished study of students' and tutors' perceptions of directiveness, Irene Clark found that tutors view their tutorials as less directive than students do in terms of contributing ideas, making corrections, and the degree and influence of conversation. She attributes this result partly to the tutor training "that had emphasized the importance of allowing students as much opportunity as possible to develop their own ideas, urging consultants to guide and suggest rather than lead" (n.d., 16). While such training is necessary, to a degree, it contributed to tutor views or tutorials that countered those of the students, even if one considers that students may have, conversely, overestimated the contributions of the tutor. It is troublesome that tutors feel the need to see themselves as less directive than they likely are, for, given the challenges and complexity of tutoring, tutors should not be made to feel inadequate when they cannot live up to an orthodoxy of nondirective pedagogy, whatever reasons, pedagogical or political, may underlie it.

While presenting a fully developed method of tutor training is beyond the scope of this paper, I would like to offer a few possibilities. The watchword in tutor training should not be nondirective peership, but flexibility. Tutors should learn to shift between directive and nondirective methods as needed, and develop some sense of a sliding scale.

- More student knowledge, less tutor knowledge = more nondirective methods.
- Less student knowledge, more tutor knowledge = more directive methods.

As it stands, this scale is admittedly reductive. It would also have to account for what educationists call "the affective domain," that is, the various personality traits of tutors and students. Timid students, despite a lot of knowledge, might require both nondirective and directive methods, nondirective questioning to draw forth what they know, directive prodding to make them take responsibility for the text. Likewise, less knowledgeable but gregarious students might benefit from nondirective questions to question a hasty but wrongheaded enthusiasm, or directive warnings when they are stubbornly blundering into moves that could result in a disastrous response to the assignment.

Clark's study further lends credence to a more flexible approach. In addition to suggesting that training influenced tutors to perceive their sessions as more nondirective than they might have been, Clark found that students who rated themselves as "good" writers viewed tutorials as less directive, while students who rated themselves as "adequate" or "poor" writers saw the sessions as more directive. I would maintain that there is a good chance that these perceptions were accurate, that more able students needed less direction than the less able. It's common sense. However, whether out of political timidity or an excessive commitment to egalitarian principles, writing centers have not wanted to admit it—until recently.

Clark's NWCA study, coupled with the earlier sporadic efforts cited above and more recent voices, indicates that centers are beginning to be more courageous in describing their work. In a recent case study of a complex tutorial between a male Ph.D. student tutor and a female student in first-year composition, Jane Cogie (2001) demonstrates how, from session to session and moment to moment, tutorial methods shift from directive to nondirective and, as a result, so does the authority of the participants. When Ken, the tutor, in a directive move, tells Janelle, the student, that she seems to be critiquing a "stereotype," the term turns up in her revision as an organizing principle and point of focus, greatly expanded. Similarly, when he *tells* her that interviews are a valid method of research, she is able to expand the paper significantly. Ken's moves here are directive, yet Janelle's use of his directives makes them her own. We have here not plagiarism, but teaching and learning. Cogie concludes:

> The point here is that given the dual need for guidance and authority in most students, any strategy involves risk. Fostering student authority is not a matter of following a single approach and avoiding another. The authority of students may grow from moves as diverse as asking them tough questions, providing summaries or terms to help them conceptualize points and build confidence, and helping them negotiate assignment demands, gain the necessary situated knowledge, or try out aspects of the writing process. (47)

Fortunately, I think the kind of tutoring I am calling for and Cogie describes has been going on for a long time in many centers, without being widely acknowledged. While centers have always valued and elicited students' input, they have also had the good sense to place student needs before orthodoxy. I turn for evidence here to Mickey Harris's recent professional memoir, delivered as the Exemplar's address at the CCCC 2000 and subsequently published in CCC (2001). On the one hand, in discussing the early days of her center at Purdue, Harris describes a very safe house, happily recounting tales of tutors dragging in old sofas, decorating the lab, and raising funds to buy pizzas. She relates ways in which she trained tutors not to dominate tutorials. On the other hand, she speaks of finding "crevices where the conversation permits [her] to adopt a mentor role" (436), and her summary of what went on in her lab shows a sensible mixture of nondirective and directive methods that drew upon the students' authority without stifling the tutors'.

> When students had no idea how to begin an assignment—or even what it was asking for—we addressed that with questions and suggestions for strategies, and we learned how to help writers acquire the strategic knowledge they needed to achieve goals such as how to add more content or organize what they had written. . . . We supplied information they didn't have (answering such questions as "So what goes in an introduction?" "What is my instructor

telling me to do here?" "How do I cite this in MLA format?" "What goes in a personal statement for this application?") and tried to re-explain whatever parts of our explanations they didn't get. (432)

Here it is evident that Harris's staff is exercising their power and authority ("suggestions," "supplied information," "answering questions"). At the same time, Harris states how "some deep personal discomfort with rules and power structures led [her] to revel in creating and strengthening the guidelines for a non-hierarchic place like our Writing Lab" (435). This is not to say Harris is not practicing what she preaches, or that she contradicts herself, but rather to show how she maintained the safe house atmosphere without divesting her staff of the power and authority needed to serve students.

I suspect many other centers were doing the same, but just not talking about it. This may have been partly, as Clark and Healy (1996) charge, out of fears of being seen as contributing to some faculty's notions of plagiarism, or out of an overly simplified notion of peership and a misreading of collaborative learning theory as always egalitarian learning. Whatever the reason, nondirective, nonhierarchical methods not only have held sway, but also given rise to the dogmatic dicta that disturb commentators such as Shamoon and Burns (1995). This would be relatively harmless, a group of writing center directors keeping "our little secret," as Beth Boquet (1999) has called it, that sometimes tutors do more than ask questions, sometimes they do write on students' papers, sometimes they do question the quality of assignments they see—in other words, sometimes they wield power and exercise authority. The problem, rather, is that when tutors are trained as if this does not happen, or hear the same espoused and nodded at approvingly at writing center conferences, they feel guilty or deficient for failing to live up to the doctrine—Bokser (2000) and Palmeri (2000) are cases in point and very likely not alone.

All this is not to say centers should become authoritative, dictating to students what they should do or not do, but if they are to confront and negotiate the inevitable presence of power and authority, like their tutors, they will need to take responsibility for what they know and do not know. They will need to educate faculty in the ways in which directive tutoring is not plagiarism, but help. They will also need to take authority for what some faculty expect of them—help in grammatical and stylistic matters—without worrying that they will be stereotyped as fix-it shops or grammar garages. Finally, they will need to continue to educate faculty about what they don't know, and encourage faculty to clarify their expectations and provide students with instruction in the way of disciplinary convention, even if only in the form of copies of successful papers from past students furnished to the center. Power and authority are not nice words, but they don't have to be bad ones, either, when the actions they represent are addressed honestly and responsibly. Writing centers can ill afford to pretend power and authority do not exist, given the important responsibility they have for helping students achieve their own authority as writers in a power-laden environment such as the university.

References

Bokser, J. (2000). Dilemmas of collaboration for the tutor with work experience. *Writing Lab Newsletter* 24(9), 5–9.

Boquet, E. (1999). "Our little secret": A history of writing centers, pre- to post-open admissions. *College Composition and Communication* 50(3), 463–482.

Brannon, L., & North, S. (2000). The uses of the margins. *The Writing Center Journal* 20(2), 7–12.

Brooks, J. (1991). Minimalist tutoring: Making students do all the work. *Writing Lab Newsletter* 19(2), 1–4. Reprinted in C. Murphy & S. Sherwood (Eds.), *The St. Martin's sourcebook for writing tutors* (4th ed.) (pp. 128–132). New York, NY: St. Martin's Press.

Bruffee, K. A. (1983). Peer tutoring and the "conversation of mankind." In G.A. Olson (Ed.), *Writing center theory and administration* (pp. 3–15). Urbana, IL: NCTE.

Clark, I. L. (1990). Maintaining chaos in the writing center: A critical perspective on writing center dogma. *The Writing Center Journal* 11(1), 81–95.

Clark, I. (n.d.). Non-directive tutoring: A retrospective.

Clark, I. L., & Healy, D. (1996). Are writing centers ethical? *Writing Program Administration* 20(1/2), 32–48.

Cogie, J. (2001). Peer tutoring: Keeping the contradiction productive. In J. Nelson & K. Evertz (Eds.), *The politics of writing centers* (pp. 37–49). Portsmouth, NH: Boynton/Cook Heinemann.

Davis, K. (1995). Life outside the boundary: History and direction in the writing center. *Writing Lab Newsletter* 20(2), 5–7.

Gillam, A., Callaway, S., & Winkoff, K.H. (1994). The role of authority and the authority of roles in peer writing tutorials. *The Journal of Teaching Writing* 12(2), 161–198.

Grimm, N. (1999). *Good intentions: Writing center work for post-modern times*. Portsmouth, NH: Boynton/Cook Heinemann.

Harris, M. (2001). Centering on professional choices. *College Composition and Communication* 52, 429–440.

Hawkins, T. (1980). Intimacy and audience: The relationship between revision and the social dimension of peer tutoring. *College English* 42, 64–68.

Hemmeter, T. (1990). The "smack of difference": The language of writing center discourse. *The Writing Center Journal* 11(1), 35–48.

Leverenz, C. S. (2001). Graduate students in the writing center: Confronting the cult of (non) expertise. In J. Nelson & K. Evertz (Eds.), *The politics of writing centers* (pp. 50–61). Portsmouth, NH: Boynton/Cook Heinemann.

Murphy, C., Law, J., & Sherwood, S. (1996). *Writing centers: An annotated bibliography*. Westport, CT: Greenwood Press.

North, S. (1984). The idea of a writing center. *College English* 46, 433–446.

Palmeri, J. (2000). Transgressive hybridity: Reflections on the authority of the peer writing tutor. *Writing Lab Newsletter* 25(1), 9–11.

Shamoon, L. K., & Burns, D.H. (1995). A critique of pure tutoring. *The Writing Center Journal* 15(2), 134–151.

Silver, M., with contributions by Bruffee, K. A., Fishman, J., & Matsunobu, J. T. (1978). Training and using peer tutors. *College English* 40, 442–449.

Trimbur, J. (1987). Peer tutoring: A contradiction in terms? *The Writing Center Journal* 7(2), 21–28.

Minimalist Tutoring:
Making the Student Do All the Work

Jeff Brooks _____

SEATTLE PACIFIC UNIVERSITY

In presenting the philosophy of minimalist tutoring, Jeff Brooks argues that "the goal of each tutoring session is learning, not a perfect paper." In contrast to those who view the tutor as a proofreader and editor, Brooks sees the tutor as a commentator and guide and contends that "fixing flawed papers is easy; showing the students how to fix their papers is complex and difficult." Like Stephen North, he believes that the tutor's job is to improve the writer, not the writer's text; "our primary object in the writing center session is not the paper, but the student," he says. For tutors to achieve the goals of minimalist tutoring, Brooks advocates a hands-off approach to students' papers—one that avoids editing the papers for errors in favor of emphasizing structure, organization, logical reasoning, and stylistic control. He explains the assumptions that guide this model and describes the techniques and strategies of forms of minimalist tutoring that he terms "basic," "advanced," and "defensive." This essay first appeared in 1991 in Writing Lab Newsletter.

A writing center worst case scenario: A student comes in with a draft of a paper. It is reasonably well-written and is on a subject in which you have both expertise and interest. You point out the mechanical errors and suggest a number of improvements that could be made in the paper's organization; the student agrees and makes the changes. You supply some factual information that will strengthen the paper; the student incorporates it. You work hard, enjoy yourself, and when the student leaves, the paper is much improved. A week later, the student returns to the writing center to see you: "I got an A! Thanks for all your help!"

⚡This scenario is hard to avoid, because it makes everyone involved feel good: the student goes away happy with a good grade, admiring you; you feel intelligent, useful, helpful—everything a good teacher ought to be. Everything about it seems right. That this is bad points out the central difficulty we confront as tutors: we sit down with imperfect papers, but our job is to improve their writers.

When you "improve" a student's paper, you haven't been a tutor at all; you've been an editor. You may have been an exceedingly good editor, but you've been of little service to your student. I think most writing center tutors agree that we must not become editors for our students and that the goal of each tutoring session is learning, not a perfect paper. But faced with students who want us to "fix" their papers as well as our own desire to create "perfect" documents, we often find it easier and more satisfying to take charge, to muscle in on the student's paper, red pen in hand.

To avoid that trap, we need to make the student the primary agent in the writing center session. The student, not the tutor, should "own" the paper and take full responsibility for it. The tutor should take on a secondary role, serving mainly to keep the student focused on his own writing. A student who comes to the writing center and passively receives knowledge from a tutor will not be any closer to his own paper than he was when he walked in. He may leave with an improved paper, but he will not have learned much.

A writing teacher or tutor cannot and should not expect to make student papers "better"; that is neither our obligation, nor is it a realistic goal. The moment we consider it our duty to improve the paper, we automatically relegate ourselves to the role of editor.

If we can't fix papers, is there anything left for us to do? I would like to suggest that when we refuse to edit, we become more active than ever as educators. In the writing center, we have the luxury of time that the classroom teacher does not have. We can spend that time talking and listening, always focusing on the paper at hand. The primary value of the writing center tutor to the student is as a living human body who is willing to sit patiently and help the student spend time with her paper. This alone is more than most teachers can do, and will likely do as much to improve the paper as a hurried proofreader can. Second, we can talk to the student as an individual about the one paper before us. We can discuss strategies for effective writing and principles of structure, we can draw students' attention to features in their writing, and we can give them support and encouragement (writing papers, we shouldn't forget, is a daunting activity).

Assumptions

All of this can be painfully difficult to do. Every instinct we have tells us that we must work for perfection; likewise, students pressure us in the same direction. I have found two assumptions useful in keeping myself from editing student papers:

1. The most common difficulty for student writers is paying attention to their writing. Because of this, student papers seldom reflect their writers' full capabilities. Writing papers is a dull and unrewarding activity for most students, so they do it in noisy surroundings, at the last minute, their minds turning constantly to more pressing concerns. It is little wonder that so much student writing seems haphazard, unfocused, and disorganized. A good many errors are made that the student could easily have avoided. If we can get students to reread a paper even once before handing it in, in most cases we have rendered

an improvement. We ought to encourage students to treat their own writings as texts that deserve the same kind of close attention we usually reserve for literary texts.

Our message to students should be: "Your paper has value as a piece of writing. It is worth reading and thinking about like any other piece of writing."

2.   While student writings are texts, they are unlike other texts in one important way: the process is far more important than the product. Most "real-world" writing has a goal beyond the page; anything that can be done to that writing to make it more effective ought to be done. Student writing, on the other hand, has no real goal beyond getting it on the page. In the real world when you need to have something important written "perfectly," you hire a professional writer; when a student hires a professional writer, it is a high crime called plagiarism.

This fairly obvious difference is something we often forget. We are so used to real-world writing, where perfection is paramount, that we forget that students write to learn, not to make perfect papers. Most writing teachers probably have a vision of a "perfect" freshman paper (it probably looks exactly like the pieces in the readers and wins a Bedford prize); we should probably resign ourselves to the fact that we will seldom see such a creature. Most students simply do not have the skill, experience, or talent to write the perfect paper.

Basic Minimalist Tutoring

Given these assumptions, there are a number of concrete ways we can put theory into practice. Our body language will do more to signal our intentions (both to our students and to ourselves) than anything we say. These four steps should establish a tone that unmistakably shows that the paper belongs to the student and that the tutor is not an editor.

1.   Sit beside the student, not across a desk—that is where job interviewers and other authorities sit. This first signal is important for showing the student that you are *not* the person "in charge" of the paper.
2.   Try to get the student to be physically closer to her paper than you are. You should be, in a sense, an outsider, looking over her shoulder while she works on her paper.
3.   If you are right-handed, sit on the student's right; this will make it more difficult for you to write on the paper. Better yet, don't let yourself have a pencil in your hand. By all means, if you must hold something, don't make it a red pen!
4.   Have the student read the paper aloud to you, and suggest that he hold a pencil while doing so. Aside from saving your eyes in the case

of bad handwriting, this will accomplish three things. First, it will bypass that awkward first few moments of the session when you are in complete control of the paper and the student is left out of the action while you read his paper. Second, this will actively involve the student in the paper, quite likely for the first time since he wrote it. I find that many students are able to find and correct usage errors, awkward wording, even logic problems without any prompting from me. Third, this will help establish the sometimes slippery principle that good writing should sound good.

I am convinced that if you follow these four steps, even if you do nothing else, you will have served the student better than you would if you "edited" his paper.

Advanced Minimalist Tutoring

Of course, there is quite a bit more you can do for the student in the time you have. You can use your keen intelligence and fine critical sense to help the student without directing the paper. As always, the main goal is to keep the student active and involved in the paper. I have three suggestions:

1. Concentrate on success in the paper, not failure. Make it a practice to find something nice to say about every paper, no matter how hard you have to search. This isn't easy to do; errors are what we usually focus on. But by pointing out to a student when he is doing something right, you reinforce behavior that may have started as a felicitous accident. This also demonstrates to the student that the paper is a "text" to be analyzed, with strengths as well as weaknesses. This is where the tutor can radically depart from the role of editor.

2. Get the student to talk. It's her paper; she is the expert on it. Ask questions—perhaps "leading" questions—as often as possible. When there are sentence-level problems, make the student find and (if possible) correct them. When something is unclear, don't say "This is unclear"; rather, say, "What do you mean by this?" Instead of saying, "You don't have a thesis," ask the student, "Can you show me your thesis?" "What's your reason for putting Q before N?" is more effective than "N should have come before Q." It is much easier to point out mistakes than it is to point the student toward finding them, but your questions will do much more to establish the student as sole owner of the paper and you as merely an interested outsider.

3. If you have time during your session, give the student a discrete writing task, then go away for a few minutes and let him do it. For instance, having established that the paper has no thesis, tell the student to write the thesis while you step outside for a few minutes. The fact that you will return and see what he has accomplished (or

not accomplished) will force him to work on the task you have given him probably with more concentration than he usually gives his writing. For most students, the only deadline pressure for their paper is the teacher's final due date. Any experienced writer knows that a deadline is the ultimate energizer. Creating that energy for a small part of the paper is almost the best favor you can do for a student.

Defensive Minimalist Tutoring

So far, I have been assuming that the student is cooperative or at least open to whatever methods you might use. This, of course, is not a very realistic assumption. There are many students who fight a non-editing tutor all the way. They know you know how to fix their paper, and that is what they came to have done. Some find ingenious ways of forcing you into the role of editor: some withdraw from the paper, leaving it in front of you; some refuse to write anything down until you tell them word for word what to write; others will keep asking you questions ("What should I do here? Is this part okay?"). Don't underestimate the abilities of these students; they will fatigue you into submission if they can.

To fight back, I would suggest we learn some techniques from the experts: the uncooperative students themselves.

1. Borrow student body language. When a student doesn't want to be involved in his paper, he will slump back in his chair, getting as far away from it as possible. If you find a student pushing you too hard into editing his paper, physically move away from it — slump back into your chair or scoot away. If a student is making a productive session impossible with his demands, yawn, look at the clock, rearrange your things. This language will speak clearly to the student: "You cannot make me edit your paper."

2. Be completely honest with the student who is giving you a hard time. If she says, "What should I do here?" you can say in a friendly, non-threatening way, "I can't tell you that — it's your grade, not mine," or, "I don't know — it's *your* paper." I have found this approach doesn't upset students as it might seem it would; they know what they are doing, and when you show that you know too, they accept that.

All of the suggestions I have made should be just a beginning of the ideas we can use to improve our value to our students. I hope that they lead to other ideas and tutoring techniques.

The less we do *to* the paper, the better. Our primary object in the writing center session is not the paper, but the student. Fixing flawed papers is easy; showing the students how to fix their own papers is complex and difficult. Ideally, the student should be the only active agent in improving the paper. The tutor's activity should focus on the student. If, at the end of the session, a paper is improved, it should be because the student did all the work.

A Critique of Pure Tutoring[1]

Linda K. Shamoon and Deborah H. Burns _____

UNIVERSITY OF RHODE ISLAND

In a counterpoint to Jeff Brooks's minimalist approach, Linda Shamoon and Deborah Burns examine and critique the student-centered, nondirective practices espoused by university writing centers. These practices, they argue, generally begin as guidelines but often harden into orthodoxy. While nondirective tutoring can help students learn to depend on their own resources as writers, Shamoon and Burns point out that advanced graduate students tend to write, and learn, under the directive tutoring of thesis and dissertation advisors. Such advisors "seem authoritative, intrusive, directive and product-oriented. Yet these practices created major turning points for a variety of writers." In a similar way, master musicians often teach through a process of demonstration and directive critique, first showing student musicians how to perform a piece and then guiding the students through a performance of their own. This article, which originally appeared in The Writing Center Journal *in 1995, is important in unambiguously stating that directive tutoring, particularly when it involves discipline-specific pieces of writing, is often an effective teaching strategy. In view of these insights, Shamoon and Burns argue that writing center practices need to encompass both directive and nondirective tutoring strategies.*

In our writing center and probably in yours, graduate teaching assistants and undergraduate peer tutors conduct student-centered, one-on-one tutoring sessions. We train these tutors to make use of process-centered writing pedagogy and top-down, writer-centered responses to papers. During the tutoring sessions, tutors are always careful not to appropriate the students' writing and not to substitute their ideas for those of the students. Thus, tutors let students set the agenda, and they resist word-by-word editing of any text. While this cluster of practices has helped us establish a growing clientele and a good reputation, we have begun to wonder about the *orthodoxy* of these practices, especially as we reflect upon our personal experiences and upon stories from faculty in writing across-the-curriculum (WAC) workshops who tell us that they "really" learned to write during one-on-one tutoring sessions which were directive and appropriative. In an effort to understand these experiences more clearly, we have turned to research on expertise, social and cognitive development, and academic literacy. These sources have convinced us that directive tutoring, a methodology completely opposite our current tutoring practices, is sometimes a suitable and effective mode of instruction. As a result, we are currently struggling with radically oppositional practices in tutoring, and we are contemplating the places of these oppositional practices in our writing center.

The Orthodoxy of Current Practice

The prevailing approach to writing center tutoring is excellently explained and contextualized in several texts, among them Irene Clark's *Writing in the Center: Teaching in a Writing Center Setting* and Emily Meyer and Louise Z. Smith's *The Practical Tutor*. From these sources tutors learn to use a process approach, to serve as an audience for the student writers, and to familiarize students with the conventions of academic discourse (Clark, *Writing* 7–10; Meyer and Smith 31–32, 47). This approach emphasizes a student-centered, non-directive method, which suggests that "in order for students to improve in their writing, they must attribute their success to their own efforts and abilities, not to the skill of the tutor" (Clark, *Writing* 7). To encourage active student participation, tutors learn about "legitimate and illegitimate collabora-tion" (Clark, *Writing* 21). True collaboration occurs when the participants are "part of the same discourse community and meet as equals" (21). Tutors learn that illegitimate collaboration happens when the tutor takes over a student's writing by providing answers rather than by asking questions. Illegitimate col-laboration, says Clark, creates dependency: "[T]utor dominated conferences, instead of producing autonomous student writers, usually produce students who remain totally dependent upon the teacher or tutor, unlikely ever to assume responsibility for their own writing" (41). These ideas and others from books about tutoring, along with related concepts from articles in *The Writing Center Journal* and *Writing Lab Newsletter,* provide the bases for current writing center practices.

Upon reflection, however, we find that sometimes these sources become more than simply the research backdrop to writing center practice; sometimes they form a writing center "bible." This bible contains not only the material evidence to support student-centered, non-directive practices, but also codes of behavior and statements of value that sanction tutors as a certain kind of professional, one who cares about writing and about students, their authen-tic voices and their equal access to the opportunities within sometimes dif-ficult institutions. These codes and appeals seem less the product of research or examined practice and more like articles of faith that serve to validate a tutoring approach which "feels right," in fact so right that it is hard for prac-titioners to accept possible tutoring alternatives as useful or compelling. For example, Jean Kiedaisch and Sue Dinitz, in "Look Back and Say 'So What?': The Limitations of the Generalist Tutor," note that while those tutors who know the discipline and can supply special information for students' papers may be effective, such tutors may not always be available. Kiedaisch and Dinitz conclude, "If we can't ensure that students writing for upper level courses can meet with a knowledgeable tutor, should we be alarmed about relying on generalist tutors? We think not" (73). Kiedaisch and Dinitz may be drawn to this conclusion because the alternative model examined in the study—that of a knowledgeable tutor supplying "special information"—is simply too far outside orthodox writing center practice to be acceptable.

The power of this orthodoxy permeates writing center discourse, where we sometimes find statements that come more from a range of assumed values rather than from researched findings. For example, we read online a writing center tutor's "confession" that she showed a model essay to a student rather than let the student get frustrated at having no readily available, familiar written format to help tame his chaos of ideas. Well over a hundred entries followed assuring the tutor that models have a place in tutoring, as long as they do not transgress upon the authentic voice of the student ("Imitation/Modeling"). These assurances could be interpreted as obviating the sin of appropriating the student's paper. In addition, Evelyn Ashton-Jones, in "Asking the Right Questions: A Heuristic for Tutors," argues that to promote cognitive growth of students, tutors must engage in a version of "Socratic dialogue" and not "lapse into a 'directive' mode of tutoring" (31–33). Quoting Thom Hawkins, she labels the directive tutor as "shaman, guru, or mentor," and Socratic tutors as "architects and partners" (31). In our culture who would not rather be an architect than a shaman? Finally, in discussing the need for students to be active learners during a tutoring session, Clark asserts that students should never be "disciples sitting in humility at the feet of a mentor" (*Writing* 7).[2] The language and tone here forbid challenge. The idea that one cannot be extremely appreciative of expertise and also learn actively from an expert is an ideological formation rather than a product of research.

In these instances and others, ideology rather than examined practice ("things that go without saying") seems to drive writing center practice. First, writing is viewed as a process tied to cognitive activities occurring in recursive stages. Although these stages have been labeled in numerous taxonomies, Jack Selzer finds that most enumerations include invention, organization, drafting, and revision (280). As a result, tutoring sessions often follow a ritual that begins by noting where a writer is with a text and proceeds by "walking" through the remaining stages. Second, writing center practice assumes that process strategies are global and transferable (Flower and Hayes 365–87). The extreme non-hierarchical, presumably democratic version of this assumption is that anyone who is familiar with the writing process can be of help to anybody. In practice, tutors from any discipline who seem to be good writers help all students, allowing for peer tutoring across the curriculum (Haring-Smith 175–88). A third assumption is that the students possess sole ownership of their texts ("Teaching Composition"; Brannon and Knoblauch; Sommers 149–50). In practice, then, the tutors' mission is to help clarify what is in the text and to facilitate revision without imposing their own ideas or their own knowledge and, in so doing, without taking ownership of the text. Thus, tutors follow a script that is question-based and indirect rather than directive. Fourth and closely related, the prevailing wisdom assumes that one-on-one conferencing can best help students clarify their writing to themselves (Murray, "Teaching" 144). In practice, then, tutoring is conducted in private. Finally, there is the assumption that all texts are interpretive and that the best writing contains statements of meaning or an authentic voice (Schwegler; Murray, *A Writer;* Elbow). In practice, then, much of the tutors' discussion and indirect questioning aims at getting students to voice and substantiate overall statements of meaning. Once this has been achieved, students are often sent home to revise their texts in light of this understanding. In sum, tutoring orthodoxy is: process-based, Socratic, private, a-disciplinary, and nonhierarchical or democratic.

Many points in this characterization of writing have been challenged by social-constructionist views. Social-constructionists characterize writing as a social act rather than as a process of personal discovery or individual expression. Kenneth Bruffee calls writing displaced conversation, implying that writing occurs not in isolation but in response to ideas found in other texts and other forms of communal conversation (*Short Course* 3). Furthermore, Bruffee cites Oakeshott's belief that education is primarily an "initiation into the skill and partnership of this conversation in which we learn to recognize the voices, to distinguish the proper occasions of utterance, and in which we acquire the intellectual and moral habits appropriate to conversation" (638). Patricia Bizzell sharpens the critique by adding that students

> need composition instruction that exposes and demystifies the institutional structure of knowledge, rather than that which covertly reintroduces discriminatory practices while cloaking the force of convention in concessions to the "personal." The cognitive focus of process-oriented composition studies cannot provide the necessary analysis. (112)

In these ways, social-constructionists challenge the private, a-disciplinary nature of writing, but according to Robert J. Connors there is little in the *practice* of teaching or tutoring writing that has changed because of social constructionist views. Connors maintains that, in the classroom, social constructionists still base teaching and tutoring upon stages in the writing process. Thus, the social constructionist critique has broadened our understanding of the contexts of writing, but it has not formed an alternative set of practices.

The Challenge from Experience and from Writing across the Curriculum Faculty

The more serious challenge to current tutoring orthodoxy starts for us with some of our personal experiences as we learned to write in our discipline. When Deborah Burns was completing a thesis for her M.A. in English Literature, she was tutored by her major professor. She reports the following experience.

> The most helpful writing tutoring I ever received at the university came from the director of my Master's thesis. I wrote what I thought was a fairly good draft of my thesis, then shared it with my director for comments. I remember, at first, being surprised at the number of problems my director found with my draft. He added transitions when needed, showed me how to eliminate wordiness, and formalized my vocabulary. In addition, he offered specific suggestions for rewriting entire paragraphs, and he always pointed out areas where I had lost

focus. The most important thing he did for me was to write sentences that helped locate my work in the field of Dickens studies. For example, Dickens critics had thoroughly examined family relationships in the novels, but few worked on alcoholism and its effects on children, the central idea of my thesis. My director's specific suggestions helped me to foreground my unique way of examining some of Dickens's novels. I learned that I was so immersed in the research and articulation of the new ideas I wanted to explore in my thesis, I had neither the time nor the experience to fully understand how to write an extended piece of scholarly work in the discourse community. At first, I was confused about my perceived inability to write like the scholar I was supposed to be, but I soon realized (especially at my thesis defense) that I was fortunate to have my director as a person who *showed* me how to revise my draft so that it blended with conventional academic discourse. After I watched my director work with my text, and after I made the necessary changes, my thesis and other academic writing was much less of a mystery to me.

For many years Burns puzzled over the direct intervention made by her director while she composed her Master's thesis. The intervention had been extremely helpful, yet it went against everything she had learned in composition studies. Her director was directive, he substituted his own words for hers, and he stated with disciplinary appropriateness the ideas with which she had been working. Furthermore, Burns observed that other graduate students had the same experience with this director: he took their papers and rewrote them while they watched. They left feeling better able to complete their papers, and they tackled other papers with greater ease and success. Clearly, several features of the graduate director's practice violated current composition orthodoxy. His practices seem authoritative, intrusive, directive, and product-oriented. Yet these practices created major turning points for a variety of writers. For Burns and for others, when the director intervened, a number of thematic, stylistic, and rhetorical issues came together in a way that revealed and made accessible aspects of the discipline which had remained unexplained or out of reach. Instead of appropriation, this event made knowledge and achievement accessible.

This challenge to current tutoring practices has been further extended by conversations with faculty from a variety of disciplines during our WAC workshops. We have held faculty workshops semiannually for the last three years, and it is not unusual for faculty members to remember suddenly that at some point late in college or in graduate school, during a one-on-one conference, a professor they respected took one of their papers and rewrote it, finally showing them "how to write." During our first workshop, a colleague from animal science reported that in graduate school his major professor took his paper and rewrote it while he watched. In the colleague's own words, "He tore it to shreds, but I sure learned a lot." When he made this statement, there were looks of recognition and sympathetic murmuring from others in the room. Just recently, in a WAC faculty writing circle, a colleague from nursing reported that in order to complete her doctoral proposal she has sat through numerous

revising sessions with the most accessible member of her doctoral committee, each time learning more about writing, about critical theory, and about
how to tie the theory to her research methods. In these examples and others,
professors were acting like tutors, working one-on-one with student authors
to improve their texts, but their methods were hardly nondirective. Over and
over in the informal reports of our colleagues we find that crucial information
about a discipline and about writing is transmitted in ways that are intrusive,
directive, and product-oriented, yet these behaviors are not perceived as an
appropriation of power or voice but instead as an opening up of those aspects
of practice which had remained unspoken and opaque.

While we do not pretend that these informally gathered stories carry the same
weight as research data, we are struck by the repeated benefits of a tutoring style
that is so opposite to current orthodoxy. As we discuss these revelations further
with WAC faculty, we find that the benefits of alternative tutoring practices are
frequent enough to make us seriously question whether one tutoring approach
fits all students and situations. Surely, students at different stages in their education, from beginning to advanced, are developing different skills and accumulat-
ing different kinds of information, thus making them receptive to different kinds
of instruction and tutoring. In fact, in "The Idea of Expertise: An Exploration
of Cognitive and Social Dimensions of Writing," Michael Carter sets forth a
five-stage continuum of cognitive learning that characterizes the progress from
novice to expert. Carter explains that novices and advanced beginners utilize
global, process-based learning and problem-solving strategies; that intermediate
and advanced students shift to hierarchical and case-dependent strategies; and
that experts draw intuitively upon extensive knowledge, pattern recognition,
and "holistic similarity recognition" (271–72). If students are exercising different
cognitive skills at different stages in their learning, it makes sense that they may
be responsive to different kinds of information and tutoring styles at different
stages, too. Our personal and WAC experiences suggest that, at the very least,
for intermediate and advanced students, and perhaps on occasion for beginners,
too, one tutoring approach does not fit all.

An Alternative Mode of Practice: Master Classics in Music

Since we have encountered so many positive alternative representations of the
tutoring of writing, we have started to ask ourselves when such practices are
helpful and exactly how they can be best characterized. Interestingly, in order
to find answers we have had to look outside the discipline. This is not surprising since, according to Michael Agar, most of us sometimes have difficulty
seeing alternatives to our own ways of thinking, especially to everyday notions
that seem based on common sense.

> There are two ways of looking at differences. . . . One way is to figure out that
> the differences are the tip of the iceberg, the signal that two different systems
> are at work. Another way is to notice all the things that the other [system]

lacks when compared to you[rs], the so-called *deficit theory* approach. . . . The deficit theory does have its advantages. But it's a prison. It locks you into a closed room in an old building with no windows. . . . (Agar 23, emphasis in original)

In other words, within a strong system generally held notions and behaviors so permeate our lives that only they seem legitimate or make sense, while all other notions and behaviors seem illegitimate. In order for alternative practices to look sensible, they must be appreciated from within another strong system. One such system that may be found outside of writing instruction is the practice of master classes in music education. Master classes are a form of public tutoring that is standard practice in music education (Winer 29). The circumstances and conduct of master classes are almost totally opposite those seen in nondirective tutoring practices.[3]

During a master class an expert music teacher meets with a group of students studying the same specialty, such as piano, voice, strings, brass, etc. The students vary in their achievement levels, from novice to near-expert. Several students come to the session prepared to be tutored on their performance of a piece or a portion of a piece, while others may come as observers. The tutorial typically begins with one student's performance; then the master teacher works over a section of the piece with the student, suggesting different ways to play a passage, to shape a tone, to breathe, to stand or sit, or even to hold an instrument. On occasion, the master teacher will play the passage herself and ask the student to play it with her or immediately after her. Then, as a typical end-of-the-tutorial strategy, the master teacher has the student play the whole passage or the piece again. At this time it is not unusual for those who are observing to respond with a new sense of understanding about the music or the technique.

When a master class is at its best, the emotional tone is compelling. The atmosphere is charged with excitement, with a sense of community, and with successive moments of recognition and appreciation. Excitement comes from the public performances, which are often anxiety provoking for the performer; but there is relaxation, too, for no one expects the perfection of a formal performance. Instead, a sense of community animates the participants, who are willing to have their performances scrutinized in order to improve, and everyone recognizes those moments during the tutorial when increased mastery passes into the hands of the student. Indeed, all the participants have a sense of high expectation, for they have access to someone who has mastery, who wants to share this knowledge with them, and who, by showing them about a limited passage of music, reveals a world of knowledge, attitude, and know-how.

Examples of such master classes can be found in the documentary *From Mao to Mozart: Isaac Stern in China*, a film about violinist Isaac Stern's 1979 visit to China. The film, which won an Academy Award for the best documentary of 1980, includes several excerpts from master classes on the violin offered by

Stern to a variety of students in China. In one scene, Stern works with a young, extremely able violinist who is having trouble following his precise suggestions. Suddenly, Stern says he will share a secret with her. He plays a passage from her solo piece and then pulls out an extra shoulder pad hidden under his suit jacket. This extra padding enables him to hold his violin in a position that facilitates his playing. Later, the student replays the passage while Stern pushes up and positions her violin as if she, too, were wearing the secret padding. Her performance suddenly improves so much that the audience recognizes the change and bursts into applause. Throughout this episode, there is a sense of delight, of the sharing of important information, and of appreciation.

What strikes us as important about master classes is that they feature characteristics exactly opposite current tutoring orthodoxy. They are hierarchical: there is an open admission that some individuals have more knowledge and skill than others, and that the knowledge and skills are being "handed down." This handing down is directive and public; during tutoring the expert provides the student with communally and historically tested options for performance and technical improvement. Also, a good deal of effort during tutoring is spent on imitation or, at its best, upon emulation. Rather than assuming that this imitation will prevent authentic self-expression, the tutor and the student assume that imitation will lead to improved technique, which will enable freedom of expression. Finally, there is an important sense of desire and appreciation. The students have sought out the expert because they already have recognized the value of her knowledge and skills, and because she seeks to share this expertise with students, both to preserve and to expand the discipline and its traditions. Mutual appreciation and mutual desire seem to be at the center of this kind of teaching. In music master classes, sitting at the feet of the master is one way of learning.

Reflections upon Alternative Tutorial Practices

Although the master class model has much to offer writing centers, it is not immune to abuse. History is littered with examples of directive, authoritative "tutoring" gone awry, from sports coaching to religious cults. Nor are all music master classes as successful as those portrayed in the documentary about Isaac Stern. The famous German conductor Wilhelm Furtwangler, for example, was known to belittle and physically abuse his students and orchestra members (Fenelon 116). But such cases represent alternative practices run amok, when authoritative has become authoritarian, when directive has become dictatorial, and when imitative has become repressive. The challenge for writing centers is to know the best features of these alternative pedagogies in order to broaden current practice. We need to know enough about these practices to prevent abusive application and to secure their benefits for students and their tutors.

Music is not the only discipline to use alternative tutoring practices. In art education, the studio seminar is an important and widely practiced form of public tutorial. According to Wendy Holmes, a professor of art history at the

University of Rhode Island, studio seminar is the crucial intermediate course for art majors, when they start exploring, locating, and solving artistic problems on their own, whether in sculpture, painting, or other media. During studio time, students work on their own projects, and the instructor "visits" and tutors each student individually, suggesting ideas, options, or techniques for the project; and during seminar time, students display their work to each other and to the instructor for public commentary, analysis, and reflection. Studio seminar is a mix of private and public tutoring that is directive. In pharmacy practice internships, senior pharmacy majors are placed in real-world settings to observe their professors in action, to apply their newly acquired professional knowledge, and to receive guided practice in a mix of private and public tutoring (Hume). Nursing students take "clinicals," courses which provide the same combination of observation and guided practice as do medical internships and residencies (Godfrey). All these examples include practices that are more similar to the music master class than to nondirective writing tutoring. Emulative learning is conducted in a hierarchical environment to facilitate new information or masterly behavior within a domain. While these examples of alternative practices are most commonly found at intermediate or advanced levels, they are sometimes usefully applied with novices, too (as we explain below).

These instances of public tutoring that are the norm within certain disciplines provide an opportunity to reflect upon the constellation of conditions that make directive tutoring fruitful. Three strands of research are important: research on the development of expertise (including connections to imitation and modeling) helps explain the links between directive tutoring and cognitive development; theoretical explanations of subjectivities help us understand directive tutoring and social development; research on academic literacy helps us understand directive tutoring and disciplinary development.

As we have already noted, research about expertise helps elucidate the connections between cognitive skills development and alternative tutoring practices for all learners, from novice to near-expert. Specifically, Carter explains that experts have extensive "repertoires" for problem solving, repertoires built on domain-specific knowledge and experience. He points out that chess grand masters have about "50,000 meaningful chess configurations in their repertoires" (269). Carter argues that novices in all domains build up such repertoires, gradually shifting their modes of thinking from global, general purpose strategies to the hierarchical, domain-specific strategies used by experts in the field (269). Similarly, in her review of the literature on the cognitive aspects of expertise, Geisler points to students in physics solving "thousands of word problems" as they build up domain-specific problem solving repertoires (60). Geisler explains that the changes which characterize the cognitive move from novice to expert include the development of abstract representations of specific cases, the replacing of literal description with abstract discourse, and the rehearsal of extended arguments to support solutions to problems (9–54).

With this research in mind, we turn first to intermediate stages of development, followed by a look at the needs of novices. We find that master classes, studio seminars, clinicals, and other representations of directive tutoring enable committed intermediate and advanced students to observe, practice, and develop widely valued repertoires. When the studio instructor turns the student's attention away from the student's own painting and toward the painting of a master, the student sees how an expert has solved the same problem of light, color, and form. When the studio instructor dabs some pigment on the student's canvas and transforms the impact of the picture, the student observes how experts handle the major elements of the discipline. Throughout the studio seminar, the student has time to practice similar solutions and try out others. Thus, directive tutoring provides a particularly efficient transmission of domain-specific repertoires, far more efficient and often less frustrating than expecting students to reinvent these established practices. At its best, directive tutoring provides a sheltered, protected time and space within the discipline for these intermediate and advanced students to make the shift between general strategies to domain strategies. This cognitive shift seems to depend upon observation and extensive practice—often in emulation of the activities of the tutor-expert—leading to the accumulation of expert repertoires and tacit information.

Novice writers can also benefit from observing and emulating important cognitive operations. In "Modeling: A Process Method of Teaching," Muriel Harris explains that for novice writers, too, composing skills and writing behaviors may be learned through imitation, and that productive patterns of invention or editing may come to replace less useful ones through observation and "protected" practice. In fact, using some of the same techniques that we are arguing for in this article, Harris reports a case study in which she turned to modeling after observing the nonproductive composing habits of a novice writer named Mike.

> Scrambling for a better technique [than free writing], I seized on modeling. . . . In preparation I explained [to Mike] the strategies we would use for the next few sessions. We would begin by having him give me a topic to write on for fifteen to twenty minutes. I would begin by thinking about the rhetorical situation, the "who," "what," "why," plus a few operators to achieve my goal. After these few minutes of planning, I would start writing and keep writing. . . . When I was done, we would reverse roles, and I would give him a topic. As much as possible, he would try to copy the behavior he had observed. All of these instructions were preceded by brief explanations of what he would observe and the principles he would try to use. My intent was to model a pattern of behavior for Mike to observe and try out and also to monitor his attempts by listening to his protocol and observing his actions. (78)

After three such sessions, Harris reports that "Mike's writing improved noticeably." We note that in these sessions Harris was being directive, telling the student what to observe, what topics to write on, and what behaviors to imitate. We note, too, that the modeling continued for several sessions, with Harris providing a repeated, fixed focus upon specific writing repertoires, and that the student engaged in several learning activities—observing, imitating, and practicing—always guided by Harris' supportive words. We take this to be a version of directive tutoring at its best, with periods of observation and protected practice focused upon important skills development. As Harris says, "And what better way is there to convince students that writing is a process that requires effort, thought, time and persistence than to go through all that writing, scratching out, rewriting and revising with *and for* our students?" (81, emphasis ours).

Cognitive development, however, is not the only change students undergo as they engage in formal education. Recent work in cultural criticism suggests that as students strive to attain academic knowledge or a new understanding of a profession or a career, they inevitably occupy a new subject position, one that may be well-served by directive tutoring practices. These points are most easily explained with respect to intermediate and advanced students, but the ideas apply to beginners as well. Most intermediate or advanced students are highly motivated, active learners, already working with a significant amount of domain knowledge and with the representations of the field given to them by their instructors. As they master this information, they typically start to see themselves as members of a domain community. For example, Faigley and Hansen note that students who successfully completed an advanced course in psychology "felt confident that they could write a publishable report, suggesting that they viewed themselves at the end of the course as fledgling members of the field, able to think and write like psychologists" (144). Similarly, Geisler states, "Professional identity becomes part of personal identity" (92). Bizzell notes that admission to the "academic discourse community is as much social as cognitive, that it is best understood as an initiation" (125). In other words, as intermediate and advanced students get a sense of a domain, they start to occupy a subject position as a *participant* in the domain that is both confirmed by others and assumed by the student. But, as Robert Brooke suggests, this experience of shifting subjectivities and the transformation of identity is *not* necessarily limited to intermediate or advanced students. Brooke found that students in an *introductory* level English class who were encouraged to imitate the drafting processes of their teacher were also receptive to other aspects of being a writer, including the expressions of attitudes, values, and stances towards experiences that lie at the heart of a writer's identity. By the end of the semester several of the students in Brooke's study came to view themselves as writers, and they accepted this identity as new and exciting (32–35). All of these researchers draw attention to the social dimensions of learning and to the important connections between domain processes and social identity.

Directive tutoring supports these connections. Not only does directive tutoring support imitation as a legitimate practice, it allows both student *and* tutor to be the subjects of the tutoring session (while nondirective tutoring allows only the student's work to be the center of the tutoring session). For example, when the master musician rephrases a passage for the intermediate or advanced violin student, the tutor's phrasing, tone, and body language become the subject of the session—her skills *and* her way of being a musician—but the student does not necessarily feel that his musicianship has been appropriated. Instead, the student, too, will have his turn as musician in this master class, and this confirms his musicianship. The interaction with the master teacher establishes that he, too, is a musician. The social nature of directive and emulative tutoring serves to endorse the student's worth as an emerging professional. Similarly, directive tutoring of writing presents more than a demonstration of steps in the writing process. It models a writer's attitudes, stances, and values. In so doing, it unites the processes of writing with the subjectivity of being a writer. As Brooke points out, not all students, particularly not all novices, would choose to assume the subjectivity of their writing tutor or teacher, but when they do, they encase writing processes in the values, attitudes, and acts of interpretation that make writing a socially meaningful experience (37–38). There is much to be gained by unifying the processes of writing with the writer herself. Directive tutoring displays this unity, even for novices.

Finally, in light of research on academic literacy, we speculate that directive tutoring lays bare crucial rhetorical processes that otherwise remain hidden or are delivered as tacit knowledge throughout the academy. According to Geisler, academic literacy and achievement of professionalism are tied not only to domain content and personal identity but also to mastery of rhetorical processes (88–92). These processes of reasoning, argumentation, and interpretation support a discipline's socially constructed knowledge base. Those students who learn to recognize these rhetorical processes seem also to come to understand a discipline. Geisler argues that the current system of education is constructed to keep these rhetorical processes hidden from students, usually until sometime during graduate school, thus creating a "great divide" among those who have mastered such processes and those who have not (89–90). Geisler charges that academicians and professionals are complicit in hiding these crucial rhetorical processes from most students and the public, thus ensuring their own social status and power over others. Her book is an attempt to place before the public the argument that rhetorical processes must be made more prominent in education if we are to give all students access to academic literacy and a share in the wealth of our society. Although Geisler does not present a method for revealing rhetorical processes earlier in education, she does present a fascinating case study in which such processes were made public (214–29). In a philosophy class, students had a chance to hear their instructor build an argument for a comparative reading of several texts, tear down that structure, and then rebuild it. When the teacher honestly shared his rhetorical processes in this manner, Geisler found that the students gained both a wide appreciation of a discipline and also an ability to express themselves within it (226–27).

We argue that directive tutoring, at its best, is similarly empowering. Directive tutoring displays rhetorical processes in action. When a tutor redrafts problematic portions of a text for a student, the changes usually strengthen the disciplinary argument and improve the connection to current conversation in the discipline. These kinds of changes and the accompanying metalanguage or marginalia often reveal how things are argued in the discipline. Thus, directive tutoring provides interpretive options for students when none seem available, and it unmasks the system of argumentation at work within a discipline. In fact, we speculate that when faculty have not developed an appreciation of the connections between the social construction of disciplinary knowledge and related rhetorical processes, they treat knowledge of the discipline as self-evident and absolute rather than as changing and socially negotiated. Directive tutoring is based upon the articulation of rhetorical processes in order to make literate disciplinary practice plain enough to be imitated, practiced, mastered, and questioned.

Implications for the Writing Center

Alternative tutoring practices are provocative for the writing center, especially if it is to develop into the kind of writing community Stephen North calls for in "The Idea of a Writing Center," a place where all writers — novices and experts — receive support for their writing. We need to keep in mind the crucial cognitive, social, and rhetorical changes students undergo as they strive to become proficient writers in the academy. The writing center could better help to facilitate these developments by serving as a site where directive tutoring provides a sheltered and protected time and space for practice that leads to the accumulation of important repertoires, the expression of new social identities, and the articulation of domain-appropriate rhetoric. Furthermore, if the crucial difference between novice and advanced expertise is the development of rhetorical practices, then writing centers could be the site where instructors from a variety of disciplines articulate and demonstrate these practices, so that students may observe, emulate, question, and critique them.

Many writing centers are already providing elements of these practices. For example, Muriel Harris reports that professors from across the curriculum participate in writing centers, talking about the features of domain-specific writing ("Writing Center and Tutoring" 168–69.) Kiedaisch and Dinitz, as well as Leone Scanlon, supply examples of knowledgeable students from a variety of domains tutoring in writing centers. At the University of Rhode Island a writing center tutor is present during a physics laboratory, on hand for conversation and consultation as students gather and record data in their lab notebooks, as they write up their lab reports, and as they revise their drafts in light of the instructor's responses. Finally, Louise Smith describes two writing programs that draw on experts for writing instruction. One program at Queens College pairs faculty members with advanced undergraduates, and another at the University of Massachusetts/Boston fosters collaboration between faculty and tutors to disseminate theory and research about composition.

Although these applications of public and domain-based tutoring are interesting and impressive, they are piecemeal and seem prompted by concerns other than critically broadening orthodox tutoring practices. We probably do not know the best systematic application in the writing center of directive, public, and emulative tutoring; we probably do not yet know the writing center equivalent of master classes. We do know, however, at least some of the features that should be part of this application. The writing center can be a site where ongoing conversation about the rhetoric of a domain occurs *in* the rhetoric of the domain. For example, the writing center can be a site where professors work occasionally and *publicly* on their writing and on others' writing. Also, the writing center can be a site where the proficient (such as graduate students and seniors) and the novice converse about "intersubjective knowledge" (Geisler 182), or that kind of discourse which externalizes and argues for domain-appropriate abstractions, which externalizes and argues for domain-appropriate linkages to case-specific data, and which provides opportunities for reflection and critique. This is exactly the kind of discourse now hidden from the novices; the writing center is the place to make it public, directive, and available for imitation, appreciation, and questioning. Finally, the writing center can be a site where experts and novices meet often to externalize tacit information—those values, assumptions, and options that inform all texts within a discipline.

Unless writing center research and methods are enlarged to include these practices, writing centers are in danger of remaining part of the social arrangements which, according to Geisler, encourage the a-rhetorical accumulation of domain knowledge and which keep expert rhetorical processes at a distance from the lay public and the novice:

> Our current educational sequence provides all students with a naïve understanding of the more formal components of expertise but withholds an understanding of [the] tacit rhetorical dimension. In this way . . . a great divide has been created—not a great divide between orality and literacy as literacy scholars originally suggested, but rather a great divide with experts on one side with a complete if disjoint practice of expertise, and lay persons on the other side. (89–90)

Current writing center and tutoring practices support this social arrangement by making an orthodoxy of process-based, Socratic, private, a-disciplinary tutoring. This orthodoxy situates tutors of writing at the beginning and global stages of writing instruction, it prevents the use of modeling and imitation as a legitimate tutoring technique, and it holds to a minimum the conduct of critical discourse about rhetorical practices in other fields. If writing center practices are broadened to include *both* directive and non-directive tutoring, the result would be an enrichment of tutoring repertoires, stronger connections between the writing center and writers in other disciplines, and increased attention to the cognitive, social, and rhetorical needs of writers at all stages of development.

Notes

[1] The authors wish to thank Meg Carroll, Rhode Island College, and Teresa Ammirati, Connecticut College, for the use of selected resources from their writing centers.

[2] Clark does not universally dismiss imitation, modeling, or other directive techniques. In "Collaboration and Ethics in Writing Center Pedagogy," she suggests that "imitation may be viewed as ultimately creative, enabling the imitator to expand previous, perhaps ineffective models into something more effective which ultimately becomes his or her own. . . . Sometimes a suggestion of a phrase or two can be wonderfully instructive" (8–9).

[3] The term "master class" may lead to some confusion about the differences between teaching and tutoring. We are referring to "tutoring" as one-on-one instruction, coaching, and responding; and "teaching" as one-to-whole group instruction, coaching, and responding.

Works Cited

Agar, Michael. *Language Shock: Understanding the Culture of Conversation.* New York: Wm. Morrow, 1994. Print.

Ashton-Jones, Evelyn. "Asking the Right Questions: A Heuristic for Tutors." *The Writing Center Journal* 9.1 (1988): 29–36. Print.

Bizzell, Patricia. "College Composition: Initiation into the Academic Discourse Community." *Academic Discourse and Critical Consciousness.* Pittsburgh: U of Pittsburgh P, 1992. Print.

Brannon, Lil, and C. H. Knoblauch. "On Students' Rights to Their Own Texts: A Model of Teacher Response." *College Composition and Communication* 33 (1982): 157–66. Print.

Brooke, Robert. "Modeling a Writer's Identity: Reading and Imitation in the Writing Classroom." *College Composition and Communication* 39 (1988): 23–41. Print.

Bruffee, Kenneth A. "Collaborative Learning and the 'Conversation of Mankind.'" *College English* 46 (1984): 635–52. Print.

---. *A Short Course in Writing: Practical Rhetoric for Teaching Composition through Collaborative Learning.* 3rd ed. New York: HarperCollins, 1993. Print.

Carter, Michael. "The Idea of Expertise: An Exploration of Cognitive and Social Dimensions of Writing." *College Composition and Communication* 41 (1990): 269–86. Print.

Clark, Irene. "Collaboration and Ethics in Writing Center Pedagogy." *The Writing Center Journal* 9.1 (1988): 3–11. Print.

---. *Writing in the Center.* Dubuque: Kendall/Hunt, 1985. Print.

Connors, Robert J. Address. URI/Trinity College Second Summer Conference on Writing. Kingston, May 1994. Print.

Elbow, Peter. *Writing without Teachers.* New York: Oxford UP, 1973. Print.

Faigley, Lester, and Kristine Hansen. "Learning to Write in the Social Sciences." *College Composition and Communication* 36 (1985): 140–49. Print.

Fenelon, Fania. *Playing for Time.* New York: Atheneum, 1977. Print.

Flower, Linda, and John R. Hayes. "A Cognitive Process Theory of Writing." *College Composition and Communication* 32 (1981): 365–87. Print.

Geisler, Cheryl. *Academic Literacy and the Nature of Expertise: Reading, Writing, and Knowing in Academic Philosophy.* Hillsdale: Erlbaum, 1994. Print.

Godfrey, Deborah. Professor of Nursing. University of Rhode Island. Personal interview. 29 July 1994. Print.

Haring-Smith, Tori. "Changing Students' Attitudes: Writing Fellows Programs." *Writing across the Curriculum: A Guide to Developing Programs.* Ed. Susan H. McLeod and Margot Soven. Newbury Park: Sage, 1972. 177–88. Print.

Harris, Muriel. "Modeling: A Process Method of Teaching." *College English* 45 (1983): 74–84.

---. "The Writing Center and Tutoring in WAC Programs." *Writing across the Curriculum: A Guide to Developing Programs*. Ed. Susan H. McLeod and Margot Soven. Newbury Park: Sage, 1972. 154–74. Print.

Holmes, Wendy. Professor of Art History. University of Rhode Island. Personal interview. 15 July 1994.

Hume, Anne. Professor of Pharmacy Practice. University of Rhode Island. Personal interview. 15 July 1993.

"Imitation/Modeling as a Teaching Method." Writing Center Discussion List. Web. 19–30 May 1994. Available e-mail: WCENTER@UNICORN.ACS.TTU.EDU

Kiedaisch, Jean, and Sue Dinitz. "Look Back and Say 'So What?': The Limitations of the Generalist Tutor." *Writing Center Journal* 14.1 (1993): 63–74.

Meyer, Emily, and Louise Z. Smith. *The Practical Tutor.* New York: Oxford UP, 1987. Print.

Murray, Donald M. "Teaching the Other Self: The Writer's First Reader." *College Composition and Communication* 33 (1982): 140–47. Print.

---. *A Writer Teaches Writing.* Boston: Houghton Mifflin, 1968. Print.

North, Stephen. "The Idea of a Writing Center." *College English* 46 (1984): 433–46. Print.

Scanlon, Leone. "Recruiting and Training Tutors for Cross-Disciplinary Writing Programs." *The Writing Center Journal* 6 (1986): 37–41. Print.

Schwegler, Robert A. "Meaning and Interpretation." URI/Trinity College 2nd. Summer Conf. on Writing. Kingston, May 1994.

Selzer, Jack. "Exploring Options in Composing." *College Composition and Communication* 35 (1984): 276–84. Print.

Smith, Louise Z. "Independence and Collaboration: Why We Should Decentralize Writing Centers." *The Writing Center Journal* 7.1 (1986): 3–10. Print.

Sommers, Nancy. "Responding to Student Writing." *College Composition and Communication* 33 (1982): 148–66. Print.

Soven, Margot. "Conclusion: Sustaining Writing Across the Curriculum Programs." *Writing across the Curriculum: A Guide to Developing Programs*. Ed. Susan H. McLeod and Margot Soven. Newbury Park: Sage, 1972. 189–97. Print.

Stern, Isaac. *From Mao to Mozart: Isaac Stern in China.* Dir. Murray Lerner. Harmony Film Group, 1980. Film.

"Teaching Composition: A Position Statement." *College English* 46 (1984): 612–14. Print.

Winer, Deborah G. "Close Encounters: Pros and Cons of Master Classes." *Opera News* 54 (1989): 28–31. Print.

Tutoring Style, Tutoring Ethics: The Continuing Relevance of the Directive/Nondirective Instructional Debate

Steven J. Corbett _____

UNIVERSITY OF WASHINGTON AT SEATTLE

Steven J. Corbett examines the theoretical, practical, and philosophical issues surrounding minimalist tutoring and discovers a significant discrepancy between "what we actually do and what we say we do" in this essay originally published in 2008 in Praxis. Corbett states that minimalist tutoring, as part of the directive/nondirective debate, "raises issues involving tutor authority, tutor-tutee (and even instructor) trust, tutor training, and writing process versus product—all relevant concerns in any writing instruction situation." He contends that "when diving deeply into a discussion of directive/nondirective tutoring, we soon begin to realize that—as in any education situation—we are dealing not just with instructional but also political issues." Corbett contends that this debate is more a continuum of practices than a polarity, and he argues that "tutors can better serve (and be better served) if they are encouraged to broaden their instructional repertoires" beyond a rigid adherence to either directive or nondirective modes.

A New Look at the Directive/Nondirective Debate

Arguably, no single issue in writing center theory and practice gets at the heart of one-to-one or small-group instruction like the question of directive/nondirective teaching methods. At the 2007 International Writing Centers Association Conference in Houston, Texas, writing center legends Muriel Harris, Jeanne Simpson, Pamela Childers, and Joan Mullin discussed the "core assumptions" surrounding four hot topics in writing center theory and practice, including *minimalist tutoring as standard.* Conversation buzzed around the idea that when considering what has become the default instructional mode in one-to-one tutoring—the minimalist approach—writing center practitioners and theorists need to consider what we actually do versus what we say we do. The question of how and when tutors should use techniques like open-ended questioning versus just telling students what they think they should do, or what the tutors might do themselves if they were in the tutee's position, raises issues involving tutor authority, tutor-tutee (and even instructor) trust, tutor training, and writing process versus product—all relevant concerns in any writing instruction situation. Yet, despite all the critical questions and considerations the directive/nondirective debate raises, several session participants wondered if we in writing center circles have made more of this issue than we really need to.

When diving deeply into a discussion of directive/nondirective tutoring, we soon begin to realize that—as in any education situation—we are dealing not just with instructional but also political issues. Much has been written on the minimalist approach (for example, Ashton-Jones; Brooks; Harris) and on subsequent critiques of this approach (for example, Clark "Collaboration and Ethics," "Writing Centers and Plagiarism," "Perspectives"; Clark and Healy; Shamoon and Burns "A Critique," "Plagiarism"; Grimm; Wingate; Latterell; Boquet "Intellectual Tug-of-War," *Noise*; Carino; Geller et al.). I will analyze several key texts that comment on and critique general assumptions and influential arguments surrounding this debate, especially Irene Clark and Dave Healy's 1996 "Are Writing Centers Ethical?" I will argue that one-to-one contexts demand a close reconsideration of our typically nondirective, hands-off approach to tutoring. Tutors can better serve (and *be* better served) if they are encouraged to broaden their instructional repertoires, if directors and coordinators encourage a more flexible notion of what it means to teach (and learn) one-to-one. Granted, this is an idealistic claim. I will thus begin to illustrate why—precisely because "instructional flexibility" is easier said than done—we should continue to carefully scrutinize tutoring style and method via the directive/nondirective continuum.

Hands Off or On? The Directive/Nondirective Instructional Continuum

When diving deeply into a discussion of directive/nondirective tutoring, we soon begin to realize that—as in any education situation—we are dealing not just with instructional but also political issues. Clark and Healy's essay tracks the history of the nondirective (or noninterventionist) approach in the "orthodox writing center." It describes how in the 1970s and early 1980s writing centers began to replace grammar drills and skills with what would become the higher-order concerns (HOCs) and lower-order (or later-order) concerns (LOCs) approach to tutoring. Along with this new instructional focus, however, came a concurrent concern—fear of plagiarism. The fear of plagiarism goes hand-in-hand with the idea of intellectual property rights, a political and personal issue pertinent to tutors, students, instructors, and program directors. This "concern with avoiding plagiarism, coupled with the second-class and frequently precarious status of writing centers within the university hierarchy, generated a set of defensive strategies aimed at warding off the suspicions of those in traditional humanities departments" like English (Clark and Healy 245). For Clark and Healy, the resulting restraint on tutor method soon took on the practical and theoretical power of a moral imperative. They describe how influential essays from Evelyn Ashton-Jones, Jeff Brooks, and Thomas Thompson cemented the hands-off approach to one-to-one instruction.[1]

In an ironic twist, Clark and Healy note that "by being so careful not to infringe on other's turf—the writer's, the teacher's, the department's, the institution's—the writing center has been party to its own marginality and silencing" (254). In answer to this perceived marginality and silencing, they offer essays by Marilyn Cooper, Shamoon and Burns, and Muriel Harris, as well as the work of Vygotsky, that value the pedagogical feasibility of modeling and imitation and an epistemology that moves writers outside their texts to some degree. Cooper, for example, in her close reading of Brooks, argues "when writing center sessions remain resolutely focused on how a student can fix a paper, it is difficult for tutors to focus instead on what students know and need to know about writing" (337). For Cooper, and others, a strict minimalist approach forecloses the act of collaboration that could take place in a one-to-one, collaborative negotiation that takes both the tutor's and the tutee's goals into consideration. This echoes comments made during the 2007 IWCA session I mentioned above. Respondents felt that a strict minimalist approach can be manipulative and still leaves the tutor very much in control of the session. Cooper would have us instead make room for the "really useful knowledge" that may involve listening to student experience or offering ways of reading assignment prompts or even syllabi that make room for the writer's creativity or risk taking, rather than, as Brooks would have us, "'always focusing on the paper at hand'" (347).

In short, tutors need to be aware of the rhetorical complexity — both interpersonal and intertextual — that any given tutorial can entail. Clark and Healy point to an earlier work of Harris's from *College English* in 1983, "Modeling: A Process Method of Teaching," in which she advances a directive approach. In describing the benefits of intervening substantially in students' writing processes, Harris asks "what better way is there to convince students that writing is a process that requires effort, thought, time, and persistence than to go through all that writing, *scratching out, rewriting, and revising* with and for our students?" (qtd. in Clark and Healy 251; emphasis added). Harris, early on, like Shamoon and Burns, understood the value and importance of the ancient rhetorical tradition of modeling and imitation *in the service of invention*. In order to perform such moves as "scratching out" and "rewriting," tutors must have some confidence in their ability (the theoretical and practical feasibility and timeliness involved) in offering more direct suggestions on issues of style and correct usage.[2]

Negotiating the Fine Line between Talk, Teaching, and Our Best Intentions

Harris, however, has always understood the value of both directive and non-directive tutoring strategies, and scholars like Nancy Grimm, Anne DiPardo, and Carol Severino concur. In her concise yet theoretically sophisticated 1999 monograph *Good Intentions*, Grimm juxtaposes the implications of Brian Street's autonomous and ideological models of literacy with the work we do. Arguing that our traditional hands-off approach to one-to-one instruction is often misguided, she writes:

> Writing center tutors are supposed to use a nondirective pedagogy to help students "discover" what they want to say. These approaches protect the status quo and withhold insider knowledge, inadvertently keeping students from nonmainstream cultures on the sidelines, making them guess about what the mainstream culture expects or frustrating them into less productive attitudes. These approaches enact the belief that what is expected is natural behavior rather than culturally specific performance. (31)

Like Cooper five years earlier, Grimm calls for writing center practitioners to move away from a focus on the paper to the cultural and ideological work of literacy: negotiating assignment sheets to see if there might be any room for student creativity or even resistance; making students aware of multiple ways of approaching writing tasks and situations, in order to make tacit academic understandings explicit; rethinking tired admonishments regarding what we can *not* do when tutoring one-to-one. Grimm illustrates what a tough job this really is, though, in her analysis of DiPardo's "'Whispers of Coming and Going': Lessons from Fannie."

While Grimm, drawing on Street and Lisa Delpit, forcefully argues for the importance of moving past our infatuation with nondirective tutoring, she may be inadvertently pointing to why it is also perhaps just as important for us to continue to value some of our nondirective strategies—suggesting the truly subtle nature of this issue. DiPardo's essay describes and analyzes the tutorial relationship between Morgan, an African American tutor, and Fannie, a Navajo student who just passed her basic writing course and is attempting the required composition course. Both DiPardo and Grimm speculate that Morgan's repeated attempts to prod and push Fannie toward what Morgan believed was realization or progress only pushed Fannie away from any productive insights. The tutorial transcript presented by DiPardo illustrates how Morgan dominated the conversation, often interrupting Fannie (though unfortunately we do not get micro-level analysis like how long pauses were after questions, etc.), how Morgan appropriated the conversation, attempting to move Fannie toward her idea of a normal academic essay. While this approach may ostensibly resemble the directive approach advocated by Grimm, Delpit, and others, what it leads Grimm and DiPardo to conclude is that tutors must be encouraged to practice "authentic listening": "As DiPardo's study illustrates, without authentic listening, the very programs designed to address social inequality inadvertently reproduce it, 'unresolved tensions tugged continually at the fabric of institutional good intentions' (DiPardo 1992, 126)" (Grimm 69). Ironically, "authentic listening," or allowing the student to do most of the talking during one-to-ones to enable them to be more in control of the tutorial discourse, is one of, perhaps the most fundamental of, nondirective strategies.

Something as fundamental as asking the tutee at the beginning of the tutorial what phase their draft is in could go a long way toward setting up just how hands on or off a tutor can be. Carol Severino, drawing on Ede and Lunsford, associates directive tutoring with hierarchical collaboration and nondirective tutoring with dialogic collaboration. But her analysis of two conferences involving two different tutors with the same student points just as much toward our assumptions of what a good tutorial is *supposed* to sound like. The student is Joe, an older African American returning student taking a class titled "Race and Ethnicity in Our Families and Lives." Severino analyzes the transcripts of sessions between Joe and Henry, a high school teacher in his thirties working on his MA in English, and Joe and Eddy, a younger freshman with less teaching experience. Like the sessions that DiPardo and Grimm analyze above, Henry uses his teacherly authority, from the very start of the conference, by asking closed or leading questions that persuasively direct the flow of the rest of the tutorial. In contrast, during the session between Joe and Eddy, Eddy starts off right away asking Joe open-ended questions like how he feels about the paper, and where he wants to go from there. For Severino, this sets a more conversational, peerlike tone that carries through the rest of the tutorial. Although obviously privileging the nondirective/dialogic approach, Severino concludes by asserting that it is difficult to say which of the above sessions was necessarily "better" (especially since we do not hear Joe's point of view, and, importantly, we do not know what phase or draft Joe's paper is in). Instead, she urges those who prepare/educate tutors to avoid prescriptive tutoring dictums that do not take into consideration varying assignment tasks, rhetorical situations, and student personalities and goals—the "always" and "don't" that can close off avenues for authentic listening and conversation. The problem with Severino's analysis, is that we do not get a clear enough picture of exactly what was going on during the tutorial. As with Fannie above, we do not know how Joe felt about the interaction. Perhaps he found greater value in Henry's more directive approach.

Reconsidering Our Best Intentions: Conclusion

This discussion of directive and nondirective tutoring suggests that if we keep our pedagogy flexible and attuned to one writer at a time, we may better anticipate when to urge a closer rethinking of content or claim, when to pay attention to conventions and mechanics, and how and when to do both. In short, tutors need to be aware of the rhetorical complexity—both interpersonal and intertextual—that any given tutorial can entail. This complexity means that tutor coaches should stay wary of the all-too-tempting sort of rules of thumb that lead to Geller et al.'s caution regarding "premature cognitive commitments" or Severino's denouncement of prescriptive dictums that can unintentionally cement a strained social relationship between tutor and tutee. Geller et al. write: "Familiar memes—don't write on the paper, don't speak more than the student-writer, ask non-directive questions—get passed among cohorts of writing tutors as gospel before they even interact with writers in an everyday setting" (21). As Harris and Shamoon and Burns suggest, we should reevaluate nondirective tutoring in light of the historical precedents that may no longer serve exigencies that originally produced them (for example, fear of plagiarism, or writing centers struggling to find their institutional identity). We should reevaluate the importance of the classical-rhetorical idea of imitation and style in the service of invention—but with a heightened sensitivity to when to provide models for imitation, and when to nudge students toward agency in their own inventive processes. If our best intentions more closely match our best practices, we might find ways to further question and more rigorously examine these reconsidered notions. An understanding and appreciation of the range and scope of the directive/nondirective continuum can provide one possible starting point for such examinations.

Adding the idea of modeling, a willingness to sometimes take a more hands-on approach to tutoring, can complement a tutor's instructional repertoire. Tutor coaches (be they directors or more experienced co-workers) can offer suggestions—or models or examples—of when it might be more or less appropriate to be more or less directive or nondirective. Something as fundamental as asking the tutee at the beginning of the tutorial what phase their draft is in could go a long way toward setting up just how hands-on or -off a tutor can be.

Finally, we should (and often do) realize that sometimes it's all right to give a pointed suggestion, to offer an idea for a subtopic, to give explicit direction on how to cite MLA sources, to practice along a continuum of instructional choices both socially collaborative and individually empowering.

Notes

[1] Ashton-Jones juxtaposes the "Socratic dialogue" with the "directive" mode of tutoring. Drawing on Tom Hawkins, she characterizes the directive tutor as "shaman, guru, or mentor," while Socratic tutors are given the more co-inquisitive label "architects and partners." Personally, I feel that it could be a good thing if a tutor-tutee relationship develops to the point that the tutee looks to the tutor as somewhat of a "mentor." Brooks, in arguing that students must take ownership of their texts, associates directive tutors with editors, good editors perhaps sometimes, but editors nonetheless. Brooks goes so far as to advise that if a tutee seems unwilling to take an active role in the tutorial, tutors simply mimic the tutee's unengaged attitude and action. And Thompson urges tutors to avoid having a pen in hand during tutorials. In the name of the Socratic method, he also urges tutors "not to tell students what a passage means or give students a particular word to complete a thought" (Clark and Healy 246).

[2] One problem with the literature on the directive/nondirective debate is the fact that no one really talks about what stage of an essay draft a tutee is in. The stage makes a great difference in how a tutor should approach the tutorial. For example, if a student is in the early phases of a draft, then perhaps tutors can take a more minimalist approach, asking questions, trying not to get too hands-on. If the student is working on a "final" draft, then it would be more appropriate for a tutor to get involved in some of the more hands-on "scratching out" and "rewriting" Harris speaks of. Thus, one of the key queries that should be asked in the first round of questions foregrounding a tutorial is something like "What stage is this draft in?" which of course will lead to further follow-up questions.

Works Cited

Ashton-Jones, Evelyn. "Asking the Right Questions: A Heuristic for Tutors." *The Writing Center Journal* 9.1 (1988): 29–36. Print.

Barnett, Robert W., and Jacob S. Blumner, eds. *The Allyn and Bacon Guide to Writing Center Theory and Practice*. Needham Heights: Allyn and Bacon, 2001. Print.

Boquet, Elizabeth H. "Intellectual Tug-of-War: Snapshots of Life in the Center." Briggs and Woolbright Urbana: NCTE, 2000. 17-30. Print.

---. *Noise from the Writing Center*. Logan: Utah State UP, 2002. Print.

Briggs, Lynn Craigue, and Meg Woolbright, eds. *Stories from the Center: Connecting Narrative and Theory in the Writing Center*. Urbana: NCTE, 2000.

Brooks, Jeff. "Minimalist Tutoring: Making the Students Do All the Work." *Writing Lab Newsletter* 15.6 (1991): 1–4. Print.

Buranen, Lise, and Alice M. Roy, eds. *Perspectives on Plagiarism and Intellectual Property in a Postmodern World*. Albany: SUNY UP, 1999. Print.

Carino, Peter. "Power and Authority in Peer Tutoring." *The Center Will Hold: Critical Perspectives on Writing Center Scholarship*. Eds. Michael A. Pemberton and Joyce Kinkead. Logan: Utah State UP, 2003. 96–116. Print.

Clark, Irene Lurkis. "Collaboration and Ethics in Writing Center Pedagogy." *The Writing Center Journal* 9.1 (1988): 3–12. Print.

---. "Perspectives on the Directive/Non-Directive Continuum in the Writing Center." *The Writing Center Journal* 22.1 (2001): 33–58. Print.

---. "Writing Centers and Plagiarism." Buranen and Roy 155–67. Print.

Clark, Irene Lurkis, and Dave Healy. "Are Writing Centers Ethical?" Barnett and Blumner 242–59. Print.

Cooper, Marilyn M. "Really Useful Knowledge: A Cultural Studies Agenda for Writing Centers." Barnett and Blumner 335–49. Print.

Delpit, Lisa. "The Silenced Dialogue: Power and Pedagogy in Educating Other People's Children." *Harvard Educational Review* 58.3 (August 1988): 280–97. Print.

DiPardo, Anne. "'Whispers of Coming and Going': Lessons from Fannie." Barnett and Blumner 350–67. Print.

Geller, Anne Ellen, Michele Eodice, Frankie Condon, Meg Carroll, and Elizabeth H. Boquet. *The Everyday Writing Center: A Community of Practice.* Logan: Utah State UP, 2007. Print.

Grimm, Nancy Maloney. *Good Intentions: Writing Center Work for Postmodern Times.* Portsmouth: Boynton/Cook, 1999. Print.

Harris, Muriel. *Teaching One-to-One: The Writing Conference.* Urbana: NCTE, 1986. Print.

Latterell, Catherine G. "Decentering Student-Centeredness: Rethinking Tutor Authority in Writing Centers." Briggs and Woolbright 104–20. Print.

Severino, Carol. "Rhetorically Analyzing Collaborations." *The Writing Center Journal* 13 (1992): 53–64. Print.

Shamoon, Linda K., and Deborah H. Burns. "A Critique of Pure Tutoring." *The Writing Center Journal* 15.2 (1995): 134–51.

---. "Plagiarism, Rhetorical Theory, and the Writing Center: New Approaches, New Locations." Buranen and Roy 183–92.

Wingate, Molly. "What Line? I Didn't See Any Line." *A Tutor's Guide: Helping Writers One to One.* Ed. Ben Rafoth. Portsmouth: Boynton/Cook, 2000. 9–16. Print.

Kairos and the Writing Center: Modern Perspectives on an Ancient Idea

Carl Glover

MOUNT ST. MARY'S UNIVERSITY

Carl Glover examines the relevance of the ancient Greek idea of kairos, *or "the opportune moment," to tutoring as an actively "involved experience." Glover finds that a "kairos-consciousness," or a readiness to respond appropriately to the opportunities created in the tutor-client relationship, can provide for an "ethically grounded" experience capable of synthesizing "antithetical elements." For tutors, kairos involves a type of "double vision" that looks for a balance between the abilities of the writer and the demands of the paper.* Kairos *thus is a way in which tutors can be attuned to "the cues in moments of insight" in which the writer is engaged in "discovery" and "holds the primary responsibility for the progress of the paper."*

Kairos, the ancient rhetorical concept of "timeliness" or "the opportune moment," has important implications for the work of tutors and directors in the modern writing center. This chapter begins with a brief historical survey of this concept, followed by a discussion of its applications to writing center work. Although the primary emphasis is on the more obvious uses of *kairos,* related to timeliness and the opportune moment, the chapter also explores the more mystical ways in which *kairos* is treated as a concept of time itself, independent from the normal flow of time.

In the ancient Greek language, according to the Liddell and Scott *Greek-English Lexicon, kairos* has several basic definitions. The most useful ones for our study include: "exact or critical time, season, or opportunity" and "due measure, proportion, fitness" (859–60). In his analysis of *kairos,* Richard Onians suggested that the term is not a mere abstraction but is derived from archery. *Kairos* is the shaft or opening through which the archer must shoot the arrow to accurately hit the target. The archer must exercise "due measure and proportion" in aiming the arrow and drawing the bow string; he must hit a "vital part of the body" to fell his prey; he must release the arrow at the "exact or critical time" to strike a moving target (343–45).

The concept of *kairos* was an ideal valued highly by the ancient Greeks, so it is not surprising that Kairos was considered a Greek god. According to Posidippus, a third century BC epigrammatist, a statue crafted by the sculptor Lysippus depicts Kairos as a young man, standing on tiptoe with winged feet, and with a strikingly long lock of hair in front yet bald at the back of his head. This unique hairstyle, in Posidippus's view, gave Kairos the character of decision, because the lock of hair was a "symbol that one must take the favorable opportunity by the forelock" (Delling 457). Once Kairos has raced by on his winged feet, he cannot be grasped by the hair from behind. When the opportune moment has passed, it can no longer be seized.

The earliest written record of the word *kairos* is attributed to Hesiod in his *Works and Days,* dating from around 800 BC (*Oxford Classical Dictionary* 421–22). In a passage devoted to navigational advice, Hesiod cautioned, "Observe [due] measures. Timeliness [kairos] is best in all matters" (694). Of the Seven Sages, four of whom lived in the latter half of the seventh to the early sixth centuries BC, four wrote about *kairos.*

Solon advised "Seal your words with silence, and your silence with kairos" (Diels and Krantz 63 16). Bias held that "[b]y kairos you will have eulabeian [discretion, circumspection]: a good hold of things" (Diels and Krantz 65 11). DeVogel added this paraphrase: "By acting at the right moment you will act prudently" (115 note 3). The apothegm "Know your time" is attributed to Pittacus (Diels and Krantz 64 12). Chilon was credited with the maxim "All good things belong to kairos" (Diels and Krantz 61 13).

References to *kairos* abound in Pindar. Some have the character of sage advice, as in *Olympian* 13.47: "Yet measure due *[kairos]* is meet in all things, and the fitting moment is the best aim of knowledge." Other references to *kairos*, however, point to a fundamental, self-conscious attempt by the poet to ground his composition in a rhetorical *kairos*. In describing this new method of composition, Pindar wrote, "If thy utterance hitteth the critical moment, twining together in brief space the cords of many themes, less blame followeth from mankind; for tiresome satiety blunteth lively expectation" (*Pythian* 1.81). For Pindar, *kairos* combines both the "critical moment" of a story and the "due measure" the poet must use to avoid saturating the audience with too much information. The poet's first task is to attain knowledge of *kairos*, the opportune moment, "the instant in which the intimate connection between things is realized" (Untersteiner 111). A knowledge of *kairos* then allows the poet to arrange things "in accordance with their significance" (Gundert qtd. in Untersteiner 111).

Although Pythagoras left no writings, accounts of his work are attested to by many writers in the ancient world. In his ethically based cosmological system, *kairos* functions as the force that joins opposites together in harmony. According to this Pythagorean system, *kairos* is a generative element, because all matter in the universe springs from this harmony of opposing forces. The same *kairos* that brings harmony to opposing elements in the generation of the universe also unites individuals in harmony and justice. In his *Life of Pythagoras*, Imblichus highlighted Pythagoras's notion of the link between *kairos* and human relations: "[Pythagoras] taught about the relations towards parents and benefactors. He said that the use of the opportune time *[kairos]* was various. For those of us who are angry or enraged, some are so seasonably, and some unseasonably. . . . He further observed that to a certain extent opportuneness *[kairos]* is to be taught" (Guthrie *Sourcebook* 102). This passage calls attention to a fundamental problem in rhetorical pedagogy addressed later by Isocrates and of concern to writing center directors today. To what extent can *kairos* be taught? Can a Pythagorean *kairos*, firmly anchored in universal ethical principle, be "various" enough to address all situations? The previous passage seems to admit the possibility of teaching *kairos*, perhaps even reducing it to exercises in a handbook for writing center tutors, but all the while maintaining a sense of the limitations of such efforts. Life's contingencies are simply too numerous, complex, and unpredictable to reduce to a series of previously rehearsed "opportune" responses. Perhaps Pythagoras's notion can be taken to suggest a pedagogy based on a "*kairos*-consciousness," a readiness to respond appropriately to the opportunities created in the tutor–client relationship.

The *kairos* that brings harmony to opposing forces in the Pythagorean system is similar to Empedocles's notion of *kairos*, which synthesizes antithetical elements, such as love and strife. The difference between the two is that in the Pythagorean system *kairos* functions within an established framework of an ethically grounded cosmological system, whereas for Empedocles antithesis becomes the foundation for a relativistic epistemology predicated on *kairos*, the "situational context." According to Richard Enos, the harmony of antithetical elements brought about by *kairos* is best translated as "balance" (44). In

Empedocles's view, all knowledge is probable because it is attained only through the senses, which are unreliable. No two people experience the same event in the same way. *Kairos,* based on this relativistic epistemology, maintains a balance among sense perceptions necessary for evaluating probable knowledge.

For the sophists, lifestyle factors such as travel over rugged terrain, agonistic speech performances before live audiences, and the ever-present exchange of ideas with student traveling companions fostered a *"kairos* consciousness." Responding appropriately to moments of opportunity was a mode of living necessary for the sophists' survival. *Kairos,* for the sophist Gorgias, is an irrational or nonrational force that resolves the antitheses in a relativistic world, but when used rhetorically *kairos* becomes the principle by which the rhetor determines the greater or lesser degree of probable truth. In addition, for Gorgias, *kairos* also becomes a prompting toward speaking, a moment of crisis or urgency to fill the void created by conflicting ideas, a seizing of an opportunity to speak in a moment of decision.

Despite fundamental differences between the sophistic emphasis on relativism and situational context and Plato's ideal rhetoric based on a priori principles, Plato's system, like that of the sophists, becomes functional through *kairos.* The use of *kairos* is clearly described in the *Phaedrus,* when Socrates outlined an ideal rhetoric: "It is only when he has . . . grasped the concept of the propriety of time [kairos] — when to speak and when to hold his tongue. . . . It is only then, and not until then that the finishing and perfecting touches will have been given to his science" (271d–72b).

Isocrates provided a middle ground between the practical orientation of the sophists and the philosophical position of Plato. In *Against the Sophists,* Isocrates disdained those who reduce the rules of rhetoric to handbooks, failing to take into consideration the doctrine of *kairos.* In his view, *kairos* is the first principle of rhetoric and cannot be reduced to rule-governed procedures. According to Isocrates, "Oratory is good only if it has the qualities of fitness for the occasion [*kairos*], propriety of style, and originality of treatment" (12–13).

Despite this seemingly rich history of *kairos,* I hasten to point out that during the first century BC, Dionysius of Halicarnassus wrote, "No orator or philosopher has up to this time defined the art of the 'timely' [*kairos*], not even Gorgias of Leontini, who first tried to write about it, nor did he write anything worth mentioning" (Sprague 63). Dionysisus' words notwithstanding, the evidence from ancient Greece indicates that *kairos* was an important concept in the development of Greek rhetoric and epistemology.

Kairos and the Modern Writing Center

All of the ideas from ancient Greece surveyed thus far (timeliness, the opportune or critical moment, due measure, discretion, appropriateness, moments of insight or connection, harmonizing of opposites, a tool for selecting among alternatives, knowing when to speak and when to be silent) are relevant to a critical consciousness essential for writing center work.

The discussion of *kairos* in the writing center begins by exploring applications of this concept to the work of tutors. All of the ideas raised apply to directors as well, but because directors must assume additional responsibilities, their concerns are addressed separately.

Tutors must make an immediate judgment concerning how best to help their clients. In a sense, they must find the *kairos* point of the tutoring session, which requires a kind of double vision that looks for a balance between the abilities of the client and the demands of the paper. The tutor must take the following questions into consideration in those moments of decision early on in the tutoring session:

> *Time constraints:* What are realistic goals for the tutor and client to reach given the time allotted? Is the appointment for thirty minutes, one hour, or in rare cases, is it open-ended?

> *The needs of the client:* Has this client visited the writing center before? For this paper? Has the client worked with the same tutor on this or other papers? Has the client worked with another tutor on a previous draft of this paper? What strengths and weaknesses are immediately obvious to the tutor? How can the tutor help to build confidence in the writer using the strengths apparent in the paper? What opportunities for tutoring or growth do the writer's weaknesses present?

> *The demands of the assignment:* What does the assignment ask the writer to do? What writing and thinking skills are called for? Is the writer asked to analyze, synthesize, summarize, paraphrase? Does the assignment suggest an organizational pattern? Must the paper be obviously thesis driven? Is the writer required to make a formal argument?

> *The* kairos *of the paper itself:* Does the paper contain a point of resonance for the writer to build on? Does it suggest a new focus or direction for revision? Does it offer a new way of interpreting the assignment?

Setting the Stage for Moments of *Kairos*

Perhaps the best way to frame this discussion is in the Platonic sense of *kairos:* knowing when to speak and when to be silent and knowing how much to say or how little to say. This is the *kairos* of due measure. Establishing the proper atmosphere certainly helps make moments of *kairos* possible in writing center appointments. Opening the session with a warm greeting and small talk helps set the tone for a relaxed and attentive atmosphere. It is essential for the client to realize early in the appointment that the tutor has an open mind, open to possibilities for revision. The direction the appointment takes should not be controlled entirely by the tutor, but it is an open-ended process of continuing negotiation between tutor and client.

After breaking the ice with informal talk, the tutor might begin by asking two simple questions: "What can I help you with today?" and "Can you tell me the assignment in your own words?" Moments of *kairos* may develop merely through the process of talking the paper out.

There are several approaches to addressing the paper itself. Some tutors begin by quickly skimming the paper to get an overall sense of it before beginning the conversation with the client. Others have the client read the paper aloud or the tutor reads the paper aloud to the client. Clearly, this oral treatment of the paper allows both client and tutor to "hear" the paper, to be attentive to its strengths and weaknesses, and to look for opportunities for revision. I do not recommend that tutors read papers silently, pausing to point out grammatical errors or other problems. This approach limits the possibility for meaningful interaction to occur, disabling the flow of *kairos*.

During an appointment, an attentive tutor might recognize a moment of *kairos* when the "light bulb" goes off, either for the client or for the tutor or for both. This might occur, for example, when a connection between ideas is realized, or when a new direction for the paper is discovered. Tutors must learn to recognize these moments, to be attentive to the cues inherent in moments of insight. During these moments, the client may grow more inquisitive or animated in discussion. Or perhaps the client's body language might signal some form of intellectual breakthrough. This may be the right time to ask leading questions. In some cases, the identification of a weakness in the paper or a problem with surface error might become an opportunity, a moment of *kairos*, when learning takes place.

Not only must tutors know when to speak and how much to say, they also need to learn how to make the best use of silence. This is possibly the most difficult aspect of a *kairos* consciousness, because our natural tendency is to feel uncomfortable with moments of awkward silence and fill the void with our own words. By allowing moments of silence to occur in a writing center appointment, the tutor lets the client know that the tutor will not provide all the "answers," but that the client holds the primary responsibility for the progress of the paper.

Kairos and Writing Center Directors

Because writing center directors either currently serve or have served as writing center tutors, the aforementioned discussion of *kairos* applies to their work as well. In addition, directors must also develop a sense of *kairos* to effectively carry out their leadership responsibilities in writing centers.

A *Kairos* of Tutor Selection   First of all, when selecting tutors, writing center directors must choose the best tutors in keeping with their centers' particular mission statements and goals. To be sure, the process of tutor selection varies among writing centers. Some prospective tutors must complete a training course, often for academic credit, before assuming their roles as tutors. Others might require a minimum grade point average or even a master's degree for professional tutors. Whatever selection procedure directors follow, the moment of *kairos* for many of them comes in the interviewing process.

While interviewing potential tutors, the director should look for certain traits indicative of a *kairos* consciousness: attitude, energy level, ability to focus, personality. Whereas tutors' writing and editing skills are essential, these other factors may contribute more to their ability to recognize moments of *kairos* in a writing center appointment.

The *Kairos* of Tutor Training Tutor training programs vary from full-blown courses — complete with session observation, practice tutoring, and taped tutorials — to a few workshops and on-the-job training. Whatever the training program involves, directors should develop a program that is most specifically appropriate to the strengths and weaknesses of the individual tutor. A one-size-fits-all training program might seem to be the most cost-effective and time-efficient approach to training tutors, especially at larger schools, but a training program with *kairos* in mind will better serve the clients and the institution as a whole.

Clearly, a training program centered on the needs of the individual tutor is more time consuming and labor intensive, but the results are worthy of the extra effort.

The key to a *kairos*-based training program is careful observation of the tutors, both during training itself and during live tutoring sessions. New tutors at larger writing centers should be paired with mentors, or experienced tutors, for exchanging feedback, for assessing strengths and weaknesses, and for planning ways to grow and improve. The tutor–mentor relationship will set the stage for the opportune moment for growth and discovery in the training process.

A *Kairos* of Writing Center Practice

Directors must take care in formulating writing center policies and procedures to avoid interfering with moments of *kairos*. Without a doubt, the nondirective approach favored by many writing centers has great merit. This "client-centered" approach, influenced by the theories of psychotherapist Carl Rogers, allows writers to discover for themselves, through response to questions, the direction their papers ought to take. This method of tutoring allows the students to maintain ownership of their own texts. When carried too far, however, this approach can be counterproductive. For example, I know of a few writing centers who mandate a rather extreme hands-off approach to tutoring, forbidding tutors to hold pencils or pens in their hands, thus avoiding the temptation to mark on the clients' texts. Unfortunately, the *kairos* of the moment might demand a well-placed word or two, a mark of punctuation, or a circle and arrow connecting ideas on the paper. It is impossible to make such a mark, to respond to this opportune moment, without a writing implement in hand. The policy should not be whether or not to make marks on papers (and this should be done only with the client's permission), but *when* is it appropriate to write on a paper, and *what* and *how much* should be written. Tutors with a sense of *kairos* will learn the right time and the right way to intervene in a paper. Directors should not handcuff their tutors, but should develop writing center practice with *kairos* in mind.

Writing center directors fill a variety of roles within academic institutions, and the administrative challenges vary from institution to institution.

Whatever the nature of this role, be it tenured or tenure track academic professional or administrative staff, the director must develop a sense of *kairos* in terms of the overall structure of the institution. The director must know when to either support or challenge the status quo in regard to the dictates of the institutional situation.

Kairos as a Concept of Time

The reemergence of *kairos* as a philosophical concept in the twentieth century results in part from the influence of theologian Paul Tillich, who introduced the term in his writings in connection with the religious socialist movement in Germany after World War I. For Tillich, as for the writers of the Old and New Testaments, time is an empty form, an abstract, objective reflection that can receive any kind of content (*Protestant Era* 33). The quantitative measure of time is *chronos* and the qualitative measure of time is *kairos*. The relationship between *chronos* and *kairos* becomes dynamic when *kairos,* "an outstanding moment in the temporal process," breaks into *chronos*, the temporal dimension, "shaking and transforming it and creating a crisis in the depth of human existence" (45). According to Tillich, moments of *kairos* are the turning points when "the eternal judges and transforms the temporal" (47).

Awareness of *kairos* for Tillich is a matter of vision. Although psychological and sociological observation and analysis "serve to objectify the experience and to clarify and enrich the vision," they cannot create the experience of kairos ("Kairos" 370–71). To capture this vision, this *kairos* consciousness, one must be actively engaged in "involved experience" (370):

> The consciousness of the kairos is dependent on one's being inwardly grasped by the fate and destiny of the time. It can be found in the passionate longing of the masses; it can become clarified and take form in small circles of conscious intellectual and spiritual concern; it can gain power in the prophetic word; but it cannot be demonstrated and forced; it is deed and freedom, as it is fate and grace. (*Protestant Era* 48)

In Tillich's view, *kairos* also has the character of decision. These moments of decision are not abstract, metaphysical notions, but are concrete decisions "possible only in a concrete, material world" (142).

In the Old Testament, time is measured in terms of its content. For example, in the familiar "Catalogue of the Seasons" in Ecclesiastes 3:1–9, time is defined by its content:

1. For everything there is a season, and a time for every matter under heaven:
2. a time to be born, and a time to die; a time to plant, and a time to pluck up what is planted;
3. a time to kill, and a time to heal; a time to break down, and a time to build up; etc.

The Hebrew word for time in the previous passage is *'eth,* which is translated in the Septuagint, the Greek version of the Old Testament, as *kairos.* What is the character of *kairos* in this passage? Following Tillich, these verses present *kairos* as "a moment," a "point of time," and a "time of crisis and decision." At first glance, this notion of *kairos* seems to apply, especially to crisis situations involving death, killing, and war. On the other hand, most of the other pairs mentioned are clearly not critical or decisive times: "to weep," "to laugh," "to mourn," "to dance," "to embrace," "to refrain from embracing," "to seek," "to lose," "to rend," "to sew." These occasions are the normal human emotions and reactions that make up everyday life. In addition, few of these experiences or events occur within a "moment" or a "point of time." Certainly war and peace extend beyond a moment's duration.

It can be concluded, then, that *kairos* as an interruption in the normal flow of time, can be either brief or last for an extended period. It can include both life-changing events and brief moments of insight, those "aha" moments, mentioned previously, that spring forth during our daily routines. All of us have experienced from time to time those moments when *kairos* breaks into our normal experience of the passage of time. For example, when I meet an old friend whom I have not seen for a long time, we spend some time together, perhaps consuming a few of our favorite beverages, and share our thoughts about old times and what is going on in our lives today. It seems that only a few minutes have passed, but in fact we have been together for maybe two or three hours. We have lost track of time, not because of inattentiveness, but because the normal flow of time as we experience it has been broken into by a moment of *kairos.* I would hope that occasionally a writing center conference would produce this type of moment of *kairos* for our tutors and clients.

What about those moments of crisis, or those life-changing experiences, or those profound extended moments of *kairos* that Tillich wrote about? Those are rare in writing center work, but they can happen. I offer an example from my own experience. When Greg first came to our writing center as a sophomore, he was a wayward youth in search of a direction. He had little interest in academics and seemed to be merely going through the motions. Although he had good ideas, he had a great deal of difficulty expressing himself in writing. He came to see me, the director of our writing center, because he was required to; as a freshman, he had failed the college's writing proficiency requirement. I assigned him to work with Deb, one of our professional tutors. Over the course of the next three years, Greg was transformed both as a writer and as a person. His thirst for knowledge was kindled and he became a strong writer. He also developed a sense of direction for his life. It was almost as if in the *kairos* of the present, he made sense of his past and envisioned a promising future. Although I realize that a number of factors might have contributed to Greg's transformation, he told me on more than one occasion that working with Deb in our writing center changed his life.

These life-altering extended moments of *kairos* are rare in writing center work, but they do occur, perhaps without our ever knowing it. But when tutors and directors discover these cases, they are richly rewarded, knowing that their work has borne fruit.

Works Cited

Delling, Gerhard. "Kairos." *Theological Dictionary of the New Testament*. Ed. Gerhard Kittel. Trans. and Ed. Geoffrey W Bromley. Grand Rapids: Eerdmans, 1975. Print.

DeVogel, C. J. *Pythagoras and Early Pythagoreanism*. The Hague: Royal VanGorcum, 1959. Print.

Diels, Hermann, and Walter Kranz. *Die Fragmente der Vorsokratiker*. Berlin: Weidmannsche, 1956. Print.

Enos, Richard Leo. "The Epistemology of Gorgias Rhetoric: A Re-examination." *Southern Speech Communication Journal* 42 (1976): 35–51. Print.

Guthrie, Kenneth Sylvan. *The Pythagorean Sourcebook*. Ed. David R. Fideler. Grand Rapids: Phanes, 1987. Print.

Hesiod. Works *and Days*. Trans. Hugh G. Evelyn-White. Loeb Classical Library. New York: Putnam's, 1920. Print.

Holy Bible. Revised Standard Version. Camden: Thomas Nelson, 1959. Print.

Isocrates. *Isocrates II*. Trans. George Norlin. Loeb Classical Library. Cambridge: Harvard UP, 1968. Print.

Liddell, Henry George, and Robert Scott, eds. *A Greek-English Lexicon*. Revised by Sir Henry Stuart Jones and Robert McKenzie. Oxford: Clarendon, 1968. Print.

Onians, R. B. *The Origins of European Thought*. Cambridge: Cambridge UP, 1951. Print.

Pindar. *The Odes of Pindar*. Trans. John Sandys. Loeb Classical Library. Cambridge: Harvard UP, 1961. Print.

Plato. *Phaedrus*. Trans. W C. Helmbold and W. G. Rabinowitz. Indianapolis: Bobbs-Merrill, 1956. Print.

Sprague, Rosamund Kent, ed. *The Older Sophists: A Complete Translation by Many Hands of the Fragments in Die Fragmente der Vorsokratiker*. Columbia: South Carolina UP, 1972. Print.

Tillich, Paul. "Kairos and Kairoi." *Systematic Theology*. Chicago: U of Chicago P, 1948. Print.

---. *The Protestant Era*. Trans. James Luther Adams. Chicago: U of Chicago P, 1948. Print.

Untersteiner, Mario. *The Sophists*. Trans. Kathleen Freeman. New York: Philosophical Library, 1954. Print.

Identifying Our Ethical Responsibility: A Criterion-Based Approach

David Bringhurst _____
WRIGHT STATE UNIVERSITY

David Bringhurst examines the many constituencies the writing center serves—institutional, student, and professional—in terms of ethical responsibilities that define the writing center's "pedagogy and self-image." Typically, ethics and the writing center are examined on a situational basis—for example, in terms of a single issue (plagiarism) or a single constituency (students). However, rather than advocating situational analysis, which proves to be too limiting, Bringhurst calls for a "holistic ethical approach" that recognizes the complexity of responding to all the constituencies the writing center serves. Of particular concern is the "ambivalence" some writing center professionals hold about the function of the writing center in academic institutions concerned with "maintaining the status quo" and serving as a "normalizing agent" in writing instruction. Bringhurst contends that this view leads to a too quick and simplistic advocacy for the writing center to operate at the "margins" of the academy and is based on a situational interpretation of ethics versus a holistic approach that seeks integration, affirmation, and a capacity "to fully engage" on an ethical basis with all the writing center's constituencies.

The subject of writing center ethics touches on a broad spectrum of issues. We serve many constituencies—institutional, departmental, student, and professional—and are often explicitly or implicitly asked to defend our conduct and even our existence to one or more constituencies at any given time. Concerns about plagiarism, oppression, fair labor practices, and our role within the institution and the larger professional and social communities in which we work and live constantly challenge our pedagogy and our self-image. Most of the published attempts to come to terms with our ethical responsibilities, however, focus on our responsibility to a single constituency (e.g., clients) or individual issues (e.g., plagiarism). This situational approach to ethics can be valuable, but only if we have first grounded ourselves in a holistic ethical approach that holds us accountable to all of our constituencies. At the end of the day, we must recognize that as professionals, who are not on the margin of but inside the academic institution, we have an ethical obligation to serve all of our constituents. Any solutions we propose to ethical problems must include an ethical response to each of the constituencies affected or we risk a response that is ethical for one constituent but unethical for another. Fortunately, all of these constituencies have much in common, including the aim of doing "good" for the primary constituency: students.

The writings of Michael Pemberton reflect the range of ethical issues tutors regularly confront. From dealing with students who present essay content that tutors find morally questionable, to the ethical ways tutors might deal with what they view as poorly defined or unfair assignments from faculty, Pemberton showed an awareness of the difficult decision-making process tutors must go through. Pemberton provided useful insights for tutors, but he struggled (as so many of us do) with the broader issues that confront us as writing center administrators. He attempted to establish three laws for tutoring based on the model of Asmiov's Three Laws of Robotics, but his attempt is ultimately flawed by its bias toward collaborative and process theory and its narrow focus on tutor–client interaction ("Writing Center Ethics: Three Laws" 13).

Collaborative and process theories are problematic as foundations on which to build an ethical system of tutoring. Although collaborative and process theories are dominant formative influences in writing center pedagogy today, the question of their ethical rightness is still clearly open for debate (as we will see later); thus, any ethical system based on them must be considered suspect. Moreover, Pemberton's focus on the tutor–client relationship, although useful to that relationship, ignores his own assessment that "writing center ethics are deeply embedded in institutional and situational contexts, and, as such, they resist reduction to a simple set of principles or universal guidelines" ("Writing Center Ethics: Three Laws" 13). Pemberton, himself, cautioned that "when considering whether or not to give advice or take ethical stands with students, tutors in writing centers must be attuned to circumstances that extend far beyond the narrow confines of the writing tutorial: What are the motivations and purposes and goals of the people involved—be they students, tutors, faculty, or administrators?" ("Writing Center Ethics" 10). This caution applies to other areas of ethical inquiry within the writing center as well. In the end, any ethical system we might adopt must encompass and provide guidance for our ethical relationship with each of our constituencies.

One of the most common areas where we find ourselves challenged by the motivations, purposes, and goals of our other constituencies is over the issue of plagiarism. A great deal of the scholarship on writing center ethics deals with our alleged complicity in student plagiarism. We often answer this charge by defending our pedagogy based on one of the dominant theories that influence it, be it collaborative theory, noninterventionism, or even questioning the concept of authorship itself.

Richard Behm offered one such defense in answer to charges from an English faculty member that the help his students received at Behm's writing center was tantamount to plagiarism. The faculty member contended that "one of the most important functions a university serves is certifying students, making judgments about their abilities so that employers and others may determine fitness for jobs and so on. When a student receives assistance on a draft of a paper, or even discovering ideas for a paper that is to be graded, the work is no longer solely that of the student, and thus this certifying function is subverted" (Behm 3). Behm countered that "the certifying function of education" threatens the "traditional mission of a university as a place of teaching and learning" (4–5). Behm believed that we have become overly concerned with life in the "real world" and this concern has led to an emphasis on certification and thus poisoned our methodologies. "[E]ach day in college is 'the real world,' and we are about a very important task, one that overshadows the political mandate to certify students as accountants or restaurant managers or English teachers" (5). Behm, himself, used a similarly "real-world" defense when he "contend[ed] that collaborative learning as practiced in most writing centers is not plagiarism, that it is not only ethical but also reflective of the way people really write" (9). He went on to "argue that the truly unethical act is *not* making such collaborative learning available to students, bowing to the demand to certify them instead of acknowledging the primary imperative of educating them" (10).

Behm was right that to withhold the collaborative option is unethical, but he was wrong in the implication that this is somehow an either/or scenario. Behm's theories undercut the very "traditional mission" to which he sought to return us. Certification is merely the stamp of approval, if you will, that the university has succeeded in its mission, which Behm earlier defined as teaching and learning. Whereas it is possible that we could or have let our priorities become skewed, Behm ignored the reality that the certifying function exists along a continuum that includes teaching and learning. One might argue that we know the teaching mission has been accomplished when the learner learns. But, in order to determine if learning has taken place, we must measure or assess the student in some way. It is only after teaching occurs that assessment is employed to determine whether or not learning has taken place. Once we have determined that it has taken place, certification serves to alert others that the student has learned what was required. Not to certify would be outrageously unethical because that certification, in the form of a grade or degree, has great value to the student. In many respects, it is their reason for entering the academy or, arguably, our writing centers. To ignore our primary constituency's primary motivation—a motivation, by the way, that is ethically sound—is clearly unethical.

Collaborative learning is but one theory offered as a defense against charges of complicity in student plagiarism. Both interventionist approaches to tutoring and process theory have been implemented or invoked in our defense against charges of plagiarism. Irene L. Clark and Dave Healy argued that noninterventionist policies are "a set of defensive strategies" resulting from "a concern with avoiding plagiarism, coupled with the second-class and frequently precarious status of writing centers within the university hierarchy" (245). But, as with the collaborative theory, Clark and Healy charged that there are problems with noninterventionism as an adequate solution to the problem of plagiarism. Clark and Healy believed that "a noninterventionist policy as an absolute must ultimately be judged ethically suspect, increasing the center's marginality, diminishing its influence, and compromising its ability to serve writers" (242). Like noninterventionism, invoking process theory as a defense against plagiarism has come under attack by some scholars. Shamoon and Burns posited that a defense against plagiarism based on process theory "does nothing directly to offset the charges of unethical behavior" and "has the potential to further implicate the writing center in such charges" ("Plagiarism" 185).

Both Clark and Healy and Shamoon and Burns argued that the weaknesses of these defensive approaches stem from a failure to address the assumption of validity that sole authorship has come to possess in academic circles. Not only did Clark and Healy see the noninterventionist approach to tutoring as ultimately unethical, they argued that it perpetuates a limited and limiting understanding of authorship in the academy. By privileging individual responsibility and accountability and by valorizing the individual writer's authentic "voice," the writing center has left unchallenged notions of intellectual property that are suspect at best. Furthermore, as Lisa Ede, Andrea Lunsford, Marilyn Cooper, and others have argued, the idea that writing is fundamentally a solitary activity and that individual writers can and should "own" their texts relegates the writing center to a limited bystander's role, even as it limits writers' understanding of their options and of their relationship to others. (Clark and Healy 247)

Shamoon and Burns also referred to Ede and Lunsford, but also enlisted the scholarship of Rebecca Moore Howard, whose "historical overview of concepts of plagiarism demonstrates that modern definitions of authorship and plagiarism are social constructs that have taken shape in the West during the last 300 years" ("Plagiarism" 187). They found process theory wanting as a defense against charges of plagiarism because it "discounts [tutoring] in terms of publicly identified authorship and ownership." Furthermore, they argued, "The effacing of the tutor's presence has the effect of leaving the concept of sole authorship in place, surely in the instructor's mind but probably also in the student's mind, too" ("Plagiarism" 186)

It seems, then, that our past theoretical responses to plagiarism, lacking in one way or another, are insufficient answers to the charge. Clark and Healy and Shamoon and Burns argued that it is because our attempts have left the idea of sole authorship unchallenged. This is an accurate and astute assessment, but only in the valid, but limited question of our alleged complicity in plagiarism. Despite the ubiquity of the charge, plagiarism is only a smaller ethical issue that exists in a larger ethical context. Like Pemberton's focus on the tutor–client relationship, a fixation on plagiarism as an ethical issue creates a kind of myopia that prevents us from seeing the larger issues.

Nancy Maloney Grimm challenged this myopic view by suggesting that it might be the academy itself that is unethical. She did not exculpate writing centers from their role in the academy's unethical behavior. She noted that "writing centers maintain the status quo, thereby oppressing the very students most dependent on writing center assistance" (xvii). Grimm believed that "as they presently operate, writing centers are more often normalizing agents, performing the institutional function of erasing differences" (xvii). This charge stems from her view that "because writing centers are places where assimilation into the discursive systems of the university is facilitated, one rarely hears stories about the erasures: the loss of motivation, the compromise of creativity, the silencing of family stories, the impediments to agency, the suppression of other literacies and worldviews" (xvi). It is clear from the tone of this assertion, that Grimm viewed our ethical standing in the broader terms of its complicity with, in her opinion, the unethical academy. She made this claim more explicitly when she challenged us "to move toward a more 'fair' writing center practice" and "rethink the ethical codes and policies that place limits on what tutors are allowed to do for students. Ethical codes in writing centers, particularly those that support minimalist 'hands-off' tutoring, often protect those who are favorably positioned within the institution from coming to terms with the realization that the institution itself is not fair" (114–15). This is a revolutionary idea that Clark and Healy later expanded on with their "new ethics for the writing center" (253–57). Grimm's attempt to reframe the issue, which in its essence is on target, flies off the mark and is thus undercut because she used some spurious logic and fell prey to a commonly held misconception.

Grimm employed some faulty logic when she conflated the personal experiences of her family history with what happens in academe. "My maternal and paternal grandparents," she related, "came from countries where they were forbidden to speak their native languages, where the culture of the conqueror, oppressor, colonizer attempted to override their own. . . . [I]t is that history that troubles me when I see representations of writing center work as innocent and ideologically neutral" (xvi). The connection she saw, however, is based on a false analogy. I do not think it is disrespectful to Grimm's valid feelings for her family's own lost culture to suggest that neither in scope nor in degree is what we do on a par with the experiences of her family at the hands of their "conquerors." When a people are conquered or colonized, the intention is to wipe out the conquered people's identity, including their language and history. However misguided our pedagogy might be, our actions cannot be reasonably compared to such atrocities. Implicit in the terms *conqueror* and *colonizer*, if not *oppressor,* are the acts of invasion, usually by force, and occupation. But academies do not invade the lands and homes of our students; in a sense, students invade the academy. For students come to the academy and, for the most part, do so of their own free will. Moreover, students may leave at any time. They are free agents, in any meaningful use of the term, who seek us out to learn what we have to teach.

Grimm's suspicion of the institution is clear in her somewhat Orwellian charge that writing centers are "normalizing agents." And she is right; that is precisely our job. But Grimm would have us believe that this is a negative role that obliterates culture rather than our ethical responsibility to prepare students to participate fully in the academic discourse community. The academic discourse community is but one community to which students belong. They are not isolated within the university, but rather partake of it even as they continue to be members of their family, social, and work communities. To see students as victims or even as just students is to rob them of their agency and identity. "Student" is just one role that people play, and the academy is but one stage on which they play that or any role.

Although it is true that some of our clients come to us from different cultures, our facile view of them as somehow helpless outsiders fending off the oppression of the academic system is misguided. Their presence in our centers is surely a sign of their need or desire, if not their willingness, to enter the system, to be on the inside. When we bend over backward to preserve their

"voices" in the name of ethics, we are actually abdicating our ethical responsibility to help them enter into the system as embodied by the institution. In
so doing, we effectively ensure their isolation much in the same way as our
insistence that we are on the outside tends to marginalize us. This belief in our
own marginalization—in our "outsider" status—not only helps to undercut
Grimm's case, it keeps us from grasping the full implications of what it means
to question the academy's ethics.

The psyche of writing center professionals, and thus its scholarship, is
marred by our ambivalence about our status and role within the academy.
There are tantalizing glimpses of confidence and an understanding of our place
within the academy, but our perception of our marginality keeps us from
inheriting our true place. Pemberton came close to recognizing the problem
when, if you'll remember, he said "writing center ethics are deeply embedded in institutional and situational contexts" ("Writing Center Ethics: Three
Laws" 13). He even named our constituencies when he cautioned tutors to be
aware of "the motivations and purposes and goals of the people involved—be
they students, tutors, faculty, or administrators" ("Writing Center Ethics" 10).
Clark and Healy also, in proposing their new ethics for the writing center,
pointed out that we "should be confident of [our] own expertise and insight
and should be willing to use [our] unique position in the academy to challenge
the status quo by critiquing institutional ideology and practice" (255).

Yet, despite such evidence, writing center literature is filled with references
to our marginality and status as outsiders. Shamoon and Burns played the
marginalization card in two separate contexts. In arguing that, as part of the
academy, we help create a "Fordist approach to production," they made the
point that writing center labor is "held in place—its marginal place" by that
approach ("Labor Pains" 65, 67). Although arguing that we should play a
significant role in the discussion and definition of plagiarism, they urged the
writing center "to reposition itself away from its precarious position on the
margins and toward the center of the academy" ("Plagiarism" 184). This last
affirmation of marginality is repeated in their final compelling argument for
moving us "into the center of academic life" ("Plagiarism" 191–92). In both
cases, their insistence on our marginality is particularly discordant given its
juxtaposition within such a positive message.

Clark and Healy provided an even stronger example of this strange and
ambivalent disjunction. They worry that the policy of noninterventionism is
"increasing the center's marginality" (242). They referred to "the second-class
and frequently precarious status of writing centers within the university hierarchy" (245). Even the underlying premise for their vision of a new ethics for
writing centers is built on the foundation of our supposed marginality. Their
contention "that writing centers are well positioned to question the status quo"
is based on "what Harvey Kail and John Trimbur have called 'semiautonomous'
institutional space located 'outside the normal channels of teaching and learning'" and "what Nancy Welch calls 'critical exile'" (253). Frustratingly, they

confirmed the deep-seated misapprehension that the best place from which to "challenge the status quo by critiquing institutional ideology and practice" is from the margins. (255).

Before we challenge anyone, we should first challenge our own assumptions of our place within the academy. As someone with both writing center and administrative credentials, Jeanne Simpson provided an insightful and useful place to start. Simpson debunked many of the myths we seem to have about the role of the Central Administration. Interestingly enough, she asserted that our supposed marginalization "would be a surprise to Central Administration. If a program is being funded, space provided, salaries paid, assessment and evaluation being conducted, then the assumption . . . is that it is part of the institution and that some part of the institution's mission is being addressed." Simpson further contended "that writing centers have more control over what Central Administration knows about them than is perceived" (190). According to Simpson, most issues such as "instructional quality" and "evaluation decisions (retention, promotion, tenure)" are assumed to occur at the departmental level, and "[d]epartmental affiliation is not seen . . . as a prestige issue but as a mechanical/organizational/logistical issue" (190–91).

If Simpson was right that we are not being marginalized by the administration, and I suspect she was, then perhaps the source of our marginalization occurs at the departmental level. If this is the case, we should consider why this may be so. Perhaps departments, our own as well as others in the academy, marginalize us because they only see us when there is a perceived problem, such as potential plagiarism. Perhaps it is because, when they do approach us, we respond defensively and/or approach the problem from the perspective of what they must be doing wrong to cause such a misperception. Perhaps there is an actual or perceived problem with our credentials as professionals. Perhaps we are not aligning our missions, theories, and practices with those of our department and other departments. Perhaps it is because we act marginalized because we think we're marginalized. To be honest, I really don't know.

What I do know is that we will not be able to fully and ethically engage with our constituencies—the academy, departments, students, tutors, and ourselves—until we find out. Until we view ourselves as an integral, perhaps not central, functional part of the academy, we will not be able to effectively help it or our other constituencies accomplish their mission(s). As outsiders we can rant and rave, but we cannot affect change in any meaningful way. True revolution comes from within. This is one of "the theoretical, pedagogical, and political facts of life" Clark and Healy insisted we must acknowledge (242). Another is that there will be some policies that we will just have to accept because we won't always be able to change people's minds. But even that fact of life is not so harsh. It only seems that way because we fall prey to the meta-myth, if you will, that is at the heart of our sense of marginalization. For when we feel like we are on the margins, we view those on the "inside" as our enemies. They are somehow against us, in opposition. But this is not true.

As Simpson showed us, the administration is, at worst, neutral in regard to us. Furthermore, she proposed that by educating ourselves about the needs of the administration, we can better communicate and integrate ourselves with it:

> The kind of information that writing center directors will need to gather and distribute will not be as closely related to the philosophy and daily functioning of a writing center as it will be to larger, institutional issues. Directors need to be sophisticated enough in their own administrative activities to balance the two levels of knowledge and expertise — theoretical and managerial, pedagogical and budgetary — effectively. (193)

Simpson conceded that, currently, "our professional literature and organizations" are weak in the areas of management and budget (193). Nevertheless, having identified the need, there is no reason to believe that we cannot meet the challenge.

At the departmental level, there may be frustration with us, but only to the degree that we isolate ourselves from departmental goals and missions. Directors must navigate the local terrain in their academy, but a review of some of the general codes of ethics for faculty suggest that they will find more common ground than not. According to part II of the "Statement on Professional Ethics of the American Association of University Professors":

> As teachers, professors encourage the free pursuit of learning in their students. They hold before them the best scholarly and ethical standards of their discipline. Professors demonstrate respect for students as individuals and adhere to their proper roles as intellectual guides and counselors. Professors make every reasonable effort to foster honest academic conduct and to ensure that their evaluations of students reflect each student's true merit. They respect the confidential nature of the relationship between professor and student. They avoid any exploitation, harassment, or discriminatory treatment of students. They acknowledge significant academic or scholarly assistance from them. They protect their academic freedom. (Weingartner 132)

Furthermore, part III states, "Professors acknowledge academic debt and strive to be objective in the professional judgment of colleagues" (Weingartner 132). Further confirmation of the similar beliefs and intentions we share can be found in the "Statement of Professional Ethics of the Modern Language Association of America." The Preamble states that the freedom of inquiry that scholars should enjoy "carries with it the responsibilities of professional conduct. We intend this statement to embody reasonable norms for ethical conduct in teaching, research, and related public service activities in the modern languages and literatures" (Weingartner 135). Statements 4 through 7 develop an ethic for dealing with issues of academic integrity:

> 4. Free inquiry respects the diversity of the modes and objects of investigation, whether they are traditional or innovative. We should defend scholarly practices against unfounded attacks from within or without our community.

5.   Our teaching and inquiry must respect simultaneously the diversity of our own culture and that of the cultures we study.
6.   Judgments of whether a line of inquiry is ultimately useful to society, colleagues, or students should not be used to limit the freedom of the scholar pursuing it.
7.   As a community valuing free inquiry, we must be able to rely on the integrity and the good judgment of our members. For this reason, we should not . . . plagiarize the work of others. . . . (Weingartner 135–36)

The footnote in the original explains that the definition of plagiarism used is from *The MLA Style Manual*. Points 1 and 4 in the section titled "Ethical Conduct in Academic Relationships," subsection A titled, "Obligations to Students" are particularly interesting and germane. Point 1 states, "Faculty members should represent to their students the values of free inquiry," and point 4 states, "Student-teacher collaboration entails the same obligation as other kinds of research: faculty members should acknowledge appropriately any intellectual indebtedness" (Weingartner 136). One assumes that students should conduct themselves in a similar manner. In any event, there seems to be little in these ethical declarations that is at odds with our own intentions.

Shamoon and Burns offered a professional approach to engaging faculty in discussions or debates about ethical and pedagogical issues.

> A writing center that is driven by the social-rhetorical approach does not frame questions of plagiarism as either ethical problems or as groundless charges from the uninformed. . . . Practitioners in such a writing center are ready to engage other instructors in elaborate conversations about context, about disciplinary expectations, about topical frameworks and, especially, to engage them in conversations about difference—the differing and special expectations instructors have for their specific writing assignments and for what is valued by them in student writing, including writing that is imitative and elaborative of ideas and forms of disciplinary discourse. . . . From such conversations come the potential to move the writing center off the margins of the university and into the center of academic life. ("Plagiarism" 191–92)

Note the lack of rebellion in this approach. An approach like Shamoon and Burns proposed, one that engages us in conversation about the issues that concern us, could raise the level of writing center discourse within the institution, but we must first expunge the outsider view that keeps us from understanding institutional roles, those of others as well as our own.

When we have more closely aligned ourselves with the mission of the academy and its departments, we will find ourselves better able to ethically serve students as well. This will help us to better determine whether or not the writing center methodologies proposed by some theorists meet the needs of both the academy and students. Alice M. Gillam looked at the peer tutorial processes espoused by Kenneth Brufree and Harvey Kail and John Trimbur:

> In the Brufree model, the long-range social goal seems to supercede the imme-
> diate educational goal. . . . [T]he goal of Kail and Trimbur's model is cast in
> terms which refer specifically to education, [but] this model implicitly suggests
> the larger social goal of a critically conscious and politically active citizenry.
> Notably, neither Brufree's nor Kail and Trimbur's model focuses primarily on
> explicit writing goals. (44–45)

The place where the goals of the academy and its students meet is a critical
area where, as Clark and Healy suggested, we can provide a window, not only
into the classroom, but onto the needs of our student clients (255). There is
nothing wrong with trying to expand the intellectual consciousness of our students; in fact, it is implicit in our broader educational goals. But when we paint
our theories with such a broad brush, we may overlook the fact that for many
students, these laudable goals are years away from being attainable. Students
in a developmental phase may require more emphasis on the standards of
discourse, whereas those further along the continuum may be better placed to
begin questioning the community and its structure.

   The pervasive view of our marginalization has devastating effects on our
self-image as professionals, on our ethical conduct as professionals, and ultimately on our status as professionals. But, in many ways, more importantly,
our view of ourselves as outsiders is most damaging to the one constituency
that is at the heart of our mission: students. The primary reason for this is that
the "outsider" view has a harmful (and rather ironic) effect on how we view
student autonomy or agency. The sense of marginalization that comes through
in our own scholarship is painful to confront and paralyzing in its effect. As
a profession, we seem extremely insecure with our place in the world and it
leads to some strange paradoxes. But this is both cause and effect. When we
see ourselves as outside the system, we are led into these false or, at the very
least, inadequate defenses. Only when we see ourselves as a part of the system
and not apart from it will we be able to create an ethical solution that will
answer the needs of all of our constituencies. Ultimately, it is the act of claiming our insider status that will have the greatest and most positive long-term
ethical implications for our profession and for us as professionals.

Acknowledgments

The initial drafts of this chapter were written with the assistance of the writing center in which
I work. I would like to specifically thank Dr. Joe Law for his invaluable aid in helping me
organize my thoughts and for discussing the issues with me.

Works Cited

Behm, Richard. "Ethical Issues in Peer Tutoring: A Defense of Collaborative Learning." *The
    Writing Center Journal* 10.1 (1989): 3–12. Print.
Clark, Irene L., and Dave Healy. "Are Writing Centers Ethical?" *WPA: Writing Program Admin-
    istration* 20.1–2 (1996): 32–38. Rpt. in *The Allyn and Bacon Guide to Writing Center Theory
    and Practice*. Ed. Robert W. Barnett and Jacob S. Blumner. Boston: Allyn and Bacon, 2001.
    242–59. Print.

Gillam, Alice M. "Collaborative Learning Theory and Peer Tutoring Practice." *Intersections: Theory-Practice in the Writing Center.* Ed. Joan A. Mullin and Ray Wallace. Urbana: NCTE, 1994. 39–53. Print.

Grimm, Nancy Maloney. *Good Intentions: Writing Center Work for Postmodern Times.* Portsmouth: Heinemann-Boynton/Cook, 1999. Print.

Pemberton, Michael. "Writing Center Ethics." *Writing Lab Newsletter* 18.4 (1993): 10–12. Print.

---. "Writing Center Ethics: The Three Laws of Tutoring." *Writing Lab Newsletter* 19.4 (1994): 13–14. Print.

Shamoon, Linda K., and Deborah H. Burns. "Labor Pains: A Political Analysis of Writing Center Tutoring." *The Politics of Writing Centers.* Ed. Jane Nelson and Kathy Evertz. Portsmouth: Heinemann-Boynton/ Cook, 2001. 62–73. Print.

---. "Plagiarism, Rhetorical Theory, and the Writing Center: New Approaches, New Locations." *Perspectives on Plagiarism and Intellectual Property in a Postmodern World.* Ed. Lise Buranen and Alice M. Roy. Albany: State University of New York Press, 1999. 183–92. Print.

Simpson, Jeanne. "Perceptions, Realities, and Possibilities: Central Administration and Writing, Centers." *Writing Center Perspectives.* Ed. Byron L. Stay, Christina Murphy, and Eric H. Hobson. Emmitsburg: NWCA Press, 1995. 48–52. Rpt. in *The Allyn and Bacon Guide to Writing Center Theory and Practice.* Ed. Robert W Barnett and Jacob S. Blumner. Boston: Allyn and Bacon, 2001. 189–93. Print.

Weingartner, Rudolph H. "The Moral Dimensions of Academic Administration." Ed. Steven M. Cahn. *Issues in Academic Ethics.* Lanham: Rowman & Littlefield, 1999. Print.

Tutor and Student Assessments of Academic Writing Tutorials: What Is "Success"?

Terese Thonus

CALIFORNIA STATE UNIVERSITY AT FRESNO

In this essay, which originally appeared in the journal Assessing Writing, *Terese Thonus explores Stephen M. North's assertion in "The Idea of a Writing Center"—which appears on p. 44—that the writing center's primary role and contribution is "talking to writers." However, as Thonus argues, "many studies of tutorial effectiveness lack adequate analyses of tutorial talk." Using the frameworks of interactional sociolinguistics, conversation analysis, and ethnographic research, Thonus examines the implications of "tutorial talk" in terms of related models of institutional discourse focusing on talk that is adversary-oriented, management-oriented, naturalistic and participant-oriented, expertise-oriented, and objectives-oriented. Her goal is to determine what dimensions of conversational interactions contribute to "the assessment of tutorial success." Again drawing on North and his famous statement that the job of writing center tutors is "to produce better writers, not better writing," Thonus considers "less idealized, more prag-matic conceptualizations of tutor roles and actions" in order to emphasize, in both tutoring and tutor training, the "behaviors demonstrated as constitutive of success."*

1. Introduction

The university-level writing center, established first in the U.S. as the 1960s' English Department "writing lab" (North, 1984), has developed over the decades into a sophisticated service supporting students in first-year writing programs and beyond across the full range of disciplines. Instructors who evaluate students not only according to their knowledge of subject matter but also their ability to express themselves in writing consider writing center tutorials a useful if not necessary step towards writing improvement. This is particularly true of instructors who value written expression as the mark of an "educated person," who have themselves worked as tutors, and/or who have collaborated with writing programs in developing writing assignments suitable to their own disciplines (Thonus, 2001).

Academic writing tutorials "fit the bill" as institutional discourse in that interactions pattern as diagnosis + directive + report writing phases, each pred-icated on evaluation (Agar, 1985; Thonus, 1998). They share certain features with other institutional discourse types such as medical consultations (West, 1990), health–visitor interactions (Heritage & Sefi, 1992), and psychotherapy sessions (Ferrara, 1994). Tutorials also resemble certain academic discourse genres such as advising interviews (Bardovi-Harlig & Hartford, 1993; Hartford & Bardovi-Harlig, 1992), counseling sessions (Fiksdal, 1990; He, 1998), and teacher–student writing conferences (Sperling, 1994).

Of these, tutorials most closely approximate writing conferences, yet they differ from them in two fundamental ways. First, tutors are not the tutees' classroom instructors, and thus can neither formally evaluate student papers nor model how students' instructors view the role of writing in their courses. Second, tutor training guides, such as Gillespie and Lerner (2000) and Meyer and Smith (1987), promote the notion that tutors and tutees are of equal status and that tutees have the right and obligation to "call the shots" in tutorial inter-actions. The reality of tutorial practice, however, differs markedly (Thonus, 1999a, p. 244). Because tutors are motivated, trained, and paid by the institu-tion to improve student writing, their dominance of writing center interaction is therefore predictable, and the "collaborative" dilemmas of tutorial practice understandable (Thonus, 1999b).

In contrast to course instructors, writing tutors "concentrate on broadly constituted principles such as 'good writing' rather than on institutional-, discipline-, or course-specific rules. They must remain neutral with respect to 'higher' rules and are forbidden from evaluating assignments posed by students' instructors or from hazarding a guess as to ultimate evaluations of student writing" (Thonus, 1998, p. 32). This separation of the writing center from the act of formal evaluation is key to "the idea of a writing center" (North, 1984) because an increased focus of resources and personnel on writing assessment would take away from a center's main goal, "to keep students coming in and coming back" (Johnson-Shull & Kelly-Riley, 2001, p. 27), The interaction between writing assessment and writing support is thus viewed as a "feedback loop," two ostensibly opposing forces operating to establish equilibrium: "Assessment creates and enforces a firm standard, and the Writing Center mitigates the formality by offering a flexible mechanism as a support" (op. cit., 84).

In contrast to this idealistic characterization of tutors who do not evaluate, Thonus (2001) found that tutors criticize course instructors (either tacitly or overtly) on everything from course content to assignment construction to evaluation of student writing precisely because they view themselves as colleague pedagogues. That is, it appears that tutors view instructors, not tutees, as their peers. They therefore assume the right, if not the obligation, to evaluate student writing. Thus, the argument must be made that the writing tutorial is an evaluative act in fact if not by design.

Evaluations of tutoring and of the writing center typically treat students as "clients" and ask them to rate the "services" of the center — usually once a semester at most — and often focus on "repeat clients" only. Bell (2000) termed this approach "consumer-oriented" and proposed five additional alternatives to writing center evaluation: adversary-oriented, management-oriented, naturalistic and participant-oriented, expertise-oriented, and objectives-oriented. Adding her voice to the debate, Yancey (2002) critiqued the outcomes-oriented nature of much writing center assessment: "Too often we talk about what works, but seeing what does not work is every bit as instructive, and is in fact necessary if we are to develop an adequate theory of tutor development" (op. cit., 199). Harris (2002) argued for research performed by writing center administrators that parallels classroom teacher research in its self-critical component.

The assessment of tutorial success falls within the purview of Lerner's (2002) "descriptive assessment" far more than the more "evaluative" assessment of writing centers. Unfortunately, empirical studies in this area are rare, and those that have been published lack credibility due to design flaws (e.g., Walker & Elias, 1987). A recent exception is Jones (2001), who performed a meta-analysis of the existing research on writing center assessment, examining direct and indirect ways in which tutorials can influence student writing performance and the delicate line between measurable and intangible outcomes that researchers must tread. Jones admitted that concrete evidence that writing centers actually improve student writing is difficult to substantiate, so that indirect evidence such as satisfaction surveys are often used instead.

Rarely is writing center assessment connected with assessments of the quality or change(s) in quality of students' writing. Nevertheless, students continue to consult writing center tutors on a voluntary or involuntary basis, and those who return a second time are coming back for more of what they got the first. And tutors continue to do their jobs day after day because they believe they are making a difference in student writing: "A tutor-as-causal-inquirer, in other words, intends to intervene helpfully with students" (Yancey, 2002, p. 190). It is imperative, therefore, to ask what factors students and (secondarily) tutors appeal to in accounting for the perceived "success" of writing tutorials. It is impossible to separate the notion of tutorial "success" from the enumeration of certain evaluative criteria. Whether formulated by the center itself, by tutors, by students, by course instructors and thesis directors, or by a combination of participants, these often tacit criteria are "running in the background" of every writing tutorial.

This study suggests a hybrid methodology combining ethnographic techniques and conversation analysis that may enable a more realistic means of evaluation of the effectiveness of writing tutorials.

2. Methodology

Stephen North, perhaps the original writing center theorist, proposed a methodology for assessing writing tutorials and writing centers, the analysis of tutorial talk:

> Talk is everything. If the writing center is ever to prove its worth in other than quantitative terms—number of students seen, for example, or hours of tutorials provided—it will have to do so by describing its talk: what characterizes it, what effects it has, how it can be enhanced. (1984, p. 444)

The methodology used in this study fits North's recommendation, and falls into the "naturalistic" category:

> The naturalistic element means that the evaluator seeks first-hand experience of the situation, studying it in situ without redefining, constraining, or manipulating it. The participant element means that all stakeholders or their representatives are usually involved in the evaluation. Evaluators acknowledge multiple realities and seek, by inductive reasoning, to understand the various perspectives, and, at the same time, evolve an appropriate methodology. (Bell, 2000, p. 13)

Note the connection between this approach to the assessment of writing centers and Hamp-Lyons' (2001) urging that we include all stakeholders in the assessment of writing. In order to accommodate these multiple perspectives, *interactional sociolinguistics* (Schiffrin, 1996) was selected as the primary research approach. Based on the work of Gumperz (1982), interactional sociolinguistics combines conversation-analytic and ethnographic techniques, thus permitting the concurrent analysis of linguistic and contextual factors.

2.1. Research questions. Three research questions guided this qualitative, interpretive study:

1. What linguistic and interactional features appear in conversations in these tutorials?

2. Which of these linguistic and interactional features do tutors and tutees reference when commenting on the success of the tutorials, and is the recurrence of any of these features correlated with assessments of a tutorial as "successful"?
3. What conclusions can be reached linking analysis of the tutorials with reflections upon the tutorials as regards perceived success of the tutorial and its impact on writing improvement?

Out of these questions arose the research methodology: Question (1) was answered by analysis of features and sequences of talk in tutorial transcripts, while question (2) was answered by analysis of data gathered in participant interviews. Question (3) associated the two data sets to provide an account of tutorial success and associate this with writing success.

2.2. Setting. The research site was Indiana University Writing Tutorial Services (WTS), which serves students in freshman and basic English composition classes and also graduate and undergraduate students, both native speakers (NSs) and nonnative speakers (NNSs) of English, in the full range of academic disciplines, at four campus sites.

2.3. Participants. Participants in the study were six NS and six Asian NNS undergraduate students enrolled at the university during the spring and summer terms of 1997, along with their respective tutors (Table 1).

This selection of tutorials yielded a wider selection of interactions between males and females, and NSs and NNSs of English; between tutorials in which tutors' subject-area expertise matched and differed from the content area of tutees' papers; between discipline-specific tutorials, and those with freshman composition students; and between first-time visits to WTS and repeat visits with the same tutor. In qualitative terms, this data set is an attempt to illustrate the varied contexts in which tutorial conversations occurred in this writing center.

2.4. Procedure. The participation of students and tutors in the study was solicited before their scheduled tutorials. The tutorials were then taped and transcribed (see Appendix A for transcription conventions). The student assignment sheet and paper, and the tutor's record of the tutorial were obtained as supporting documentation. Within a few days of each tutorial, the student and tutor met with the researcher separately to discuss their interaction. A second meeting with the researcher, usually a week later, was a "member check" during which participants read through the researcher's notes of the first interview, clarifying and correcting information. Participants then elaborated upon aspects of the notes and of the tutorial transcript. Finally, the researcher asked both participants in each tutorial to identify tutor behaviors they believed were most explicitly linked to tutorial success, and later, tutor and tutee interpretations of these details were compared.

Table 1
Participant information

Tutorial	Total time (minute)	Tutor gender and age	Tutee gender, language proficiency, and age	Tutor area of primary expertise	Tutee paper content area	First-time visit	Repeat visit w/same tutor
A	53	M (36)	NSF (29)	English (literature)	Political Science	no	yes
B	59	F (28)	NSM (22)	English (literature)	Math	no	yes
C	59	F (50)	NSF (19)	Education	English (composition)	no	yes
D	57	F (37)	NNSM (20)	English (literature)	English (composition)	no	no
E	59	F (32)	NNSF (20)	English (literature)	English (composition)	no	yes
F	53	M (32)	NSF (20)	Philosophy	Sociology	no	yes
G	50	F (26)	NSF (19)	English (composition)	Folklore	yes	no
H	57	F (34)	NNSF (22)	English (literature)	English (literature)	no	yes
I	55	F (22)	NNSF (21)	Sociology	Religious Studies	no	yes
J	38	F (26)	NNSM (27)	Comparative Literature	English (composition)	yes	no
K	50	M (28)	NNSF (25)	English (literature)	English (composition)	yes	no
L	53	F (25)	NSF (18)	English (literature)	English (composition)	yes	no

3. Features for Analysis

The features selected for the analysis of tutorial transcripts were discourse phases; interactional features, specifically volubility (time at talk); overlaps (simultaneous speech and interruptions); backchannels; laughter; directive type and frequency; mitigation type and frequency; and the negotiation of acceptances and rejections of evaluations and directives. In the oral discourse analysis literature, these features have been argued to depict such interactive stances as role, dominance, and expertise (e.g., Bardovi-Harlig & Hartford, 1991; Lim & Bowers, 1991; Tyler, 1995) and have been employed in analyses of tutorial talk by Blau, Hall, and Strauss (1998), Davis, Hayward, Hunter, and Wallace (1988), Seckendorf (1987), Thonus (1998, 1999a, 1999b, 2001), and Young (1992). An even more important motivation for choosing these features is that study participants referenced these and similar features in construing tutorials as "successful." The features are briefly described below.

3.1. Discourse phases. An outline of a tutorial's phases and component segments, its profile, was compiled for each of the 12 tutorials. The purposes of the profile were to "map" the interaction and to track topic nominations, which are key to understanding role and power relations in one-on-one conversations in educational settings (Rudolph, 1994; Ulichny & Watson-Gegeo, 1989; Walker & Elias, 1987). Following Agar (1985) and Hartford and Bardovi-Harlig (1992), the key phases identified were (1) the *opening*, (2) the *diagnosis*, (3) the *directive*, and (4) the *closing*.

3.2. Volubility. Volubility or participant time at talk (James & Drakich, 1993; Tannen, 1994) in the tutorials was measured by four different methods: total words, words per minute, words per turn, and ratio of tutor to student words.

3.3. Overlaps. In this analysis, *overlap* was defined as any simultaneous speech in which a conversational participant takes the floor before the first speaker has relinquished it through "completion intonation" (Jefferson, 1986). Based on the typology proposed by Roger, Bull, and Smith (1988), three kinds of overlap were identified. The first is the initiation of a contribution by a second party before the first has finished:

```
(TG - Tutor G. SG - Student G)

  TG:  Why no-, I mean why, [why
⇒ SG:                       [It doesn't work that way? I mean, I, I always, that's just the way I
       always (.) [thought
⇒ TG:             [Where would you put it in, in this paper (if you wanted to move it?
⇒ SG:                                [Well, I mean it would be the body paragraph in the
       middle, like I was going to end up talking about these (.) kind of like, because that's what I was, I thought
       we were supposed to do . . .

(Tutorial G, 98–100)
```

A second type of overlap, the *joint production* (Ferrara, 1994; Sacks, 1992) constitutes the completion of a first party's utterance by the second:

(TH - Tutor H. SH - Student H)

TH: So those yeah, that's the way, that's definitely a good way to go about it, um to identify the key concepts
       that you want to include in your thesis that are really important to your argument. ((writing)) So the
       personal and cultural memory (5s), the Kundera expressing his state of mind.   (4s)
SH: uh-huh
TH: and then Silko
⇨ SH: Speaks for her heritage?
TH: Speaks for her heritage? (4s) Yeah. So all of this into your thesis...

(Tutorial H, 19–20)

A third and less frequent type of overlap in these data is *simultaneous speech*, a main-channel overlap without taking the floor.

3.4. Backchannels. Backchannels were defined as "off-line" hearer continuers not constituting a taking of the floor (Sacks, Schegloff, & Jefferson, 1974). Because of their low volume and pitch, backchannels in these tutorial data differ noticeably from the higher volume and often higher pitch of *listener responses* (Fiksdal, 1990), which are main-channel utterances that fill turn slots. Both backchannels (*o.k., uh-huh*) and a listener response (*Got it*) are illustrated here:

(TA - Tutor A. SA - Student A)

SA: What brings me in? I'm working on a paper for my class, Ethics and Public Policy,
       and I've come up with a draft, and I'm looking for feedback on the draft.
⇨ TA: o.k.
SA: Basically, the (.) intention of the course is to develop good arguments
TA: uh-huh
SA: and we're studying ethics and public policy, and this week we were [on (.) the subject of
TA: [o.k.
SA: surrogacy, surrogate parenting.
⇨ TA: Got it.

(Tutorial A, 1–2)

Note, however, that [listener response] is not analyzed in this paper.

3.5. Laughter. Laughter has been characterized as a "conversational activity" (Jefferson, Sacks, & Schegloff, 1987) and an intentional speech act (Mao, 1997). It fills turn slots, serves as a response to previous talk, and acts as a purposeful lead-in to the next talk sequence. In addition, "laughing together is a valued occurrence which can be the product of methodic, coordinated activities" (Jefferson, 1984, p. 348). In these data, three types of laughter were identified: single-party, sequenced, and simultaneous.

3.6. Directive type and frequency. Directives offer what Fitch (1994) described as a clear "window" into participants' perceptions of role and status. This analysis recognized two types of directives, *interaction-internal directives* (IIDs) (West, 1990) and *suggestions* (D'Andrade & Wish, 1985; Searle, 1975). IIDs deal with the "here and now" of tutorial interaction, the work that will be accomplished during the tutorial by tutor or by student, e.g., *Say a little bit more about that. Maybe you could flesh that out.* In contrast, *suggestions* refer to actions the tutor wishes the tutee to perform once the tutorial is over, e.g., *But work on it a little bit, and run it by him* [the course instructor]. Directives were typed and graded according to a system of "request strategies" (Blum-Kulka, House, & Kasper, 1989). Combined with mitigation, these produced a ten-point scale from mitigated indirect (less direct) to unmitigated imperative (more direct) directives, as exemplified in Table 2.

3.7. Mitigation type and frequency. In the analysis of mitigation type and frequency, a "mitigated" utterance was one with one or more downgraders attached to it. These included tense/aspect and conditional/subjunctive syntactic downgraders and six lexical-phrasal downgraders: appealer, cajoler, hedge, downtoner, subjectivizer, and understater (Blum-Kulka et al., 1989). Moreover, upgraders such as *really*, *definitely*, and *again*, which aggravate rather than mitigate utterances, were noted (see Table 3).

3.8. Negotiation of acceptances and rejections of evaluations and directives. Gathered during participant interviews, this information amplified the utterance-level analysis of directives to focus on outcomes in sequences over multiple turns. Of interest were (a) how often and in what ways tutor and student evaluations and directives were received and (b) what impact negotiations of acceptances and rejections had on the perceived success of each tutorial.

Table 2
Directive strategies

---

1. Indirect (mitigated):
   Maybe the thesis doesn't have to say everything changed one way or the other. (Tutorial F, 195)
2. Indirect (unmitigated):
   And when you're unsure about idioms that's a good place to look. (Tutorial H, 80)
3. Interrogative (M):
   Is there like some general way you could just say what, what does that, this essay describes? (Tutorial E, 101)
4. Interrogative (U):
   And then are you going to have examples (.) of how this script works? (Tutorial B, 25)
5. First person modal (M):
   Um (.) if you decide to use this quote, I would suggest that you lop it off. (Tutorial C, 48)
6. First person modal (U):
   So I would go with that as well. (Tutorial I, 90)
7. Second person modal (M):
   I was just wondering if maybe you just want to make this um a statement rather than a question, just so you can be a little more directive with um (.) your gentle reader. (Tutorial A, 81)
8. Second person modal (U):
   You need to talk about the intro before you get into the, into the thesis. (Tutorial D, 35)

9. Imperative (M):
   So, and then, you know, in some way just to sort of like remind us. (Tutorial G, 30)
10. Imperative (U):
    So think about that when you're writing your introduction. (Tutorial L, 157)

Table 3
Mitigation strategies

---

1. Tense/aspect:
   I'm wondering if you want to um, if you want to sort of bonk the reader on the head with that sooner. (Tutorial A, 34)
2. Conditional/subjunctive:
   So, if you were to look up the prepositions, you would get good examples of how these prepositions would be used in a sentence. (Tutorial J, 64)
3. Appealer:
   Then you're going to talk about these three guys who wrote these articles, right? (Tutorial L, 149)
4. Cajoler:
   You know, you should number your pages. (Tutorial B, 34)
5. Hedge:
   So you can kind of im-, apply that strategy to your other paragraphs, too, then. (Tutorial G, 82)
6. Downtoner:
   So you probably want to use these phrases in your topic sentences. (Tutorial H, 49)
7. Subjectivizer:
   But you need to show why you're agreeing with them, it seems to me. (Tutorial K, 55)
8. Understater:
   And you can show, and you're going to split this paragraph up a little bit more to show how he's willing. (Tutorial D, 103)
9. Upgrader:
   Again, you want to, what you want to ask yourself in deciding this is "What is the point that I'm trying to get across, and what, what order would make more sense?" (Tutorial I, 81)

---

4. Results

It should first be noted that participants' interpretations of conversational features and events in their tutorials often corresponded, and that this coincided with positive tutor and student evaluations of those tutorials as "successful." Specifically, Tutorials A, G, and J were judged by both participants as "successful," and Tutorials C and I by both participants as "unsuccessful," with the others "moderately successful." Specific indicators of why these judgments arose will be uncovered by the description and discussion of results that follows.

4.1. Discourse phases. Tutorial openings were very short (1-2 turns) and at times missing (as in Tutorial C, Table 4). This marks tutorial conversations as solidly institutional: It is the *tutor's* job to "get down to business." The *diag-*

nosis phase tended to be fairly short and usually occurred only once during the tutorial. The *directive* phase occupied the majority of turns in all of the tutorials. The *closing* was rarely absent but highly variable in length, depending on how much small talk tutor and tutee engaged in. Tutors nominated the lion's share of topics, thus controlling tutorial interaction to a great extent. In Table 4, note that Student C nominated only one topic during the directive phase and one in the closing.

Table 4
Profile of Tutorial C

Opening (none)

    Diagnosis (1–21)
        T ⇨ Segment 1: Inviting S self-diagnosis (1–6)
        T ⇨ Segment 2: Discussing the assignment sheet (6–21)

    Directive (21-97)
        T ⇨ Segment 1: Cutting out quotations (21–28)
        T ⇨ Segment 2: Mechanics: word choice and spelling (28–32)
        T ⇨ Segment 3: Cutting out quotations (32–39)
        T ⇨ Segment 4: Word choice in paraphrases (39–47)
        T ⇨ Segment 5: Cutting out quotations through paraphrasing (47–63)
        T ⇨ Segment 6: Clarifying meaning (63–66)
        T ⇨ Segment 7: Mechanics: verb tense (66–72)
        T ⇨ Segment 8: Cutting out quotations (72–87)
        T ⇨ Segment 9: Mechanics: agreement (87–91)
        T ⇨ Segment 10: Cutting out quotations (91–92)
        T ⇨ Segment 11: MLA citation form (93)
        S ⇨ Segment 12: Composing a title (94–97)

    Closing (97-110)
        T ⇨ Segment 1: Small talk and praise (97–103)
        T ⇨ Segment 2: Leave-taking (103–105)
        T ⇨ Segment 3: Filling in the evaluation form (106–109)
        S ⇨ Segment 4: Comic postlude (109–110)

Characterization of discourse phases by participants fell into three categories: *interactional, rhetorical,* and (for lack of a better term) *parts of the paper.* Chosen by the majority of participants, interactional descriptions of discourse phases focused either on tutor actions, student actions, or both. Rhetorical characterizations were produced only by tutors, such as Tutor K's "return to thesis statement" and "organizing paragraphs around ideas." Parts-of-the-paper descriptions included Student D's "thesis, body, intro, and conclusion" and Tutor B's "appendix, body, intro, and conclusion." In six of the nine tutorials for which both participants offered descriptions of discourse phases, tutor and student characterizations were similar (Tutorials A, C, E, F, G, and K). Despite this overall similarity, the language used by tutors and students to characterize identical phases often diverged. Differing interpretations were also evident in tutors' and students' perceptions of actions in the tutorials. For example, Student C (Tutorial C) described two of the phases of Tutorial C as "when I first came in and told her what I wanted" (student action), while Tutor C (Tutorial C) described this as "her input and what she thought" (tutor action).

4.2. Interactional features. Few tutorials evidenced identical participant interpretations of these and other interactional features. In fact, divergent interpretations of these features occurred in even the most "successful" tutorials, though more frequently in tutorials producing the least mutual satisfaction.

4.2.1. Volubility. In all but one tutorial, tutors spoke half again as much as their tutees (a ratio of 1.5). Tutors were considerably more voluble with NNS tutees than with NS tutees.

4.2.2. Overlaps. Overlaps were not solely a phenomenon of tutor speech. Tutees were also given to overlaps, overall at a slightly higher rate than their tutors (0.26 vs. 0.23 per turn) and sometimes at an individually higher rate than their tutors, especially in NS–NS tutorials. According to Makri-Tsilipakou (1994), *affiliative* or addressee-oriented, face-saving overlaps, particularly joint productions, display cooperation and empathy between interlocutors. The majority of the overlaps in these data were interpreted by the participants as affiliative. Tutees commented that they found their tutors' overlaps "helpful," and tutors interpreted tutee overlaps as movements towards greater student authority and participation. However, there were also some *disaffiliative* overlaps, that is, overlaps bearing little or no relation to the previous speaker's utterance: Makri-Tsilipakou (1994) says that these have the best chance of being interpreted as interruptions. Following is an example of an overlap identified as an interruption, from Tutorial K:

(TK - Tutor K. SK - Student K)

TK: O.K. (.) O.K. So. how can I help you? What do you want to work on with this?
SK: Because um my problem is my because sometimes I lack um, I, I have my first um summary, because
     sometimes I lack um some words. And I because the different languages, so I tend to transfer, [translated
TK.   [uh-huh
SK: that word.   So I want yeah, 1 don't know if you can see some problems [Um my writing skill
⇒ TK: o.k.   [When you talk about (.)
     I'm sorry, O.K. When you talk about, when you talk about translating, do you write in. what is your first
     language?
SK: Um Chinese.

(Tutorial K, 19–21)

Whereas both Student K and Tutor K interpreted his overlap (*When you talk about . . .*) as an interruption, Tutor K viewed his own action with disapproval, but Student K interpreted it as signaling his interest, consistent with her NNS positive politeness culture, which views apparently face-threatening acts by role superiors more positively than in Western cultures.

4.2.3. Backchannels. With three exceptions, students backchanneled more often than their tutors (an average of 1.17 vs. 0.74 per turn). NNS students (especially Student H and Student K) backchanneled far more frequently than their NS peers.

4.2.4. Laughter. Laughter was not a common feature of conversational turns in these writing tutorials (0.14 per turn for tutors vs. 0.25 for students). Not only did tutors in two NNS tutorials (I and K) not laugh, but the mean rates for both tutors and students were considerably lower than those for participants in NS tutorials.

4.3. Directive type and frequency. Tutor directives were frequent in all these tutorials. The typical pattern was an adjacency pair of one speaker's proposal (evaluation or suggestion) followed by acceptance or rejection of that proposal by the other participant. Evaluation–suggestion sequences were frequently expanded by a third element, the grounder (Blum-Kulka et al., 1989), which strengthens directives by "promising" the outcome students might expect if they take the tutor's recommended course of action. As the parentheses in the formula below imply, the only obligatory element of an evaluation–suggestion sequence in these tutorials was the suggestion; the other elements were optional.

- (Evaluation) (Acceptance or rejection of the evaluation)
- Suggestion (+ grounder)
- (Acceptance or rejection of the suggestion)

Overall, the most common directive strategy employed in these tutorials was the second-person (2p) modal formula (e.g., in Tutorial B "You should number your pages"). Of 784 directives, nearly 40% were phrased in this way, compared to just over 30% for the next most frequent category, imperatives. This attests to the fact that most tutor suggestions were formulated with a modicum of politeness and attention to potential face threat (see also Thonus, 1999a). However, imperatives were more common in NNS tutorials. The overall frequency of tutor directives in tutorials with NS and NNS students was remarkably similar, although the tutorials with the highest directive frequency (Tutorial H) and the lowest (Tutorial E) were both NNS tutorials.

In their interviews, tutors repeatedly used the adjective *directive* as they characterized and criticized their own interactional contributions. Their use of this adjective referred not only to uttering directives frequently but also to "repeatedly providing too much assistance to students" rather than asking "Socratic questions."

Tutor comments regarding their directiveness and its outcomes fell into three categories: (a) avoiding the "teacherly voice"; (b) being too directive; (c) and warranting directiveness through the offering of *accounts* ("culturally acceptable justification for what is considered to be unacceptable behavior," Rubin & Rubin, 1995, p. 27). Tutor A, who led one of the "successful" tutorials, reported that he avoided directiveness by adopting "a voice that makes the tutee feel somewhat more comfortable than if I were using a sort of teacherly voice." He labeled as "Grundyesque" a more directive tutoring approach forced as a response to students who expected their tutors to ask all the questions. In contrast, in one of the least successful tutorials, Tutor C labeled her utterances in one excerpt "dictatorial" and "teacher-ish," a tone she claimed to have gained through years of holding teacher–student conferences.

Of the 12 tutors, Tutor F provided the most extensive critique of his own "directiveness." He felt that doing "more constructive work than Socratic work" was a decision harmful to the student: "The authority you have as an instructor—when you say that, it's as good as said. Someone's going to walk away thinking, 'The instructor or tutor responded to that. I'm on to something.' You want them to be on to it because of their winnowing out the wheat from the chaff. You don't want them to be on it because you said, 'I like it.'"

Other tutors besides Tutor F described themselves as "directive" but went on to offer accounts for their behavior. Certain similarities emerge in these accounts: Suggestions were offered, for example, for the student's own good, so that skills would transfer to other tutorials. Other accounts for directiveness included Tutor B's reference to "time running out" and Tutor J's explanation that the tutorial was "more advice-filled than the norm" because of Student J's lack of familiarity with WTS and with her as a tutor.

During the second interview of each participant pair, tutors and students were asked to rank a set of tutor directives along a continuum of forcefulness. In only one of the 12 tutorials [were] tutor and student ranking of directives identical (Tutorial G), and in only one did both participants opt out of the exercise (Tutorial C). As was the case for interactional features, similar or identical rankings of directives were evident in tutorials considered the most "successful" (A, G, and J), whereas divergent ranking was a necessary but not sufficient condition for lack of mutual satisfaction.

4.4. Mitigation type and frequency. On average, half of the directives tutors issued were mitigated. However, more mitigated than unmitigated directives were uttered in NS tutorials than in NNS tutorials, a full 10-percentage-point difference (52% vs. 42%). Tutors were more likely to use multiple mitigated directives in tutorials with NS students, and much more likely to use downgraders in NS tutorials than in NNS tutorials.

4.5. Negotiation of acceptances and rejections of tutor evaluations and suggestions. Evaluation–suggestion sequences were analyzed for evidence of tutor–student negotiation. The following example of an evaluation–suggestion sequence is from Tutorial D:

> Tutor evaluation (negative): It's not quite the one you made it in there.
> Student acceptance (backchannel): *yeah.*
> Student self-evaluation (negative): *The explanation is not really direct.*

Tutor acceptance (listener response): *Yeah.*
Tutor suggestion: But basically try to relate more directly to the quotation.
Tutor grounder: And that'll be kind of neat because it explains about . . .
Student acceptance (listener response): *Yeah, but I'm just a bit confused.*

Although tutor–student negotiations of evaluations and directives seemed to indicate asymmetry, such negotiations were more likely to lead to mutual satisfaction.

4.6. Some general findings. Despite the institutional discourse context that places discernible constraints upon the participants, the wide range of tutor and student conversational behavior evidenced in these interactions cannot be directly linked to a single contextual variable. Rather, tutorial success appears to be contingent on a network of factors.

Not surprisingly, symmetry of tutor and tutee perceptions correlates with judgment of the tutorial as "successful." Manifest lack of symmetry indicates conversational "difficulty" (Obeng, 1994) and produces a lack of mutual satisfaction with the tutorial session, whereas relative symmetry in tutor and student talk may indicate parallel orientations to the conversation and predict tutorial success. Of the 12 tutorials, certain interactions emerged as more symmetrical than others in terms of the linguistic and interactional features examined. For example, student involvement in the introduction of topics seen in Tutorials J and K contrasted with tutor dominance of topic initiation and the monotopicality and topic recursiveness of Tutorials C and F. Tutorial G, with its high frequency of both tutor and student laughter and small talk, and Tutorial A, with its high frequency of comic interludes, joint productions, and small talk, may attest to a common orientation on the part of tutor and student: "We can do this together, and this can be fun."

Though symmetrical, lower than average tutor and student rates of volubility, overlap, backchannels, and laughter, and specifically low rates or absence of backchannels and laughter (Tutorial I) may indicate low involvement and investment of both participants in the interaction, and this low involvement seemed to correlate with less mutual satisfaction with the interaction. Mismatches in volubility (Tutorials D, E, and K), overlaps (Tutorials B and E), backchannels (Tutorials H, K, and L), and laughter (Tutorials B and H) may signal differing perceptions of conversational roles and expectations of the other party.

Remarkably, personal familiarity of tutor with tutee seemed to offer no guarantee of mutual satisfaction. Of the most successful tutorials (A, G, and J), G and J were first-time tutorials, whereas A was a repeat visit for Student A with the same tutor (Tutor A). At the other end of the continuum, in Tutorials C and I, Student C and Student I had previously worked with their respective tutors, thus suggesting that rather than increasing the likelihood of a positive outcome, familiarity created certain participant expectations that were not fulfilled. A striking similarity among Tutorials A, G, and J is that none qualified as subject-area matches, an attribute they shared with the least successful tutorials (C and I). In addition to familiarity and subject-area match, gender, age, student language proficiency, and tutor subject-area expertise were ineffective predictors of either tutorial success or inadequacy.

4.7. Identifying the attributes of "successful" tutorials. During the second participant interview, tutors and tutees were asked to list the tutor behaviors they viewed as most contributing to the success of the tutorials. This activity was based on the assumption that mutual satisfaction indicates success, and that satisfaction is at least partly motivated by equivalent and positive interpretations of reciprocally nominated tutor and student behaviors. Successful tutor behaviors most often cited by both tutors and tutees were (a) helping with the definition and the construction of a thesis statement (Tutorials A, F, H, K, and L); (b) clarifying and expanding essay content around it (B, D, F, H, J, and K); (c) emphasizing student ownership of the paper (A, D, E, and G); and (d) encouraging further contact between the tutee and the course instructor (F, K). To illustrate, Tutor A and Student A agreed that Tutor A had "reassured" his tutee and placed responsibility for its success squarely on her shoulders. Student A specifically recalled Tutor A's technique of "paraphrasing her," and both tutor and tutee remembered Tutor A's focus on key words and his questioning of Student A's main ideas. In contrast to the relative symmetry of participant perceptions in Tutorial A, those in Tutorial C were highly asymmetrical. In fact, what Student C found most helpful about the tutorial was not even mentioned by Tutor C, and vice-versa. While Tutor C congratulated herself on helping Student C with appropriate use of quotations and on praising her while warning of possible stumbling blocks, Student C rejected both tutor actions as "not helpful." In fact, the only tutorial advice she said she liked was Tutor C's "correcting and clarifying sentences," an action Tutor C did not view as "real tutoring."

The hybrid methodology of this study, combining conversation analysis (linguistic analysis of tutorial transcripts) and naturalistic enquiry (interviews with participants) revealed some necessary but not sufficient conditions for the success of tutorials in this context. Ten attributes will be discussed. While all have emerged from the analysis of the data, the first four came principally from the interview data and the remaining six came principally from the tutorial data.

1.   *The tutor is a student, actively engaged in academic writing in his or her discipline.* In interviews, students identified their tutors' current writing experience as part of "knowing writing." For example, Student A said of her tutor, "He's in the college atmosphere, and I think he understands what is expected in the college atmosphere, especially in the writing process." The two tutorials judged least successful by participants were those with "adjunct" or non-student tutors, Tutor C and Tutor I, who were not concurrently enrolled in university classes.

2. *The instructor "surrogate" role is declined by the tutor, and this abdication is welcomed by the student.* The student views the tutor's role as distinct and less authoritative than that of his or her course instructor and realizes that tutorial conversations differ from other instructional conversations. Discussion of this issue arose most frequently in interviews with participants in Tutorials A, G, and J, those judged "most successful" according to a number of other criteria. For example, Tutor A explained that he did not view himself as a "surrogate" for the instructor: "I represent a reader . . . I'm certainly not in the position of speaking as the final reader, but I think I can make some educated guesses about things I probably have in common with that reader." Student A reasoned that the differences between her tutors and her instructor created "a comfort zone" in tutorials. The relaxed atmosphere was "not unprofessional, but it's less professional [than talking to a professor], more on a friendship basis." Avoiding the instructor role was more difficult for tutors who had taught or were currently teaching the same courses in which their tutees were enrolled (Tutor D, Tutor E, Tutor K, and Tutor L).

3. *Tutor authority and expertise are not openly negotiated.* In what may appear a direct challenge to the abdication of instructor surrogacy, Tutor D believed her student had constructed her as "a type of teacher, which means that there's a greater respect and you don't want to interact as much." In his interview, Student D supported her: "If tutors are in WTS already, I think they're qualified to guide us in our papers, or else they wouldn't be there." In contrast, this excerpt from Tutorial C, one of the least successful tutorials, illustrates open negotiation of Tutor C's expertise. Note Student C's ironic utterance *I'm not the expert*:

(TC - Tutor C. SC - Student C)

TC: Um so (.) how you, how do you want to handle that, as far as the quotation? (.) Since I, since I heard you say, and I'm trying to restate it, but I thought I heard you say that you thought that this quote, this first quote (.) is not precisely what, what you wanted to say (.)
SC: No, that's not what I said ((laugh)).
TC: Then I didn't hear you correctly. Go ahead.
SC: I just, I, I don't think there's a problem with the quote.   Like, that's just
TC: o.k.
SC: what I think.   But you know, I'm not the expert, so. I du-, I just guess I just
TC: o.k.
SC: don't think that I understand why you think that there's a serious problem there.

(Tutorial C, 55–57)

4. *The tutor's diagnoses and the student's self-diagnoses correspond and are agreed upon early in the session.* Tutorial I, judged one of the least successful, was instructive in this regard. Because it was a repeat tutorial, and because Student I returned with a draft on a different subject than she and Tutor I had worked on during their previous session,

Tutor I reported being caught off guard. Because Student I did not agree with Tutor I's concept of the audience for her paper, she did not accept her tutor's diagnoses. This created havoc in the tutorial. Tutor I said: "I had a tough time because she wrote this draft for a reader who knows Muslim terminology, and that made it difficult for me to make meaning as I read. Because my familiarity with the text was none, absolutely none, I couldn't get my head inside what she was possibly thinking." Student I argued: "You don't really need to explain everything . . . the language or terminology of it. Like if you say *sheikh*, you don't have to say 'Sheikh is a learned person.' You just basically assume that your reader knows it . . . . I kept telling her that when I'm writing this paper the paper is for an audience of this class who has read the book, and they know what I'm talking about."

5. *Turn structure more closely resembles that of "real" conversation rather than an ask-and-advise service encounter comprised of restricted question + answer adjacency pairs.* This contrast is illustrated with the two examples which show the turn structure, Tutorial E, which was rated highly, and Tutorial F, which was rated less favorably. Tutorial E was replete with "real" questions for student information or opinion that TE did not already know or suspect: In contrast to Tutorial E, Tutorial F may be characterized as a series of question–answer adjacency pairs with only minimal elaboration.

6. *Average to high rates of interactional features (volubility, overlaps, backchannels, laughter) signal involvement of both parties. Overlaps and backchannels are welcomed if they serve affiliative purposes.* Tutorials in which both tutor and student demonstrated high and roughly equal rates of interactional features were rated as among the most successful. For example, in such tutorials both tutors and tutees commented that they found their interlocutor's overlaps "helpful." Student F commented of her tutor's overlaps, "He's incorporating what I'm saying," and Student D said of his tutor, "She's finishing my thought." In such tutorials, tutors also interpreted student overlaps as moves towards greater authority and participation. For example, Tutor H explained her student's overlaps as "She's just trying to restate what she means."

7. *The international features of the tutorial are markedly characterized by movements toward solidarity, including such features as simultaneous laughter, affiliative overlaps, and small talk.* Looking only at the first point on this list, both tutors and students viewed simultaneous laughter as positive. Here, Tutor A and Student A laughed simultaneously about "a third person saying this, or asking these questions" (Why? So what?):

(TE - Tutor E, SE - Student E)

TE: And is that author (.) um do you know like where the author's from? [Is this, do you
SE: [Hmm
TE: get any information [in there, in the article? I mean, not maybe specifically what
SE: [No ((laugh)).\
TE: country, but is this author from inside the   Muslim world? [Did you find
SE: no   [No.
TE: that out?
SE: Just talk about the right and Muslim   (2s) [No. (4s)
TE: uh-huh   [o.k.
SE: Because I was just wondering whether (.) you know you were saying outsiders view the veil as oppressive,
[but
TE: [Oh, you think the author may be an outsider?
TE: Well then, yeah, that was, that was my question, of if, not that I, I think the author is an outsider but
     wondering where you would place the author as inside or outside?

(Tutorial E, 49–51)

(TF - Tutor F. SF - Student F)

TF: How would it, I mean, do they have like no economy at all? (.)
SF: Mmm, not really. [I mean
TF: [What, I guess we need to define "economy" then
SF: Hold on. Uh-huh.
TF: Yeah. Well what does it, what do you mean by when you say, "The economy helps you understand social
     structures"? What's going on there?
SF: Um (.) they're not working in the job force. I mean, they're not [um there's no job
TF: [o.k.
SF: force...

(Tutorial F, 47–49)

(TA - Tutor A. SA - Student A)

TA: ((laugh)) That's [good! I like that!
SA: [((laugh)) Someone else was here, I know who was it, or give me some hint or of like,
     --?-- "Do I need to go on or what?" She said, "Well answer these two questions: 'Why? So what?'"
TA: [((laugh))
SA: [(((laugh))
TA: So what? Who cares? Why am I here?

(Tutorial A, 59–60)

According to Student A, their simultaneous laughter was yet another indication of "the circle" of their communication in the tutorial: "We were both laughing because we know the context and where those questions come from, and we just think it's funny." Tutor A's utterances *So what? Who cares? Why am I here?* extended the laughter, he reported, "making sport, having a little existential crisis, making a joke." Both participants interpreted laughter as a move towards "peerness."

8. *Negotiation of acceptances and rejections of tutor evaluations and directives most often results in student acceptances. Acceptances are overt and clearly marked, and rejections, if in evidence, are supported by accounts.*

With the exception of those in Tutorial C, outright student rejections are rare in these data. NNS tutees were especially likely to mask their rejections. For example, here Tutor J suggests that Student J compose by talking into a tape recorder:

(TJ - Tutor J, SJ - Student J)

TJ: So if you're having trouble writing it down, one thing that you can do is, is take a step back from the words that you've chosen before and talk to yourself. Say, "O.K. This doesn't make sense. What can I say (.) differently? How can I express this story differently?" Um you might try opening up a new screen on your computer and [trying again without looking at the old words. Or you could try talking into a tape recorder.
SJ: [uh-huh
TJ: [I know that that feels silly, but you could play it back then and hear the story being told. (2s) O.K.?
SJ: oh [((laugh)) o.k.
       O.K., I will try. (.) Yeah, I will try. [((laugh))
TJ: [o.k.
       (2s) Good...

(Tutorial J, 59-60)

Student J construed his first laugh as an attempt to "soften" Tutor J's suggestion and his second laugh as a falsehood: "I'm not going to try."

9.   *Tutor mitigation of directives is frequent (for NS tutorials).* As mentioned above, more mitigated than unmitigated directives were uttered in NS tutorials than in NNS tutorials, and the least number of downgraders appearing in any NS tutorial was greater than the largest number in any NNS tutorial. These findings support Young's (1992) argument that NS and NNS tutees operate within different politeness cultures and Thonus' claim that suggestions "without such polite accoutrements" as mitigations are more comprehensible and thus more desired by NNS tutees (Thonus, 1999a, 1999b).

10. *Symmetrical interpretations of discourse phases, directive forcefulness, and tutor and student behaviors contributing to success indicate that tutor and student have achieved some degree of intersubjectivity, the understanding of the other's intent.* Results suggest that symmetrical interpretations of discourse phases and directive forcefulness were strongly linked by participants to perceptions of tutorial success, and that lack of symmetry was associated with less than enthusiastic evaluations of the interactions.

5. Conclusion

This investigation arose out of the expressed need for concrete evaluation of an ongoing academic support service. Thus, the research results were immediately and practically applicable to the achievement of the mission of the enterprise, and the findings deserve consideration for use in evaluating the effectiveness of other tutoring contexts. The study thus qualifies as a case of applied linguistics *in* education rather than applied linguistics *of* education (J. Heritage, personal communication, October 12, 1995).

Writing tutors are constantly involved in tradeoffs between communicative and social goals, juggling comprehensibility, politeness, and effective practice (cf. Thonus, 1999b). Explicit statements by tutors and tutees regarding what contributed to tutorial success have indicated that the conventional perceptions of current tutorials as peer collaboration, while providing some guidelines for tutor behavior, also limit definitions of "successful" behaviors to certain prescribed actions (Thonus & Plummer, 1999) in ways that may not be helpful.

A focus on tutorial process is important and cannot be ignored, but given the current funding climate in higher education, a focus on tutorial outcomes is imperative. While this shift in emphasis from process to product may appear reversionary in terms of writing tutorial and composition theory, it also displays an interest in client (=student and instructor) expectations of a service, particularly one as institutionally accountable as a writing center. To contrast "good" and "bad" tutorials is essential, but to distinguish between "excellent" tutorials and "the rest" requires training tutors in specific interactional and pragmatic features that research of this type suggests are most conducive to success. And though no clear mechanism for doing so has yet been proposed, it is hoped that participant assessments of tutorial success will influence and result in positive instructor assessments of student writing.

Acknowledgments

This article is based on my 1998 dissertation, *What makes a writing tutorial successful: An analysis of linguistic variables and social context* (Indiana University, Bloomington). I acknowledge the guidance and inspiration of my committee—Albert Valdman, Kathleen Bardovi-Harlig, Samuel Obeng, and Ray Smith—and the staff of the Campuswide Writing Program and Writing Tutorial Services. Furthermore, I thank the 24 tutor and student participants who so graciously agreed to be taped and interviewed for this study. Finally, I acknowledge the financial support of the National Council of Teachers of English Research Foundation, Grant-in-Aid #97-32, and the Department of English, East Carolina University, and the Department of Linguistics, California State University, Fresno for research release time.

References

Agar, M. (1985). Institutional discourse. *Text*, 5, 147–168.

Bardovi-Harlig, K., & Hartford, B. S. (1991). Saying "no" in English: Native and nonnative rejections. *Pragmatics and Language Learning (Monograph Series)*, 2, 41–57.

Bardovi-Harlig, K., & Hartford, B. S. (1993). The language of comembership. *Research on Language and Social Interaction*, 26, 227–257.

Bell, J. H. (2000). When hard questions are asked: Evaluating writing centers. *The Writing Center Journal*, 21, 7–28.

Blau, S., Hall, J., & Strauss, T. (1998). Exploring the tutor/client conversation: A linguistic analysis. *The Writing Center Journal, 19*, 19–48.

Blum-Kulka, S., House, J., & Kasper, G. (Eds.). (1989). *Cross-cultural pragmatics: Requests and apologies.* Norwood, NJ: Ablex.

D' Andrade, R., & Wish, M. (1985). Speech act theory in quantitative research on interpersonal behavior. *Discourse Processes, 8*, 229–259.

Davis, K. M., Hayward, N., Hunter, K. R., & Wallace, D. L. (1988). The function of talk in the writing conference: A study of tutorial conversation. *The Writing Center Journal, 8*, 45–51.

Edwards, J. A. (1993). Principles and contrasting systems of discourse transcription. In J. A. Edwards & M. D. Lampert (Eds.), *Talking data: Transcription and coding in discourse research* (pp. 1–31). Hillsdale, NJ: Erlbaum.

Ferrara, K. (1994). *Therapeutic ways with words.* Oxford, England: Oxford University Press.

Fiksdal, S. (1990). *The right time and pace: A microanalysis of cross-cultural gatekeeping interviews.* Norwood, NJ: Ablex.

Fitch, K. L. (1994). The issue of selection of objects of analysis in ethnographies of speaking. *Research on Language and Social Interaction, 27*, 51–93.

Gillespie, P., & Lerner, N. (2000). *The Allyn & Bacon guide to peer tutoring.* Boston, MA: Allyn & Bacon.

Gumperz, J. J. (1982). *Discourse strategies.* Cambridge, England: Cambridge University Press.

Hamp-Lyons, L. (2001). Fourth-generation writing assessment. In T. Silva & P. K. Matsuda (Eds.), *On second language writing* (pp. 117–127). Hillsdale, NJ: Erlbaum.

Harris, M. (2002). Writing center administration: Making local, institutional knowledge in our writing centers. In P. Gillespie, A. Gillam, L. F. Brown, & B. Stay (Eds.), *Writing center research: Extending the conversation* (pp. 75–89). Hillsdale, NJ: Erlbaum.

Hartford, B. S., & Bardovi-Harlig, K. (1992). Closing the conversation: Evidence from the academic advising session. *Discourse Processes, 15*, 93–116.

He, A. W. (1998). *Reconstructing institutions: Language use in academic counseling encounters.* Norwood, NJ: Ablex.

Heritage, J., & Sefi, S. (1992). Dilemmas of advice: Aspects of the delivery and reception of advice in interactions between health visitors and first-time mothers. In P. Drew & J. Heritage (Eds.), *Talk at work: Interaction in institutional settings* (pp. 359–417). Cambridge, England: Cambridge University Press.

James, D., & Drakich, J. (1993). Understanding gender differences in amount of talk: A critical review of research. In D. Tannen (Ed.), *Gender and conversational interaction* (pp. 281–312). Oxford, England: Oxford University Press.

Jefferson, G. (1984). On the organization of laughter in talk about troubles. In J. M. Atkinson & J. Heritage (Eds.), *Structures of social action: Studies in conversation analysis* (pp. 346–369). Cambridge, England: Cambridge University Press.

Jefferson, G. (1986). Notes on "latency" in overlap onset. *Human Studies, 9*, 153–183.

Jefferson, G., Sacks, H., & Schegloff, E. A. (1987). Notes on laughter in the pursuit of intimacy. In G. Button & J. R. E. Lees (Eds.), *Talk and social organisation* (pp. 152–205). Clevedon, England: Multilingual Matters.

Johnson-Shull, L., & Kelly-Riley, D. (2001). An assessment office within a writing center: The Butterfly Effect. In R.H. Haswell (Ed.), *Beyond outcomes: Assessment and instruction within a university writing program* (pp. 25–36). Norwood, NJ: Ablex.

Johnson-Shull, L., & Kelly-Riley, D. (2001). Writes of passage: Conceptualizing the relationship of writing center and writing assessment practices. In R. H. Haswell (Ed.), *Beyond outcomes: Assessment and instruction within a university writing program* (pp. 83–91). Norwood, NJ: Ablex.

Jones, C. (2001). The relationship between writing centers and improvement in writing ability: An assessment of the literature. *Education, 122,* 3–20.

Lerner, N. (2002). Insider as outsider: Participant observation as writing center research. In P. Gillespie, A. Gillam, L. F. Brown, & B. Stay (Eds.), *Writing center research: Extending the conversation* (pp. 53–71). Hillsdale, NJ: Erlbaum.

Lim, T.-S., & Bowers, .1. W. (1991). Facework: Solidarity, approbation, and tact. *Human Communication Research, 17,* 415–450.

Makri-Tsilipakou, M. (1994). Interruption revisited: Affiliative vs. disaffiliative intervention. *Journal of Pragmatics, 21,* 401–426.

Mao, L. (1997, April). *Laughter as a signaling mechanism in invitational discourse.* Paper presented at the Eleventh Annual International Conference on Pragmatics and Language Learning, University of Illinois, Urbana-Champaign.

Meyer, E., & Smith, L. Z. (1987). *The practical tutor.* Oxford, England: Oxford University Press.

North, S. M. (1984). The idea of a writing center. *College English, 46,* 433–446.

Obeng, S. (1994). Verbal indirection in Akan informal discourse. *Journal of Pragmatics, 21,* 37–65.

Roger, D., Bull, P. E., & Smith, S. (1988). The development of a comprehensive system for classifying interruptions. *Journal of Language and Social Psychology, 7,* 27–34.

Rubin, H. J., & Rubin, I. S. (1995). *Qualitative interviewing: The art of hearing data.* Thousand Oaks, CA: Sage.

Rudolph, D. E. (1994). Constructing an apprenticeship with discourse strategies: Professor–graduate student interactions. *Language in Society, 23,* 199–230.

Sacks, H. (1992). Lectures on conversation (Vol. 2). Oxford, England: Blackwell.

Sacks, H., Schegloff, E., & Jefferson, G. (1974). A simplest systematics for the organization of turn-taking for conversation. *Language, 50,* 696–753.

Schiffrin, D. (1996). Interactional sociolinguistics. In S. L. McKay & N. H. Hornberger (Eds.), *Sociolinguistics and language teaching* (pp. 307–327). Cambridge, England: Cambridge University Press.

Searle, J. R. (1975). Indirect speech acts. In P. Cole & J. L. Morgan (Eds.), *Speech acts. Syntax and semantics 3* (pp. 59–82). New York, NY: Academic Press.

Seckendorf, M. H. (1987). *Writing center conferences: An analysis* (Doctoral dissertation, State University of New York, Albany).

Sperling, M. (1994). Discourse analysis of teacher–student writing conferences: Finding the message in the medium. In P. Smagorinsky (Ed.), *Speaking about writing: Reflections on research methodology* (pp. 205–234). Thousand Oaks, CA: Sage.

Tannen, D. (1994). The relativity of linguistic strategies: Rethinking power and solidarity in gender and dominance. In D. Tannen (Ed.), *Gender and conversational interaction* (pp. 165–188). Oxford, England: Oxford University Press.

Thonus, T. (1998). *What makes a writing tutorial successful: An analysis of linguistic variables and social context* (Doctoral dissertation, Indiana University).

Thonus, T. (1999a). How to communicate politely and be a tutor, too: NS-NNS interaction and writing center practice. *Text, 19,* 253–279.

Thonus, T. (1999b). Dominance in academic writing tutorials: Gender, language proficiency, and the offering of suggestions. *Discourse and Society, 10,* 225–248.

Thonus, T. (2001). Triangulation in the writing center: Tutor, tutee, and instructor perceptions of the tutor's role. *The Writing Center Journal, 21,* 57–82.

Thonus, T., & Plummer. L. (1999, April 16-18). *Methodology as mythology: Tutors' directive instruction.* Paper presented at the National Writing Centers Association, Bloomington, IN.

Tyler, A. (1995). The coconstruction of cross-cultural miscommunication: Conflicts in perception, negotiation, and enactment of participant role and status. *Studies in Second Language Acquisition, 17,* 129–152.

Ulichny, P., & Watson-Gegeo, K. A. (1989). Interactions and authority: The dominant interpretive framework in writing conferences. *Discourse Processes, 12,* 309–328.

Walker, C. P., & Elias, D. (1987). Writing conference talk: Factors associated with high- and low-rated writing conferences. *Research in the Teaching of English, 21,* 266–285.

West, C. (1990). Not just "doctors' orders": Directive-response sequences in patients' visits to women and men physicians. *Discourse and Society, 1,* 85–112.

Yancey, K. B. (2002), Seeing practice through their eyes: Reflection as teacher. In P. Gillespie, A. Gillam, L. F. Brown, & B. Stay (Eds.), *Writing center research: Extending the conversation* (pp. 189–201). Hillsdale, NJ: Erlbaum.

Young, V. H. (1992). *Politeness phenomena in the university writing conference* (Doctoral dissertation, University of Illinois, Chicago).

Appendix A. Transcription conventions

Transcription style in the presentation of tutorial data is what Edwards (1993) terms *vertical*, a running arrangement of text in which utterance and nonutterance materials are presented as they occurred in real time. Additional symbols are drawn from Bardovi-Harlig and Hartford (1993) and He (1998).

Utterances are represented by conventional American English spellings for words and parts of words. Filled pauses (*um, hmm*) and listener responses (*Uh-huh, o.k., Huh?*) are represented and treated as words. Conventional punctuation (periods, commas, question marks) signals basic intonation contours, and exclamation points mark emphatic statements. Overlaps between participant contributions are symbolized by square brackets ([ ]) aligned vertically, as in this example:

```
TG:   Oh, so how all [of them relate to lecture, and not just how the leprechaun, [or just, just
      the
SG:                  [That's kind of what I was doing                              [Yeah,
TG:   [the leprechaun [relates,
SG:   [leprechaun.    [uh-huh
```

Joint productions and interruptions are sequenced spatially:

```
SG:   So that's why
TG:                        What's manifest function mean?
SG:   Manifest function
TG:                        I mean is this something that you explain in your paper?
```

Backchannels are inserted on the line just below that of the speaker who has the floor, as illustrated by SG's *o.k.* and *uh-huh* and TG's *yeah*:

```
TG:   O.K. umn so let's see. So what you're going to do then, let's just review here,      (.) is (.)
SG:                                                                        o.k.
TG:   add the collector's, I think that the main thing that you need to be doing is adding the collector's
      interpretation to [each of these paragraphs because
SG:                      [uh-huh
      I give the informant's,            pretty much.
TG:                         yeah
```

These symbols code nonutterance (nonlinguistic, paralinguistic) material:

(.)	Short pause (1-2 seconds)
(5s)	Timed pause (2+ seconds)
(( ))	Additional observation: laugh, cough, sigh, etc.
»	Hand striking or pounding a surface

These marks reflect analytical and display concerns:

| --?-- | Undecipherable or doubtful hearing |
| ⇨ | Turn(s) focused for analysis |

Writing Center Assessment: Searching for the "Proof" of Our Effectiveness

Neal Lerner _____

MASSACHUSETTS INSTITUTE OF TECHNOLOGY

Neal Lerner examines the challenge of seeking "proof" of effectiveness in writing center work—specifically, asking what the writing center accomplishes, and if that accomplishment aligns with what writing center professionals say and think they are accomplishing. In this article from The Center Will Hold *(Pemberton & Neuleib 2003), Lerner emphasizes three issues associated with assessment in the writing center—first, what he deems an "evaluative conscience" in which writing centers over the last twenty years have been criticized in some circles for their inability or unwillingness to prove that what they do actually is effective; second, an analysis of several studies of writing center "effectiveness" in relation to the broader context of calls for assessment in higher education; and third, examples of actual assessment strategies carried out in the writing center Lerner directs. Lerner's overall effort is to "offer a clearer understanding of research to provide evidence of writing center effects" and to "put into a critical context the common call to investigate how well we are doing."*

Two words that haunt writing center professionals are "research" and "assessment." The first is too often held out as something others do to us, something we do not have time for, or something that is lacking in our field. The second is tied to our financial and institutional futures—if we cannot assess how well we are doing whatever it is we are supposed to be doing, we are surely doomed.

In this chapter, I reclaim these two words in several ways. First, I review the history of calls for our field to answer the assessment bell, calls that act as a sort of evaluative conscience, laying on 20 plus years of guilt about our inability or unwillingness to prove ourselves to our institutions and, ultimately, to ourselves. Next, I offer a critique of the few published studies of writing center effects, pointing out the logical and methodological complications of such work. Then, I turn to the larger assessment movement in higher education, particularly the work being done to study students' first year in college or university. I take from that research not only useful assessment tools that might be adapted to writing center settings, but also important cautions about the nature of assessment work and its potential pitfalls. Finally, I offer some examples of real live assessment from the writing center I direct at my institution, not necessarily as exemplars for the field, but instead as indications that the work I call for can, indeed, be clone. Overall, my intent here is to offer a clearer understanding of research to provide evidence of writing center "effects," its uses and limitations, and to put into a critical context the common call to investigate how well we are doing.

Evaluate or Else

For any of us engaged in writing center work, it always seems obvious that one-to-one teaching of writing is effective, and this belief has a long history. In 1939, E. C. Beck wrote in *English Journal* that "perhaps it is not too much to say that the conference method has established itself as the most successful method of teaching English composition" (594). Nevertheless, as writing centers moved from "method" to "site"—as Beth Boquet (1999) describes the evolution of the free-standing writing center—frequent calls for "accountability" followed, usually in response to threats from budget-conscious administrators or misguided faculty. However, the attempts to provide this accountability (or simply call for it) that have appeared in our literature often say more about our field's uneasiness with evaluation research than about the effectiveness of the work we do.

One source of uneasiness is with the use of statistics beyond the simple counting of numbers of students or appointments. In 1982, Janice Neuleib explained this uneasiness by noting that "many academics tend to wring their hands when faced with the prospect of a formal evaluation. English teachers especially have often not been trained in statistics, yet formal evaluation either explicitly or implicitly demands statistics" (227). For Neuleib, "formal" evaluation is necessary because "[good] tutoring and all that goes with it cannot be appreciated without verifiable evaluation techniques" (232).

While Neuleib's call is nearly 20 years old at the time of this writing, it is difficult to say that the field has answered her charge with a rich body of statistical research. The reasons for this absence are many, but most important, in my view, is composition's orientation toward qualitative or naturalistic studies of students' composing processes, as Cindy Johanek has pointed out (2000, 56). While I am aware that qualitative evidence can lend a rich and nuanced perspective to our evaluation studies (and have performed and will continue to perform such studies myself), I join Johanek in calling for additional research methods, namely quantitative or statistical ones, to understand more fully the work we do. Statistical evidence also lends itself to short forms, perfect for bullet items, PowerPoint presentations, and short attention spans—in other words, perfect for appeals to administrators and accrediting bodies. I would also argue that despite Neuleib's statement about our fear of numbers, our field is often under the sway of numerology, given the ways we have always counted who comes through our doors and why.

Nancy McCracken of Youngstown State identified the need to evaluate in 1979: "Many of us have had to expend so much effort convincing our funders of the need for a writing lab in the first place that I think that we have not adequately addressed the need for evaluation and the key issues involved" (1). To answer this charge, McCracken relied upon "error analysis of writing samples done at the start and at the end of the term" (1). This analysis (or counting, really) included "total number of words and paragraphs and rates of occurrence of focus-errors [errors identified by student and tutor from starting sample] (1–2). While the pre-test, post-test design is encouraging, what is troubling here is a powerful focus on the text itself and the reduction of student writing into primarily mechanical features. It is difficult to imagine that the tutor[1] identified invention or revision strategies as a student's primary need and could evaluate progress on those tasks based on two writing samples; however, McCracken tells us that "demanding thorough diagnosis and evaluation has profoundly altered our staff's perceptions of their function and their effectiveness. It is enormously satisfying for the tutor to see clear evidence of progress where before it was only vaguely sensed" (2). Some students might surely have made "progress" of a sort, but McCracken does not provide accounts of how many students improved or how much improvement occurred in individual cases. Instead, we are left with one possible approach to proving the assumption that McCracken identifies and that many of us hold dear: "We have all had to discover ways to demonstrate what we know is the tremendous effectiveness of the writing lab experience for our students" (1).

A broad survey of the evaluative methods of this period was offered by Mary Lamb in 1981. Lamb surveyed 56 writing centers nationwide and found six "methods of evaluation": (1) basic statistics (i.e., usage data—nearly all centers reported this accounting); (2) questionnaires or surveys of students and faculty (used by half of the centers); (3) pre- and post-tests, usually of mechanical skills (only four centers collected writing samples in this method; the others used "objective" tests of English mechanics); (4) follow-up reports of students' grades who used the center (18% used this method); (5) external evaluations (14% of the centers surveyed used this method); (6) reports of staff publications and professional activities (7% used this method).

Since that time, I cannot imagine that the terrain has changed much. Ticking off the numbers of students who come through our doors and subdividing them according to categories that would make a census taker proud are about as easy as it gets and, for many of us, are adequate to the level of accountability to which we are held—at least the current level of accountability. But I am reminded of my first semester as a writing center director when I met with my division director and presented some nice tables on how many students we had worked with. "But of the hours you are open, during how many of those are your staff actually working with students?" Gulp! It seems my criteria for evaluation did not quite match up with my boss's criteria. That's not a good thing when it comes time for budget allocations (my staff salary budget was cut 40% by the end of that semester). I would also maintain that justifying our existences based upon how many students we work with will never get us very far. "Voluntary" writing centers (in other words, excluding those which students are required to attend or those centers that also run computer labs and count every time a student downloads an mpeg as a "contact") typically see no more than 10 to 15 percent of their student bodies, based on responses to that inquiry I and others have posted to the listserv WCenter over the last five years. That is not exactly a selling point. Thus, counting works fine when our supervisors give our annual reports about as close a reading as you might expect for columns of numbers subdivided by myriad categories. But when the inevitable budget crunch occurs, when the axe-wielding Provost is hired or a "back-to-basics" English chair rises from the ranks, those nifty tables and charts just won't cut it. In those cases we need to be ready with real evidence, convincing data, and a grasp of how to produce those figures.

Finally, the audience for our assessment efforts need not only be those who pull the purse strings. As Nancy Grimm points out in this volume, writing centers are uniquely positioned to investigate the ways that students—particularly non-mainstream students—encounter the cultures of higher education. With this research agenda, writing centers can move beyond simply defending their budgets and instead make significant contributions to these students, to our institutions, and to the knowledge in our field.

A Review of Some Evaluation Studies, or How to Lie with Statistics

The number of published statistical studies on writing center effects is quite few.[2] Two accounts that have appeared in *The Writing Lab Newsletter* are Stephen Newmann's "Demonstrating Effectiveness" (1999) and my own "Counting Beans and Making Beans Count" (1997). Both studies asked the same question: "Do students who use the writing center get higher first-year composition grades than students who do not?" Both studies used the same methods: compare students' grades who use the writing center with those who do not, but try and position students at similar starting points by using SAT Verbal scores. The assumption here is that two students with an SAT Verbal of 450 would end up with about the same grade in first-year composition (FYC). However, if one of those students visits the writing center, that student's grade would be higher than the student with the same SAT score who did not visit. Thus, the hope is that the "intervention" of the writing center pays off in tangible results, namely higher course grades.

Both Newmann and I did report such results. Newmann writes that "the lower SATs [of students who were tutored] and smaller percentage of As [for students who were not tutored] suggested that the Writing Program helped less able students who were willing to work harder to perform as well as their peers" (9). My claim was that "students at the lowest end of the SAT verbal benefited the most [from writing center visits]; on a one-hundred point scale, the mean grade of this group was five points higher than students within the same SAT verbal range who did not come to the Writing Center" (3).

Two studies, similar methods, similar triumphant results; unfortunately, both are about as statistically and logically sound as the flat tax. Three assumptions underlie both studies: (1) that students with lower SAT scores are at a disadvantage in-first-year composition courses; in other words, that there is a strong relationship between SAT Verbal scores and final grades in FYC; (2) that a student's final grade in FYC is an indication of her or his writing ability; and (3) that students will receive the same grade in FYC regardless of the instructor. The first assumption is fairly easy to disprove. For my institution, for the combined first-year classes from 1996 to 1999 or 488 students, the correlation between students' SAT Verbal scores and FYC averages[3] was equal to .12. In non-mathematical terms, this result says that the relationship between the two scores was extremely weak (a correlation of zero indicates no relationship; correlations of −1.00 or 1.00 indicate the strongest relationship possible). In fact, the correlation between SAT Math and FYC grades was higher (.20) than the one for SAT Verbal! Thus, for my institution at least, trying to predict FYC grades based upon students' SAT Verbal scores just does not work.

The second assumption — that there is a strong relationship between a student's FYC grade and his or her writing ability — is one that should be troubling to anyone who has taught the course. Sure, some students benefit tremendously and flourish in terms of their writing. Others come to us with considerable skill and leave at about the same level. Many are somewhere in between. In other words, tying writing center effects to FYC grades is troubling territory when we really do not know for sure if the grade is a fair assessment of the goals that the writing center holds for its student visitors.

The third assumption — that grading is consistent across FYC sections — is also troubling. When I conducted the study I refer to above, my division director and I realized that one instructor gave almost all of her students very high grades (and very few had visited the writing center!). I do not bring this up to condemn that colleague — perhaps she was working on a contract system or some other method that allowed almost all of her students to meet her criteria for high grades — but my point is that FYC grades in most places (or at least in my institution) are not particularly consistent across sections/instructors.

So, are the difficulties inherent in these sorts of studies[4] the primary reason why we generally avoid conducting them in the first place? Perhaps. However, we do not have to look far in order to understand how to make powerful statistical arguments. In the last two years, I have become increasingly involved in research on and the development of academic activities for students' first-year, and in particular, first-year seminar courses. That body of literature is a valuable resource for ideas and justifications for research on writing center effects.

If They Can Do It, So Can We — Learning from Studies of First-Year Seminar

What is perhaps most interesting about the literature on first-year seminar and other programmatic attempts to provide support for first-year students is how the descriptions often echo writing center themes. For example, Betsy Barefoot, the Co-Director of the Policy Center on the First Year of College, has described a dilemma familiar to many of us:

> A pervasive and central problem is that many of the programs and activities that constitute the "first-year experience" are in a continuous battle for slams within the academy . . . never becoming a central, sustainable part of the institution's fabric. First-year programs often have a single champion rather than broad-based institutional support and frequently operate with a minimal budget or no budget. (quoted in Cusco 2000, 2)

In response to this need to "institutionalize" first-year programs, many researchers have engaged in an impressive array of studies; however, what distinguishes much of this work from writing center assessment are the efforts to de evaluative research to the goals the institution holds for its students, whether those are simply retention or are part of larger general education goals. Barefoot (2000), again, offers the following three observations about administering and evaluating first-year seminar courses. I, however, have substituted "writing centers" for "first-year seminars" to demonstrate the applicability to our field:

> [Writing centers] are not a magic bullet that will change student behavior. [They] can serve as one piece of a comprehensive [educational] program—a linchpin of sorts to give coherence to the curriculum and co-curriculum.
>
> [Writing center] effects can be multiplied through connections with other structures and programs such as learning communities, advising, orientation, and residence life.
>
> Assessment of [writing center] outcomes is important. If [writing centers] are to survive the vicissitudes of changing administrations and fluctuating resources, there must exist some evidence that the [writing center] is doing for students and for the institution what it was designed to do. (3–4)

Thus, we need to think broadly about research on writing center effects, not just about how many students came through our doors or if those students were satisfied, but about how do our writing centers contribute to the teaching and learning goals that our institutions hold dear? How do we begin to investigate such matters?

A Framework for Research on Writing Center Effects

M. Lee Upcraft and John Schuh (2000) lay out a comprehensive eight-part framework for assessing students' first-year experience, one that I will adapt to writing center work. Assessment should include the following: (1) keep track of who participates, (2) assess student needs, (3) assess student satisfaction, (4) assess campus environments, (5) assess outcomes, (6) find comparable institution assessment, (7) use nationally accepted standards CO assess, and (8) assess cost-effectiveness. For many of these points, I will also show some of the assessment attempts I have been making in my own writing center.

1. Keep track of who participates. As Mary Lamb pointed out in 1981, counting who comes through our doors is something that nearly every writing center does and reports on, and is often the extent of our evaluative attempts. In the five years that the MCPHS [Massachusetts College of Pharmacy and Health Sciences] Writing Center has been open, I have faithfully submitted those usage reports to my dean. Certainly, demonstrating usage can provide persuasive evidence that we are meeting our goals. For example, if a writing center was targeted to certain student populations (e.g., first-year students or non-native English speakers) reporting on how many of *those* students were served can be a much more impressive and meaningful number than percent of total student body (which, as I pointed out earlier, is quite low in most cases). For instance, the MCPHS Writing Center was primarily intended to meet the needs of students in first-year composition, and we usually find that between 50 to 70 percent of the first-year class comes through our doors—a much more impressive number than percentage of the whole student body. We also have consistently found that 60 to 75 percent of the writers we see self-identify as non-native English speakers, a persuasive number to show administrators who are concerned about providing academic support for this growing population at my college. Thus, we need to keep counting, but our counting needs to have a specific focus and should not be the extent of our evaluative efforts.

2. Assess student needs. Upcraft and Schuh (2000) ask, "What kinds of services and programs do first year students really need, based on student and staff perceptions, institutional expectations, and research on student needs? Put another way, how do we know if what we offer 'fits' our first-year students?" (1). This is a powerful question when considered in light of our field's often-stated desire to be "student-centered." How much do we know about the needs of writers who come to our centers, and, perhaps more importantly, the needs of writers who *do not* visit us? How does writing center work fit into current theories of student learning and development (see, for example, Haswell 1991; Baxter Magolda 1999)? I cannot say that I have fully engaged in researching these powerful questions; however, this past academic year I did survey FYC students and had particular questions for students who did not visit the Writing Center. What I found was that the primary reason for students not visiting was that the hours were inconvenient (40% of the responses), followed closely by "Did not need to receive feedback from a tutor" (32%) and "Primarily worked with classroom teacher" (24%). However, 86% of the students who did not visit agreed with the statement that "The Writing Center is for any student engaged in any writing task," and 82% indicated that they would make use of an online Writing Center if one were available. These findings indicate that in terms of students' needs, we can do a better job of scheduling available hours or of creating online services, but that we are not limited by students' remedial definition of our work. Thus, feedback from students who did not use our services this past academic year gives valuable input on the assessment of current efforts and indications for future ones.

   3. Assess student satisfaction. This area of evaluation is one that many writing center directors pursue, and we often find that students are highly satisfied with our services, particularly if we survey them right after a session is completed. However, it is difficult to sort out if writers are just trying to be supportive of their peers who work in the writing center or if they were genuinely satisfied. James Bell's (2000) approach to this dilemma was to survey writing center users at three different points after their session: immediately afterward, two weeks later, and two months later. He found that satisfaction remained high over time: "Two months after a 45-minute conference all impact might be expected to have dissipated, but three-quarters of the clients agreed or strongly agreed that they could still apply what they had learned, and two-thirds agreed or strongly agreed that it would continue to help them in the future" (22). Bell's assessment protocol is a practical and powerful example for our field to follow.

   One other important constituency often left unassessed is faculty. What are faculty perceptions of the writing center? At the end of the 2000–01 academic year, I distributed a survey to faculty[5] and found results that were encouraging: On a five-point Likert scale (5 = strongly agree and 1 = strongly disagree), the highest mean rating, 4.9, was for "I feel comfortable referring my students to the MCPHS Writing Center." The two next highest responses were for "Students who utilize the Writing Center make discernible improvements in their writing" (4.5) and "I view the Writing Center as a valuable resource even for competent writers" (4.5). Faculty also indicated they were aligned with our intent to help all student writers by showing fairly strong disagreement (2.5) with the statement "The main function of an effective writing center is to serve primarily the weakest student writers." The survey also provided a public relations opportunity to let faculty know that the Writing Center is concerned about meeting their needs, including our availability to help faculty with their writing in progress, a survey item that was met with surprise by quite a few responders.

   In addition to our own surveying, a great opportunity for writing centers is to connect with larger institutional efforts at surveying student satisfaction.

Offices of Institutional Research, Student Affairs, or other campus entities are increasingly using instruments such as the College Student Experiences Questionnaire (Pace and Kuh 1998) to investigate student satisfaction with a wide variety of their educational experiences. While specific questions about writing centers will likely not appear on the national standardized surveys, they will contain questions about academic support services, or they often have the ability to be customized. Thus, important allies for any writing center director are those survey creators and administrators on your campus. Assessment of writing center satisfaction should be seen as part of a larger institutional effort.

4. Assess campus environments. In the context of first-year programs, Upcraft and Schuh (2000) note, "It is critical to take a look at first-year students' collective perceptions of the campus environments within which they conduct their day-to-day lives. For example, what is the campus climate for first-year women? What is the academic environment, both inside and outside the classroom?" (2). As applied to writing centers, these can be powerful questions, particularly as we look not merely at "effects," but at the environment of the writing center itself. What is the students' perception of the writing center? How is space used by students and staff? What determines the flow of traffic? What is the writing center climate for different student groups: women, men, non-traditional students, non-native English speakers? It is often claimed that writing centers are "safe havens" of sorts,[6] but how systematic have been our attempts to understand this environment from the perspective of writers, tutors or faculty?[7]

5. Assess outcomes. While many institutions increasingly describe their work with students in terms of "outcomes," writing centers have been slow to take up this challenge, partially because of fears that outcomes talk might reduce the complexity of the work we do to "measurable" gains outside of the goals we hold for our centers. However, consider Upcraft and Schuh's (2000) broad categorization of outcomes as applied to first-year programs: "Of those students who participate in [our] services . . . , is there any effect on their learning, development, academic success, transition to college, retention, or other intended desired outcomes, particularly when compared with non-participants?" (2). In other words, it is important to think broadly of writing center outcomes, not in terms of the narrowest measures—students' command of mechanical skills—but in terms of such things as students' development as writers and success as college students, as well as the ways the writing center contributes to the professional development and future success of its tutors.

Researching these sorts of outcomes is quite challenging, of course, but also quite necessary to establish writing centers as essential academic components. A natural effect of such work might also be to have us broaden our individual missions vis-à-vis our institutions. After all, the goals we hold for our writing centers—whether articulated formally in mission statements or less formally in our promotional materials and annual reports—provide the first focus for our assessment efforts. But those goals themselves can often be broadened to include not just our effect on student writers, but our effect on the entire institution. Such is the strategic work of making writing centers central to the conversation about writing at our institutions, to paraphrase Stephen North's charge (1984, 440).

In terms of the outcomes measures I have pursued, I cannot say I have quite measured up to the challenge I offer. Nevertheless, I have collected and analyzed a broad range of writing center data and have plans for continued analysis.[8] For example, in order to investigate the achievement differences between first-year students who used the writing center and those who did not, I combined four years' worth of data on first-year students, as shown in the table below:

Table 1
First-Year Students, 1996–99

	Mean SAT Verbal	Mean H.S. GPA	Mean FYC GPA	Mean First-Year GPA
WC Users (307)	487	3.23	3.07	2.73
WC Non-Users (181)	499	3.11	2.78	2.42

All of the above differences between writing center users and nonusers are statistically significant,[9] with the exception of SAT Verbal scores. In other words, the two groups did not start at different levels according to SAT Verbal scores, but those who did visit the Writing Center at least once during the academic year had First-Year Composition grades and end-of-first-year GPAs that were higher than students who did not visit the writing center.

Alert readers are by now remembering the condemnation of my own and other studies several pages earlier. However, I need to frame the results above in a somewhat different way. SAT Verbal scores *are* a measure of *some* ability; it is just a statistical reality that they have little relationship to FYC grades. However, by showing that SAT Verbal scores were not significantly different for writing center users and non-users, I am showing that these two groups were starting from a similar footing, according to this measure (and let me add that it is a measure that administrators will recognize immediately). My previous cautions about relying on FYC grades and about studies that do not take into account teacher effects are well worth considering here. However, my argument for positive writing center effects is bolstered by "big" numbers. By looking at data across multiple years, multiple students, and multiple teachers, but applying the single variable of writing center usage, I am making a pretty convincing argument that this single factor — visiting the writing center — has a pretty powerful relationship not just to students FYC grades but to their overall first-year GPA, despite the broad variation in those other factors over the four years for which I am accounting. In terms of the single outcome of students' grades, visiting the writing center makes a difference.[10]

One other way of considering the contribution of writing center visits is through the statistical technique of multiple regression, which calculates the contribution of several factors on some outcome. In my case, I used multiple regression to find out how well the factors of students' SAT Verbal score, SAT Math score, high school GPA, and number of writing center visits can predict first-year GPA. Writing center visits were a statistically significant variable in the entire equation,[11] lending more support to the idea that the writing center makes a difference.

One common critique of such findings is that students who visit the writing center get better grades because they are more motivated. To explore this hypothesis, I used the results of the Learning and Study Strategies Inventory (LASSI, H&H Publishing), a self-reporting instrument of "readiness" to learn, which we had first-year students complete during summer orientation for the 1999-2000 academic year. Two of the LASSI measures address "attitude" and "motivation," so I compared the scores of students who visited the writing center that academic year with those who did not. What I found was that neither of those factors—as well as the eight other LASSI measures—showed statistically significant differences between the two groups. In other words, according to that instrument and for that academic year, writing center users were not more motivated than non-users.

My use of the LASSI (unfortunately, for only a single academic year because we have not administered it since then) is an example of how we can connect our writing center assessment efforts to larger institutional attempts to collect data. Many institutions, including my own, administer the CIRP survey (The Higher Education Research Institute) to incoming freshman every fall. The CIRP provides a great deal of demographic data, as well as an indication of students' high school study habits and attitudes.[12] Tremendous possibilities exist to use these data to compare students who use the writing center with those who do not, as well as to compare these groups according to results of satisfaction surveys, such as those I mentioned earlier.

One more obvious area for writing center outcomes research is the specific contribution writing centers make to students' development as writers. In 1981, Mary Lamb expressed surprise that only four of the 56 centers she surveyed collected "pre- and post-test samples of writing" (77). I doubt that situation has changed much since, usually because centers are not set up to collect such data, and a whole host of complexities would surround such a procedure (e.g., sorting out non-writing-center influences on students' development, creating the logistics to collect consistent samples, coordinating the grading/evaluation of the samples). I can report that I did make an attempt at such a study, using the diagnostic essay that a group of first-year students wrote during freshman orientation, comparing that essay to a similar writing task—a required Writing Proficiency Exam that students wrote within a year after completing FYC—and then calculating whether writing center visits would make a difference in students' "improvement" over the two tasks. While I did find that the grades on the later writing sample were significantly higher than the first (grading was done by two independent raters), writing center visits were not a significant factor. Several complications confound these findings, however. Students knew that the diagnostic essay did not "count," so perhaps that writing effort was less than characteristic. Graders also knew which essay was the diagnostic and which was the proficiency exam, thus biasing their judgment that the latter task could he of superior quality. Finally, while I did control for teacher effects with this sample—all students were from my sections of FYC—only one out of 46 students did not visit the writing center; thus, I could not separate students into two clear groups. Perhaps almost all benefited from their writing center experience! Nevertheless, the research design I used holds promise for future efforts at examining the effects of writing center visits on students' actual writing, whether on a single task or on multiple tasks.

One approach to understanding the effects of writing center sessions would be to examine the influence of conference dialogue on student writing or to ask, "Are there components of the tutor–writer conversation that get incorporated into a student's subsequent draft?" This question has been explored in the context of elementary and high school students' writing conferences with their teachers (see Vukelich and Leverson 1987; Sperling 1991), but not on the college level or in writing center settings. It would be one way to understand not just writing center effects, but the process of learning that we believe goes on in writing center sessions.

An additional area of writing-center effects are the benefits that tutors—whether peer or professional—draw from their work. Molly Wingate (2001) has reported on the ways that her undergraduate tutoring staff at Colorado College benefit from their writing center work, including higher grade-point averages and more satisfaction and higher rates of annual giving as alumnae as compared to the rest of the student body (9–10). Indeed, the acknowledgment of the writing center as an ideal place for the training of composition teachers is long standing (see, for instance, Almasy and England 1979; Clark 1988; Zelenak et al. 1993). Thus, our understanding of writing center "outcomes" can be broadened far beyond students' command of English mechanics or grades in first-year composition, and can instead be expressed in ways that administrators, colleagues, and students will understand and value.

6. Find comparable institution assessment. While we often recognize the particulars of the local context within which our writing centers are situated, we also often seek comparisons with similar institutions. In times of particular need—budget cuts or salary justifications—the requests appear on WCenter with a strong sense of urgency. Research on writing center effects should similarly be considered within the scope of other institutions, whether that is the results of our efforts or our methods. Our field is a relatively young one in this sense — national "benchmarks" do not necessarily exist, accreditation efforts have primarily stalled, and the central collection and dissemination of writing center data is logistically challenging. One hopeful sign in this direction is the creation of a Writing Centers Research Project at the University of Louisville. . . . This "think tank," archive, and research center is a new venture and one that will certainly raise the possibility for the kinds of cross-institutional comparisons that Upcraft and Schuh (2000) call for in terms of first-year programs.

7. Use nationally accepted standards to assess. Similar to the item above, our field has not necessarily created national standards that might be used to gauge our effects. The International Writing Centers Association has created a useful self-study document, . . . and efforts have recently linked writing center assessment experts to the Writing Programs Administrator consultant–evaluator program. However, the political terrain of calls for "standards" can be quite rocky; in the history of our field such calls are usually associated with back-to-basics movements, attacks on non-standard literacy practices, and a pedagogical focus on mechanics. One useful framework in this debate is Alexander Astin's (1993) notion of "talent development" as the preferred goal of our institutions. In Astin's words, "The fundamental premise underlying the talent development concept is that true excellence lies in the institution's ability to affect its students and faculty favorably, to enhance their intellectual and scholarly development, to make a positive difference in their lives" (6–7). Astin contrasts this view of "excellence" with long-held notions of institutional assessment based upon the amount of resources held (including high-quality students and faculty, library holdings, campus facilities) and the reputation accorded the institution, usually according to the amount of resources. Thus, in the national-ranking view that predominates, institutions that add little more than networking possibilities for their graduates continue to be held in much higher regard than institutions that move students much farther along the developmental continuum, and assessment efforts are focused on the former and ignore the latter.

The applicability of Astin's ideas of "talent development" fits well with the goals of our writing centers, where our efforts are focused on the development of students' writing processes and on our tutors' professional development. If we are to develop standards for writing center excellence, such a view should predominate, particularly given the paucity of resources many writing centers are facing. Perhaps even our long-standing attempts to escape the label of "remediation" can be reconsidered when we realize that working with the most underprepared writers allows for the greatest amount of development, a charge that few other campus entities embrace as fully as writing centers do.

8. Assess cost effectiveness. This final component is one that makes most of us take pause. In the context of first-year programs, Upcraft and Schuh (2000) ask: "Are the benefits students and the institution derive from the programs and services targeted to first-year students worth the cost and how do we know?" While we are reluctant to ask that question in terms of writing centers, and are quick to acknowledge the difficulties in calculating costs and benefits, budget-conscious administrators always have—and always will—ask such a question. However, by engaging in the assessment procedures outlined in this framework, we will be in a much stronger position to argue for the benefits of our work and to show the relative costs. These need not merely be in reductive terms, i.e., dollars and cents. Instead, we need to think broadly about our contributions to institutions, considering our writing centers' contributions to campus life and climate, to general education outcomes, to our institutions' commitment to academic excellence. Given the paucity of most of our budgets, the work we do comes at a relative bargain—now it is incumbent upon us to demonstrate that bargain with sustained research and assessment.

And in the End

My intention in this chapter has been to demonstrate that research on writing center effects does not require an additional graduate degree or a small army of assessment "experts." Collaborating with colleagues across our institutions can serve the dual purpose of capitalizing on local expertise and sending the message that the writing center is serious about assessment. For institutions with graduate programs, writing center assessment can provide an important venue for graduate students to put into practice the methods they are learning in the classroom (see, for example, Olson, Moyer, and Falda 2001).

In 1979, Nancy McCracken wrote, "No matter the size of the writing lab, for several different purposes and at several different points in its development, the director has to justify the lab's existence" (1). That need has not gone away in the intervening 22 years, but hopefully now we can avoid the defensiveness of "justification" and instead begin to assess our work in ways that we feel are meaningful and useful.

Notes

[1] McCracken (1979) tells us that it is the tutor who is making that initial "diagnosis" of student error, for one of the benefits of her system is that "lab staff members who are trained in careful diagnosis of writing problems become superior tutors" (2).

[2] While published studies are few, the number conducted is likely quite large. When I gave a talk on this subject at the 2000 International Writing Centers Association conference in Baltimore and asked my audience how many had conducted such studies, nearly all the hands in the room went up. The fact that so few of these studies see the light of publication is perhaps an indication of our uneasiness with statistical methodologies.

[3] FYC average represents a student's mean grade from the two-semester composition sequence. Students' grades were fairly consistent from one semester to the next, and the difference between these two grades was not statistically significant for the four years I calculated.

[4] For two additional published statistical studies, each with its own set of flaws, see Roberts (1988); Waldo (1987). For a more thorough critique of my own study, see Lerner (2001).

[5] Number of faculty surveys returned was 28 or roughly 28% of the total full-time faculty during the 2000–01 academic year.

[6] The claim of "writing center as safe house" is a long-standing one as demonstrated by the following comment from a 1951 CCCC workshop on "Organization and Use of a Writing Laboratory"; "The writing laboratory should be what the classroom often is not—natural, realistic, and friendly" (18).

[7] For an example of one attempt to describe the writing center environment, see Connolly, DeJarlais, Gillam, and Micciche (1998).

[8] I am grateful for the help of my colleagues Lila Foye and Xiangqian Chang in performing these statistical analyses.

[9] My test of statistical significance indicates that there was a five percent or less probability that the differences between these mean scores were due to chance alone. That is the usual accepted level of "error" in studies such as these (Johanek 2000, 107).

[10] To account for students who made a single writing center visit per course requirement, I also ran the analysis for two groups: 1) students who had visited the writing center two or more times and 2) those who had visited once or not at all. The former group's expository writing grades and first-year GPA were significantly higher than the latter. It is also interesting to note that, when dividing the two groups up this way, the one-or-no-visits group had a mean SAT Verbal that was significantly larger than the two-or-more-visits group!

[11] Regression equation adjusted R^2 = .29; P value for each variable: SAT Verbal = .016, SAT Math = 1.15×10^{-10}, High School GPA = 1.42×10^{-12}, Writing Center Visits = 1.12×10^{-8}.

[12] For the 2000-01 academic year CIRP results, see Sax, Astin, Korn, and Mahoney (2000).

References

Almasy, R., & England, D. (1979). Future teachers as real teachers: English education students in the writing laboratory. *English Education, 10*, 155–162.

Astin, A. W. (1993). *Assessment for excellence: The philosophy and practice of assessment and evaluation in higher education.* Phoenix, AZ: Oryx Press.

Barefoot, B. O. (2000). The first-year experience—Are we making it any better? *About Campus, 4*(6), 12–18.

Baxter Magolda, M. B. (1999). *Creating contexts for learning and self-authorship: Constructive-developmental pedagogy.* Nashville, TN: Vanderbilt University Press.

Beck, E. C. (1939). Composition-teaching in a state teachers college. *English Journal, 28*, 593–597.

Bell, J. H. (2000). When hard questions are asked: Evaluating writing centers. *The Writing Center Journal, 2*(1), 7–28.

Boquet, E. (1999). "Our little secret": A history of writing centers, pre– to post–open admissions. *College Composition and Communication, 50*(3), 463–482.

Clark, I. L. (1988). Preparing future composition teachers in the writing center. *College Composition and Communication, 39*(3), 347–350.

Cuseo, J. B. (17 June 2000). Assessment of the first-year experience: six significant questions. Policy Center on the First Year of College. Retrieved from http://www.sc.edu/fye/resources/assessment/pdf/Cuseo6Qs.web.pdf

Grimm, N. (2003). In the spirit of service: Making writing center research a "featured character." In M.A. Pemberton & J. Neuleib (Eds.), *The center will hold: Critical perspectives on writing center scholarship.* Logan, UT: Utah State University Press.

Haswell, R. H. (1991). *Gaining ground in college writing: Tales of development and interpretation.* Dallas, TX: Southern Methodist University Press.

Higher Education Research Institute. (2000). *The cooperative institutional research program (CIRP)*. Los Angeles, CA: Higher Education Research Institute, UCLA Graduate School of Education.

Johanek, C. (2000). *Composing research: A contextualist paradigm for rhetoric and composition*. Logan, UT: Utah State University Press.

Lamb, M. (1981). Evaluation procedure for writing centers: Defining ourselves through accountability. In T. Hawkins & P. Brooks (Eds.), *Improving Writing Skills*. New Directions for College Learning Assistance, No. 3. San Francisco, CA: Jossey-Bass.

McCracken, N. (1979). Evaluation/accountability for the writing lab. *The Writing Lab Newsletter, 3*(6), 1–2.

Neuleib, J. (1982). Evaluating a writing lab. In M. Harris (Ed.), *Tutoring writing: A sourcebook for writing labs*. Glenview, IL: Scott Foresman.

Newmann, S. (1999). Demonstrating effectiveness. *The Writing Lab Newsletter, 23*(8), 8–9.

North, S. (1984). The idea of a writing center. *College English, 46*, 433–446.

Olson, J., Moyer, D.J. & Falda, A. (2001). Student-centered assessment research in the writing center. In P. Gillespie, A. Gillam, L. F. Brown, & B. L. Stay (Eds.), *Writing center research: Extending the conversation*. Mahwah, NJ: Erlbaum.

Pace, C. R., & Kuh, G. D. (1998). *College student experiences questionnaire* (4th ed.) Bloomington, IN: Indiana University.

Pemberton, M. A., & Neuleib, J. (Eds.) (2003). *The center will hold: Critical perspectives on writing center scholarship*. Logan, UT: Utah State University Press.

Sperling, M. (1991). Dialogues of deliberation: Conversation in the teacher–student writing conference. *Written Communication 8*(2), 131–162.

Upcraft, M. L., & Schuh, J. H. (2000, May 26). Assessing the first-year student experience: A framework. Policy Center on the First Year of College. Retrieved from http://www.brevard.edu/fyc/FYA_contributions/UpcraftRemarks.htm

Vukelich, C., & Leverson, L. D. (1987). Two young writers: The relationship between text revisions and teacher/student conferences. In J.E. Readence & R. S. Baldwin (Eds.), *Research in literacy: Merging perspectives*. Thirty-Sixth Yearbook of the National Reading Conference. Rochester, NY: National Reading Conference.

Wingate, M. (2001). Writing centers as sites of academic culture. *The Writing Center Journal, 21*(2), 7–20.

Zelenak, B., Cockriel, I., Crump, E. & Hocks, E. (1993). Ideas in practice: Preparing composition teachers in the writing center. *Journal of Developmental Education, 17*, 28–30, 32, 34–35.

Exporting Writing Center Pedagogy: Writing Fellows Programs as Ambassadors for the Writing Center

Carol Severino and Megan Knight
UNIVERSITY OF IOWA

In this essay, originally published in the 2007 collection Marginal Words, Marginal Work? Tutoring the Academy in the Work of Writing Centers, *Carol Severino and Megan Knight discuss the* Writing Fellows Program *they established at the University of Iowa and its implications for campus and community outreach. Writing Fellows are "ambassadors" from the writing center to external constituencies. They are assigned to instructors across the curriculum to work individually with students on their drafts for course assignments. Writing Fellows also work with instructors to become familiar with their goals for the course and how writing assignments relate to these goals—as well as to aid instructors with the design of writing assignments. Severino and Knight discuss the implications of a program like this to broaden our understanding of tutoring practices and implications, extend the benefits of the writing center, and build a sense of community between the writing center and other parts of the university.*

In the middle of the vast sprawl of the University of Iowa campus sits the Writing Center, a single carpeted room housing a bank of computers and a dozen tables surrounded by chairs. In a sense, the Writing Center is its own country in the middle of a larger country, like the Vatican in Italy or Andorra in Spain. It has its own rules and protocols, some of them quite distinct from what goes on elsewhere on campus. After all, where else can a student go for help on any writing task, from a job application to a psychology paper to a dissertation on pharmacokinetics? Where else can an instructor turn for advice on writing response strategies and one-on-one conference dynamics? Where else is it possible for a student to get assistance on an assignment from a teacher who is not grading her performance?

For the students and teachers who have discovered the Writing Center and taken advantage of all it has to offer, it has served as a valuable resource. But the fact remains that on a campus of this size, such a small place can be easily overlooked. A primary question for those of us working in the Writing Center, then, has been: How do we get word out about the services and resources we have available for the campus community? We face a real challenge in making our little country visible on the large map of the University of Iowa.

Until recently, our options and strategies have been limited. Our main channels for reaching the campus population have been indirect: we could dispatch information, publicizing our services electronically (via the weekly online newsletter for department chairs or through the Writing Center's website) or in print (in the Campus Orientation Manual and in brochures, posters, and flyers). From there, we could only hope that instructors and academic advisors would spread the word further, telling students about the Center or perhaps even referring them to us; we anticipated that those instructors might then find out still more about us from the students they referred. Instructors might request more information, at which point we could dispatch an emissary to their classrooms in the form of a Writing Center tutor who could fill those students in directly on our services—a good outreach method, but one whose success depends too much on the interest and initiative of busy, often overcommitted instructors.

These publicity and outreach efforts, then, were often hit and miss, leaving the majority of faculty and students with incomplete or even incorrect knowledge of basic writing center procedures, such as how tutors prioritize and attend to a draft's macro issues (adherence to the assignment, organization, argumentation, thesis) before micro issues (grammar, punctuation, and citation and documentation style), and how they elicit students' input to foster collaboration rather than simply editing students' papers for them. Many faculty and students still believed the myth that the Writing Center was a fix-it shop rather than a site for intellectual exchange among writers.

Ultimately, in order for the Writing Center to serve its purpose, its constituents have had to come to us—until now. In 2003 when we started a Writing Fellows Program, we found we had created a new means both of bringing the campus community to us and of exporting Writing Center philosophy and practice across the UI campus. To paraphrase Irene Clark on Writing Center outreach, Mohammed can go to the mountain as well as the mountain coming to Mohammed (quoted in Barnett & Blumner, 1999, p. xii). Writing Fellows—undergraduates trained in peer tutoring—now fan out as Writing Center ambassadors across campus and across town, working with other students in a range of courses, helping to demonstrate clearly the nature of what happens in the Writing Center to greater numbers of faculty and students.

Here is how the program works as outreach: Writing Fellows are assigned to instructors across the curriculum to work with their students on drafts of two course papers. Students in "fellowed" courses submit their drafts to the Fellows two weeks before they are due to their instructors. Fellows spend that first week analyzing the drafts according to the demands of the assignment, commenting in the margins, and composing "commenting letters" to their dozen or so assigned students, explaining what they see as the strengths and weaknesses of their drafts. Then they return the drafts with the commenting letters and set up conferencing appointments. The second week, they meet individually with their assigned students to discuss strategies for revision. (See www.uiowa.edu/~writingc/teachers/writing_fellows for more information on the workings of the UI program.)

In this narrative, we use excerpts from Fellows' commenting letters and from faculty and student evaluations to illustrate how the Writing Fellows Program at the University of Iowa serves an ambassadorial function, effectively communicating to students and faculty what the Writing Center does while helping to foster what Barnett and Rosen call "a campus-wide writing environment" (1999, p. 2).

Beginning a Writing Fellows Program

Three years ago, responding in part to the University President's call to make the University of Iowa "The Writing University" by raising our academic writing programs to the level and visibility of our well-known creative writing programs, we founded our Writing Fellows Program modeled after Writing

Fellows programs established first at Brown in 1980 and then spreading to other institutions, both large and small (Haring-Smith, 1992). At the 2002 National Conference for Peer Tutors of Writing, UI Writing Center Director Carol Severino heard an impressive presentation by the University of Wisconsin Writing Fellows and arranged for a site visit to the Wisconsin Writing Center, where Center Director Brad Hughes and Fellows Director Emily Hall and several Fellows and professors who have worked with Fellows explained the function and benefits of the program. The goals of Fellows programs are to improve student writing and writing processes, to promote collaborative learning, and to encourage instructors to use writing to learn in their courses (Haring-Smith, 1992). Because Iowa has no required writing courses beyond first-year Rhetoric and no larger University-wide WAC program of faculty development, we anticipated that the Writing Fellows Program could extend writing instruction beyond the departments of Rhetoric and English and encourage instructors in departments across the College to consider writing instruction part of their professional responsibility.

As a writing-across-the-curriculum (WAC) program related to a Writing Center (WC), the Writing Fellows/Writing Center connection at the University of Iowa follows a long tradition of WAC/WC partnership; as Joan Mullin points out, Writing Centers beget Writing Across the Curriculum Programs or vice versa (2001). In fact, at the University of Memphis, the writing center tutors are considered ambassadors for the WAC program (Johnson & Speck, 1999)—the reverse of Iowa's situation in which the (WAC) Fellows serve as ambassadors for the Writing Center. Our Writing Center is housed within the Rhetoric Department, which is responsible for teaching academic writing, speaking, and reading to first-year students and is known for the interdisciplinary scholarship and teaching of its faculty. A Rhetoric faculty member and the Writing Center Director, Severino is also the Writing Fellows director; Mary Trachsel, cofounder of the program, was the Chair of the Rhetoric Department. The Writing Fellows Assistant Director Megan Knight is also a Rhetoric faculty member, as are most of the commenting mentors, whose role it is to consult with the Fellows on patterns in the students' drafts, the content of their commenting letters, and on strategies for tutoring. The Fellows are paid through the Honors Program, which also helps with Fellows recruiting and funding; hence, the Program is a collaboration between the Rhetoric Department and the Honors Program, with funding for the Fellows supplied by the Provost's Office and the College of Liberal Arts and Sciences.

In Fall 2003, our inaugural year, we began with fifteen Writing Fellows in six courses in six different disciplines (see Severino & Trachsel, 2005, about this first year and its implications for WAC); in two years, we have doubled in size, serving twice as many courses with twice as many Fellows. About half our current Fellows are newly recruited and taking the Fellows course while they comment and conference, whereas the other half are experienced, having taken the course in 2004 or 2003.

The key elements in starting a Fellows program are:

1. Recruiting tutors.
2. Establishing a training course or program for them (see Soven, 2005, for a textbook specific to Fellows).
3. Finding stipends for them. Our Fellows receive $600 for fellowing their first semester and $700 for each subsequent semester in which they work. Expanding the number of Fellows, of course, involves more money for stipends, which involves persistent arguments based on positive evaluations from faculty and students served by the program. (See www.uiowa.edu/~writingc/teachers/writing_fellows for examples of such evaluations and Appendix A for resources and web pages for starting Fellows Programs.)
4. Recruiting committed and versatile faculty willing to make adjustments in their assignment procedures and to meet with Fellows periodically to discuss their assignments, students' responses to them, and commenting strategies.

Our Writing Fellows are honors students who have made it through a rigorous application process, including submission of a personal statement, two papers, and a transcript (they must have GPAs of 3.33 or more), as well as a 30-minute interview. During their first semester in the program, they take an Honors seminar (Writing Theory and Practice 143:102) taught by the program's directors. The course prepares Fellows for their new role, giving them hands-on strategies for commenting on papers and serving as peer tutors; it also introduces pedagogical concepts such as direct and indirect approaches to tutoring and acquaints them with the program's origins and philosophy through Fellows Program histories such as Margot Soven's essay (2001) whose appendix contains useful template forms for recruiting tutor and faculty. In addition, the class provides a community environment in which Fellows can meet one another, swap stories, and exchange tips and ideas.

At the same time, these beginners, along with their experienced counterparts, are actively working as Fellows, making the seminar a kind of on-the-job training. Each semester, Fellows are assigned to courses according to major or area of interest whenever possible. Because the program only works with courses that have small enrollments (20–40 students), Fellows generally work in teams of two or three, and each Fellow is responsible for a dozen or so students in his or her assigned class. All the students in an instructor's course are required to use Fellows, not only those who want to or those whom the instructor believes need the assistance. In the cases of both the commenting letters they write and individual conferences they participate in, the Fellows are modeling Writing Center practice and thus serving as its ambassadors—the emphasis on global/macro rather than micro issues, as their letters do, and the emphasis on collaboration, as the conferences invite.

Writing Center Tutors Versus Writing Fellows

What is the difference between Writing Fellows and Writing Center tutors? In contrast to the undergraduate Writing Fellows, all our Writing Center tutors are graduate student teaching assistants fulfilling part of their assistantship by tutoring both undergraduate and graduate students in the Writing Center. Undergraduate Writing Fellows tutor only undergraduate students whose instructors have agreed to work with Fellows; they usually conference with their students outside the Writing Center. In contrast, graduate student tutors work within the walls of the Writing Center with any students, undergraduate or graduate, who come to the Center regardless of whether their instructors recommended it. Fellows' students are obligated to participate in the program, whereas WC tutors' students sign up for tutoring on a more or less voluntary basis. Writing Center tutors work with writers from multiple courses during any stages of the writing process, from brainstorming to editing, not solely on revising drafts, as do the Fellows.

However, the most important difference between Fellows and tutors is how the former must work closely with course instructors to become familiar with their goals for the course and how their writing assignments relate to these goals. Sometimes the Fellows give instructors feedback on assignment drafts so that they make their assignment goals more clear and explicit to their students. Writing Center tutors rarely have such formal opportunities to provide such input on assignments before they are distributed. Nor do Writing Center tutors write formal commenting letters to students unless they are working as e-mail tutors.

The Commenting Letter

We spend a great deal of time during the Fellows' course studying and developing good commenting letter form. In keeping with Writing Center practice, we focus on a student-centered process approach that begins with students' filling out a cover sheet to accompany their drafts. On the cover sheet, the writers indicate what they felt went well in their drafts and what they feel still needs work, and which aspects of the drafts they would like help with from their Fellows. The cover sheet means that the first word comes from the student, and the Fellows' marginalia and the tone of their commenting letters create a sense of collaborative "conversation." (See Appendix B for a Sample Cover Sheet.)

Fellows are encouraged to make their feedback as specific as possible, focusing on the concerns the writer identifies on the cover sheet. For example, here is an excerpt from a Fellow's response to a draft for an assignment in a course on the History of the Deaf Community; the assignment asks students to situate and compare two stories in two different historical contexts. Notice how Fellow Julia LaBua responds directly to the student's cover sheet, shaping her feedback in response to the writer's concerns. LaBua comments that the student's thesis is not yet specific enough and needs to compare and contrast content from the stories.

Dear _____, Your first draft begins to explore how the two stories reflect the time period in which they were written, and the implications of that historical context on how the deaf were perceived. You commented on the cover sheet that you haven't delved into these themes and topics enough yet; I think your self-analysis is right on. You have some of the bones; now it's time to expand on them and perhaps bring in some of the other themes you see the two stories sharing. One thing that will help you do this is to strengthen and expand on what seems to be your thesis statement: "It is interesting to note the differences between each author's attitudes in how they recognized the conditions of deafness and blindness." Think about some specific ways you can show that with examples from the stories and your analysis of them.

Writing Fellows are trained according to the advice of Donald Daiker (1989) to begin each letter with praise, even if it is simply to encourage the student by saying she or he is off to a good start. More commonly, Fellows are able to praise particular features of the draft, such as its level of development or the student's thoroughness in addressing a certain element of the assignment. Fellows are then taught to provide suggestion's for revision, restricting themselves to the three or four features they think the writer might improve. Most commonly, Fellows seem to find themselves urging the writer to come up with a more strongly worded or clearly defined thesis or main point. Depending on how well the student has fulfilled in the draft the macro demands of the assignment, they might also point out one or two patterns of error such as pronoun/antecedent agreement or wordiness and model an editing process with one or two problematic sentences from the student's paper. Often with lower-order concerns and error patterns, they mention in the commenting letter that during the conference they can discuss particular grammar and style rules and more examples of their application. They then close by reiterating what they see as the draft's strengths, encouraging the writer to begin the revision process before the conference.

As a more complete example, here in its entirety is a Fellow's response to a student's draft in an interdisciplinary course called Cultural Diversity and Identity. The assignment asks students to apply the course readings on racism to their own experiences. Laura Goettsch's letter starts with praise, critiques the three features of thesis, focus, and overgeneralizations, and reminds the student about the conference:

Dear _____, I think you're off to a great start with this assignment. It seems that you have a good grasp of the readings and have begun to incorporate how those readings have affected you over the course of this class. I do have a few suggestions that you might like to look over:

1. Thesis: I've identified the line on your paper that I thought was meant to be your thesis. As a reader, I felt like you had a lot of ideas in your paper that weren't covered by the main claim/thesis you made in your introduction. I wonder if you can expand your thesis to include more. Some questions to think about: What ideas and themes do I discuss in my paper? What am I trying to

prove about these ideas? What conclusions do I draw in my paper? How can I combine all of the main themes into a concise statement of intent for my paper?

2. Themes analysis: I feel like you have a pretty good grasp of the readings, but as a reader, I want to know more. While you offer a lot of description of the readings, I wonder if you can concentrate more on the themes the authors identify. On the second page, I've marked a section where I think you do this really well. Here are some questions you could ask yourself about the rest of the paper: What are the main themes and ideas that each author is trying to create from their paper? How are those ideas interrelated? How have those ideas affected you during your own reading and during class? How can you center your paper on the themes rather than summarizations of the text?

3. Generalizations: I felt as a reader that you really have strong feelings about the racism and its future. However, I often felt a little bewildered by some of the broad generalizations in your paper. Some questions you could consider asking yourself: Do I support the claims I make in my paper? Am I avoiding generalizations that don't adequately describe how I'm feeling? How can I make my points without drawing too broad of a conclusion? How can I identify when I do create broad generalizations in my paper?

Overall, I think you definitely have begun to create all the necessary building blocks to create a well-written and clear paper. You have examples from all of the readings and you've begun to apply them to your own experiences of personal growth. I'm looking forward to working with you in person during our conferencing session. If you have any questions, feel free to contact me. Otherwise, I will see you sometime in the next couple of days.

The Conference

Hand in hand with the letters are those one-on-one meetings that Fellows hold with their peers twice a semester. Again, these meetings are modeled closely after those that take place in the Writing Center every day; in fact, Fellows spend some time during their first semester on the job observing graduate student tutors working in the Writing Center as a way of gaining an understanding of how conferencing dynamics work and gathering some strategies to use in their own one-on-one meetings. Fellows are encouraged to adopt a hands-off approach when possible, making room for the writer to set the agenda and inviting a collaborative approach. A conference will generally begin with discussion of any new revisions the writer may have made since receiving the commenting letter or by addressing some of the writer's questions or concerns; the commenting letter can serve as a point of reference if there is a lull in the conversation. The conference provides the revising student ideal opportunities to try out and verbalize new and connecting ideas for the next draft with the Fellow's support.

In these conferences, Fellows perform a delicate balancing act, tapping into all they have in common with their student peers while at the same time taking advantage of their training and authority as tutors. To extend the metaphor, it is as if Fellows as ambassadors have the advantage of dual citizenship: they are simultaneously members of the undergraduate student community and of the teaching community. Students who might be hesitant to make use of the Writing Center itself, perhaps out of a sense of intimidation at the idea of working on their writing with the graduate students and faculty who staff the Center, may find conferencing with an undergraduate peer a more comfortable introduction to Writing Center practices.

Fellows as Ambassadors

As one form of their diplomacy as ambassadors, Writing Fellows' face-to-face conferences give reluctant students who are "Fellowed" a taste of what the Writing Center offers, which may encourage them to make use of the Center. Many students think they might like to use the Writing Center, but keep putting it off as one might procrastinate making any appointment (for a haircut, a chiropractic adjustment, etc.), whereas others simply have never considered seeking feedback on their writing. As one student in an interdisciplinary music history course called World of the Beatles noted in her Writing Fellows program evaluation, "[The program] can definitely segue a person into taking advantage of the services that the writing center provides for students."

On a related note, students whose Fellows decide to conference with them in the actual Writing Center, as opposed to the norm of a coffeehouse or the student union, are most likely to make these connections. One such student, whose Fellow always meets her students in the Writing Center, noted the Writing Center/Writing Fellows association on her evaluation, stating that participating in the Fellows program would lead her to the Writing Center. She wrote that her Fellow was "extremely helpful to me on both my papers. Her comments helped me focus on what needed to be improved and helped me revise my paper before and after my conference with her. My conferences were also beneficial in focusing and revising my papers. I intend to seek the writing center more often to help with future assignments and recommend this group and center highly to friends, peers, and colleagues."

A second form of diplomacy the Writing Fellows provide is a critique of myths about receiving writing feedback as being "remedial." Unlike some students who protest the Fellows requirement in their courses even though they usually find their Fellows helpful, this next student praises the requirement for acquainting her with the Writing Center. Here she implies that before being Fellowed, she saw the Writing Center as mainly for problem writers: "Feeling that I was a good writer already, I would have never used the Writing Center but for it being required in this course." A center-phobic student in the same course similarly recognized the eventual beneficial effect of a required program: "I believe having to go through the Writing Fellows forced me to produce better papers as an end result, as most students (myself included) are somewhat reluctant to go to the actual writing center."

A third form of diplomacy Fellows enact is helping students demystify and rehearse for their Writing Center appointments. In one case, a student already had scheduled an appointment at the Writing Center for help with a paper in another course (not the Political Science course in which she was being Fellowed) when she met according to schedule with her Fellow to talk about her draft. She asked her Fellow, Lindsey Schneider, what she should expect from the Writing Center tutor because she had never been there before. Lindsey notes, "We discussed how she could prepare for her session by coming up with questions and relating some of the difficulties she was having with the paper I was working with her on to her other assignment. She told me that meeting with me beforehand helped her get more out of her writing center session because she had a better idea of how to discuss her writing with others." Thus, Fellow and student did a writing center run-through to prepare the student for her appointment.

Other students use Writing Center services at the same time that they are being Fellowed, either to supplement the Fellow's feedback, or out of curiosity, as a check on its quality and accuracy. A few Fellowed students use the Writing Center to compare the Fellow's feedback with that of a graduate student they consider more "professional," experienced, or knowledgeable about the discipline. For example, one student in English Literature—who became a Fellow herself the following year—sent her drafts to the e-mail tutor after she revised them according to her Fellow's feedback. A student in English Poetry also sought out feedback on a Fellowed draft from a graduate student tutor in our evening appointment program.

Likewise, both Fellows candidates and hired Fellows are inspired to use the Writing Center for help with their own projects and to witness writing tutors in action. When they are applying to the program, they seek both e-mail and face-to-face feedback on their statements of purpose for their applications to the program. One candidate, who wanted to be knowledgeable about the tutoring process when she came for her Fellows interview, enrolled in our program of twice-a-week sessions with the same tutor all semester in order to find out firsthand what the feedback and revision process was like. When they are appointed as Fellows and take Writing Theory and Practice, they seek e-mail and face-to-face assistance with their papers for that and other courses.

The versatility and the visibility of our Writing Center have benefited from the Fellows' outreach. Some instructors visit the Writing Center for the first time when they attend the Program's opening orientation reception. At that reception and when we are recruiting them, we urge instructors to explain Writing Center services on their syllabus and to send us their students in non-Fellowed courses. Consequently, the number of upper-level students in our Enrollment, Appointment, and E-mail Tutoring programs is increasing. As Leahy notes about his Writing Fellows Program, which was spawned by the Writing Center at Boise State University, the program "has brought us into partnerships with faculty and students that we have not been able to address in any other way" (1999, p. 72). In our first two years, we have already worked twice with three professors and will work for the second or third time with four others in the Fall. The majority of the 25 professors who have worked with us are eager to work again with Fellows.

The Ripple Effect

So how does this program serve as outreach and create a ripple effect that helps spread the Writing Center's practices and processes across campus? How does the program act as a stone thrown in the middle of the university pond? First, and most simply, the program works to change students' and faculty's perceptions of and attitudes about the writing process. Students are reminded (as they have probably heard before) that anything they write will be better if they approach the process in stages, allowing their ideas to mature and change over time. There is no better way to force revision than to create deadlines other than the final one, something that anyone who has ever pulled an all-nighter can attest to. Second, the Program combats students' all-too-common fears of the writing process and concerns about their own abilities by reassuring them that there is merit to their work. And third, it encourages them to consider global issues: How clear is my main point? Have I supported my ideas? Does my paper flow smoothly from one point to the next?—before the sentence-level concerns that too many students (and instructors) unfortunately still seem to believe are all that's needed for good writing. And finally, the program models the feedback and revision process. Students who receive feedback on their work see firsthand the value of using a process approach and the value of collaborative learning, lessons we hope they will apply to other areas of study. Their peers—friends, classmates, roommates—will have opportunities to see this modeled by students who have had the benefit of being Fellowed, in turn.

Professors whose courses are Fellowed likewise see how much better their students' work is when it goes through a drafting process and receives the benefit of constructive critical feedback along the way. When asked on their faculty Fellows evaluations about whether the papers they received that semester were better than those submitted by comparable classes they've taught, instructors responded positively. A professor of African American Literature wrote, "In general the papers were better organized. Evidence of scrutiny of word choices and continuity of theme were more obvious. Overall, papers presented stronger arguments." An Anthropology professor agreed: "The papers were better. They all met the minimum expectations of structure that I have for college level work. No paper came in garbled the way some last minute papers have always come in in the past." An Art History professor favorably contrasted the drafts and final papers: "Particularly looking from drafts to final versions, the improvements in organization and expression were sometimes dramatic."

And a Political Science professor enumerated many improvements on both local and global features: "I felt the papers were better in several ways. First, there were fewer sentence fragments. Second, the writers' voice was more 'active' with fewer nominalizations. Third, and most important, papers were organizationally coherent. . . . Another way of saying the same thing: there was much less 'stream of consciousness' writing, in which students bring up ideas as they occur to them, but don't relate them to one another in a coherent fashion."

In the best-case scenarios, these instructors are inspired to incorporate elements of the program into future courses and to use elements of the commenting process in their own responses to student work. For example, the Anthropology professor we worked with last spring will present the commenting/conferencing model to the teaching assistants he is supervising when he teaches a large lecture course in the fall. A Geography professor who added an additional fifteen students to his already overenrolled class in International Child Labor—too many students for his three Writing Fellows to handle—became a Writing Fellow himself for the second assignment, writing commenting letters on drafts and conferencing individually with his students (perhaps inspired by Severino, who helped Fellow the first paper, and Trachsel, the Rhetoric Department Chair at the time, who helped Fellow the second).

Haring-Smith's vision for a Writing Fellows program was that the Fellows' responses would serve as models for the faculty (1992). Leahy claims that such modeling is better than the usual WAC faculty development workshops: "The direct and immediate modeling of response is of value to instructors. It is, in a way, more efficient than teaching faculty in workshops about responding to student writing" (1999, p. 74). And in all cases, the ambassador/emissary role of the Fellows serves to communicate the value of the Writing Center—its presence and its practices—to a wider audience on the University of Iowa campus. More importantly, it fosters the kind of "campus-wide writing environment" (Barnett & Rosen, 1999) that is key to constructing The Writing University.

The University as Writing Center

The Writing Fellows Program functions as more than a means of bringing the UI population to our doorstep: it is also a way of bringing the Writing Center to the University, modeling Center philosophy and practice, and breaking down the borders that separate one "country" from another. Of course, we couldn't fit the entire population of the UI community into our tiny space— nor would we want to. In truth, our goal is not merely to let the campus community know about our resources and invite instructors and students to take advantage of them; it is also to demonstrate to them the value of adopting our practices and philosophy as their own.

Fellows function as ambassadors not only for the Center itself, then, but for what it represents pedagogically, as well. In a visionary sense, the perfect outcome would be a university that is a Writing Center—one where the presence of an actual Writing Center would be rendered moot, because teachers and students would as a matter of course make use of just the kinds of writing and response strategies we suggest. Until then, the Writing Fellows Program is helping to put us on the map.

Appendix A: Resources for Starting a Writing Fellows Program

Aarons, V., & Salomon, W. (1989). The writing center and writing across the curriculum: Some observations on theory and practice. *Focuses*, 2(2), 91–102.

Bruffee, K. (1984). Peer tutoring and the conversation of mankind. In G. Olson (Ed.), *Writing centers: Theory and administration* (p. 315). Urbana, IL: NCTE.

Dever, B., Cramer P., France A., Mahon F., Ogawa, M. J., Raabe, T., & Rogers, B. (1995). Writing lab consultants talk about helping students writing across the disciplines. *Writing Lab Newsletter*, 19(9), 810.

Dinitz, S., & Howe, D. (1989). Writing centers and writing across the curriculum: An evolving partnership. *The Writing Center Journal*, 10(1), 45–51.

Hubbuch, S. M. (1988). A tutor needs to know the subject matter to help a student with a paper: __Agree__Disagree__Not Sure. *Writing Center Journal*, 8(2), 23–30.

Jolliffe, D., & Brier, E. (1988). Studying writers' knowledge in academic disciplines. In D. Jolliffe (Ed.), *Writing in academic disciplines* (pp. 35–77). Norwood, NJ: Ablex.

Kiedaisch, J., & Dinitz, S. (1993). Look back and say 'so what': The limitations of the generalist tutor. *Writing Center Journal*, 14(1), 63–74.

Kinkead, J., Alderman, N., Baker, B., Freer, A., Hertzke, J., Hill, S. M., Obry, J., Parker, T., & Peterson, M. (1995). Situations and solutions for tutoring across the curriculum. *Writing Lab Newsletter*, 19(8), 1–5.

Leahy, R. (1992). Writing assistants in writing-emphasis courses: Toward some working guidelines. *Writing Lab Newsletter*, 16(9–10), 11.

Pemberton, M. (1995). Rethinking the WAC/Writing center connection. *The Writing Center Journal*, 15(2), 116–133.

wac.colostate.edu: This site lists and provides links to detailed descriptions of at least 16 different writing fellows programs. You can also access issues of WAC publications such as *Across the Disciplines*, *The WAC Journal*, and *Academic Writing*.

www.wisc.edu/writing/wf/main.html: The University of Wisconsin Writing Fellows web page, with access to the faculty handbook and to samples from the Fellows handbook.

Appendix B: Sample Cover Sheet

Name:
Title of Paper:

What do you like most about this draft?

What did you find most difficult while writing this assignment?

List some aspect(s) of this draft you would like me to pay special attention to when commenting on your paper.

Anything else you need me to know?

References

Barnett, R., & Blumner, J. (1999). Introduction. In R. Barnett & J. Blumner (Eds.), *Writing centers and writing across the curriculum programs: Building interdisciplinary partnerships* (pp. ix–xiii). Westport, CT: Greenwood.

Barnett, R., & Rosen, L. M. (1999). The WAC/writing center partnership: Creating a campus-wide writing environment. In R. Barnett & J. Blumner (Eds.), *Writing centers and writing across the curriculum programs: Building interdisciplinary partnership* (pp. 1–12). Westport, CT: Greenwood.

Daiker, D. (1989) Learning to praise. In C. Anson (Ed.), *Writing and response: Theory, practice, and research* (pp. 103–113). Urbana, IL: NCTE.

Haring-Smith, T. (1992). Changing students' attitudes: Writing Fellows Programs. In S. McLeod & M. Soven (Eds.), *Writing across the curriculum* (pp. 175–188). Newbury Park, CA: Sage.

Johnson, S., & Speck, B. (1999). The writing center as ambassador plenipotentiary in a developing WAD program. In R. Barnett & J. Blumner (Eds.), *Writing centers and writing across the curriculum programs: Building interdisciplinary partnerships* (pp. 13–31). Westport, CT: Greenwood.

Leahy, R. (1999). When a writing center undertakes a writing fellows program. In R. Barnett & J. Blumner (Eds.), *Writing centers and writing across the curriculum programs: Building interdisciplinary partnerships* (pp. 71–88). Westport, CT: Greenwood.

Mullin, J. (2001). Writing centers and WAC. In S. McLeod, E. Miraglia, M. Soven, & C. Thaiss (Eds.), *WAC for the new millennium: Strategies for continuing writing across the curriculum programs* (pp. 179–199). Urbana, IL: NCTE.

Severino, C., & Trachsel, M. (2005). Starting a writing fellows program: Crossing disciplines or crossing pedagogies? *International Journal of Learning, 11*, 449–455.

Soven, M. (2001). Curriculum-based peer tutors and WAC. In S. McLeod, E. Miraglia, M. Soven, & C. Thaiss (Eds.), *WAC for the new millennium: Strategies for continuing writing across the curriculum programs* (pp. 200–232). Urbana, IL: NCTE

Soven, M. (2005). *What the writing tutor needs to know.* Belmont, CA: Thompson/Wadsworth.

A Writing Center–Education Department Collaboration: Training Teachers to Work One-on-One

Jacob S. Blumner
UNIVERSITY OF MICHIGAN AT FLINT

In this essay, originally published in the online writing center journal Praxis, *Jacob Blumner explores the role that professional development can play in the knowledge base of the student-tutor and in the student-tutor's education. He emphasizes collaborations between the writing center and campus and community groups as especially beneficial in this process and describes how one such collaboration with an education department enhanced the preparation of students studying to be teachers and of students learning to be tutors. Blumner states that "collaboration between education programs and writing centers should be studied to bring another layer of research and scholarship to writing centers," especially as both education department and writing center scholarship emphasize ways to individualize curricula. He concludes that this type of "interdisciplinary collaboration" enriches learning and encourages students and student-tutors to reconceptualize traditional models of teaching writing whether in the classroom or the writing center.*

Writing centers regularly work to serve an entire campus community, developing satellite centers to make their services more convenient and establishing an online presence to serve tech-savvy students. Some units outside of arts and sciences, such as business or health science, establish writing centers to better focus on their students' specific disciplinary writing needs. Many centers do community outreach that varies from providing a "grammar hotline" to collaborating with public schools and outside agencies on projects ranging from high school writing centers to corporate consulting. All of these activities support the main mission of a writing center: helping students become better writers. But writing centers can do more.

An often overlooked or underdeveloped element of the writing center is the professional development of the student-tutor and the place it plays in the student-tutor's education. For many that development is implicit; the egalitarian nature of writing centers has tutors collaborating on the projects listed above, as well as having them present and publish their work. Tutors take on additional responsibilities in writing centers, giving them valuable experience with things such as administration and marketing. This model of active professional development should be closely examined, and writing centers should target student populations who will most benefit from the experience of being tutors. In this particular case, I am advocating for a program that recruits and trains education students from all disciplines to tutor in the writing center.

Education students stand uniquely to benefit from the experiences of tutoring in a writing center. Once these students become teachers, they will need to work individually with their students. Certainly education students have the experience of working individually with a faculty member, and if they are fortunate, through their experiences in school, they will work individually with students through classroom internships or student teaching. But methods classes and student teaching provide little training and practice for working one-on-one with students. Though some programs may train future teachers how to conference individually with students, none provide the opportunity to gain as much experience as working in a writing center. Additionally, writing centers provide a special environment for conferences because peer tutoring dramatically reduces the authoritarian nature of student–teacher conferences, thus enabling the tutor and writer to really focus on what matters—the learning process. Writing center tutors learn how to work specifically on the writing—not the grade, something on which teachers of writing should be focused. In a writing center, education students will be able to work with a variety of students from diverse backgrounds, and if they intend to teach high school, they can see what kinds of experiences and attitudes students have in and about college. They will also see the diverse kinds of writing demanded in college in all disciplines. So when they begin teaching high school, they will have a better understanding of what the future may hold for their students.

The collaboration between education programs and writing centers should be studied to bring another layer of research and scholarship to writing centers. Collaboration between education programs and writing centers seems natural. They share some common roots and literature. Both education and writing center scholarship draw on Vygotsky's zone of proximal development theory to individualize curricula for students, a theory that also supposes a collaborative process for education. Irene L. Clark applies Vygotsky's theory to writing center pedagogy, arguing, "tutors should focus on 'functions that have not yet matured, but are in the process of maturation'" (92). Education majors who tutor will learn Vygotsky's theory and extensively practice pushing writers into the zone through collaborative tutoring sessions. This will eventually enable them as teachers to apply the same theory in their classrooms. (See Doolittle for an overview of Vygotsky's zone of proximal development in the classroom.)

Dovetailing nicely with Vygotsky's zone of proximal development is John Dewey's philosophy of education (see Lampert-Shepel). In *Democracy and Education*, Dewey argues against authoritarian teaching methods and for experiential-based education, claiming, "When an activity is continued into the undergoing of consequences, when the change made by action is reflected back into a change made in us, the mere flux is loaded with significance. We learn something." Essentially, Dewey claims students learn best through action and reflection, both central practices to writing center pedagogy. In tutoring sessions, writers act by drafting, revising, and editing, and they reflect by discussing rhetorical decisions with the tutor. In every session, tutors must facilitate the action and reflection, maximizing learning by pushing writers into their zone of proximal development. Education majors who tutor can take their developed knowledge of talking and working with writers to their classrooms, finding insightful ways to help writers learn through experience and reflection.

The roots between English education and writing centers are particularly extensive, including the scholarship of James Britton, Peter Elbow, Donald Murray, Nancy Atwell, Stephen Tchudi, and Mike Rose. In fact, Irene Clark and Joyce Moyers have written about writing centers participating in English teacher training. But the collaboration should not stop with future English teachers. In her 1989 article, "Writing across the Curriculum: The Second Stage, and Beyond," Susan McLeod advocated integrating writing across the curriculum into the fabric of a university so it will become an ingrained, accepted component of the academic curriculum. Once integrated, Writing across the Curriculum will be better placed to help shape writing instruction. Writing centers also need to strive for integration into the curriculum, instead of remaining on the academic periphery. For many institutions, the writing center is what Muriel Harris calls the de facto WAC center. Faculty and administrators turn to the writing center for assistance with writing issues that range from improving a writing assignment to helping a program develop a curricular map for writing throughout a major or program. Writing centers have much to offer, and if they are better integrated into the academic fabric, they will be better positioned to serve faculty and students in ways that move beyond traditional tutorial sessions.

Writing centers have much to gain from education programs and students, as well. First, much of the research that writing center scholars rely on comes from education or English education scholars. An infusion of education students as tutors will bring an infusion of that theory and practice. The collaboration between education programs and writing centers should be studied to bring another layer of research and scholarship to writing centers, something writing center scholars, such as Beth Boquet, note is vital to writing center legitimacy and survival. The collaboration will add to the diversity of majors in the writing center and will lay the foundation for connections to the public schools and the community. With education majors as tutors, and in collaboration with schools of education, writing centers can reach out beyond the university walls. Writing centers can collaborate with local schools to develop writing centers within them, drawing on graduated tutors who become teachers. Potentially, the collaboration can serve as another training ground for education-major tutors who, while still students, can work in the local schools' centers. Tutors can serve as mentors for students in the public schools, and the university writing center can host workshops or other programs for local schools and the community. Additionally, education-major tutors can lead community outreach projects involving Head Start programs, adult and community education programs, and community writing groups, as well as hosting workshops for community members. So it seems perfectly sensible to create a bridge between education and writing centers.

Writing centers need to move beyond the traditional role of a physical entity providing services to students who come through their doors or bringing their services to the occasional classroom. What might such a program look like? I think it could take many forms, depending on local contexts and conditions, but here are some possibilities. Despite the heavy course load education students already have, programs could include a tutor-training course as an elective because these courses are based heavily on pedagogy and on integrating practice (i.e., tutoring). If this is not an option, students could participate in an intensive tutor-training workshop so that they would be adequately prepared to work with students and their writing. Education programs could make tutoring an elective internship or a service-learning component of one of their courses. This would enable education programs to add educational components that would tie the students' experience in a writing center to what they will be doing in a classroom. Some education programs may be fortunate enough to create these kinds of collaborations with local high school writing centers so that their students would have the experience of tutoring the student population they may be teaching in the future. The programmatic possibilities are endless and exciting.

There are challenges that are real, but they can be overcome or avoided. Education programs, through state mandates, allow for few elective courses, so fitting a tutor-training course into the curriculum would be difficult. Strong arguments would have to be made to demonstrate how tutoring writing would benefit all education students, not just those intending to teach English. Peggy Broder's "Writing Centers and Teacher Training" is a good starting point for demonstrating the benefits to education students. In her essay, Broder details how working in a writing center provides valuable experience for future writing teachers and extrapolates some of the benefits to all teachers. WAC scholarship and state mandates for writing success could also be harnessed to argue for such a program. The National Commission on Writing released a report in April 2003 titled **"The Neglected R,"** in which they wrote, "We strongly endorse writing across the curriculum. The concept of doubling writing time is feasible because of the near-total neglect of writing outside of English departments" (31). Support from reports like "The Neglected R" and innovative programs, such as mentor programs in which tutors go into public schools to work with students, will entice education majors from disciplines other than English to participate. Ultimately, this will positively affect education at the primary and secondary levels, and potentially contribute to a seamless move for students from public school to the university.

With the success of these programs, writing center directors would have to safeguard against the writing center becoming an arm of the education program, designed only to serve education students and those writers seeking help, but I think with attention that can be avoided.

The benefits of enriching writing center activity and personnel while developing a meaningful interdisciplinary collaboration with education programs outweigh the risks described above. As universities adapt to changes in student populations and curricular demands, writing centers need to follow suit. Writing centers need to move beyond the traditional role of a physical entity providing services to students who come through their doors or bringing their services to the occasional classroom. Changes in general education programs, the continuing push for greater accountability through assessment and accreditation, an increasing emphasis on interdisciplinarity, and more coursework in online and electronic environments make the need for integration and collaboration within a university more important so that campus communities can create more integrated educational experiences for students.

Works Cited

Boquet, Beth. "'Our Little Secret': A History of Writing Centers, Pre- to Post-Open Admissions." *CCC* 50 (1999): 463–82. Print.

Broder, Peggy F. "Writing Centers and Teacher Training." *Writing Program Administration* 13.3 (1990): 37–45. Print.

Clark, Irene Lurkis. "Collaboration and Ethics in Writing Center Pedagogy." *The St. Martin's Sourcebook for Writing Tutors*. Ed. Christina Murphy and Steve Sherwood. New York: St. Martin's, 1995. 88–96. Print.

---. "Preparing Future Composition Teachers in the Writing Center." *CCC* 39 (1988): 347–50. Print.

Dewey, John. *Democracy and Education*. New York: Macmillan, 1944. *Institute for Learning Technologies*. Web. 15 March 2006.

Doolittle, P. E. "Vygotsky's Zone of Proximal Development as a Theoretical Foundation for Cooperative Learning." *Journal on Excellence in College Teaching* 8.1 (1997): 83–103. Print.

Harris, Muriel. "A Writing Center without a WAC Program: The De Facto WAC Center/Writing Center." *Writing Centers and Writing across the Curriculum Programs*. Ed. Robert W. Barnett and Jacob S. Blumner. Greenwood Press, 1999. 89–104. Print.

Lampert-Shepel, E. "Reflective Thinking in Educational Praxis: Analysis of Multiple Perspectives." *Educational Foundations* 13.3 (1999): 69–88. Print.

McLeod, Susan. "Writing across the Curriculum: The Second Stage, and Beyond." *CCC* 40 (1989): 337–43. Print.

Moyers, Joyce K. "The Tutor-Trained Teacher: The Role of the Writing Center in Teacher Education." Dallas: Conference on College Composition and Communication, 1981. *ERIC Document Reproduction Service*. ED 199739. Web. 3 Jan. 2006.

National Commission on Writing. *The Neglected R*. April 2003. Web. 3 Jan. 2006.

AFFIRMING DIVERSITY

"Whispers of Coming and Going": Lessons from Fannie
Anne DiPardo _____
THE UNIVERSITY OF IOWA

Anne DiPardo's essay, a case study of her work with Fannie, a Native American student, was chosen the outstanding work of scholarship for 1993 by the National Writing Centers Association. DiPardo profiles Fannie's development over a number of writing center tutorials. Through details about Fannie's past and dialogue between Fannie and DiPardo, the reader comes to know Fannie well enough to care about her. The essay also explores the corresponding development of Morgan, a peer tutor, as she struggles with the collaborative techniques she attempts to incorporate in her work with Fannie. DiPardo's essay emphasizes multicultural sensitivity by encouraging tutors to question the assumptions they make about students and to seek clues to the "hidden corners" of a student's past, personality, and methods of learning. DiPardo supports the notion of reflective practice in tutoring by encouraging tutors to be "perennially inquisitive and self-critical" while learning from the students they attempt to teach. Perhaps the essay's greatest value is the insight it offers into an individual student and tutor as they negotiate a relationship. This essay first appeared in The Writing Center Journal *in 1992.*

> *As a man with cut hair, he did not identify the rhythm of three strands, the whispers of coming and going, of twisting and tying and blending, of catching and of letting go, of braiding.*
> —Michael Dorris, A Yellow Raft in Blue Water

We all negotiate among multiple identities, moving between public and private selves, living in a present shadowed by the past, encountering periods in which time and circumstance converge to realign or even restructure our images of who we are. As increasing numbers of non-Anglo students pass through the doors of our writing centers, such knowledge of our own shape-shifting can help us begin—if *only* begin—to understand the social and linguistic challenges which inform their struggles with writing. When moved to talk about the complexities of their new situation, they so often describe a more radically chameleonic process, of living in noncontiguous worlds, of navigating between competing identities, competing loyalties. "It's like I have two cultures in me," one such student remarked to me recently, "but I can't choose." Choice becomes a moot point as boundaries blur, as formerly distinct selves become organically enmeshed, indistinguishable threads in a dynamic whole (Bakhtin 275; Cintron 24; Fischer 196).

Often placed on the front lines of efforts to provide respectful, insightful attention to these students' diverse struggles with academic discourse, writing tutors likewise occupy multiple roles, remaining learners even while emerging as teachers, perennially searching for a suitable social stance (Hawkins)—a stance existing somewhere along a continuum of detached toughness and warm empathy, and, which like all things ideal, can only be approximated, never definitively located. Even the strictly linguistic dimension of their task is rendered problematic by the continuing paucity of research on the writing of nonmainstream students (see Valdés, "Identifying Priorities"; "Language Issues")—a knowledge gap which likewise complicates our own efforts to provide effective tutor training and support. Over a decade has passed since Mina Shaughnessy eloquently advised basic writing teachers to become students of their students, to consider what Glynda Hull and Mike Rose ("Rethinking," "Wooden Shack") have more recently called the "logic and history" of literacy events that seem at first glance inscrutable and strange. In this age of burgeoning diversity, we're still trying to meet that challenge, still struggling to encourage our tutors to appreciate its rich contours, to discover its hidden rigors, to wrestle with its endless vicissitudes.

This story is drawn from a semester-long study of a basic writing tutorial program at a west-coast university—a study which attempted to locate these tutor-led small groups within the larger contexts of a writing program and campus struggling to meet the instructional needs of non-Anglo students (see DiPardo, "Passport"). It is about one tutor and one student, both ethnic minorities at this overwhelmingly white, middle-class campus, both caught up in elusive dreams and uncertain beginnings. I tell their story not because it is either unusual or typical, but because it seems so richly revealing of the larger themes I noted again and again during my months of data collection—as unresolved tensions tugged continually at a fabric of institutional good intentions, and as tutors and students struggled, with ostensible good will and inexorable frustration, to make vital connections. I tell this story because I believe it has implications for all of us trying to be worthy students of our students, to make sense of our own responses to diversity, and to offer effective support to beginning educators entrusted to our mentorship.

"It, Like, Ruins Your Mind": Fannie's Educational History

Fannie was Navajo, and her dream was to one day teach in the reservation boarding schools she'd once so despised, to offer some of the intellectual, emotional, and linguistic support so sorely lacking in her own educational history. As a kindergartner, she had been sent to a school so far from her home that she could only visit family on weekends. Navajo was the only language spoken in her house, but at school all the teachers were Anglo, and only English was allowed. Fannie recalled that students had been punished for speaking their native language—adding with a wry smile that they'd spoken Navajo anyway, when the teachers weren't around. The elementary school curriculum had emphasized domestic skills—cooking, sewing, and, especially, personal hygiene. "Boarding school taught me to be a housemaid," Fannie observed in one of her essays, "I was hardly taught how to read and write." All her literacy instruction had been in English, and she'd never become literate in Navajo. Raised in a culture that valued peer collaboration (cf. Philips 391–93), Fannie had long ago grasped that Anglo classrooms were places where teachers assume center stage, where students are expected to perform individually: "No," her grade-school teachers had said when Fannie turned to classmates for help, "I want to hear *only* from *you*."

Estranged from her family and deeply unhappy, during fifth grade Fannie had stayed for a time with an aunt and attended a nearby public school. The experience there was much better, she recalled, but there soon followed a series of personal and educational disruptions as she moved among various relatives' homes and repeatedly switched schools. By the time she began high school, Fannie was wondering if the many friends and family members who'd dropped out had perhaps made the wiser choice. By her sophomore year, her grades had sunk "from As and Bs to Ds and Fs," and she was "hanging out with the wrong crowd." By mid-year, the school wrote her parents a letter indicating that she had stopped coming to class. When her family drove up to get her, it was generally assumed that Fannie's educational career was over.

Against all odds, Fannie finished high school after all. At her maternal grandmother's insistence, arrangements were made for Fannie to live with an aunt who had moved to a faraway west-coast town where the educational system was said to be much stronger. Her aunt's community was almost entirely Anglo, however, and Fannie was initially self-conscious about her English: "I had an accent really bad," she recalled, "I just couldn't communicate." But gradually, although homesick and sorely underprepared, she found that she was holding her own. Eventually, lured by the efforts of affirmative action recruiters, she took the unexpected step of enrolling in the nearby university. "I never thought I would ever graduate from high school," Fannie wrote in one of her essays, adding proudly that "I'm now on my second semester in college as a freshman." Her grandmother had died before witnessing either event, but Fannie spoke often of how pleased she would have been.[1]

Fannie was one of a handful of Native Americans on the campus, and the only Navajo. As a second-semester first-year student, she was still struggling to find her way both academically and socially, still working to overcome the scars of her troubled educational history. As she explained after listening to an audiotape of a tutorial session, chief among these was a lingering reluctance to speak up in English, particularly in group settings:

> *Fannie:* When, when, I'm talking . . . I'm shy. Because I always think
> I always say something not right, with my English, you know.

(Pauses, then speaks very softly.) It's hard, though. Like with my friends, I do that too. Because I'll be quiet—they'll say, "Fannie, you're quiet." Or if I meet someone, I, I don't do it, let them do it, I let that person do the talking.

A. D.:   Do you wish you were more talkative?

Fannie: I wish! Well I am, when I go home. But when I come here, you know, I always think, English is my second language and I don't know that much, you know.

A. D.:   So back home you're not a shy person?

Fannie: (laughing uproariously) No! (continues laughing).

I had a chance to glimpse Fannie's more audacious side later that semester, when she served as a campus tour guide to a group of students visiting from a distant Navajo high school. She was uncharacteristically feisty and vocal that week, a change strikingly evident on the tutorial audiotapes. Indeed, when I played back one of that week's sessions in a final interview, Fannie didn't recognize her own voice: "Who's that talking?" she asked at first. But even as she recalled her temporary elation, she described as well her gradual sense of loss:

Sometimes I just feel so happy when someone's here, you know, I feel happy? I just get that way. And then (pauses, begins to speak very softly), and then it just wears off. And then they're leaving—I think, oh, they're leaving, you know.

While Fannie described their week together as "a great experience," she was disturbed to find that even among themselves, the Navajo students were speaking English: "That bothered me a lot," she admitted, surmising that "they're like embarrassed . . . to speak Navajo, because back home, speaking Navajo fluently all the time, that's like lower class." "If you don't know the language," Fannie wrote in one of her essays, "then you don't know who you are. . . . It's your identity . . . the language is very important." In striking contrast to these students who refused to learn the tribal language, Fannie's grandparents had never learned to speak English: "They were really into their culture, and tradition, and all of that," she explained, "but now we're not that way anymore, hardly, and it's like we're losing it, you know." Fannie hoped to attend a program at Navajo Community College where she could learn to read and write her native language, knowledge she could then pass on to her own students.

Fannie pointed to the high drop-out rate among young Navajos as the primary reason for her people's poverty, and spoke often of the need to encourage students to finish high school and go on to college. And yet, worried as she was about the growing loss of native language and tradition, Fannie also expressed concerns about the Anglicizing effects of schooling. Education is essential, she explained, but young Navajos must also understand its dangers:

I mean like, sometimes if you get really educated, we don't really want that. Because then, it like ruins your mind, and you use it, to like betray your people, too . . . That's what's happening a lot now.

By her own example, Fannie hoped to one day show her students that it is possible to be both bilingual and bicultural, that one can benefit from exposure to mainstream ways without surrendering one's own identity:

If you know the white culture over here, and then you know your own culture, you can make a good living with that . . . when I go home, you know, I know Navajo, and I know English too. They say you can get a good job with that.

Back home, Fannie's extended family was watching her progress with warm pride, happily anticipating the day when she would return to the reservation to teach. When Fannie went back for a visit over spring break, she was surprised to find that they'd already built her a house: "They sure give me a lot of attention, that's for sure," she remarked with a smile. Many hadn't seen Fannie for some time, and they were struck by the change:

Everybody still, kind of picture me, still, um, the girl from the past. The one who quit school—and they didn't think of me going to college at all. And they were surprised, they were really surprised. And they were like proud of me too . . .'cause none of their family is going to college.

One delighted aunt, however, was the mother of a son who was also attending a west-coast college:

She says, "I'm so happy! I can't wait to tell him, that you're going to college too! You stick in there, Fannie, now don't goof!" I'm like, "I'll try not to!"

"I Always Write Bad Essays": Fannie's Struggles with Writing

On the first day of class, Fannie's basic writing teacher handed out a questionnaire that probed students' perceptions of their strengths and weaknesses as writers. In response to the question, "What do you think is good about your writing?" Fannie wrote, "I still don't know what is good about my writing"; in response to "What do you think is bad about your writing?" she responded, "Everything."

Fannie acknowledged that her early literacy education had been neither respectful of her heritage nor sensitive to the kinds of challenges she would face in the educational mainstream. She explained in an interview that her first instruction in essay writing had come at the eleventh hour, during her senior year of high school: "I never got the technique, I guess, of writing good essays," she explained, "I always write bad essays." While she named her "sentence structure, grammar, and punctuation" as significant weaknesses, she also added that "I have a lot to say, but I can't put it on paper . . . . It's like I can't find the vocabulary." Fannie described this enduring block in an in-class essay she wrote during the first week of class:

From my experience in writing essays were not the greatest. There were times my mind would be blank on thinking what I should write about.

In high school, I learned how to write an essay during my senior year. I learned a lot from my teacher but there was still something missing about my essays. I knew I was still having problems with my essay organization.

Now, I'm attending a university and having the same problems in writing essays. The university put me in basic writing, which is for students who did not pass the placement test. Of course, I did not pass it. Taking basic writing has helped me a lot on writing essays. There were times I had problems on what to write about.

There was one essay I had problems in writing because I could not express my feelings on a paper. My topic was on Mixed Emotions. I knew how I felt in my mind but I could not find the words or expressing my emotions.

Writing essays from my mind on to the paper is difficult for me. From this experience, I need to learn to write what I think on to a paper and expand my essays.

"Yes," her instructor wrote at the bottom of the page, "even within this essay—which is good—you need to provide specific detail, not just general statements." But what did Fannie's teacher find "good" about this essay—or was this opening praise only intended to soften the criticism that followed? Fannie had noted in an interview that she panicked when asked to produce something within 45 minutes: "I just write anything," she'd observed, "but your mind goes blank, too." Still, while this assignment may not have been the most appropriate way to assess the ability of a student like Fannie, both she and her instructor felt it reflected her essential weakness—that is, an inability to develop her ideas in adequate detail.

At the end of the semester, her basic writing teacher confided that Fannie had just barely passed the course, and would no doubt face a considerable struggle in first-year composition. Although Fannie also worried about the next semester's challenge, she felt that her basic writing course had provided valuable opportunities. "I improved a lot," she said in a final interview, "I think I did—I know I—did. 'Cause now I can know what I'm trying to say, and in an afternoon, get down to that topic." One of her later essays, titled "Home," bears witness to Fannie's assertion:

> The day is starting out a good day. The air smells fresh as if it just rained. The sky is full with clouds, forming to rain. From the triangle mountain, the land has such a great view. Below I see hills overlapping and I see six houses few feet from each other. One of them I live in. I can also see other houses miles apart.
>
> It is so peaceful and beautiful. I can hear birds perching and dogs barking echos from long distance. I can not tell from which direction. Towards north I see eight horses grazing and towards east I hear sheep crying for their young ones. There are so many things going on at the same time.

It is beginning to get dark and breezy. It is about to rain. Small drops of rain are falling. It feels good, relieving the heat. The rain is increasing and thundering at the same time. Now I am soaked, I have the chills. The clouds is moving on and clearing the sky. It is close to late afternoon. The sun is shining and drying me off. The view of the land is more beautiful and looks greener. Like a refreshment.

Across from the mountain I am sitting is a mountain but then a plateau that stretches with no ending. From the side looks like a mountain but it is a long plateau. There are stores and more houses on top of the plateau.

My clothes are now dry and it is getting late. I hear my sister and my brother calling me that dinner is ready. It was a beautiful day. I miss home.

"Good description," her instructor wrote on this essay, "I can really 'see' this scene." But meanwhile, she remained concerned about Fannie's lack of sophistication: "Try to use longer, more complex sentences," she added, "avoid short, choppy ones." Overwhelmed by the demands of composing and lacking strategies for working on this perceived weakness, Fannie took little away from such feedback aside from the impression that her writing remained inadequate. Although Fannie was making important strides, she needed lots of patient, insightful support if she were to overcome her lack of experience with writing and formidable block. Only beginning to feel a bit more confident in writing about personal experience, she anticipated a struggle with the expository assignments that awaited her:

She's having us write from our experience. It'll be different if it's like in English 101, you know how the teacher tells you to write like this and that, and I find that one very hard, 'cause I see my other friends' papers and it's hard. I don't know if I can handle that class.

Fannie was trying to forge a sense of connection to class assignments—she wrote, for instance, about her Native American heritage, her dream of becoming a teacher, and about how her cultural background had shaped her concern for the environment. But meanwhile, as her instructor assessed Fannie's progress in an end-of-term evaluation, the focus returned to lingering weaknesses: "needs to expand ideas w/examples/description/explanation," the comments read, not specifying how or why or to whom. Somehow, Fannie had to fill in the gaps in her teacher's advice—and for the more individualized support she so sorely needed, she looked to the tutorials.

"Are You Learnin' Anything from Me?": The Tutorials

Morgan, Fannie's African American tutor, would soon be student teaching in a local high school, and she approached her work with basic writers as a trial run, a valuable opportunity to practice the various instructional strategies she'd heard about in workshops and seminars. Having grown up in the predominantly Anglo, middle-class community that surrounded the campus,

Morgan met the criticisms of more politically involved ethnic students with dogged insistence: "I'm first and foremost a member of the *human* race," she often said, going on to describe her firm determination to work with students of all ethnicities, to help them see that success in the mainstream need not be regarded as cultural betrayal. During the term that I followed her—her second semester of tutoring and the first time she'd worked with non-Anglo students—this enthusiasm would be sorely tested, this ambition tempered by encounters with unforeseen obstacles.

Morgan's work with Fannie was a case in point. Although she had initially welcomed the challenge of drawing Fannie out, of helping this shy young woman overcome her apparent lack of self-confidence, by semester's end Morgan's initial compassion had been nearly overwhelmed by a sense of frustration. In an end-of-term interview, she confessed that one impression remained uppermost: "I just remember her sitting there," Morgan recalled, "and talking to her, and it's like, 'well I don't know, I don't know' . . . . Fannie just has so many doubts, and she's such a hesitant person, she's so withdrawn, and mellow, and quiet. . . . A lot of times, she'd just say, 'well I don't know what I'm supposed to write. . . . Well I don't like this, I don't like my writing.'"

Although Fannie seldom had much to say, her words were often rich in untapped meaning. Early in the term, for instance, when Morgan asked why she was in college, Fannie searched unsuccessfully for words that would convey her strong but somewhat conflicted feelings:

Fannie: Well . . . (long pause) . . . it's hard . . .
Morgan: You wanna teach like, preschool? Well, as a person who wants to teach, what do you want outta your students?
Fannie: To get around in America you have to have education . . . (unclear).
Morgan: And what about if a student chose not to be educated—would that be ok?
Fannie: If that's what he wants . . .

At this point Morgan gave up and turned to the next student, missing the vital subtext—how Fannie's goal of becoming a teacher was enmeshed in her strong sense of connection to her people, how her belief that one needs an education "to get around" in the mainstream was tempered by insight into why some choose a different path. To understand Fannie's stance towards schooling, Morgan needed to grasp that she felt both this commitment *and* this ambivalence; but as was so often the case, Fannie's meager hints went unheeded.

A few weeks into the semester, Morgan labored one morning to move Fannie past her apparent block on a descriptive essay. Fannie said only that she was going to try to describe her grandmother, and Morgan began by asking a series of questions—about her grandmother's voice, her presence, her laugh, whatever came to Fannie's mind. Her questions greeted by long silences, Morgan admitted her gathering frustration: "Are you learnin' anything from me?" she asked. Morgan's voice sounded cordial and even a bit playful, but she was clearly concerned that Fannie didn't seem to be meeting her halfway. In the weeks that followed, Morgan would repeatedly adjust her approach, continually searching for a way to break through, "to spark something," as she often put it.

The first change—to a tougher, more demanding stance—was clearly signaled as the group brainstormed ideas for their next essays. Instead of waiting for Fannie to jump into the discussion, Morgan called upon her: "Ok, your turn in the hot seat," she announced. When Fannie noted that her essay would be about her home in Arizona, Morgan demanded to know "why it would be of possible interest to us." The ensuing exchange shed little light on the subject:

Fannie: Because it's my home!
Morgan: That's not good enough . . . that's telling me nothing.
Fannie: I was raised there.
Morgan: What's so special about it?
Fannie: (exasperated sigh) I don't know what's so special about it . . .
Morgan: So why do you want to write about it, then?

Morgan's final question still unanswered, she eventually gave up and moved to another student. Again, a wealth of valuable information remained tacit; Morgan wouldn't learn for several weeks that Fannie had grown up on a reservation, and she'd understood nothing at all about her profound bond with this other world.

Two months into the semester, Morgan had an opportunity to attend the Conference on College Composition and Communication (CCCC), and it was there that some of her early training crystallized into a more definite plan of action, her early doubts subsumed by a new sense of authoritative expertise. Morgan thought a great deal about her work with Fannie as she attended numerous sessions on peer tutoring and a half-day workshop on collaborative learning. She returned to campus infused with a clear sense of direction: the solution, Morgan had concluded, was to assume an even more low-profile approach, speaking only to ask open-ended questions or to paraphrase Fannie's statements, steadfastly avoiding the temptation to fill silences with her own ideas and asides. As she anticipated her next encounter with Fannie, she couldn't wait to try out this more emphatic version of what had been called—in conference sessions and her earlier training—a "collaborative" or "nondirective" stance.

Still struggling to produce an already past-due essay on "values," Fannie arrived at their first post-CCCC tutorial hour with only preliminary ideas, and nothing in writing. Remembering the advice of Conference participants, Morgan began by trying to nudge her towards a focus, repeatedly denying that she knew more than Fannie about how to approach the piece:

Morgan: What would you say your basic theme is? And sometimes if you keep that in mind, then you can always, you know, keep that as a focus for what you're writing. And the reason I say that is 'cause when you say, "well living happily wasn't . . ."

Fannie: (pause) . . . Well, America was a beautiful country, well, but it isn't beautiful anymore.

Morgan: Um hm. Not as beautiful.

Fannie: So I should just say, America was a beautiful country?

Morgan: Yeah. But I dunno—what do you think your overall theme is, that you're saying?

Fannie: (long pause). . . . I'm really, I'm just talking about America.

Morgan: America? So America as . . . ?

Fannie: (pause) . . . Um . . . (pause)

Morgan: Land of free, uh, land of natural resources? As, um, a place where there's a conflict, I mean, there, if you can narrow that, "America." What is it specifically, and think about what you've written, in the rest. Know what I mean?

Fannie: (pause) . . . The riches of America, or the country? I don't know . . .

Morgan: I think you do. I'm not saying there's any right answer, but I, I'm—for me, the reason I'm saying this, is I see this emerging as, you know, (pause) where you're really having a hard time with dealing with the exploitation that you see, of America, you know, you think that. And you're using two groups to really illustrate, specifically, how two different attitudes toward, um the richness and beauty of America, two different, um, ways people have to approach this land. Does that, does this make any sense? Or am I just putting words in your mouth? I don't want to do that. I mean that's what I see emerge in your paper. But I could be way off base.

Fannie: I think I know what you're trying to say. And I can kind of relate it at times to what I'm trying to say.

Morgan: You know, I mean, this is like the theme I'm picking up . . . (pause) I think you know, you've got some real, you know, environmental issues here. I think you're a closet environmentalist here. Which are real true, know what I mean? (pause) And when you talk about pollution, and waste, and, um, those types of things. So I mean, if you're looking at a theme of your paper, what could you pick out, of something of your underlying theme.

Fannie: (pause) . . . The resources, I guess?

Morgan: Well I mean, I don't want you to say, I want you to say, don't say "I guess," is that what you're talkin' about?

Fannie: Yeah.

Morgan: "Yeah?" I mean, it's your paper.

> *Fannie:* I know, I want to talk about the land . . .
> *Morgan:* Ok. So you want to talk about the land, and the beauty of the land . . .
> *Fannie:* Um hm.
> *Morgan:* . . . and then, um, and then also your topic for your, um, to spark your paper . . . what values, and morals, right? That's where you based off to write about America, and the land, you know. Maybe you can write some of these things down, as we're talking, as focusing things, you know. So you want to talk about the land, and then it's like, what do you want to say about the land?

What *did* Fannie "want to say about the land"? Whatever it was, one begins to wonder if it was perhaps lost in her tutor's inadvertent appropriation of these meanings—this despite Morgan's ostensible effort to simply elicit and reflect Fannie's thoughts. While Fannie may well have been struggling to articulate meanings which eluded clear expression in English, as Morgan worked to move her towards greater specificity, it became apparent that she was assuming the paper would express commonplace environmental concerns:

> *Fannie:* I'll say, the country was, um, (pause), more like, I can't say perfect, I mean was, the tree was green, you know, I mean, um, it was clean. (long pause) I can't find the words for it.
> *Morgan:* In a natural state? Um, un-, polluted, um, untouched, um, let me think, tryin' to get a . . .
> *Fannie:* I mean everybody, I mean the Indians too, they didn't wear that (pointing to Morgan's clothes), they only wore buffalo clothing, you know for clothing, they didn't wear like . . . these, you know, cotton, and all that, they were so . . .
> *Morgan:* Naturalistic.
> *Fannie:* Yeah. "Naturalistic," I don't know if I'm gonna use that word . . . I wanna say, I wanna give a picture of the way the land was, before, you know what I'm, what I'm tryin' to say?

The Navajos' connection to the land is legendary—a spiritual nexus, many would maintain, that goes far beyond mainstream notions of what it means to be concerned about the environment. However, later in this session, Morgan observed that Fannie was writing about concerns that worry lots of people—citing recent publicity about the greenhouse effect, the hole in the ozone layer, and the growing interest in recycling. She then brought the session to a close by paraphrasing what she saw as the meat of the discussion and asking, "Is that something that you were tryin' to say, too?" Fannie replied, "Probably. I mean, I can't find the words for it, but you're finding the words for me."

Morgan's rejoinder had been, "I'm just sparkin', I'm just sparkin' what you already have there, what you're sayin'. I mean I'm tryin' to tell you what I hear you sayin'."

Morgan laughed as, in an end-of-term interview, she listened again to Fannie's final comment: "I didn't *want* to find the words for her," she mused; "I wanted to show her how she could find 'em for herself." Still, she admitted, the directive impulse had been hard to resist: "I wanted to just give her ideas," Morgan observed, adding that although Fannie had some good things to say, "I wanted her to be able to articulate her ideas on a little higher level."

Although it was obvious to Morgan that the ideas in Fannie's paper were of "deep-seated emotional concern," she also saw her as stuck in arid generalities: "'I don't know, it's just such a beautiful country,'" Morgan echoed as she reviewed the audiotape. While Morgan emphasized that she "didn't wanna write the paper for her," she allowed that "it's difficult — it's really hard to want to take the bull by the horns and say, 'don't you see it this way?'" On the one hand, Morgan noted that she'd often asked Fannie what she was getting out of a session, "'cause sometimes I'll think I'm getting through and I'm explaining something really good, and then they won't catch it"; on the other hand, Morgan emphasized again and again that she didn't want to "give away" her own thoughts.

Although Morgan often did an almost heroic job of waiting out Fannie's lingering silences and deflecting appeals to her authority, she never really surrendered control; somehow, the message always came across that Morgan knew more than Fannie about the ideas at hand, and that if she could, she would simply turn over pre-packaged understandings. While her frustration was certainly understandable, I often had the sense that Morgan was insufficiently curious about Fannie's thoughts — insufficiently curious about how Fannie's understandings might have differed from her own, about how they had been shaped by Fannie's background and cultural orientation, or about what she stood to learn from them.

When asked about Fannie's block, a weary Morgan wrote it off to her cultural background:

> You know, I would have to say it's cultural; I'd have to say it's her you know, Native American background and growing up on a reservation . . . maybe . . . she's more sensitive to male-female roles, and the female role being quiet.

On a number of occasions Morgan had speculated that Navajo women are taught to be subservient, a perception that contrasted rather strikingly with Fannie's assertion that she wasn't at all shy or quiet back home.[2] Hoping to challenge Morgan's accustomed view of Fannie as bashful and retiring, in a final interview I played back one of their sessions from the week that a group of Navajo students were visiting the campus. Fannie was uncharacteristically vocal and even aggressive that morning, talking in a loud voice, repeatedly seizing and holding the floor:

Fannie: You know what my essay's on? Different environments. Um, I'm talking, I'm not gonna talk about my relationship between my brothers, it's so boring, so I'm just gonna talk about both being raised, like my youngest brother being raised on the reservation, and the other being raised over here, and they both have very different, um, um, (Morgan starts to say something, but Fannie cuts her off and continues) characteristics or somethin' like that. You know, like their personalities, you know.

Morgan: Um. That's good. (Morgan starts to say something more, but Fannie keeps going.)

Fannie: It's funny, I'm cutting, I was totally mean to my brother here. (Morgan laughs.) Because, I called, I said that he's a wimp, you know, and my brother, my little brother's being raised on the reservation, is like, is like taught to be a man, he's brave and all that.

Luis: (a student in the group) That's being a man?!

Fannie: And . . .

Luis: That's not being a man, I don't find.

Fannie: (her voice raised) I'm sorry — but that's how I wrote, Ok?! That's your opinion, I mean, and it's . . .

Luis: I think a man is sensitive, caring, and lov —

Fannie: (cutting him off) No, no . . .

Luis: . . . and able to express his feelings. I don't think that if you can go kill someone, that makes you a man.

Fannie: I mean . . .

Luis: That's just my opinion (gets up and walks away for a moment).

Fannie: (watching Luis wander off) Dickhead.

Morgan listened with a widening smile to the rest of this session, obviously pleased with Fannie's sometimes combative manner and unflagging insistence that attention be directed back to her. "Ha! Fannie's so much more forceful," Morgan exclaimed, "and just more in control of what she wants, and what she needs." When asked what she thought might have accounted for this temporary change, Morgan sidestepped the influence of the visiting students:

> I would love to think I made her feel safe that way. And that I really um, showed her that she had, you know, by my interactions with her, that she really had every right to be strong-willed and forceful and have her opinions and you know, say what she felt that she needed to say, and that she didn't have to be quiet, you know. People always tell me that I influence people that way. You know? (laughs). "You've been hangin' around with Morgan too much!"

Hungry for feedback that she'd influenced Fannie in a positive way, Morgan grasped this possible evidence with obvious pleasure. Fannie was not a student who offered many positive signals, and it was perhaps essential to Morgan's professional self-esteem that she find them wherever she could. In this credit-taking there was, however, a larger irony: if only she'd been encouraged to push a little farther in her own thinking, perhaps she would have found herself assisting more often in such moments of blossoming.

Conclusion: Students as Teachers, Teachers as Students

When Morgan returned from the CCCC with a vision of "collaboration" that cast it as a set of techniques rather than a new way to think about teaching and learning, the insights of panelists and workshop leaders devolved into a fossilized creed, a shield against more fundamental concerns. Morgan had somehow missed the importance of continually adjusting her approach in the light of the understandings students make available, of allowing their feedback to shape her reflections upon her own role. At semester's end, she still didn't know that Fannie was a nonnative speaker of English; she didn't know the dimensions of Fannie's inexperience with academic writing, nor did she know the reasons behind Fannie's formidable block.

Even as Morgan labored to promote "collaborative" moments—making an ostensible effort to "talk less," to "sit back more," to enact an instructional mode that would seem more culturally appropriate—Fannie remembered a lifetime of classroom misadventure, and hung back, reluctant. Morgan needed to know something about this history, but she also needed to understand that much else was fluid and alive, that a revised sense of self was emerging from the dynamic interaction of Fannie's past and present. Emboldened by a few treasured days in the company of fellow Navajos, Fannie had momentarily stepped into a new stance, one that departed markedly from her accustomed behavior on reservation and campus alike; but if her confidence recalled an earlier self, her playful combativeness was, as Fannie observed in listening to the tape, a new and still-strange manifestation of something also oddly familiar, something left over from long ago.

Rather than frequent urgings to "talk less," perhaps what Morgan most needed was advice to *listen more*—for the clues students like Fannie would provide, for those moments when she might best shed her teacherly persona and become once again a learner. More than specific instructional strategies, Morgan needed the conceptual grounding that would allow her to understand that authentically collaborative learning is predicated upon fine-grained insight into individual students—of the nature of their Vygotskian "zones of proximal development," and, by association, of the sorts of instructional "scaffolding" most appropriate to their changing needs (Bruner; Applebee and Langer). So, too, did Morgan need to be encouraged toward the yet-elusive understanding that such learning is never unilateral, inevitably entailing a reciprocal influence, reciprocal advances in understanding (Dyson). As she struggled to come to terms with her own ethnic ambivalence, to defend herself against a vociferous chorus proclaiming her "not black enough," Morgan had reason to take heart in Fannie's dramatic and rather trying process of transition. Had she thought to ask, Morgan would no doubt have been fascinated by Fannie's descriptions of this other cultural and linguistic context, with its very different perspectives on education in particular and the world in general (John; Locust). Most of all, perhaps, she would have been interested to know that Fannie was learning to inhabit both arenas, and in so doing, enacting a negotiation of admirable complexity—a negotiation different in degree, perhaps, but certainly not in kind, from Morgan's own.

Having tutored only one semester previously, Morgan was understandably eager to abandon her lingering doubts about her effectiveness, eager for a surefooted sense that she was providing something worthwhile. Her idealism and good intentions were everywhere apparent—in her lengthy meditations on her work, in her eager enthusiasm at the CCCC, in her persistent efforts to try out new approaches, and in the reassurance she extended to me when I confessed that I'd be writing some fairly negative things about her vexed attempts to reach Fannie. Morgan had been offered relatively little by way of preparation and support: beyond a sprinkling of workshops and an occasional alliance with more experienced tutors, she was left largely on her own—alone with the substantial challenges and opportunities that students like Fannie presented, alone to deal with her frustration and occasional feelings of failure as best she could. Like all beginning educators, Morgan needed abundant support, instruction, and modeling if she were to learn to reflect critically upon her work, to question her assumptions about students like Fannie, to allow herself, even at this fledgling stage in her career, to become a reflective and therefore vulnerable practitioner. That is not to suggest that Morgan should have pried into hidden corners of Fannie's past, insisting that she reveal information about her background before she felt ready to do so; only that Morgan be respectfully curious, ever attentive to whatever clues Fannie might have been willing to offer, ever poised to revise old understandings in the light of fresh evidence.

Those of us who work with linguistic minority students—and that's fast becoming us all—must appreciate the evolving dimensions of our task, realizing that we have to reach further than ever if we're to do our jobs well. Regardless of our crowded schedules and shrinking budgets, we must also think realistically about the sorts of guidance new tutors and teachers need if they are to confront these rigors effectively, guiding them towards practical strategies informed by understandings from theory and research, and offering compelling reminders of the need to monitor one's ethnocentric biases and faulty assumptions. Most of all, we must serve as models of reflective practice—perennially inquisitive and self-critical, even as we find occasion both to bless and curse the discovery that becoming students of students means becoming students of ourselves as well.

Notes

¹ "Fannie" was the actual name of this student's maternal grandmother. We decided to use it as her pseudonym to honor this lasting influence.

² Morgan's assumption is also contradicted by published accounts of life among the Navajo, which from early on have emphasized the prestige and power of female members of the tribe. Gladys Reichard, an anthropologist who lived among the Navajos in the 1920s, reported that "the Navajo woman enjoys great economic and social prestige as the head of the house and clan and as the manager of economic affairs, and she is not excluded from religious ritual or from attaining political honors" (55). Navajo women often own substantial property, and children retain the surname of the matrilineal clan; the status accorded women is further reflected in the depictions of female deities in Navajo myths (Terrell 57, 255).

Acknowledgments

Special thanks to Sarah Warshauer Freedman for encouragement and sage advice throughout this project. Thanks also to Don McQuade, Guadalupe Valdés, and the members of my fall 1991 writing research class at The University of Iowa. This work was supported by a grant from the NCTE Research Foundation.

Works Cited

Applebee, Arthur, and Judith Langer. "Reading and Writing Instruction: Toward a Theory of Teaching and Learning." *Review of Research in Education*. Vol. 13. Ed. E. Z. Rothkopf. Washington, DC: American Educational Research Association, 1986. Print.

Bakhtin, Mikhail Mikhailovich. *The Dialogic Imagination: Four Essays by M. M. Bakhtin*. Ed. Michael Holquist. Trans. Caryl Emerson and Michael Holquist. Austin: U of Texas P, 1981. Print.

Bruner, Jerome. "The Role of Dialogue in Language Acquisition." *The Child's Conception of Language*. Ed. A. Sinclair. New York: Springer-Verlag, 1978. Print.

Cintron, Ralph. "Reading and Writing Graffiti: A Reading." *The Quarterly Newsletter of the Laboratory of Comparative Human Cognition* 13 (1991): 21–24. Print.

DiPardo, Anne. "Acquiring 'A Kind of Passport': The Teaching and Learning of Academic Discourse in Basic Writing Tutorials." Diss. UC Berkeley, 1991. Print.

---. *'A Kind of Passport': A Basic Writing Adjunct Program and the Challenge of Student Diversity*. Urbana: NCTE, 1993. Print.

Dorris, Michael. *A Yellow Raft in Blue Water*. New York: Holt, 1987. Print.

Dyson, Anne. "Weaving Possibilities: Rethinking Metaphors for Early Literacy Development." *The Reading Teacher* 44 (1990): 202–13. Print.

Fischer, Michael. "Ethnicity and the Postmodern Arts of Memory." *Writing Culture: The Poetics and Politics of Ethnography*. Ed. J. Clifford and G. E. Marcus. Berkeley: U of California P, 1986. Print.

Hawkins, Thom. "Intimacy and Audience: The Relationship between Revision and the Social Dimension of Peer Tutoring." *College English* 42 (1980): 64–68. Print.

Hull, Glynda, and Mike Rose. "Rethinking Remediation: Toward a Social-Cognitive Understanding of Problematic Reading and Writing." *Written Communication* 6 (1989): 139–54. Print.

---. "This Wooden Shack: The Logic of an Unconventional Reading." *College Composition and Communication* 41 (1990): 287–98. Print.

John, Vera P. "Styles of Learning—Styles of Teaching: Reflections on the Education of Navajo Children." *Functions of Language in the Classroom*. Ed. Courtney B. Cazden and Vera P. John. 1972. Prospect Heights: Waveland, 1985. Print.

Locust, Carol. "Wounding the Spirit: Discrimination and Traditional American Indian Belief Systems." *Harvard Educational Review* 58 (1988): 315–30. Print.

Philips, Susan U. "Participant Structures and Communicative Competence: Warm Springs Children in Community and Classroom." *Functions of Language in the Classroom*. Ed. Courtney B. Cazden and Vera P. John. 1972. Prospect Heights: Waveland, 1985. Print.

Reichard, Gladys. *Social Life of the Navajo Indians*. 1928. New York: Columbia UP, 1969. Print.

Shaughnessy, Mina. "Diving In: An Introduction to Basic Writing." *College Composition and Communication* 27 (1976): 234–39. Print.

Terrell, John Upton. *The Navajo: The Past and Present of a Great People*. 1970. New York: Perennial, 1972. Print.

Valdés, Guadalupe. *Identifying Priorities in the Study of the Writing of Hispanic Background Students*. Grant. No. OERI-G-008690004. Washington, DC: Office of Educational Research and Improvement, 1989. Print.

---. *Language Issues in Writing: The Problem of Compartmentalization of Interest Areas Within CCCC*. Paper presented at the Conference on College Composition and Communication. 21–23 March, 1991. Print.

Vygotsky, Lev. *Mind in Society*. Cambridge, MA: Harvard UP, 1978. Print.

Learning Disabilities and the Writing Center
Julie Neff
UNIVERSITY OF PUGET SOUND

In order to assist students with learning disabilities, writing center tutors need to understand the challenges these students face in writing academic papers. As Julie Neff points out in her article, students with learning disabilities often score above average on intelligence tests and do excellent work in some courses, but they may not perform well in courses that emphasize particular skills, such as math, reading, or writing. Students with learning disabilities may amass a wealth of specific knowledge about a discipline but have trouble accessing that knowledge without assistance. Such students may need help brainstorming about topics, with the tutor asking probing questions and writing down the students' answers. Others may have difficulty at the strategic level. Because of the variety of learning disabilities, Neff suggests, tutors must remain open-minded and modify tutoring techniques to meet individual student writers' specific needs. This essay, which first appeared in NCTE's 1994 collection Intersections: Theory-Practice in the Writing Center, *provides a place for tutors to start building an understanding of students with learning disabilities.*

Since September 1984, when Stephen North's now famous article, "The Idea of a Writing Center" appeared in *College English,* a picture of the writing conference has developed: the writer and the writing advisor sit side by side, the writer holding the pencil, the writing advisor asking probing questions about the development of the topic; or the student types text into a computer as the writing advisor fires questions designed to help the student think through the writing problem; or, in a revising session, the advisor points to a word or phrase that seems to be "wrong" for this particular paragraph as the student jots notes so she can later correct the text. In these conferences, the writing advisor tells the student to check punctuation and spelling and gives the student a handout to help with the process. After all, the writing center is not a "fix-it" shop for student papers; it is a place for writer to meet reader in order to receive a thoughtful response.

Behind these pictures of writing center conferences lie some basic assumptions: students can improve their ability to invent, organize, draft, revise, and edit based on the responses of a thoughtful reader. Even though the conference is in many ways collaborative, most of the responsibility for composing and transcribing is placed on the student writer. Recent theory and pedagogy in rhetoric and composition support these pictures of the collaborative writing conference, e.g., Bruffee, Harris, Ede, and Lunsford.

But one group of students does not and cannot fit into this pedagogical picture: students with learning disabilities. Though their particular disabilities vary, these students need a different, more specific kind of collaboration than the average student who walks through the doors of the writing center.

What Is a Learning Disability?

Although there is still some disagreement about the precise definition, learning disabilities are generally a varied group of disorders that are intrinsic to the individual.

The Learning Disabilities Act of 1968, which has only changed in small ways since it was drafted, defines a learning disability as "a disorder in one or more of the basic psychological processes involved in understanding or in using spoken or written languages." Individuals with learning disabilities are likely to experience trouble with "listening, thinking, talking, reading, writing, spelling, or arithmetic." Learning problems that are primarily due to a physical condition, like visual or hearing impairment, retardation, emotional dysfunction, or a disadvantaged situation, are not considered to result from learning disabilities. While these other problems sometimes accompany a learning disability, they are not the cause or the result of the disability. Nor are learning disabilities the result of social or economic conditions. People who have learning disabilities are born with them, or they have acquired them through a severe illness or accident, and the disability will continue to affect them over their lifetimes. Although many people overcome their learning disabilities, they do so by learning coping strategies and alternate routes for solving problems. People with learning disabilities cannot be "cured." However, with help, those with learning disabilities can learn to use their strengths to compensate for their weaknesses.

A learning disability is the result of a malfunction in the system in one or more areas. We cannot look into the brain and see the malfunction, but we can see the results in a student's performance on a discrete task. The Woodcock-Johnson Test of Cognitive Ability, one of the most widely used tests for measuring learning disabilities, uncovers discrepancies between capacity and performance. Although the requirements differ from state to state, two standard deviations between potential and performance on the Woodcock-Johnson test (or similar tests such as the WAIS-R, TOWL, or WRAT) suggest that a student is learning disabled, as does an extreme scatter of subtest scores.

Some learning disabilities are truly debilitating in that the individual is unable to cope with or overcome the problems. However, many people with learning disabilities are able to function at the highest levels in one area while having difficulty in another. In fact, many people who are learning disabled in one area are gifted in another. Dyslexic and slow to read, Albert Einstein was learning disabled, as was Thomas Edison (Lovitt 1989, 5). Although these are two of the most well-known cases, they are not exceptional ones. According to specialists at a learning disabilities clinic, Another Door to Learning, one successful businessman claimed his learning disability has contributed to his success because it allowed him to view problems from a different perspective. Often learning-disabled students who come to college score in the above-average range of standard IQ tests and have finely honed skills for compensating for and adapting to their particular disability.

What Do We Know about the Brain?

While no one yet knows the precise causes of a learning disability, the materials drafted by the National Joint Committee on Learning Disabilities presume that the disability, which manifests itself in problems with the acquisition and use of listening, speaking, reading, writing, reasoning, mathematical or spatial skills, grows out of some sort of brain dysfunction.

Although researchers know much more now than they did a decade ago, the debate over just how the brain works continues. Some scientists believe that the brain is bicameral, with the left side responsible for language and reason, and the right side responsible for nonverbal, intuitive activities—the mystical if you will (Bergland 1985, 1). Others believe that the bicameral model over-simplifies the workings of the brain and is more misleading than it is useful.[1]

Richard Bergland (1985) explains that in the last several years a new "wet model" of the brain has emerged, one that is based on the theory that the brain runs on hormones. The idea that the brain is a gland run by hormones has resulted in a new, burgeoning field of medicine known as neuroendocrinology which gives credence to the idea that the learning disability has a physiological basis.

Meantime, over the past decade, cognitive psychology has moved away from the Platonic idea that human rationality grows out of pure intelligence. Instead, researchers are seeing the brain as "a knowledge medium," a storehouse for great quantities of knowledge about the world. This view of the brain represents a paradigm shift from the Platonic view, which asserts that only by reasoning with formal rules we can come to general understanding: if worldly knowledge is more important than pure reason, we have a model of human rationality that relies on information in the brain and vast associative connections that allow the human mind to turn a fragment of information into a considerable amount of knowledge. Human cognition consists not of pure reason but is instead composed of the information stored in the brain and the brain's ability to connect those pieces of information. Worldly knowledge, according to Jeremy Campbell (1989), has become far more important than pure logic.

How Does This Theory Help Us Understand a Learning Disability?

The idea of the brain as a knowledge machine, and as an organ run by hormones, can help us understand a learning disability. The brain processes enormous amounts of information. The brains of learning-disabled persons have these same properties; but often learning-disabled persons have trouble accessing and retrieving the information, and occasionally gathering and storing it. This is not because they are unintelligent but because of a physiological problem. Judy Schwartz, author of the book *Another Door to Learning,* says that individuals not only have to have basic information, they have to know they have it. The substance and assumptions are inside the learning-disabled person's brain, but he or she may not know the information is there. To access what is known, he or she must consciously learn how to tap the information through self-cuing or other methods. In these circumstances, the writing center can be helpful.

Misconceptions about Learning Disabilities

Although brain theory and research support the idea that a learning disability has a physiological basis, many people, including educators, continue to have a number of misconceptions about people with learning disabilities. Some see the learning-disabled students as "special education" students who are now being mainstreamed. Some see them as manipulative individuals looking for an excuse for bad spelling and punctuation. Some see "learning disability" as a euphemism for "retarded." Others claim that learning disabilities do not actually exist.[2]

Since a learning disability has a physiological basis and is not due to low intelligence, social situations, or economic conditions, a learning disability is not unlike other kinds of disabilities that have a physiological basis. Renee must use a wheelchair because she was born with an imperfect spine. This defect, not caused by low intelligence, social situation, or economic factors, is a physiological problem that Renee overcomes by taking a slightly different route to accomplish her goals. Renee can reach the second floor, but she won't use the stairs; she'll use the elevator. Similarly, the learning-disabled student can master the material; but she may need to write the exam on a computer, and she may also need extra time to access the information she has.

A Case Study

Although learning disabilities vary widely, it may be easier to understand how a learning disability affects an individual by looking at a specific student with a specific disability. When Barb was in middle school, her mother asked her to take a roast from the refrigerator and put it in the oven at 350 degrees so it would be ready when she got home from work. The roast was in the baking dish, seasoned, and covered with plastic wrap. At the appropriate time, Barb did exactly as she was asked. The roast was done perfectly when her mother came home, but it was coated with melted plastic.

Why hadn't Barb removed the plastic? She had taken cooking in school and often baked cakes and cookies at home. Even though she has 20/20 vision, Barb couldn't comprehend the plastic. Because the plastic exists in space, Barb's spatial problems kept her from seeing it until her mother tied it to language by saying, "This roast is covered with melted plastic." Barb replied, "I'm sorry. I didn't notice it."

Barb has a disability that affects her ability to access and create reliable images and thus to understand things spatially. She understands and gains access to her world and spatial relationships by building and shaping images with language, which in turn gives her access to images.

Barb needed written or oral directions to remove the plastic. As soon as she had words, Barb could grasp the situation and accomplish the task. According to Carol Stockdale of Another Door to Learning, the image was recorded, but Barb only had access to it through language. Barb often said, "Well, I know that," but, in fact, she did not know it consciously until she had the language to refine the image.

In middle school, Barb was placed in an English class that taught grammar as a discrete subject: two weeks for literature, two weeks for grammar. Barb's spoken English was excellent; her speech included sophisticated syntax and vocabulary, and she was most successful with the reading and discussion of the literature. But the spatial quality of the grammar drills confounded Barb. Because she failed to grasp the spatial task of retrieving the mechanics of written English, spatial labels like "adverb" meant nothing to her. While she could use an adverb correctly in spoken and written English, she could not "see" the term "adverb" any more than she could see the plastic wrap.

When Barb started high school, her classes were content rich; they stressed worldly knowledge. Although she continued to have difficulty with math and chemistry, she found that her writing and especially the mechanics improved as she took courses in history, literature, and art and music history. In these courses, she was learning the language that would allow her to store and retrieve information. The more information she had the better she became at making connections, and these connections were as apparent in the classroom as in the kitchen.

Because Barb was coping well with her reading and writing in her high school classes, she did not anticipate that "driving class" would be a problem. But as Barb sat behind the wheel of the family sedan to have a practice session with her mother, her mother realized that learning to drive, a spatial task, would be much more difficult than learning art history.

Barb edged the car toward the pavement from the gravel shoulder of the road. "Turn the car a little to the left, Barb, and as you pick up speed, ease onto the pavement," her mother said patiently. Barb eased the car onto the grey cement at about 20 mph. But soon she was back on the gravel, and then a minute later she had drifted to the left side of the road. Many novice drivers drift, but Barb remained unaware of both the drift and resulting position. "Barb, you're driving on the wrong side of the road! Do you realize what could have happened?!" Barb's mother exclaimed.

"I'm sorry," Barb replied calmly; "I didn't notice." And indeed she did not notice, even though she saw. Barb had not yet used language which "uncovered" the images before her eyes to build and access the images that would allow her to drive safely.

Though she had never thought much about it before, Barb's mother realized that driving is in many ways a spatial task. According to Jeremy Campbell's theories, Barb's brain was capable of storing and connecting great amounts of information; her learning disability kept her from accessing it.

Carol Stockdale, a learning-disabilities specialist who had worked with Barb, suggested several strategies for conquering the problem. Barb walked around the car, touching it and measuring it against herself to see how big it was, all the time having a conversation with herself that translated the spatial into verbal dimensions. She went back to the country road near her home to look at the lines that marked the road and to touch the road and the gravel on the shoulder of the road and to say, "These are the lines that mark the lane, and these are the rocks that mark the side where I do not want to drive." As she found her way to all of her usual spots—the store, the school, the hardware store—she developed an internal conversation: "Turn right at the Exxon sign; turn left at the blue house on the corner."

Navigating through Space

And so Barb learned to use verbal clues to navigate through space. Understanding how to learn to drive gave Barb insight into conquering all kinds of spatial problems. Although she continued to have difficulty with mathematics and foreign language in high school, her ability to write academic papers about topics in her language-based academic courses—history, literature, and art history—continued to improve.

When Barb went to college, she needed help with kinds of structures that were new to her, and she needed specific models to understand the shapes of analytical papers particular to certain courses. She also needed these models translated into language. For Barb, looking at something was not seeing it, at least not until she had shaped and refined the image with language.

More and more confident of her ability to know the world through language, Barb was increasingly comfortable with difficult ideas, for instance, in her college philosophy class: "Plato uses serval [sic] arguments to prove the existence of the forms: the first argument occurs in the Meno when Socrates shows that learning is merely a recollection of previous knowledge of forms by questioning a slave boy about the Pythagorean theorem." Despite the misplaced letter in the word "several," and the misplaced first phrase, the sentence involves sophisticated content communicated in an equally sophisticated sentence structure. This sentence is not the work of a basic writer or a person unable to deal with the intellectual challenges of higher education. Still, because of her difficulty accessing spatial information, Barb needed help with organization, mechanics, and new kinds of writing tasks.[3]

The Role of the Writing Center

Although learning-disabled students come to the writing center with a variety of special needs, they have one thing in common: they need more specific help than other students.

Often writing center directors do not know what kind of a learning disability the student has, but because the spatial systems and language systems overlap and act reciprocally, students who are dyslexic and students who are spatially impaired may demonstrate many of the same problems with spelling, grammar, development, and organization.[4] Therefore, they will need similar kinds of assistance.

By changing the picture of the writing conference, the writing center director can ensure that learning-disabled students, no matter what the disability, are being appropriately accommodated. The writing advisors still need to be collaborators, but they also may need to help the students retrieve information and shape an image of the product. They may be called upon to demonstrate organization or to model a thesis sentence when the students cannot imagine what one might look like. The advisors may have to help the students call up detail in ways that would be inappropriate for the average learner. They may need to help with the physical production of texts. And they may need to help with correcting mechanics when the papers are in their final stages.

Paradoxically, and at the same time, the writing advisor must help the students be independent through self-cuing; creating a dependent atmosphere does not foster the students' ability to cope, does not develop the students' self-esteem, and does not help the students become better writers. The writing advisor must treat learning disabled persons as the intelligent, resourceful persons they are. Conferences without respect and understanding are seldom successful.

Prewriting

Many of the discovery techniques commonly used in the composition class and in the writing center may not be productive for students with learning disabilities because, though these students may have the information, they may have no way to access it. The picture of the eager student freewriting to discover ideas needs to be amended when one works with learning-disabled students. Freewriting is almost impossible for most because they do not know, and can't imagine, what to write. Students with language retrieval problems may not be able to call up any words at all to put on the paper. This holds true for students with either spatial impairments or language difficulties.

For learning-disabled students, freewriting leads from one generalization to another or from one specific to another. Because they do not see the relationship between the specific and the general, without intervention they are locked in a non-productive cycle, unable to succeed unless it is by accident. And if they do succeed by accident, they do not understand their success. According to Carol Stockdale at Another Door to Learning, many learning disabled students have no way of intentionally creating order.

Freewriting is also frustrating for persons who are learning disabled because it requires them to write without knowing where they are going. Just as Barb had trouble understanding the road, other learning-disabled students need to know where they are going so they will know when they get there. Unable to recognize what is relevant and what is not, they find the freewriting an exercise in futility, while other students may find it a way to create knowledge.

In the writing center, directed conversation can take the place of freewriting. Because these students have trouble accessing what they know, they are unlikely to realize they know great amounts of information. Here, the writing advisor plays an important role. Nowhere else on most campuses can writers find an individual who will ask the leading question that can unlock trapped information.

In some cases, the writing advisor may need to ask students like Barb specific, seemingly obvious questions to help them unlock the ideas in their minds and then take notes for them as they generate ideas for their papers. In essence the writing advisor is helping them see the plastic wrap.

Here is an example of a writing conference that respects the student's intelligence and at the same time helps him gain access to what he knows, and helps him find an organizational pattern for it.

Writing Advisor: Hi David, how are you? Have a seat.
David: Not good. I have another paper to write for my Intro to Fiction class.
Writing Advisor: Hmmm, you did well on your last paper, didn't you?

David:	Yes, but this time I don't have anything to write about.
Writing Advisor:	Now just think back to that first paper. As I recall, you didn't have a topic for that one either the first time we talked.
David:	I guess you're right, but this time I really don't know what to write about.

The writing advisor knows that David has a learning disability. Understanding the brain as Jeremy Campbell explains it, as the great storehouse of knowledge, she suspects that David knows a great deal about the potential topic; she knows she will need to help David gain access to the tremendous information he does have.

Writing Advisor:	What is the assignment?
David:	To write a 3–4 page paper about *The Great Gatsby*.
Writing Advisor:	David, I know you're worried about this paper, but I also know from the last paper we talked about how smart you are and how much you actually know. So let's just chat for a few minutes about the book without worrying about the paper.

The writing advisor turns her chair toward David and takes off her glasses. She realizes that despite David's high scores on standard I.Q. tests and good study habits many of his teachers have considered him "slow," careless, or lazy. She wants to be sure she treats him as the intelligent person he is. She begins with the obvious questions that will help him focus on the book and what he knows.

Writing Advisor:	Who wrote *The Great Gatsby*?
David:	F. Scott Fitzgerald. He was married to Zelda. And he also wrote *Tender Is the Night*. Some people think he stole his stories from Zelda's journals. Don't you think that's right?
Writing Advisor:	I do think it's "right." I did know she had a big influence on him. . . .
David:	I mean he was drunk a lot and Zelda was the one who was writing all this stuff about their life. It's not fair.
Writing Advisor:	I agree. This whole idea of fairness . . . was there anything in *Gatsby* that wasn't fair?
David:	Yes, I don't think Tom was fair in the way he treated Daisy. He had an affair and he lied to her. Gatsby wasn't all that good either. He made his money illegally.
Writing Advisor:	Do you think that was fair?

David:	I guess not, at least not for the people he took advantage of.
Writing Advisor:	I wonder if a word like "honesty" or "integrity" might help get at what we're talking about.
David:	"Integrity," that's it.

When the writing advisor saw David lean forward, his eyes bright, she knew it was time to write something down. She took out a piece of paper and a pencil, wrote "integrity" in the middle of the page and showed it to David. She continues to take notes so that David can work at connecting the information without worrying about the physical production of text.

Writing Advisor:	Tell me who has it and who doesn't.
David:	Tom doesn't and Gatsby doesn't. [The writing advisor wrote "Tom" on the left side of the page and "Gatsby" under it and connected each word to "integrity" with a line.]
Writing Advisor:	Tell me why you don't think they have integrity.

David recounted example after example and the tutor noted each one under the appropriate name. As he talked, David included other characters and decided whether each had integrity or not and gave appropriate examples. In each case the tutor noted the information David produced and drew lines around similar information.

Writing Advisor:	This is going to be a wonderful paper. Can you see the development taking shape? Look at the connections you've made.
David:	Yes, but I'm not sure how to start the introduction.
Writing Advisor:	Well, what kinds of things will your reader need to know in order to follow you through the paper?

By the time David had listed the kinds of things that he would include in the introduction, almost an hour had passed. The writing advisor wanted to conclude the session on a reassuring note, and she wanted David to know that he could teach himself to self-cue.

Writing Advisor:	David, you know so much about your topic, and you have really good ideas. All I did was ask you questions. Eventually you'll be able to ask yourself those same questions. But now, why don't you do some writing, and then we'll have another appointment, if you like, to look at transitions, mechanics, and those sorts of things. It's fun seeing the connections in your mind unfold.

| David: | I think I can write a draft now. Will you be able to help me with spelling later in the week? |
| Writing Advisor: | Sure, I'll see you when the draft is done, and we'll look at all kinds of things. |

Because the act of calling up the words and getting them onto paper is so difficult for some learning-disabled students, the student may be unable to concentrate on the ideas and instead only focuses on the production of text. The writing advisor may need to do the typing or the drafting so the student is free to concentrate on answering the fairly specific, sometimes leading, questions proposed by the writing advisor. The writing advisor will know when to do the typing by asking the student, "Would you like me to record so you can work on generating the words?"

Organization

Even after generating a page or two of material, students may still not be able to distinguish the important information from the supporting detail. Again writing advisors should understand that they must help the student over or around the problem. The advisors will probably say what they think is the most important element; once they say it, the students may be able to agree or disagree even though they cannot invent or articulate the idea on their own. The writing advisors might draw a map of the ideas and support for the student, or color-code the information to help with organization. The writing advisors should always be doing and saying at the same time. With learning-disabled students, just pointing seldom helps.

The writing advisor might need to model a thesis sentence for the student, asking simple questions like "What is your paper about?" "Rice," the student replies. "What about rice?" Students are often delighted and surprised when they come up with the single statement that will set the paper spinning.

The advisor may need to be just as explicit about the paper's development: "What is your first point going to be?" As the student responds, the advisor takes down the information, and then asks, "And what is your second point?" "And your third?" Showing students how to create an overview of the information and then teaching them how to categorize information will help the students manage the spatial qualities of organization.

Simply using a model like the five-paragraph essay to teach organization is unlikely to produce successful writing. Since structure grows out of content, the students may be successful one time with a five-paragraph essay, but when they try to apply the formula the next time, the formula may not work. They may be further hindered by being unable to let go of the formula or image.

A student like Barb may not be able to see paragraph breaks until the writing advisor says, "Notice how long this paragraph is," while at the same time pointing to the too-long paragraph. She may even need to say, "This is a paragraph." But the instant the advisor points it out, Barb will say, "Well, I know that." And after saying so, she does indeed know it.

Proofreading and Editing

Frank Smith (1982) makes the distinction between composition and transcription, between the composing of thought and the mechanics of getting the language down on paper according to certain conventions. Spelling and punctuation need to be done with the students so that they feel part of the process; most importantly, the editing must be specific and hands-on and must involve detailed explanations of what the advisor is doing. The writing advisor cannot expect the students to make the changes based on a rule or principle. The explanation must be specific, and it may need to be written as well as said: "Look at the beginning of this sentence. You have five words before your subject. How about a comma?" Students may agree that something is so, but they may be unable to hold the thought in their minds or recall it later.

Encouraging students to be independent through the use of a spell checker and grammar checker is essential, but the writing advisor may need to sit at the computer with students explaining how it works and its limitations. Telling students to put text through a spell check is seldom enough. The advisor may need to read the paper aloud to the students so they can catch errors: a final proofreading by the writing advisor is also appropriate for the learning-disabled students because these students may not be able to see the mistakes until they are pointed out to them.

Wheelchair-bound students can get to the third floor, but they may not be able to take the stairs. Their only routes are the elevator or the ramp. It's not that students with a learning disability can't get it, it's that they can't get it the same way the normal learner can.

Other Kinds of Organization That Affect Writing

Learning-disabled students sometimes have as much trouble coping with the organization of the writing and research time as they do with the organization of the text. Writing advisors can help by showing the students how to use a study planning sheet that contains small but regular accomplishments, and which will lead to the accomplishment of a larger task. It is not enough to tell students to do it; the writing advisors need to demonstrate the strategy, especially the first time. They should also ask the students to refer to the list on a regular basis; the markers of accomplishment need to be tangible.

Social Interaction

Many, but not all, learning-disabled students have trouble in social situations. A visit to the writing center may be one of these social situations. The student's behavior may be inappropriate: he interrupts another conversation, she stands too close or talks too much. Many people with learning disabilities are unable to "read" the nonverbal behavior of others. So even if the writing advisor frowns or looks away, the inappropriate behavior continues. Being explicit but positive will help the individual change this behavior: "Marty, please stop talking; I have something important to tell you." "Glad to see you, Sara. I'll sit here; you sit across from me; that will be a comfortable distance. I'll be ready to talk to you in a minute."

Despite the need for specific instructions and clear questions, the writing advisor must remain positive and encouraging. Often teachers and others misunderstand learning disabilities and accuse students of being lazy or dumb. As a result, college students with learning disabilities often have low self-esteem and may be defensive or uncertain of their own academic ability. Writing advisors can make a major contribution to a learning-disabled student's success if they are positive, encouraging, and specific about the writing, the revision, and the writing process.

Working with these students in the writing center is sometimes difficult because it means modifying or changing the usual guidelines, and it may mean more and longer appointments, for instance, appointments that last an hour instead of a half hour, and a writing advisor may need to proofread. Writing centers may need to change the rules and policies that govern these sessions and change the training that staff receive. But the students have a right to services, and writing centers have a responsibility to help learning-disabled students succeed.[5] Writing centers have always been places that help students reach their full potential, and this philosophy should extend to students with learning disabilities.

Most learning-disabled students need more support and help rather than less. And writing centers can provide that assistance. For these students, writing center professionals need a new picture of the writing conference that includes the writing advisor's becoming more directly involved in the process and the product. With adequate help and support, students with a learning disability can produce better papers, and they can also become better writers.

Notes

[1] At the October 1991 meeting of the International Conference on Learning Disabilities, the debate over the left brain–right brain model continued in the conference sessions. The debate is interesting in that writing center professionals often use the model to explain parts of the composing process.

[2] The same law that defines a learning disability guarantees the rights of the learning-disabled person. It is just as illegal to discriminate against a learning-disabled person as it is to discriminate against a person of an ethnic minority or a person with a physical disability. Recently a professor at the University of California Berkeley refused to accommodate a student's request for untimed tests. The student filed suit, and the faculty member was required to pay monetary damages to the student. Faculty members and institutions can be held accountable for blatant discrimination. (Heyward).

[3] Barb's is not an unusual case. As the diagnosis of learning disabilities has improved, students can be helped sooner and can be taught compensatory strategies that lead to success in high school as well as in college. In 1978 when statistics on learning disabilities were first

kept, 2.6 percent of all freshmen reported having a disability. In 1988, it was 6 percent. In ten years of record keeping, the number had more than doubled. Still, many experts in the field believe that 6 percent is much too low and the number of learning disabled students is actually between 10 and 20 percent. Many cases have gone undetected.

[4] Because problems with spelling and mechanics are the easiest to recognize and fix, many educators have believed that these are the only problems that learning-disabled students have with writing. But a University of Connecticut study showed that 51 percent of the students had trouble with organization compared to 24 percent who had trouble with proofreading (McGuire, Hall, Litt).

[5] In 1993, the American Disabilities Act (ADA), which makes discrimination against a learning-disabled person illegal, became law.

References

Bergland, R. (1985). *Fabric of mind.* New York, NY: Penguin.

Brinkerhoff, L. (1991, October 11). *Critical issues in LD college programming for students with learning disabilities.* Paper presented at the International Conference on Learning Disabilities, Minneapolis, MN.

Campbell, J. (1989). *The improbable machine.* New York, NY: Simon & Schuster.

Hammill, D. D., Leigh, J. E., McNutt, G., and Larsen, S. C. (1981). A new definition of learning disabilities. *Learning Disability Quarterly, 4*(4), 336–342.

Heyward, L., & Associates. (Ed). (1992). *Association on handicapped student service programs in postsecondary education disability accommodation digest, 1*(2), 6.

Heyward, S. (1991). "Provision of academic accommodations." *Postsecondary LD Network News 12,* 7.

Levy, N. R., & Rosenberg M. S. (1990). Strategies for improving the written expression of students with learning disabilities. *LD Forum, 16*(2), 23–26.

Lipp, J. (1991). Turning problems into opportunities. *Another Door to Learning Newsletter,* 1–3.

Longo, J. (1988). The learning disabled: Challenge to postsecondary institutions. *Journal of Developmental Education, 11*(3), 10–12.

Lovitt, T. (1989). *Introduction to learning disabilities.* Needham Heights, MA: Allyn & Bacon.

McGuire, J. (1989, October 11). *Access and eligibility.* Paper presented at the International Conference on Learning Disabilities. Minneapolis, MN.

McGuire, J., Hall, D., and Litt, A. V. (1991). "A field-based study of the direct service needs of college students with learning disabilities." *Journal of College Student Development 32,* 101–108.

National Clearinghouse on Postsecondary Education for Individuals with Handicaps 8.2 (1989), 4.

Philosophy take-home exam. Smith College, 1991.

"The Rehabilitation Act of 1971." (1977, May 4). *Federal Register,* 93–112.

Schwartz, J. (1991, October 13). Personal interview.

Schwenn, J. (1991, October 12). *Stereotyped football players: Poor students or undiagnosed learning disabilities?* Paper presented at the International Conference on Learning Disabilities, Minneapolis, MN.

Smith, F. (1982). *Writing and the writers.* Hillsdale: Erlbaum.

Stockdale, C. (1991, October 13). Personal interview.

U.S. Congress, 1969. *Children with Specific Learning Disabilities Act of 1969.* Washington, DC: U.S. Government Printing Office.

Woodcock, R., & Johnson, M. B. (1989). *Woodcock-Johnson tests of achievement.* Allen: Teaching Resources.

Queering the Writing Center

Harry Denny _____

ST. JOHN'S UNIVERSITY

Harry Denny urges writing centers to adopt some of the insights and methods of queer theory. As he argues, writing centers that alert student writers to the role language plays in constructing knowledge and social identity can help these writers "gain a modicum of agency" in using language to construct their own knowledge and identity. In this approach, Denny explains, tutors empower a student writer to express ideas that defy, critique, or clash with those held by privileged members of the academic culture, including the tutors themselves. Ideally, by "queering sessions—seeking strategic occasions to subvert conventional dynamics," a tutor and student collaborate in the discovery of creative ways to meet writing assignments without betraying the student's own vision. In this essay, which originally appeared in The Writing Center Journal *in 2005, contemporary writing center and queer theorists share key goals, Denny contends, including their ongoing effort to bring to light the normalizing forces of society and to equip people with different perspectives or identities to resist these forces.*

Writing centers are sites around which folklore circulates. Staff meetings, classrooms, newsletters, and journals are filled with tales of individual and collective actualization, celebrating one-to-one teaching as deeply social, collaborative, and empowering. Legends from the writing center also speak to the tensions inherent in the spaces, reflecting divisions of tutoring as prescriptive versus directive, banking versus dialogic, and peer-driven versus expert-owned. Following their review of writing center theory, history, and practice, Paula Gillespie and Neal Lerner advise. "What is most important is to understand where our practices come from and to unravel the various influences on those practices" (154). Knowing these conditions of possibility makes for more effective tutoring, and this awareness also speaks to a politics about learning and the production of writers. Gillespie and Lerner describe commonplace mindsets about writing centers as garrets for skills-building and testing, as generative spaces for confidence and collaboration, and as critical arenas in which to problem-pose institutional and social discursive practices (147–150). For each domain, the tutorial and the social actors in and surrounding it are implicated in a certain identity politics. In the storehouse writing center, skill-building and knowledge transmission posit the writer as a vessel in need of filling, and identity becomes conferred as a sort of membership card or rite of passage. In the generative writing center, the writer emerges from social interaction, and identity becomes a negotiation of assimilation, separation, and subversion. In the critical/activist writing center, consciousness-raising produces writers aware of the constellation of subject positions and power dynamics cutting through them, and identity becomes a strategic decision grounded in context. Regardless of the roots of writer self-awareness—as expression of inner self, as maturation, or as invocation—the production of identity is central to the mission of writing centers. Producing better writers, to extend Stephen North's aphorism, involves understanding the manufacture and dynamics of identity, a process that involves on-going self-discovery and reconciliation with collective identities and discourse communities. Just as the writing process is individual and recursive, so too is the process of coming to terms with and reinventing one's identity. Writing centers inevitably find themselves at the crossroads of that journey for students, tutors, and the other professionals that inhabit their spaces.

Nevertheless, in stories and theories from the writing center, the bodies attached to those narratives and critical projects often lack interrogation and understanding, in spite of the warm embrace and supportive environment that is cultivated. What does it mean to claim an identity as a writer? When unpacking the sign "writer," what other kinds of markers lurk under its veneer? As tutors and teachers champion a writer-identity, what others are sutured to it? When a writer-identity is nurtured, what other forms of identity get eclipsed? In what ways are writer-identities tied to contexts and spaces? How might they transcend those spaces? How does becoming a writer mesh with the other identities emerging, circulating, and falling away in writing centers? What role do tutors play in these sets of relations, especially as tutors continually construct themselves as well? Composition classrooms and writing centers are spaces where negotiation of academic, social, cultural, and political identities are ubiquitous, yet research has not produced adequate theory and practice to help tutors and writers navigate identity production and its politics. This article seeks to begin conversations that might lead to better awareness of the interplay of identity, discursive practice and composition, most specifically in the writing center.

Alongside the need for talk about identity politics (and perhaps as a consequence of its absence) is the need to include the perspective of lesbian, gay, bisexual, and transgender studies (or what some have come to call "queer theory"). This intellectual work foregrounds identity and the experiences of constructing and assuming codes of self, community and nationality for autonomy and pride. Such attention to the politics of identity and their material consequences dovetails with progressive scholarship from/about writing centers and composition studies, and this article draws out those occasions when queer theory may inform our critical lens on tutorials and the positioning of the writing center. Writing and speaking about homosexuality are activities that produce discomfort, yet these feelings are familiar terrain for people in writing centers. Like queer people, writing center professionals continually confront our marginality: we daily encounter students and faculty alike who approach our spaces with uneasiness. Though some might understand writing centers as "safe harbors" of progressive politics and pedagogy, our spaces are also liminal zones, transitory arenas always both privileged and illegitimate. Writing centers are known as cutting-edge and institutional backwaters; they are celebrated and denounced; they are noisy and silent/ed; they are spaces where much organic, lasting learning happens, but spaces where often no record of achievement or assessment gets granted. Writing centers are places overflowing with structuring binaries: directive/nondirective, editing/tutoring, expert/novice, teacher/student, graduate student/undergraduate, professional/ peer, women/men, "American"/ESL, advanced/basic, faculty/administrator, administrator/secretary, faculty/lecturer, lecturer/teaching assistant, teaching assistant/tutor, white/people of color, black/Asian, latino/black, straight/gay, etc. These binaries and their negotiations of which side is privileged and which is illegitimate are ubiquitous in sessions. Queer theory advances awareness of the presence and multiplicity of these binaries as means for constructing individual and collective existences as well as knowledge of the politics involved in navigating and subverting them.

On one level, this article calls attention to the ways that queer theory can inform what we do in writing centers, but on another level, it cautions against an identity politics that positions any epistemology as offering a totalizing way of knowing. As individual lenses, atomized sensitivities to the dynamics of class, gender, race, and nationality do not correct society's tendency toward myopia, but these partial perspectives do come together to change/challenge the individual's comprehension of the world. For example, one can examine the material consequences of class struggle in most writing centers: we find students whose struggles with academic literacy reflect the effects of under-funded primary and secondary schools or the effect of working-class culture where academic intellectual capital holds little sway. Such claims, while useful, are reductive because more cogent analysis factors in the variety of structuring dynamics and institutions that produce students' identities (as well as everyone else's sense of self). Besides the effects of postindustrial economics, students, tutorials, and writing centers constantly engage the dynamics of patriarchy, racial supremacy, nationalism, and psychological/cognitive development as they work to produce better writing and identity construction.

Sexuality is another lens through which we must view the writing center, but it is an interpretive gaze that has received little attention in writing center theory and practice. This call to queer the writing center is not an appeal to recognize gays in the midst and celebrate us as oracles of some standing. As feminist Donna Haraway would say, we must situate our knowledge in relation to other ways of theorizing, and this article offers queer theory as one among the many critical voices that shape and analyze writing center work. Eve Sedgwick puts the issue another way:

> An understanding of virtually any aspect of modern Western culture must
> be, not merely incomplete, but damaged in its central substance to the degree
> that it does not incorporate a critical analysis of modern homo/heterosexual

definition; and . . . the appropriate place for that critical analysis is to begin from the relatively decentered perspective of modern gay and antihomophobic theory. (1)

By Sedgwick's view, queer theory and its attention to the operation and liminality of binaries in our culture starts with the production and regulation of sexuality. Its symptomatic practices extend out to, though do not necessarily determine, other discursive rituals around gender, race, nationality, and class. As a critical starting point for exploring any aspect of U.S. culture, queer theory analyzes practices that inscribe meaning, making certain bodies and ways of doing visible and marked and others illusory, invisible or unmarked. Like the predication of sexual identities on their oppositions (identity being codependent on what it is not), this article hopes to start a conversation about writing centers engaged in a perpetual tango of identity invoked and differed.

Queer Theory Meets Writing Center Theory: From Liberation Activism to Critical Practice

Queer theory comes out of a history of political struggle and is located at the intersection of sexuality studies and feminist, critical race, social, cultural, and literary theories. In response to AIDS and homophobic activism, the lesbian and gay movement reclaimed the meaning of "queer." This practice was part of a larger history and set of rhetorical moves in which contemporary civil rights and identity movements have long engaged. People of African descent have shifted between signs of self-naming from "negro" to "Afro-American," "black," and "African American," and other people of color have followed similar paths and cycles of recoding. After questioning their own identity and place in society, the women's and feminist movements of the late 1960s and 1970s challenged the popular signifiers of sex and gender. Naturalized expectations of women's roles and status started to give way to a new era of opportunities and challenges. Just as racial minorities and women worked to open up meanings and spaces available to their communities, organization began to happen for lesbians and gay men, eventually culminating in increased visibility and place for diversity of sexual expression and identity. At the peak of a second wave of gay liberation activism in the late 1970s, the AIDS crisis launched an ongoing struggle over knowledge construction that had material consequences for public health and community self-identification. Activism around HIV/AIDS challenged governmental authority to speak for and about people living with the illness themselves or in their community, particularly when its policies had deleterious effects. The complexity of the epidemic provided occasions to question the symbolic meaning of sexual practices and identity, especially as they might aid in education to reduce HIV infection across communities defined by and overlapping sexual, racial and class boundaries. Against the backdrop of that health crisis, the gay community also fought continuing neoconservative and evangelical moves to parlay public anxiety about the epidemic and wider progressive change in the culture as an occasion to roll back the advances of the New Left and its Great Society policies and programs.

This lesbian and gay activism became associated with a loosely networked national social movement known as Queer Nation. Though its political and cultural influence waned during the 1990s, Queer Nation's questioning of sexual morés and practices took up and built on contemporary forms of social criticism and theory. The product of this marriage was queer theory, a school of criticism that has gained widespread visibility in humanities and social science scholarship. Despite its conventional usage as an umbrella term for lesbian, gay, bisexual and transgender (LGBT) studies, queer theory represents a specific set of intellectual and cultural commitments. More precisely, it reads against the grain of dominant codings of language and considers ways in which language and epistemology construct and constrain possibilities for (sexual) identity and their implications for public and private practices. For example, Cindy Patton analyzes governmental and healthcare systems' discursive responses to the HIV pandemic, and she shows how AIDS is used to reinscribe marginalizing codes of sexism, racism, homophobia, and nationalism (*Globalizing Aids; Inventing Aids; Sex and Germs: The Politics of Aids*). Patton argues these clashes over definitions and their manufacture have tangible effects for gay communities, ghettos, and developing countries in terms of access to treatment, drugs, and public engagement of the epidemic. Through dialogue, forced at times, each of the social actors (gay activists, doctors, Pharmaceutical researchers, public health officials) has come to appreciate how the discursive practices around HIV/AIDS had an impact on pedagogy for HIV education and for research methods around the epidemic, from transmission routes differing for communities to treatment protocols requiring revision to meet the unique physiology of different populations. Without protest, HIV prevention and AIDS would have continued to be framed in terms of identities, not in relation to practices and bodily composition. By resisting dominant usage and challenging the circulation of privileged ways of knowing, Patton's research and wider queer scholarship seek to render visible those practices that enforce marginalization of minority identities, practices that often result in greater suffering and death.

Foundational scholarship on writing centers pursues a similar agenda of challenging hegemonic practices and championing pedagogies of empowerment. Stephen North, Ken Bruffee, and Andrea Lunsford champion dialogic, collaborative, and process-oriented interaction between tutors and students, and the ideal product is student-centered pedagogy. This approach to teaching builds writers who understand composition as recursive and who engage in conversation with a larger academic community. Christina Murphy challenges the politics at the root of collaborative pedagogy theory where knowledge emerges from community consensus. This theory, she notes, neglects to interrogate the dynamics of power, leaving unexplored the question of whether participants in collaboration ever have equal status or equitable opportunity.

Marilyn Cooper also challenges unfettered assimilation of "standard" codes, and she appeals for tutorials to foster critical awareness of academic discourse communities. Building on the work of Antonio Gramsci and Paulo Friere, Cooper calls for writing center tutors to act as "organic intellectuals" who teach students to question their conditions of existence, particularly in relation to social and cultural dynamics at play in academic life. From a feminist perspective, Meg Woolbright argues for tutors (and students by implication) to question gendered practices of domination and control within conferences. She applauds the different pedagogical environment that writing centers foster:

> Both feminist and writing center commentators advocate teaching methods
> that are nonhierarchical, cooperative, interactive ventures between students
> and tutors talking about issues grounded in the students' own experience.
> They are, above all, conversations between equals in which knowledge is con-
> structed, not transmitted. (69)

Anis Bawarshi and Stephanie Pelkowski complement Marxist and feminist awareness of forces of domination by foregrounding attention to the colonialist tendencies of writing center theories and practices. When writing center scholarship and practitioners speak to/about marginal populations, pedagogy and discourse frequently reifies these subjects as "other," positioning groups exterior to the political and cultural majority usually without validating their discourse practices as legitimate alternatives and often suggesting their inferiority. The language majority population often couches its discourse in racial and national terms, further confounding tensions and exacerbating divisions. Like the other critical pedagogues, Bawarshi and Pelkowski endorse instruction that highlights questioning and demystifying academic discourse practices.

Explorations of how knowledge, power, and identity happen are crucial parts of cultural studies, feminist and postcolonial critiques of writing center theory, and queer theory seeks to complement their critical interventions. It also extends knowledge of practices of domination to an appreciation for the physics and elasticity of social and cultural codes. By becoming more aware of the codes constituting their identities and the codes' implications for academic life, students gain a modicum of agency. However, that sense of empowerment is always confounded by dominant interests' resistance to challenges to the status quo. Knowledge of and being able to act on codes does not diminish the reality and effect of their existence when these codes privilege certain ways of writing and speaking over others. "Standard" vernaculars will always exist to mark status, and crises that erupt over their challenge testify to their sway and staying power. Learning to code-switch between "standard" discourse practices and community-based ones does not necessarily translate into practical empowerment: Speaking a white, middle-class, academic vernacular enables outsiders to gain access to that discourse community, but such code-switchers do not eliminate the ubiquitous presence of racism, sexism, and nationalism and their marginalizing effects. Subject positions are not seamless, natural signs; claiming them—claiming an identity—depends on the acquisition and deferral of codes. Identities become compilations of codes, sets of signs that depend on their oppositions for meaning. Identifying under the signs "writer" or "student" suggests a conscious (or unconscious) reaction to *not* being a "writer" or "student." In that moment of claiming an aspect of identity, subjects also depend on rejected or deferred possibilities. This mutually constituting dance of identity assumed and resisted is a primary focus of queer theory scholarship and offers insight for writing center studies.

In supporting writers, we never just sit side by side with them as purely *writers*: they come to us as an intricately woven tapestry, rich in the authenticity and texture of identities, but this cloth often requires something extra to be legitimated in the academy. Tutorials become spaces where students and tutors alike shore up, build anew, and deconstruct identities and the ways of knowing that are sutured to them. As students learn to construct essays with an attention to audience that forces them away from safe confines of the personal and local, their ways of knowing confront a complex interplay of the dominant, the oppositional, the subversive, and the self. On top of those negotiations, students must also examine the lenses through which they are viewed. The speech and writing patterns of nonnative English language learners are often seen as being at odds with "standard" academic English, and practitioners get marked as ESL, an other in the classroom. The vernaculars that first-generation students from the urban areas use are frequently judged as too "street," and they are positioned as needing "remediation." Women's prose in patriarchal classrooms can be disregarded as too emotional or personal, so they are told to be more dispassionate. For gay people coming to terms with their sexuality, exploration of desire and its expression (and the homophobia that often reacts to it) are shunted aside, and they are encouraged to maintain separate worlds of the personal and the public. Students come to tutoring in possession of rich cultural capital that doesn't translate easily for use in the academy, and schooling often assumes students possess intellectual capital for effective operation in its discourse communities. Both populations need to negotiate beyond the familiar and to contemplate the unseen and unknown; however, this dialectic rarely happens.

As students develop critical awareness of and agency over identity and its implications for academic life, students also realize their proximity to and stakes for acquiring that knowledge are not equitable across populations. The journey to speaking and writing "standard" English is not the same for everyone, and the travelogues of those experiences usually take on a telling rhetoric rooted in highly moralistic and meritocratic narratives. Some are initiated into practices of passing and coming out that are analogous to rituals queer people often experience as rites for claiming sexual identity. Fostering a critical relation to dominant practices initiates students into a doubting consciousness that itself is a powerful political act in a society increasingly anti-intellectual and unquestioning of the status quo. Queer people, by coming to terms with their sexuality on some level, continually perform such counter-hegemonic activity, and those lessons learned can be taken up in mentoring writers. In *Textual Orientations*, Harriet Malinowitz writes about the transformative possibilities of a pedagogy rooted in foregrounding sexual minorities' epistemologies (for ourselves and the dominant):

> Sexual identity informs heterosexuals' epistemologies, too, though in ways that may be less immediately apparent to them—just as most socially dominant or validated identities are more dimly perceived as players in people's meaning-making operations than are the identities of Others. Heterosexuals, like white people, insofar as that part of their identity is not regularly challenged or scrutinized, are free to regard it as a significant fact demarcating their selfhood; it is possible for them to experience it instead as part of a seamless garment of "humanness"—which is to say, they frequently do not "view" or "see" it until it is touched by the discourse of the Other. (24)

For mainstream society, ways of knowing seem natural, but their very contingency becomes apparent when their assumptions come into proximity to others marked by racial, gender, class, sexual, national and other forms of difference. The seamless narratives that construct dominant people's "humanness" become provisional lenses to be invoked and chosen. Epistemologies become interpretive gazes that open up possibilities for vision and revision. In writing center sessions, the practice of questioning our assumptions about ways of knowing is underutilized. For example, at Stony Brook, where I teach, tutors frequently encounter immigrant and international students who struggle with well-worn debates about affirmative action, women's place in society, and civil liberties, yet when tutors mentor such students, they fail to understand that white, middle-class, liberal, and "American" perspectives are not necessarily shared by people new to mainstream culture in the United States. Similarly, students from working-class neighborhoods of New York City are often at a loss in our writing center when tutors push them to view issues and the world from beyond the perspective of home in Bensonhurst or Flushing Meadows. For both types of sessions, proximity becomes a crucial tipping point for piercing the naturalized; only by queering their conversation does a different sort of learning happen.

    Challenging hegemonic or dominant epistemologies and practice is not exclusive to queer theory, but it adds pedagogical value by deconstructing privileged practices in relation to their companion subordinate forms. For every privileged epistemology, action, and identity, queer theory assumes a companion set of marginalized ways of knowing, doing, and being. This form of criticism has its genesis in Michel Foucault's study of language, medicine, psychology, incarceration, education and sexuality. The production and deconstruction of "problem" writers in writing centers is analogous to Foucault's genealogy of sexuality and knowledge of its "deviant" forms. In *The History of Sexuality*, he traces the historical emergence of discourse about sexual beings as an allegory of the appearance of contemporary intellectual inquiry, modes of thinking that underlie modes of academic study and teaching. What we understand today as homosexual and heterosexual identities are not formations that step outside of historical contexts and culture; rather, these identities are the product of a set of discourses rooted in time and place or the result of people putting their sexual practices into discourse. As scientists and psychologists came to replace priests as culturally sanctioned counselors, sexual diversity came into relief, and categories came into existence (utterances were related and weighed). "Normal" sexuality was not so much a set of activities in and of itself so much as an opposition to a set of activities it was not—the "abnormal." Heterosexuality emerged and predicated itself on knowing and being opposed to homosexuality (or better, the set of discourses we have come to associate with same-sex desire). In our contemporary epistemology, sexuality is a tango of encoding and decoding meaning, a perpetual dance of signifying the other that extends to additional modes of inquiry.

These discursive operations—the interplay of oppositions—are not always readily apparent to society because dominant codes seek to naturalize themselves and turn attention to discordant forms. To deflect awareness of those constructing logics of the social and cultural, public attention often turns to individuals: those out of step with or unlike the dominant become problems requiring correction; institutionalized practices and ways of thinking remain stable and continue the unfettered production of individuals. Homosexuals become curious figures needing explanation (or to be explained away): pop culture wonders aloud what made them *that way*. Women become suspect creatures if professional and public existence challenges dominant codes of femininity and roles of motherhood and supporter. People of color become problematic when they step out of submissive roles and segregated spaces of popular culture and consumption. In their own corner of the academic world, writing centers become sites where problems are individualized and made legible, if not on the bodies of students, then at least on the surface of their papers. In *Good Intentions*, Nancy Grimm champions awareness of the gulf between the dominant culture and those from the subaltern, and she argues success in college is often predicated on one's ability to master and practice institutional codes and ways of thinking:[1]

> The dominant ideology of individual liberalism that structures the system of higher education and the writing programs and writing centers within it has historically distracted our attention from systemic influences on our work and instead focused our attention on the individual student who is expected to change, to become normal. As [Iris Marion] Young explains, within an individualist ideology, we hold individuals rather than institutions accountable. Sometimes we blame students for not trying hard enough or not setting the right priorities or not learning enough in high school and sometimes we blame teachers for creating unfair obstacles or for having unfair attitudes or for not preparing students for college or sometimes we blame parents for not having the "right" family values. (108)

Failing to code themselves as "normal" or perform within a band of normative expectations, students are often dissected in all manner intellectual, philosophical, and psychological. Students become the target of critical attention as *individuals*, and systemic dynamics and institutions escape culpability. Though Grimm and Young do not couch their analyses in queer theory, their appeal is similar: writing center practitioners must *queer* the dynamics that put forth particular codes of identity and intellectual practice as "normal" and others as not. Administrators, teachers, and tutors too often deride the literacy practices and educational capital that students bring to writing centers, making students personify those problems while larger social and cultural logics go unexamined. Instead, writing mentors ought to help students bridge the multiple literacies to which they have access and those dominant forms they require for academic success.

Queer theory explores discourse practices that privilege particular epistemologies, ontologies, and practices, and it also foregrounds the mutually constituting nature of forces of domination, privilege, and normativity for all those marked as marginal. For queer activists and scholars, pedagogical practice is rooted in a subversive agenda to demystify and denaturalize structuring dynamics. As with most people who lack status in our society, sexual minorities develop mechanisms to cope with forces of domination. Queer folk create subcultures comprised of neighborhoods and support networks, and we develop ways to integrate with larger society, making strategic decisions about when to invoke our identities and experiences and when to proselytize about who we are. For many people of color and women, their bodies encode their identity and speak for them, yet for working-class people, religious minorities, and queer people, our legibility can confound. Regardless of visibility, these marginalized people share techniques for navigating public space beyond the safe confines of home and community. In writing centers, people from the margins are frequently the majority population, yet tutors and other writing center professionals often do not tap these students' own innate social and cultural literacies as resources for aiding their academic work. Having learned how to survive in a society marked by racism, sexism, class-bias, nationalism and homophobia, students marked as other have sophisticated tools, yet writing center staff and the students' instructors usually do not mentor them on ways to manipulate these devices for use in the academy. I next discuss two such practices, "passing" and "coming out," that are central to the gay community and that can advance our critical understanding of tutorials, as well as the institutional positioning of writing centers.

"Passing" in the Writing Center

In *Our Kind of People*, Lawrence Otis Graham recounts the history and politics of race within the American black community. Though conventional treatments explore interracial dynamics, Graham charts the complexity of competing perceptions and relationships to race and racialized identity between

African Americans themselves. One dynamic he examines is the politics of passing, and this social practice seems to have had its earliest articulation and most explicit expression within African American communities where complexion enabled some light-skinned blacks to pass as (and assume the privileges and power of being) white. A hierarchy based on skin tone was built upon this foundation, and blacks with lighter tones assumed privileged status over those with darker complexion. These dynamics then dovetailed with social cleaving around class, and Graham argues all sorts of community-based institutions arose in response to an individual's ability to pass among the white mainstream, both economically and racially.

Like African Americans, the gay community has its own history of constructing itself in relation to the larger heterosexual population. In the early twentieth century, lesbian couples in nascent urban gay ghettos could survive without social harassment if one partner passed as a straight man by performing conventions of masculine dress and behaviors (D'Emilio and Freedman; Peiss and Simmons). The other partner would assume traditional gender expectations of women of the period, and thus to the dominant society, the couple could appear as "normal" or heterosexual. For gay men from the late nineteenth century on through gay liberation to today, social spaces like the fashion world, entertainment, and the arts would become safe arenas where they could be "out" or visible, so long as they conformed to specific codes of conduct (e.g., being fey, campy, etc.) and expressed no overt attraction toward other men. For men outside those historically safe spaces, passing as a straight male became (and still remains) a highly valued trait: To ensure personal safety and job security, these men seek to blend in with and be indistinguishable among heterosexual men. Each of these occasions for passing requires individuals to acquire particular types of cultural capital as well as knowledge of their relative value to both privileged and marginal populations. For people of color, playing upon race themselves presupposes awareness of American ranking of populations by skin tone; for lesbians, knowledge of the gendering of romantic relationships and bodies enables manipulation of male and heterosexual privilege; and for gay men, attention to codes of masculinity permits agency in decisions to be visible.

Learning these codes and practices of passing and developing ways of coping with this knowledge does not happen only for queer people and people of color. Students, particularly those positioned as marginal, "at risk," or in need of "remediation," come to writing centers (or are sent to them) wanting to learn and acquire those skills, markers, and insights that enable them to pass in the academy—both in terms of performance and identity. Writing centers champion this work, facilitating students' acquisition of these forms of capital. This knowledge helps students navigate between margin and center; it helps the other signify like the privileged mainstream. Regardless of whether tutors or administrators embody dominant society in part or whole (white, male, middle-class, straight, American), codes of privilege and their rules of usage are often natural to or already learned by us. Epistemology, ontology and dominant practices are stable to us because they have come to operate smoothly through us. For successful academics and students, this "second nature" that many experience as comfort and security with academic discourse is a consequence of position and the ease with which practices of normalization have worked. We know, intuitively at least, elements of genre, effective argumentation, critical thinking, grammar and usage, and this knowledge allows us to approach communication moments with classes and peers with a greater likelihood of success. For students who lack this capital, academic conversations can be inhibited because of conventions of which they often have minimal knowledge. For students from the margins, acquiring these codes and rules holds real material implications. On the upside, learning and performing the codes of privilege (passing) creates the possibility for greater economic and political power, but on the downside, refusal (not passing) can be tantamount to a resistant embrace of the status quo. This latter move can be heretical in a society that predicates status and social mobility on college-sanctioned education and continual self-improvement.

For tutors and directors from marginalized backgrounds, our language use allows us to pass even if our identities, bodies, or complexions call into question our natural fit in the academy. We have experienced that very cultural negotiation that has been so widely written about and that many of our students engage. Richard Rodriguez talks about moving between two worlds of language growing up in Los Angeles and ultimately being forced to pass in dominant English-speaking culture. Other authors of color write about the false choice of picking one language culture over another, of necessarily being forced to pass. bell hooks provides powerful examples in her work of learning to move between her rural working-class, African-American community of childhood and passing among elite circles in the academy. Mike Rose, as a working-class Italian American, also writes about his quest to acquire the codes of passing in mainstream linguistic communities as well as tutoring to those on the margins. In learning to signify and code-switch, Rose had to traverse a social and cultural landscape marked by codes of class to become a celebrated academic. In learning to pass, these academics demonstrate the intensely personal and difficult journey that students from the margins encounter: They must face and come to terms with their social position and cultural practices, they must make difficult decisions about personal and professional futures, and they must negotiate their relationship between margin and center. In sum, students must make strategic decisions to bracket, albeit temporarily, stratifying dynamics of class, race, gender, and sexuality at play and interpret such success stories as case studies in the virtue and possibility of meritocracy winning out. Just as queer people must always already occupy a calculated relation to public space, so too must first-generation college students act in assuming a position in academic discourse communities. Dominant culture posits their integration as endorsement of meritocracy and elides the dynamics that students must overcome and paper over.

To pass, to invoke the literacy codes and identity practices of the dominant, presupposes that doing so is desirable or even an act over which individuals have agency, and it assumes the dominant yields space for the marginal possessing the right codes/conduct. For people of color and women, their bodies usually speak their marginality before their words are audible, and many would argue class and sexuality articulate their presence in nonverbal ways, of course not always approaching the legibility and history that race and sex possess in our culture. For those students who are marked by social cleaving, whose bodies speak before spoken, their ability to code-switch competes with bodily encoding over which they have little power to influence dominant society's reception. When these students come to college, academic discourse practices operate as a set of codes intended to democratize, but these codes also often separate and exclude. No separatist discourse and epistemology (e.g., afrocentric or gynocentric) will ever upset the hegemony of dominant academic discourse patterns (e.g., Eurocentric, middle-class, liberal, etc.), so having the ability to invoke those codes is a pragmatic necessity born of the economic and political necessity to have access to the privilege that they carry. However, conventions of academic discourse are widely seen as amorphous at best, and they are continually under assault as being too discipline-specific or not field-dependent enough (as movements toward and away from WAC/WID indicate). At the same time as students from the margins are taught a restrictive set of communication conventions in the academy, our popular culture embraces diversity of expression from spoken word to music and visual arts. For young people, consumption of culture focuses not on the normative, but looks to the margins. As suburban and rural youth revel in a "ghettoized" Christina Aguilera and don FuBu and Eminem-inspired dress, the academic mainstream teaches them to bracket these urban, ethnic, working-class impulses in their official language. Larger cultural and social forces foster a mixed message: Blend, but don't blend too much. Though these admonitions celebrate a veneer of diversity that enables an illusive individuality, they simultaneously condemn codings of difference that approach a tipping point of potential paradigm shift. Blending in signifies assimilation and a lack of recognition by the dominant; one gets the privileges and benefits (proximity, safety, material success). Not passing signifies a separation and an abundance of recognition by the mainstream; one gets the benefits of self-actualization and risks the costs (distance, violence, and economic loss). For women and people of color, the politics and consequences of this dynamic long have been known, but for queer people, knowledge and testing of the limits of passing are still dawning as the recent public debate over "gay marriage" attests. (At what point does mirroring the structures of heterosexual culture transform into assimilation? How are special rights eclipsed for equity's sake rather than for being co-opted?)

The passing that is taught in writing centers also possesses a problematic logic: We teach students to move toward and privilege the academic discourse community, and we subtly disabuse movement back to home discourse communities. We foster passing as and discourage coming from. Assimilation is lauded just as separation is viewed as suspect. Boundary incursions between home and academic discourse spaces are seen as violations tantamount to threats to national security (at least as we receive it in the national political rhetoric of "homeland security"). In my writing center and larger writing program, culturally privileged faculty, staff and students alike bemoan nonnative English speakers using their first (or second or third or fourth) languages outside classrooms ("They'll never learn to speak like us if they keep doing that"), but crosscultural conversations that enable discovery and dialogue between identities and linguistic usage rarely happen. Students of color and those with working-class backgrounds are implored not to write like they speak, yet talk about and validation of the dynamics and politics of English dialects are illusive. Ironically enough, despite my university's location in the New York City suburbs, a metro-region that celebrates its immigrant roots and multiethnic character (even though its history has a more dubious record), actual practiced appreciation for that heritage and flavor can be vexing. Continual talk and learning are required to bridge the experiential gulf between students, tutors, and professors, and that reflective work promises to transcend the educational outcomes for all participants. If writing centers accept the mission to enable students and tutors to learn about and reconcile competing discourse community expectations, they must be wary of only fostering the passing part of the equation. Writing center professionals must encourage awareness that knowledge and expression are *not* socially constructed but are coerced and appropriated. Communication conventions in the academy are not the results of tidy agreements, but the souvenirs of clashes and encounters between margin and center.

For students who use writing centers to engage this confounding game, a kind of queer reading must guide their instruction to pass in the academy. In teaching and fostering this rhetorical identity, tutors often inadvertently encourage a unidirectional passing. "They" get to pass in "our" world. Mentors do not encourage students to become aware that identities are invoked; they are assemblages to which individuals must have a critical relation and assemblages that can be moved between and piled on one another. Tutors risk creating, in the vein that Richard Rodriguez talks about, separate worlds and languages that possess implicit privileging and distancing. Students should not come to see that their "home" or "private" worlds and languages are less legitimate or valuable. Instead, they need to read communication situations and make strategic decisions about conforming, resisting or subverting the existing patterns or conventions. Blending in by speaking and writing like the dominant has obvious material consequences (good grades, less conflict, greater integration), as does resistance have clear material effects (poor grades, more conflict, and less integration). A third way means taking on a subversive approach to communication, by assessing constraints (What is possible? What is not?) and self-consciously manipulating codes. Students could invoke dialects as part of introductions and descriptions of personal experiences, or they can trade upon identity as a means to push frames of reference for their audience and subject matter. Confessionals for their own sake and dialects deployed without strategic referent usually do not impress academic audiences, but they can be won over when these strategies serve as evidence of personal engagement with content material and effective argumentation. This coming to read the communication situation for safety and possibility for subversion is a hallmark of queer theory; the lesson is that identity can be invoked to the degree and extent that the individual chooses and over which she has agency.

By queering sessions—seeking strategic occasions to subvert conventional dynamics—the limits of the ordinary can be tested by students and tutors. Their bodies and performance also may serve pedagogical ends that challenge normalized academic discourse practices. While tutors of color embody difference in most academic exchanges, racialized approaches to critical thinking only become legible when individuals encounter the other in physical as well as intellectual proximity. Discourses trumpeting sexism become harder to defend when one's tutor is a woman or when the tutor pushes a student to consider a different lens through which to view the world. Rhetoric that regurgitates conditioned liberalism (or conservativism) can be checked by tutors who seek out oppositional viewpoints. Queering tutorials involves what Nancy Welch calls an engagement of the mirror stage and movement to learning-to-play. In this view, tutors and students work together to find "potential spaces" where students can develop a relationship with academic writing, not by necessarily conforming or resisting convention, but by mutually exploring creative ways to experiment and play (Welch 54). Welch's theory undermines the standard duality that tutors face and offers a third way: Assimilation and resistance give way to subversive or queer play. The ideal/real dialectic visioning of the world moves toward a sort of harmony.

Welch's use of Lacanian psychoanalytics also helps to bring into relief the queer place that writing centers themselves ought to occupy at most colleges and universities. Just as students and tutors need help reconciling idealized visions of themselves and the world with a reality replete with contradictions and tensions, so too must writing centers confront a gulf between theory and practice, between ideal and real. Welch argues against a false binary of "ideals and theories" on the one hand and a *real politik* of institutionality on the other hand; instead, she lauds space overbrimming in "activity, questioning, and change that a writing center in pursuit of the practical would eclipse" (54). This writing center would be an arena where noise, as Beth Boquet explains, would be literal and figurative, disruptive, improvised, and energizing. For many writing center practitioners, the reality is often quite different: like many of the students we serve, we feel a pressure to pass, to blend in, and to not chafe. As contingent staff or untenured faculty, we fear real material consequences if we fail to conform or adapt to conventions of pedagogy and performance, or, more directly, if we fail to pass. We fear budget cuts for recalcitrant activity; we fear the loss of tenure if we do not play well with senior colleagues; we fear further marginalization when we countervail administrative edicts. Hallways and panel presentations at regional and national conferences are chocked full of this folklore, so such anxiety is often real and not the stuff of academic urban legends. But as Welch notes, we need not slip into reifying dualisms of assimilation and resistance. Perhaps there is a liminal, queer zone where writing center practitioners seek out "what disrupts and what exceeds" and develop ways of identifying writing centers as integrative spaces where oppositions commingle and come into an uneasy existence (Welch 57). Just as gay people must come to terms with how and if they can articulate their identity by knowing what is possible in their local context of safety and needs, so too must directors navigate between idealism and abject resignation to pragmatism. Writing center directors and staff must find strategic occasions to evangelize and give testimonials of what we do, not just to build the faith among the unconverted, but to destabilize conventional wisdom of what we do and who we are.

"Coming out" in the Writing Center

Intertwined with the public visibility of queers is the ritual of coming out, a speech act that marks discursive movement away from the private domain of the closet. In American culture, being queer never just involves the sex acts in which one engages or the community to which one identifies, but also requires a particular and perpetual practice of naming and renaming ourselves to others. This coming out narrative has its origins with the production of homosexuality that Michel Foucault famously wrote about. As reviewed above, concepts of heterosexuality emerged in relation to articulation of homosexuality; the normal has been predicated on the abnormal. The production of these identities is not done through positivistic observation but through dialogue, conversations where uttering one's thoughts on self make them true and real. Foucault charts the genealogy of those confessionals and argues where once priests conferred meaning on them, sociologists and psychiatrists assumed scientific authority over interpretation and subsequent pathologization of individuals' identities. As a consequence of identity movements' (civil rights, women's, lesbian and gay liberation, etc.) actions during the twentieth century, agency over self-definition has shifted from pastors, scientists and physicians to individuals themselves. Though we no longer sanction most public expressions of homosexual identity as threats to public or mental health, its presence or proximity still does not pierce the dominant heteronormativity of society. Coming out challenges the unmarked and naturalized discourses of compulsory heterosexuality and upsets normative assumptions about interlocutors. Putting homosexuality into discourse is just as productive as failing to do so; not complicating the discursive practices of heterosexuality enables its existence as a normal that elides its mutually constitutive abnormal. Coming out does not undermine the practices of heteronormativity; rather, coming out brings into relief discursive relations with the other. By putting one's sexuality into discourse when dialoguing with others—by saying, "I am . . ."—a person integrates her private and public sense of self and forces her interlocutors to perform their own negotiation of identity on some conscious or unconscious level. The audience must reconcile being and not being.

This experience of coming out is ubiquitous to writing center tutorials, yet our scholarship has not talked about them in those terms. Though sessions likely do not involve cathartic proclamations of one's sexual identity ("Yes! Yes! Yes! I am gay and proud of it" or "Hi, my name is Harry, and I'm a homosexual"), conferences do turn on confessional moments that are intimately woven with students' and tutors' sense of self in relation to writing center ritual. Common tutorial practice centers on starting sessions with ice breaking and self-assessment talk. Tutors draw students out with background information on their majors, course-work, prior experiences with writing, assignments, and thoughts on their composition strengths and weaknesses, each turn becoming more intimate in the level of disclosure. Before turning to collaborative learning, students must offer themselves up for analysis and interpretation by laying their writing sins and self on the table for absolution. Students are compelled to come out, to mark themselves, as writers with particular sets of needs that individualize themselves in a context, where no one else is being marked as different or coming out themselves. If sharing writing is an intimate and vulnerable act, then tutors' rituals of enacting public self-analysis of students' ways of producing writing is doubly so. Writing centers are sites where to traverse them means coming out as someone wanting help and support. Then, once in the writing center, students are expected to continue coming out and confessing in greater detail their needs and expectations. Like the parish priest or therapist of bygone days (for gay people), the tutor is positioned as a confessant who aids the confessor in coming to terms with her thoughts and expression. Students must put into discourse what they feel they are doing well and, often more important, what they think they are not doing well and struggling with. Once discursively expressed, tutors are positioned to validate or repudiate students' practices, and the tutors are then empowered to assist students with coming to terms and developing plans for dealing with their knowledge. Their mentorship is predicated upon the degree to which students can offer up discourse for interpretation and act upon it. This dialogic tutoring does not just facilitate collaborative learning about concrete issues; it also aids students' integration within academic communities, ideally with a critical sensibility to the process.

This coming-out practice is not necessarily problematic so much as it presupposes students' experience and comfort with self-disclosure to others with whom they are not necessarily familiar. Since students require a certain level of trust and security to confess and reflect upon self to a public figure like a tutor, creating a safe space is crucial for effective work in sessions. However, such safety comes with proximity to people like oneself, but writing centers are not always staffed by individuals who look and act like the students they serve. Embracing diversity in writing centers is a never-ending project because student bodies are in perpetual flux. Mirroring student demographics does not address inevitable experiential gaps between tutors and students, even if their physical identities are alike. As tutors become more attuned to generalized traits associated with specific groups of students, such awareness may unintentionally reify stereotypes and be patronizing. At the same time, knowledge of cross-cultural differences can offer cues to interaction styles and expectations so long as that knowledge does not take on the feel of recipes for action with particular types of people. Cultural and social resistance to the practice of confession may be not only an issue of one's identity—coming from a community where speaking to (or speaking in particular ways to) "outsiders" is not a routine practice—but also a factor of one's experience in academic discourse communities. For many students, collaborative writing, active learning, and recursive process are educational rituals that are not well known or comfortable. Because students frequently reach writing centers while participating in first-year composition programs, their awareness of conventional practices and the reasoning behind them is often nonexistent or immature, as Nancy Sommers has explained so well. For students, in this sense, offering up their experience (or lack thereof) is a fruitful enterprise, yet obtaining that knowledge requires an uncomfortable disclosure, an act most would find tenuous.

Such risk can be mitigated if tutors themselves engage in a sort of coming out, thereby fostering a transactional dialogue in which knowledge is shared and consumption and transmission of it is not one-sided. By narrativizing their own concurrent experiences with joining academic discourse communities, tutors help students demystify the process as well as make their own struggles less individual and isolating. Tutors, thus, mark experiences that are often deemed transparent and uncomplicated. To know that someone else has experienced one's anxieties offers a degree of consolation and validation, particularly if tutors are careful not to diminish a student's own journey as hackneyed. The experience of coming out is not exclusive to mentoring modes and practices of academic conversations. Tutors also must contend with disclosing their own components of identity, be they racial/ethnic, religious, class, sexual, or political. Although racial and gender codes are usually obvious to interlocutors, less mature students may not understand their import for shaping messages and epistemologies. Ethereal markers of identity have an impact on communication, but students frequently lack the cultural capital to consider them. At the risk of imparting political correctness (from either the right or left), tutors can help students complicate their frames of reference and audience awareness, and tutors can also foster sensitivity and appreciation for diversity. Disclosures of unmarked components of identity are precarious enterprises because tutors place themselves in vulnerable positions for rejection or verbal abuse by students. As anyone else, tutors also require a modicum of safety to come out, thus making conferences critical occasions for understanding and appreciating interactants' willingness and ability to engage such talk.

Just as tutorials have an interplay and negotiation of self-disclosure that marks and encodes aspects of academic and personal identity, writing centers must engage in a sort of perpetual disclosure. As an institutional space, the writing center obviously cannot speak in the conventional sense, yet its visibility and reputation on campus articulate and inscribe meaning. Like Beth Boquet recalls in connection with her space, the noises and vibe that permeate a writing center's walls signify in ways that affirm or confound perceptions of students, faculty and administrators. Directors share urban legends about students and faculty alike coming to writing centers, discovering what we do, and proclaiming testimonials. We also share the disaffected narratives where our spaces are described as recalcitrant, unrelenting, and lacking in utility. Depending on the specifics, either type of folklore posits promise or ruin. To contend with and shore up such perceptions, writing center leaders must also engage in a never-ending campaign of building knowledge of and community for writing centers. At one school where I once worked as a graduate student tutor, my colleagues and I would jokingly refer to our introductory classroom visits as "We're the writing center, and we're okay" speeches. In retrospect, those presentations were not entirely different from diversity presentations where lesbians and gay men speak to classes about their experiences as sexual minorities.

As I later took professional and faculty positions in writing centers, those consciousness-raising sessions with students about writing centers expanded to committee and department meetings as well as to university administrators. Today, I find myself coming out more frequently as a writing center person and educating students and colleagues about that aspect of my professional identity than I have ever felt compelled to do as a gay man. Inevitably as agendas are being set, perspectives being solicited, or new business being invited, I find myself at times sheepishly inching my hand up or murmuring, "The writing center could use . . . " or "In the writing center we try to . . ." In building up to making a case for tenure, I already must explain all those hours dedicated to service and teaching, explaining once again what the tutors and I do and why they require ongoing training and support. In coming out as a writing center person, in marking myself as dissimilar from other junior faculty who don't share such responsibilities, I wonder if I am marginalized as a consequence and to what effect. Only time will tell. Until I have a better sense of perspective, I find affirmation and absolution in the stories of/from writing center colleagues around the country. Like the secluded, closeted gay person out there in the world, reading about the experiences and theories of others makes me feel less alone, less adrift.

Towards an Interrogation and Integration of Identity, or Queering Identity in the Writing Center

To queer people, contending with our liminality—living somewhere between being in or out, or existing as figures somewhere between normal or abnormal—is crucial to our quest for acknowledgement and safety. Such experiences in the borderlands parallel the lives in and spaces of writing centers: students, tutors, administrators, and the centers themselves. They seek to validate and to be validated, they seek knowledge and practices and to be known, they want the security to explore. As tutors and directors, we surely can foster that kind of work for students, but we must also help students understand their interlocutors, be they embodied or abstract. We need not reify abstractions; rather, we must explore through dialogue and reflection the practices and dynamics of audience and rhetorical context. Tutors and faculty must articulate and reflect on their own experiences and processes of coming to terms with life in the academy as individuals with a complex sets of markers constituting who we are. By speaking to those negotiations, we all learn about the possibilities and pratfalls of consciousness-raising and learning the rules of the academic game. This discursive play is just as central as teaching writing, critical thinking, argumentation, and the like. Students discover that writing and identifying never stand alone outside a context or community; they are always already constructed in relation to both. Mentoring students toward that realization is among our better offerings to academic communities.

Composition and writing center theories laud collaboration, attention to agency in the writing process, and awareness of cognitive, social and cultural dynamics in student learning. Queer theory is not just about seeing the homosexuals in writing centers or noticing the sexual politics that circulate through our spaces; queer theory involves appreciation for how epistemology has an impact on students, tutors, staff and on the institutional position of the writing center. With these insights on the nexus of queer theory and writing center pedagogy, tutors can work with students to discover how they invoke identity in the writing and tutoring process, and those insights influence critical awareness of liminal dynamics elsewhere. Queer people use passing as a technique to "fit in" in spaces where security it not assured. To many subaltern students, acquiring those codes to pass, in both performative and identity senses, confers a degree of safety, even if only provisional. Passing without a critical relation or sense of its limitations invokes the metaphor of the closet where the mainstream gets to ignore the other in its midst, a figure who is marginalized and not seen. As students master the codes and practices of dominant society (particularly in the communication of knowledge, arguments, and ideas), they must nurture awareness of their own identities and experiences. That wisdom can flesh out (not necessarily trump) theories and information students acquire in their coursework. When our students' knowledge begins to challenge and expand the parameters of discourse and community, so too will the rules that govern those fields begin to shift. As Muriel Harris writes, "Tutorial instruction . . . introduces into the educational setting a middle person, the tutor, who inhabits a world somewhere between student and teacher. . . . Students readily view a tutor as someone to help them surmount the hurdles others have set up for them" (qtd. in Permberton and Kinkead 8). Indeed, that middle person, a writing mentor, helps students navigate an academic terrain that can be uninviting and exclusionary. Discovering well-worn paths and learning new routes to self-understanding and awareness of the world is a hallmark of intellectual life, and tutors model and facilitate this complicated and intensely personal work.

Notes

[1] My use of the term *subaltern* comes from Jennifer Terry's appropriation of Gayatri Spivak's work in postcolonial studies. Terry extends the subaltern from Spivak's usage as a term to understand identities, subject positions and voices of colonized people in developing countries to sexual minorities in the U.S.

Works Cited

Bawarshi, Anis, and Stephanie Pelkowski. "Postcolonialism and the Idea of a Writing Center." *Writing Center Journal* 19.2 (1999): 41–59. Print.

Boquet, Elizabeth H. *Noise from the Writing Center*. Logan: Utah State UP, 2002. Print.

Bruffee, Ken. "Peer Tutoring and the Conversation of Mankind." *Writing Centers: Theory and Administration*. Ed. Gary A. Olson. Urbana: NCTE, 1984. 3–15. Print.

Cooper, Marilyn M. "Really Useful Knowledge: A Cultural Studies Agenda for Writing Centers." *Writing Center Journal*. 14.2 (1994): 95–97. Print.

D'Emilio, John, and Estelle B. Freedman. *Intimate Matters: A History of Sexuality in America*. 2nd ed. Chicago: U of Chicago P, 1988. Print.

Foucault, Michel. *The History of Sexuality: An Introduction, Vol. 1*. New York. Random House, 1978. Print.

Gillespie, Paula, and Neal Lerner. *The Allyn and Bacon Guide to Peer Tutoring*. 2nd ed. Boston: Pearson, 2003. Print.

Graham, Lawrence Otis. *Our Kind of People: Inside America's Black Upper Class*. New York: HarperCollins, 2000. Print.

Grimm, Nancy Maloney. *Good Intentions: Writing Center Work for Postmodern Times*. Portsmouth: Heinemann, 1999. Print.

Haraway, Donna. "Situated Knowledges: The Science Question in Feminism and the Privilege of Partial Perspective." *Simians, Cyborgs, and Women: The Reinvention of Nature*. New York: Routledge. 1991. 183–201. Print.

hooks, bell. *Talking Back: Thinking Feminist, Thinking Black*. Boston: South End Press, 1989. Print.

Lunsford, Andrea. "Collaboration, Control, and the Idea of a Writing Center." *Writing Center Journal* 12.1 (1991): 3–11. Print.

Malinowitz, Harriet. *Textual Orientations: Lesbian and Gay Students and the Making of Discourse Communities*. Portsmouth: Boynton/Cook, 1995. Print.

Murphy, Christina. "The Writing Center and Social Constructionist Theory." *Intersections: Theory-Practice in the Writing Center*. Ed. Joan A. Mullin and Ray Wallace. Urbana, IL: NCTE, 1994. 25–38. Print.

Murphy, Christina, and Steve Sherwood, eds. *The St. Martin's Sourcebook for Writing Tutors*. 2nd ed. Boston: Bedford/St. Martin's, 2003. Print.

North, Stephen M. "The Idea of a Writing Center." *College English* 46 (1984): 433–46. Print.

Palton,.Cindy. *Globalizing Aids*. Minneapolis: U of Minnesota P, 2002. Print.

---. *Inventing Aids*. New York: Routledge, 1990. Print.

---. *Sex and Germs: The Politics of AIDS*. Boston: South End, 1985. Print.

Peiss, Kathy, and Christina Simmons, eds. *Passion & Power: Sexuality in History*. Philadelphia: Temple UP, 1989. Print.

Pemberton, Michael A., and Joyce Kinkead. "Introduction: Benchmarks in Writing Center Scholarship." *The Center Will Hold: Critical Perspectives on Writing Center Scholarship*. Ed. Michael A. Pemberton and Joyce Kinkead. Logan: Utah State UP, 2003. 1–20. Print.

Rodriguez, Richard. *The Hunger of Memory*. New York: Bantam Doubleday Dell, 1982. Print.

Rose, Mike. *Lives on the Boundary*. New York: Penguin, 1989. Print.

Sedgwick, Eve Kosofsky. *Epistemology of the Closet*. Berkeley: U of California P, 1990. Print.

Sommers, Nancy. "Revision Strategies of Student Writers and Experiences of Adult Writers." *College Composition and Communication* 31 (1980): 378–88. Print.

Spivak, Gayatri Chakravorty. "Subaltern Studies Deconstructing Historiography." *Other Worlds: Essays in Cultural Politics*. New York: Routledge, 1988. 197–221. Print.

Terry, Jennifer. "Theorizing Deviant Historiography." *differences* 3 (1991). 55–74. Print.

Welch, Nancy. "Playing with Reality: Writing Centers after the Mirror Stage." *College Composition and Communication* 51.1 (1999): 51–69. Print.

Woolbright, Meg. "The Politics of Tutoring: Feminism within the Patriarchy." *Writing Center Journal* 13.1 (1993): 16–31. Print.

Young, Iris Marion. *Justice and the Politics of Difference*. Princeton: Princeton UP, 1990. Print.

Reassessing the "Proofreading Trap": ESL Tutoring and Writing Instruction

Sharon A. Myers _____

TEXAS TECH UNIVERSITY

Sharon A. Myers explores the practical and ethical challenges tutors face when working with second-language writers. Although Myers acknowledges the writing center profession's deep roots in nondirective (or minimalist) tutoring, she argues that tutors cannot expect ESL writers to learn in the same ways or at the same rates as native writers. She calls for tutors' recognition that so-called sentence-level errors actually involve deeper levels of creating and processing meaning. By helping ESL students correct these errors, then, tutors can help students gain deeper insights into English syntax—an important step in becoming better readers and writers of the language. Such learning often takes a long time—"years, not months"—and may not become immediately apparent to either the student or the tutor. Myers takes particular issue with writing center scholars and others who view sentence-level revision for ESL students as unethical. As she says, "The central insight in foreign language pedagogy in the last thirty years is that, in fact, language acquisition emerges from learners wrestling with meaning in acts of communicating or trying to communicate. That is exactly what ESL students are doing in writing centers, person to person." This article, which first appeared in The Writing Center Journal *in 2003, serves as a thought-provoking challenge to tutors who attempt to apply nondirective approaches to ESL students. It may also provide theoretical support for tutors who tend to take a more directive approach in working with second-language writers.*

ESL writers present a common dilemma to writing centers — the desire for sentence-level interventions from their tutors. Our staff often experience such interventions as contradicting the aim of writing centers, formulated by Stephen North as making "sure that writers, and not necessarily their texts, are what get changed by instruction" (438). The job of writing center tutors, North stated, "is to produce better writers, not better writing" (438). The sentence-level demands of ESL students, however, are seen as "editing." Eric Hobson expresses this attitude in an article about writing center pedagogy in which he complains that during the period between the late 70s and early 80s,

> writing courses dealt with writing (e.g., invention, drafting, revision, development of authors' voices, etc.) while writing center staff were allocated the demanding and ethically questionable task of "cleaning up" writers' editing skills, of eradicating minority dialects . . . and of "dealing with" nonnative writers. (155–66)

It is easy to understand why, faced with cutting through the confused syntactic and lexical tangles entwined in the sentences of second-language texts, writing specialists might much prefer to discuss issues of content and organization. Giving students correct grammar or more appropriate vocabulary is perceived as "fixing" the paper, something understood to violate the autonomy of the writer and the integrity of the work's authorship.

As someone who has worked with ESL writers for more than fifteen years, the attitude that sentence-level errors are mechanical, relatively unimportant ephemera has always seemed problematic to me, though I have heard it expressed or implied by conscientious tutors many times. It is a good example of the professional disjunction between composition specialists and ESL specialists that Paul Matsuda has described in *College Composition and Communication,* and a good example of the need to go outside of composition studies to improve what Matsuda refers to as "institutional practices" appropriate to second-language learners. It is wrong to assume, he explains, "that ESL writing can be broken down neatly into a linguistic component and a writing component and that the linguistic problems will disappear after some additional instruction in remedial language courses" (715). I want to show, in this article, that it is indeed the "linguistic" component (vocabulary and syntax) as much or more than what is considered the "writing" (rhetorical) component that ESL students need most, and that their "errors" are persistent evidence of normal second-language learning and processing, not some failure on the part of students. Many international graduate students, in particular, usually have a good idea of what they want to say, but are often at a loss as to how to say it. That is, they may have fewer whole-essay problems than native English speaking students, but still need a great deal of support. Even in cases in which a student is producing multiple drafts, the organization of such drafts may require macro-organizing language such as "Arguments against phenomenon X depend on four assumptions," or "The perspective that informs most research on X is . . . ," or "I would like to discuss two alternatives and their implications . . . ," or other language to signal sequencing of information across a text, provide background for contrast, or announce the dimensions in which the topic will be presented (e.g., whether the writer is going to evaluate, analyze, report, or critique). The language and the writing are inseparable.

There are a number of causes underlying the frustrations felt by both ESL students and tutors in writing centers. These include the unrealistic expectations about language learning embedded in our institutional arrangements for ESL students; the historic deemphasis of sentence pedagogies; a conception of culture which excludes the structure of languages; ethical confusion; the understanding of errors as something to be eliminated rather than as artifacts of processing (and often of developmental progress); and the failure to recognize the depth of the "sentence-level" problems involved in second-language processing.

Unrealistic Expectations

Writing is arguably the most advanced and difficult of the modes, and usually the last acquired. Even among first-language learners, relatively few achieve the ability to write good formal academic prose at the university level. While the ability to speak a given language does not necessarily predict a person's ability to write in it, it is useful to note something about the time involved in spoken second-language acquisition in order to adjust the dimensions in which we need to perceive our students' struggles. The Foreign Service Institute has estimated that a minimum level of professional speaking proficiency (entailing the ability to fluently support opinions, hypothesize, and explain complex phenomena) in a foreign language relatively remote from English may require a native English speaker 2,400 hours of intensive training under the ideal conditions provided by the Foreign Service. A superior level may entail hundreds of hours more. According to Liskin-Gasparro, attaining a superior level in a more closely related language, such as Spanish or French, is estimated to take 720 hours (qtd. in Omaggio-Hadley 26). By comparison, four semesters of foreign language classes in a U.S. university provide 200–300 hours of instruction. Assuming that these estimations of the time it takes English learners to learn to speak foreign languages at professional levels would at least approximate the time it takes for speakers of other languages to speak with the same proficiency in English, it is not realistic to expect that many ESL students will speak fluently at advanced levels. I don't believe the ability to write at advanced levels is achieved much faster or that writing center tutors should be led to believe that students should. Writing is denser than speech and in academic settings requires very high levels of reading comprehension, a formal register, sophisticated paraphrasing ability and a specialized vocabulary. Very few ESL students who walk into a writing center are likely to have such high levels of proficiency. As Williams notes, it is not realistic to believe that they "should have put their second language problems behind them and be ready to take on the challenges of the composition classroom without further support" (qtd. in Matsuda 715). Students from China and Korea, for example, may have "studied" English for as long as eleven years in their home countries, but that "study" may have consisted of rote memorization of isolated words in vocabulary lists and "grammar" tests based on discrete items conforming to "rules" whose limitations are unknown to them. Immigrant students who enter U.S. high schools may never have had their needs to understand English as a foreign language attended to adequately, given the patchwork of requirements and variable quality of ESL teacher-training programs across the states and the strong political resistance to funding the needs of bilingual students. Even now, very few TESL or Applied Linguistics teacher preparation programs offer full courses in second-language composition. As a result, immigrant students often come into writing centers with second-language issues in addition to all the problems associated with "basic" writers in other populations.

The acquisition of a second language is a major achievement in a human life. It takes years of work. The depth and scale of the achievement are not always appreciated by U.S. writing tutors, few of whom have ever mastered any language other than their own at the level of sophistication demanded of ESL writers in academic settings, and who may actually, therefore, consider the control of agreement conventions in language, for example, a minor problem (more about agreement conventions further on).

The Historic Turn from Sentence-Level Pedagogies

In his history of "The Erasure of the Sentence" in composition studies, Robert J. Connors attributes the fall of the sentence as a focus of instruction to the strong movements away from formalism, behaviorism, and empiricism that have defined much of composition theory for the last twenty years. He laments the loss of useful sentence pedagogies as many writing specialists rejected everything about all three *isms* (or what they associated with those *isms*) with the kind of extremism unfortunately typical in education. With good reason, form was dethroned and meaning crowned. No one wants a return to the bad old days of the five-paragraph jello mold garnished with topic sentences, but like Connors, I think that ignoring the sentence, which is a central feature of writing in the texts of both native and nonnative speakers, is a disservice to both populations. In the case of ESL students, whose greatest and most consistent difficulties are baldly manifested in the boundaries of the sentences itself, it seems like an eerie kind of denial.

More problematic than the historic deemphasis of the sentence, however, is the separation of instruction in vocabulary and syntax with instruction in rhetoric. An article representative of dichotomizing sentence-level errors ("language") from "writing" in work with ESL students is "Avoiding the Proofreading Trap: The Value of the Error Correction Process" by Jane Cogie, Kim Strain, and Sharon Lorinskas published in *Writing Center Journal* (Spring/Summer, 1999). Constructing their analysis in just that framework, they interpret the persistence of the primary problems of ESL students and the persistence of the student need/demand for help with them (articulated or not) as a source of frustration and stress. Student demands for direct help in what the authors seem to consider a secondary level of writing are actually construed, as their title indicates, as a "trap" which must be "avoided" through techniques of indirect error correction. But there is no getting away from the fact that students need control of a great deal of lexis and syntax in the first place. They need a lot of vocabulary and a lot of experience, both in comprehension and production, to get to any level where "ideas" even become comprehensible. Meaning does not flow from such knowledge and experience, but the ability to express meaning does.

Language and Culture

Jane Cogie introduces the article by noting her appreciation of Judith Power's interpretation of the role of writing center instructors as "cultural informants":

> The cultural informant role endorsed by Powers gives writing center tutors flexibility for meeting specific needs of ESL students not met by the nondirective writing center ideal. With their many cultural, rhetorical, and linguistic differences, ESL students often lack the knowledge to engage in the question and answer approach to problem-solving used in most writing centers. . . . The read-aloud method for discovering sentence-level errors, frequently productive for native speakers, provides little help to ESL students who lack the ear to hear their own errors. The value of the cultural informant role, then, is that it validates sharing information about English that these students have no way of knowing on their own. (7)

Over time, however, Cogie feels disillusioned, as "too often this role, at least when sentence-level errors were concerned, tended to translate into the tutor editing and the student observing" (7). Like Purcell, whom she cites, she wishes to "shift the focus of the ESL session from difficult-to-resist, sentence-level errors to more meaningful idea-related issues . . ." (8). Cogie describes a tutor who felt that in her role as "cultural informant," she was merely editing, giving the student her "language," but not her "ideas" (8). But just as instruction in vocabulary and syntax ("language") cannot be separated from instruction in rhetoric ("writing"), language and culture are inseparable.

Writing instructors are indeed cultural informants. Culture refers not only to the contours of personal space, the educational roles of teacher and student, the sense of time, the politeness conventions and the discourse conventions of a given group, but to language and its forms. Culture includes the way that a given language determines, subordinates, complements, coordinates, pluralizes, counts, modalizes, interrogates, lexicalizes. In fact, the greatest problem many ESL writers have is in controlling the syntax and lexis of the English language. By "lexis," I mean not only words—what we usually think of as "vocabulary"—but multiword units such as "in some ways," "on either side of," phrases such as "make arrangements for," and frequently co-occurring words such as "highly significant" or "closely linked." If we want to help non-English speakers write in English, we need to acknowledge the central role of language in writing—including all the redundant syntactic forms needed for "ideas" to take shape. Writing instructors and tutors schooled in modern composition theory, well aware of the failings and absurdities of traditional writing instruction reifying form over content, are wary of reducing the concept of writing to "good grammar." But what "English grammar" means to a native speaker of English, even one who grows up with a dialect of English unused in formal instruction, is very different from what it means to a second-language learner. The need to learn the many complex ways a language determines, subordinates, coordinates, lexicalizes and so on are often demeaned in composition literature, pooh-poohed as mere "sentence-level grammar" resulting in "sentence-level errors." These language structures should not be somehow divorced from culture or our roles as cultural informants. Errors in vocabulary and syntax occur within the structural constraints of a language and constitute "culture" just as much as every other feature of language below (phonetic) or above (rhetorical) the sentence level. Enabling the members of a different culture to express themselves in a new culture is work that cultural informants do. Being a culture informant includes being a language informant.

Ethical Perspectives: Writing Process and Language Learning Process

One concern of writing tutors is expressed in the area of Cogie et al.'s article subtitled "Ethical Rationale" (9). The authors cite an example in which a writing tutor (Kate Gadbow) "helps a Japanese M.A. student more than she intends" on a master's thesis (9). After graduating, the student interviewed for U.S. jobs and was rejected. As a result, Gadbow believes, the student had to relinquish her "career goals" and go back to Japan. Gadbow reports that her student "was harmed by her focus as a tutor on helping her to graduate rather than on helping her become more proficient in English" (10). Cogie then comments: "Certainly not all ESL sessions that fail to promote independence in the writer have such momentous consequences" (10). It may not be the case that Gadbow's editing role resulted in the student's failure to find work in the U.S. An alternative explanation could be that the student failed on the basis of her oral proficiency and/or listening comprehension, rather than her writing. In any case, second-language learners are inevitably dependent on people who know how to speak and write the second language, in order to learn how to speak and write it themselves. The learning takes a very long time and very, very many engagements with the language, not just a series of sessions with a writing tutor. In fact, the tutor may have provided much of the input the student will finally need to make particular vocabulary or structures available for spontaneous production at a later date when the student's growing and changing inner version of the language (often characterized as "interlanguage") is ready to absorb them.

While I would interpret the case of the Japanese student differently than Gadbow, fear is understandable in tutors who believe that such consequences might be possible if, according to their best lights, they "fail to promote independence" in the ESL writers they work with. But what does independence mean? Learning is slow and occurs through processes neither entirely understood nor under the control of either the tutor or the learner. It is frustrating for ESL students to have a native informant of the language resist informing them, particularly one who is employed, ostensibly, to pay attention to their language and help them write. And not only resist, but suggest through this resistance (even though it may not be intended) that it is somehow dishonest or lazy to expect the tutors to do so. This resistance is confusing, but most second-language learners are insecure about their language learning themselves and not in a position to question their tutors' methods.

If an ESL student's text is corrected by a tutor who flags an error and then offers alternatives, the fact that the student returns on another day and makes the same mistake is not evidence that the student is irresponsible nor is it irresponsible of the tutor to correct it again. Some features of language are learned before others. Students are not uniformly ready at all times to internalize everything pointed out to them, and much of language acquisition — that is, language that is internalized and available for production — takes place at an unconscious level. There are far too many things to remember to hold everything in conscious memory. Moreover, although we don't understand exactly how they work, there is substantial evidence for the existence of developmental patterns in second-language learning, which may well supersede the dictates of formal instruction (see Rod Ellis's *Study of Second Language Acquisition*). It is also important to keep in mind that students may require many exposures to words or patterns, and perhaps multiple communicative engagements with them as well, before they are internalized. Repeating a correction is not a capitulation to some stubborn student trait; it is simply acknowledging the real nature of what is a genuinely long and messy process. It may appear to the tutor that the student is passive, that is, not "responding to instruction," but the student is not necessarily passive at all. A great deal of language learning is receptive. Nor can the student necessarily fully learn features of the language in the time dimension in which the tutor is teaching. Checking writing samples across periods of six months or a year may show improvement barely noticeable over a thirteen-week semester—and some language features and levels of fluency do take years, not months, to achieve. This or that exposure to some language feature may be just one or two frames in the time-lapse movie in which the human brain captures the unfolding contours of a foreign language. The students can't be rushed into an exclusive focus on the issues of mature language use we have come to consider the "writing process." Some of the ethical tension writing tutors experience also seems to be a result of underestimating how much idiosyncrasy is embodied in every human language.

Treatment of "Error"

Cogie et al.'s article is intended to provide student "tutors and their trainers a collection of practical strategies for developing bit by bit the error awareness ESL students need to self-edit" (10). In fact, students are very often painfully aware of their errors, but are not sure or simply do not know how to fix them. I don't think tutors need to spend a lot of time to develop "strategies" to increase the students' (already sometimes paralyzing) awareness of their errors, or that doing so necessarily enables students to self-edit. (To give Cogie credit, she does appreciate the importance, in the affective domain, of assessing a student's proficiency and level of confidence, and advises restraint accordingly.) Most student "errors" however, are lexical, and if they don't have the appropriate word or lexical phrase, no editing will provide it. A great many tangles in "syntax" are a result of circumlocutions—vocabulary problems, not grammar problems. While I agree that there is a place for helping students self-edit, insofar as they can, I think that so much focus on errors is only helpful in proportional relation to the students' proficiency (the lower the proficiency, the less useful it is) and that for any level of proficiency it is not as important as learning more and more language in the first place. Accuracy, as Michael Lewis has often pointed out (*The Lexical Approach,* 164–72), is the last thing any second-language learner ever acquires, and then it is relative. I don't find any shame in directly helping students identify what is not working, but even then, that is only a small part of what they need and what we can provide, which is a repertoire of things that do work. They are not engaged merely in "editing" but in learning a new language.

Before discussing other ways we might help ESL students with "sentence-level" problems, I would like to consider the four suggestions offered by Cogie et al.: using a learner's dictionary, minimal marking, error logs, and self-editing checklists. They write that their rationale is to provide, in the absence of "native-speaker-like-intuitions," these "'more mechanical proofreading strategies' Muriel Harris and Tony Silva suggest are 'necessary'" (9). What Harris and Silva actually wrote, however, was "Therefore, some recourse to more mechanical rule-based proofreading strategies *or to outside help, such as a native speaker reader, will probably be necessary*" (535, emphasis mine). Comments on the four strategies Cogie et al. suggest follow:

Learner's dictionaries. The use of learner's dictionaries (see Appendix) is the least controversial of Cogie et al.'s suggestions. Such dictionaries are aimed at the needs of nonnative speakers. They use phonetic spellings and information about how to stress lexical items such as compounds and idioms. They also provide a great deal of lexical grammatical information, such as the countability or noncountability of nouns and the gradability of adjectives. They may have a limited vocabulary for definitions so that learners don't have to continually look up new words. Kim Strain points out to a student that a learner's dictionary can provide information, for example, about what verbs are transitive or intransitive (16–17). The dictionary can indeed be useful if the student knows that a violation of the verb's transitiveness or intransitiveness has occurred. If this is pointed out, then the student can look to the dictionary for some examples. If it is not, then the only way a student could "edit" his or her paper would be to look up every single verb. Strain writes that the student may need "a firmer sense of the grammatical pattern for transitive and intransitive verbs." But there is no "grammatical pattern" to get a sense of. You just have to know what verbs are transitive and what verbs are not. There is no rule establishing this pattern.

Minimal marking. Minimal marking (in this case, two checks by a text line with two errors and one check by a line with one error) doesn't seem very helpful. It tells the student, "There are two errors here." What kind of errors? Nouns? Verbs? If verbs, is it a problem with tense? Aspect? Person? Valency (patterns of transitivity)? Agreement? Register (formal/informal)? Mode (a spoken rather than written form)? Are my errors concerned with articles? Pronouns? Word order? Lexical choice? The possibilities for a nonnative speaker are a veritable black hole. I think we owe it to the student to at least identify the nature of errors and not just to enumerate them. Whose independence does this minimal marking really support? Richard Haswell's minimal marking scheme (which Cogie et al. cite) is intended for "regular freshman composition sections" (603). Such sections are primarily made up of native speakers of English. Haswell proposes that "[b]ecause the teacher responds to a surface mistake only with a check in the margin, attention can be maintained on more substantial problems" (601). But what may be a minor problem for a native speaker can be a substantial problem indeed for a second-language student. One rationale he gives for this minimal marking is that "[i]t shows the student that the teacher initially assumed that carelessness and not stupidity was the source of the error" (601). However, this rationale does not necessarily apply to the errors of nonnative speakers either quantitatively or qualitatively, as it is not carelessness that accounts for most of their problems.

Error log bogs. The value of error logs may be the most questionable of all Cogie et al.'s recommendations because, given the extremely long time it takes to learn a language, the cost/benefit ratio seems much more likely to be enhanced by spending more time learning more language (meaning more words and lexical phrases) than on the study of errors. The number of times a student is asked to have recourse to a dictionary, for example, has to be embedded in a realistic estimate of how many times it will actually be useful and at what point the student will become so frequently and hopelessly distracted from the flow of the text that he or she just chucks it. Time estimates have to be based on how much time the student has to spend on a piece of writing in the context of everything else the student has to do, and not only on the time available for individual instruction in the writing center. Sometimes it is simply more economical to point out an error and supply a correction or an alternative way to express something. A lexical notebook, such as those proposed by Michael Lewis (*Implementing* 75–85), would probably be more valuable than an error log and more likely to be referred to in the future. Lewis recommends having students keep notebooks of collocations such as "population increase/decrease"; polywords such as "in accordance with"; and phrasal verbs such as "look up to," that are clustered around themes and topics of importance to each student. If there is no time, the same thing can be done verbally, with the student repeating examples from a dictionary or examples supplied by the tutor. There is substantial evidence that phonological memory influences both grammar and vocabulary acquisition (see Nick C. Ellis).

I refer to error log "bogs" because I think it is easy to get bogged down in spending time and attention to the nature and analysis of wrong use of language when that time and attention could be employed in the service of learning correct use that eliminates errors in a much more productive way. Most learner errors are quite predictable, without the need for logs of them. They are either lexical, in which case they are tied to word idiosyncrasies and not amenable to "sentence-level" grammar anyway, or predictable in the sense that they are the same errors all second-language learners make while they are learning English. A great deal of variation is predictable on the basis of first languages, described in *Learner English: A Teacher's Guide to Interference and Other Problems* by Michael Swan and Bernard Smith, who list and discuss the sources of common problems typical of English learners from nineteen different language groups. Students who come from languages that do not have articles, for example, strongly tend to omit articles; students whose first languages have articles tend to use them too much in English. Writing down "missing definite article" under a column labeled "Name/Description of Error" could get pretty redundant for Korean students, for example. There are so many dimensions of article use that govern whether or not an article belongs in front of a given noun in a given context that simply putting it in front of the noun in the "Correction" column, even in the context of a phrase, is not always guaranteed to elucidate anything for the student except that he or she should have used it in that place in that sentence in the context of that paper. Why not just correct it in the paper in the first place?

Very often, not having the English necessary to express something, students simply translate directly from their mother tongues. Filling up an error log with all the infelicities this produces does not address the cause of the error, which is simply lack of the language needed in the first place. Such "errors" cannot be reverse engineered in an error log.

Self-editing checklists. The authors propose self-editing checklists, handouts given to students which ask them to record their three most frequent errors (to check against their current paper) and to check all verbs for subject-verb agreement, modals, tenses, and voice (all extremely complicated phenomena from a second-language perspective). While I am skeptical of such checklists for the same reasons I question the value of error logs, I think there may be a place for self-editing checklists for very advanced students, but only for certain problems which can be simply defined and identified. One that comes to mind is the comma splice. A list of example comma splices which have appeared in the student's own texts, matched by a corresponding repair might be useful to list, contributing to the sense of what comma splices look and "sound" (read) like. Probably the most useful suggestion on the checklist provided by the authors is the final one, which advises the ESL student to "ask a knowledgeable friend to read over your paper and look for problem areas" (22). The authors note that this should be a friend outside of the writing center. I would note that that such friends would be very likely to provide the vocabulary and grammar correction that the tutors in the writing center are not comfortable providing.

Looking Below the "Surface" of the Sentence. The major question for writing instructors and for tutors is always, first of all, where to begin on ESL papers full of errors in syntax and vocabulary. The authors advise distinguishing between "local errors" and "global errors," a distinction which usually refers to prioritizing errors that obscure meaning (global errors) over "errors that do not significantly hinder communication of a sentence's message (local errors)" (Hendrickson 360). This is a useful distinction and a legitimate instructional strategy, but the distinction cannot be made mechanically through an a priori definition of errors, such as "Global errors include incorrect verb tense, verb incorrectly formed, incorrect use or formation of a modal . . . awkward word order . . . ," and so on (Cogie et al. 15), while "Local errors include incorrect subject-verb agreement, incorrect or missing article, problem with the singular or plural of a noun, wrong word choice . . ." (Cogie et al. 16). Whether or not an error is global or local depends first and foremost on its context. "Awkward word order" in the sentence of a given text does not necessarily interfere with meaning at all; it may be, simply, awkward. On the other hand, the distinction between singular and plural in a noun phrase could very much affect meaning, and "wrong word" choices probably obscure meaning more than any other single mistake. Rather than refer to these arbitrary and misleading categories, a tutor would be better advised to simply ask herself or himself, during the reading of a text, what, if anything, most confuses meaning here? Or, what, if anything, makes the meaning most difficult to process, even if it is recoverable? In some contexts, it may indeed be even the misuse or omission of a single definite or indefinite article.

Related to these distinctions is the practice of waving away what native speaking tutors or instructors define as "local" or "surface" errors, "minor irritants" that the students should be able to clear up relatively easily. In reality these errors often reflect extremely complex problems for second-language learners. Subject-verb agreement often falls into this category. Isn't it strange how, despite all the times they are shown and told, the students, even very advanced ones, just keep failing to make their subjects and verbs agree? It appears to be so simple.

The belief that it is simple is an instance of what Paul Westney points out as instructor (not student) error in teaching pedagogical "rules," which is the assumption that because they look simple to us, they are simple to a nonnative speaker (80–83). Subject-verb agreement is a difficult feature of English. First of all, the student has to know whether a given noun is countable in order to make it agree with a verb. The "countable/noncountable" distinction made of English nouns is bizarre to students whose languages do not contain it. A furniture is a furniture is a furniture. On what basis is the student supposed to be able to figure out that it is not? Again, it is lexical, something particular to a word, not "sentence-level" grammar that determines what to do. There is nothing about words that flags their countability, and the semantic concept is so alien it is hard to remember even if the countability of a particular noun has been brought to the student's attention on some other occasion. In addition to this pitfall, the tricky English anachronism of the third person "s" lies in wait to ambush subject-verb agreement in the sentences of even the most advanced students. On one level, the third person "s" is probably hard to keep in memory precisely because it doesn't affect meaning very much; it is a redundant feature, since the noun clause has already declared its identity and number. Meaning has already been established, so there is no strong semantic demand for the information, only the abstract grammatical convention of repeating it. This is not natural or obvious to nonnative speakers at all, nor is it easy to keep in mind. Compounding the problem of subject-verb agreement are both the phonological and orthographic properties of the "s" inflection. The "s" is often deemphasized in the speech of natives, from whom students get much of their input. Because it is deemphasized, it is often not heard, and as a result, not imitated. If students tend to drop it in speech, they tend to drop it in writing. The "s" inflection is realized in three different morphemes: /s/, /z/, and /ez/. These have to be rendered as "s" or "es" in writing independent of their pronunciation, and are sometimes confounded with the apostrophed "s" and "es" forms of the possessive incarnation of the "s" inflection. Unless, of course, the noun takes an irregular plural. This is a feature of individual nouns, and not a rule-governed phenomenon. Compound nouns, too, are a real minefield for nonnative speakers trying to produce agreement. Zalewski illustrates the difficulties with compound nouns by noting that sometimes there is no formal singular or plural distinction at all, as in the word "Japanese" in an example where a writer explains that Americans shrug to express "I don't know," followed by the sentence, "On the other hand, Japanese shakes the head from side to side" (695). The ambiguity of this and other problems in number and person, she writes, "constitute a serious textual breakdown not only because trying to solve them costs the reader a lot of processing effort but also because ultimately their disambiguation turns out to be impossible" (697). Such problems, she writes, "have all too often been viewed as *local* and thus deemphasized in form-focused instruction" (697, emphasis added).

As for "incorrect or missing articles," insofar as they embody anaphoric relations (those which refer back to previous discourse), their significance (and therefore the choice of whether or how to use them) can span across hundreds of pages or years of shared knowledge; their use is not at all confined to the insides of sentences or to the local demands of a noun phrase. Using "an" in front of the word "experiment," for example, may obscure the fact that the writer is referring to the one known to the addressee and the writer, which was described six pages ago. Another one of Zalewski's student texts illustrates extrasentential links expressed by articles at the paragraph level. The student is writing about arranged marriages (notes in italics are mine):

> There is a go-between who take care of between a boy and a girl. Before they meet, they can get personal histories of each other. Then, a go between (*In native discourse the "a" here would be "the" since the go-between has already been introduced in the previous sentence*) gives them a meeting. In a meeting (*again, this would be "the," because the meeting has already been mentioned*), a go-between (*should be "the," previous mention*) introduces a boy and a girl (*as before, previous mention: should be "the boy" and "the girl"*) to each other. In almost case, meetings are dinner parties. Their parents often go with them to a meeting (*the meeting previously described, not just any meeting: should be "the" meeting*). (694)

These are not sentence-level links. Importantly, they are also errors which seriously hamper the ability of a reader to process meaning.

I mention each of these different issues concerning subject-verb agreement and definite/indefinite articles to illustrate how deeply complex they are for nonnative speakers. And they represent only two features of syntax that are often misconstrued as merely "surface" or "local." In fact, both connect to very large regions of language structure and use.

Teaching Language Versus Documenting Errors

I think it is both possible and desirable for writing center staff to fill the role of "foreign/second-language teachers" as well as writing instructors. In fact, writing tutors are perfectly positioned to facilitate the language learning these students need in order to develop their ability to write in English. The central insight in foreign language pedagogy in the last thirty years is that, in fact, language acquisition emerges from learners wrestling with meaning in acts of communicating or trying to communicate. That is exactly what ESL students are doing in writing centers, person to person.

What needs to occur is a shift in emphasis from carving up whatever language the students have managed to summon up for their texts and then asking them to autopsy it, to giving the students more and more language from which to make choices, establishing more and more links for them from the language they have to new language they need. Facilitating learning by providing correct language input rather than focusing on incorrect language can be done in a principled way, informed by insights into writing processes staff already have, but conditioned by an understanding of language-acquisition processes that are no less real or important, such as the time dimension in which acquisition takes place and the many layers of complexity learners face such as those illustrated above.

Writing tutors need to acknowledge and respond to the central role of lexis in language learning. They should also be equipped with much better knowledge of the pedagogical grammar of English as a second/foreign language. It is not the same grammar used to teach native speakers. Rather than just pointing out an error, tutors can provide alternative language: "Another way to say that is . . ."; "One way of putting it is . . ."; "Some other phrases you can use are. . . ." Much of writing (and much of speech, for that matter) consists of stringing together lexical phrases, not filling in grammatical slots. We use, and learn, much of language in words and word "chunks," not in abstract rules (Nick C. Ellis; Kirsner; Lewis; Little; Nattinger and DeCarrico; Tschirner). Language can be given verbally (asking the student to repeat), dictated with the student taking it down in writing, or offered through the use of a collocation dictionary (see Appendix). In some contexts, a lexical notebook might be appropriate; in another, just inserting a correction directly into the student's text as a reformulation might be the best course of action (see Myers for one version of using reformulation as composition feedback).

Modern corpus linguistics and discourse analysis provide interesting language frames that can be used to help writers. Nattinger and DeCarrico, for example, advocate acquainting students with written discourse forms at both global and sentence levels. In formal essays, for example, these frames include lexical phrases for topic nomination such as "[T]he goal of this paper is to . . ."; phrases for agreement and disagreement ("X does not support Y . . ."); or contrast (". . . is unlike . . . with respect to . . .") (172). Learning sentence heads (such as "It is possible that . . . ," or "The research suggests that . . .") enrich the writing repertoire, as do frames, such as "Evidence of . . . indicates . . . ," or "One interpretation of . . . is . . . ," or "An alternative interpretation is. . . ."

Reporting verbs (e.g., suggest, imply, point out, note) are used much more in writing than in speech, and can be presented to students as alternatives in sentence-level contexts. Consciousness-raising exercises can be advised, such as suggesting that a student note reporting verbs they find when they read English text outside of the writing center. Subordination and coordination, the bane of ESL students, can be practiced in sentence-combining exercises such as those popular in the 1970s and '80s (de Beaugrande; Broadhead; Strong).

Much of the language students need is writing-specific, and the writing center is an ideal place to give it to them. Most of all, showing is better than telling: "Here are some examples of acceptable student essays written by students in your field," or "Here are some examples of acceptable texts written by students who have been given assignments similar to yours." With the permission of student writers, writing centers could have files of such examples. Students need to get a sense of what such texts look like and "sound" like. This would be especially useful to international students, who are often even less familiar with what they are expected to produce than are the U.S. students.

Grammar instruction needs to be based on a principled examination of what is genuinely teachable and learnable, not just shunted off to traditional reference grammars based on Latin language paradigms aimed at native speakers that so many writing specialists just assume are useful (see Appendix for a recommendation). Tutors need to relinquish the attitude that giving second-language students the language they need is "unethical" or "immoral." Filling in an article somewhere it is needed and pointing out the context is one drop in the waves of the language ocean carving out its shape on the shoreline of the student's memory. One drop, or even fifteen, are not all that significant. Likewise, repeating some words or other instruction is not a sign of pathological student "dependence." Repetition plays an important role in language learning. Nor should native English speaking students be used as models in designing instruction for ESL students.

I am well aware that there are students who would be happy to let writing tutors do all their work for them; that there are students who are lazy or manipulative or both. Members of this minority show up regularly in my classes, and while I give everybody the benefit of the doubt to begin with, it doesn't take very long to identify them. Tutors who have multiple sessions with such students soon identify them, too. I just flatly tell these students that they need to go home and work on the text more before I will be willing to help them with it, or I point out a few "global" errors and note that it is sloppy in regard to X, Y, and Z, too, and to come back after they have paid more attention to it. But most students, especially ESL students, genuinely want to learn and are willing to work hard. I think we owe second-language students second-language writing instruction more broadly conceived than error documentation. There is indeed a "trap." It is created by the contradictions between what ESL learners need and are capable of and what an uninformed perspective leads us to suppose they need and are capable of. Nancy Grimm's admonition in regard to students with different backgrounds (in her example, an African American student and a young woman from a conservative Christian background) could apply as well to ESL students who enter the writing center:

When the proofreading issue is contextualized within an ideological model of literacy, it becomes . . . complicated. Rather than refusing to engage in this task because individual writers are supposed to be able to do it for themselves, writing centers need more complex understandings of the issues involved. (20)

A much more relaxed attitude about "error," one reflecting an appreciation of second-language acquisition processes, and better training in the pedagogical grammar of English as a second language would go a long way toward preventing either students or tutors from feeling frustrated or "trapped" in any part of the tutoring process.

Works Cited

Biber, Douglas, Stig Johansson, Geoffrey Leech, Susan Conrad, and Edward Finegan. *Longman Grammar of Spoken and Written English*. Essex: Longman, 1999. Print.

Broadhead, Glenn J. "Sentence Patterns: Some of What We Need to Know and Teach." *Sentence Combining: A Rhetorical Perspective* Ed. Donald A. Daiker, Andrew Kerek, and Max Morenberg. Carbondale: Southern Illinois UP, 1985. 61–75. Print.

Cogie, Jane, Kim Strain, and Sharon Lorinskas. "Avoiding the Proofreading Trap: The Value of the Error Correction Process." *The Writing Center Journal* 19.2 (1999): 7–31. Print.

Connors, Robert J. "The Erasure of the Sentence." *College Composition and Communication* 52:1 (2000): 96–128. Print.

de Beaugrande, Robert. "Sentence Combining and Discourse Processing: In Search of a General Theory." *Sentence Combining: A Rhetorical Perspective.* Ed. Donald A. Daiker, Andrew Kerek, and Max Morenberg. Carbondale: Southern Illinois UP, 1985. 61–75. Print.

Ellis, Nick C. "Sequencing in SLA: Phonological Memory, Chunking, and Points of Order." *Studies in Second Language Acquisition* 18 (1996): 91–126. Print.

Ellis, Rod. *The Study of Second Language Acquisition.* Oxford: Oxford UP, 1994. Print.

Gadbow, Kate. "Foreign Students in the Writing Lab: Some Ethical and Practical Considerations." *The Writing Lab Newsletter* 17.3 (1992): 1–5. Print.

Grimm, Nancy. "The Regulatory Role of the Writing Center: Coming to Terms with a Loss of Innocence." *The Writing Center Journal* 17.1 (1996): 5–29. Print.

Harris, Muriel, and Tony Silva. "Tutoring ESL Students: Issues and Options." *College Composition and Communication* 44.4 (1993): 525–37. Print.

Haswell, Richard H. "Minimal Marking." *College English* 45 (1993): 600–4. Print.

Hendrickson, James M. "Error Correction in Foreign Language Teaching: Recent Theory, Research, and Practice." *Methodology in TESOL: A Book of Readings.* Ed. Michael H. Long and Jack C. Richards. New York: Newbury House, 1987. 355–69. Print.

Hill, Jimmie, and Michael Lewis, eds. *Dictionary of Selected Collocations.* Hove: Language Teaching Publications, 1997. Print.

Hobson, Eric H. "Writing Center Pedagogy." *A Guide to Composition Pedagogies.* Ed. Gary Tate, Amy Rupiper, and Kurt Schick. New York: Oxford UP, 2001. 165–82. Print.

Huckins, Thomas N., and Leslie A. Olsen. *Technical Writing and Professional Communication for Nonnative Speakers of English.* 2nd ed. New York: McGraw-Hill, 1991. 514–30. Print.

Kirsner, Kim. "Second Language Vocabulary Learning: The Role of Implicit Processes." *Implicit and Explicit Learning of Languages.* Ed. Nick C. Ellis. San Diego: Academic Press, 1994. 283–311. Print.

Leki, Ilona. *Understanding ESL Writers: A Guide for Teachers.* Portsmouth: Boynton/Cook, 1992. Print.

Lewis, Michael. *The Lexical Approach: The State of ELT and a Way Forward.* Hove: Language Teaching Publications, 1993. Print.

---. *Implementing the Lexical Approach: Putting Theory into Practice.* Hove: Language Teaching Publications, 1997. Print.

Liskin-Gasparro, Judith E. *ETS Oral Proficiency Testing Manual.* Princeton: Educational Testing Service, 1982. Print.

Little, David. "Words and Their Properties: Arguments for a Lexical Approach to Pedagogical Grammar." *Perspectives on Pedagogical Grammar.* Ed. Terence Odlin. Cambridge: Cambridge UP, 1994. 99–122. Print.

Matsuda, Paul Kei. "Composition Studies and ESL Writing: A Disciplinary Division of Labor." *College Composition and Communication* 50.4 (1999): 699–721. Print.

Myers, Sharon. "Teaching Writing as a Process and Teaching Sentence Level Syntax: Reformulation as ESL Composition Feedback." *TESL-EJ* 2.4 (1997): 11–16. Print.

Nattinger, James R., and Jeanette S. DeCarrico. *Lexical Phrases and Language Teaching.* Oxford: Oxford UP, 1992. Print.

North, Stephen M. "The Idea of a Writing Center." *College English* 46.5 (1984): 433–46. Print.

Omaggio-Hadley, Alice. *Teaching Language in Context.* 3rd ed. Boston: Heinle & Heinle, 2001. Print.

Powers, Judith K. "Rethinking Writing Center Conferencing Strategies for the ESL Writer." *The Writing Center Journal* 13.2 (1993): 39–47. Print.

Purcell, Katherine. "Making Sense of Meaning: ESL and the Writing Center." *The Writing Lab Newsletter* 22.6 (1998): 1–5. Print.

Strong, William. *Sentence-Combining: A Composing Book.* New York: Random House, 1973. Print.

Swan, Michael, and Bernard Smith. *Learner English: A Teacher's Guide to Interference and Other Problems.* Cambridge: Cambridge UP, 1987. Print.

Tschirner, Erwin. "From Lexicon to Grammar." *The Coming Age of the Profession: Issues and Emerging Ideas for the Teaching of Foreign Languages.* Ed. Jane Harper, Madeleine Lively, and Mary Williams. Boston: Heinle & Heinle, 1998. 113–28. Print.

Westney, Paul. "Rules and Pedagogical Grammar." *Perspectives on Pedagogical Grammar.* Ed. Terence Odlin. Cambridge: Cambridge UP, 1994, 72–96. Print.

Williams, Jessica. "ESL Composition Program Administration in the United States." *Journal of Second Language Writing* 4 (1995): 157–79. Print.

Zalewski, Jan P. "Number/Person Errors in an Information-Processing Perspective: Implications for Form-Focused Instruction." *TESOL Quarterly* 27.4 (1993): 691–703. Print.

APPENDIX: Resource Recommendations

LEARNERS' DICTIONARIES

Collins Cobuild learners' dictionaries are good references and can be found on the Cobuild website: <http://www..collinslanguage.com/>. They provide information about whether a verb takes a gerund and/or an infinitive, for example, and about how common or uncommon a word is (information much appreciated by students who do not want to sound old-fashioned or weird). They are based on a corpus of over 250 million words taken, not from traditional definitions and examples, but from real-world speech and writing. Word pragmatics are noted, explaining word function (advising or agreeing, for example). Discourse organizing functions are noted, along with attitudes the words express, or whether they are used for emphasis. Style is described (American or British, rude, journalistic, literary, technical, spoken or written, technical, formal or informal), and authentic examples are given in complete sentences. All nouns are identified as count or noncount, and adjectives as graded or not and how (that is, inflected for comparison, as in "slow, slower, slowest"). Verbs that only occur in the passive voice are noted, and transitive and intransitive verbs are noted as is information, for example, about whether an intransitive verb is followed by a prepositional phrase or by a specified adverb. Patterns in the use of titles are given, as well as the patterns in which number and other word classes are expressed. Such an advanced learner's dictionary is also a good reference for tutors, who need to learn "word grammar" themselves, or at least know where to find it if they are not familiar with the pedagogical grammar of English as a foreign language. The advanced learner's dictionary is now on CD-ROM with a thesaurus, grammar information, and a five-million-word word bank for examples.

An online dictionary much favored by my ESL university students is *Wordsmyth* <http://www.wordsmyth.net/>. Examples of how English expresses things, whether found in a dictionary or provided by a native speaker, are the most useful. The students need to learn the right way to use the language to express their meanings, not just how to recognize (in the cases where recognition is even possible) that they have used some word or expression in the wrong way.

COLLOCATION DICTIONARIES

Another good resource for ESL writers is the *Dictionary of Selected Collocations* edited by Jimmie Hill and Michael Lewis. This is a resource enabling students to learn what is often of most use to them as writers: what words go with what words. This collocation dictionary is based on contemporary work in corpus linguistics. Our ability to analyze the patterns of language has been boosted many orders of magnitude over traditional analyses by the use of computers, and it is only recently that these findings are emerging into dictionaries and grammars. The collocation dictionary does not define words, but gives students probable combinations based on frequency studies of huge corpora of authentic written and spoken language. This book is of great value to second-language students. Entries are given on the categories of nouns, verbs, adjectives, and adverbs (mostly nouns). For example, if a student is writing about a career, the dictionary provides a list of words and phrases which most commonly cluster around that word, including a list of verbs that come before the noun, a list (in the most common tense) of which come after it, and a list of adjectives and phrases which contain the noun. Here is their example entry (11) ("sb" is an abbreviation for "subject"):

CAREER

V: abandon, be absorbed in, be destined for ~ in, boost, carve out, change, choose, concentrate on, cripple, cut short, damage, determine, develop, devote oneself to, embark on, end, enter upon, further, give up, hamper, have a ~ in (banking), help, hinder, interrupt, launch out on, launch sb on, map out, plan, predict, promote, pursue, put an end to, ruin, sacrifice, salvage, set sb on, spoil, start, take up, wreck ~

V: ~ blossomed, had its ups and downs

A: amazing, brilliant, chequered, colourful, demanding, difficult, disappointing, distinguished, entire, fine, flourishing, glittering, golden, good, great, honourable, ill-fated, meteoric, modest, promising, splendid, steady, strange, successful, turbulent, unusual, varied ~

P: outset of, peak of, pinnacle of, springboard for, summit of ~, a ~ change

In a different example, starting from a verb or adjective, the student would find, after the word "convinced": "absolutely, almost, easily, half-, more or less, not altogether, not entirely, practically, totally _convinced_ about/of . . ." (230).

Another useful reference for collocations is the Collins Cobuild English Collocations on CD-ROM, available through the same website of the Cobuild dictionaries noted above.

GRAMMAR REFERENCE

A good modern resource grammar for tutors is the *Longman Grammar of Spoken and Written English* by Douglas Biber et al. Unlike descriptions in traditional grammars, those in the *Longman Grammar* are based entirely on empirical data.

Addressing Racial Diversity in a Writing Center: Stories and Lessons from Two Beginners

Nancy Barron and Nancy Grimm _____
MICHIGAN TECHNOLOGICAL UNIVERSITY

Through an extended dialogue about their attempts to address racial diversity in a writing center context, Nancy Barron and Nancy Grimm illustrate the difficulties in overcoming the reluctance of peer tutors—socialized to ignore racial differences—to openly discuss issues arising from the students' race. Aware that a writer's linguistic background and training, willingness to seek assistance or share candid opinions, and attitude toward authority figures may hinge at least in part on race, Barron and Grimm argue for open discussion of racial issues. Originally published in The Writing Journal *in 2002, this essay focuses on the significant impact racial openness will have on writing and writing center interactions rather than maintaining the "colorblindness" (the assumption that race doesn't matter) they believe most writing centers practice.*

> *Narrative provides a way to speak things otherwise unspeakable, to give voice to that which would otherwise go unheard.*
>
> —*Briggs and Woolbright*

The academic essay, even the collaborative academic essay, is generally written in a single voice. Although we share the same first name and the same theoretical commitments, we do not share similar histories and perspectives. One of us is Mexican-American (or Chicana or Latina), a new assistant professor with many years of experience being a student of color in Anglo institutions (Nancy Barron), and one of us is white (or Anglo or Caucasian), of Irish/Lithuanian heritage, a long-time writing center director from a working-class background (Nancy Grimm). Although our shared commitments as literacy educators allow us to sometimes use *we* to signify our unity in purpose, we also employ our individual *I*'s to mark our different racial, generational, and cultural perspectives. The work we discuss in this article would not have been possible if we shared the same voice and history. In foregrounding our differences as well as our mutual vision, we create a sometimes bumpy ride for the reader, interfering with modernist expectations of coherence, yet exposing the seams we think our readers need to see in order to understand how the fabrics of our personal and professional lives connected. We move as well between narrative and exposition, between practice and theory, in order to "give voice to that which would otherwise go unheard."

A Story to Begin, Nancy Barron

During an unexpected free moment in the Writing Center, another writing coach, a young African-American woman, wanted to discuss her response to an assignment with me. I remember the topic had something to do with color, class, and societal conflict. I listened as she gave a quick summary of the class readings and then a more careful analysis from her own position as a black young woman with a middle-class upbringing. Because of my own experience as a student and teacher of color, I asked a few questions along the way. I was curious to know when she saw her analysis specific to her own experience and when she felt the conflicts she described as issues of color for a larger community. She paused, thought quickly, and emphasized, "Now that's something I would've done, but that's not all black people."

Throughout her ten- to fifteen-minute explanation, she revealed her conscious attempts of placing herself among a larger community. Her earlier controlled demeanor changed to excitement as she articulated her arguments faster and without hesitation to a point where she half-jokingly made statements about student race relations at the university. She reminded me of Cornel West in her preacher-style explanation and of an independent confident young person with an ease of language and comfort in sharing her ideas. Her discussion came to an end with an "and that's that" head-nodding conclusion. We both laughed at her very physical conclusion of her lengthy and punctuated response to an assignment designed to prompt such thinking. Here was a student willing to make connections and conclusions on a topic hardly discussed openly. I commented to the writing coach, "Well. Just type up what you just told me and you're done." I started to ask how the topic was connected with the rest of the course when the writing coach responded quickly and sharply, "Yeah right. I'm going to write all of that for the assignment."

I asked why not, and she let me know she was the only black student in the classroom. I thought aloud, trying to think of any way she could bring up some of her key correlations with the texts and her perspective that I had heard only minutes before. But her experience came through once again when she said that even if she submitted an anonymous entry to the class electronic discussion list, the anonymity wouldn't last very long. She asked, "How many white kids would even consider what I just said? It would be so obvious who said what."

I fell silent. My head raced to the past, to the present, looking for any familiar instances in my own experience that would help me create an alternative to her decision. I think my silence and looking away prompted pity from the writing coach who was well aware of my own studies about racial legacies tin higher education. She let me know, as she may to her mother, that in fact she was learning, and, like all of her other assignments, she thought about their implications. But, she added, for her to sit down and write "like a black person" in a class where she was the only black student, she smiled, looked away, and shook her head, "No."

One way to think about the writing coach's decision not to participate is to consider her present student position. She knows she's an involuntary minority (a concept John Ogbu uses to distinguish between voluntary immigrants to this country and those who are here due to slavery or conquest), she knows she's black, and she's had experience being alone in academic discussions. But her situation isn't an issue of standing alone. To stand alone on an issue of color when you are the colored is also to possibly sever ties, to insult, to ostracize oneself, not only in the classroom, but also in all aspects of campus life. Educator Laurel Johnson Black reminds us that before students of color come to college, "'twelve years of preparation' separate children into those who may speak and those who ultimately may not—and sometimes cannot" (Black 111). There is no question that this writing coach could speak. She was articulate, a thinker, and managed her undergraduate schooling where black students make up 1.5% of the student body. She had a history of attending schools with "Caucasians," as she called her Anglo classmates. She learned how African Americans were heard among Anglo students, and maintained a pretty good grasp for which topics were sensitive, controversial, and potentially risky for her to take on.

What struck me then and now is how insightful the writing coach was. She had study habits, homework practice, on her side. She connected her experience with the assignment. She expanded the topic by offering a response that included her studies and her personal experiences. She clearly had something to say. The assignment invited this sort of response, as good assignments should. Yet, her instructor was not to know of her analysis or close reading of the text. A great loss not only for the instructor, but also for the other nonblack students in class.

Most students of color know they represent a larger group of color regardless of their economic class, or experiences with the assignments. Whether her ideas were articulated face to face, or written in electronic entries, in the end she'd be the black person taking a side, not offering a perspective like the other Anglo students. I understood her decision, but I found myself wondering when and how does nonmainstream thinking, like this student's, get to the place where others can learn from and question, thereby giving her a chance to rethink her central concepts. I was bothered about our session for a few terms afterwards, and finally I saw that the ideas, the connections, the conclusions the writing coach discussed on that day in fact were heard, were listened to, were questioned, by a writing coach in the Writing Center. The student had taken a risk with a non–African American. She shared her position as a black young woman to someone not in the same position. She tested her ideas, listened and responded to questions. She, as she told me, learned. Did I? I'd like to think so, but I got caught up trying to find openings in the "color wall" that keeps most people on "*their*" side.

Two terms after this spur-of-the-moment conversation, she officially signed up for a regular weekly appointment with me to work on course assignments for a rhetoric course. During our sessions, she almost always raised her position as a black woman as she learned to interpret speeches, talks, and articles by analyzing rhetorical moves. I found myself rethinking how I was listening. When should I encourage her to write from the risky position of color? What would her writing gain? What would the topic gain? What happens to her thinking and main ideas when she chooses not to? I wished her instructor could hear the amount of analytical thinking the student did taking on the assignment and readings. Her writing, unfortunately, yet typically for most involuntary minorities I've worked with, showed less than half of what I had heard during our sessions. The rest of her thinking became the invisible foundation buried under her "white prose," as we later called her writing. Black describes what motivates such decisions:

> Rather than "slip" and begin speaking in a way that is comfortable and familiar, rather than further set themselves apart as "other," one strategy is to respond minimally. In doing so, the student can focus on what the teacher is saying — it's a wise learning strategy. But in not responding as "fully" as the teacher may expect, the student is also not doing all those things that teachers are looking for engaging themselves with the material (and the teacher!); demonstrating by repeating back to the teacher that they have been listening and understand this new information; indicating a willingness to develop the writing using their own ideas. It is a double bind. (108)

I now ask myself what practices keep students like her knowing when they can and cannot contribute their perspectives? I knew that this student's ability to split off aspects of her identity was connected to her need to present a unified self in her papers. To suggest that she represent both worlds was to risk sliding into incoherence. Successful students present themselves as unified with the instructor's views. But because her story makes its way into mine and because my story makes its way into print, her story begins to make its ripples, to disturb the sense that we are doing all we can, that students like her are simply resistant to suggestion.

From experiences like the one shared in this story, we know that many students of color have developed strategies for managing academically on a campus that pretends to be colorblind. Colorblindness is a way of avoiding the mess of racial history by pretending that racial differences don't exist. Students of color are supposed to write as though their color didn't matter. Students like the one in our story learn to disguise their lived experiences and the way their interpretations have been formed by their experiences. A writing coach's attempts to get such a student to say more, to develop her ideas, to include more detail are likely to be frustrated. Students like the one in this story may challenge our good intentions by clearly expecting us to comment only on their sentence structure and organization. They may ask a writing coach to help them find the "right" phrases, but the writing coach, unaware of his or her participation in the colorblind pretense, may wonder what they *mean* by "right" phrase. The student in the story has good reason to disregard efforts to encourage her to include more of her thinking. Her experience has taught her that if she needs a writing center at all, it's to help her write "white."

We suspect that many writing center workers have encountered students from diverse cultures who have implicitly been expected to engage in literacy in ways that deny their differences. Bilingual students are supposed to write as though English were their only language. Bidialectical students are not supposed to use their "nonstandard" dialect in school. Bicultural students are supposed to interpret what they read from the perspective of mainstream culture. Writing centers might be the best place on campus to glimpse the extent to which difference really matters in writing, yet too often the writing center is the place where acculturation is supposed to occur, a place where students are supposed to learn to read and write as if they have no differences. Students who bring differences of color, class, and culture are expected to make themselves over to match the institutionalized image of the typical student, while white middle-class students' sense of complacency is reinforced by the familiar values and routines of university life.

For some time now, higher education has theoretically endorsed the idea of multiculturalism. Diversity in students, in faculty, in curriculum is generally accepted as a good thing. In practice, however, teachers, tutors, and administrators have struggled with meaningfully instantiating diversity. A commitment to multiculturalism allows institutions to acknowledge the variability of culture and race, yet the dominant culture's framework continues to guide institutional practices. Generally, writing center workers are at a loss to convince diverse students that their differences are indeed valued. Like it or not, many writing centers would agree with what Stephen North observed in 1984: "We cannot change [the] context [in which the writer is trying to operate]: all we can do is help the writer learn how to operate in it and other contexts like it" (441).

Lately, some writing center scholars have been pushing against the real and imagined limitations on the writing center's ability to affect the context within which students write (Bawarshi and Pelkowski, 1999; Grimm, 1999; Condon and Condon, 2000). With these scholars, we take diversity arguments seriously, but we have found that it's far easier to theorize about diversity in a scholarly article or conference paper than to meaningfully instantiate *productive diversity* in a writing center program. In this article, we want to share the short version of what happened in one Writing Center when we started moving from theoretical ideals to actual changes in the training program for Writing Center coaches (tutors). We take the term *productive diversity* from literacy scholars Kalantzis and Cope who articulate a new vision of literacy education, one that moves beyond superficial multiculturalism and into a deeper understanding of pluralism. Kalantzis and Cope are members of The New London Group (an international group of literacy scholars). The New London Group argues that moving beyond token forms of multiculturalism means leaving behind forms of pedagogy that involve "overwriting existing subjectivities with the language of the dominant culture" (The New London Group 18). Instead, they argue for *productive diversity* which "means that the mainstream—be that the culture of the dominant group or institutional structures such as education—is itself transformed." (Kalantzis and Cope 124). Knowing that institutional structures resist change, we looked for a way to begin transforming the practice of the Writing Center where we work. Like most writing centers, our program is strongly influenced by the mainstream values of the institutional structure. Most of the assignments that students bring to the Writing Center expect them to demonstrate the dominant group's values and practices, and most of the undergraduate and graduate writing coaches who work in our Writing Center take these expectations for granted.

In looking for a place to begin nibbling away at the structures and expectations that prevent change, we knew that we wanted the Writing Center itself to become a place where interactions like the one in our opening story occur more frequently. We believe that the personal transformations that occur in the Writing Center will eventually lead to larger social changes. Few Writing Center employees chose tutoring as their life work. Most of them graduate and go on to become corporate employees, business owners, members of the armed forces, and faculty members. They take the Writing Center experience with them into these contexts. The student in the story we began with harbors no illusions about the context she currently operates within, and we harbor no illusions that we can transform that context before she graduates. But we wanted to begin a process that would begin to ripple through that context. With The New London Group, we believe that we "we can instantiate a vision through pedagogy that creates in microcosm a transformed set of relationships and possibilities" (19).

Like most writing centers, we already appeared to address diversity in our tutor training. We focused on how to work productively with the many international students who use our Writing Center. Our training also included information about working with students who have learning disabilities. We regularly worked through the Myers/Briggs Personality Inventory so that we could understand the potential for personality differences to undermine Writing Center relationships. The aspect of diversity that was missing from our training program was also the one most shied away from in our professional literature and conferences—racial diversity. *The Writing Center Resource Manual*, published by the NWCA Press [and edited by Bobbie Bayliss Silk], and most tutor-training books contain no mention of race as a factor that affects literate activity. Yet, in our bookcases, these writing center books sit right next to books by literacy theorists such as Shirley Brice Heath, James Gee, Brian Street, and Mike Rose, all of whom provide evidence of the profound ways that social legacies affect our literacy practices and our worldview. From our Writing Center experience, we know that differences in identity and lived experiences, far more than differences in style or grammar, can undermine the best of communicative intentions. In America, race has a powerful influence on perspective and experience.

In identifying race as our focus in our revised approach to training, we understand it to be a social construct rather than a biological or genetic fact. We also understand race in the twenty-first century as a much more complex topic than the historical binary construction of black and white. But while we understand racial identity as far more fluid than it may have been fifty years ago, our experience with this project confirms three precepts proposed by race theorists Omi and Winant: "1. Old-fashioned racism still exists; 2. The traditional victimology of racism is moribund; and 3. To oppose racism one must remain conscious of race" (157).

In the remainder of this article, we reflect on our experience of moving in one Writing Center from a theoretical commitment to productive diversity to actual social change. While we cannot provide a neat five-step process for others to follow, we will structure our discussion around four of the lessons we learned from this experience. In deliberately trying to address race in our training over the last six years, the biggest challenge was accepting that we were a lot further from the goal of productive diversity than we imagined. The personal transformations that productive diversity calls for do not happen easily, nor do they occur by reading a book. Addressing race in a writing center program is not a one-time event, but a continual process, one that we remain engaged in today.

Lesson 1: Expect the Unexpected.

We wish we could recommend a particularly effective starting place for focusing attention on the ways that race affects literacy practices, but all we can do is describe where we began and why. We started making changes in an unusual year when the turnover in our staff was minimal. Most of our graduate and undergraduate students had already had one year of work experience and orientation to the theories that inform our practices. That particular year, we happened to have three students of color on the staff, remarkable because students of color (Native American, African American, and Latino) represent only 3.6 percent of the total enrollment at our university. The experience of the staff and the advantage of having students of color on the staff cleared away typical excuses for not introducing something new in training—too much to do with a new staff, too high of a turnover, too far from the "real" focus of Writing Center work.

Knowing we had an experienced staff (at least in writing center terms), we decided to focus some of our weekly writing center meetings on revisionist accounts of US history. At the beginning of the year, we presented three texts to the staff members: Ronald Takaki's *A Different Mirror*, James Loewen's *Lies My Teacher Told Me*, and Joel Spring's *Deculturalization and the Struggle for Equality*. To us, history offers the best explanation for the ways relationships are structured today. We believe many of these untold histories live in the memory of our students' teachers, parents, and grandparents. At the time, we assumed that exposure to this revisionist history in Writing Center training would show our Writing Center coaches how much color (and class) still affects opportunity structures in spite of the American belief in equality of opportunity. We hoped that these histories would sensitize our white middle-class coaches to the different experiences and memories that students of color bring to literacy education. We hoped that as a result of reading these histories, they might question some of the faulty assumptions that structure race relations on campus and begin to enter conversations that explored real differences. We hoped that the readings would expose (and began to fill) some gaps in their education. We hoped the historical perspective would make them more cautious about the assumptions they brought to tutoring sessions when working with students of color and more careful about clarifying the positions from which they entered these conversations.

We approached the texts as we have many other texts we bring to tutor training. We asked the writing coaches to pair up, choose a chapter, offer a summary of that chapter, and attempt to make connections to writing center practice. Initially, our concern was for the two African-American undergraduate coaches. Would they be put on the spot as we discussed issues of color? Would they feel pushed to become the spokesperson for "their people"? How could we call attention to issues of color without making them living specimens during the meetings?

Our concerns were misplaced. What we were unprepared for was the outburst among the mainstream members of the group. Their responses weren't necessarily spiteful (though, on occasion, maybe some were more than spiteful), but mostly they reacted in defense of their schooling, their knowledge, their identities. They became defensive at the idea of systemic domination and injustice. Many covered their uncomfortable views through denial. How could it be, the more confident and extroverted of the group asked, that their understandings were of privilege? How could they all be lumped together as a group known as white? One coach questioned, "Who is Takaki (author of one of the texts) anyway?" and another reminded us flatly, "Yeah, anyone can have a book published." Attempts to connect any of the readings to current practice were also stonewalled. Coaches questioned the relevance of the revisionist perspective for education today. In their minds, these histories didn't matter in post–civil rights time. There were no longer laws that kept students of color outside the university. As students, they considered themselves equal. Most of the coaches were youthful, and most of them behaved as though they had been exposed to something fearful, something that made them feel vulnerable. When we asked why this history had not been a part of their education, they countered that such history would frighten school children. They questioned the wisdom of exposing children to information for which they were not responsible. They argued that if in fact this revisionist history were true, then the history books would be too big, and there would be too much to cram into a course.

While we were caught in this unexpected whirlwind, we discovered an invaluable article by Beverly Tatum, called "Talking about Race, Learning about Racism: The Application of Racial Identity Development Theory in the Classroom." In Tatum's work, we found explanations for the reactions we were encountering, and we recommend this article to anyone undertaking a similar project. Tatum sees racial issues as emotional as well as intellectual. She warns that if these emotional responses are not addressed, they "can result in student resistance to oppression-related content areas" (Tatum 2). She points out that "such resistance can ultimately interfere with the cognitive understanding and mastery of the material" (Tatum 2). Tatum presents racial identity development theories that helped us understand the various reactions we encountered. Reading Tatum also assured us that everyone would grow with increased exposure and experience with people outside their own group. (Just recently, we also discovered Helen Fox's new book *When Race Breaks Out*, another invaluable resource.)

Tatum helped us make sense of the uncharted territory. Reading her reminded us that many of the undergraduates were encountering challenges to their belief systems for the first time. Beliefs about colorblindness, equality of opportunity, and individual effort seep into education from the earliest grades, reinforcing one another and keeping the lid on Pandora's Box. These beliefs keep white Americans comfortable, and they protect white Americans from accepting responsibility for honest dialogue about racial differences. Raising questions about race in tutor training means opening the Box. We learned to accept that the nice undergraduates on our staff, the ones we carefully screened and hired, would use these beliefs to defend themselves against the discomfort of dialogue about race. We learned that under the inevitable stress created by change, we can revert to familiar beliefs ourselves. We learned that if writing center training does not directly engage these beliefs, they are strong enough to undermine the best of intentions.

Rather than rush through the process or shut it down, we decided to move more slowly, finding time for individual conversations and inviting coaches to join us on a conference proposal reflecting on the experience. Many responded, and the process of writing the proposals and papers proved invaluable for reflecting on the highly charged experience. Through this process, we developed a more fine-grained understanding of the responses that initially confused us. For example, we discovered that one of the white coaches who seemed bored by the topic was from a multiracial family and had participated for several years in one of the few interracial campus groups, the gospel choir. Initially we had interpreted her boredom as a cover for discomfort when in fact she was, because of her greater contact with racial differences, at a different stage in identity development than many of the other white students. We also learned that another coach whose name and appearance suggested Latino heritage had been raised by his Polish mother. Learning that he knew little about his father's family helped us understand his discomfort with the discussions.

> **Nancy Grimm:** Engaging in this process with our coaches taught me that I, too, was unprepared to enter conversations about racial diversity. Helen Fox writes, "How is it that whites have no stories about how learning about race has affected our engagement with our students, our understanding of our material, our values and beliefs, our soul? Why are bookstores full of stories about the ways people of color have been affected by race relations yet carry nothing, or nearly nothing, about the experiences of whites?" (16). Fox recommends beginning our conversations about race by starting with our own stories about race. Reading Fox's advice makes me uncomfortably aware of the privileges I assumed when I instigated this project and the unacceptable interpretations I made of many of the coaches' responses. Although at this point I cannot recommend a particularly apt time or method for introducing race as a topic for writing center training, this experience has taught me how important it is to start with my own stories rather than assume that the histories written by and about *Others* will do the job for me. Following Fox's advice is a dose of humble pie. I realized I began learning about race as a college student/waitress in restaurant kitchens where Black and Latino workers prepared the food I carried and served to the front white (although not "segregated") part of the establishment. And I began interacting socially with the kitchen workers for the same sort of adolescent reasons I started smoking—because they were fun, and this experience was cool, risky, different, and therefore exciting. I quit smoking and learned to think about, rather than exoticize, racial difference much later in life.

Lesson 2: Find a Buddy with Similar Commitments Whom You Can Trust with Your Naiveté.

At the time of our work on this project, one of us (Nancy Barron) worked as a graduate student writing coach. This institutional placement combined with being a person of color offered access to conversations and relationships where some of the racial tensions were circulating and where some of the changes were occurring. Neither of us had experience initiating this sort of project, but because we shared a similar vision of literacy education and also valued our differences in perspective, we began turning to one another for motivation and insight. Because this project troubled workplace interactions, we needed a buddy whom we trusted to sort out our interpretations and decisions.

Nancy Barron: One advantage to being a person of color is that I'm allowed to not only knock but often I am let into the entry way of other students of color. The rest is up to me. Once I'm allowed to ask questions and to listen, I have to work hard to maintain my welcome, to sense when I should leave. Some Anglos may think people of color have it easy with other people of color. If this were true, we'd be a mighty force and some insecure person's nightmare. My calling card is just that. I'm allowed to call, but I'm not guaranteed a conversation. I have to earn their trust. At the same time, some people of color often seem to believe that there isn't much point trying to work with Anglos. I know I've heard many times, "Anglos don't listen." "They've already made up their minds." "They think they know everything." Sure, I've met Anglos who fit these descriptions, and it's problematic to simply say I've met people of color who fit these descriptions as well. However, to say as a statement, "'Anglos' or 'Whites' don't listen," is to say my experience with Nancy Grimm never happened. When I look back at our work, I realize my desire to work with others was put to the test. Was I patient enough? Was I expecting Nancy Grimm to understand my experience even though I didn't understand hers? If it's true that Anglos think they know everything, then I've lived a dream. In my dream I've met and worked with individuals who were as tangled up in our U.S. history as I am. If we are going to make change— positive encompassing change—we must work together in the face of the system, not because of it.

Nancy Grimm: My work with Nancy Barron provided the motivation as well as the guidance to continue with this project. Without her insights, suggestions, and stories of her experiences, I would have given up at an early stage. As a Writing Center director, one of my responsibilities is to maintain motivation and a collective sense of purpose among staff members. There were moments throughout this project when it was clear that our discussions about race were creating divisions as well as confusion. It was so much easier to maintain the status quo, to hire students who were most like me, to train them to enact a monolingual, monocultural writing center pedagogy. Nancy Barron's stories and cajoling helped me to maintain perspective and to think structurally about what was happening rather than take the conflicts personally. She reminded me to understand the coaches' responses historically, to remember that most of them were born long after Martin Luther King's time. Even with her guidance, there were moments of discouraging clarity when I understood better than before all the forces that keep us *out of this* uncharted territory.[3]

One thing our collaboration taught us was to pay attention to the many ways we are not the "same." If these differences are not addressed, then the conflicting assumptions that guide our behaviors can undermine the trust needed for honest collaboration. Even in the one institutional inheritance we ostensibly shared—the same religious faith—we learned how strongly our racial heritages contributed to different understandings of the traditions and tenets of that faith.

Although we share similar scholarly interests, our collaboration is also sustained by friendship, by meals shared together, by experiences with one another's families. The regularity and depth of these exchanges has created trust, the foundation for any sort of transformation. Productive diversity will not come about as easily among people who share only a workplace in common. Our collaboration may be an example of the transformative potential of productive diversity, but we caution that the transformations in our individual perspectives did not happen "naturally." We learned to ask honest, hard questions of one another, and we learned to listen carefully and openly to the response. "What were you thinking?" "Why did you say that?" "Can you unpack this for me?" Gradually, we each gained a more developed sense of how race contributes to the frames we used to understand Others.

> **Nancy Grimm:** Answering the questions Nancy Barron asked me meant letting go of an initial bristle of anger sparked by childhood memories of the "What do you think you're doing?" questions often posed (sometimes only implied) by adults responding to my trespassing against invisible class boundaries. It meant letting go of the protected hierarchy provided by hard-won academic credentials. It meant remembering the times as a student when I wanted to ask similar questions but didn't because it was safer to remain invisible, guessing at the answers. It meant the hard work of unpacking the assumptions and intentions and expectations that now formed my interactions at school. It meant the exhilaration of discovering that, yes, this was it all along. This is what made the journey long and hard, the always wondering what they were thinking, who taught them that, how they knew they were right so much of the time. It confirmed the appeal of Writing Center work, the way I could sometimes anticipate the questions that were in a student's head because I, too, had had those questions once. It meant the difficult work of making the tacit explicit. Above all, it created the satisfying achievement of a richer perspective on how school and literacy work.

Lesson 3: Be Clear for Yourself about What Is Motivating the Focus on Race.

From the beginning of our project, we shared a commitment to understanding more about the ways that diversity affects literacy education, and we were both committed to a vision of education that involved more than acculturation. Although we knew we each shared this commitment, we did not do enough to share it with the staff. Instead, we started making changes without clarifying adequately enough why we were making changes and what vision of the future we held. The undergraduates on our staff are both practical and intelligent, and they quickly recognized that we had made a shift and were moving in an unfamiliar direction. They began to put the brakes on, and we (again assuming they shared our unarticulated commitments) were frustrated by their resistance. We came slowly to recognize that we needed to be clear about the vision of learning we held. Together, we imagine a writing center as a place where people can come together across their differences to share interpretations inevitably informed by racial, class, social, and cultural identities, where in learning about difference, our own perspectives become transformed, and thus we begin to communicate, to solve problems, to teach, and to coexist more fully. However, even if the entire staff of a writing center subscribed to this vision, there are many reasons why they would not consider race as a confounding issue. Because writing center theory encourages us to think in terms of individuals rather than systems, because Americans believe that literacy education is the road to equity, because liberal ideology encounters racism by pretending that color makes no difference, because we are living in the post–civil rights era, it is easier to believe that race doesn't affect what we do in writing centers or that writing centers can't affect the work that racism does.

> **Nancy Grimm:** As the Writing Center director, I should have worked harder to clarity why we were taking this new direction in tutor training. Instead, I mistakenly assumed that the staff would readily align themselves with this desire to make the Writing Center a place where more conversations like the one in our opening story would take place. I was able to theorize about diversity, to make intellectual arguments for an ideological model of literacy (Street), but I didn't work hard enough on making arguments that made sense to mainstream undergraduates who as writing coaches were already carrying more responsibility for literacy education than many faculty do. What's more, most of these undergraduates were engineering and science majors, accustomed to thinking in practical rather than theoretical terms. In retrospect, I credit their challenges and resistance with forcing me to clarify the ways that race (and all diversity) intersects with literacy. I can't say I've finished this process of clarification, but I have learned how important it is to distinguish between individual acts of racism and structural racism. Rather than lead undergraduate coaches to believe I am holding them individually responsible for racism, I need to show how the Writing Center is implicated in institutional structures that remain oppressive to students of color. Equally important, I need to show the mainstream students how a commitment to productive diversity can benefit them.

It is difficult for those of us who are white to see the invisible social structures and assumptions that impede productive engagements with difference. Yet, at mainstream institutions, students of color rarely find their cultural beliefs represented in the curriculum and even more rarely do they find spaces where their primary literacy practices can be accepted as significant communicative acts. if they want to provide performances that earn good grades, they develop coping mechanisms that do not include making effective use of the writing center, at least not the writing center as most mainstream practitioners think of it. Members of the dominant group have difficulty conceptualizing systematic oppression because it lies outside of their lived experience. If we were starting over again, we would distinguish between systematic oppression and individual acts of racism. Political theorist Iris Marion Young helps us make it clear that structural oppression occurs when "the oppressed group's own experience and interpretation of social life finds little expression that touches the dominant culture, while that same culture imposes on the oppressed group its experience and interpretation of social life" (Young, *Justice* 60).

According to Young, oppression is "embedded in unquestioned norms, habits, and symbols, in the assumptions underlying institutional rules and collective consequences of following those rules" (41). Oppression in a structural sense has more to do with "often unconscious assumption and reactions of well-meaning people in ordinary interactions, media and cultural stereotypes, and structural features of bureaucratic hierarchies and market mechanisms—in short the normal processes of everyday life" (41). Oppression, then, doesn't need a military. Structural oppression is continuous and embedded in basic transactions and opinion. Young says the "systemic character of oppression implies that an oppressed group need not have a correlate oppressing group" (41). People just doing their jobs, without reflecting about how they currently and potentially affect the system, end up perpetuating oppression because they "do not understand themselves as agents of oppression" (42). Young concludes, "for every oppressed group there is a group who is *privileged* in relation to that group" (42). Young explains how, "[o]ften without noticing," the dominant groups "project their own experience as representative of humanity as such" (59).

> **Nancy Barron:** Initially, this idea was very difficult for me to comprehend because I tried to understand it as an oppressed individual might. But, the more I considered how much *I* unconsciously will my Anglo friends to be more like me, to be more Mexican when it comes to issues of death, to be more Latino when it comes to closeness and physical boundaries, I know, I, too, project my sense of humanity onto individuals from very different worldviews. The difference is that I'm surrounded by responses, by behaviors, by words and actions that rotund me not in the majority.

Young also makes it explicit that, in matters of race, "The stereotypes confine [students of color] to a nature which often is attached in some ways to their bodies," so it isn't that a person of color says the wrong things but rather what that person looks like that will maintain the stereotype. Young also says, "Those living under cultural imperialism" are defined "from the outside, positioned, placed, by a network of dominant meanings they experience" from elsewhere, from people "with whom they do not identify and who do not identify with them" (59).

> **Nancy Barron:** In a Latino community, my university colleagues looked like the oppressors, the ones who never listened but always knew what was right for everyone. At the same time, these colleagues persistently assumed everyone saw them as individuals, and not connected to a larger group.

In addition to Young, we found Patricia Williams helped us to explain to the staff the insidious effects of colorblindness—the habit of pretending not to notice color because it "doesn't (or shouldn't) matter." Patricia Williams tells a story about her nursery-school-aged son who responded to his teachers' queries about the color of trees, grass, sky with the comment, "It makes no difference." His teachers advised Williams to take him to have his eyes tested. When the expert pronounced his vision sound, Williams began to analyze her son's "problem" differently. She realized that he had heard his teachers admonish his classmates who were fighting about whether a black person could be the good guy in the playground games. "It doesn't matter whether you're black or white or red or green or blue," they insisted. Her son must have concluded that if his color didn't matter (in spite of his painful experience on the playground), then neither did the color of the sky, the clouds, or the flowers. Williams writes,

> My son's anxious response was redefined by his teachers as physical deficiency. This anxiety redefined as deficiency suggests to me that it may be illustrative of the way in which the liberal ideal of color-blindness is too often confounded. That is to say, the very notion of blindness about color constitutes an ideological confusion at best, and denial at its very worst. I recognize, certainly, that the teachers were inspired by a desire to make whole a division in the ranks. But much is overlooked in the move to undo that which clearly and unfortunately matters just by labeling it that which "makes no difference"; the dismissiveness, however unintentional, leaves those in my son's position pulled between the clarity of their own experience and the often alienating terms in which they must seek social acceptance. (4)

The poignant story Williams tells about her son shows the way that well-intentioned white Americans avoid the harsh reality that color still makes a difference in post–civil rights times, and it also shows the effect of the avoidance on a student of color whose confusion is then cast as deficit.

> **Nancy Grimm:** I will never forget one of the first times we discussed the fallacies of colorblindness around a Writing Center table. One African-American student told about how when he walked across the campus at dusk, from the library to the residence hall, white women would quickly cross to the other side of the street — the side without a sidewalk. As we listened, another young African-American man who sat next to me sadly nodded his head, and he trembled as though his body were racked by fever. Although I didn't look over at him, I felt his trembling and thought about how I knew him as a responsible, warm, bright student, one who had worked for several years in the Writing Center. Outside the Writing Center, particularly at dusk, his color mattered far more than his character. Since that time, another African-American writing coach has told about how he regularly hears car door locks click when he walks through town. These stories, written as they are on their bodies of young men I care for, illustrate how painfully false the notion of colorblindness is.

Writing center coaches need both the theoretical and narrative-based arguments for addressing race, but perhaps most important is convincing them of the value that expanded communicative repertoire will have for them. Moves toward diversity in the writing center need to be rooted in a sense that the mainstream has something to gain from leaving colorblindness behind. Again, we turn to The New London Group who insist that the existing "formalized, monolingual, monocultural, and rule-governed" project of literacy pedagogy will not hold up to today's challenges (9). Their proposed pedagogy involves a new conception of students, one that imagines them as "as active design-ers—makers—of social futures" (7).

If race is to be a topic in writing center training, the undertaking has more hope of succeeding if student coaches are invited into the project as design-ers rather than as recipients of an imposed diversity experience. To move beyond the belief that racism is a thing of the past, but also to gain from the significant progress toward racial democracy that has been achieved since the 1950s, we need to invite students into productive exchanges about issues of color in order that they might decide how to achieve a broader communicative repertoire. We find this vision reinforced in Kalantzis and Cope, who clarify that learning need not be a matter of "development" in which the old self is left behind (as from a homely caterpillar to a beautiful moth), but rather a matter of *expanding repertoire*, "starting with a recognition of lifeworld experi-ence and using that experience as a basis for extending what one knows and what one can do" (124). Because so many writing center administrators are white, because the professional organization is predominantly white, most of our programmatic and professional decisions have been based on assumptions informed by white experience that has rarely been challenged. To change this status quo, students who work in writing centers need to understand their role as designers of a new world.

Lesson 4: Address the Extent to Which Relationships with Self, Family, Friends, and Institutions Are Structured by Racial Beliefs and Assumptions.

We didn't realize until we were in the middle of this project the extent to which we were not only challenging the self-complacency of individuals but also threatening individuals' relationships with family, friends, and institu-tions. This was far more than an academic project. Provoking the kind of transformation called for by productive diversity in a tutor-training program involves tinkering with something as fundamental as people's identities and the ways these identities have been formed in relationship with others. Person-ally held beliefs about race, whether they are articulated or not, are connected with one's relationship with parents, siblings, friends, neighbors, extended family, former teachers, schools, churches, places of employment. We did not understand when we began how much was at stake, yet we learned that if change was going to occur, we needed to offer new ways of conceptualiz-ing these relationships. We also needed to pay attention to the relationships among staff members rather than look at what happened between the staff and the students who used the Writing Center. Most importantly, we needed to replace the familiar understandings that were being threatened with new understandings. If we could not suggest ways to restructure belief systems and renegotiate relationships, then our effort would unravel, and we would end up reinforcing attitudes we are trying to replace.

Theorists such as John Ogbu and Iris Marion Young (again) helped us think about how to renegotiate beliefs about race within relationships. Ogbu helps us make the useful distinction between voluntary and involuntary minorities, clarifying that the large group of *voluntary* minorities (which often include the immediate family and ancestors of many of the undergraduate coaches) were willing to give up languages and identities in order to "become" American, believing that their sacrifices would benefit succeeding generations. An important difference is that the voluntary minority *chooses* to come to the U.S. by immigration. As a result, they have a homeland to compare their U.S. experiences with, and they see discriminatory practices as temporary (368). Voluntary minorities believe in education and they tend to push their children to better themselves since they have the opportunity to take full advantage of the U.S. educational system.

The involuntary minority, on the other hand, is part of the U.S. experience because of conquest or colonization. Ogbu's groups of involuntary minorities include the Native Americans who were colonized, African Americans who were brought as slaves, and the Mexican Americans who were incorporated after the Treaty of Guadalupe Hidalgo of 1848. These three groups do not have the same identification with the dominant American culture; they tend to compare themselves *against* the Anglo mainstream. In general, they do not believe discriminatory practices are temporary because the glass ceilings and limited opportunities are evident throughout generations and in their communities. And, as Ogbu says, "they see no justifiable reason for their inferior education—except discrimination" (375).

According to Ogbu, sometimes schooling is perceived as "a linear acculturation, [where] involuntary minority students feel that they have to choose between academic success and maintaining their minority identity and cultural frame of reference" (378). It is important that those of us with a family history of voluntary immigration be able to understand and explain this significant difference when objections are raised by family or friends. Additionally, it is important for understanding the literacy choices that involuntary minorities face in a writing center. For some students, it's great to get individual attention; for others that individual attention can seem like an interrogation or even dismissal of family belief systems and familiar ways with words.

To provide guidance to coaches who have never before been aware of the dangers of projecting their own experiences onto others, we again turned to a point made by Young. In an essay titled "Asymmetrical Reciprocity," Young argues that when people try to put themselves in another's position, they inevitably put *themselves* in the other's position. This is particularly problematic in matters of race. Young says, "When privileged people put themselves in the position of those who are less privileged, the assumptions derived from their privilege often allow them unknowingly to misrepresent the other's situation" (*Intersecting* 48). We find it helpful to share Young's caution as well as her recommendation that we approach communication across differences with a stance of *wonder*. According to Young, "a respectful stance of wonder toward other people is one of openness across, awaiting new insight about their needs, interests, perceptions or values. Wonder also means being able to see one's own position, assumptions, perspective as strange, because it has been put in relation to theirs" (56). Young's insistence on recognizing the asymmetry in positions is a useful corrective to an overemphasis on the peerness of relationships in the writing center. Young emphasizes that the value of assuming *asymmetry* is that people enlarge their thinking in two ways: (a) their own thinking becomes relativized, and (b) they develop an enlarged understanding of the world, one that is unavailable given the limits of our own perspectives. Recognizing these gains is important, given that confrontation with difference can be unsettling and disruptive.

Nancy Grimm: While I was often discouraged and conflicted about this undertaking, I learned through it that racial encounters were occurring every day in the Writing Center, too often in unproductive ways. I learned to pay more attention to the ways Writing Center experiences were affecting the students of color on the staff, and my newly developed awareness has made it impossible to go back to pretending that race doesn't matter. I learned to look for small instances of change rather than institutional change. I learned that as a visible campus representative of academic literacy, my words, my presence, my responses matter to students of color, just as much as my silence, my absence, my complicity also matter. Nancy Barron was persistent in teaching me to recognize that I, too, was a member of a race and a culture, and that my actions and reactions either reinforced or challenged the beliefs that students of color hold about the mainstream. I am encouraged when six years after our beginning, long after the original group of writing coaches has graduated, the undergraduates of color regularly apply to work in the Writing Center. I am encouraged when I see our increasing number of international students working side by side with writing coaches of color. I am encouraged when I hear mainstream coaches respond to cultural inquiries from international students by saying "As a white American" rather than representing their experience as universal. I am encouraged when a Native-American writing coach gives the Writing Center a medicine wheel and a map of the US showing Native tribes. I am encouraged when at our predominantly white institution, an African-American walk-in coach reads an essay about how unnecessary affirmative action is, and the mainstream student writer has the lived experience of wondering about how the shape and tone of his argument are affecting his audience. Our Writing Center has become a place where students of color are employees, students who are often bidialectical and bicultural and sometimes bilingual. This signifies to Writing Center users and to faculty in unmistakably visual terms that literacies are always multiple, situated, and ideological.

Productive diversity, the transformation in mainstream practices envisioned by the new literacy scholars, is the sort of goal that needs to be kept visible on the horizon for a long, long time. The old autonomous versions of literacy make it too easy to maintain racial divisions, to hold individuals responsible for long-standing social ills, to separate certain lived experiences from textual representation, to imagine that justice can be achieved by reading a book, to think that we can intellectually rather than experientially challenge structural racism. It is comfortable to retreat to this old programming when the going gets rough. It is equally easy for others to challenge, misinterpret, and weaken efforts to change. The dialectical relationship between a theoretical commitment and transformed practice is central to this effort. Again and again, we returned to theorists for the interpretive frameworks and conceptual understandings to take into practice and to clarify our arguments. Again and again, we question how to practically live our commitments. The balance is fragile. Courtney Cazden turns to the Australian Aboriginal metaphor of *ganma*, literally a place where fresh and salt water meet to nourish richly diverse forms of life, "biologically in the literal situation, culturally and intellectually in the metaphorical" (321). The metaphor reminds us of the unequal power relation: salt water can easily overcome fertile land, while fresh water can do little harm to the ocean. A writing center can be an institutional site where diverse forms of thinking can be encouraged, yet the salt water of mainstream institutional life is always abundantly present and can quickly overwhelm the fresh water. The work of maintaining the fragile balance happens in one relationship at a time.

In spite of our best efforts to address the challenges we encountered, we also learned to accept that sometimes a particular individual's identity may be too fragile, and change will not occur when a person feels too vulnerable. Transformation, if it is going to happen at all, will happen in multidirectional ways, in no predictable time frame, and often in spaces beyond the institutional gaze. We believe the writing center provides a space for hope, a place to begin. Our concluding story shows the unpredictability of knowing if or how or where or when these attempts will lead to the kinds of transformations that make dialogue across differences possible. One thing we learned for sure was that the more we changed our thinking and interpretations of others' responses, the better we listened and the more we understood.

A Story to Conclude, Nancy Barron

A number of years ago, an Anglo male writing coach, whom I thought seemed to respect me, got into a rant and became extremely frustrated as he tried to convince me that the Great Lakes' Indians were only trouble, lived in the past, demanded rights that weren't theirs. The focus was on Indian fishing rights (he came from generations of Anglo fishermen). Now, it's important to understand that the student was a third-year undergraduate, a mainstream Anglo, and known for his arrogance. And, I was a graduate student, from the west, so fishing rights were something I had read and heard about, but I had never experienced the clashes before. And, my own undergraduate university provided slightly traumatic memories—janitors printing KKK paraphernalia for their group, a physical assault on campus during the middle of the day against an African-American woman student.[4] I had internalized my own defense, my low expectations of *Them*, the ones who are always so sure they know much. But I was aware of my weak tendencies, and worked hard to remember he was a kid, a human capable of listening. I tried and still try to untangle the tight construction I have of disrespectful Anglos.

The young face tried to let me know I was okay since the Indians out in the southwest were different. (He saw me connected with Indians because I explained to him once what it meant to be mestizo.) He fit my Anglo stereotype of letting me know he knew who I was. Always so confident and sure they know, always in control. His eyes narrowed as he said authoritatively, rudely and with a clenched mouth, "*They* [the desert people] don't cause trouble like the ones up here!" His words, and, worse, his look caused my stomach to turn, my heart became heavy, and my head insisted I say something. I challenged him to take the department's Ojibwe culture class so that he might learn about fishing rights from an Ojibwe perspective. Before I could finish, he raised his voice to a near shout. His flushed young face transfigured under a baseball cap with a fishing-lure logo. I heard and felt, "I'd go in there and tell them, 'I hate you Indians!'" I shut down. I looked down and mentally searched for a song to hum so I couldn't hear him anymore.

My head sometimes races when my eyes send images that don't make sense, words that don't fit the image before me. Had I been younger, in my early twenties, I probably would've concluded he was just a *white boy*. An ignorant son of a racist who'd *never* change. That's how they are. *Asi son los Anglo Sajones.* But I was older, so I searched for reasons, for any past memory that might explain what my eyes saw and my ears heard. I didn't and couldn't make myself talk to him after I saw and felt his deep anger. Every time I saw him, I averted my eyes. My body did not want his image, and I didn't have the practice to take on a kid I used to respect. I knew, in my head, his hate was not new. He most likely heard similar conclusions from friends, family, other nonnative fishers. But I wasn't ready, simply wasn't capable of dealing with the force of his hate. Regardless of what stage he was in, regardless of my own experience working with youthful ignorance, I felt disappointed, discouraged, and disabled.

We became mutually uncomfortable around each other, and although we had plenty of opportunity to talk things out, I *couldn't* as well as wouldn't. I was bruised and absolutely heavy with the image of his disgust toward an entire people. Believe it or not, I once really liked this kid. I liked his cockiness, his arrogance that I wrote off as his youthful immaturity. But I never expected to see such anger that seemed to be generations old. I never expected and couldn't accept that the intelligent immature kid was capable of crushing me with what I considered his distorted hate. This kid and I weren't complete strangers. We had entered the stage of conversations where we shared insights of education, of individuals, of jobs, of movies.

He ended up quitting the Writing Center that same year, and I never saw him again anywhere on campus or in the community, which is unusual for a small campus of 6,000 and a small town in the upper peninsula. I thought he left the area. My colleagues and peers would bring up his name and usually shake their heads as they'd recount a memory or two about his behavior. His behavior had been "a problem" but I used to find his shallow thinking honest, not purposefully hurtful. As for his explosion, I was always mixed. In some ways, he was too honest for me. There was a part of me that wanted to remember the kid who hid his hatred from me. The kid who didn't play games, but let you know how he read an article, an assignment. He'd come to me regularly to complain about an African student. She was too confident, too outspoken for being an international student. She wasn't humble, happy to be in the U.S. She was too direct, knew what she wanted from her studies, and challenged him politically, socially, and continuously during their sessions. He was always pink (mostly from frustration) at the end of their sessions, and we always debriefed. I wasn't sure why he came to me, but I decided he chose to, so I made sure I was honest. My focus was on his reactions. Why did he carry a script for international students to follow? He couldn't answer except "everyone knows that," meaning his conclusions were tacit and probably reinforced by media, friends, and family. I'd turn the script around and demand he behave as I would like for him, too. Not a chance. There was my opening to shove the mental mirror in front of him. With the African student, lie began to reflect. I could almost hear his soul snap out of its rigid structure—he began to change. And, like most people, I made the mistake of thinking change meant he was now open. He would leave behind his ignorance as if it were a bad habit. I failed to acknowledge I was dealing with a mindset, a philosophy of sorts, a worldview. A heavy and deep worldview.

I believe I'm a lucky person when it comes to issues of color because I've been fortunate to see people change with my own eyes. Two-and-a-half years after his rage and my incompetence to battle the results of his rage, I walked into the room where I was to defend my dissertation. Among the group present in the audience was the same kid. He sat off to my right, under a baseball cap with some kind of fishing logo. He came to my dissertation defense on literacy assumptions and involuntary minorities—issues of color that included the local Ojibwe. I saw him, had a memory flash, my stomach began to react, my eyes turned away, my head raced once again. I wondered for a few moments whether he would interrupt my presentation, but he didn't. He said, as he left in a hurry, "I wanted to see what you had to say." And I thought I'd never see him again.

A few weeks later, I ran into him at a local tourist spot at one of the most northern points in the peninsula (Brockway Mountain). It's one of my favorite spots because Lake Superior feels superior, and the land feels rugged. I'm told it's a good place to catch the northern lights. The hawks and bald eagles soar near there on windy days, so, for me, this place is unique and of its own. On this day, however, there was no wind. No birds. No waves. Superior was humbled as the sunlight shone white on the smooth lake. It was pure chance (or was it?) to see that the same kid whose tight face held a lethal mouth with venomous words now held a nervous smile. We took each other's hands as a welcome and clearly a relief. He let me know he was traveling with his current job and meeting "all kinds of different people." My eyes saw what seemed a sincere expression, apologetic almost, and definitely relieved as he told me about his future plans that included working with people from different backgrounds.

I retell this story for a few reasons. The first is to point out that I did nothing unusual or *extra* to work with this kid. In fact, I was overwhelmed during the time I could have said or done something to address my feelings about his words, how he affected me, and so on, but I didn't. And I was in a position to do so. Everything was set up for me to *educate* him. But I basically said nothing, hardly made eye contact. In many ways, I did what I ask academics *not* to do. I advocate for academics to work on letting students know when they disagree with their opinions. It's very important for involuntary minority students to hear the words from their instructors. Instead, I made the young Anglo kid invisible, something I think involuntary minorities have practice with—especially with Anglo men. So, I know *I* had nothing to do with his attempts to meet different people, to find courage and attend my dissertation defense knowing he'd be sitting among many people who thought poorly of him. Yet, he came, for whatever reasons. On the mountain, he let me know he wasn't the same, for whatever reasons. I saw the same kid, a little older, but the same one who still wore fishing insignia on his baseball caps. His outburst, as upsetting as it was, fit a type. He behaved liked mainstream males are expected to. His behavior on the mountain, as awkward yet warm as it was, fit a type I'm unfamiliar with. I believe he's moved to different stage; he's changed ever so slightly, but he changed. And for whatever reasons, he's kept me in mind and made sure I knew he had changed. He may or may never know how much his actions have confused my memories. He's made me think, reflect, and construct more space for future behaviors like his that I may run into.

My understandings have and hopefully will continue to change. The images I saw in the past, I see in the present, but differently. The colors, the tribes of cultural differences still look the same, but they don't feel the same. My eyes send similar images to my head, and, clearly, with practice, my head, ears, stomach, and heart filter the same images from the past a little differently. It's probably important to remember I'm an involuntary minority telling a story about an Anglo male mainstream student. Our roles weren't typical since I'm the authority, and he, my subordinate. The teacher and the student, the colored and the opaque, the woman and the man, the older and the younger. We took risks. And we both ended up uncomfortable, and I temporarily shut down. And I'd do it again knowing that change hardly comes when we want it to or how we'd like for it to be. Risks are important. The Writing Center is set up to work with students individually. Risks are there, but hidden most of the times. There is no guarantee, no script, no way to control the person in front or the person within exactly as we'd like to. But there is time to make room, to make spaces for memory. When we recall what we know is possible, then the present isn't always as new, always as surprising. With more practice with diversity, more practice remembering it's not easy, more practice asking what all might be happening that I can't see, maybe, just maybe, we'll arrive at more humane confusion and recognize our dependence on each other.

Notes

[1] The Writing Center where we have worked together is located at a technological university in a remote rural area where students of color account for less than four percent of the total student population. Stories from universities and colleges with a greater representation of diversity may be quite different. We hope this article serves as an invitation to share more about how racial diversity is addressed in different writing center contexts.

[2] We recognize Sylvia Matthews as an influential partner on the work that led to this article. Sylvia teaches the tutor training course at our Writing Center and was involved in many of the experiences and discussions we write about here.

[3] In *Because of the Kids: Facing Racial and Cultural Differences in Schools*, readers will find another useful story about the challenges of collaborating across racial differences.

[4] This incident became for me a central memory of my first year at university. It was during spring term, 1988. On a sunny Friday afternoon, an Anglo woman and man approached and shoved a young African-American woman student until they knocked her down, saying, "We don't want any of you niggers on this campus." An Asian-American student saw and heard what happened. He approached, shouting at the couple to leave the student alone to which they replied, "We don't want any of you Chinks, either." The word spread quickly on campus, and by the following Monday there was a student-initiated information meeting on the incident. The tension, fear, and anger was thick and heavy, reminding me of the black and white race-related documentaries I had seen about the States in the 1950s. The student leaders let us know what happened, that the couple were not students (meaning they were local community members), that the African-American student did not want to return to campus, and that all students of color should never walk alone on campus, especially not at night, and especially not in the parking lot. I became afraid, for the first time, to continue my studies. I also became angry that I became afraid, and I continued my studies.

Works Cited

Bawarshi, Anis, and Stephanie Pelkowski. "Postcolonialism and the Idea of a Writing Center." *The Writing Center Journal* 19.2 (1999): 41–58. Print.

Black, Laurel Johnson. *Between Talk and Teaching: Reconsidering the Writing Conference*. Logan: Utah State UP, 1998. Print.

Briggs, Lynn Craigue, and Meg Woolbright, eds. *Stories from the Center: Connecting Narrative and Theory in the Writing Center*. Urbana: NCTE, 2000. Print.

Cazden, Courtney B. "Four Innovative Programmes: A Postscript from Alice Springs." *Multiliteracies: Literacy Learning and the Design of Social Futures*. Ed. Bill Cope and Mary Kalantzis. New York: Routledge, 2000. Print.

Condon, Frankie, and Michael Condon. "The Resisting Center: Race, Inequality, and the Activist Writing Center." National Writing Centers Association Conference, 2000. Print.

Fox, Helen. *"When Race Breaks Out": Conversations about Race and Racism in College Classrooms*. New York: Peter Lang, 2001. Print.

Grimm, Nancy Maloney. *Good Intentions: Writing Center Work for Postmodern Times*. Portsmouth: Heinemann, 1999. Print.

Kalantzis, Mary, and Bill Cope. "Changing the Role of Schools." *Multiliteracies: Literacy Learning and the Design of Social Futures.* Ed. Bill Cope and Mary Kalantzis. New York: Routledge, 2000. Print.

Loewen, James W. *Lies My Teacher Told Me: Everything Your American History Textbook Got Wrong.* New York: The New Press, 1995. Print.

The New London Group. "A Pedagogy of Multiliteracies." *Multiliteracies: Literacy Learning and the Design of Social Futures.* Ed. Bill Cope and Mary Kalantzis. New York: Routledge, 2000. Print.

North, Stephen M. *"The Idea of a Writing Center."* College English 46.5 (1984): 433-46. Print.

Obidah, Jennifer E., and Karen Manheim Teel. *Because of the Kids: Facing Racial and Cultural Differences in Schools.* New York: Teachers College P, 2001. Print.

Ogbu, John U. "Minority Status, Cultural Frame of Reference, and Schooling." *Literacy: Interdisciplinary Conversations.* Ed. Deborah Keller-Cohen. Cresskill: Hampton P, 1994. 361–84. Print.

Omi, Michael, and Howard Winant. *Racial Formation in the United States from the 1960s to the 1990s.* 2nd ed. New York: Routledge, 1994. Print.

Silk, Bobbie Baylis, ed. *The Writing Center Resource Manual.* Emmitsburg: NWCA Press, 1998. Print.

Spring, Joel. *Deculturalization and the Struggle for Equality: A Brief History of the Education of Dominated Cultures in the United States.* 2nd ed. New York: McGraw-Hill, 1997. Print.

Street, Brian V. *Literacy in Theory and Practice.* Cambridge: Cambridge UP, 1984. Print.

Takaki, Ronald. *A Different Mirror: A History of Multicultural America.* Boston: Little, Brown, 1993. Print.

Tatum, Beverly Daniel. "Talking about Race, Learning about Racism: Application of Racial Identity Development Theory in the Classroom." *Harvard Educational Review* 62 (1992): 1–24. Print.

Williams, Patricia J. *Seeing a Color-Blind Future: The Paradox of Race.* New York: The Noonday P, 1997. Print.

Young, Iris Marion. *Intersecting Voices: Dilemmas of Gender Political Philosophy, and Policy.* Princeton: Princeton UP, 1997. Print.

---. *Justice and the Politics of Difference.* Princeton: Princeton UP, 1990. Print.

EXPLORATIONS: THE MULTIMODAL WRITING CENTER

Preserving the Rhetorical Nature of Tutoring When Going Online

Lisa Eastmond Bell
ROCKY MOUNTAIN WRITING CENTERS ASSOCIATION

In this essay, originally published in The Writing Center Director's Resource Book *in 2006, Lisa Bell examines "the rhetorical differences among face-to-face tutoring, asynchronous OWLing, and synchronous online tutoring" and the tutoring methods needed to carry out each mode effectively. Analyzing differences and similarities among these approaches, Bell states that the learning process of the tutorial—no matter what the mode—must involve a "dialectical engagement" that encompasses "exchange, clarification, justification, and meaning making." At risk in online environments is the shift in the tutorial from a focus on organizing and expressing ideas to textual editing functions. Bell explores this dichotomy and offers suggestions on ways to retain the "rhetorical nature of tutoring" in online environments that support the exchange of ideas and the engagement of the writer and tutor in the writing process.*

There were thirty-seven broken links on the OWL and several emailed papers waiting in the in-box when I arrived as the new writing center coordinator. With only two weeks before the start of fall semester and no staff hired, the OWL was the least of my worries. None of the new staff would know enough about tutoring, let alone online tutoring, to answer OWLs, so I took it upon myself to send replies to submissions. Not wanting to ruffle feathers, I answered the OWL as previously done in the center. This meant inserting into the emailed text my comments in all blue caps. I was not an expert in computer communication, but I knew enough to suspect my all-caps responses were equivalent to a tutor standing on a chair with a bullhorn to address the adjacent writer. Also, because of the campus's open enrollment status, some students' papers were riddled with errors, and the many patterns of errors were part of what needed to be addressed in the tutorial. It was difficult to see how to help and still provide a learning experience without falling into the editing trap. Again, I found myself textually screaming, shouting out comma rules left and right.

The promised turnaround time of twenty-four hours made it difficult to get a weekend in without a couple hours of work tutoring online. However, I had no immediate access to the OWL to change the policy in writing. Three weeks into the semester, I opened our email account to find twenty-one papers wait-ing for me. I spent the day responding and then made plans to shut the OWL down until a better format was in place.

The new format not only had to be practical and functional, it needed to better reflect what the tutors did in the center. The online work, as it stood, felt a very distant cousin to what I had known as a tutor and administrator in face-to-face sessions. I wanted to tell jokes, confirm understanding with eye contact, and hear the student own the paper by reading it aloud. I knew that before bringing the OWL beast back online, I had to understand what structure I was dealing with and how it related to tutoring in the physical "sit down and talk" sense. I had to understand the rhetorical differences brought about by changes in tutoring mediums and environment. There was research to be done. My reviews of literature uncovered little more than lore—other people's stories with mostly not so happy endings. There were "how tos" but few "whys." I felt, as did SUNY Albany's Karen Rowan, the excitement sur-rounding online tutoring "is best served as an appetizer to a substantial entrée of research and scholarship" (10).

Yet online tutorials were and are taking place at an alarming rate consid-ering the lack of research. We haven't determined how the service is being accepted by student writers and tutors or how the tutoring process itself has been altered by online mediums. As Sara Kimball suggested, "In working with student writers online, we are not merely transporting what we do in face-to-face conversation in our real-life writing center into cyberspace" (30). Clearly, we lack an understanding of what we are doing when we take writing center work online. As a writing center coordinator, I felt the need to acknowledge the rhetorical differences among face-to-face tutoring, asynchronous OWLing, and synchronous online tutoring and discover what tutoring and training methods are needed to address these issues in order to continue writer-cen-tered tutoring and explore the future of writing center work.

Certainly, I needed answers. Returning to the theoretical foundations of writing center work, there were three guiding principles on which I decided to build our center's face-to-face and OWL work. First, as Stephen M. North observed, was "to produce better writers, not better writing" (438). Second was to encourage writers to gain the skills and confidence that would help them improve their writing. As Mary M. Dossin asserted, "Tutoring is only valid when it is part of the learning process" (14). Finally, as Joan Hawthorne suggested, "Our rationale is to work with rather than for the writer" (qtd. in Moe 15).

The next step in the discovery process was returning to examine the famil-iar. Revisiting the recognizable would help me rethink the future of our OWL. Although some decisions had already been made (a note in the OWL com-mittee folder said they had decided to disable the chat capabilities for OWL because it [wasn't] being used"), I felt we could change the tide if proven necessary.

Looking at the familiar aspects of writing center work, I started with the basics of tutorials. Ideally, face-to-face, writing tutors work one-on-one with writers for approximately twenty minutes to an hour, depending on the assignment. They focus first on the broad issues of organization and content and second on sentence-level revision issues, keeping in focus the task of creating better writers and not simply better papers. As far as OWLing, over the past decade we have seen everything from Multi-Object Oriented (MOO)s to whiteboards to web cams. However, due to costs, time, and training, synchronous tutoring programs are the exception rather than the rule in web work. By and large, the majority of OWL tutorials are of the asynchronous email variety. Essentially, writers email their papers to the tutors along with answers to a short survey about their class, assignment, stage in the writing process, due date, and concerns. Tutors open these email submissions and respond to each writer's work either at an appointed time or on the basis of other workloads in the center.

Online tutorials must complement rather than replace traditional tutorials. Justin Jackson was correct in writing of Purdue's OWL, "I am not arguing that online tutorials can ever replace f2f [face-to-face] tutorials; they cannot" (1). Sitting in an office responding to student papers online all day was not a familiar form of tutoring to me. It seemed, rhetorically, vastly different from f2f tutorials. Just as Mary Wislocki explained, "Like many writing center directors, I had found that developing my OWL was a complicated business, especially since it seemed to challenge rather than reinforce well-worn writing center practices and values" (71). This is possibly because "the paper doesn't communicate by itself—the person communicates" (Coogan qtd. in Capossela 245), and without the writer present in some form, the learning process, the dialectical engagement—exchange, clarification, justification, meaning making— does not seem entirely intact. My questions to all but one or two writers went unanswered. Eye contact was impossible. I began to feel as if I was not running a writing center online but a much used and abused "fix-it" center.

Tutoring is a discussion-based, dialectical exchange. Tutors and writers move through the motions of communication, written and oral, in order to clarify and hone arguments and ideas. Tutorials often get noisy because writers and tutors are busy making meaning. Tutors and writers talk through text and wade through words, looking for the best way to express ideas to certain discourse communities. They grapple with the ideas, assignment, and structure, then address sentence-level and stylistic concerns, making their way through the writing process, prewriting to proofreading. Throughout these global-to-local, process-based sessions, ideally tutors clarify the roles of writers and tutors, and they rely heavily on methods of questioning and reader response to facilitate discussion. They also redefine and clarify words, phrases, and ideas while reading the silences, facial expressions, and body movements of writers. For these reasons, the presence of the writer is vital to a tutoring session because "both the writer and the tutor are real individuals, with real writing needs; it is an ongoing dialogue that needs . . . direct and indirect questioning, and the writer's response" (Jackson 1–2). My attempts at tutoring through asynchronous email exchange felt different because they lacked the vital presence of the writer.

Online mediums often omit a writer's presence or at least alter the connections between author, audience, and text, minimizing the importance of the writer's learning process. In online tutorials, tutors are not always able to read the student without an opening discussion or visual social cue, although many try to simulate it in a brief survey to be completed before sending a paper in for a tutorial. For me, as an online tutor, the survey did not provide enough of the writer's presence. The survey gave me about as much insight into the writer as a personal ad gives one about a prospective date. I didn't want a sound byte. I wanted information beyond the surface, motives, and methods. Kimball noted that the "lack of information about participants' attitudes and intentions makes a difference in a medium that seems like conversation" (9). One clear example of problems that occur when the writer is omitted is evident in Holly Moe's 2000 review of an online tutoring service. For her piece, Moe posed as a student and e-mailed a paper to the service that, in her absence, was forced to make assumptions about the text and author's intentions. According to Moe, the tutor "misread the prompt and offered me all the wrong solutions. Furthermore, he or she edited my sentences, changing my voice and meaning" (15). Moe's experience confirms that "the most frightening prospect of the online tutorial is that all one is left with is the writing and not the writer, the product and not the process" (Jackson 2).

This shift to editing rather than tutoring is especially easy because writing centers serve students from across the disciplines, and tutors certainly do not and cannot comprehend the content of such a wide range of texts. For this reason alone, tutors may assume that student authors "know what they are talking about" and revert to looking at formulaic concepts of structure, style, grammar, and usage. Additionally, tutors have to work a lot harder to maintain a global-to-local approach because only the text is present through e-mail, and editing is a lot easier to do when there is no writer there to remind you that writing is about communicating ideas just as much as it is about the technical transmittance of ideas.

What I have found after working both as an instructor and short-lived asynchronous tutor is that basic parts of face-to-face tutorials are altered significantly in asynchronous OWLing. Questions posed to student writers become little more than the sort of questions instructors pose in the margins of a paper. "How do you think that this relates to X?" is no longer a conversation-inducing question, but becomes "make this relate to X." "What is the main point of this paragraph?" is no longer a question to help engage writers in the revision process and the analysis of essay organization. Instead, it seems to tell writers that their paragraph is currently pointless. Also, when the question is posted via e-mail, the time factor makes an immediate reassuring tutor response such as "that's what I got out of the paragraph, too" almost impossible, disrupting the feedback that is so vital to the learning process.

Many of these shifts in tutoring practices when moving from face-to-face to online tutoring (synchronous and asynchronous) are never resolved because of a lack of shared time and space within a tutorial. David Coogan, of Illinois Institute of Technology, pointed out that email tutorials

> change the meaning of tutorial work by challenging the rhetorical constraints of face-to-face conferencing. In other words, by replacing talk with asynchronous writing, email disrupts the most familiar boundaries in the writing center: shared space and limited time. As a result, email changes the conference's discipline by slowing it down (from 30 minutes to several days), and by collapsing the self into the text where it becomes a rhetorical construct, not a social given. Interpreting student text, rather than the student, becomes email tutoring's centerpiece. (171)

Clearly, when time and space elements are altered online, defaulting to a text-focused tutorial is understandably common.

Consequently, another problem that comes with the rhetorical shift of putting tutorials online is the misunderstanding of both the tutor's and the writer's roles within a tutorial. Some writing center directors see the posting or email submission of papers as equal to the student who comes into the center, unfamiliar with the tutoring process, and asks to drop off a paper and pick it up again in a few hours after it has been "corrected." Clearly, these students do not recognize their role in the process of revising their own papers. Likewise, I've had students admit to signing up for online synchronous tutorials so they won't miss watching their favorite sitcom during that same hour. I can imagine them pajama clad, TV blaring in the background, typing with one hand and eating popcorn with the other, only taking in tutor questions during commercial breaks. Their understanding of their own involvement as an active participant is very different than what we would except from them. If we return to the idea that we want "to work with rather than for the writer" (Hawthorne qtd. in Moe 15), then it is obvious that roles must be clarified. In face-to-face tutorials, the sharing of physical space and time encourages (but doesn't guarantee) a writer's involvement. However, this feeling of responsibility and involvement produced by the writer's environment is not always duplicated online. In either situation, fortunately, if the writer is present, then roles can be clarified by the tutor at any time during a session.

Although we may worry about shifts in roles and understanding of involvement, some writers are comfortable with the lack of conversation even if it means a lack of learning. According to Patricia Ericsson and Tim McGee, "Not only did the kind of help our OWL users wanted work against the creation of a dialogue, email technology itself may promote 'one shot' interactions." Eric Hobson illustrated this idea with the story of a student and a tutor sitting in the same computer lab, completing a tutorial. The tutor didn't realize the student was a few computers down, but the student said he or she had purposely chosen to have an online tutorial so he or she could leave when desired, just get specific questions answered, and not have to talk about themselves, the audience, or even the purpose of the text (487). Certainly, this scenario is not unique to asynchronous OWLing. Synchronous online tutoring has its own difficulties keeping dialectical discussions in place. My OWL tutors admit they are more directive in online tutorials, and if they don't admit it, I can show them transcripts of their tutorials. They justify this approach complaining that typing is so much slower than talking, and without nonverbal cues and voice inflection to guide communication, they are better off directly telling the writer what needs to be done. This justification is unsettling because it is very different from what we claim as theoretical foundations. Because online tutoring is so slow and communication is potentially so difficult, tutors often "cut to the chase" leaving out discussion, which should be the heart and soul of the tutorial. These situations say a lot about what is going on in some online tutorials and seems to point to a lack of training or at least the need to review with tutors the rhetorical nature of their work and the goal of providing learning experiences.

Certainly, just as a physical writing center is only as good as its tutors, the same is true for an OWL. As Jackson explained, "Much like the f2f [face-to-face] tutorial, each tutor must identify his other strengths as an online tutor [and] understand the limits and opportunities of the online 'dialogue'" (2). Tutor training is not the same face-to-face as online, but there is still the need to read theory and lore, to observe sessions, and to be mentored. Online tutors also need the opportunity to reflect, to review tutorial transcripts and make adjustments that bring them more in line with the theoretical foundations of their writing center's work. Whereas face-to-face tutors may have training on the importance of body language, online tutors may need a module on the use of emoticons (i.e., smiling faces) or the language of online chat. Will a tutor know how to respond when the writer types "brb" (be right back) or "lol" (laugh out loud)? Will they know that they need not shout responses through the bullhorn of capitalization?

However, whereas some techniques need to be introduced or reexamined, some methods still hold true in online tutoring. We may teach the value of questioning, but stress the wait time, acknowledging the time it takes to type. Additionally, reader response and modeling are common tutoring methods that work well when adapted for online instruction as long as writers know that models are teaching tools and not to be appropriated verbatim. Likewise, although OWL tutors may not be able to model the use of a handbook or pull handouts off the shelf, they can be trained to hyperlink to web guides and online handouts. These adaptations to tutoring are essential if our goal of strengthening and supporting writers is to remain intact, and tutors are to see the connections between their face-to-face and online tutorials. Devising and dispensing such tutor training may bear cost and time constraints, so as

Muriel Harris and Michael Pemberton suggested, "directors have to see tutor preparation as part of building successful OWLs" (538).

One cannot claim that OWL work is easy. There are problems with authorial presence, understanding of roles, lack of shared time and space, and a need for additional and adapted tutor training. If online tutoring mediums and student involvement are so rhetorically different on OWLS and so difficult to preserve online, then why do we OWL at all? Although I shut down our OWL during my first semester on the job, our online tutoring was only gone for a month. When I brought the service back, I was more satisfied with the alignment of our face-to-face and online work. In the synchronous whiteboard format, both the writer and text are presenting in the tutorial. This format takes, on average, more time than email tutorials, but remains closer to the rhetorical nature of our face-to-face tutoring with a discussion-based, dialectical approach. Additionally, tutoring online has helped us achieve our commitment to serving all students, including those learning via distance education courses or those with work and family commitments that keep them off campus. Moreover, our web presence gives us validity in the face of an administration concerned with keeping a growing college on the cutting edge of technology. In response to our commitment to the rhetorical nature of tutoring, they have been willing to grant us just enough funding to let us choose quality over convenience. Finally, our online synchronous work, although uncomfortable at times, has provided a way to grow and develop in both theory and practice. OWLers are the adolescents of writing center work—awkward and confused, but excited by the possibilities of the future.

Being involved with OWLS means being committed to evolution and being willing to see things and accept them in a new light. Cynthia Selfe explained this need for an open mind, saying, it is unwise to see ourselves "for or against technology—rather than to understand the complex ways in which technology has become linked with our conception of literacy and, possibly, to shape the relationship between these two phenomena in increasingly productive ways" (36–37). Undoubtedly, online work is changing writing center theory and practice in many promising ways. For example, as David Healy indicated:

> Online conferencing makes the "Your place or mine?" question obsolete. In doing so, it may fundamentally alter the way both clients and consultants perceive their relationship to the institution because the meeting place is no longer physically tied to the institution at all. . . . And might the conversations that take place online be less directly implicated in institutional hierarchy because the institution is less obviously present in those conversations? (544)

Additionally, directors, tutors, and students are experimenting with tutorials through the use of everyday communication methods, such as Instant Messenger and text messaging. Clearly, the possibilities with the work are fascinating.

Yet not all writing center directors have had or will have, anytime soon, the luxury of choosing how to develop and shape their online presence. While at my institution, I have been fortunate to have the flexibility of deciding how and when we will use technology in our center and how web work will help us better meet our goals, not all directors have the technical support, the programs available, and the time to reflect and explore, let alone maintain such services. They must work within the confines of overworked web support services and budgets too limited for additional training. As Hobson observed, "Not every center's clientele have access to the technology needed to make such projects expedient; not every center can determine its future and fate to the extent needed to follow suit; not every center's mission or philosophical foundation is commensurate with the assumptions contained in many online writing center projects" (481). So although my program has adapted and adopted certain boundaries and rhetorical structures for our work, it is not to say that those other different programs are off the mark. As Wislocki explained, "[A] multiplicity of voices and opinions—as well as expressions of frustration and enthusiasm—are the healthy sounds of an engaged community talking the emerging field of OWLs into existence." (74). While I consider ideal circumstances for OWL work, I recognize that they don't exist yet, although we may strive to approximate them by increasing our research, reflection, and experimentation.

The possibilities that accompany alternative mediums for tutoring are endless as new hardware and software are continually emerging, and undoubtedly, online practices will change with the ever-advancing medium. However, we cannot simply avoid research and reflection and wait for someone else to figure out how to preserve the rhetorical nature of our work. It is through experimentation that writing centers will discover the previously unknown pathways for transmitting their services online. With the presence of text messaging, web cams, and so forth, these pathways are making themselves clearer. As Michael D. McMaster, a social theorist, explained, "To make the shift in thinking [into the information age], we need the willingness to unlearn the old and the courage to grapple with the new and unfamiliar" (qtd. in Murphy and Law 190). In essence, the near future of online tutoring is full of experimentation and offers plenty of room for research in both that which is currently being done via OWLs and the many possibilities that are to come.

The links on our center's OWL all currently work, and our online tutoring numbers are steadily climbing, but I am still asking questions. After over a decade of OWL work in writing centers, we must look back. If we were building the first OWLs in this day, how would they be different? Would we be thinking outside the email box? Surely, "attempting only to replicate familiar face-to-face tutorial settings in an electronic, text-oriented environment can lead to frustration and to defeat as OWL planners find themselves unable to simulate all characteristics of effective tutorials" (Harris and Pemberton 522), but now that we have more experience, what can we see for the future of this work and the preservation of our theoretical foundations? In examining the rhetorical nature of tutoring programs and working to preserve the essential aspects of the tutoring process, we are acknowledging not only what we have and what we want, but why writing center work is key to the learning process in the first place.

Works Cited

Capossela, Toni-Lee, ed. *The Harcourt Brace Guide to Peer Tutoring.* Orlando: Harcourt Brace, 1998. Print.

Coogan, David. "Email Tutoring, a New Way to Do Work." *Computers and Composition* 12.2 (1995): 171–81. Print.

Dossin, Mary M. "The ESL Quandary." *Writing Lab Newsletter* 20 (1996): 14–15. Print.

Ericsson, Patricia, and Tim McGee. "The Online Tutor as Cross-Curricular Double Agent." *Kairos* 2.2. Web. 14 May 2003.

Harris, Muriel, and Michael Pemberton. "Online Writing Labs (OWLs): A Taxonomy of Options and Issues." *The Allyn and Bacon Guide to Writing Center Theory and Practice.* Ed. Robert Barnett and Jacob Blumner. Needham Heights: Allyn and Bacon, 2001. 521–40. Print.

Healy, David. "From Place to Space: Perceptual and Administrative Issues in the Online Writing Center." *The Allyn and Bacon Guide to Writing Center Theory and Practice.* Ed. Robert W. Barnet and Jacob S. Blumner. Needham Heights: Allyn and Bacon, 2001. 541–54. Print.

Hobson, Eric, ed. *Wiring the Writing Center.* Logan: Utah State UP, 1998. Print.

Jackson, J. A. "Interfacing the Faceless: Maximizing the Advantages of Online Tutoring." *Writing Lab Newsletter* 25.2 (2000): 1–7. Print.

Kimball, Sara. "Cybertext/Cyberspeech: Writing Centers and Online Magic." *The Writing Center Journal* 18 (1997): 30–49. Print.

Moe, Holly. "Web Study of Smarthinking.com." *Writing Lab Newsletter* 25 (2000): 13–16. Print.

Murphy, Christina, and Joe Law. "Writing Center and WAC Programs as Infostructures: Relocating Practice With Futurist Theories of Social Change." *Writing Centers and Writing across the Curriculum Programs Building Interdisciplinary Partnerships.* Ed. Robert Barnett and Jacob S. Blumner. Westport: Greenwood, 1999. Print.

North, Stephen M. "The Idea of a Writing Center." *College English* 46 (1984): 433–46. Print.

Rowan, Karen. Rev. of *Taking Flight with OWLS: Research into Technology Use in Writing Centers.* Ed. James Inman and Donna Sewell. *Writing Lab Newsletter* 25 (2000): 9–10. Print.

Selfe, Cynthia. *Technology and Literacy in the Twenty-First Century: The Importance of Paying Attention.* Carbondale: Southern Illinois UP, 1999. Print.

Wislocki, Mary. Rev. of *The OWL Construction and Maintenance Guide.* Ed. James Inman and Clint Gardener. *The Writing Center Journal* 24 (2003): 71–75. Print.

Words, Images, Sounds: Writing Centers as Multiliteracy Centers

David Sheridan
MICHIGAN STATE UNIVERSITY

Looking toward the future in this essay from The Writing Center Director's Resource Book *(2006), David Sheridan examines the integration of digital media into traditional modes of communication that have emphasized textual studies and print-based composition. His central question is*

"What model for the relationship between technology and rhetoric should writing centers embrace?" and he argues that writing centers need to be decisively involved in shaping the technologies that are shaping literacy in contemporary global society. This transformation will necessitate that writing centers redefine and expand their understandings of rhetoric and communication and will have an impact on the ways tutors are trained and carry out their functions in working with students on nontraditional, multimodal projects that will call on the tutor to possess new "categories of knowledge and skills."

> *If schools are to equip students adequately for the new semiotic order . . . then the old boundaries between "writing" on the one hand, traditionally the form of literacy without which people cannot adequately function as citizens, and, on the other hand, the "visual arts," a marginal subject for the especially gifted . . . should be redrawn. This will have to involve modern computer technology, central as it is to the new semiotic landscape.*
>
> *— Gunther Kress and Theo van Leeuwen*

> *Nowhere is there greater potential for achieving a degree of success in this exceedingly complex venture [of fostering computer-mediated literacy] than there is in the numerous computer-supported writing centers that have been set up in schools and institutions across the country.*
>
> *— Cynthia Selfe*

Imagine that Jane, a first-year writing student, comes to the writing center seeking help. When her peer consultant asks about the nature of her project, she says that her class is taking a "service learning" approach. The class has been divided into small groups, each of which has been assigned a different community partner. Jane's community partner, a nonprofit organization serving homeless people, has asked the student writers to produce a Web site. The proposed site will educate readers about the organization and about homelessness in general. The community partner envisions a visually rich site that integrates brief chunks of text with photographs and design elements to achieve a professional but emotionally engaging experience for readers.

As conversation continues, it becomes clear that Jane, although interested in the written components of her evolving Web site, is more concerned about design issues: color scheme, layout, typography, photographs. She is worried that she does not have the technical or visual skills to integrate design elements effectively.

What is the appropriate response of a writing center to a student with this set of needs? Should peer consultants offer support for the rhetorical use of visual materials and design elements? Should they guide clients through the use of Web-authoring applications like Dreamweaver and photo-editing applications like Photoshop? Or should consultants limit themselves to a discussion of writing, narrowly conceived?

Gunther Kress (echoing a host of other literacy theorists) observed: "[T]he land-scape of communication is changing fundamentally" (["Crossroads"] 67). As the New London Group put it, in order to "participate fully in public, community, and economic life," we are all increasingly asked to employ "multiliteracies" (9). The electronic media (i.e., radio, film, and TV) of the twentieth century asked us to be consumers of multimodal compositions, a role requiring us to expand our notion of "literacy" to include the meaning-making practices necessary to parse "texts" that communicate through the integration of written and spoken words, music and other sounds, and an array of visual elements. The emergent technologies of the twenty-first century increasingly ask us to be *composers* of multimodal texts. We are asked to produce Web pages, PowerPoint slides, desktop-published documents, and even digital videos—compositions that encourage and even necessitate attention to design, visual communication, and media in ways that the traditional academic essay, printed on 8½" × 11" paper with one-inch margins, historically has not.

John Trimbur and others suggested that writing centers will increasingly define themselves as "multiliteracy centers," in part to reflect these fundamental changes in the semiotic landscape (29). This chapter introduces basic theoretical and practical issues involved in this redefinition. I begin with four key questions that writing centers need to face as they move toward a multiliteracy approach:

1. What model for the relationship between writing and other modes of communication should writing centers embrace?
2. What model for the relationship between technology and rhetoric should writing centers embrace?
3. To what extent should writing centers lead and to what extent should they follow as their home institutions adopt multiliteracy pedagogy?
4. How should writing centers change existing practices of tutor recruit-ment and training?

After exploring these questions, I sketch more fully what multiliteracy consult-ing looks like in practice.

What Model for the Relationship between Writing and Other Modes Should Writing Centers Embrace?

> One of the key ideas informing the notion of Multiliteracies is the increas-ing complexity and interrelationship of different modes of meaning. We have already identified six major areas in which functional grammars . . . are required—Linguistic Design, Visual Design, Audio Design, Gestural Design, Spatial Design, and Multimodal Design. Multimodal Design, however, is of a different order to the others as it represents the patterns of interconnection among the other modes. (New London Group 25)

Fundamental to the notion of multiliteracies is the interconnectedness of dif-ferent semiotic components. Web pages and other new media forms commu-nicate their message through the integration of words, images, and sounds.

Different elements "cooperate" to convey the "totality of the information," to borrow Roland Barthes's language (16). To support new media composing effectively, then, multiliteracy centers need to move away from models that see the written word as the exclusive or even the privileged mode of communication. Multiliteracy consultants need to engage composers in conversations about all media components.

Imagine, for instance, how a consulting session might look if the consultant conceives of her role narrowly, as one of engaging the client in matters related to writing. In this conversation, we can imagine Jane's disappointment as she is told that although her concerns about design and about photographs are certainly important, they fall outside the purview of the writing center. But even the conversation about writing, narrowly conceived, is likely to be plagued with dead ends and false starts: "As a reader, I don't get a very vivid picture of the conditions in this shelter," the consultant might say. To which the client might respond, "Oh, that's because alongside that text there will be a photograph that powerfully depicts the material conditions of the shelter." At another point the consultant might say, "As a reader, I find these short chunks of text tedious. This experience of your text is fragmented. It's hard to make connections." The client might respond, "Each of the chunks is the amount that will fit on a standard computer monitor. To help readers make connections, we plan to use color coding and hyperlinks."

In new media, the semiotic whole is greater than the sum of its parts. Words are inextricably linked to other media elements, making it difficult to talk about them in isolation. A multiliteracy consultant meeting with Jane would embrace the chance to explore the rhetorical dimensions of all elements, including photographs, color, layout, and navigation scheme.

What Model for the Relationship between Technology and Rhetoric Should Writing Centers Embrace?

> Those with a knowledge of literacy, its myriad manifestations and its ramifications, must become actively involved in shaping the complex of technology that, in turn, shapes our literacy, our cultures, and ourselves. (Haas and Neuwirth 330)

For some, I suspect, it is relatively easy to understand why writing centers should be willing to engage students in conversations about the rhetorical use of images and other media components in Web pages and PowerPoint presentations. We have become accustomed to a broadening of the words "rhetoric" and "literacy" to include "visual rhetoric" and "visual literacy." But what about technology? Should writing consultants guide students through the process of editing their digital photographs in Photoshop or creating Web pages in Dreamweaver? Isn't that a job for IT support on campus?

Literacy theorists have been exploring the link between technology and literacy for some time. As hybrid terms like *computer-mediated literacy*

(Selfe), *cyberliteracy* (Gurak), and *electracy* (Ulmer) suggest, many theorists who examine the relation between rhetoric and technology come to the conclusion that the two are intimately related. Haas and Neuwirth warned against the "computers are not our job" attitude common in English studies (325), and Beebe and Bonevelle, speaking about writing centers specifically, concluded, "The more tutors know about the software programs that their tutees use, the more effectively tutors can help tutees" (50). Because technology and literacy are inextricably linked, I am arguing here that multiliteracy centers should include support for technical dimensions of the composing process.

For instance, let's imagine that Jane has expressed to her consultant that she hopes the photographs provided by her community partner will serve as visual critiques of stereotyping found in the mass media. In discussing the rhetorical goals for these photographs, the client and consultant will need to discuss possibilities for editing them. Perhaps a photograph of a woman in a shelter is dark and grey and taken from such a distance that her facial features are not discernable—realities that tend to undermine the ability of viewers to identify with her. Can the photograph be lightened? Can it be blown up? Can the color be adjusted?

Answers to these questions need to account for technological realities. Whether or not a photograph can be blown up, for instance, is a decision that needs to take into account the resolution of the original image. Deciding to lighten a photograph assumes the composer knows that photo-editing applications allow this operation, as well as how much a photo can be lightened, under what circumstances, and, of course, how to do it. A multiliteracy consultant who knows photo-editing applications can talk with her client about what kinds of revisions are possible, can guide her client through the process of making those revisions, and can talk about the rhetorical effectiveness of those revisions once they are made.

The interrelatedness of technology and rhetoric saturates almost every dimension of digital composing. Questions like "Can I superimpose words over an image?," "Can I have two columns?," and "Can I use a particular font?," all imply both an understanding of the rhetoric of design as well as technologies related to composing and to the medium of delivery.

Separating technical and rhetorical dimensions of multimodal communication artificially segments the composing process. It also ignores current realities about how students define their needs. Many students view multimodal communication as a purely technical challenge: They know what they want to say, they just need to make the computer work. Multiliteracy consultants can help students come to a more sophisticated understanding of multimodal communication by foregrounding the interrelationship of technical and rhetorical concerns. If students need to go to separate sources to get technical and rhetorical help, then many of them, for pragmatic reasons, will simply skip the rhetorical support altogether.

To What Extent Should Writing Centers Lead and to What Extent Should They Follow as Their Home Institutions Adopt Multiliteracy Pedagogy?

At Michigan State, changes in writing center and instructional practices usually involve a recursive process. Student composers and writing instructors come to the center with various needs: Can someone here help me with this PowerPoint presentation? Can someone show me how to make a Web page? The special needs of these students and instructors are occasions for reinterrogating the mission and practice of the center. They force us to ask: Are there existing resources on campus for these students? Should we offer new kinds of support? (Web document A).

But as we have extended our services to include support for certain kinds of composing, some instructors have adopted new classroom practices. Instructors who know that their students can receive support for Web authoring at the center might feel more comfortable assigning a Web essay. Increasing services, then, has created an increased demand for those services.

Writing centers can respond to demand, but can also be agents of institutional change, advocating for the kinds of composing and teaching they feel are important (Bruffee). As part of its mission to foster a culture of writing across campus, MSU's center, like many centers, works with instructors of writing-intensive courses across the curriculum who seek to integrate writing into their courses in pedagogically effective ways. Consistent with this approach is the invitation to help instructors integrate technology effectively (Web document B). Instructors are invited to sit down with writing center consultants or faculty to discuss all aspects related to teaching with technology, from framing new media assignments to confronting logistical considerations about labs and equipment. Additionally, the center offers a series of whole-class presentations that explore basic issues related to digital composing (Web document C). The center works with instructors to create generative composing environments for students through a combination of whole-class, small-group, and one-on-one support services. In this model, then, demand is not just a preexisting entity that writing centers react to; it is a function, in part, of the kinds of teaching and composing practices centers can enable.

How Should Writing Centers Recruit and Train Multiliteracy Tutors?

Multiliteracy consultants need to have three categories of knowledge and skills. They need to develop a sophisticated understanding of consulting pedagogy, including both traditional models for providing peer support as well as an understanding of how these models need to be adapted when consulting moves into a digital environment. They need to develop an understanding of multimodal rhetoric. And they need to understand the technical processes that are involved in composing digital media (Web document D).

In order to develop a cadre of consultants who have knowledge in these three areas, a multifaceted approach to recruitment and training is necessary. At MSU, multiliteracy consultants, or digital writing consultants (DWCs), are part of the general consulting pool and go through the same training process as other consultants. This training is aimed at helping students build practical yet theoretically sophisticated models for writing centers and for peer consulting. To this end, trainees read extensively in writing center scholarship, observe consulting sessions, and reflect on and synthesize what they observe and read by engaging in a variety of forms of discussion (classroom, electronic, and paper based).

Within any given cadre of consultants, some subset [is] interested in becoming a DWC. Occasionally, this subset includes students who are formally trained in a field (e.g., graphic design) related to composing with new media. More often, some students have learned relevant skills as part of a previous job or have taught themselves because of personal interest. Others have little or no experience as new media composers. DWCs go through supplemental training that varies according to the needs of the center and the backgrounds of the consultants, but usually includes some combination of specialized reading, additional observations of experienced DWCs, and opportunities to engage in multimodal projects. At various times we have provided this supplemental training through "special topics" courses, as well as through less formal self-paced programs (see Web document E).

Before coming to Michigan State, I helped to develop a multiliteracy program through the University of Michigan's Sweetland Writing Center. To recruit students with the appropriate skill sets, we made a point of contracting graphic design majors. However, we discovered that the academic schedules and goals of these students were different from those of the liberal arts students who typically entered Sweetland's Peer Tutoring Program. To recruit effectively, we invited a graphic design professor to teach a version of our tutor-training course that had been modified slightly to reflect the interests of the design majors. As writing centers seek effective multiliteracy consultants, they may need to consider alternative recruitment strategies like this.

As writing center administrators structure consultant training and recruitment programs, I submit that it is useful to conceive of this task as establishing a particular kind of culture. Patti Stock explained that the MSU Writing Center

> has taken upon itself the ambitious task of creating a culture of writing and continuous inquiry. . . . Taking advantage of the opportunities that exist when individuals with different but related goals teach and learn from one another for their mutual benefit . . . the Center is developing a practice we call consultative teaching. A combination of collaborative learning, peer tutoring, service learning, student research, and jointly conducted student–faculty research, the practice of consultative teaching recognizes students as knowledgeable individuals with valuable ideas and experiences to contribute to the learning situation. (12)

Supplemental web resources are available at <http://www.msu.edu/~sherid16/wedr>.

A multiliteracy center is at its best when it is based on a professional and intellectual community in which consultants are encouraged to reflect on their practice as both composers and consultants. As composers, DWCs at MSU embrace opportunities to engage in multimodal communication, producing in any given semester a variety of educational and publicity materials — Web sites, flyers, handouts, PowerPoints, videos, posters, brochures, logos — for the center and its collaborators. We workshop our compositions formally and informally at multiple points throughout the composing process, seeking constructive feedback about both rhetorical and technical issues. Our experiences as composers inform our consulting practices.

As consultants, DWCs are encouraged to be reflective practitioners and are provided a range of formal and informal venues to talk with others about their work. For instance, we seek out opportunities to explore our evolving understanding of multiliteracy consulting at professional conferences, viewing these presentations as occasions to articulate our ideas more fully, to establish a wider context for them through research, and to solicit constructive feedback from others in the writing center community.

DWCs are able to provide effective support for peers because they have an abiding interest in both the practice and theory of multiliteracy composing and consulting. This interest is kindled and developed, in part, by the general culture of the center. When a student walks in seeking help with a Web project, the conversation that our consultants facilitate is energized by an ongoing personal and professional investment in understanding new media.

Multiliteracy Consulting

As I have described it so far, a multiliteracy center is technology-rich space staffed by consultants who have sophisticated understandings of peer-consulting pedagogy, multimodal rhetoric, and composing technologies. These consultants engage students in conversations about rhetorical choices they make concerning not just words, but images and other media elements as well. But what does multiliteracy consulting look like in practice? To make these ideas more concrete, let's imagine that Mark, a preservice elementary school teacher, comes to the writing center seeking help with his Web-based teaching portfolio. He envisions a portfolio that contains written statements about his teaching philosophy, examples of lesson plans that he has created, and photographs of students with [whom] he has worked.

When Tanya, Mark's multiliteracy consultant, learns that Mark will be working on a Web project, she invites him to sit down at one of the consulting tables. Tanya explains that they can move to a computer workstation later if necessary. The conversation begins with general discussion about the nature of the project and the rhetorical situation: Is this an assignment? Are there any guidelines? Who are the target audiences? What are the primary rhetorical purposes?

Mark explains that this is his own initiative, not an assignment. He's heard from friends who have gotten teaching jobs that a good digital portfolio is one way to stand out as a job candidate. His primary audience is an interview team. His purpose is to persuade his audience that he is a creative teacher with a thorough understanding of contemporary educational theory.

After this preliminary discussion, Tanya hands Mark an oversized sheet of paper containing the empty window of a Web browser. She explains that this browser window is approximately the size of a computer monitor with a resolution of 800 × 600 pixels. Tanya asks Mark to sketch out the homepage of his portfolio as he imagines it might look. The sketch that Mark comes up with includes a banner across the top and central photograph. Superimposed across the bottom of the photo are links to the various sections of his portfolio: teaching philosophy, lesson plans, professional activities, and resume.

When Tanya asks about the photograph, Mark takes a stack of glossy prints out of his backpack and spreads them on the table. Some are of students sitting in rows, some of individual students, some of students working in small groups. "If you could only select one," Tanya asks, "which one do you think best represents your teaching philosophy?" Mark identifies one that shows five students working in a loose circle on the classroom floor. Paint, glue, scissors, and colored paper are scattered around them. Mark explains that this photo reflects his vision for collaboration and active learning. But he remarks that the photo looks dull and cluttered; the students in the circle appear too small, and other students in the background and on the periphery distract from the message he hopes to convey. Tanya promises that some of those problems can be resolved and suggests that this might be a good time to find a workstation.

Tanya has Mark sit down at a computer and positions herself slightly off to the side so that she can see the screen but does not have control over the keyboard. They begin with the photograph, Tanya guiding Mark through the process of scanning the photo and opening it in Photoshop. With Tanya's help, Mark selectively blurs elements in the photograph that are extraneous, which has the effect of making the students in the circle more prominent. After each change, Mark and Tanya discuss the rhetorical implications.

At some point, the conversation turns to matters of design and color. Repeatedly in this conversation, Mark has used "kid friendly" and "professional" to describe the overall style he hopes to employ throughout his site. He decides that he can achieve both of these goals by committing to a few warm colors and favoring clean shapes surrounded by lots of white space. And so the conversation continues.

In this imagined multiliteracy consulting session, I have tried to show how principles that have become fundamental to traditional consulting practice, such as a "minimalist" or "nondirective" approach to consulting, can be translated into a multiliteracy consulting session. Tanya does not do Mark's work for him, nor does she lecture him about what he should do; instead, she keeps him actively engaged in the composing process by asking strategic questions and by making sure he is always in control of the technology. Additionally, I have tried to show that a "rhetorical" approach that emphasizes the relationship between rhetorical decisions to key contextual elements such as audience and purpose is equally appropriate for multiliteracy consulting. A rich understanding of the rhetorical situation can inform decisions about navigation schemes, photographs, and other media elements in addition to writing. In this approach, "content" is not applied narrowly to the written components of a project; all media elements are seen as contributing to the overall rhetorical effect.

The Multiliteracy Center and the University

Writing centers are often overtasked and underresourced. Developing a multiliteracy program can seem overwhelming. I have tried to suggest here that a multiliteracy program can grow incrementally, building on existing models and practices. In any cadre of consultants, a few will already possess some of the skills needed to consult with clients about multimodal projects. Basic Web authoring, PowerPoint, and desktop publishing can be done on standard personal computers that many writing centers will have already purchased for other purposes.

As multiliteracy programs grow, writing centers will need to tap into resources and seek out forms of collaboration that might differ from conventional practice. Writing centers will need to cultivate relationships with IT support, graphic design, and computer science. They will need to seek out funds that have been earmarked for technology at the departmental, college, university, state, and federal levels.

The landscape of communication is changing, and so are the composing practices of the students that writing centers have traditionally served. English studies, composition theory, and the academy in general have been moving away from a narrow commitment to the study of "writing" toward a semiotic approach that examines signifying practices more generally. Writing centers continue to focus narrowly on the written word at the risk of increasing obsolescence. What I have tried to offer here are some first thoughts about how writing centers might respond to the composing practices of the twenty-first century.

Works Cited

Barthes, Roland. "The Photographic Message," *Image-Music-Text*. Trans. Stephen Heath. New York: Hill and Wang, 1977. 15–31. Print.

Beebe, Randall L., and Mary J. Bonevelle. "The Culture of Technology in the Writing Center: Reinvigorating the Theory-Practice Debate." *Taking Flight with OWLs*. Ed. James A. Inman and Donna N. Sewell. Mahwah: Lawrence Erlbaum, 2000. 41–51. Print.

Bruffee, Kenneth. "Peer Tutors as Agents of Change." *Proceedings of the Seventh Annual Conference on Peer Tutoring in Writing*. Ed. Stacy Nestleroth. University Park: Pennsylvania State UP, 1990. 1–6. Print.

Gurak, Laura J. *Cyberliteracy: Navigating the Internet with Awareness*. New Haven: Yale UP, 2001. Print.

Haas, Christina, and Christine M. Neuwirth. "Writing the Technology That Writes Us: Research on Literacy and the Shape of Technology." *Literacy and Computers: The Complications of Teaching and Learning with Technology*. Ed. Cynthia Selfe and Susan Hilligoss. New York: MLA, 1994. 319–35. Print.

Kress, Gunther. "'English' at a Crossroads: Rethinking Curricula of Communication in the Context of the Turn to the Visual." *Passions, Pedagogies, and 21st Century Technologies*. Ed. Gail E. Hawisher and Cynthia Selfe. Logan: Utah State UP, 1999. 66–88. Print.

Kress, Gunther, and Theo van Leeuwen. *Reading Images: The Grammar of Visual Design*. London: Routledge, 1996. Print.

New London Group, The. "A Pedagogy of Multiliteracies: Designing Social Futures." *Multiliteracies: Literacy Learning and the Design of Social Futures*. Ed. Bill Cope and Mary Kalantzis. London: Routledge, 2000. Print.

Selfe, Cynthia. "Redefining Literacy: The Multilayered Grammars of Computers." *Critical Perspectives on Computers and Composition Instruction*. Ed. Gail E. Hawisher and Cynthia Selfe. New York: Teachers College P, 1989. 3–15. Print.

Stock, Patricia. "Reforming Education in the Land-Gant U: Contributions from a Writing Center." *The Writing Center Journal* 18.1 (1997): 7–30.

Trimbur, John. "Multiliteracies, Social Futures, and Writing Centers." *The Writing Center Journal* 20.2 (2000): 29–32. Print.

Ulmer, Gregory L. *Internet Invention: From Literacy to Electracy*. New York: Longman, 2003. Print.

New Media Matters: Tutoring in the Late Age of Print

Jackie Grutsch McKinney _____

BALL STATE UNIVERSITY

Jackie Grutsch McKinney explores the changes that will be required in tutoring and tutor training as the traditional print-based writing center of the twentieth century becomes the new media-based multiliteracy center of the twenty-first century. As the predominance of print wanes and new means of communication technology mark a seismic shift in both writing instruction and tutoring, writing center professionals must recognize and respond to the changes ahead and the potential challenges and opportunities. In this essay published in The Writing Center Journal *in 2009, McKinney provides a historical and theoretical background for the emergence of new media, considers the implications of the shifts in theory and practice that writing centers must make (including redefining the work of tutors), and explores "how to tutor new media." Tutors will need to be given ways to understand, appreciate, and talk about "the interactivity of modes" and their own sense of "the gestalt in students' new media texts."*

At the turn of the century, John Trimbur predicted that writing centers would become "Multiliteracy Centers," drawing on the terminology of the New London Group (30). These re-envisioned centers, he suggested, would provide help for students working on a variety of projects: essays, reports, PowerPoint presentations, Web pages, and posters. His prediction has proved true to some degree—most notably in the state of Michigan. The University of Michigan's Sweetland Writing Center opened a Multiliteracy Center in 2000 within its writing center, a place where students "could receive one-to-one support as they worked on digital projects such as websites, PowerPoint presentations, and other forms of communication that depend on multiliteracies" (Sheridan, "Sweetland" 4). Additionally, at Michigan State, digital writing consultants worked with students on digital texts as early as 1996 (see Sheridan, "Words" and DeVoss). Institutions outside of Michigan have responded to new media writing also. The Worcester Polytechnic Institute—where Trimbur works—named its writing center the Center for Communication Across the Curriculum, with "workshops" in writing, oral presentation, and visual design (Trimbur 29), and the Center for Collaborative Learning and Communication was created at Furman University (Inman). Many other centers have not changed names but have begun tutoring students on a variety of texts.

However, in one of the few published articles on writing centers and new media, titled "Planning for Hypertexts in the Writing Center . . . or Not," Michael Pemberton asks if writing centers should open their doors to students working on hypertexts. Although he answers "maybe"—he believes directors should decide based on their local needs and constraints—the bulk of his argument seems to say "no" more loudly than "yes," as seen here:

> Ultimately, we have to ask ourselves whether it is really the writing center's responsibility to be all things to all people. There will always be more to learn. There will always be new groups making demands on our time and our resources in ways we haven't yet planned for. And there will never be enough time or enough money or enough tutors to meet all those demands all of the time. If we diversify too widely and spread ourselves too thinly in an attempt to encompass too many different literacies, we may not be able to address any set of literate practices particularly well. (21)

Now—twenty years after Stephen Bernhardt urged us to *see* student texts; after Craig Stroupe, more recently, argued for the visualization of English studies; after Diana George showed us how visual literacy has been a part of writing instruction since the 1940s; and after Gunther Kress argued convincingly that the revolution in writing dominated by the image is not coming, it is already here—the writing center community seems divided on whether writing centers should work with new media.

Though at first blush I thought that Pemberton's argument was short-sighted, upon reflection, I think this sort of response actually speaks to an understandable uncertainty: We are fairly sure that we do good work with paper essays, pencils, and round tables. We are just not sure that we can do good work when those things change into new media texts, computer screens and speakers, mice and keyboards, and computer desks. The argument follows that if we are not certain we can do good work, then we should not do it at all.

I agree with Pemberton that we shouldn't take on work that we are not prepared for. But our agreement only goes so far, because I *do* think it is our job to work with all types of writing in the writing center—including new media. In this article, then, I suggest that writing centers need to offer tutoring in new media texts, but not the same tutoring we've always done. I begin by briefly defining *what* new media are (or, really, how I will use the term) and outlining *why* I think writing center tutors should work with new media texts. The bulk of this essay is devoted to *how* to tutor new media, since I see that as the crux of the issue, so in the last part, I describe the ways that writing center directors and staffs wanting to work with new media can evolve their practices to do so.

What Is New Media?

Scholars use the term "new media" in a handful of ways that both overlap and diverge, which can make matters complicated. Are new media texts digital? Can they be print? Are they the same as multimodal texts? Or are they employing a different rhetoric? Cynthia Selfe, Anne Wysocki, and Cheryl Ball each offer definitions of new media that I find helpful, not because they agree with one another, but rather because I can see from the sum of their individual definitions the exciting range of new media texts.

For Cynthia Selfe, new media texts are digital. She defines new media texts as "texts created primarily in digital environments, composed in multiple media, and designed for presentation and exchange in digital venues" ("Students" 43). Although such texts contain alphabetic features, she claims that "they also typically resist containment by alphabetic systems, demanding multiple literacies of seeing and listening and manipulating, as well as those of writing and reading" ("Students" 43). She would use "new media" to describe a web portfolio or another text viewed on screen that would contain alphabetic texts and other modes, too.

Anne Wysocki, though, sees new media as any text that in its production calls attention to its own materiality:

> I think we should call "new media texts" those that have been made by composers who are aware of the range of materialities of texts and who then highlight the materiality: such composers design texts that help readers/consumers/viewers stay alert to how any text—like its composers and readers—doesn't function independently of how it is made and in what contexts. ("Openings" 15)

This attention to materiality means the text might or might not be digital. As Wysocki writes, "new media texts do not have to be digital; instead, any text that has been designed so that its materiality is not effaced can count as new media" (15). An example of a new media text that isn't digital is Wysocki et al.'s *Writing New Media* itself. Design choices in this text, such as the horizontal orientation of the page numbers, make readers "stay alert" to how the writers are playing with the usual conventions of a book. The key term for Wysocki's conception of new media, then, is materiality.

A third definition of new media conies from Cheryl Ball in "Show, Not Tell: The Value of New Media Scholarship" She writes that new media are "texts that juxtapose semiotic modes in new and aesthetically pleasing ways and, in doing so, break away from print traditions so that written text is not the primary rhetorical means" (405). For Ball, then, like Selfe, new media is multimodal and digital. Unique to Ball's definition, however, is that what's "new" in new media is the way in which these texts make arguments—the primacy of nontextual modes. New media texts make fundamentally different types of arguments. She illustrates this difference in her article through analysis of two web texts. One relies on print conventions to make its linear argument; the other radically departs from print conventions as it asks readers to compose the argument by dragging and dropping audio, still images, and text to play together in an order determined by the viewer/reader.

Combined, the three definitions show a range of texts that are "new" in significant ways: 1) their digital-ness; 2) their conscious materiality or form; 3) their multimodality; and/or 4) their rhetorical means. Of course, texts that fall under the category of *new* media by one or more of these definitions have existed for some time, but it is only recently that students, especially in writing classrooms, have been regularly asked to read or compose new media texts. The norm in colleges and universities for decades has been typed, double-spaced, thesis-driven texts 8½-by-11-inch, stapled, white paper. Thus, in this article, when I say that we should train tutors to work with new media, I mean the sorts of texts that would fit any of the three (Wysocki's, Selfe's, or Ball's) definitions outlined above. Practically speaking, this would mean that tutors would also be trained to work with texts that are not traditional, paper, alphabetic, text-only, academic print essays or assignments. Increasingly common, new media assignments in first-year composition (FYC) include PowerPoint presentations or slidecasts; video essays and documentaries; audio essays or podcast series; posters, collages, and other visual arguments; websites or hypertexts; and comic books, animations, or graphic novels. These are the sorts of texts we must be prepared to work with in the writing center in the twenty-first century in addition to the more traditional texts that have been the norm.

Why Tutor New Media?

Pemberton suggests four ways of dealing with new texts in writing centers: 1) ignore them since they will rarely appear; 2) use specialist tutors; 3) treat new media texts like other texts; or 4) train all tutors to work with them.[1] The last of these is the approach I will argue for; I believe the writing center is the place to tutor students with their new media texts. I think all tutors should be trained to work with these texts and that these texts have unique features, which means some of our traditional tutoring practices will not work (more on this later). Here, I will briefly defend my belief that we should take on the task of tutoring new media. Many readers, I imagine, will not need convincing, as writing centers around the country already work with new media writing. For these readers, this section might help them articulate this new work to colleagues or administrators who question the evolution of their writing centers. Other readers might find themselves more resistant to offering what they perceive as yet another service when demands on their resources and time are already too high. I can empathize with this position but do my best to articulate how I do not think tutoring new media is something we can or should opt out of. It is not another thing—it is *the* thing we have always done, just in new forms, genres, and media.

Reason #1: New media is writing. Writing has irrevocably changed from the early days of writing centers. Early writing centers in the 1960s and 1970s developed peer tutoring techniques when student texts were written by hand or with typewriters. Adding another mode—even a simple image—to paper texts was difficult and usually avoided. The 1980s and 1990s brought us personal computers with word processing, but for the earlier part of this period, the texts writing centers worked with did not radically change. Word processors made texts that looked like they came from typewriters; texts were composed on screen but printed and distributed on paper.

Fast forward to the 2000s. Student texts now are nearly always composed on screen. Most students have their own computers—laptops are popular. Many texts that students compose, even for FYC, never leave the screen. Students write reading responses in a course management system, like BlackBoard. They post the response to the course discussion board where the instructor and other students respond. Likewise, longer writing assignments—essays and web pages—can be "turned in" and "turned back" without ever being printed out. In fact, when Microsoft Word 2007 was released, it sported a new default typeface created for onscreen viewing, replacing the long-reigning Times New Roman, because of the frequency with which texts—even word-processed texts—were viewed on screen.

In these ways, we have witnessed a fundamental change in the textual climate. Before, putting a text on paper—and writing for that linear, left-to-right, top-to-bottom, page-to-page form—was *the* way to write. That has changed. Now, there are many ways to communicate through writing; consequently, putting a text to paper is now a rhetorical choice that one should not make hastily. We ought to really think through whether a paper essay, say, is the best way to reach our audience or purpose. If we decide to compose paper essays knowing we have the wide range of available textual choices, we are deeming the paper essay the best way to meet our rhetorical ends. Many of us, perhaps, have spent our lifetimes writing paper essays because that was how

MCKINNEY / NEW MEDIA MATTERS

arguments were made—academically if not otherwise. The paper essay was the default. This is no longer the case even in academic circles. Many academic conference presentations are not paper essays read to the audience but arguments presented with PowerPoint slideshows, videos, animations, and print or digital posters, suggesting that many academic writers, upon weighing their rhetorical choices, are no longer choosing paper essays.

I think it is unreasonable to grant that writers have a wide range of options for meeting their rhetorical ends—even academically—yet to insist that we will only help with those texts that writing centers have historically worked with, namely, paper essays and assignments. New media is "new," as the earlier definitions show, yet it is still writing. More than that, it is a type of writing that academia and the greater public value more and more.

Sending students with new media texts to another center or a specific tutor, as some centers have done, could give the message that new media is not writing, that it is not something the writing center values. Some universities might be in the position, as the University of Michigan was, to create a separate center for new media texts. But many of us struggle, annually, to keep one center open. Many of us also struggle to run one center, and most of us would not find additional compensation for willingly increasing our workload, I imagine. However, preparing all tutors to work with new media texts requires no second space or additional staffing. It does not necessarily require great investments in new technology or technology training. Most writing centers are likely adequately outfitted with at least one, if not several, computers on which to view digital texts. We might very well want to acquire large monitors or projectors to enable viewing of certain texts (e.g., slidecasts, video essays, or PowerPoint presentations), but these texts can be viewed on small screens for the purpose of tutor response.

Reason #2: The line between new media and old media is blurry. Though I attempted a clear-cut definition of new media texts in the previous section, it is often the case that a text straddles the old media/new media line. A writing center that officially works with only essays, reports, and other such alphabetic texts will increasingly, if not already, find multimodality and digitality a part of such texts. Pemberton's question about hypertexts is a good example. He meant, I think, to question whether writing centers ought to work with digital texts composed in HTML and viewed in web-browsers, otherwise known as web pages. Yet many programs now, including Microsoft Word and PowerPoint, allow for hypertext links (not to mention color, images, charts, sound, animation, and video), so traditional essays are quickly becoming less, well, traditional. If we say we do not work with hypertexts, would we then not work with essays that contain links? Or what of a webpage that contained an essay with no links? When is it an essay and when is it hypertext?

I think a writing center that sets out to determine when a traditional essay becomes a new media text—in order to say "yes" we work with these or "no" we don't work with those—will find this an increasingly difficult task. Likewise, a writing center that asserts that it can only help with the "writing" part of a new media text is also on shaky ground. The alphabetic text in a new media text is subsumed into the whole and must be read in context of the whole composition.

Reason #3: If we don't claim it for writing, others will subsume it as technology. If we surrender the composition of web texts or other new media texts to computer science or another department on campus, we allow new media composition to be lost to the technology. As Danielle DeVoss writes, "Writing center theory and practice must . . . evolve so we can situate ourselves as crucial stakeholders, working towards more complex and critical use of computing technologies and computer-related literacies" (167). If composing new media texts [is] just about mastering the technology; then we can be convinced (or others will try to convince us) that new media is better left to those on campus who know the most about technology. For example, if creating a website is only about learning HTML or CSS, then we could let the computer science department teach it. Yet, if we consider new media as texts composed consciously in multiple modes, we would have to acknowledge that we are responsible for and good at teaching composing.[2] We ought to speak up about how creating digital texts involves more than mastering a software program just as loudly as we speak up about how writing in general is more than mastering MLA format or rules for comma usage.

New media texts are texts—written for particular occasions, purposes, and audiences. As such, writers of new media still need human feedback. Related to this, the "CCCC Position Statement on Teaching, Learning, and Assessing Writing in Digital Environments," a guide for classroom instruction of digital writing, advises, "Because digital environments make sharing work especially convenient, we would expect to find considerable human interaction around texts; through such interaction, students learn that humans write to other humans for specific purposes." The statement reminds us that digital texts are rhetorical and therefore need rhetorical feedback—of the ilk a writing center typically provides—not just technical troubleshooting. The evolved writing center secures a spot for humans to meet other humans over texts, digital or not. Working with students on their new media texts asserts our stake as composing professionals in the new media age.

How to Tutor New Media

In the previous two sections I argued, perhaps paradoxically, that there is something new and different about new media writing, yet that it is writing and therefore we should tutor writers working on it. For me, there is enough that is "new" about new media that I had to ask myself how well our traditional tutoring practices address it. Trimbur is clear, too, that the change in types of projects we see in the center will change our tutoring. He writes,

> The new digital literacies will increasingly be incorporated into writing centers not just as sources of information or delivery systems for tutoring but as productive arts in their own right, and writing center work will, if anything, become more rhetorical in paying attention to the practices and effects of design in written and visual communication — more product-oriented and perhaps less like the composing conferences of the process movement. (30)

I have to agree with Trimbur that it would be foolish not to prepare my tutors to work with these texts. What I have come to believe is that accepting new media texts necessitates rethinking our dominant writing center ideas and revising our common practices. Practices vary from center to center, from tutor to tutor. Still, there are some practices espoused repeatedly in the literature of the field and tutor training manuals that seem to compose our general tenets. Many of these practices will have to change. Although such radical reimaginings of writing center work may seem daunting, we could see this as an occasion to reconsider how well we are responding to all texts, to all writers — an occasion to improve the work we do.

Up to this point, I have been concerned with arguing that we ought to work with new media; now I complicate that. I think it would be irresponsible not to think through (and follow through with) consequent changes to our practices. In what follows, I look at the often-espoused practices for tutoring writing, particularly the ways we read student texts and the ways we respond.

How we read student texts. Ever since Stephen North published his writing center manifesto, "The Idea of a Writing Center," writing center scholars and practitioners have been guided by this statement: "in a writing center the object is to make sure that writers, and not necessarily their texts, are what get changed by instruction. In axiom form it goes like this: our job is to produce better writers, not better writing" (37). What follows this writing center mantra is important; he writes, "In the center, we look *beyond* or *through* that particular project, that particular text, and see it as an occasion for addressing our primary concern, the process by which it is produced" (38, emphasis added). This idea has been translated into practice in various ways. For one, Christina Murphy and Steve Sherwood, in *The St. Martin's Sourcebook for Writing Tutors*, describe tutoring in terms of "pretextual," "textual," and "posttextual," [see p. 19] where the goal of tutoring is, indeed, to get beyond the text. In these three stages, the tutor is to first talk about the paper with the client, then read the paper with the client, and finish by moving from the paper and dealing with the client's issues in writing in general.

Another way to "look beyond" particular projects is to not physically look at them. This comes in the form of a hands-off policy in relation to student texts. We train our tutors to leave the text in front of the client or between tutor and client. As Leigh Ryan and Lisa Zimmerelli suggest in *The Bedford Guide for Writing Tutors*, "Give the student control of the paper. Keep the paper in front of the student as much as possible. If you are working at a computer, let the writer sit in front of the screen as well as control the keyboard" (19). When a student hands a tutor a paper, the tutor often quickly puts it down on the table. Irene Clark and Dave Healy note that this practice, which they call the pedagogy of noninterventionalism, exists because of an ethical concern in some centers. If tutors hold the paper, write on the paper, or otherwise "own" the paper, they may be unwittingly helping the student too much, i.e., plagiarizing or editing. Linda Shamoon arid Deborah Burns, in turn, call this hands-off practice "The Bible," an orthodoxy that has attained the force of an ethical or moral code within writing center studies (175).

Likewise, tutors are encouraged to use a read-aloud method for tutoring. Tutors read the student text aloud to the client or request the client to do so. However, this common approach of reading texts in writing centers might not be helpful for students with new media texts. The intertwining of multiple modes may be lost if the tutor looks *through* the text or does not look *at* the paper or *at* the screen. Furthermore, there is no way to "read aloud" visual elements or sounds. Consequently, the tutor may just skip over these elements thereby privileging the verbal, perhaps to the detriment of the student.

For example, several years ago one of my composition students, "Amy," took her final project to the writing center for help. She was working on her "book," a type of portfolio project that asked students to rethink their semester's work in terms of a consistent theme and design. She had decided to use divider pages featuring Winnie the Pooh throughout her book. It was an odd choice as a design feature that became downright inappropriate when one of her "chapters" was an essay on Hitler. The baffling juxtaposition of Pooh and Piglet and the horrific details in her essay surely did not escape her tutor; however, the tutor did not say anything to Amy about this choice quite possibly because the tutor was working under the typical assumption that the alphabetic text was her domain, or because the tutor never even saw this visual element since Amy held the book and read aloud to the tutor. Amy might have received a similar silence had she used certain types of online tutoring which ask writers to cut and paste their text into email forms or whiteboards, allowing tutors to see only the alphabetic text.[3]

How we read texts in writing centers is especially problematic for certain new media texts, such as digital texts, which offer the reader a choice in navigation—where to start, when to go back, where to go next. A tutor must look at a hypertext and interact with it to read it, which begs the question: how would one—or why would one—read aloud a website? The first step in evolving writing center practice, then, is insisting that tutors look at texts to see student writing. Stephen Bernhardt's suggestion to composition teachers that they ought to look *at* student texts instead of *through* them seems just as important for writing centers now. If we don't, Bernhardt warns that we are ensuring our own irrelevance as the gap widens between the literacies we have traditionally taught and the ones students need: "Classroom practice which ignores the increasingly visual, localized qualities of information exchange can only become increasingly irrelevant" (77). Doing so, we ask tutors to consider the materiality of texts from the resolution of images to the quality of paper for a resume.

Secondly, instead of asking tutors to read aloud, we can ask tutors to talk aloud as they negotiate a text — a subtle yet important change. In reading aloud, the tutor may be tempted to skip over nonverbal elements since the elements are, well, not verbal. In fact, in my own tutoring experience, I have worked with students who quickly turn the page past charts or graphs as if they are inconsequential to the text at hand. However, if the tutor talked through the text, he or she would instead render a reading of it, showing the student how it could be read in its entirety. For instance, imagine Amy taking her book to a talk-aloud session. The tutor right away would begin with the materiality of the text. "Wow, this is quite a big document. I see it has lots of pages. This, here, seems to be a title. Is this a collection of writings of sorts?" And then, "I'm noticing as we go through this that you've used Winnie the Pooh on each divider page. Why is that?"

This tactic would be immensely helpful for hypertexts, too. The tutor could talk through the links and her expectations for how to negotiate the pages. "OK, we've read through this page on Senator Clinton. I'd like to go back to the page on Moveon.org, but I don't see how I'd do that." Or, "The first thing I notice is these images changing — fading into one another. They all seem connected by their subject — all protesters of sorts? This makes me think this website is about protesting even though the title says, 'Citizens of America.'" This sort of talking aloud would let students see how a reader makes meaning by reading the various modes in the text: images, text, layout, color, movement, and so forth.

How we talk about student writing. In a typical writing center session, tutors are trained to read through the student's text and then to set an agenda on what issues to tackle during the remainder of the session. Many tutors are trained to focus the tutorial on higher order concerns (HOCs) first. These are defined as "the features of the paper that exist beyond the sentence-level; they include clarity of thesis or focus, adequate development and information, effective structure or organization, and appropriate voice and tone" (McAndrew and Reigstad 42). Only after working through the "higher order" issues does the tutor turn to lower order concerns (LOCs), which primarily manifest on the sentence level. All in all, this practice makes sense. It is only logical to work students through revisions that might necessitate substantial changes first before tackling what is happening on a micro-level.

Nonetheless, there may be a problem with this practice for new media texts since tutors are not trained to see other modes, such as visual elements, as contributing to the overall meaning of the text. That is, they are not trained to see that visual elements can be and often are a higher order concern and should be attended to as such. For instance, a tutor, Bryan, told me last year of a student he worked with who was composing a scholarship essay. The student had selected an apple clip art border for his text that he felt was fitting for the type of scholarship—a scholarship for future teachers. These apples, which Bryan felt inappropriate for the genre, were really the only thing he remembered about the essay, yet were not something he discussed with the student since he said he wanted to discuss "the more important issues" first. Clearly, this is just one example, but I believe it does speak to the way we set agendas—what we decide to talk about with writers.

Tutors do not typically broach the subject of formatting without direct questioning from the student because issues of formatting, if they are seen at all, are seen as LOCs or because tutors usually work with drafts and may assume the students will know how to "fix" such elements by the final copy. The visual aspects of a text may not even be on the tutor's radar, let alone other modes such as sound, color, or motion. In numerous tutoring manuals, there is little acknowledgement that visual elements or document design are important for tutors to read and discuss with students.[4] The closest are Ryan and Zimmerelli's *Bedford Guide*, which states that lab reports should have headings, includes a page on PowerPoint presentations, and asks tutors to consider if resumes are "pleasing to the eye" (87), and Bertie Fearing and W. Keats Sparrow's "Tutoring Business and Technical Writing Students," which focuses mainly on issues of voice, diction, economy, emphasis, and parallelism, but also devotes one paragraph to typography, headings, and lists. Beyond this, there is little about the multimodality of academic essays and more often than not nothing about considering the multimodality of any other type of assignment. Even when telling tutors how to work with typically visually heavy forms—manuals, instructions, memos, proposals, progress and feasibility reports—McAndrew and Reigstad do not show tutors how to give feedback on the nonverbal elements. Obviously, if writing centers are going to work with new media texts—those texts which purposely employ various modes to make meaning—tutors will have to be trained to know when and how the interaction of various modes are HOCs.

Furthermore, unless trained otherwise, tutors might not suggest the use of nontextual modes in revision planning with the student. There are moments as readers when the use of a diagram, illustration, or image could help with our comprehension of ideas, and there are times when the use of a bulleted list, graph, or chart allows a writer to present ideas succinctly. Tutors, as readers of and responders to texts, need to be able to describe to clients their expectations in terms of verbal and other elements and plot out the tutoring sessions to reflect that. Tutors need to be able to talk about new media texts, which requires both a broader understanding of rhetoric (of how new media texts are rhetorical) and a new set of terms about the interactivity between modes and the effects of that interactivity.

Several composition scholars have theorized how we might respond to or assess classroom-assigned new media writing. Several of them emphasize the rhetorical nature of new media, thereby arguing that we can respond to new media in ways similar to how we respond to other texts, as they are all rhetorical. For example, in "Looking for Sources of Coherence in a Fragmented World," Kathleen Blake Yancey argues that we need new ways of talking about digital writing. "Without a new language, we will be held hostage to the values informing print, values worth preserving for that medium, to be sure, but values incongruent with those informing the digital" (89–90). To that end, she offers a heuristic for readers to ask of digital texts: What arrangements are possible? Who arranges? What is the intent? What is the fit between intent and effect? (96). Though she sees digital composition as different, she sees rhetoric as "being at the heart" of all the writing composition teachers assign and assess (90).

Likewise, Madeleine Sorapure's "Between Modes: Assessing Student New Media Compositions" suggests teachers look for the use of the rhetorical tropes of metaphor and metonymy when assessing students' new media compositions, thereby focusing on the relationship of modes. She writes,

> Focusing assessment on the relations of modes might alleviate part of what Yancey described as the "discomfort" of assessment: that part that comes from our sense that we are not the most qualified people on campus to judge the effectiveness of the individual modes of image, audio, or video in a multimodal composition. But I think we are indeed qualified to look at the relations between modes and to assess how effectively students have combined different resources in their compositions. (4)

I think Sorapure's idea is on the right track. We don't need to be, say, filmmakers to respond to video in new media compositions. However, we do need to be able, at a minimum, to respond to how the video relates to the whole of the text. As Yancey, Sorapure, and others suggest, new media texts are rhetorical. We can talk about how the text is motivated, how it is purposeful, how it is written to a particular audience. These conversations can be similar to the conversations we have about old media texts.[5] Yet if we do read rhetorically to determine how well a text meets its ends, our tutors need to be able to explain how a text has or has not done so. I do not think our language for talking about texts is adequate in and of itself for this task.

Instead, I have increasingly drawn on other fields to give tutors ways to talk about the interactivity of modes and their sense of the gestalt in students' new media texts. Teaching tutors these terms will give them a vocabulary to describe the relationships between modes; without such an understanding, many times students and tutors assume that images, graphics, animation, or other modes are decoration or supplementation (although they probably won't use that term) for the real mode of writing: the words. I've tutored more than one student who assumed that visuals always make sense to readers, that other modes don't need interpretation like words do.

As a start, I think it appropriate to teach tutors Karen Schriver's terms for the relationships between modes, Robin Williams's principles of good design, and Cynthia Selfe's criteria for visual assessment. Each of these, I believe, gives more concrete language for tutors or teachers responding to new media. The space of this article will not permit me to draw out extended examples of each of the terms; I hope that readers interested in these ideas will look to the primary texts. However, I will briefly look at a sample new media text to see how this terminology as a whole might help a tutor respond to such a text.

Relationships between modes: Karen Schriver. Schriver's terms were intended to describe how visuals work with alphabetic text, though they easily translate to the relationships between different modes, too, such as sound, video, and color.

Redundant:	"substantially identical content appearing visually and verbally in which each mode tells the same story; providing a repetition of key ideas" (412)
Complementary:	"different content visually and verbally, in which both modes are needed in order to understand the key ideas" (412)
Supplementary:	"different content in words and pictures, in which one mode dominates the other, providing the main ideas, while the other reinforces, elaborates, or instantiates the points made in the dominant mode (or explains how to interpret the other)" (413)
Juxtapositional:	"different content in words and pictures, in which the key ideas are created by a clash or semantic tension between the ideas in each mode; the idea cannot be inferred without both modes being present simultaneously" (414)
Stage-setting:	"different content in words and pictures, in which one mode (often the visual) forecasts the content, underlying theme, or ideas presented in the other mode" (414)

Principles of design: Robin Williams. Williams's four basic design principles come from her work, *The Non-Designer's Design Book*, where she tries to simplify design concepts for those who must design on paper or screen but do not do so as their primary occupation. Using this sort of text draws on the field of graphic design, which has multimodal composition at its heart.

Contrast:	difference created between elements for emphasis; elements must be made quite different or else the elements simply *conflict* with one another (63)
Repetition:	how consistently elements (e.g., typeface, color, pattern, transition) are used; repetition unifies (49)

| Alignment: | how elements line up on a page, the visual connection between elements; "every item should have a visual connection with something else on the page" (31) |
| Proximity: | how closely elements are placed on page or screen: related items should be close to one another, unrelated items should not be (15–17) |

Visual assessment criteria: Cynthia Selfe. The last set of terms comes from a chapter of *Writing New Media* in which Selfe, drawing on the work of Gunther Kress and Theo van Leeuwan, gives assignments and rubrics for helping writing instructors incorporate new media into their classes. This set of terms is helpful in looking, literally, at the gestalt of a new media text.

Visual impact:	"the overall effect and appeal that a visual composition has on an audience" ("Toward" 85)
Visual coherence:	"the extent to which the various elements of a visual composition are tied together, represent a unified whole" ("Toward" 86)
Visual salience:	"the relative prominence of an element within a visual composition. Salient elements catch viewers' eye [*sic*]; they are conspicuous" ("Toward" 86)
Visual organization:	"the pattern of arrangement that relates the elements of the visual essay to one another so that they are easier for readers/viewers to comprehend" ("Toward" 87)

Using the new terminology to respond to a new media text. Figure 1—which can be viewed at http://www.clarion.edu/80053.jpg—is a poster created by the Writing Center staff at Clarion University. They produce these posters collaboratively as a staff and sell customized versions via their website. This one, the "Criminal Justice Poster," is one of my favorites. I selected this text to model a new media response because it fits within the very general definition of new media that I have used throughout this article, because it consciously takes advantage of its materiality as a poster, and because it relies on multiple modes to make its argument. It also is exchanged as a digital text first—composed digitally and bought from digital previews before it is printed poster-size. In addition, I wanted to select a text which a reader of this article could see in its entirety.

So, first off, what kind of relationship do we see between the modes here? The composer has used text, photograph, color, and typography to make this text. The image of the handcuffed person is in a *complementary* relationship with the text, "Don't let your writing get so out of hand it has to be put behind bars." The image helps give the reader context. Though the text is a threatening command (do this or else), the orange, bright blue, and green colors and typography are more playful than foreboding. Perhaps this *juxtaposition* is purposeful to play up the humor of the poster, or perhaps it takes away from the effect. This could be something to discuss with the writer.

We can also look at the principles of design at work here. *Contrast* is evident in the change in typeface. The composer wanted to emphasize the word "Don't," so it appears larger than the other words. The different colors, sizes, and weight of the other words and background signal difference, perhaps of importance. "Don't let your writing" is in one typeface; the rest of the text is in a very similar sans serif typeface, which makes for a *conflict*. *Repetition* is evident in the color choices; the background colors are also used for the type. The words "Don't" and "writing" are actually repeated and faded into the background. There are varied *alignments* here. Mostly, the text is center-aligned and shares the same base line. However, "Don't" and "let your" don't share a common baseline. The (mostly) center alignment makes the words on the left margin and right margin nearly line up. Further, there is no consistent alignment within the colored blocks; the text sits near the bottom in blue and green squares but floats to the top in orange. There are two sentences here and the *proximity* is very close between them, signaling to the reader that these ideas are closely related. The image breaking through the first sentence makes the reader understand the picture as part of the message of that first sentence.

Finally, we could look at this as a visual argument. Using Selfe's terms, we would probably acknowledge that the overall *visual impact* is quite striking. This is a poster that stands out because of the image and bright (though not garish) colors. The purpose of a poster is to call attention to itself, and this poster has the potential to do that. The *visual coherence* is also quite strong because of the repetition of colors and type. The poster will be customized in the white box with the purchaser's logo or information. There is a possibility that there will be less coherence when that element is introduced if there are different types or colors. The elements that are *visually salient* are the word "Don't" and the photograph. Both hold key positions—one in the top left corner and one across the center of the poster. The quick in-a-glance message provided by these two elements is, "don't end up in cuffs"—pretty powerful! The placement of the prominent "Don't" at the top invites the reader to start there and move down; thus the *visual organization* of elements tells the reader how to use the text.

At this point, I should mention two things. First, I am not implying that a tutor would or should go through reading/responding to a text as extensively as this during a session. Like other sessions, the tutor and student would discuss what seems most pressing. I, for one, would probably talk to this composer about how color and type relate to text and image and the overall alignment—another tutor might focus on other elements. Which brings me to my second point: not everyone using these terms is going to come to the same reading. The reader's job with new media is still interpretation. Responding to new media requires close interaction with the text and ways to talk about what we read/view/interact with.

Summary and Closing Thoughts

This article has been about reconsidering how we train tutors to read and respond to texts. The subject here has been new media texts. I've asked us to reconsider how we tutor and how we talk to students about their writing. The impetus for these evolved practices is the arrival of increasing numbers of new media texts assigned in university classes. As new media texts consciously and purposefully employ multiple modes to make meaning, they require us to direct our attention to texts differently. Current practices won't suffice, as they limit us to the alphabetic text. Thus, I believe it is imperative to train all tutors in these evolved practices because they will change the ways we respond to all texts, considering more than we have before, perhaps in significant ways. In short, here's the 28-word, visually arranged version of this article:

Twentieth-Century Tutoring	Twenty-First-Century Tutoring
Read aloud	Talk aloud
Getting beyond the text	Interacting with the text
Zoomed in: talk about words	Zoomed out: talk about whole

It strikes me that writing center studies is at a crossroads, a moment in time where tough decisions regarding the scope of our practices need to be made. Certainly, changes in composing technologies have asked us to push beyond the writing center practices that developed in the 1970s writing center boom. I, for one, do not think this is a time for conservatism, for preserving the tradition for the sake of tradition. Though I understand the impulse as a writing center director to say, "Not one more thing! We do enough!," to me, tutoring new media is not another thing. Writing has evolved with new composing technologies and media, and we must evolve, too, because we are in the writing business. A radical shift in the way that writers communicate both academically and publically necessitates a radical reimagining and re-understanding of our practices, purposes, and goals.

Finally, I want to address one of the concerns that I discussed earlier: that we are not sure that we can do a good job of tutoring new media, so perhaps we shouldn't try. I think we need to remember that writing centers are largely based on the idea that talk among peers will help. We've never been concerned about expert tutors or perfection, and our feathers get ruffled when others (students or professors) expect this. If we evolve the practices in the ways I suggest, tutors will not be experts in new media composing, but they will be able to offer a response. And that is what we do.

Notes

[1] Pemberton focuses exclusively on hypertexts, not all new media.

[2] For more on this, see Grutsch McKinney.

[3] This could also hold true for tutoring via email or chat. The texts may be copied and pasted into an email and the tutor will not see the text as it will materialize for its intended audience, for example, how it prints out on the page.

[4] In addition to this essay by Jackie Grutsch McKinney, the *Sourcebook* also includes document design-themed essays by Lisa Eastmond Bell (p. 326), David Sheridan (p. 334), and Christina Murphy and Lory Hawkes (p. 361).

[5] For example, see JoAnn Griffin's schema in "Making Connections with Writing Centers" for discussing audience, purpose, form, context, organization, unity/focus, detail/support, style, and correctness of alphabetic essays, audio essays, and video essays (pp. 155–56).

Works Cited

Ball, Cheryl. "Show, Not Tell: The Value of New Media Scholarship." *Computers and Composition* 21.4 (2004): 403–25. Print.

Bernhardt, Stephen A. "Seeing the Text." *College Composition and Communication* 37.1 (1986): 66–78. Print.

Conference on College Composition and Communication. "CCCC Position Statement on Teaching, Learning, and Assessing Writing in Digital Environments." Adopted 25 Feb. 2004. Web. 15 Dec. 2007.

Clark, Irene, and Dave Healy. "Are Writing Centers Ethical?" *WPA: Writing Program Administration* 20.1/2 (1996): 32–48. Print.

DeVoss, Danielle. "Computer Literacies and the Roles of the Writing Center." *Writing Center Research: Extending the Conversation*. Ed. Paula Gillespie, Alice Gillam, Lady Falls Brown, and Bryon Stay. Mahwah: Erlbaum, 2002. 167–85. Print.

Fearing, Berne E., and W. Keats Sparrow. 'Tutoring Business and Technical Writing Students in the Writing Center." *Writing Centers: Theory and Administration*. Ed. Gary A. Olson. Urbana: NCTE, 1984. 215–56. Print.

George, Diana. "From Analysis to Design: Visual Communication in the Teaching of Writing." *College Composition and Communication* 54.1 (2002): 11–39. Print.

Griffin, JoAnn. "Making Connections with Writing Centers." *Multimodal Composition: Resources for Teachers*. Ed. Cynthia Selfe. Kresskill: Hampton P. 2007. 153–66. Print.

Grutsch McKinney, Jackie. "The New Media (R)evolution: Multiple Models for Multiliteracies." *Multiliteracy Centers*. Ed. David Sheridan and James Inman. Cresskill: Hampton, 2010. Print.

Hassett, Michael, and Rachel W. Lott. "Seeing Student Texts." *Composition Studies* 28.1 (2000): 29–47. Print.

Inman, James. "At First Site: Lessons From Furman University's Center for Collaborative Learning and Communication." *Academic Writing* 2 (2001): n. pag. Web. 15 Dec. 2007.

Kress, Gunther. *Literacy in the New Media Age*. New York Roulledge, 2003. Print.

McAndrew, Donald, and Thomas J. Reigstad. *Tutoring Writing: A Practical Guide for Conferences*. Portsmouth: Boyton/Cook, 2001. Print.

Murphy, Christina, and Steve Sherwood. *The St. Martin's Sourcebook for Writing Tutors*. 2nd ed. Boston: Bedford/St. Martin's, 2003. Print.

North, Stephen M. "The Idea of a Writing Center." *College English* 46.5 (1984): 433–46. Print.

Pemberton, Michael. "Planning for Hypertexts in the Writing Center . . . or Not." *Writing Center Journal* 24.1 (2003): 9–24. Print.

Ryan, Leigh, and Lisa Zimmerelli. *The Bedford Guide for Writing Tutors.* 4th ed. Boston: Bedford/ St. Martin's, 2006. Print.

Schriver, Karen A. *Dynamics in Document Design.* New York: Wiley Computer P, 1997. Print.

Selber, Stuart. *Multiliteracies for a Digital Age.* Carbondale: Southern Illinois UP, 2004. Print.

Selfe, Cynthia. "Students Who Teach Us: A Case Study of a New Media Text Designer." Wysocki et al. 43–66. Print.

---. "Toward New Media Texts: Taking Up the Challenges of Visual Literacy." Wysocki et al. 67–110. Print.

Shamoon, Linda K., and Deborah H. Burns, "A Critique of Pure Tutoring." *Writing Center Journal* 15.2 (1995): 134–51. Print.

Sheridan, David. "The Sweetland Multi-Literacy Center." *Sweetland Newsletter.* Oct. 2002. Web. 15 Dec. 2007.

---. "Words, Images, Sounds: Writing Centers as Multiliteracy Centers." *The Writing Center Director's Resource Book.* Ed. Christina Murphy and Byron Stay. Mahwah: Erlbaum, 2006. 339–50. Print.

Sorapure, Madeleine. "Between Modes: Assessing Student New Media Compositions." *Kairos* 10.2 (Spring 2006). Web. 15 Dec. 2007.

Stroupe, Craig. "Visualizing English: Recognizing the Hybrid Literacy of the Visual and Verbal Authorship on the Web." *College English* 62.5 (2005): 607–32. Print.

Trimbur, John. "Multiliteracies, Social Futures, and Writing Centers." *Writing Center Journal* 20.2 (2000): 29–31. Print.

Williams, Robin. *The Non-Designer's Design Book* Berkeley: Peachpit P. 2003. Print.

Wysocki, Anne Frances. "Opening New Media to Writing: Openings and Justifications." Wysocki et al. 1–42. Print.

Wysocki, Anne Frances, Johndan Johnson-Eilola, Cynthia L. Selfe, and Geoffrey Sirc. *Writing New Media.* Logan: Utah State UP, 2004.

Yancey, Kathleen Blake. "Looking for Sources of Coherence in a Fragmented World." *Computers and Composition* 21.1 (2004): 89–102. Print.

The Future of Multiliteracy Centers in the E-World: An Exploration of Cultural Narratives and Cultural Transformation

Christina Murphy and Lory Hawkes _____

MARSHALL UNIVERSITY

DEVRY UNIVERSITY

Christina Murphy and Lory Hawkes discuss the transformation of writing centers to multiliteracy centers as a cultural narrative of "new historicism" in which one paradigm replaces another with significant implications for interpretation and action. In this essay, originally featured in the 2010 collection Multiliteracy Centers: Writing Center Work, New Media, and Multimodal Rhetoric, *Murphy and Hawkes offer a contemporary "Idea of a Writing Center," which is responsive to the "texture of social change" that the panoply of e-literacies provide. They contend that this paradigmatic and historical transition to multiple semiotic modes will require new models of tutor training as tutors become "digital content specialists" within this e-world of contemporary communication. In this reconfiguration, tutors are not just consultants who help others produce but rather producers who create sophisticated tools to support students working on both digital and nondigital projects. Peer tutors are reconfigured as "digital content specialists" who "use the principles of e-literacies, cognitive theory, and composition pedagogy" to design multimodal learning environments customized to the needs of individual learners.*

Brook Thomas (1989) is among many contemporary critics who call for a new historical discourse that enables the modern era to understand its relationship to history as a repetitive texture of change. Within this texture, new ideas replace old ideas as sociopolitical and socioeconomic realities shift frames of understanding and interpretation and, thus, the tensions between ascending and declining paradigms generate the mythologies by which old ideas tenuously cling to power.

For Writing Centers, the course of events has been no different from what Thomas describes as a "new historicism." The process of new paradigms replacing old has been one that has had both beneficial and limiting effects for the development of Writing Centers within academics. The old paradigms have had a decidedly negative effect in devaluing the types of contributions that Writing Centers can make to higher education and thus have worked to keep Writing Centers from reaching their full potential. However, the current century provides new opportunities for Writing Centers to reestablish themselves both within and outside academics as multiliteracy centers Focused on the e-literacies or (a) digital technology (digital literacies), (b) images and design (visual literacies), (c) using the Internet to search for information (information literacies), and (d) the capacity to work electronically in international settings and groups (global literacies). Decidedly, the future of the Writing Center will be shaped by its digital awareness and the contributions of digital content specialists to student engagement and instruction via electronic methods.

The significance of this shift in emphases and priorities is highly significant for Writing Centers in that they are the academic units best positioned by their philosophies and histories to capitalize on the importance of e-literacies for the transformation of academics in the 21st century. Thus, the movement from traditional Writing Centers focused on the values and mechanisms of the print culture of the 20th century to multiliteracy centers in the 21st century is truly a significant achievement. It is also a movement that will prove to be transformative for Writing Centers and for the professionals who staff them and that will shape their strategic visions and goals.

One of the most significant changes will be in the ethos that many Writing Centers and Writing Center professionals have demonstrated in the 20th century, specifically in terms of concepts of marginalization and rebellion. Liz Rohan (2002), for example, speaks of the fragile ethos that affects Writing

Center professionals who labor within an academy that regards their work as inferior or antithetical to the work of the classroom. In the classroom, teacher scholars teach, create, and discover new knowledge, whereas in the Writing Center, tutors offer sympathy and support, deal with writing problems, and provide instructional services and retention initiatives to the academy. It is no wonder, then, that Stephen North's (1984) essay, "The Idea of a Writing Center," remains the single most famous and most cited essay in Writing Center scholarship largely because, in essence, North's essay is a call for an understanding by the academy of the type of work that Writing Center professionals actually do. North's essay is also a consummate martyrdom narrative in which North is pleading for Writing Center professionals to be understood, accepted, and valued by English departments. Despite that North repudiated this essay in 1994 with "Revisiting 'The Idea of a Writing Center,'" in which North stated that his ideas had been both romantic and naive, still Writing Center professionals continue to position their discussions and definitions of Writing Center work along the polarities of North's sense of martyrdom and devaluation, or along Kevin Davis's (1995) call to rebellion, in which positioning Writing Centers on the boundary of the academy as subversive agents for change is the most positive direction and philosophical stance that Writing Centers can pursue.

In essence, North and Davis exemplify the long tradition of marginalization and protest against marginalization that has characterized Writing Center work and scholarship for decades. In essence, too, this process has been permitted—if not encouraged—by the fact that, for a number of decades, the debate has been oddly positioned philosophically. Thus, much of Writing Center scholarship and practice have been focused on defending the Writing Center against challenges and questions by other academics or asserting the value or traditional methods of tutoring via one-on-one sessions in a print-culture setting. Little attention has been paid to redefining the tutor as a digital content specialist or the student as one whose learning will be best shaped and best served by electronic methods. In essence, little attention has been paid to finding new academic and cultural paradigms for the Writing Center and its instructional methods and value. Also, the broader national conversation on Writing Centers has not taken into account the instructional implications of changes in societal philosophies.

In essence, Writing Center theorists have not fully explored the implications of social systems theories to Writing Center practices or potentials. Thus, as Victoria E. Bonnell and Lynn Hunt (1999) indicate in their "Introduction" to *Beyond the Cultural Turn*, in the push-pull of ideas and paradigms, it is difficult to determine whether paradigms shape or are shaped by social realities. No doubt there is some interplay, but as Mehdi Farashahi, Taieb Hafsi, and Rick Molz (2005) point out, empirical research and its outcomes drive social realities more than philosophies and paradigms drive the empirical investigations and achievements of science and technology. This conclusion has enormous implications for Writing Center professionals, who must move arguments away from such limited concepts as institutional status—especially within English departments—toward the realities of social change (and thus social roles) driven by science and technology. The ultimate outcome of such a shift in perspective will be the realization that the future of the Writing Center is not as a Writing Center but. as a multiliteracy center with expanded pedagogical possibilities and new roles for Writing Center specialists. In this view, Writing Centers will assume their rightful and credible role as a knowledge-making academic resource that fosters the major educational and societal goals of multimodal literacy. Writing Centers will also assume their rightful role as multiliteracy centers engaged in the type of instruction and communication (as well as philosophical and pragmatic design) that Howard Rheingold (1998) describes as "computer-mediated communication that is a many-to-many medium" (p. 121).

If, as David Bawden (2001) contends, the mastery of reading and writing to achieve understanding demonstrates literacy, for decades Writing Center educators have been making the university system of instruction work by diagnosing flaws in reading and writing and in devising creative methods to offer cognitive solutions. All of these initiatives have been pursued amid a growing diversity of students, from students coping with cultural challenges, to learning difference students, to physically challenged students, to academically underprepared students. These educators wisely selected print materials for distribution to students; used dialogue, interpretation, and coaching; and provided feedback in face-to-face and computer-mediated venues to help students learn effective techniques of expression. To be able to deal with the range of students and determine their problems, Writing Center educators have had to be conversant with composition pedagogy as well as with finding effective pragmatic and interpersonal ways to influence students into working through their frustrations with the system of assignments and grading. On the one hand, these educators retaught composition techniques by customizing examples, language exercises, or writing sessions. In doing so, they had to understand the purpose of the composition, align reteaching with the stated goals of the assignment, and yet keep the student writer engaged. These mini-sessions demanded content mastery of composition pedagogy and Writing Center pedagogy as they matched the right approaches to each student's skills, interests, and concerns. As content specialists. Writing Center professionals had the ability to customize information into a hierarchy of learning experiences to promote knowledge building.

Clearly, these modes dominated Writing Center interactions for most of the 20th century; however, in the new paradigm of the 21st century, Writing Center educators become digital content specialists. Drawing on Norman Fairclough's (1993) view of discourse as a socially accepted system of using language to think and act in ways that identify a person as a member of a socially meaningful group, David Bawden (2001) argues that digital literacy provides a means

of grasping the nature of that discourse identity and of interacting with others to improve social perspective and standing. By this process, Bawden does
not mean merely computer literacy (the ability to wield the processes of the
computer to do one's work or accomplish a process) or information literacy
(an understanding of how to gain and use information, as well as the societal
implications of using technology and accessing information). Instead, he envisions digital literacy as a multimedia fluency of expression based on the ability
to acquire and evaluate what one reads and how one chooses to respond in a
dynamic cyberenvironment. Citing Paul Gilster's (1999) 10 core competencies
for digital literacy, Bawden notes that Glister and others regard digital literacy
as "an essential life skill . . . as a survival skill" (pp. 247–248). Similarly, in
"Assessing Multiliteracies and the New Basics," Mary Kalantzis, Bill Cope, and
Andrew Harvey (2003) endorse the life-long value of developing multiliteracies and the resultant impact on the individual. They also advocate significant
curricular changes:

> The need for flexibility, autonomy, collaboration, problem-solving skills, broad
> knowledgeability, and diverse intelligence are all underlined by changes to the
> traditional area of literacy. Yet the trend to multiliteracies is simply a very visible
> example of broader trends within the new economy, which suggest the need for
> new orientations to knowledge. Learning will increasingly be about creating a
> kind of person, with kinds of dispositions and orientations to the world, and not
> just persons who are in command of a body of knowledge. (p. 23)

A digital content specialist, then, can empower student investigation and
knowledge-making by building user interfaces to combine information in
an effective presentation and navigational hierarchy. This outcome can be
accomplished in two ways to help mediate gaps in understanding and help
promote authorship. First, the digital content specialist can customize infor-
mational displays to enhance the user's experience. For example, for the visually impaired student who has trouble understanding the concept of privacy
for an essay the student is writing, the digital content specialist could create a
domain of large typography augmented with sound and slow-moving, simple
slide shows to illustrate the concept by juxtaposing key phrases with pictures
from recent news stories (also enlarged for easier reading). Second, for the
student with learning disabilities who may have trouble reading an assigned
essay, the digital content specialist could build an interface that presents the
essay in hypertext episodes with a few questions voiced by streaming audio
to build comprehension at the end of each episode. The interface would have
programmed controls that enabled the student to move slowly or quickly
through the essay by touching the screen or selecting a Next button, and these
controls would give the student feedback on overall comprehension either
textually or aurally with a voice synthesizer.

Four technological innovations will improve the Writing Center's digital self-
awareness and make the digital content specialist an important contributor to

the well-being of the university by finding ways to use software systems to enhance student learning. The first innovation has already been in place for some time and may include hypertext editors or object-oriented interface development environments (IDES) that are licensed for use on the university network. These may be high-end software suites, course-delivery systems, proprietary programs, or open-source applications. Although these software products may already exist on many campuses, their use for Writing Centers has not been fully explored. With an editor or an IDE, the digital content specialist can merge pictures with text and imbed sounds to create mood and motivation for further exploration. Using newer animation software, the digital content specialist can portray a process or capture a series of visual images to make a research strategy more vivid. Equally exciting is the improved ability to carry a signal. With improved bandwidth, stream-ing video and audio are possible. If the student learns better with spoken instructions or attends better to visual demonstration, customized instruc-tion can be crafted to be sent over the university networks or to reside on a Writing Center workstation.

More than ever before, self-paced learning opportunities are possible as a result of object-oriented IDEs. With rudimentary knowledge of hypertext navigation and scripting language or the use of a high-end scripting editor included in the university's network software, the digital content specialist can provide access to handouts on the university networks juxtaposed with files or handouts from other universities organized by theme, topic, approach, rhetorical or instructional strategy. and so forth. Because self-publishing is also a form of learning and an opportunity to revise and improve written content, digital content specialists can work with students who want to publish their web pages, whether the publication is for personal satisfaction or part of a larger collection of work in a cyber portfolio—which can augment students' resumes for job consideration.

In a similar vein, IDEs also enable digital content specialists to create writ-ing experiences out of everyday things. With an understanding of composi-tion pedagogy and Writing Center pedagogy, a digital content specialist could import an image of Michael Jackson into a text editor, offer a sound clip from a recent broadcast from the pop star, link to his web page and then to a news story about the 2005 trial, and ask the student to write a response based on the combined sensory experience of the media to determine whether the two sites present a biased or unbiased view of the case. The student would be able to experience the news through sight, sound, and text and to cre-ate his or her own text to evaluate the given text. The context would have a richness of sensory experience by putting a human face together with dif-fering reports that require responsible, citizen-based judgment. Additionally, the Macromedia Suite, which includes Flash software, provides a simple way to create computer-rendered movies playable on a web page. Thus, a further learning context could be explored by sequencing images from the trial with excerpts from the news headlines and then asking students to express their reactions to the media's influence.

A second digital innovation currently underutilized on university campuses is the large online learning system like WebCT™, Blackboard™, and eCollege™, as well as other open-source systems. These large delivery systems emulate hypertext editors with proprietary programming to provide a visual IDE in which to fashion course syllabi, assignments, and exams. These learning systems have robust multimedia capabilities that can be creatively blended to provide a multisensory learning experience. These learning systems provide liberal storage area for streaming media and graphics. Finally, these learning systems all have color adjustments to increase contrast between the background and foreground text and a means of increasing the size of the typography should visual accommodation be necessary. Because the university network renders files quickly and because students in the university are familiar with the access techniques, digital content specialists could use the Chat feature to stage self-help sessions For study skills, research, and time management. The archived discussions (threaded discussions) could be used as a knowledge management system to offer answers to the most frequently asked questions. The streaming audio and video capabilities could be used as a convenient means to play one of the Writing Center's prerecorded tutorials.

The third technological innovation is wireless technology that permits the broadcast of a signal that is then interpreted and rendered by a personal device, whether that is a cell phone or a personal [digital] assistant. Wireless technology, coupled with the improved vibrant color displays on small monitors, means that learning is both portable and personal. Learning experiences can now become mobile outreaches so that user interfaces developed in hypertext design environments can be downsized, simplified, and broadcast to students on their personal devices and on demand. A digital camera that is connected to a university network could be a streaming media recorder of events simultaneously transmitted by a web cam. These events could be the source and the spur for practice writings. Podcasting, or the use of video transmitted through wireless technology to personal data devices, could be a new way of letting students know what might be available as help in the multiliteracy center.

The fourth technological innovation that is recasting the potential of user interface design in the hands of digital content specialists is both a technology and a social reaction to software gerrymandering. The growth of extensible markup language (XML) web services is remarkable. XML is the new generation of hypertext scripting that enables a designer to concentrate on content so that the designer can customize elements or objects referenced by the script. In essence, the XML scripting language permits the designer to create the interface and the meta-language. that produces the interface. XML is the scripting language of choice to produce a reusable code web service that is shared with the larger Internet developer community. The digital content specialist with knowledge of XML, style sheets, and object technology can create tutorials, rich media reports, and utilities that can be shared with colleagues. The Web service, as a module of working code, would be reusable scripting to perform an often-repeated function, or it might prove to be a utility program for a much-repeated function. Web services can be accessed easily and applied quickly to networks, and web services are resources to the technical community. The model of global sharing of web services emulates the vision of Ted Nelson, who envisioned the global digital lending library called Xanadu. As both literacy and multiliteracy instruction continue to increase and complexify in this highly technological era and global society, one major question and opportunity for digital content specialists to consider is whether the Xanadu model could be extended to multiliteracy centers and universities that share archives of reusable interfaces categorized by learning experience and user.

The opportunities to advance, customize, and individualize learning experiences through the use of such a design would transform many aspects of student-centered learning and even further permit the multiliteracy center to address the broad range of issues associated with mediating knowledge in both a global and technological era. Not surprisingly, social theorist Rita Süssmuth (1998) has commented that the potential to mediate knowledge through technology and other means that accomplish socioeconomic ends is an aspect of "the future-capability of society" (p. 27) that educators and all agents within society must be aware of in the design and operation of social systems. Specifically, Süssmuth states that "any attempt to explore the future-capability of society" must be equated with "operative capability" and understood in terms of "the ability to shape events" (p. 27). Reconfirming this premise, she writes, "Most of all, however, future-capability refers to the ability of society and the individual to cope with change and to integrate future framework conditions into human coexistence" (p. 27).

Given the issues that Süssmuth raises, we return to our original questioning of what models and modes of thoughts will best serve Writing Centers in the 21st century, and we find that the question is rooted in a broad range of concerns associated with social transformations. Clearly, Writing Centers are becoming virtual communities, and this progression will mark the dynamic evolution of Writing Centers into multiliteracy centers. This is a progression that is not only predictable, but that is related to other progressions in society. Fundamentally, it is a progression centered in efforts to define what constitutes community in contemporary times, from Robert D. Putnam's (2000) exposition of this issue in his award-winning book, *Bowling Alone: The Collapse and Revival of American Community*, to the discussions of the abstractions that bring communities together via shared concepts and beliefs that Benedict Anderson (1991) explores in *Imagined Communities*. Although social critics Guy Debord (1995) and Jean Baudrillard (1988) question the implications and values of the even more abstract communities created and mediated by technology, their questions and concerns provide a means for the digital content specialists that Writing Center professionals are becoming to design and actualize multiliteracy centers that contribute to the enrichment of communication across an extensive range of settings and experiences. Ultimately, they contribute to community formation and to what Thomas M. Carr, Jr. (1990), calls "the resilience of rhetoric."

Both of these aspects are issues that Sherry Turkle (1984, 1995), a major theorist on e-literacies, explores in *The Second Self. Computers and the Human Spirit and in Life on the Screen: Identity in the Age of the Internet.* Turkle's key premises have great significance for Writing Center professionals as they seek to become digital content specialists who use the principles of e-literacies, cognitive theory, and composition pedagogy to carry out their roles within multiliteracy centers. Specifically, Turkle emphasizes that, under earlier models of computer-mediated communication, the boundaries between the computer and the person using the computer were clear and mechanistic. People acted on computers by giving commands to machines—largely so because the vast potential of the computer for different modes of communication and interaction had not yet been fully explored. Within the new model of e-literacies, individuals use computers to enter into dialogues, navigate simulated worlds, and create virtual realities. As a professor in the Program in Science, Technology, and Society at MIT, Turkle exemplifies the types of knowledges and emphases that Writing Center professionals will be exploring in the e-worlds of the 21st century. The connections between technology and society, between the individual's cognitive processes and the cognitive processes required for communicating in the global world of the Internet, and the implications for the types of learners Writing Center professionals will be encountering and instructing are of profound consequence. They will require a deeper understanding not only of our traditional views of what constitutes literacy, but also of our views of identity, knowledge, and community formation. They will also transform our traditional understandings of tutoring and replace them with highly integrated theories of language, learning, and social practices mediated through both the social environment and the various symbol systems of the e-literacies.

The types of social contributions to communication and to community formation that digital content specialists can generate within a multiliteracy center are key aspects of what Nathaniel Branden (1997) describes as knowledge structures in the information age. As Branden indicates,

> We now live in a global economy characterized by rapid change, accelerating scientific and technological breakthroughs, and an unprecedented level of competitiveness. These developments create a demand for higher levels of education and training than were required of previous generations. (p. 221)

Branden further explains that the issue of competency within such times of rapid change and highly complex technologies creates a need for those skilled at responding to and mastering these issues. In other words, it calls for people who can educate others to be responsive to the potentials of technologies to achieve positive and constructive aims within a global society. It calls for digital content specialists who combine multiple perspectives on social cognition and social interaction into a global world made instantly and complexly accessible via technology.

This is the society that Thomas L. Friedman (2005) describes as "flat," in the sense that the digital revolution has created a highly connected world in which rapid and extensive technical advances have instantaneously connected individuals, organizations, and institutions with billions of other people across the planet. To develop, interpret, and structure knowledge within this "flat" and connected world will require expertise beyond the level of traditional instruction provided in today's institutions of higher education. It will also require a rethinking and a transformation of the traditional Writing Center, a task that will fall to theorists and practitioners alike to envision and carry out. It will no longer be productive to be bogged down in the types of arguments over "good intentions" and the types of "noise" that should be coming from the Writing Center, as Nancy Maloney Grimm (1999) and Elizabeth H. Boquet (2002) have called on the Writing Center community to contemplate over the last few years. It will no longer be sufficient to debate issues of marginalization and rebellion within academic structures or to fret over the threat of the outsourcing of writing programs and Writing Centers to corporate entities. What will be necessary are new cultural narratives and cultural transformations for the Writing Center as it becomes the multiliteracy center and thus a major educational resource for the 21st century.

Clearly, many of our most important tasks and contributions for the Writing Center will remain, although modified and enhanced by the requirements of a digital age. By improving outcomes and enriching educational experiences, Writing Center professionals as digital content specialists will continue to contribute to student recruiting/retention and to the significance of universities as community partners and leaders in knowledge creation and dissemination. By helping students achieve their goals, deal with frustrations brought about by literacy inadequacy, or shape new modes of expression, Writing Center professionals as digital content specialists will provide a socioeconomic boost to students who might otherwise fail in the university and consequently Fail in their life's aspirations of a degree and a career. Digital content specialists stand at the epicenter of pedagogical transformation to a new world of astounding possibilities brought about by an understanding of their roles in knowledge-making. To act as agents of change within education and educational systems has been a time-honored tradition that Writing Center professionals have fulfilled for well over a century of accomplishment. The next chapter that Writing Center professionals will write in the cultural narrative of the Writing Center will be as digital content specialists who have understood, accepted, and enacted the relationship between social structures and social life — in other words, who have understood the social construction of reality.

They will have understood, too, the value of information and communication technologies to the educational process and will have developed ways in which to integrate this knowledge into their tutoring and pedagogy. Perhaps greatest of all, they will have recognized, as Gunther Kress (2003) points out, the differences between—and different demands of—academic and professional literacies. Academic literacies may well circumscribe and limit definitions of what constitutes literacy and also may well identify these definitions with issues of class, culture, and social control, as Nancy Maloney Grimm (1999) contends. In contrast, professional literacies often work within the broadest of multicultural and multiliteracy contexts to incorporate a vast range of techniques for achieving communication via the integration of language, image, design, and conceptual frameworks. Further, professional literacies provide for more varied means of individualizing communication and learning than do academic literacies and, as such, resonate with what social systems theorist Don Tapscott (1996) envisions as the central social trend of the 21st century—the "molecularization" of knowledge that permits for knowledge and instructional strategies to be highly individualized. The old concept of mass instruction via classrooms and lecture halls is rapidly being replaced by educational methods in which the individual is an active and interactive creator in the instructional process. In a related manner, the actual space of the classroom, lecture hall, or Writing Center is being replaced by virtual space, in which instruction does not need to be located in a physical space, but can be virtually located and universally accessible via the Internet.

What lies ahead for the Writing Center as a multiliteracy center is building on these social systems trends to create highly individualized instructional methods by using technology to respond to each learner's skills and interests and by centering these methods within the e-literacies that will define the 21st century. The implications of a shift like this will be enormous in the impact on Writing Center professionals who will need to become—and be trained to become—digital content specialists who are adept at using technology and who understand the implications of technology for knowledge creation. There is no question this is more than a paradigmatic shift or a philosophical redefinition and refocusing. As social systems theorist Gunther Kress (2003) indicates, it is the emergence of a new era of communication that represents the decline of the print culture and its values, a philosophy and methodology that have held sway over our culture and our educational systems for centuries.

That Writing Center professionals can play a lead role in defining this shift and these revolutionary changes for society is an exciting prospect; it is also a testament to the adaptability, flexibility, and resiliency of Writing Centers in responding to change—a major capability that Don Tapscott and Art Caston (1993) claim is the key to survival and relevance in contemporary times. Tapscott and Caston contend that social institutions responsive to this shift as electronic technologies become the predominant mode of communication and knowledge generation will survive, whereas those that have "severe difficulties embracing the change" or that "remain constrained by traditional approaches" will be doomed to irrelevance and eventual elimination. Fortunately for

Writing Centers, the path seems clear, in that the rapid advancement of technology has clearly demonstrated that knowledge of the e-literacies is now an educational imperative for those who wish to operate successfully in academic and professional settings and who wish to contribute to the advancement of society as citizens or civic leaders.

Thus, we end where we began with a focus on the need for a "new historicism" for the Writing Center field. The cultural narrative that needs to be advanced for Writing Centers is of the significant role that Writing Centers can play in centralizing the e-literacies within education. The new cultural narrative must emphasize, too, that the multiliteracy center can emerge from the Writing Center because Writing Centers provide a solid base—in terms of structure, history, and educational values—on which to construct the newer model of writing instruction in a highly technological, global society. Students will need to learn to construct and communicate via multimodal texts, and certainly the instructional models and practices of Writing Centers demonstrate their openness, versatility, and flexibility in responding to educational challenges and opportunities. In the 20th century, Writing Centers demonstrated their enormous ability to respond innovatively to societal shifts that redefined educational emphases and audiences (Murphy, 1991). In the 21st century, this same creativity and authenticity will enable Writing Centers to respond to the societal challenges created by the vast array and broad impact of the information and communication technologies. The best setting and method for responding to these challenges and opportunities will be the development and emergence of the Writing Center as the multiliteracy center in which multimodal instruction and learning can be fostered and explored.

We see the greatest challenge to this vision resting with the training of the Writing Center professionals who will direct and work within the multiliteracy center. Certainly, changes of this sort will produce divisions within the profession as to how the centers should proceed and where the heart and values of such centers should reside. One of the key issues will be, too, how Writing Center professionals will be trained to use the new information and communication technologies wisely and well. There is no question that Writing Center professionals have been adept over the years at shaping [heir centers to their institutions. Thus, Louise Wetherbee Phelps (1991) is correct in arguing that disciplinary knowledge emerges from practical inquiry and common practice, and this principle is important in recognizing how the training and common practice of Writing Center professionals as digital content specialists will occur. It is a question of institutional identity and purpose, and these facets will guide the transformation of the Writing Center into the multiliteracy center, as well as shape and guide the types of local knowledge that multiliteracy center professionals will need in developing their programs, responding to various audiences and constituencies, and navigating the often turbulent waters of defining a meaningful and effective institutional role in times of rapid societal and educational change. In other words, in those times in which a "new historicism" is emerging that redefines potential and enables the actualization of an even greater level of achievement.

References

Anderson, B. (1991). *Imagined communities: Reflections on the origin and spread of nationalism.* London, England, and New York, NY: Verso.

Baudrillard, J. (1988). In M. Poster (Ed.), *Selected writings.* Palo Alto, CA: Stanford University Press.

Bawden, D. (2001). Progress in documentation Information and digital literacies: A review of concepts. *Journal of Documentation, 57*(2), 218–259.

Bonnell, V. E., & Hunt, L. (1999). introduction. In V. E. Bonnell & L. Hunt (Eds.), *Beyond the cultural turn* (pp. 1–34). Berkeley, CA: University of California Press.

Boquet, E. H. (2002). *Noise from the writing center.* Logan, UT: Utah State University Press.

Branden, N. (1997). Self-esteem in the information age. In F. Hesselbein, M. Goldsmith, & R. Beckhard (Eds.), *The organization of the future* (pp. 221–229). San Francisco, CA: Jossey-Bass.

Carr, T. M., Jr. (1990). *Descartes and the resilience of rhetoric.* Carbondale, IL: Southern Illinois University Press.

Davis, K. (1995). Life outside the boundary: History and direction in the writing center. *Writing Lab Newsletter, 20*(2), 5–7.

Debord, Guy. (1995). *The society of the spectacle* (D. Nicholson-Smith, Trans.). Cambridge, MA: Zone Books.

Fairclough, N. (1993). *Discourse and social change.* Cambridge, England: Polity Press.

Farashahi, M., Hafsi, T. & Molz, R. (2005). Institutionalized norms of conducting research and social realities: A research synthesis of empirical works from 1983 to 2002. *International Journal of Management Reviews, 7*(1), 1–24.

Friedman, T. L. (2005). *The world is flat: A brief history of the twenty-first century.* New York, NY: Farrar, Strauss & Giroux.

Gilster, P. (1999). *Digital literacy.* New York, NY: Wiley.

Grimm, N. M. (1999). *Good intentions: Writing center work for postmodern times.* Portsmouth, NH: Heinemann-Boynton/Cook.

Kalantzis, M., Cope, B., & Harvey, A. (2005). Assessing multiliteracies and the new basics. *Assessment in Education, 10*(1), 15–26.

Kress, G. (2003). *Literacy in the new media age.* New York, NY: Routledge.

Murphy, C. (1991). Writing centers in context: Responding to current educational theory. In R. Wallace & J. Simpson (Eds.), *The writing center: New directions* (pp. 276–288). New York, NY: Garland.

North, S. (1984). The idea of a writing center. *College English, 46*(5), 433–446.

North, S. (1994). Revisiting "the idea of a writing center." *The Writing Center Journal, 15*(1), 7–19.

Phelps, L. W. (1991). Practical wisdom and the geography of knowledge in composition. *College English, 53*(8), 863–885.

Putnam, R. D. (2000). *Bowling alone: The collapse and revival of American community.* New York, NY: Simon Schuster.

Rheingold, H. (1998). Virtual communities. In F. Hesselbein, M. Goldsmith, R. Beckhard, & R. F. Schubert (Eds.), *The community of the future* (pp. 115–122). San Francisco, CA: Jossey-Bass.

Rohan, L. (2002). Hostesses of literacy: Librarians, writing teachers, writing centers, and a historical quest for ethos. *Composition Studies. 30*(2), 60–77.

Süssmuth, R. (1998). The future-capability of society. in F. Hesselbein, M. Goldsmith, R. Beckhard, & R. F. Schubert (Eds.), *The community of the future* (pp. 27–33). San Francisco, CA: Jossey-Bass.

Tapscott, D. (1996). *The digital economy: Promise and peril in the age of networked intelligence.* New York, NY: McGraw-Hill.

Tapscott, D. & Caston, A. (1995). *Paradigm shift: The new promise of information technology.* New York, NY: McGraw-Hill.

Thomas, B. (1989). The new historicism and other old-fashioned topics. in H. A. Veeser (Ed.), *The new historicism* (pp. 182–203). New York, NY: Routledge.

Turkle, S. (1984). *The second self: Computers and the human spirit.* New York, NY: Simon & Schuster.

Turkle, S. (1995). *Life on the screen: Identity in the age of the internet.* New York, NY: Simon & Schuster.

PART

III

Resources for Further Inquiry

The burgeoning interest in writing centers over the past several decades has created a wealth of informative resources for tutors. In addition to scholarly journals and books, tutors can find support for their work in professional organizations, electronic networks like WCenter, and Web sites dedicated to providing online resources for tutors.

Because writing center work has always respected the value of individual narratives and case studies, scholarship in the field often includes examples drawn from tutors' actual practice. This approach helps make writing center scholarship accessible to novice tutors, who will appreciate the conversational style of the journals, books, and electronic networks. They will also find much to identify with in the case studies and narrative examples these resources often explore.

INTERNATIONAL WRITING CENTERS ASSOCIATION (IWCA)

The primary professional organization for writing center personnel is the International Writing Centers Association (IWCA). The IWCA promotes writing center causes and provides educational materials and support services related to writing center practice. The organization sponsors the IWCA Press, which publishes books on writing center theory and practice, including its manual, the *International Writing Centers Association Handbook*; hosts the Summer Institute for writing center professionals; and provides links to The Writing Centers Research Project and to Writing Center Surveys.

Among its many services, the IWCA publishes a national directory of high school, community college, and college and university writing centers; sponsors a national conference; lends support to its regional organizations and conferences; awards outstanding scholarship on writing centers; offers information and assistance through its committees and subcommittees on a range of writing center issues; and provides a free "starter kit" for setting up a writing center. For tutors, the IWCA provides links that have been developed by various universities to a range of topics—including such issues as organization of essays, questions to get writers started in a tutoring session, approaches to aid students in writing introductions and conclusions, ways in which tutors can respond to drafts and provide appropriate critiques, discussion groups on tutoring ESL students, writing styles and citation styles for various disciplines, and so forth. Information on IWCA and its regional affiliates is available on the IWCA home page at <http://writingcenters.org>.

NATIONAL CONFERENCE ON PEER TUTORING IN WRITING (NCPTW)

The National Conference on Peer Tutoring in Writing (NCPTW) is the major conference devoted exclusively to issues associated with peer tutoring. "The NCPTW offers peer tutors the opportunity to contribute in professional and scholarly ways to the larger writing center community and is dedicated to providing forums for tutors to share and present research at national and international conferences." The NCPTW sponsors an annual conference on peer-tutoring theory and practice; the conference is often held in conjunction with the International Writing Centers Association (IWCA) annual conference. Information on the NCPTW can be found at <http://www.ncptw.org>.

ONLINE RESOURCES

Many writing centers provide online information about tutoring and related writing concerns. One of the most comprehensive resources is the Online Writing Lab (OWL) at Purdue University. This OWL provides download-able files on ESL instruction, grammar, spelling, punctuation, general writing concerns, documentation, professional writing, writing across the curriculum, PowerPoint presentations, hypertext, and use of Internet search engines <http://owl.english.purdue.edu>.

The University of Richmond offers an extensive series, "Training for Tough Tutorials," that can be found at <http://writing2.richmond.edu/training/tough /index.html>.

The Appalachian College Association offers an online tutoring manual that includes such topics as the student–tutor relationship, tutorials with students representing a broad range of needs, ESL strategies, research strategies, and documentation styles. "Tutor.edu: A Manual for Writing Center Tutors" is at <http://ww3.montreat.edu/tutor>.

Electronic Networks and Blogs

WCenter is the leading electronic network for online discussions of writing center work, but new discussion venues include two blogs — PeerCentered and an International Writing Centers Association (IWCA) Forum.

WCenter lets writing center personnel share information, seek answers to inquiries, pose questions for further investigation, and establish a sense of community. WCenter provides an important way for writing center person-nel to share the immediacy of the work and concerns. It serves as one con-firming example of Jeanne Simpson's view that "the writing center movement has expanded because writing center people have learned to communicate, to form a network, to transmit information, and to exchange assistance" ("What Lies Ahead for Writing Centers: Position Statement on Professional Concerns," *The Writing Center Journal* 5.2 and 6.1 [1985]: 35-39). Subscribe to WCenter by contacting Elizabeth Bowen at <elizabeth.bowen@ttu.edu>.

PeerCentered is a site that encourages peer writing consultants and others to chronicle their experiences in writing centers and at writing center conferences. Bloggers and readers can find the site at <www.peercentered.org>.

The IWCA Forum covers a broad range of subjects but also has one blog devoted to Peer Tutors. The website for the Forum is <http://www.writingcenters .org/board/index.php>.

JOURNALS

Writing center work has two major print journals devoted exclusively to its concerns: *Writing Lab Newsletter*, edited by Muriel Harris of Purdue University, and *The Writing Center Journal*, edited by Melissa Ianetta from the University of Delaware and Lauren Fitzgerald from Yeshiva University. Both journals are sponsored by the International Writing Centers Association.

The Writing Lab Newsletter provides news on conferences and meetings as well as columns, letters, and scholarly articles on writing center practice. It regularly publishes a column on peer tutoring as well as articles by peer tutors. The newsletter is respected for its accessible style and its capacity to convey the voices of writing center personnel at work. In contrast, *The Writing Center Journal* publishes more theoretical and scholarly articles. Both journals have searchable online archives, offering full-text articles. The *Writing Lab Newsletter*'s archives can be accessed at <http://www.writinglabnewsletter .org/new/>. Readers can access *The Writing Center Journal*'s archives at <http:// www.louisville.edu/a-s/writingcenter/wcenters/wcj.html>.

Two online journals—*Praxis: A Writing Center Journal* and *Dangling Modifier*—also devote their issues to a discussion of writing center concerns. Sponsored by the University of Texas's Undergraduate Writing Center, *Praxis* publishes articles on a variety of topics related to consulting in or administering a writing center. *Dangling Modifier*, a publication produced by Pennsylvania State University Writing Center in conjunction with the National Conference on Peer Tutoring in Writing, publishes brief articles on topics related to peer tutoring. Readers can find *Praxis* on the Web at <http://projects.uwc.utexas .edu/praxis/?q=> and *Dangling Modifier* at <http://www.ulc.psu.edu/Dangling _Modifier/index.php>.

Other national journals that occasionally include articles on writing centers and tutoring are *College English; Composition Studies; College Composition and Communication (CCC); JAC: A Journal of Composition Theory; English Journal; Research in the Teaching of English; Journal of Basic Writing; The Journal of Teaching Writing; Kairos: A Journal of Rhetoric, Technology, and Pedagogy; Writing Assessment;* and *Teaching English in the Two-Year College.*

BOOKS AND ARTICLES

The following selected list of books and articles can serve as additional resources for discussions of rationales, strategies, theories, and techniques of tutoring:

Books

Barnett, Robert W., and Jacob S. Blumner, eds. *The Allyn & Bacon Guide to Writing Center Theory and Practice*. Boston: Allyn and Bacon, 2001. Print.

---. *The Longman Guide to Writing Center Theory and Practice*. New York: Pearson Longman, 2008. Print.

Boquet, Elizabeth H. *Noise from the Writing Center*. Logan: Utah State UP, 2002. Print.

Breuch, Lee-Ann Kastman. *Virtual Peer Review: Teaching and Learning about Writing in Online Environments*. Albany: State U of New York P, 2004. Print.

Briggs, Lynn Craigue, and Meg Woolbright. *Stories from the Center: Connecting Narrative and Theory in the Writing Center*. Urbana: NCTE, 2000. Print.

Bruce, Shanti, and Ben Rafoth, eds. *ESL Writers: A Guide for Writing Center Tutors*. Portsmouth: Boynton/Cook, 2004. Print.

Capossela, Toni-Lee. *The Harcourt Brace Guide to Peer Tutoring*. New York: Harcourt, 1998. Print.

Childers, Pamela B. *The High School Writing Center: Establishing and Maintaining One*. Urbana: NCTE, 1989. Print.

Childers, Pamela B., Anne Ruggles Gere, and Art Young. *Programs and Practices: Writing across the Secondary School Curriculum*. Portsmouth: Boynton/Cook, 1994. Print.

Clark, Irene Lurkis. *Writing in the Center: Teaching in a Writing Center*. Dubuque: Kendall/ Hunt, 1985. Print.

Coogan, David. *Electronic Writing Centers: Computing in the Field of Composition*. Westport: Greenwood, 1999. Print.

Denny, Harry. *Facing the Center: Toward an Identity Politics of One-to-One Mentoring*. Logan: Utah State UP, 2010. Print.

Donaldson, A. J., & Topping, K. J. *The Peer-Tutor Training Handbook for Higher and Further Education*. Dundee: Centre for Paired Learning, University of Dundee, 1996. Print.

Dvorak, Kevin, and Shanti Bruce. *Creative Approaches to Writing Center Work*. Cresskill, NJ : Hampton, 2008. Print.

Elmborg, James K., and Sheril Hook. *Centers for Learning: Writing Centers and Libraries in Collaboration*. Chicago: Association of College and Research Libraries, 2005. Print.

Flynn, Thomas, and Mary King, eds. *Dynamics of the Writing Conference: Social and Cognitive Interaction*. Urbana: NCTE, 1993. Print.

Geller, Anne Ellen, Michele Eodice, Frankie Condon, Meg Carroll, and Elizabeth H. Boquet. *The Everyday Writing Center: A Community of Practice*. Logan: Utah State UP, 2007. Print.

Gillespie, Paula, Alice Gillam, Lady Falls Brown, and Byron L. Stay, eds. *Writing Center Research: Extending the Conversation*. Mahwah: Erlbaum, 2002. Print.

Gillespie, Paula, and Neal Lerner. *The Allyn & Bacon Guide to Peer Tutoring*. Boston: Allyn & Bacon, 2000. Print.

Grego, Rhonda C., and Nancy S. Thompson. *Teaching/Writing in Thirdspaces: The Studio Approach*. Carbondale: Southern Illinois UP, 2007. Print.

Grimm, Nancy Maloney. *Good Intentions: Writing Center Work for Postmodern Times*. Portsmouth: Boynton/Cook, 1999. Print.

Harris, Muriel. *Teaching One-to-One: The Writing Conference*. Urbana: NCTE, 1986.

---. *Tutoring Writing: A Sourcebook for Writing Labs*. Glenview: Scott, Foresman, 1982. Print.

Haviland, Carol, Maria Notarangelo, Lene Whitley-Putz, and Thia Wolf, eds. *Weaving Knowledge Together: Writing Centers and Collaboration*. Emmitsburg: NWCA P, 1998. Print.

Hewett, Beth L. *The Online Writing Conference: A Guide for Teachers and Tutors*. Portsmouth: Boynton/Cook, 2010. Print.

Hewett, Beth L., and Christa Ehmann. *Preparing Educators for Online Writing Instruction: Principles and Processes*. Urbana: NCTE, 2004. Print.

Hobson, Eric H., ed. *Wiring the Writing Center*. Logan: Utah State UP, 1998. Print.

Inman, James A., and Donna M. Sewell, eds. *Taking Flight with OWLS: Examining Electronic Writing Center Work*. Mahwah: Erlbaum, 2000. Print.

Johnson, T. R., and Tom Pace. *Refiguring Prose Style: Possibilities for Writing Pedagogy*. Logan: Utah State UP, 2005. Print.

Kent, Richard. *A Guide to Creating Student-Staffed Writing Centers Grades 6-12*. Peter Lang, 2006. Print.

Kinkead, Joyce A., and Jeanette G. Harris, eds. *Writing Centers in Context: Twelve Case Studies*. Urbana: NCTE, 1993. Print.

Lerner, Neal. *The Idea of a Writing Laboratory*. Carbondale: Southern Illinois UP, 2009. Print.

Macauley, William J., and Nicholas Mauriello, eds. *Marginal Words, Marginal Works? Tutoring the Academy in the Work of Writing Centers*. Cresskill: Hampton, 2007. Print.

Maxwell, Martha, ed. *When Tutor Meets Student*. Ann Arbor: U of Michigan P, 1994. Print.

McAndrew, Donald A., and Thomas J. Reigstad. *Tutoring Writing: A Practical Guide for Conferences*. Portsmouth: Boynton/Cook, 2001. Print.

Meyer, Emily, and Louise Z. Smith. *The Practical Tutor*. New York: Oxford UP, 1987. Print.

Mullin, Joan, and Ray Wallace, eds. *Intersections: Theory-Practice in the Writing Center*. Urbana: NCTE, 1994. Print.

Murphy, Christina, and Byron L. Stay, eds. *The Writing Center Director's Resource Book*. Mahwah: Erlbaum, 2006. Print.

Murphy, Christina, and Joe Law, eds. *Landmark Essays on Writing Centers*. Mahwah: Erlbaum, 1995. Print.

Murphy, Christina, Joe Law, and Steve Sherwood, eds. *Writing Centers: An Annotated Bibliography*. Westport: Greenwood, 1996. Print.

Myers-Breslin, Linda, ed. *Administrative Problem-Solving for Writing Programs and Writing Centers*. Urbana: NCTE, 1999. Print.

Nelson, Jane, and Kathy Evertz, eds. *The Politics of Writing Centers*. Portsmouth: Boynton/Cook, 2002. Print.

Nicholas, Melissa. *(E)merging Identities: Graduate Students in the Writing Center*. Southlake: Fountainhead, 2008. Print.

Olson, Gary A., ed. *Writing Centers: Theory and Administration*. Urbana: NCTE, 1984. Print.

Pemberton, Michael A., and Joyce Kinkead, eds. *The Center Will Hold: Critical Perspectives on Writing Center Scholarship*. Logan: Utah State UP, 2003. Print.

Rabow, Jerome, Tiffani Chin, and Nima Fahimian. *Tutoring Matters: Everything You Always Wanted to Know about How to Tutor*. Philadelphia: Temple UP, 1999. Print.

Rafoth, Ben, ed. *A Tutor's Guide: Helping Writers One to One*. New York: Heinemann, 2000. Print.

Reigstad, Thomas J., and Donald McAndrew. *Training Tutors for Writing Center Conferences*. Urbana: NCTE, 1984. Print.

Rice, Jeff, and Marcel O'Gorman, eds. *New Media/New Methods: The Academic Turn from Literacy to Electracy*. West Lafayette: Parlor, 2008. Print.

Ryan, Leigh. *The Bedford Guide for Writing Tutors*. Boston: Bedford, 1994. Print.

Selber, Stuart. *Multiliteracies for a Digital Age*. Carbondale: Southern Illinois UP, 2004. Print.

Sheridan, David M., and James Inman. *Multiliteracy Centers: Writing Center Work, New Media, and Multimodal Rhetoric*. Cresskill: Hampton, 2010. Print.

Silk, Bobbie Bayless, ed. *The Writing Center Resource Manual*. Emmitsburg: NWCA, 2002. Print.

Spigelman, Candace, and Laurie Grobman. *On Location: Theory and Practice in Classroom-Based Writing Tutoring*. Logan: Utah State UP, 2005. Print.

Stay, Byron L., Christina Murphy, and Eric H. Hobson, eds. *Writing Center Perspectives*. Emmitsburg: NWCA P, 1995. Print.

Steward, Joyce, and Mary Croft. *The Writing Laboratory: Organization, Methods, and Management*. Glenview: Scott, Foresman, 1982. Print.

Waldo, Mark L. *Demythologizing Language Differences in the Academy: Establishing Discipline-based Writing Programs*. Mahwah: Erlbaum, 2004. Print.

Wallace, Ray, and Jeanne Simpson, eds. The *Writing Center: New Directions*. New York: Garland, 1991. Print.

Articles

Bawarshi, Anis, and Stephanie Pelkowski. "Postcolonialism and the Idea of a Writing Center." *Writing Center Journal* 19.2 (1999): 41–59. Print.

Bishop, Wendy. "Writing from the Tips of Our Tongues: Writers, Tutors, and Talk." *Writing Center Journal* 14.1 (1993): 30–44. Print.

Behm, Richard. "Ethical Issues in Peer Tutoring: A Defense of Collaborative Learning." *Writing Center Journal* 10.1 (1989): 3–13. Print.

Blau, Susan R., John Hall, and Tracy Strauss. "Exploring the Tutor/Client Conversation: A Linguistic Analysis." *Writing Center Journal* 19.1 (1998): 19–49. Print.

Boquet, Elizabeth, Betsy A. Bowen, Catherine Forsa, Devin Hagan, and Mary A. McCall. "Record and Reflect: iPod Use in Writing Center Staff Development." *Praxis: A Writing Center Journal* 6.1 (2008): n. pag. Web.

Bowden, Darsie. "Inter-Activism: Strengthening the Writing Center Conference." *Writing Center Journal* 15.2 (1995): 163–81. Print.

Carino, Peter, and Doug Enders. "Does Frequency of Visits to the Writing Center Increase Student Satisfaction?" *Writing Center Journal* 22.11 (2001): 82–103. Print.

Carter, Shannon. "Tutoring Writing Is Performing Social Work Is Coloring Hair: Writing Center Work as Activity System." *Praxis: A Writing Center Journal* 3.2 (2006): n. pag. Web.

Cogie, Jane, Kim Strain, and Sharon Lorinskas. "Avoiding the Proofreading Trap: The Value of the Error Correction Process." *Writing Center Journal* 19.2 (1999): 7–33. Print.

Donahue, Tiane. "Cross-Cultural Analysis of Student Writing: Beyond Discourses of Difference." *Written Communication* 25.3 (2008): 319–52. Print.

Gill, Judy. "The Professionalization of Tutor Training." *The Writing Lab Newsletter* 30.6 (2006): 1–5. Print.

Graesser, A. C., et al. "Collaborative Dialogue Patterns in Naturalistic One-to-One Tutoring." *Applied Cognitive Psychology* 9 (1995): 495–522. Print.

Grimm, Nancy. "Attending to the Conceptual Change Potential of Writing Center Narratives." *The Writing Center Journal* 28.1 (2008): 3–21. Print.

---. "Rearticulating the Work of the Writing Center." *College Composition and Communication* 47.4 (1996): 523–48. Print.

---. "The Regulatory Role of the Writing Center: Coming to Terms with a Loss of Innocence." *Writing Center Journal* 17.1 (1996): 5–30. Print.

Gruber, Sibylle. "Coming to Terms with Contradictions: Online Materials, Plagiarism, and the Writing Center." *Writing Center Journal* 19.1 (1998): 49–73. Print.

Harris, Muriel. "Talking in the Middle: Why Writers Need Writing Tutors." *College English* 57.1 (1995): 27–42. Print.

Healey, Dave. "Tutorial Role Conflict in the Writing Center." *Writing Center Journal* 11.2 (1991): 41–51. Print.

Hemmeter, Thomas. "The 'Smack of Difference': The Language of Writing Center Discourse." *Writing Center Journal* 11.1 (1990): 35–49. Print.

Joyner, Michael. "The Writing Center Conference and the Textuality of Power." *Writing Center Journal* 12.1 (1991): 80–90. Print.

Kennedy, Barbara L. "Non-native Speakers as Students in First-Year Composition Classes with Native Speakers: How Can Writing Tutors Help?" *Writing Center Journal* 13.2 (1993): 27–39. Print.

Kimball, Sara. "Cybertext/Cyberspeech: Writing Centers and Online Magic." *Writing Center Journal* 18.1 (1998): 30–50. Print.

MacDonald, R. B. "Group Tutoring Techniques: From Research to Practice." *Journal of Developmental Education* 17.2 (1993): 12–18. Print.

Mattison, Michael. "Someone to Watch Over Me: Reflection and Authority in the Writing Center." *Writing Center Journal* 27.1 (2007): 29–51. Print.

Murphy, Christina. "On Not 'Bowling Alone' in the Writing Center, or Why Peer Tutoring is an Essential Community for Writers and for Higher Education." *The Writing Center Director's Resource Book*. Ed. Christina Murphy and Byron L. Stay. Mahwah: Erlbaum, 2006. 273–81. Print.

---. "The Writing Center and Social Constructionist Theory." *Intersections: Theory-Practice in the Writing Center*. Ed. Joan Mullin and Ray Wallace. Urbana: NCTE, 1994. 25–38. Print.

Nelson, R. R. "Peer Tutors at the College Level: Maneuvering within the Zone of Proximal Development." *Journal of College Reading and Learning* 36.2 (1995–96): 43–51. Print.

Raines, Helen Howell. "Tutoring and Teaching: Continuum, Dichotomy, or Dialect?" *Writing Center Journal* 14.2 (1994): 150–63. Print.

Rihn, Andrew. "The Tutor as Academic Ambassador." *Dangling Modifier* 16.2 (2010): n. pag. Web.

Shepley, Nathan. "Places of Composition: Writing Contexts in Appalachian Ohio." *Composition Studies* 37.2 (2009): 75–90. Print.

Sherwood, Steve. "Apprenticed to Failure: Learning from the Students We Can't Help." *Writing Center Journal* 17.1 (1996): 49–58. Print.

---. "Humor and the Serious Tutor." *Writing Center Journal* 13.2 (1993): 3–13. Print.

Singley, Carol J., and Holly W. Boucher. "Dialogue in Tutor Training: Creating the Essential Space for Learning." *Writing Center Journal* 8.2 (1988): 11–22. Print.

Szubinska, Barbara, and Sherry Robinson. "Revising the Writing Center: A Self-Study." *Writing Lab Newsletter* 26.4 (2001): 12–14. Print.

Thompson, Isabelle. "Scaffolding in the Writing Center: A Microanalysis of an Experienced Tutor's Verbal and Nonverbal Tutoring Strategies." *Written Communication* 26.4 (2009): 417–53. Print.

Thonus, Terese. "Tutors as Teachers: Assisting ESL/EFL Students in the Writing Center." *Writing Center Journal* 13.2 (1993): 13–27. Print.

Villanueva, Victor. "Blind: Talking about the New Racism." *Writing Center Journal* 26.1 (2006): 3–19. Print.

Walker, Kristen. "The Debate over Generalist and Specialist Tutors: Genre Theory's Contribution." *Writing Center Journal* 18.2 (1998): 27–47. Print.

GRAMMAR HOTLINE DIRECTORY

A *Grammar Hotline Directory* is published annually by Tidewater Community College. The directory lists email, Web sites, and telephone services in the United States and Canada that provide free answers to short questions about writing and grammar. The Web site is <http://www.tcc.edu/students/resources/writcent/gh/hotlinol.htm>. Or for more information, write to Writing Center and Grammar Hotline, Tidewater Community College, 1700 College Crescent, Virginia Beach, VA 23453. Phone (757) 822-7170, Fax (757) 822-7171 (Attn: Writing Center), or email writcent@tcc.edu.

ABOUT THE AUTHORS

Christina Murphy is the former Dean of the College of Liberal Arts and Professor of English at Marshall University in Huntington, West Virginia. She has served as the President of the National Writing Centers Association and has published widely on writing center issues. Her coedited books on writing centers include *Landmark Essays on Writing Centers* (1995), *Writing Center Perspectives* (1995), *Writing Centers: An Annotated Bibliography* (1996), *The Theory and Criticism of Virtual Texts: An Annotated Bibliography* (2001), and *The Writing Center Director's Resource Book* (2006). She also has published over one hundred articles and book chapters in a range of journals and essay collections. Murphy has served as the editor of two national journals, *Composition Studies* and *Studies in Psychoanalytic Theory*, and of the regional journal *English in Texas*. Her short stories and poems have appeared in over fifty journals and five anthologies, and she has received an Editor's Choice award and Special Mention for a Pushcart Prize.

Steve Sherwood is the Director of the William L. Adams Center for Writing at Texas Christian University. Currently an at-large representative to the International Writing Centers Association Executive Board, he is a past president of the South Central Writing Centers Association. His essays have appeared in *The Writing Center Journal*, *Journal of Teaching Writing*, *Dialogue*, *Writing Lab Newsletter*, *Writing Center Perspectives*, *Wiring the Writing Center*, *The Writing Center Resource Manual*, *English in Texas*, *Weber Studies*, *Rendezvous*, and other publications. With Christina Murphy and Joe Law, he compiled *Writing Centers: An Annotated Bibliography* (1996), for which Murphy, Law, and Sherwood received a 1997 International Writing Centers Association award. In 2003, Sherwood's novel *Hardwater* won the George Garrett Fiction Prize, sponsored by the Texas Review Press, which published the novel in 2005.